Financial Aid
for Asian Americans
2012-2014

RSP FINANCIAL AID DIRECTORIES
OF INTEREST TO MINORITIES

College Student's Guide to Merit and Other No-Need Funding
Selected as one of the "Outstanding Titles of the Year" by *Choice,* this directory describes 1,300 no-need funding opportunities for college students. 490 pages. ISBN 1588412121. $32.50, plus $7 shipping.

Directory of Financial Aids for Women
There are 1,400+ funding programs set aside for women described in this biennial directory, which has been called "the cream of the crop" by *School Library Journal* and the "best available reference source" by *Guide to Reference.* 552 pages. ISBN 1588412164. $45, plus $7 shipping.

Financial Aid for African Americans
Nearly 1,300 funding opportunities open to African American college students, professionals, and postdoctorates are described in this award-winning directory. 490 pages. ISBN 1588412172. $42.50, plus $7 shipping.

Financial Aid for Asian Americans
This is the source to use if you are looking for funding for Asian Americans, from college-bound high school seniors to professionals and postdoctorates; more than 900 sources of free money are described here. 350 pages. ISBN 1588412180. $40, plus $7 shipping.

Financial Aid for Hispanic Americans
The 1,100 biggest and best sources of free money available to undergraduates, graduates students, professionals, and postdoctorates of Mexican, Puerto Rican, Central American, or other Latin American heritage are described here. 446 pages. ISBN 1588412199. $42.50, plus $7 shipping.

Financial Aid for Native Americans
Detailed information is provided on nearly 1,400 funding opportunities open to American Indians, Native Alaskans, and Native Pacific Islanders for college, graduate school, or professional activities. 506 pages. ISBN 1588412202. $45, plus $7 shipping.

Financial Aid for Research and Creative Activities Abroad
Described here are more than 1,000 scholarships, fellowships, grants, etc. available to support research, professional, or creative activities abroad. 422 pages. ISBN 1588412067. $45, plus $7 shipping.

Financial Aid for Study and Training Abroad
This directory, which the reviewers call "invaluable," describes nearly 1,000 financial aid opportunities available to support study abroad. 362 pages. ISBN 1588412059. $40, plus $7 shipping.

Financial Aid for Veterans, Military Personnel, & Their Families
According to *Reference Book Review,* this directory (with its 1,100 entries) is "the most comprehensive guide available on the subject." 436 pages. ISBN 1588412091. $40, plus $7 shipping.

High School Senior's Guide to Merit and Other No-Need Funding
Here's your guide to 1,100 funding programs that *never* look at income level when making awards to college-bound high school seniors. 416 pages. ISBN 1588412105. $29.95, plus $7 shipping.

Money for Graduate Students in the Arts & Humanities
Use this directory to identify 1,000 funding opportunities available to support graduate study and research in the arts/humanities. 292 pages. ISBN 1588411974. $42.50, plus $7 shipping

Money for Graduate Students in the Biological Sciences
This unique directory focuses solely on funding for graduate study/research in the biological sciences (800+ funding opportunities). 248 pages. ISBN 1588411982. $37.50, plus $7 shipping.

Money for Graduate Students in the Health Sciences
Described here are 1,000+ funding opportunities just for students interested in a graduate degree in dentistry, medicine, nursing, nutrition, pharmacology, etc. 304 pages. ISBN 1588411990. $42.50, plus $7 shipping.

Money for Graduate Students in the Physical & Earth Sciences
Nearly 900 funding opportunities for graduate students in the physical and earth sciences are described in detail here. 276 pages. ISBN 1588412008. $40, plus $7 shipping.

Money for Graduate Students in the Social & Behavioral Sciences
Looking for money for a graduate degree in the social/behavioral sciences? Here are 1,100 funding programs for you. 316 pages. ISBN 1588412016. $42.50, plus $7 shipping.

Financial Aid for Asian Americans 2012-2014

Gail Ann Schlachter

R. David Weber

A List of Scholarships, Fellowships, Grants, Awards, Internships, and Other Sources of Free Money Available Primarily or Exclusively to Asian Americans, Plus a Set of Six Indexes (Program Title, Sponsoring Organization, Residency, Tenability, Subject, and Deadline Date)

Reference Service Press
El Dorado Hills, California

ISBN 10: 1588412180
ISBN 13: 9781588412188

10 9 8 7 6 5 4 3 2 1

Reference Service Press (RSP) began in 1977 with a single financial aid publication *(The Directory of Financial Aids for Women)* and now specializes in the development of financial aid resources in multiple formats, including books, large print books, disks, CD-ROMs, print-on-demand reports, eBooks, and online sources. Long recognized as a leader in the field, RSP has been called by the *Simba Report on Directory Publishing* "a true success in the world of independent directory publishers." Both Kaplan Educational Centers and Military.com have hailed RSP as "the leading authority on scholarships."

Reference Service Press
El Dorado Hills Business Park
5000 Windplay Drive, Suite 4
El Dorado Hills, CA 95762-9319
    (916) 939-9620
    Fax: (916) 939-9626
    E-mail: info@rspfunding.com
Visit our web site: www.rspfunding.com

Manufactured in the United States of America
Price: $40.00, plus $7 shipping.

ACADEMIC INSTITUTIONS, LIBRARIES, ORGANIZATIONS AND OTHER QUANTITY BUYERS:
Discounts on this book are available for bulk purchases. Write or call for information on our discount programs.

Contents

Introduction

WHY THIS DIRECTORY IS NEEDED

Despite our country's ongoing economic problems and increased college costs, the financial aid picture for minorities has never looked brighter. Currently, billions of dollars are set aside each year specifically for Asian Americans, African Americans, Hispanic Americans, and Native Americans. This funding is open to minorities at any level (high school through postdoctoral and professional) for a variety of activities, including study, research, travel, training, career development, and creative projects.

While numerous print or online listings have been prepared to identify and describe general financial aid opportunities (those open to all segments of society), those resources have never covered more than a small portion of the programs designed primarily or exclusively for minorities. As a result, many advisors, librarians, scholars, researchers, and students are often unaware of the extensive funding available to Asian Americans and other minorities. But, with the ongoing publication of *Financial Aid for Asian Americans,* that has all changed. Here, in just one place, Asian American students, professionals, and postdoctorates now have current and detailed information about the special resources set aside specifically for them.

Financial Aid for Asian Americans is prepared biennially as part of Reference Service Press' four-volume *Minority Funding Set* (the other volumes in the set cover funding for African Americans, Hispanic Americans, and Native Americans). Each of the volumes in this set is sold separately, or the complete set can be purchased at a discounted price. For more information, contact Reference Service Press's marketing department or visit www.rspfunding.com/prod_prodalpha.html.

No other source, in print or online, offers the extensive coverage provided by these titles. That's why the Grantsmanship Center labeled the set "a must for every organization serving minorities," *Reference Sources for Small and Medium-Sized Libraries* called the titles "the absolute best guides for finding funding," and *Reference Books Bulletin* selected each of the volumes in the *Minority Funding Set* as their "Editor's Choice." *Financial Aid for Asian Americans,* itself, has also received rave reviews. *Al Jahdid* called the directory "an excellent resource," the Miami-Dade Public Library System included it in its list of "Essential Titles for the College Bound," and *Small Press* found it both "inclusive" and "valuable." Perhaps *Choice* sums up the critical reaction best: "a unique and valuable resource; highly recommended."

WHAT'S UPDATED?

The preparation of each new edition of *Financial Aid for Asian Americans* involves extensive updating and revision. To make sure that the information included here is both reliable and current, the editors at Reference Service Press 1) reviewed and updated all relevant programs covered in the previous edition of the directory, 2) collected information on all programs open to Asian Americans that were added to Reference Service Press' funding database since the last edition of the directory, and then 3) searched extensively for new program leads in a variety of sources, including printed directories, news reports, journals, newsletters, house organs, annual reports, and sites on the Internet. We only include program descriptions that are written directly from information supplied by the sponsoring organization in print or online (no information is ever taken from secondary sources). When that information could not be found, we sent up to four collection letters (followed by up to three telephone or email inquiries, if necessary) to those sponsors. Despite our best efforts, however, some sponsoring organizations still failed to respond and, as a result, their programs are not included in this edition of the directory.

The 2012-2014 edition of *Financial Aid for Asian Americans* completely revises and updates the previous (sixth) edition. Programs that have ceased operations have been dropped from the listing. Similarly, programs that have broadened their scope and no longer focus on Asian Americans have also been removed from the listing. Profiles of continuing programs have been rewritten to reflect current requirements; nearly 75 percent of the continuing programs reported substantive changes in their locations, requirements (particularly application deadline), benefits, or eligibility requirements since the 2009-2011 edition. In addition, more than 250 new entries have been added to the program section of the directory. The resulting listing describes the 925 biggest and best sources of free money available to Asian Americans, including scholarships, fellowships, grants, awards, and internships.

WHAT MAKES THIS DIRECTORY UNIQUE?

The 2012-2014 edition of *Financial Aid for Asian Americans* will help Americans with origins from Asia or subcontinent Asia and Pacific island nations (e.g., Japan, China, the Philippines, Vietnam, Korea, Laos, Cambodia, Taiwan, Burma, Thailand, Malaysia, Indonesia, Singapore, Brunei, Macao, Hong Kong, India, Pakistan, Bangladesh, Tonga) tap into the billions of dollars available to them, as minorities, to support study, research, creative activities, past accomplishments, future projects, professional development, work experience, and many other activities. The listings cover every major subject area, are sponsored by more than 750 different private and public agencies and organizations, and are open to Asian Americans at any level, from college-bound high school students through professionals and postdoctorates.

Not only does *Financial Aid for Asian Americans* provide the most comprehensive coverage of available funding (925 entries), but it also displays the most informative program descriptions (on the average, more than twice the detail found in any other listing). In addition to this extensive and focused coverage, *Financial Aid for Asian Americans* also offers several other unique features. First of all, hundreds of funding opportunities listed here have never been covered in any other source. So, even if you have checked elsewhere, you will want to look at *Financial Aid for Asian Americans* for additional leads. And, here's another plus: all of the funding programs in this edition of the directory offer "free" money; not one of the programs will ever require you to pay anything back (provided, of course, that you meet the program requirements).

Further, unlike other funding directories, which generally follow a straight alphabetical arrangement, *Financial Aid for Asian Americans* groups entries by intended recipients (undergraduates, graduate students, or professionals/postdoctorates), to make it easy for you to search for appropriate programs. This same convenience is offered in the indexes, where title, sponsoring organization, geographic, subject, and deadline date entries are each subdivided by recipient group.

Finally, we have tried to anticipate all the ways you might wish to search for funding. The volume is organized so you can identify programs not only by intended recipient, but by subject focus, sponsoring organization, program title, residency requirements, where the money can be spent, and even deadline date. Plus, we've included all the information you'll need to decide if a program is right for you: purpose, eligibility requirements, financial data, duration, special features, limitations, number awarded, and application date. You even get fax numbers, toll-free numbers, e-mail addresses, and web sites (when available), along with complete contact information.

WHAT'S EXCLUDED?

While this book is intended to be the most comprehensive source of information on funding available to Asian Americans, there are some programs we've specifically excluded from the directory:

- *Programs that do not accept applications from U.S. citizens or residents.* If a program is open only to foreign nationals or excludes Americans from applying, it is not covered.

- *Programs that are open equally to all segments of the population.* Only funding opportunities set aside primarily or exclusively for Asian Americans are included here.

SAMPLE ENTRY

(1) **[49]**

(2) **BRUCE LEE SCHOLARSHIP**

(3) US Pan Asian American Chamber of Commerce
Attn: Scholarship Coordinator
1329 18th Street, N.W.
Washington, DC 20036
(202) 296-5221   Toll-free: (800) 696-7818
E-mail: info@uspaacc.com
Web: www.uspaacc.com

(4) **Summary** To provide financial assistance for college to Asian Pacific American high school seniors who have persevered over adversity.

(5) **Eligibility** This program is open to high school seniors of Asian or Pacific Islander heritage who are U.S. citizens or permanent residents. Applicants must be planning to enroll full time at an accredited postsecondary educational institution in the United States. Along with their application, they must submit a 500-word essay on the adversities they have overcome. Selection is based on academic excellence (GPA of 3.3 or higher), character, ability to persevere and prevail over adversity, community service involvement, and financial need.

(6) **Financial data** The maximum stipend is $5,000. Funds are paid directly to the recipient's college or university.

(7) **Duration** 1 year.

(8) **Additional information** Funding is not provided for correspondence courses, Internet courses, or study in a country other than the United States.

(9) **Number awarded** 1 or more each year.

(10) **Deadline** March of each year.

DEFINITION

(1) **Entry number:** The consecutive number that is given to each entry and used to identify the entry in the index.

(2) **Program title:** Title of scholarship, fellowship, grant, award, internship or other source of free money described in the directory.

(3) **Sponsoring organization:** Name, address, and telephone number, toll-free number, fax number, e-mail address, and/or web site (when information was available) for organization sponsoring the program.

(4) **Summary:** Identifies the major program requirements; read the rest of the entry for additional detail.

(5) **Eligibility:** Qualifications required of applicants, plus information on application procedure and selection process.

(6) **Financial data:** Financial details of the program, including fixed sum, average amount, or range of funds offered, expenses for which funds may and may not be applied, and cash-related benefits supplied (e.g., room and board).

(7) **Duration:** Period for which support is provided; renewal prospects.

(8) **Additional information:** Any unusual (generally nonmonetary) benefits, features, restrictions, or limitations associated with the program.

(9) **Number awarded:** Total number of recipients each year or other specified period.

(10) **Deadline:** The month by which applications must be submitted.

- *Money for study or research outside the United States.* Since there are comprehensive and up-to-date directories that describe the available funding for study, research, and other activities abroad, (see the list of Reference Service Press titles opposite the directory's title page), only programs that fund activities in the United States are covered here.

- *Very restrictive programs.* In general, programs are excluded if they are open only to a limited geographic area (less than a state) or offer limited financial support (less than $500). Note, however, that the vast majority of programs included here go way beyond that, paying up to full tuition or stipends that exceed $20,000 a year!

- *Programs administered by individual academic institutions solely for their own students.* The directory identifies "portable" programs—ones that can be used at any number of schools. Financial aid administered by individual schools specifically for their own students is not covered. Write directly to the schools you are considering to get information on their offerings.

- *Money that must be repaid.* Only "free money" is identified here. If a program requires repayment or charges interest, it's not listed. Now you can find out about billions of dollars in aid and know (if you meet the program requirements) that not one dollar of that will ever need to be repaid.

HOW THE DIRECTORY IS ORGANIZED

Financial Aid for Asian Americans is divided into two sections: 1) a detailed list of funding opportunities open to Asian Americans and 2) a set of six indexes to help you pinpoint appropriate funding programs.

Financial Aid Programs Open to Asian Americans. The first section of the directory describes more than 900 sources of free money available to Asian Americans. The focus is on financial aid aimed at American citizens or residents to support study, research, or other activities in the United States. The programs listed here are sponsored by more than 750 different government agencies, professional organizations, corporations, sororities and fraternities, foundations, religious groups, educational associations, and military/veterans organizations. All areas of the sciences, social sciences, and humanities are covered.

To help you focus your search, the entries in this section are grouped into the following three chapters:

- **Undergraduates:** Included here are nearly 400 scholarships, grants, awards, internships, and other sources of free money that support undergraduate study, training, research, or creative activities. These programs are open to high school seniors, high school graduates, currently-enrolled college students, and students returning to college after an absence. Money is available to support these students in any type of public or private postsecondary institution, ranging from technical schools and community colleges to major universities in the United States.

- **Graduate Students:** Described here are more than 400 fellowships, grants, awards, internships, and other sources of free money that support post-baccalaureate study, training, research, and creative activities. These programs are open to students applying to, currently enrolled in, or returning to a master's, doctoral, professional, or specialist program in public or private graduate schools in the United States.

- **Professionals/Postdoctorates:** Included here are nearly 125 funding programs for U.S. citizens or residents who 1) are in professional positions (e.g., artists, writers), whether or not they have an advanced degree; 2) are master's or professional degree recipients; 3) have earned a doctoral degree or its equivalent (e.g., Ph.D., Ed.D., M.D.); or 4) have recognized stature as established scientists, scholars, academicians, or researchers.

Within each of these three chapters, entries appear alphabetically by program title. Since some of the programs supply assistance to more than one specific group, those are listed in all relevant chapters. For example, the Asian American Architects and Engineers Foundation Scholarships support both undergraduate or graduate study, so the program is described in both the Undergraduates *and* Graduate Students chapters.

Each program entry has been designed to give you a concise profile that, as the sample on page 7 illustrates, includes information (when available) on organization address and telephone numbers (including toll-free and fax numbers), e-mail addresses and web site, purpose, eligibility, money awarded, duration, special features, limitations, number of awards, and application deadline.

The information reported for each of the programs in this section was gathered from research conducted through the beginning of 2012. While the listing is intended to cover as comprehensively as possible the biggest and best sources of free money available to Native Americans, some sponsoring organizations did not post information online or respond to our research inquiries and, consequently, are not included in this edition of the directory.

Indexes. To help you find the aid you need, we have constructed six indexes; these will let you access the listings by program title, sponsoring organization, residency, tenability, subject focus, and deadline date. These indexes use a word-by-word alphabetical arrangement. Note: numbers in the index refer to entry numbers, not to page numbers in the book.

Program Title Index. If you know the name of a particular funding program and want to find out where it is covered in the directory, use the Program Title Index. To assist you in your search, every program is listed by all its known names, former names, and abbreviations. Since one program can be included in more than one place (e.g., a program providing assistance to both undergraduate and graduate students is described in both the first and second chapter), each entry number in the index has been coded to indicate the intended recipient group (for example, "U" = Undergraduates; "G" = Graduate Students). By using this coding system, you can avoid duplicate entries and turn directly to the programs that match your eligibility characteristics.

Sponsoring Organization Index. This index makes it easy to identify agencies that offer funding primarily or exclusively to Asian Americans. More than 750 organizations are indexed here. As in the Program Title Index, we've used a code to help you determine which organizations sponsor programs that match your educational level.

Residency Index. Some programs listed in this book are restricted to Asian Americans in a particular state or region. Others are open to Asian Americans wherever they live. This index helps you identify programs available only to residents in your area as well as programs that have no residency requirements. Further, to assist you in your search, we've also indicated the recipient level for the funding offered to residents in each of the areas listed in the index.

Tenability Index. This index identifies the geographic locations where the funding described in *Financial Aid for Asian Americans* may be used. Index entries (city, county, state, region) are arranged alphabetically (word by word) and subdivided by recipient group. Use this index when you are looking for money to support your activities in a particular geographic area.

Subject Index. This index allows you to identify the subject focus of each of the financial aid opportunities described in *Financial Aid for Asian Americans*. More than 200 different subject terms are listed. Extensive "see" and "see also" references, as well as recipient group subdivisions, will help you locate appropriate funding opportunities.

Calendar Index. Since most financial aid programs have specific deadline dates, some may have closed by the time you begin to look for funding. You can use the Calendar Index to determine which programs are still open. This index is arranged by recipient group (Undergraduates, Graduate Students, and Professionals/Postdoctorates) and subdivided by month during which the deadline falls. Filing dates can and quite often do vary from year to year; consequently, this index should be used only as a guide for deadlines beyond 2014.

HOW TO USE THE DIRECTORY

Here are some tips to help you get the most out of the funding opportunities listed in *Financial Aid for Asian Americans.*

To Locate Funding by Recipient Group. To bring together programs with a similar educational focus, this directory is divided into three chapters: Undergraduates, Graduate Students, and Professionals/Postdoctorates. If you want to get an overall picture of the sources of free money available to Asian Americans in any of these categories, turn to the appropriate chapter and then review the entries there. Since each of these chapters functions as a self-contained entity, you can browse through any of them without having to first consulting an index.

To Find Information on a Particular Financial Aid Program. If you know the name of a particular financial aid program, and the group eligible for that award, then go directly to the appropriate chapter in the directory (e.g., Undergraduates, Graduate Students), where you will find the program profiles arranged alphabetically by title. To save time, though, you should always check the Program Title Index first if you know the name of a specific award but are not sure in which chapter it has been listed. Plus, since we index each program by all its known names and abbreviations, you'll also be able to track down a program there when you only know the popular rather than official name.

To Locate Programs Sponsored by a Particular Organization. The Sponsoring Organization Index makes it easy to identify agencies that provide financial assistance to Asian Americans or to identify specific financial aid programs offered by a particular organization. Each entry number in the index is coded to identify recipient group (Undergraduates, Graduate Students, Professionals/Postdoctorates), so that you can easily target appropriate entries.

To Browse Quickly Through the Listings. Look at the listings in the chapter that relates to you (Undergraduates, Graduate Students, or Professionals/Postdoctorates) and read the "Summary" paragraph in each entry. In seconds, you'll know if this is an opportunity that you might want to pursue. If it is, be sure to read the rest of the information in the entry, to make sure you meet all of the program requirements before writing or going online for an application form. Please, save your time and energy. Don't apply if you don't qualify!

To Locate Funding Available to Asian Americans from or Tenable in a Particular City, County, or State. The Residency Index identifies financial aid programs open to Asian Americans in a specific state, region, etc. The Tenability Index shows where the money can be spent. In both indexes, "see" and "see also" references are used liberally, and index entries for a particular geographic area are subdivided by recipient group (Undergraduates, Graduate Students, and Professionals/Postdoctorates) to help you identify the funding that's right for you. When using these indexes, always check the listings under the term "United States," since the programs indexed there have no geographic restrictions and can be used in any area.

To Locate Financial Aid Programs Open to Asian Americans in a Particular Subject Area. Turn to the Subject Index first if you are interested in identifying funding programs for Asian Americans that are focused on a particular subject area (more than 200 different subject fields are listed there). To make your search easier, the intended recipient groups (Undergraduates, Graduate Students, Professionals/Postdoctorates) are clearly labeled in the more than 225 subject listings. Extensive cross-references are also provided. Since a large number of programs are not restricted by subject, be sure to check the references listed under the "General programs" heading in the index, in addition to the specific terms that directly relate to your interest areas. The listings under "General programs" can be used to fund activities in any subject area (although the programs may be restricted in other ways).

To Locate Financial Aid Programs for Asian Americans by Deadline Date. If you are working with specific time constraints and want to weed out the financial aid programs whose filing dates you won't be able to meet, turn first to the Calendar Index and check the program references listed under the appropriate recipient group and month. Note: not all sponsoring organizations supplied deadline information; those programs are listed under the "Deadline not specified" entries in the index. To identify every relevant financial aid program, regardless of filing date, go the appropriate chapter and read through all the entries there that match your educational level.

To Locate Financial Aid Programs Open to All Segments of the Population. Only programs available to Asian Americans are listed in this publication. However, there are thousands of other programs that are open equally to all segments of the population. To identify these programs, talk to your local librarian, check with your financial aid office on campus, look at the list of RSP print resources on the page opposite the title page in this directory, or see if your library subscribes to Reference Service Press' interactive online funding database (for more information on that resource, go online to: www.rspfunding.com/esubscriptions.html).

PLANS TO UPDATE THE DIRECTORY

This volume, covering 2012-2014, is the seventh edition of *Financial Aid for Asian Americans.* The next biennial edition will cover the years 2014-2016 and will be issued in mid-2014.

OTHER RELATED PUBLICATIONS

In addition to *Financial Aid for Asian Americans,* Reference Service Press publishes several other titles dealing with fundseeking, including the award-winning *Directory of Financial Aids for Women; Financial Aid for the Disabled and Their Families;* and *Financial Aid for Veterans, Military Personnel, and Their Families.* Since each of these titles focuses on a separate population group, there is very little duplication in the listings. For more information on Reference Service Press' award-winning publications, write to the company at 5000 Windplay Drive, Suite 4, El Dorado Hills, CA 95762, give us a call at (916) 939-9620, fax us at (916) 939-9626, send us an e-mail at info@rspfunding.com, or visit our expanded web site: www.rspfunding.com.

ACKNOWLEDGEMENTS

A debt of gratitude is owed all the organizations that contributed information to the 2012-2014 edition of *Financial Aid for Asian Americans.* Their generous cooperation has helped to make this publication a current and comprehensive survey of awards.

ABOUT THE AUTHORS

Dr. Gail Ann Schlachter has worked for more than three decades as a library manager, a library educator, and an administrator of library-related publishing companies. Among the reference books to her credit are the biennially-issued *Directory of Financial Aids for Women* and two award-winning bibliographic guides: *Minorities and Women: A Guide to Reference Literature in the Social Sciences* (which was chosen as an "outstanding reference book of the year" by *Choice)* and *Reference Sources in Library and Information Services* (which won the first Knowledge Industry Publications "Award for Library Literature"). She was the reference book review editor for *RQ* (now *Reference and User Services Quarterly)* for 10 years, is a past president of the American Library Association's Reference and User Services Association, is the former editor-in-chief of the *Reference and User Services Association Quarterly,* and is currently serving her fifth term on the American Library Association's governing council. In recognition of her outstanding contributions to reference service, Dr. Schlachter has been named the University of Wisconsin School of Library and Information Studies "Alumna of the Year" and has been awarded both the Isadore Gilbert Mudge Citation and the Louis Shores/Oryx Press Award.

Dr. R. David Weber taught history and economics at Los Angeles Harbor College (in Wilmington, California) for many years and continues to teach history as an emeritus professor. During his years of full-time teaching there, and at East Los Angeles College, he directed the Honors Program and was frequently chosen the "Teacher of the Year." He has written a number of critically-acclaimed reference works, including *Dissertations in Urban History* and the three-volume *Energy Information Guide.* With Gail Schlachter, he is the author of Reference Service Press' *Financial Aid for the Disabled and Their Families,* which was selected by *Library Journal* as one of the "best reference books of the year," and a number of other financial aid titles, including the *College Student's Guide to Merit and Other No-Need Funding,* which was chosen as one of the "outstanding reference books of the year" by *Choice.*

Financial Aid Programs Open to Asian Americans

Undergraduates •

Graduate Students •

Professionals/Postdoctorates •

Undergraduates

Listed alphabetically by program title and described in detail here are 383 scholarships, grants, awards, internships, and other sources of "free money" set aside for college-bound high school seniors and continuing or returning undergraduate students of Asian origins (including those of subcontinent Asian and Pacific Islander descent). This funding is available to support study, training, research, and/or creative activities in the United States.

year at an accredited college or university in the United States and have a GPA of 3.0 or higher. Selection is based on academic ability.

Financial data The stipend is $2,000.

Duration 1 year.

Additional information This program was established by the Association of National Advertisers (ANA) in 2001. The American Association of Advertising Agencies (AAAA) assumed administration in 2003.

Number awarded 3 each year.

Deadline Deadline not specified.

[22]
ANGELFIRE SCHOLARSHIP

Datatel Scholars Foundation
4375 Fair Lakes Court
Fairfax, VA 22033
(703) 968-9000, ext. 4549   Toll Free: (800) 486-4332
Fax: (703) 968-4625   E-mail: scholars@datatel.com
Web: www.datatelscholars.org

Summary To provide financial assistance to graduating high school seniors, continuing college students, and graduate students who will be studying at a Datatel client school and are veterans, veterans' dependents, or refugees from southeast Asia.

Eligibility This program is open to 1) veterans who served in the Asian theater (Vietnam, Cambodia, or Laos) between 1964 and 1975; 2) their spouses and children; 3) refugees from Vietnam, Cambodia, or Laos; and 4) veterans who served in Operation Desert Storm, Operation Enduring Freedom, and/or Operation Iraqi Freedom. Applicants must attend a Datatel client college or university during the upcoming school year as a full- or part-time undergraduate or graduate student. They must first apply to their institution, which selects 2 semifinalists and forwards their applications to the sponsor. Along with their application, they must include a 1,000-word personal statement that discusses how the conflict has affected them personally, summarizes how the conflict has impacted their educational goals, and describes how being awarded this scholarship will help them achieve their goals. Selection is based on the quality of the personal statement (60%) and academic merit (40%).

Financial data The stipend is $1,700. Funds are paid directly to the institution.

Duration 1 year.

Additional information Datatel, Inc. produces advanced information technology solutions for higher education. It has more than 750 client sites in the United States and Canada. This scholarship was created to commemorate those who lost their lives in Vietnam or Iraq and is named after a memorial administered by the Disabled American Veterans Association in Angelfire, New Mexico.

Number awarded 10 each year.

Deadline Students must submit online applications to their institution or organization by January of each year.

[23]
ANS ACCELERATOR APPLICATIONS DIVISION SCHOLARSHIP

American Nuclear Society
Attn: Scholarship Coordinator
555 North Kensington Avenue
La Grange Park, IL 60526-5592
(708) 352-6611   Toll Free: (800) 323-3044
Fax: (708) 352-0499   E-mail: outreach@ans.org
Web: www.ans.org/honors/scholarships/aad.html

Summary To provide financial assistance to undergraduate students (particularly Asian Americans, other minorities, and women) who are interested in preparing for a career dealing with accelerator applications aspects of nuclear science or nuclear engineering.

Eligibility This program is open to students entering their junior year in physics, engineering, or materials science at an accredited institution in the United States. Applicants must submit a description of their long- and short-term professional objectives, including their research interests related to accelerator aspects of nuclear science and engineering. Selection is based on that statement, faculty recommendations, and academic performance. Special consideration is given to members of underrepresented groups (women and minorities), students who can demonstrate financial need, and applicants who have a record of service to the American Nuclear Society (ANS).

Financial data The stipend is $1,000 per year.

Duration 1 year (the junior year); may be renewed for the senior year.

Additional information This program is offered by the Accelerator Applications Division (AAD) of the ANS.

Number awarded 1 each year.

Deadline January of each year.

[24]
ANSP RESEARCH EXPERIENCES FOR UNDERGRADUATES FELLOWSHIPS

Academy of Natural Sciences of Philadelphia
Attn: REU Coordinator
1900 Benjamin Franklin Parkway
Philadelphia, PA 19103-1195
(215) 299-1000   Fax: (215) 299-1028
E-mail: reucoordinator@ansp.org
Web: www.ansp.org/research/opportunities/reu.php

Summary To provide undergraduate students from any state (particularly Asian Americans, other minorities, women, and individuals with disabilities) with an opportunity to participate in a research internship during the summer at the Academy of Natural Sciences of Philadelphia.

Eligibility This program is open to U.S. citizens and permanent residents who are entering their sophomore, junior, or senior year at a college or university. Applicants must be interested in working on a research project under the mentorship of an academy scientist in biogeochemistry, botany, database programming, entomology, evolutionary systematics (molecular studies), fisheries, ichthyology, malacology, natural history and museum studies, paleontology, phycology, science library research, or stream ecology. Applications are encouraged from women, minorities, and students with disabilities.

Financial data The program covers travel to and from Philadelphia, housing, supplies, field trips, and research, and provides a stipend of $350 per week.

Duration 10 weeks, beginning in June.

Additional information This program is funded by the National Science Foundation as part of its Research Experiences for Undergraduates (REU) Program.

Number awarded Varies each year.

Deadline February of each year.

[25]
APAICS SUMMER INTERNSHIPS

Asian Pacific American Institute for Congressional
  Studies
Attn: Summer Internship Program
1001 Connecticut Avenue, N.W., Suite 530
Washington, DC 20036
(202) 296-9200   Fax: (202) 296-9236
E-mail: apaics@apaics.org
Web: www.apaics.org

Summary To provide an opportunity for undergraduate students with an interest in issues affecting the Asian Pacific Islander American communities to work in Washington, D.C. during the summer.

Eligibility This program is open to Asian American and Pacific Islander students currently enrolled in an accredited undergraduate institution; recent (within 90 days) graduates are also eligible. Applicants must be able to demonstrate interest in the political process, public policy issues, and Asian American and Pacific Islander community affairs; leadership abilities; and oral and written communication skills. They must be 18 years of age or older; U.S. citizens or permanent residents; and interested in working in Congress, federal agencies, or institutions that further the mission of the Asian Pacific American Institute for Congressional Studies (APAICS). Preference is given to students who have not previously had an internship in Washington, D.C.

Financial data The stipend is $2,500 for interns from the continental United States or $3,000 for interns from Hawaii.

Duration 8 weeks, starting in June.

Number awarded Varies each year; recently, 9 interns were selected for this program.

Deadline January of each year.

[26]
APIO SCHOLARSHIP PROGRAM

Asian Pacific Islander Organization
P.O. Box 2391
Billings, MT 59103
Web: www.apio.org/scholarship.htm

Summary To provide financial assistance to Asian and Pacific Islanders who are studying designated fields in college.

Eligibility This program is open to Asian and Pacific Islander students who have completed at least 15 semester hours of credit at an accredited 2- or 4-year college or university. Applicants must be working on a degree in a field related to natural resources (e.g., agricultural business, agronomy, botany, environmental science, forestry, geology, horticulture, plant science, rangeland management, soil science, or agricultural, civil, or environmental engineering). Along with their

application, they must submit a 1-page personal statement on their background, personal and career goals, and extracurricular activities. Selection is based on academic achievement, personal strengths, leadership abilities, career goals, and work experience. U.S. citizenship is required.

Financial data The stipend is $1,000.

Duration 1 year.

Additional information The Asian Pacific Islander Organization (APIO) was established in 1998 as a professional society of employees of the Natural Resources Conservation Service of the U.S. Department of Agriculture.

Number awarded 3 each year.

Deadline February of each year.

[27]
APPRAISAL INSTITUTE MINORITIES AND WOMEN EDUCATIONAL SCHOLARSHIP PROGRAM

Appraisal Institute
Attn: Appraisal Institute Education Trust
200 West Madison Street, Suite 1500
Chicago, IL 60606
(312) 335-4133   Fax: (312) 335-4134
E-mail: educationtrust@appraisalinstitute.org
Web: www.appraisalinstitute.org

Summary To provide financial assistance to Asian Americans, other minorities, and women who are majoring in real estate or allied fields.

Eligibility This program is open to members of groups underrepresented in the real estate appraisal profession. Those groups include women, American Indians, Alaska Natives, Asians and Pacific Islanders, Blacks or African Americans, and Hispanics. Applicants must be full- or part-time students enrolled in real estate courses within a degree-granting college, university, or junior college. They must have a GPA of 2.5 or higher and be able to demonstrate financial need. U.S. citizenship is required.

Financial data The stipend is $1,000. Funds are paid directly to the recipient's institution to be used for tuition and fees.

Duration 1 year.

Number awarded At least 1 each year.

Deadline April of each year.

[28]
ARKANSAS CONFERENCE ETHNIC LOCAL CHURCH CONCERNS SCHOLARSHIPS

United Methodist Church-Arkansas Conference
Attn: Committee on Ethnic Local Church Concerns
800 Daisy Bates Drive
Little Rock, AR 72202
(501) 324-8045   Toll Free: (877) 646-1816
Fax: (501) 324-8018   E-mail: mallen@arumc.org
Web: www.arumc.org

Summary To provide financial assistance to Asian American and other minority Methodist students from Arkansas who are interested in attending college or graduate school in any state.

Eligibility This program is open to ethnic minority undergraduate and graduate students who are active members of local congregations affiliated with the Arkansas Conference of the United Methodist Church (UMC). Applicants must be currently enrolled in an accredited institution of higher education in any state. Along with their application, they must submit a transcript (GPA of 2.0 or higher) and documentation of participation in local church activities. Preference is given to students attending a UMC-affiliated college or university.

Financial data The stipend is $500 per semester ($1,000 per year) for undergraduates or $1,000 per semester ($2,000 per year) for graduate students.

Duration 1 year; may be renewed.

Number awarded 1 or more each year.

Deadline September of each year.

[29]
ARKANSAS MINORITY TEACHERS SCHOLARSHIPS

Arkansas Department of Higher Education
Attn: Financial Aid Division
114 East Capitol Avenue
Little Rock, AR 72201-3818
(501) 371-2050   Toll Free: (800) 54-STUDY
Fax: (501) 371-2001   E-mail: finaid@adhe.edu
Web: www.adhe.edu

Summary To provide funding to Asian American and other minority undergraduates in Arkansas who want to become teachers in the state.

Eligibility This program is open to minority (African American, Native American, Hispanic, or Asian American) residents of Arkansas who are U.S. citizens or permanent residents and enrolled full time as juniors or seniors in an approved teacher certification program at an Arkansas public or independent 4-year institution. Applicants must have a cumulative GPA of 2.5 or higher and be willing to teach in an Arkansas public school for at least 5 years after completion of their teaching certificate (3 years if the teaching is in 1 of the 42 counties of Arkansas designated as the Delta Region, or if the teaching is in a critical subject shortage area, or if the recipient is an African American male teaching at the elementary level).

Financial data Loans up to $5,000 per year are available. The loan will be forgiven at the rate of 20% for each year the recipient teaches full time in an Arkansas public school (or 33% per year if the obligation is fulfilled in 3 years). If the loan is not forgiven by service, it must be repaid with interest at 10%.

Duration 1 year; may be renewed for 1 additional year if the recipient remains enrolled full time with a GPA of 2.5 or higher.

Additional information Recently, the critical subject shortage areas included art (K-12), foreign language (French, German, Spanish), mathematics (secondary), middle childhood (4-8 mathematics and science, 4-8 English language arts or social studies), science (secondary life or physical), or special education (deaf education, visually impaired, instructional specialist).

Number awarded Varies each year; recently, 97 of these forgivable loans were approved.

Deadline May of each year.

[30]
ARSENIO AND CO BIT SIY SCHOLARSHIP

Organization of Chinese Americans-Wisconsin Chapter
Attn: Scholarship Committee
P.O. Box 301
Dousman, WI 53118
(414) 258-2410   E-mail: ocawischolarship@yahoo.com
Web: www.ocawi.org

Summary To provide financial assistance to high school seniors who are children of members or business affiliates of the Wisconsin Chapter of the Organization of Chinese Americans (OCA-WI) and interested in attending college in any state.

Eligibility This program is open to graduating high school seniors whose parent has been an OCA-WI member or business affiliate for at least 2 years and who are planning to enroll full time at an accredited college or university in any state. Applicants must have a GPA of 3.0 or higher. Along with their application, they must submit a personal statement that includes information on their future college and career plans; a list of scholastic awards, honors, extracurricular activities, and honor societies and offices; and a description of their volunteer service to OCA-WI and their community. Financial need is not considered in the selection process.

Financial data A stipend is awarded (amount not specified).

Duration 1 year.

Additional information This program was established in 1993.

Number awarded 1 each year.

Deadline March of each year.

[31]
ASEI UNDERGRADUATE SCHOLARSHIPS

American Society of Engineers of Indian Origin
Attn: Southern California Chapter
P.O. Box 466
Cypress, CA 90630
E-mail: scholarships@aseisocal.net
Web: www.aseisocal.net/12.html

Summary To provide financial assistance to undergraduate students of Indian origin (from India) who are majoring in engineering, computer sciences, or related areas.

Eligibility This program is open to undergraduate students of Indian origin (by birth, ancestry, or relation). They must be enrolled full time at an ABET-accredited college or university in the United States and majoring in engineering, computer science, or allied science and have a GPA of 3.2 or higher. They must be members of the American Society of Engineers of Indian Origin (ASEI). Selection is based on demonstrated ability, academic achievement (including GPA, honors, and awards), career objectives, faculty recommendations, involvement in science fair and campus activities, industrial exposure (including part-time work and internships), and involvement in ASEI and other community activities.

Financial data Stipends range from $500 to $1,000.

Duration 1 year.

Number awarded Several each year.

Deadline August of each year.

[32]
ASIAN AMERICAN ARCHITECTS AND ENGINEERS FOUNDATION SCHOLARSHIPS

Asian American Architects/Engineers Association
Attn: Foundation
11301 West Olympic Boulevard, Suite 387
Los Angeles, CA 90064
(213) 896-9270 Fax: (866) 276-1712
E-mail: info@aaaesc.org
Web: www.aaaesc.org

Summary To provide financial assistance to members of the Asian American Architects/Engineers Association (AAa/e) who are interested in working on an undergraduate or graduate degree at a school in southern California.

Eligibility This program is open to student members of AAa/e who are U.S. citizens, permanent residents, or noncitizens enrolled full time at a college or university in southern California. Applicants must be graduating seniors, undergraduates, or graduate students working on or planning to work on a degree in architecture, civil engineering (environmental, geotechnical, structural, transportation), electrical engineering, mechanical engineering, landscape architecture or planning and urban design, or construction and construction management. Along with their application, they must submit 1) a 1-page personal statement on their involvement and service to the Asian Pacific Islander community; 2) letters of recommendation from 2 faculty members or employers; and 3) a sample of their work, which may be a design or research project, a completed project, or a proposed project, including an assignment from a class, a senior project, or an assignment from work. Financial need is not considered in the selection process.

Financial data Stipends are $2,500 or $1,500.

Duration 1 year.

Number awarded At least 3 each year: 1 at $2,500 and at least 2 at $1,500.

Deadline July of each year.

[33]
ASIAN AMERICAN COMMUNITY COLLEGE SCHOLARSHIP

Scholarship Administrative Services, Inc.
Attn: MEFUSA Program
457 Ives Terrace
Sunnyvale, CA 94087

Summary To provide financial assistance to Asian American high school seniors who are interested in attending a community college.

Eligibility This program is open to Asian American seniors graduating from high schools anywhere in the United States. Applicants must be planning to attend a community college on a full-time basis. Along with their application, they must submit a 1,000-word essay on their educational and career goals, how a community college education will help them to achieve those goals, and how they plan to serve the Asian American community after completing their education. Selection is based on the essay, high school GPA (2.5 or higher), SAT or ACT scores, involvement in the Asian American community, and financial need.

Financial data The stipend is $5,000 per year.

Duration 1 year; may be renewed 1 additional year if the recipient maintains full-time enrollment and a GPA of 2.5 or higher.

Additional information This program is sponsored by the Minority Educational Foundation of the United States of America (MEFUSA) and administered by Scholarship Administrative Services, Inc. MEFUSA was established in 2001 to meet the needs of minority students who "show a determination to get a college degree," but who, for financial or other personal reasons, are not able to attend a 4-year college or university. Requests for applications should be accompanied by a self-addressed stamped envelope, the student's e-mail address, and the name of the source where they found the scholarship information.

Number awarded Up to 100 each year.

Deadline April of each year.

[34]
ASIAN AMERICAN ESSAY SCHOLARSHIP PROGRAM

Organization of Chinese Americans-New Jersey Chapter
22 West Grand Avenue
P.O. Box 268
Montvale, NJ 07645-0268
(973) 873-8315
Web: www.oca-nj.com/essay-scholarship

Summary To recognize and reward, with college scholarships, high school seniors in New Jersey who are of Asian American descent and submit outstanding essays on what it means to be Asian American.

Eligibility This competition is open to seniors graduating from high schools in New Jersey who are of Asian American descent. Applicants must be planning to attend a college or university in any state. They must submit an essay, from 450 to 500 words, on what it means to be Asian American; essays should describe a personal experience that gave them the feeling of greatest achievement or satisfaction because of the challenges they met as an Asian American. They must also provide personal information and a list of extracurricular activities. Selection is based on theme and content (50%), organization and development (15%), grammar and mechanics (15%), style (10%), and community service and extracurricular activities (10%).

Financial data The award is $1,000.

Duration The competition is held annually.

Additional information Recipients must attend the sponsor's Asian American Heritage Month luncheon in May to accept the award.

Number awarded Approximately 15 each year.

Deadline April of each year.

[35]
ASIAN AMERICAN FOUNDATION OF OREGON SCHOLARSHIPS

Asian American Foundation of Oregon
P.O. Box 51117
Eugene, OR 97405
Web: www.aaforegon.com/scholarships.html

Summary To provide financial assistance to residents of Oregon who have been involved in Asian American cultural activities and are interested in attending college in any state.

Eligibility The program is open to residents of Oregon who have demonstrated interest and effort in Asian American cultural activities. Applicants must be graduating high school seniors or current undergraduate students at a college or university in any state. They must have a GPA of 2.5 or higher. Along with their application, they must submit a 250-word essay that describes their college plans, career interests, relationship to and interest in Asian culture, and/or future commitment to the Asian American community.

Financial data The stipend is $1,000.

Duration 1 year.

Number awarded 2 each year.

Deadline April of each year.

[36]
ASIAN AMERICAN JOURNALISTS ASSOCIATION/NBC SUMMER PARTNERSHIP PROGRAM

Asian American Journalists Association
Attn: Student Programs Coordinator
5 Third Street, Suite 1108
San Francisco, CA 94103
(415) 346-2051, ext. 102 Fax: (415) 346-6343
E-mail: programs@aaja.org
Web: www.aaja.org/programs/internships

Summary To provide an opportunity for student members of the Asian American Journalists Association (AAJA) to work as a summer intern at NBC News.

Eligibility This program is open to AAJA members who are at least sophomores and working on a bachelor's degree at a college or university in the United States. Applicants must have a serious interest in preparing for a career in broadcast journalism; production experience is not required, but it is preferred. They must be interested in working as an intern on an NBC News broadcast or at an NBC locally-owned and operated stations. Along with their application, they must submit 1) a 150-word essay on why they want to prepare for a career in broadcast journalism and what they want to gain from the experience; and 2) a 50-word essay on how they would contribute to AAJA's mission.

Financial data The stipend is $500 per week.

Duration 10 weeks during the summer.

Number awarded 3 each year.

Deadline February of each year.

[37]
ASIAN AMERICAN WRITERS' WORKSHOP INTERNSHIPS

Asian American Writers' Workshop
Attn: Internships
110-112 West 27th Street, Suite 600
New York, NY 10001
(212) 494-0061 Fax: (212) 494-0062
E-mail: desk@aaww.org
Web: www.aaww.org/aboutus_internships.html

Summary To provide summer work experience at an Asian American literary organization to college students and others.

Eligibility This program is open to individuals interested in working at an Asian American literary organization in such assignments as public programs, youth activities, development, and general administration. Preference is given to

applicants with extensive computer experience (HTML, Quark, Photoshop, Filemaker), background or interest in literature, and background or interest in nonprofit organizations. Along with their application, they must submit brief statements on 3 things that they would like to gain from this internship, 5 works of literature that have influenced them, and any skills that make them qualified for this internship.

Financial data Interns receive college credit, free enrollment in a writing workshop, membership in the Asian American Writers' Workshop, and a stipend of $500.

Duration 3 months (from June through August).

Number awarded 1 or more each year.

Deadline April of each year.

[38]
ASIAN PACIFIC FUND HUMAN CAPITAL SCHOLARSHIPS

Asian Pacific Fund
Attn: Scholarship Coordinator
225 Bush Street, Suite 590
San Francisco, CA 94104
(415) 433-6859 Toll Free: (800) 286-1688
Fax: (415) 433-2425
E-mail: scholarship@asianpacificfund.org
Web: www.asianpacificfund.org

Summary To provide financial assistance to Asian American and other minority students enrolling at any campus of the University of California who are the first member of their family to attend college.

Eligibility This program is open to members of minority groups (African American, Asian American, Latino American, or other underrepresented heritage) who are full-time incoming freshmen at a campus of the University of California. Applicants must be first-generation college students. They must have a GPA of 2.7 or higher and be able to demonstrate financial need. Preference is given to students planning to major in the liberal arts. Along with their application, they must submit essays of 250 to 500 words each on 1) their family background and the experiences or values that have led to their plans to become a college graduate; 2) a project, experience, or person related to their academic and career goals that inspired them; and 3) any unusual family or personal circumstances that have affected their achievement in school, work, or school activities.

Financial data The stipend is $1,500.

Duration 1 year; nonrenewable.

Number awarded 2 each year.

Deadline March of each year.

[39]
ASIAN PACIFIC ISLANDER AMERICAN PUBLIC AFFAIRS ASSOCIATION SCHOLARSHIPS

Asian Pacific Islander American Public Affairs Association
Attn: Community Education Foundation
185 Butcher Road
Vacaville, CA 95687
(707) 451-0130 Fax: (707) 451-0131
E-mail: info@apapa.org
Web: www.apapa.org

Summary To provide financial assistance to residents of California, especially those of Asian or Pacific Islander ancestry, who are attending college or graduate school in any state.

Eligibility This program is open to residents of California who are currently enrolled as an undergraduate or graduate student at an accredited 2- or 4-year college or university in any state. All students are eligible, but applications are especially encouraged from those who have Asian or Pacific Islander ancestry. They must have a GPA of 2.75 or higher. Along with their application, they must submit a personal statement demonstrating their commitment to the Asian Pacific Islander community. Selection is based on academic achievement, abilities, career goals, civic activities, leadership skills, and demonstrated commitment to the Asian Pacific Islander community. U.S. citizenship or permanent resident status is required.

Financial data The stipend is $1,000.

Duration 1 year; nonrenewable.

Number awarded 1 or more each year.

Deadline March of each year.

[40]
ASIAN & PACIFIC ISLANDER AMERICAN SCHOLARSHIPS

Asian & Pacific Islander American Scholarship Fund
1900 L Street, N.W., Suite 210
Washington, DC 20036-5002
(202) 986-6892   Toll Free: (877) 808-7032
Fax: (202) 530-0643   E-mail: info@apiasf.org
Web: www.apiasf.org/scholarship_apiasf_list.html

Summary To provide financial assistance to Asian and Pacific Islander Americans who are entering college for the first time.

Eligibility This program is open to U.S. citizens, nationals, permanent residents, and citizens of the Freely Associated States who are first-time incoming college students and of Asian or Pacific Islander heritage. Applicants must be enrolling full time at an accredited 2- or 4-year college or university in the United States. They must have a GPA of 2.7 or higher or the GED equivalent. In addition, they must complete the FAFSA and apply for federal financial aid.

Financial data The stipend is $2,500.

Duration 1 year.

Additional information These scholarships were first offered in 2005. Support for this program is provided by such sponsors as the AT&T Foundation, Darden Restaurants, Honda, MetLife Foundation, Target Stores, and USA Funds.

Number awarded Varies each year; recently, 256 of these scholarships were awarded.

Deadline January of each year.

[41]
ASIAN PACIFIC ISLANDERS FOR PROFESSIONAL AND COMMUNITY ADVANCEMENT SCHOLARSHIPS

Asian Pacific Islanders for Professional and Community Advancement
c/o Suwathin Phiansunthon, Scholarship Committee
P.O. Box 2694
San Ramon, CA 94583
(732) 420-7339   E-mail: info@apca-att.org
Web: www.apca-att.org/scholarship.html

Summary To provide financial assistance to Asian Pacific Islanders and other high school seniors from selected states who are interested in attending college in any state.

Eligibility This program is open to seniors graduating from high schools in Arizona, California, Colorado, Georgia, Michigan, New Jersey, Texas, and Washington, D.C. Applicants must be planning to continue their education at an accredited 2- or 4-year college or university or vocational school in any state. They must have a GPA of 2.75 or higher. Along with their application, they must submit a 750-word essay on making a difference in their community. Financial need is not considered in the selection process. Students of all ethnic backgrounds are eligible, but a goal of the sponsoring organization is to promote growth and influence on issues that impact Asian Pacific Islanders.

Financial data The stipend is $1,500.

Duration 1 year; nonrenewable.

Additional information This program was established by an organization named the Asian/Pacific American Association for Advancement at AT&T, which offered the 4A-AT&T National Scholarship Program. In 2006, that organization merged with Asians for Corporate and Community Action to form Asian Pacific Islanders for Professional and Community Advancement (APCA). Both the former and current organizations are comprised of Asian Pacific American employees of AT&T, Inc.

Number awarded Varies each year; recently, 7 of these scholarships were awarded.

Deadline April of each year.

[42]
ASIAN REPORTER FOUNDATION SCHOLARSHIPS

Asian Reporter
Attn: AR Foundation
922 North Killingsworth Street, Suite 1A
Portland, OR 97217-2220
(503) 283-0595   Fax: (503) 283-4445
E-mail: arfoundation@asianreporter.com
Web: www.arfoundation.net

Summary To provide financial assistance for college to residents of Oregon and Clark County, Washington who are of Asian descent.

Eligibility This program is open to 2 categories of students: 1) Oregon residents attending Oregon schools of higher education; and 2) residents of Oregon or Clark County, Washington attending schools of higher education in Oregon or Washington. Applicants must be of Asian descent, have a GPA of 3.25 or higher, be a graduating high school senior or current college student working on or planning to work on an undergraduate degree as a full-time student, have a record of involvement in community- or school-related activities, and be able to demonstrate financial need.

Financial data The stipend is $1,000.

Duration 1 year; nonrenewable.

Number awarded Varies each year; recently, 7 of these scholarships were awarded.

Deadline March of each year.

[43]
ASIAN STUDENTS INCREASING ACHIEVEMENT (ASIA) SCHOLARSHIP PROGRAM

Ronald McDonald House Charities
Attn: U.S. Scholarship Program
One Kroc Drive
Oak Brook, IL 60523
(630) 623-7048   Fax: (630) 623-7488
E-mail: info@rmhc.org
Web: rmhc.org/what-we-do/rmhc-u-s-scholarships

Summary To provide financial assistance for college to Asian Pacific high school seniors in specified geographic areas.

Eligibility This program is open to high school seniors in designated McDonald's market areas who are legal residents of the United States and have at least 1 parent of Asian Pacific heritage. Applicants must be planning to enroll full time at an accredited 2- or 4-year college, university, or vocational/technical school. They must have a GPA of 2.7 or higher. Along with their application, they must submit a personal statement, up to 2 pages in length, on their Asian Pacific background, career goals, and desire to contribute to their community; information about unique, personal, or financial circumstances may be added. Selection is based on that statement, high school transcripts, a letter of recommendation, and financial need.

Financial data Most awards are $1,000 per year. Funds are paid directly to the recipient's school.

Duration 1 year; nonrenewable.

Additional information This program is a component of the Ronald McDonald House Charities U.S. Scholarship Program, which began in 1985. It is administered by International Scholarship and Tuition Services, Inc. For a list of participating McDonald's market areas, contact Ronald McDonald House Charities.

Number awarded Varies each year; since RMHC this program began, it has awarded more than $37 million in scholarships.

Deadline February of each year.

[44]
ASSE UPS DIVERSITY SCHOLARSHIPS

American Society of Safety Engineers
Attn: ASSE Foundation
1800 East Oakton Street
Des Plaines, IL 60018
(847) 768-3435   Fax: (847) 768-3434
E-mail: agabanski@asse.org
Web: www.asse.org

Summary To provide financial assistance to Asian American and other minority upper-division student members of the American Society of Safety Engineers (ASSE).

Eligibility This program is open to ASSE student members who are U.S. citizens and members of minority ethnic or racial groups. Applicants must be majoring in occupational safety, health, and environment or a closely-related field (e.g., industrial or environmental engineering, environmental science, industrial hygiene, occupational health nursing). They must be full-time students who have completed at least 60 semester hours with a GPA of 3.0 or higher. Along with their application, they must submit 2 essays of 300 words or less: 1) why they are seeking a degree in occupational safety and health or a closely-related field, a brief description of their current activities, and how those relate to their career goals and objectives; and 2) why they should be awarded this scholarship (including career goals and financial need).

Financial data The stipend is $5,250 per year.

Duration 1 year; recipients may reapply.

Additional information Funding for this program is provided by the UPS Foundation.

Number awarded 2 each year.

Deadline November of each year.

[45]
ASSOCIATED CHINESE UNIVERSITY WOMEN SCHOLARSHIPS

Associated Chinese University Women, Inc.
c/o Maura Yee, Scholarship Committee
1530 Evelyn Lane
Honolulu, HI 96822
E-mail: maurayee@hawaii.rr.com
Web: www.acuwhawaii.org/main

Summary To provide financial assistance to residents of Hawaii who are of Chinese ancestry and interested in attending college in any state.

Eligibility This program is open to residents of Hawaii who are of Chinese or part-Chinese ancestry. Applicants must be attending or planning to attend an accredited 4-year U.S. college or university as a full-time student with the objective of earning a baccalaureate degree. They must have a GPA of 3.8 or higher. Along with their application, they must submit a personal statement on why they should be awarded this scholarship, including their plans for serving their community after graduation. Selection is based on academic achievement (including GPA and SAT scores), character, extracurricular activities, school and/or community service, and financial need. U.S. citizenship or permanent resident status is required.

Financial data The stipend is $2,000.

Duration 1 year.

Number awarded Up to 4 each year.

Deadline March of each year.

[46]
ASSOCIATION OF ASIAN INDIAN WOMEN IN OHIO SCHOLARSHIP

Cleveland Foundation
Attn: Scholarship Officer
1422 Euclid Avenue, Suite 1300
Cleveland, OH 44115-2001
(216) 861-3810   Fax: (216) 861-1729
E-mail: mbaker@clevefdn.org
Web: www.clevelandfoundation.org/Scholarships

Summary   To provide financial assistance to Asian Indian high school seniors in Ohio who plan to attend college in any state.
Eligibility   This program is open to graduating high school seniors in Ohio who are of Asian Indian descent. Applicants must be planning to enroll at a college or university in any state. They must be able to demonstrate financial need. Along with their application, they must submit a transcript and a 150-word essay about their goals.
Financial data   The stipend is at least $500.
Duration   1 year.
Additional information   This program is sponsored by the Association of Asian Indian Women in Ohio.
Number awarded   1 or more each year.
Deadline   April of each year.

[47]
ATSUHIKO TATEUCHI MEMORIAL SCHOLARSHIP
Seattle Foundation
Attn: Scholarship Administrator
1200 Fifth Avenue, Suite 1300
Seattle, WA 98101-3151
(206) 622-2294   Fax: (206) 622-7673
E-mail: scholarships@seattlefoundation.org
Web: www.seattlefoundation.org

Summary   To provide financial assistance to residents of Pacific Rim states who are of Japanese or other Asian ancestry and interested in working on an undergraduate degree at a college in any state.
Eligibility   This program is open to residents of Alaska, California, Hawaii, Oregon, and Washington who are graduating high school seniors or undergraduates. Applicants must be attending or planning to attend a public or private community college, 4-year college or university, or trade/vocational school in any state. They must have a GPA of 3.0 or higher, be able to demonstrate financial need, and be of Japanese or other Asian ancestry. Along with their application, they must submit a 500-word essay on the most interesting book they have read and how it influenced them.
Financial data   The stipend is $5,000 per year.
Duration   1 year; may be renewed up to 3 additional years.
Number awarded   At least 1 each year.
Deadline   February of each year.

[48]
AXA ACHIEVEMENT SCHOLARSHIPS
Organization of Chinese Americans, Inc.
1322 18th Street, N.W.
Washington, DC 20036-1803
(202) 223-5500   Fax: (202) 296-0540
E-mail: oca@ocanational.org
Web: ocanational.org

Summary   To provide financial assistance for college to Asian Pacific Americans who are entering their first year of college and can demonstrate academic merit.
Eligibility   This program is open to graduating high school seniors of Asian and/or Pacific Islander ethnicity who are entering their first year at a college, university, or community college in the following fall. Applicants must be able to demonstrate academic achievement, leadership ability, and com-
munity service. They must have a cumulative GPA of 3.0 or higher and be a U.S. citizen, national, or permanent resident. Financial need is considered in the selection process.
Financial data   The stipend is $2,000.
Duration   1 year.
Additional information   This program, established in 2004, is funded by the AXA Foundation and administered by the Organization of Chinese Americans (OCA).
Number awarded   10 each year.
Deadline   April of each year.

[49]
BEHAVIORAL SCIENCES STUDENT FELLOWSHIPS IN EPILEPSY
Epilepsy Foundation
Attn: Research Department
8301 Professional Place
Landover, MD 20785-2237
(301) 459-3700   Toll Free: (800) EFA-1000
Fax: (301) 577-2684   TDD: (800) 332-2070
E-mail: grants@efa.org
Web: www.epilepsyfoundation.org

Summary   To provide funding to undergraduate and graduate students (especially Asian Americans, other minorities, women, and individuals with disabilities) who are interested in working on a summer research training project in a behavioral science field relevant to epilepsy.
Eligibility   This program is open to undergraduate and graduate students in a behavioral science program relevant to epilepsy research or clinical care, including, but not limited to, sociology, social work, psychology, anthropology, nursing, economics, vocational rehabilitation, counseling, or political science. Applicants must be interested in working on an epilepsy research project under the supervision of a qualified mentor. Because the program is designed as a training opportunity, the quality of the training plans and environment are considered in the selection process. Other selection criteria include the quality of the proposed project, the relevance of the proposed work to epilepsy, the applicant's interest in the field of epilepsy, the applicant's qualifications, and the mentor's qualifications (including his or her commitment to the student and the project), and the quality of the training environment for research related to epilepsy. U.S. citizenship is not required, but the project must be conducted in the United States. Applications from women, members of minority groups, and people with disabilities are especially encouraged. The program is not intended for students working on a dissertation research project.
Financial data   The grant is $3,000.
Duration   3 months during the summer.
Additional information   This program is supported by the American Epilepsy Society, Abbott Laboratories, Ortho-McNeil Pharmaceutical Corporation, and Pfizer Inc.
Number awarded   Varies each year.
Deadline   March of each year.

[50]
BOOKER T. WASHINGTON SCHOLARSHIPS

National FFA Organization
Attn: Scholarship Office
6060 FFA Drive
P.O. Box 68960
Indianapolis, IN 46268-0960
(317) 802-4419   Fax: (317) 802-5419
E-mail: scholarships@ffa.org
Web: www.ffa.org

Summary To provide financial assistance to Asian American and other minority FFA members who are interested in studying agriculture in college.

Eligibility This program is open to members who are graduating high school seniors planning to enroll full time in college. Applicants must be members of a minority ethnic group (African American, Asian American, Pacific Islander, Hispanic, Alaska Native, or American Indian) planning to work on a 4-year degree in agriculture. Selection is based on academic achievement (10 points for GPA, 10 points for SAT or ACT score, 10 points for class rank), leadership in FFA activities (30 points), leadership in community activities (10 points), and participation in the Supervised Agricultural Experience (SAE) program (30 points). U.S. citizenship is required.

Financial data Scholarships are either $10,000 or $5,000. Funds are paid directly to the recipient.

Duration 1 year; nonrenewable.

Number awarded 4 each year: 1 at $10,000 and 3 at $5,000.

Deadline February of each year.

[51]
BREAKTHROUGH TO NURSING SCHOLARSHIPS

National Student Nurses' Association
Attn: Foundation
45 Main Street, Suite 606
Brooklyn, NY 11201
(718) 210-0705   Fax: (718) 797-1186
E-mail: nsna@nsna.org
Web: www.nsna.org

Summary To provide financial assistance to Asian American and other minority undergraduate and graduate students who wish to prepare for careers in nursing.

Eligibility This program is open to students currently enrolled in state-approved schools of nursing or pre-nursing associate degree, baccalaureate, diploma, generic master's, generic doctoral, R.N. to B.S.N., R.N. to M.S.N., or L.P.N./L.V.N. to R.N. programs. Graduating high school seniors are not eligible. Support for graduate education is provided only for a first degree in nursing. Applicants must be members of a racial or ethnic minority underrepresented among registered nurses (American Indian or Alaska Native, Hispanic or Latino, Native Hawaiian or other Pacific Islander, Black or African American, or Asian). They must be committed to providing quality health care services to underserved populations. Along with their application, they must submit a 200-word description of their professional and educational goals and how this scholarship will help them achieve those goals. Selection is based on academic achievement, financial need, and involvement in student nursing organizations and community health activities. U.S. citizenship or permanent resident status is required.

Financial data Stipends range from $1,000 to $2,500. A total of approximately $155,000 is awarded each year by the foundation for all its scholarship programs.

Duration 1 year.

Additional information Applications must be accompanied by a $10 processing fee.

Number awarded Varies each year; recently, 5 of these scholarships were awarded: 2 sponsored by the American Association of Critical-Care Nurses and 3 sponsored by the Mayo Clinic.

Deadline January of each year.

[52]
BROWN AND CALDWELL MINORITY SCHOLARSHIP

Brown and Caldwell
Attn: Scholarship Program
201 North Civic Drive, Suite 115
P.O. Box 8045
Walnut Creek, CA 94596
(925) 937-9010   Fax: (925) 937-9026
E-mail: scholarships@brwncald.com
Web: www.brownandcaldwell.com/_Index_scholarships.htm

Summary To provide financial assistance and work experience to Asian Americans and other minority students working on an undergraduate degree in an environmental or engineering field.

Eligibility This program is open to members of minority groups (African Americans, Hispanics, Asians, Pacific Islanders, Native Americans, and Alaska Natives) who are full-time students in their junior year at an accredited 4-year college or university. Applicants must have a GPA of 3.0 or higher and a declared major in civil, chemical, or environmental engineering or an environmental science (e.g., ecology, geology, hydrogeology). Along with their application, they must submit an essay (up to 250 words) on their future career goals in environmental science. They must be U.S. citizens or permanent residents and available to participate in a summer internship at a Brown and Caldwell office. Financial need is not considered in the selection process.

Financial data The stipend is $5,000.

Duration 1 year.

Additional information As part of the paid summer internship at a Brown and Caldwell office at 1 of more than 45 cities in the country, the program provides a mentor to guide the intern through the company's information and communications resources.

Number awarded 1 each year.

Deadline February of each year.

[53]
BUICK ACHIEVERS SCHOLARSHIP PROGRAM

Scholarship America
Attn: Scholarship Management Services
One Scholarship Way
P.O. Box 297
St. Peter, MN 56082
(507) 931-1682   Toll Free: (866) 243-4644
Fax: (507) 931-9168
E-mail: buickachievers@scholarshipamerica.org
Web: www.buickachievers.com

Summary To provide financial assistance to students (particularly Asian Americans, other minorities, and those with ties to the military) who are entering college for the first time and planning to major in specified fields related to engineering, design, or business.

Eligibility This program is open to high school seniors and graduates who are planning to enroll full time at an accredited 4-year college or university as first-time freshmen. Applicants must be planning to major in accounting, business administration, engineering (chemical, controls, electrical, environmental, industrial, manufacturing, mechanical, plastic/polymers, or engineering technology), design (graphic, industrial, product, or transportation), ergonomics, finance, industrial hygiene, labor and industrial relations, management (logistics, manufacturing, operations, or supply chain), marketing, mathematics, occupational health and safety, or statistics. U.S. citizenship or permanent resident status is required. Selection is based on academic achievement, financial need, participation and leadership in community and school activities, work experience, educational and career goals, and other unusual circumstances. Special consideration is given to first-generation college students, women, minorities, military veterans, and dependents of military personnel.

Financial data Stipends are $25,000 or $2,000 per year.

Duration 1 year; may be renewed up to 3 additional years (or 4 years for students entering a 5-year engineering program).

Additional information This program is funded by the General Motors Foundation.

Number awarded 1,100 each year: 100 at $25,000 and 1,000 at $2,000.

Deadline March of each year.

[54]
CALIFORNIA CAPITOL SUMMER INTERNSHIP PROGRAM

Asian Pacific Islander American Public Affairs Association
Attn: Community Education Foundation
185 Butcher Road
Vacaville, CA 95687
(707) 451-0130   Fax: (707) 451-0131
E-mail: info@apapa.org
Web: www.apapa.org

Summary To provide summer work experience at an office of state government in Sacramento to undergraduate and graduate student residents of California who are of Asian or Pacific Islander descent.

Eligibility This program is open to undergraduate and graduate students who are of Asian or Pacific Islander background and residents of California attending college in the state. Applicants must be interested in a summer internship in Sacramento at an office of state government. They must have a GPA of 2.75 or higher. Along with their application, they must submit a 2-page statement on their Asian or Pacific Islander background, community and public service involvement, academic and career goals, and future plans for public services and/or politics and government involvement. Selection is based on GPA, demonstrated leadership, interpersonal skills, written and verbal communication skills, and community service.

Financial data Interns receive a stipend of $1,000 upon successful completion of the program.

Duration 8 weeks, beginning in June.

Additional information Interns must also complete 20 community service hours for the sponsor's Sacramento chapter.

Number awarded 1 or more each year.

Deadline February of each year.

[55]
CALIFORNIA PLANNING FOUNDATION OUTSTANDING DIVERSITY AWARD

American Planning Association-California Chapter
Attn: California Planning Foundation
c/o Paul Wack
P.O. Box 1086
Morro Bay, CA 93443-1086
(805) 756-6331   Fax: (805) 756-1340
E-mail: pwack@calpoly.edu
Web: www.californiaplanningfoundation.org

Summary To provide financial assistance to Asian American and other undergraduate and graduate students in accredited planning programs at California universities who will increase diversity in the profession.

Eligibility This program is open to students entering their final year for an undergraduate or master's degree in an accredited planning program at a university in California. Applicants must be students who will increase diversity in the planning profession. Selection is based on academic performance, professional promise, and financial need.

Financial data The stipend is $3,000. The award includes a 1-year student membership in the American Planning Association (APA) and payment of registration for the APA California Conference.

Duration 1 year.

Additional information The accredited planning programs are at 3 campuses of the California State University system (California State Polytechnic University at Pomona, California Polytechnic State University at San Luis Obispo, and San Jose State University), 3 campuses of the University of California (Berkeley, Irvine, and Los Angeles), and the University of Southern California.

Number awarded 1 each year.

Deadline March of each year.

[56]
CANFIT PROGRAM CULINARY ARTS SCHOLARSHIPS

California Adolescent Nutrition and Fitness Program
Attn: Scholarship Program
2140 Shattuck Avenue, Suite 610
Berkeley, CA 94704
(510) 644-1533   Toll Free: (800) 200-3131
Fax: (510) 644-1535   E-mail: info@canfit.org
Web: canfit.org/scholarships

Summary To provide financial assistance to Asian American and other minority culinary arts students in California.

Eligibility This program is open to American Indians, Alaska Natives, African Americans, Asian Americans, Pacific Islanders, and Latinos/Hispanics from California who are enrolled at a culinary arts college in the state. Applicants are not required to have completed any college units. Along with their application, they must submit 1) documentation of financial need; 2) letters of recommendation from 2 individuals; 3) a 1-to 2-page letter describing their academic goals and involvement in community nutrition and/or physical education activities; and 4) an essay of 500 to 1,000 words on a topic related to healthy foods for youth from low-income communities of color.

Financial data A stipend is awarded (amount not specified).

Number awarded 1 or more each year.

Deadline March of each year.

[57]
CANFIT PROGRAM UNDERGRADUATE SCHOLARSHIPS

California Adolescent Nutrition and Fitness Program
Attn: Scholarship Program
2140 Shattuck Avenue, Suite 610
Berkeley, CA 94704
(510) 644-1533   Toll Free: (800) 200-3131
Fax: (510) 644-1535   E-mail: info@canfit.org
Web: canfit.org/scholarships

Summary To provide financial assistance to Asian American and other minority undergraduate students who are working on a degree in nutrition or physical education in California.

Eligibility This program is open to American Indians, Alaska Natives, African Americans, Asian Americans, Pacific Islanders, and Latinos/Hispanics from California who are enrolled in an approved bachelor's degree program in nutrition or physical education in the state. Applicants must have completed at least 50 semester units and have a GPA of 2.5 or higher. Along with their application, they must submit 1) documentation of financial need; 2) letters of recommendation from 2 individuals; 3) a 1-to 2-page letter describing their academic goals and involvement in community nutrition and/or physical education activities; and 4) an essay of 500 to 1,000 words on a topic related to healthy foods for youth from low-income communities of color.

Financial data A stipend is awarded (amount not specified).

Number awarded 1 or more each year.

Deadline March of each year.

[58]
CAPSTONE CORPORATION SCHOLARSHIP AWARD

National Naval Officers Association-Washington, D.C. Chapter
Attn: Scholarship Program
2701 Park Center Drive, A1108
Alexandria, VA 22302
(703) 566-3840   Fax: (703) 566-3813
E-mail: Stephen.Williams@Navy.mil
Web: dcnnoa.memberlodge.com

Summary To provide financial assistance to Asian American and other minority high school seniors from the Washington, D.C. area who have at least a 3.0 GPA and plan to attend college in any state.

Eligibility This program is open to minority seniors graduating from high schools in the Washington, D.C. metropolitan area who plan to enroll full time at an accredited 2- or 4-year college or university in any state. Applicants must have a GPA of 3.0 or higher. U.S. citizenship or permanent resident status is required. Selection is based on academic achievement, community involvement, and financial need.

Financial data The stipend is $1,000.

Duration 1 year; nonrenewable.

Additional information Recipients are not required to join or affiliate with the military in any way. This program is supported by Capstone Corporation, a minority-owned business incorporated in 1986 by former active-duty Navy officers.

Number awarded 1 each year.

Deadline March of each year.

[59]
CAPTAIN WILLIE EVANS SCHOLARSHIP

National Naval Officers Association-Washington, D.C. Chapter
Attn: Scholarship Program
2701 Park Center Drive, A1108
Alexandria, VA 22302
(703) 566-3840   Fax: (703) 566-3813
E-mail: Stephen.Williams@Navy.mil
Web: dcnnoa.memberlodge.com

Summary To provide financial assistance to Asian American and other minority high school seniors from the Washington, D.C. area who are interested in attending college in any state.

Eligibility This program is open to minority seniors graduating from high schools in the Washington, D.C. metropolitan area who plan to enroll full time at an accredited 2- or 4-year college or university in any state. Applicants must have a GPA of 2.5 or higher. Selection is based on academic achievement, community involvement, and financial need.

Financial data The stipend is $1,000.

Duration 1 year; nonrenewable.

Number awarded 1 each year.

Deadline March of each year.

[60]
CAREER DEVELOPMENT GRANTS

American Association of University Women
Attn: AAUW Educational Foundation
301 ACT Drive, Department 60
P.O. Box 4030
Iowa City, IA 52243-4030
(319) 337-1716, ext. 60   Fax: (319) 337-1204
E-mail: aauw@act.org
Web: www.aauw.org

Summary To provide financial assistance to women (particularly Asian American and other minority women) who are seeking career advancement, career change, or reentry into the workforce.

Eligibility This program is open to women who are U.S. citizens or permanent residents, have earned a bachelor's degree, received their most recent degree more than 4 years ago, and are making career changes, seeking to advance in current careers, or reentering the work force. Applicants must be interested in working toward a master's degree, second bachelor's or associate degree, professional degree (e.g., M.D., J.D.), certification program, or technical school certificate. They must be planning to undertake course work at an accredited 2- or 4-year college or university (or a technical school that is licensed, accredited, or approved by the U.S. Department of Education). Special consideration is given to women of color and women pursuing credentials in nontraditional fields. Support is not provided for prerequisite course work or for Ph.D. course work or dissertations. Selection is based on demonstrated commitment to education and equity for women and girls, reason for seeking higher education or technical training, degree to which study plan is consistent with career objectives, potential for success in chosen field, documentation of opportunities in chosen field, feasibility of study plans and proposed time schedule, validity of proposed budget and budget narrative (including sufficient outside support), and quality of written proposal.

Financial data Grants range from $2,000 to $12,000. Funds may be used for tuition, fees, books, supplies, local transportation, dependent child care, or purchase of a computer required for the study program.

Duration 1 year, beginning in July; nonrenewable.

Additional information The filing fee is $35.

Number awarded Varies each year; recently, 47 of these grants, with a value of $500,000, were awarded.

Deadline December of each year.

[61]
CARGILL ASCEND SCHOLARSHIPS

Ascend: Pan-Asian Leaders
Attn: Director of Programs
120 Wall Street, Third Floor
New York, NY 10005
(212) 248-4888   Fax: (212) 344-5636
E-mail: info@ascendleadership.org
Web: www.ascendleadership.org

Summary To provide financial assistance to members of Ascend: Pan-Asian Leaders who are college juniors working on a degree in accounting, taxation, or finance.

Eligibility This program is open to members of Ascend who are enrolled as full-time juniors at colleges and universities in the United States. Applicants must have a GPA of 3.0 or higher and a major in accounting, taxation, or finance. They must be U.S. citizens or permanent residents. Along with their application, they must submit a 500-word personal essay on how they have demonstrated leadership and teamwork in their academic studies, professional career, and/or extracurricular activities and community volunteer work; why they believe those qualities are important to be competitive in a borderless world; their career goals after graduation; and the role Ascend has played in the achievement of their academic and career goals. They must also answer questions on how they have been involved in the community and how they have made a difference. Financial need is not considered in the selection process.

Financial data The stipend is $2,000.

Duration 1 year.

Additional information Ascend was formed in 2004 as the National Asian American Society of Accountants. This program is sponsored by Cargill.

Number awarded 3 each year.

Deadline July of each year.

[62]
CARL A. SCOTT BOOK FELLOWSHIPS

Council on Social Work Education
Attn: Chair, Carl A. Scott Memorial Fund
1701 Duke Street, Suite 200
Alexandria, VA 22314-3429
(703) 683-8080   Fax: (703) 683-8099
E-mail: info@cswe.org
Web: www.cswe.org

Summary To provide financial assistance to Asian Americans and other minorities who are working on an undergraduate or master's degree in social work and are in their last year of study.

Eligibility This program is open to students from ethnic groups of color (African American, Asian American, Hispanic/Latino, or American Indian) who are in the last year of study for a social work degree in an accredited baccalaureate or master's degree program. Applicants must have a cumulative GPA of 3.0 or higher and be enrolled full time. They must demonstrate a commitment to work for equity and social justice in social work.

Financial data The stipend is $500.

Duration This is a 1-time award.

Number awarded 2 each year.

Deadline May of each year.

[63]
CARMEN E. TURNER SCHOLARSHIPS

Conference of Minority Transportation Officials
Attn: National Scholarship Program
818 18th Street, N.W., Suite 850
Washington, DC 20006
(202) 530-0551   Fax: (202) 530-0617
Web: www.comto.org/news-youth.php

Summary To provide financial assistance for college or graduate school to Asian American and other members of the Conference of Minority Transportation Officials (COMTO).

Eligibility This program is open to undergraduate and graduate students who have been members of COMTO for at least 1 year. Applicants must be working on a degree in a field related to transportation with a GPA of 2.5 or higher. Along with their application, they must submit a cover letter with a 500-word statement of career goals. Financial need is not considered in the selection process. U.S. citizenship is required.

Financial data The stipend is $3,500. Funds are paid directly to the recipient's college or university.

Duration 1 year.

Additional information COMTO was established in 1971 to promote, strengthen, and expand the roles of minorities in all aspects of transportation. Recipients are expected to attend the COMTO National Scholarship Luncheon.

Number awarded 2 each year.

Deadline April of each year.

[64]
CAROL HAYES TORIO DIETETIC TECHNICIAN SCHOLARSHIP

California Dietetic Association
Attn: CDA Foundation
7740 Manchester Avenue, Suite 102
Playa del Rey, CA 90293-8499
(310) 822-0177   Fax: (310) 823-0264
E-mail: patsmith@dietitian.org
Web: www.dietitian.org/cdaf_scholarships.htm

Summary To provide financial assistance to minority and other residents of California who are members of the American Dietetic Association (ADA) and interested in preparing for a career as a dietetic technician.

Eligibility This program is open to California residents who are ADA members and entering at least the second year of an approved Dietetic Technician Program in any state. Along with their application, they must submit a letter of application that includes a discussion of their career goals. Selection is based on that letter (15%), academic ability (25%), work or volunteer experience (15%), letters of recommendation (15%), extracurricular activities (5%), and financial need (25%). Applications are especially encouraged from ethnic minorities, men, and people with physical disabilities.

Financial data The stipend is normally $1,000.

Duration 1 year.

Number awarded 1 each year.

Deadline February of each year.

[65]
CAROL HAYES TORIO MEMORIAL UNDERGRADUATE SCHOLARSHIP

California Dietetic Association
Attn: CDA Foundation
7740 Manchester Avenue, Suite 102
Playa del Rey, CA 90293-8499
(310) 822-0177   Fax: (310) 823-0264
E-mail: patsmith@dietitian.org
Web: www.dietitian.org/cdaf_scholarships.htm

Summary To provide financial assistance to minority and other residents of California who are members of the American Dietetic Association (ADA) and interested in working on an undergraduate degree at a school in any state.

Eligibility This program is open to California residents who are ADA members and 1) entering at least the second year of

an accredited Coordinated Program (CP) or Didactic Program in Dietetics (DPD) in any state; or 2) accepted to an accredited Supervised Practice Program in any state to begin within 6 months. Along with their application, they must submit a letter of application that includes a discussion of their career goals. Selection is based on that letter (15%), academic ability (25%), work or volunteer experience (15%), letters of recommendation (15%), extracurricular activities (5%), and financial need (25%). Applications are especially encouraged from ethnic minorities, men, and people with physical disabilities.

Financial data The stipend is normally $1,000.

Duration 1 year.

Number awarded 1 each year.

Deadline February of each year.

[66]
CAROLE SIMPSON RTDNF SCHOLARSHIP

Radio Television Digital News Foundation
Attn: RTDNF Fellowship Program
4121 Plank Road, Suite 512
Fredericksburg, VA 22407
(202) 467-5214   Fax: (202) 223-4007
E-mail: staceys@rtdna.org
Web: www.rtdna.org/pages/education/undergraduates.php

Summary To provide financial assistance to Asian American and other minority undergraduate students who are interested in preparing for a career in electronic journalism.

Eligibility This program is open to sophomore or more advanced minority undergraduate students enrolled in an electronic journalism sequence at an accredited or nationally-recognized college or university. Applicants must submit 1 to 3 examples of their journalistic skills on audio CD or DVD (no more than 15 minutes total, accompanied by scripts); a description of their role on each story and a list of who worked on each story and what they did; a 1-page statement explaining why they are preparing for a career in electronic journalism with reference to their specific career preference (radio, television, online, reporting, producing, or newsroom management); a resume; and a letter of reference from their dean or faculty sponsor explaining why they are a good candidate for the award and certifying that they have at least 1 year of school remaining.

Financial data The stipend is $2,000, paid in semiannual installments of $1,000 each.

Duration 1 year.

Additional information The Radio Television Digital News Foundation (RTDNF) also provides an all-expense paid trip to the Radio Television Digital News Association (RTDNA) annual international conference. The RTDNF was formerly the Radio and Television News Directors Foundation (RTNDF). Previous winners of any RTDNF scholarship or internship are not eligible.

Number awarded 1 each year.

Deadline May of each year.

[67]
CATERPILLAR SCHOLARS AWARD

Society of Manufacturing Engineers
Attn: SME Education Foundation
One SME Drive
P.O. Box 930
Dearborn, MI 48121-0930
(313) 425-3300   Toll Free: (800) 733-4763, ext. 3300
Fax: (313) 425-3411   E-mail: foundation@sme.org
Web: www.smeef.org

Summary   To provide financial assistance to minority and other undergraduates enrolled in a degree program in manufacturing engineering or manufacturing engineering technology.

Eligibility   Applicants must be full-time students attending a degree-granting institution in North America and preparing for a career in manufacturing engineering. They must have completed at least 30 units in a manufacturing engineering or manufacturing engineering technology curriculum with a minimum GPA of 3.0. Minority applicants may apply as incoming freshmen. Along with their application, they must submit a 300-word essay that covers their career and educational objectives, how this scholarship will help them attain those objectives, and why they want to enter this field. Financial need is not considered in the selection process. Preference is given to applicants who have participated in a Science, Technology, and Engineering Preview Summer (STEPS) camp sponsored by the foundation.

Financial data   Stipend amounts vary; recently, the value of all scholarships provided by this foundation averaged approximately $2,728.

Duration   1 year; may be renewed.

Additional information   This program is sponsored by Caterpillar, Inc.

Number awarded   Varies each year; recently, 10 of these scholarships were awarded.

Deadline   January of each year.

[68]
CAUSE LEADERSHIP ACADEMY INTERNSHIPS

Center for Asian Americans United for Self Empowerment
Attn: California Asian American Student Internship
  Coalition
260 South Los Robles Avenue, Suite 118
Pasadena, CA 91101
(626) 356-9838   Fax: (626) 356-9878
E-mail: info@causeuse.org
Web: www.causeusa.org

Summary   To provide internships at sites in southern California to college students from any state interested in Asian Pacific Islander American affairs.

Eligibility   This program is open to graduating high school seniors and college undergraduates who have a GPA of 3.2 or higher and an interest in Asian Pacific Islander American affairs. Applicants must be interested in participating in a leadership academy that includes an internship placement in the office of an elected official. They should be interested in exploring a career in public office, public service, or community advocacy. Along with their application, they must be submit a 1,000-word essay on why they want to become a Center for Asian Americans United for Self Empowerment (CAUSE) intern, how the CAUSE Leadership Academy will help them

achieve their goals, and what they would like to gain from the academy. Since all assignments are in southern California, applicants should be residents of the area or prepared to live there during the summer. Selection is based on personal, academic, and extracurricular backgrounds.

Financial data   A stipend of $1,000 is paid after completion of the internship.

Duration   8 weeks during the summer.

Additional information   This program began in 1991 as California Asian American Student Internship Coalition (CASIC).

Number awarded   Varies each year.

Deadline   April of each year.

[69]
CENTER FOR STUDENT OPPORTUNITY SCHOLARSHIP

Center for Student Opportunity
Attn: Opportunity Scholarship
4903 Auburn Avenue
P.O. Box 30370
Bethesda, MD 20824
(301) 951-7101, ext. 214   Fax: (301) 951-7104
E-mail: scholarship@csopportunity.org
Web: www.csopportunity.org/ss/oppscholarship.aspx

Summary   To provide financial assistance to first-generation, low-income, and/or minority high school seniors who have participated in activities of the sponsoring organization and plan to attend selected universities.

Eligibility   This program is open to graduating high school (or home-schooled) seniors who have participated in high school activities of the sponsoring organization. Applicants must be planning to attend a 4-year college or university that has a partnership arrangement with the sponsoring organization. They must be students whose parents did not go to or graduate from college, and/or students who need financial aid or scholarships to go to college, and/or students who identify as African American/Black, American Indian/Alaska Native, Hispanic/Latino, or Asian/Pacific Islander. Along with their application, they must submit 500-word essays on 1) the challenges they have faced in their college preparation, search, and application process; and 2) why they are deserving of this scholarship. There are no minimum academic requirements.

Financial data   The stipend is $2,000 per year.

Duration   1 year; may be renewed up to 3 additional years.

Additional information   The sponsor has partnership arrangements with more than 250 universities in nearly every state; most of them are private institutions, although some public universities are included. For a list, contact the sponsor. Recipients are invited to serve as monthly guest bloggers on the sponsor's web blog to share insight and perspective about their transition to college with high school participants in the sponsor's activities.

Number awarded   1 or more each year.

Deadline   May of each year.

[70]
CENTER ON BUDGET AND POLICY PRIORITIES INTERNSHIPS

Center on Budget and Policy Priorities
Attn: Internship Coordinator
820 First Street, N.E., Suite 510
Washington, DC 20002
(202) 408-1080   Fax: (202) 408-1056
E-mail: internship@cbpp.org
Web: www.cbpp.org/jobs/index.cfm?fa=internships

Summary To provide work experience at the Center on Budget and Policy Priorities (CBPP) in Washington, D.C. to undergraduates, graduate students, and recent college graduates, especially Asian Americans or other minorities, women, and international students.

Eligibility This program is open to undergraduates, graduate students, and recent college graduates who are interested in public policy issues affecting low-income families and individuals. Applicants must be interested in working at CBPP in the following areas: media, federal legislation, health policy, housing policy, international budget project, Food Stamps, national budget and tax policy, outreach campaigns, state budget and tax policy, welfare reform, and income support. They should have research, fact-gathering, writing, analytic, and computer skills and a willingness to do administrative as well as substantive tasks. Women, international students, and minorities are encouraged to apply.

Financial data Hourly stipends are $8.50 for undergraduates, $9.50 for interns with a bachelor's degree, $10.50 for graduate students, $12.50 for interns with a master's or law degree, and $12.50 to $15.50 for doctoral students (depending on progress towards completion of degree requirements, relevant course work, and research).

Duration 1 semester; may be renewed.

Additional information The center specializes in research and analysis oriented toward practical policy decisions and produces analytic reports that are accessible to public officials at national, state, and local levels, to nonprofit organizations, and to the media.

Number awarded Varies each semester; recently, 5 interns were appointed for a fall semester.

Deadline February of each year for summer internships; June of each year for fall internships; October of each year for spring internships.

[71]
CENTRAL INTELLIGENCE AGENCY UNDERGRADUATE SCHOLARSHIP PROGRAM

Central Intelligence Agency
Attn: Human Resource Management
Recruitment and Retention Center, 4B14-034 DD1
Washington, DC 20505
(703) 371-2107
Web: www.cia.gov/careers/student-opportunities/index.html

Summary To provide funding and work experience to high school seniors and college sophomores, especially Asian Americans or other minorities and people with disabilities, who are interested in working for the Central Intelligence Agency (CIA) after graduation from college.

Eligibility This program is open to U.S. citizens who are either high school seniors or college freshmen or sopho-

mores. Seniors must be at least 18 years of age by April of the year they apply and have minimum scores of 1500 on the SAT (1000 on critical reading and mathematics and 500 on writing) or 21 on the ACT. College students must have a GPA of 3.0 or higher. All applicants must be able to demonstrate financial need (household income of $70,000 or less for a family of 4 or $80,000 or less for a family of 5 or more) and be able to meet the same employment standards as permanent employees of the CIA. This program was developed, in part, to assist minority and disabled students, but it is open to all students who meet the requirements.

Financial data Scholars are provided a salary, an optional benefits package (health, dental, and vision insurance, life insurance, and retirement), and up to $18,000 per year for tuition, fees, books, and supplies. They must agree to continue employment with the CIA after college graduation for a period 1.5 times the length of their college support.

Duration 1 year; may be renewed if the student maintains a GPA of 3.0 or higher and full-time enrollment in a 4- or 5-year college program.

Additional information Scholars work each summer at a CIA facility. In addition to a salary, they receive the cost of transportation between school and the Washington, D.C. area and a housing allowance.

Number awarded Varies each year.

Deadline October of each year.

[72]
CHEW YEE JANET LAM SCHOLARSHIP

Associated Chinese University Women, Inc.
c/o Sybil Kyi, Special Scholarships
5930 Haleola Street
Honolulu, HI 96821
(808) 373-1129   E-mail: kyis@hawaii.rr.com
Web: www.acuwhawaii.org/main

Summary To provide financial assistance to residents of Hawaii who are of Chinese ancestry and interested in majoring in education at a college in any state.

Eligibility This program is open to residents of Hawaii who are of Chinese or part Chinese ancestry. Applicants must be attending or planning to attend an accredited 4-year U.S. college or university as a full-time student with the objective of earning a baccalaureate degree. They must have a GPA of 3.8 or higher and be planning to major in education. Along with their application, they must submit a personal statement on why they should be awarded this scholarship, including their plans for serving their community after graduation. Selection is based on academic achievement (including GPA and SAT score), character, extracurricular activities, school and/or community service, and financial need. U.S. citizenship or permanent resident status is required.

Financial data The stipend is $500.

Duration 1 year.

Number awarded 1 each year.

Deadline April of each year.

[73]
CHINESE AMERICAN ASSOCIATION OF MINNESOTA SCHOLARSHIPS

Chinese American Association of Minnesota
Attn: Scholarship Program
P.O. Box 582584
Minneapolis, MN 55458-2584
E-mail: office@caam.org
Web: www.caam.org

Summary　To provide financial assistance to Minnesota residents of Chinese descent who are interested in attending college or graduate school in any state.

Eligibility　This program is open to Minnesota residents of Chinese descent who are enrolled or planning to enroll full time at a postsecondary school, college, or graduate school in any state. Applicants must submit an essay on the role their Chinese heritage has played in their work, study, and accomplishments. Selection is based on academic record, leadership qualities, and community service; financial need is also considered for some awards. Membership in the Chinese American Association of Minnesota (CAAM) is not required. Priority is given to applicants who have not previously received a CAAM scholarship.

Financial data　The stipend ranges from $1,000 to $1,500.

Duration　1 year.

Additional information　Recipients who are not CAAM members are expected to become members for at least 2 years.

Number awarded　1 or more each year.

Deadline　November of each year.

[74]
CHINESE AMERICAN CITIZENS ALLIANCE FOUNDATION ESSAY CONTEST

Chinese American Citizens Alliance
1044 Stockton Street
San Francisco, CA 94108
(415) 434-2222　　　　　　E-mail: info@cacanational.org
Web: www.cacanational.org/Essay-Contest

Summary　To recognize and reward high school students of Chinese descent who write outstanding essays on a topic related to Asian Americans.

Eligibility　This competition is open to high school students of Chinese descent. Candidates apply through their local lodge of the Chinese American Citizens Alliance and meet at a site arranged by that lodge, usually on the first Saturday in March. They are given a topic and devote the next 2 hours to writing a 500-word essay, in English, on that topic. Recently, the topic related to the census and why so many Chinese Americans do not comply with the law and participate in the U.S. Census. Selection is based on originality, clarity of thought and expression, and correctness of grammar and spelling.

Financial data　Prizes are $1,000 for first place, $700 for second place, $500 for third place, and $100 for merit awards.

Duration　The competition is held annually.

Number awarded　Varies each year; recently, prizes included 1 first place, 1 second place, 1 third place, and 10 merit awards.

Deadline　February of each year.

[75]
CHINESE AMERICAN CITIZENS ALLIANCE FOUNDATION SCHOLARSHIPS

Chinese American Citizens Alliance Foundation
Attn: Scholarships
763 Yale Street
Los Angeles, CA 90012
(213) 628-6368　　　　　E-mail: cacafoundation@gmail.com
Web: www.cacafoundation.org

Summary　To provide financial assistance to Chinese American undergraduate students at colleges and universities in California.

Eligibility　This program is open to students of Chinese descent from California who have completed the sophomore year at a college or university in the state. Applicants must provide information on their volunteer work, accomplishments and honors received in college, organizational membership and offices held, previous scholarship awards, career plans, and how they will benefit from the scholarship. Financial need is not considered. Applicants must be available for an in-person interview in Los Angeles.

Financial data　The stipend is $1,000.

Duration　1 year.

Additional information　This program, which began in 1971, currently consists of the following named scholarships: the Yoke Quong Jung Memorial Scholarship, the Huan Lin Cheng Memorial Scholarship, the Y.C. Hong Memorial Scholarship, the Collin and Susan Lai Scholarship, the Julius and Eleanor Sue Scholarship, the Robert and Edith Jung Scholarship, the James Bok Wong and Betty KC Yeow Scholarship, and the Stanley and Mary Mu Scholarship.

Number awarded　8 each year.

Deadline　June of each year.

[76]
CHIPS QUINN SCHOLARS PROGRAM

Freedom Forum
Attn: Chips Quinn Scholars Program
555 Pennsylvania Avenue, N.W.
Washington, DC 20001
(202) 292-6271　　　　　　Fax: (202) 292-6275
E-mail: kcatone@freedomforum.org
Web: www.chipsquinn.org

Summary　To provide work experience to Asian American and other minority college students or recent graduates who are majoring in journalism.

Eligibility　This program is open to students of color who are college juniors, seniors, or recent graduates with journalism majors or career goals in newspapers. Candidates must be nominated or endorsed by journalism faculty, campus media advisers, editors of newspapers, or leaders of minority journalism associations. Along with their application, they must submit a resume, transcripts, 2 letters of recommendation, and an essay of 200 to 500 words on why they want to be a Chips Quinn Scholar. Reporters must also submit 6 samples of published articles they have written; photographers must submit 10 to 20 photographs on a CD. Applicants must have a car and be available to work as a full-time intern during the spring or summer. U.S. citizenship or permanent resident status is required. Campus newspaper experience is strongly encouraged.

Financial data Students chosen for this program receive a travel stipend to attend a Multimedia training program in Nashville, Tennessee prior to reporting for their internship, a $500 housing allowance from the Freedom Forum, and a competitive salary during their internship.

Duration Internships are for 10 to 12 weeks, in spring or summer.

Additional information This program was established in 1991 in memory of the late John D. Quinn Jr., managing editor of the *Poughkeepsie Journal*. Funding is provided by the Freedom Forum, formerly the Gannett Foundation. After graduating from college and obtaining employment with a newspaper, alumni of this program are eligible to apply for fellowship support to attend professional journalism development activities.

Number awarded Approximately 70 each year. Since the program began, more than 1,200 scholars have been selected.

Deadline October of each year.

[77]
CHRISTIAN COLLEGE LEADERS SCHOLARSHIPS

Foundation for College Christian Leaders
2658 Del Mar Heights Road
PMB 266
Del Mar, CA 92014
(858) 481-0848   E-mail: LMHays@aol.com
Web: www.collegechristianleader.com

Summary To provide financial assistance for college to Christian students (especially Asian Americans and other minorities) from California, Oregon, and Washington.

Eligibility This program is open to entering or continuing undergraduate students who reside or attend college in California, Oregon, or Washington. Applicants must have a GPA of 3.0 or higher, be able to document financial need (parents must have a combined income of less than $60,000), and be able to demonstrate Christian testimony and Christian leadership. Selection is based on identified leadership history, academic achievement, financial need, and demonstrated academic, vocational, and ministry training to further the Kingdom of Jesus Christ. Special consideration is given to minority students.

Financial data A stipend is awarded (amount not specified).

Duration 1 year; may be renewed.

Additional information The foundation, formerly known as the Eckmann Foundation, was founded in 1988.

Deadline May of each year.

[78]
CHUNGHI HONG PARK SCHOLARSHIPS

Korean-American Scientists and Engineers Association
Attn: Scholarship Committee
1952 Gallows Drive, Suite 300
Vienna, VA 22182
(703) 748-1221   Fax: (703) 748-1331
E-mail: sejong@ksea.org
Web: scholarship.ksea.org/InfoUndergraduate.aspx

Summary To provide financial assistance to women who are undergraduate student members of the Korean-American Scientists and Engineers Association (KSEA).

Eligibility This program is open to women who are Korean American undergraduate students, are KSEA members, have completed at least 40 credits as a college student, and are majoring in science, engineering, or a related field. Along with their application, they must submit an essay on a topic that changes annually but relates to science or engineering; recently, students were asked to discuss the pros and cons of development vs. the environment. Selection is based on the essay (20%), KSEA activities and community service (30%), recommendation letters (20%), and academic performance (30%).

Financial data The stipend is $1,000.

Duration 1 year.

Number awarded 2 each year.

Deadline February of each year.

[79]
CIA UNDERGRADUATE INTERNSHIP PROGRAM

Central Intelligence Agency
Attn: Human Resource Management
Recruitment and Retention Center, 4B14-034 DD1
Washington, DC 20505
(703) 371-2107
Web: www.cia.gov/careers/student-opportunities/index.html

Summary To provide work experience at the Central Intelligence Agency (CIA) to undergraduates, especially Asian Americans and other minorities or people with disabilities.

Eligibility This program is open to undergraduate students, particularly minorities and people with disabilities. Applicants must be U.S. citizens, have a GPA of 3.0 or higher, be available to work in metropolitan Washington, D.C. during the summer or for a semester, and meet the same employment standards as permanent CIA employees. They must be majoring in fields such as accounting, area studies, business administration, computer science, economics, engineering, finance, foreign languages, geography, graphic design, human resources, international relations, logistics, mathematics, military and foreign affairs, national security studies, physical sciences, or political science.

Financial data Student positions offer salaries competitive with the private sector and the same benefits as permanent employees. Student trainees are also eligible to apply for the agency's tuition assistance program.

Duration Interns are required to work either 1) a combination of 1 semester and 1 summer; or 2) 2 90-day summer internships.

Number awarded Varies each year.

Deadline Applications for winter, spring, or fall may be submitted at any time, but they should be completed 6 to 9 months prior to the desired start date. Summer applications are due by October of each year.

[80]
CIE/USA-SEATTLE APA SCIENCE, ENGINEERING AND TECHNOLOGY SCHOLARSHIP AWARD PROGRAM FOR COLLEGE STUDENTS

Chinese Institute of Engineers/USA-Seattle Chapter
Attn: Scholarship Committee
15921 N.E. Eighth Street, Suite 200
Bellevue, WA 98008
(425) 653-5589   E-mail: ciescholarship@cie-sea.org
Web: cie.web.officelive.com/prodev.aspx

Summary   To recognize and reward Asian Pacific American college students in Washington who have contributed to the fields of science, engineering, and technology.

Eligibility   This award is available to students currently enrolled full time at a college or university in Washington who come from a family with an ethnic Asian Pacific background. Self-nominations are accepted, but nominations by teachers and coaches are preferred. Nomination packets must include 1) a 2-page description of applicable science, engineering, or technology projects, accomplishments, or activities; and 2) an essay by the student that includes a description of past volunteer or community service activities, a statement on their Asian Pacific family background, and a paragraph on future plans. Selection is based on that essay (20%), academic achievement (30%), volunteer and community service (25%), and extracurricular activities and accomplishments (25%).

Financial data   Awards are $600.

Duration   The awards are presented annually.

Number awarded   2 each year.

Deadline   May of each year.

[81]
CIND M. TRESER MEMORIAL SCHOLARSHIP

Washington State Environmental Health Association
Attn: Executive Secretary
103 Sea Pine Lane
Bellingham, WA 98229-9363
(360) 738-8946   Fax: (360) 738-8949
E-mail: Kerri@wseha.org
Web: www.wseha.org

Summary   To provide financial assistance to undergraduate students (particularly Asian Americans, other minorities, and those who are specially challenged) who are majoring in environmental health or other life sciences and are interested in preparing for a career in environmental health in the state of Washington.

Eligibility   This program is open to undergraduates who 1) intend to become employed in the field of environmental health in Washington following graduation and 2) are enrolled in a program either accredited by the National Accreditation Council for Environmental Health Curricula or with a curriculum comparable to the model curriculum recommended by that Council (i.e., the program must include substantial course work in biology and microbiology, organic and inorganic chemistry, epidemiology, biostatistics, and environmental health sciences). Applicants must be members of the Washington State Environmental Health Association (WSEHA). Students of color and specially challenged students are especially encouraged to apply.

Financial data   The stipend is $1,000.

Duration   1 year.

Additional information   This program was formerly known as the Ed Pickett Memorial Student Scholarship. The first scholarship was awarded in 1985. Recipients must attend the association's annual educational conference to accept the scholarship award.

Number awarded   1 each year.

Deadline   August of each year.

[82]
CJAAA SCHOLARSHIP PROGRAM

California Japanese American Alumni Association
Attn: Katherine Yoshii
P.O. Box 15235
San Francisco, CA 94115-0235
(510) 559-9277   E-mail: scholarships@cjaaa.org
Web: www.cjaaa.org/scholarship.html

Summary   To provide financial assistance to undergraduate or graduate students of Japanese American descent who are currently enrolled at campuses of the University of California.

Eligibility   This program is open to continuing or returning undergraduate or graduate students of Japanese American descent from California who are attending 1 of the 10 UC campuses. They must be U.S. citizens and may be studying in any field or discipline. A GPA of 3.0 or higher is strongly recommended but not required. Applicants interested in participating in the University of California Education Abroad Program in Japan must have a GPA of 3.5 or higher. Selection is based on academic achievement, contribution to the community, personal attributes, and financial need (in that order).

Financial data   Stipends range from $1,000 to $5,000. The Moriaki "Mo" Noguchi Memorial Scholarship of $3,000 is given to the top overall candidate. The George Kondo Award is at least $1,000 and is awarded to the applicant with the best community service record. The Yori Wada Award is $2,000 and is awarded to the applicant with the most outstanding record of public service. The stipend for a student accepted to the University of California Education Abroad Program ranges from $2,500 to $5,000.

Duration   1 year; nonrenewable.

Number awarded   8 to 10 each year.

Deadline   April of each year.

[83]
CNN-SAJA SCHOLARSHIP FOR BROADCAST JOURNALISM

South Asian Journalists Association
c/o Aseem Chhabra, Awards Committee Chair
4315 46th Street, Apartment E10
Sunnyside, NY 11104-2015
E-mail: chhabs@aol.com
Web: www.saja.org/programs/scholarships

Summary   To provide financial assistance to undergraduate and graduate broadcast journalism students of south Asian descent.

Eligibility   This program is open to students of south Asian descent (including Bangladesh, Bhutan, India, Maldives, Nepal, Pakistan, and Sri Lanka; Indo-Caribbeans are also eligible). Applicants must be currently enrolled in an undergraduate or graduate program in broadcast journalism at a college or university in North America. Selection is based on interest in broadcast journalism, participation in the sponsoring organization, reasons for entering journalism, and financial need.

Financial data The stipend is $2,000.

Duration 1 year.

Additional information This program, sponsored by CNN, began in 2007. Recipients are expected to give back to the South Asian Journalists Association (SAJA) by volunteering at the annual convention or at other events during the year.

Number awarded 1 each year.

Deadline March of each year.

[84]
COCHRAN/GREENE SCHOLARSHIP

National Naval Officers Association-Washington, D.C.
  Chapter
Attn: Scholarship Program
2701 Park Center Drive, A1108
Alexandria, VA 22302
(703) 566-3840   Fax: (703) 566-3813
E-mail: Stephen.Williams@Navy.mil
Web: dcnnoa.memberlodge.com

Summary To provide financial assistance to female high school seniors from the Washington, D.C. area who are of Asian American or other minority descent and interested in attending college in any state.

Eligibility This program is open to female minority seniors graduating from high schools in the Washington, D.C. metropolitan area who plan to enroll full time at an accredited 2- or 4-year college or university in any state. Applicants must have a GPA of 2.5 or higher. Selection is based on academic achievement, community involvement, and financial need.

Financial data The stipend is $1,500.

Duration 1 year; nonrenewable.

Additional information Recipients are not required to join or affiliate with the military in any way.

Number awarded 1 each year.

Deadline March of each year.

[85]
COLGATE "BRIGHT SMILES, BRIGHT FUTURES" MINORITY SCHOLARSHIPS

American Dental Hygienists' Association
Attn: Institute for Oral Health
444 North Michigan Avenue, Suite 3400
Chicago, IL 60611-3980
(312) 440-8944   Toll Free: (800) 735-4916
Fax: (312) 467-1806   E-mail: institute@adha.net
Web: www.adha.org/ioh/programs/scholarships.htm

Summary To provide financial assistance to Asian Americans and other minority students, along with males of any race, who are members of the Student American Dental Hygienists' Association (SADHA) or the American Dental Hygienists' Association (ADHA) and enrolled in certificate programs in dental hygiene.

Eligibility This program is open to members of groups currently underrepresented in the dental hygiene profession (Native Americans, African Americans, Hispanics, Asians, and males) who are active members of the SADHA or the ADHA. Applicants must have a GPA of 3.0 or higher, be able

to document financial need of at least $1,500, and have completed at least 1 year of full-time enrollment in an accredited dental hygiene certificate program in the United States. Along with their application, they must submit a statement that covers their long-term career goals, their intended contribution to the dental hygiene profession, their professional interests, and how their extracurricular activities and their degree enhance the attainment of their goals.

Financial data The stipend ranges from $1,000 to $2,000.

Duration 1 year; nonrenewable.

Additional information These scholarships are sponsored by the Colgate-Palmolive Company.

Number awarded 2 each year.

Deadline January of each year.

[86]
COLORADO EDUCATION ASSOCIATION ETHNIC MINORITY SCHOLARSHIPS

Colorado Education Association
Attn: Ethnic Minority Advisory Council
1500 Grant Street
Denver, CO 80203
(303) 837-1500   Toll Free: (800) 332-5939
Web: coloradoea.org/education/grants.aspx

Summary To provide financial assistance to Asian American and other minority high school seniors in Colorado who are children of members of the Colorado Education Association (CEA) and planning to attend college in any state.

Eligibility This program is open to seniors graduating from high schools in Colorado who are members of a minority ethnic group, defined to include American Indians/Alaska Natives, Asians, Blacks, Hispanics, Native Hawaiians/Pacific Islanders, and multi-ethnic. Applicants must be the dependent child of an active, retired, or deceased CEA member. They must be planning to attend an accredited institution of higher education in any state. Along with their application, they must submit brief statements on 1) their need for this scholarship; and 2) why they plan to pursue a college education.

Financial data The stipend is $1,000.

Duration 1 year; nonrenewable.

Number awarded 4 each year.

Deadline March of each year.

[87]
COLORADO EDUCATIONAL SERVICES AND DEVELOPMENT ASSOCIATION DIVERSITY SCHOLARSHIPS

Colorado Educational Services and Development
  Association
P.O. Box 40214
Denver, CO 80204
Web: www.cesda.org/664.html

Summary To provide financial assistance to high school seniors in Colorado who are planning to attend college in the state and are Asian Americans, other minorities, or first-generation college students.

Eligibility This program is open to seniors graduating from high schools in Colorado who are 1) the first member of their family to attend college; 2) a member of an underrepresented ethnic or racial minority (African American, Asian/Pacific

Islander, American Indian, Hispanic/Chicano/Latino); and/or 3) able to demonstrate financial need. Applicants must have a GPA of 2.8 or higher and be planning to enroll at a 2- or 4-year college or university in Colorado. U.S. citizenship or permanent resident status is required. Selection is based on leadership and community service (particularly within minority communities), past academic performance, personal and professional accomplishments, personal attributes, special abilities, academic goals, and financial need.

Financial data The stipend is $1,000.

Duration 1 year; nonrenewable.

Number awarded Varies each year.

Deadline March of each year.

[88]
COMMUNICATIONS INTERNSHIP AWARD FOR STUDENTS OF COLOR

College and University Public Relations Association of
 Pennsylvania
Calder Square
P.O. Box 10034
State College, PA 16805-0034
Fax: (814) 863-3428   E-mail: kathyettinger@psu.edu
Web: www.cuprap.org/default.aspx?pageid=16

Summary To provide an opportunity for Asian Americans and other students of color at institutions that are members of the College and University Public Relations Association of Pennsylvania (CUPRAP) to complete an internship in communications.

Eligibility This program is open to students of color (i.e., African Americans, Asian/Pacific Islanders, Hispanics/Latinos, and Native Americans) who have completed the first year of college and are enrolled as a degree candidate in the second year or higher. Applicants must obtain and complete a verifiable internship of at least 150 hours in a communications-related field (e.g., print media, radio, television, public relations, advertising, graphic/web design). They must be enrolled full time at an accredited 2- or 4-year college or university that is a member of CUPRAP, but they are not required to be residents of Pennsylvania. Selection is based on financial need, academic ability, communication skills, and creativity as demonstrated through work samples.

Financial data The stipend is $1,500, paid upon confirmation of employment in an internship position.

Duration The internship award is presented annually; recipients may reapply.

Additional information This internship award was first presented in 1983.

Number awarded 1 each year.

Deadline January.

[89]
COMMUNITY COLLEGE SCHOLARSHIP PROGRAM

Filipino Women's League
Attn: Community Scholarship Committee
P.O. Box 419
Pearl City, HI 96782

Summary To provide financial assistance to Hawaii high school seniors who are of Filipino descent and are interested in attending a community college in the state.

Eligibility This program is open to Hawaii residents who are graduating high school seniors, of Filipino ancestry, and enrolling full time at a community college in the state. Applicants must have a high school GPA of 3.5 or higher. Selection is based primarily on financial need; other selection criteria include scholastic achievement (measured by transcripts and SAT or ACT scores), educational goals, and extracurricular interests.

Financial data The award provides for full or partial payment of tuition (to a maximum of $1,000 per year). Payment is made directly to the financial aid office of the recipient's college.

Duration 1 year.

Number awarded 1 or more each year.

Deadline March of each year.

[90]
COMTO ROSA L. PARKS SCHOLARSHIPS

Conference of Minority Transportation Officials
Attn: National Scholarship Program
818 18th Street, N.W., Suite 850
Washington, DC 20006
(202) 530-0551   Fax: (202) 530-0617
Web: www.comto.org/news-youth.php

Summary To provide financial assistance for college to children of Asian American and other members of the Conference of Minority Transportation Officials (COMTO) and to other students working on a bachelor's or master's degree in transportation.

Eligibility This program is open to 1) college-bound high school seniors whose parent has been a COMTO member for at least 1 year; 2) undergraduates who have completed at least 60 semester credit hours in a transportation discipline; and 3) students working on a master's degree in transportation who have completed at least 15 credits. Applicants must have a GPA of 3.0 or higher. Along with their application, they must submit a cover letter with a 500-word statement of career goals. Financial need is not considered in the selection process. U.S. citizenship is required.

Financial data The stipend is $4,500. Funds are paid directly to the recipient's college or university.

Duration 1 year.

Additional information COMTO was established in 1971 to promote, strengthen, and expand the roles of minorities in all aspects of transportation. Recipients are expected to attend the COMTO National Scholarship Luncheon.

Number awarded 2 each year.

Deadline April of each year.

[91]
CONFERENCE ON ASIAN PACIFIC AMERICAN LEADERSHIP SCHOLARSHIPS

Conference on Asian Pacific American Leadership
Attn: Scholarship Committee
P.O. Box 65073
Washington, DC 20035-5073
(202) 628-1307   Fax: (877) 892-5427
E-mail: scholarships@capal.org
Web: www.capal.org/programs/scholarship-program

Summary To provide funding for summer internships in Washington, D.C. to Asian Pacific American undergraduate and graduate students.

Eligibility This program is open to Asian Pacific American (APA) undergraduate and graduate students who have secured a public sector internship within the Washington, D.C. metropolitan area at a federal government agency, a Capitol Hill legislative office, or a nonprofit organization. Applicants must demonstrate a desire to build skills and develop their commitment to public service and the APA community. Along with their application, they must submit a 750-word essay on 2 of the following topics: 1) their long-term career goals and how the summer internship experience will advance those; 2) their previous educational, community work, and internship experiences and how those experiences have influenced their long-term career goals; or 3) how they will use the experiences and knowledge that they gain during their summer in Washington to better the APA community and their local community. Selection is based on demonstrated commitment to public service, including service to the APA community; potential to benefit from the internship; demonstrated leadership and potential for continued growth in leadership skills; relevance of the proposed internship to overall public sector goals; academic achievement; and financial need.

Financial data Awardees receive a stipend of $2,000 to help pay expenses during their internship.

Duration At least 6 weeks during the summer.

Additional information This program began in 1992 with separate scholarships named for distinguished leaders of the APA community: the Asha Jaini Emerging Leader Scholarship, the Attapong P. Mellenthin Memorial Scholarship, and the Senator Paul Simon Scholarship. Recipients must agree to have a Community Action Plan (CAP) proposed, approved, and presented before their departure from Washington, D.C. at the end of the summer.

Number awarded 2 or 3 each year.

Deadline February of each year.

[92]
CONNECTICUT EDUCATION FOUNDATION SCHOLARSHIPS FOR MINORITY COLLEGE STUDENTS

Connecticut Education Association
Attn: Connecticut Education Foundation, Inc.
21 Oak Street, Suite 500
Hartford, CT 06106-8001
(860) 525-5641   Toll Free: (800) 842-4316
Fax: (860) 725-6323   E-mail: sheilac@cea.org
Web: www.cea.org/about/cef/minguidelines.cfm

Summary To provide financial assistance to Asian Americans and other minority college students in Connecticut who are interested in preparing for a teaching career.

Eligibility This program is open to minority students (Blacks, Native Americans or Alaskan Natives, Asian or Pacific Islanders, and Hispanics or Latinos) from Connecticut who have been accepted into a teacher preparation program at an accredited college or university in the state. Applicants must have earned a GPA of 2.75 or higher. Finalists may be interviewed. Financial need is considered in the selection process.

Financial data The stipend is $750.

Duration 1 year; may be renewed.

Number awarded At least 1 each year.

Deadline April of each year.

[93]
CONNECTICUT EDUCATION FOUNDATION SCHOLARSHIPS FOR MINORITY HIGH SCHOOL STUDENTS

Connecticut Education Association
Attn: Connecticut Education Foundation, Inc.
21 Oak Street, Suite 500
Hartford, CT 06106-8001
(860) 525-5641   Toll Free: (800) 842-4316
Fax: (860) 725-6323   E-mail: sheilac@cea.org
Web: www.cea.org/about/cef/minguidelines.cfm

Summary To provide financial assistance to Asian American and other minority high school seniors in Connecticut who are interested in attending college in the state to prepare for a teaching career.

Eligibility This program is open to minority seniors (Blacks, Native Americans or Alaskan Natives, Asian or Pacific Islanders, and Hispanics or Latinos) graduating from high schools in Connecticut. Applicants have been accepted at an accredited 2- or 4-year college or university in the state and be planning to enter the teaching profession. They must have a GPA of 2.75 or higher. Finalists may be interviewed. Financial need is considered in the selection process.

Financial data The stipend is $500.

Duration 1 year; may be renewed.

Number awarded At least 1 each year.

Deadline April of each year.

[94]
CONNECTICUT MINORITY TEACHER INCENTIVE PROGRAM

Connecticut Department of Higher Education
Attn: Office of Student Financial Aid
61 Woodland Street
Hartford, CT 06105-2326
(860) 947-1857   Fax: (860) 947-1838
E-mail: mtip@ctdhe.org
Web: www.ctdhe.org/SFA/default.htm

Summary To provide financial assistance and loan repayment to Asian American and other minority upper-division college students in Connecticut who are interested in teaching at public schools in the state.

Eligibility This program is open to juniors and seniors enrolled full time in Connecticut college and university teacher preparation programs. Applicants must be members of a minority group, defined as African American, Hispanic/Latino, Asian American, or Native American. They must be nominated by the education dean at their institution.

Financial data The maximum stipend is $5,000 per year. In addition, if recipients complete a credential and begin teaching at a public school in Connecticut within 16 months of graduation, they may receive up to $2,500 per year, for up to 4 years, to help pay off college loans.

Duration Up to 2 years.

Number awarded Varies each year.

Deadline September of each year.

[95]
CONNTESOL SCHOLARSHIPS

Connecticut Teachers of English to Speakers of Other
  Languages
P.O. Box 304
Norwich, CT 06360-0304
E-mail: ConnTESOL@gmail.com
Web: www.conntesol.net

Summary To provide financial assistance to Connecticut residents whose native language is not English and who are attending or planning to attend college in any state.

Eligibility This program is open to residents of Connecticut whose first language is not English. Awards are presented in 4 categories: 1) high school seniors entering a 2-year college; 2) high school seniors entering a 4-year college or university; 3) community college students transferring to a 4-year college or university; and 4) adult education students entering a college or university. Applicants must submit an essay of 250 to 500 words on how the education they are receiving in the United States is influencing their life.

Financial data The stipend is $1,000.

Duration 1 year.

Number awarded At least 4 each year (1 in each category).

Deadline April of each year.

[96]
CORA AGUDA MANAYAN FUND

Hawai'i Community Foundation
Attn: Scholarship Department
827 Fort Street Mall
Honolulu, HI 96813
(808) 537-6333   Toll Free: (888) 731-3863
Fax: (808) 521-6286
E-mail: scholarships@hcf-hawaii.org
Web: www.hawaiicommunityfoundation.org/scholarships

Summary To provide financial assistance to Hawaii residents of Filipino ancestry who are interested in attending college or graduate school to prepare for a career in the health field.

Eligibility This program is open to Hawaii residents of Filipino ancestry who are interested in enrolling full time in a health-related field (on the undergraduate or graduate school level). Applicants must be able to demonstrate academic achievement (GPA of 2.7 or higher), good moral character, and financial need. Along with their application, they must submit a short statement indicating their reasons for attending college, their planned course of study, their career goals, and what community service means to them. Preference may be given to applicants studying at a college or university in Hawaii.

Financial data The amounts of the awards depend on the availability of funds and the need of the recipient. Recently, the average value of all scholarships awarded by the foundation was $2,041.

Duration 1 year.

Number awarded Varies each year; recently, 10 of these scholarships were awarded.

Deadline February of each year.

[97]
CORRINE WILLIAMS SCHOLARSHIP

California Dietetic Association
Attn: CDA Foundation
7740 Manchester Avenue, Suite 102
Playa del Rey, CA 90293-8499
(310) 822-0177   Fax: (310) 823-0264
E-mail: patsmith@dietitian.org
Web: www.dietitian.org/cdaf_scholarships.htm

Summary To provide financial assistance to residents of California (particularly Asian Americans, other minorities, males, and those with disabilities) who are members of the American Dietetic Association (ADA) and interested in participating in specified types of programs in any state.

Eligibility This program is open to California residents who are ADA members and 1) entering the first or second year of an approved Dietetic Technician Program in any state; 2) entering at least the second year of an accredited Coordinated Program (CP) or Didactic Program in Dietetics (DPD) in any state; or 3) accepted to an accredited Supervised Practice Program in any state to begin within 6 months. Along with their application, they must submit a letter of application that includes a discussion of their career goals. Selection is based on that letter (15%), academic ability (25%), work or volunteer experience (15%), letters of recommendation (15%), extracurricular activities (5%), and financial need (25%). Applications are especially encouraged from ethnic minorities, men, and people with physical disabilities.

Financial data The stipend is normally $1,000.

Duration 1 year.

Additional information This scholarship was first awarded in 2010.

Number awarded 1 each year.

Deadline February of each year.

[98]
CRACKER BARREL-MINORITY TEACHER EDUCATION SCHOLARSHIPS

Florida Fund for Minority Teachers, Inc.
Attn: Executive Director
G415 Norman Hall
P.O. Box 117045
Gainesville, FL 32611-7045
(352) 392-9196, ext. 21   Fax: (352) 846-3011
E-mail: info@ffmt.org
Web: www.ffmt.org

Summary To provide funding to Asian Americans and other minorities who are Florida residents and preparing for a career as a teacher.

Eligibility This program is open to Florida residents who are African American/Black, Hispanic/Latino, Asian American/Pacific Islander, or American Indian/Alaskan Native. Applicants must be entering their junior year in a teacher education program at a participating college or university in Florida. Special consideration is given to community college graduates. Selection is based on writing ability, communication skills, overall academic performance, and evidence of commitment to the youth of America (preferably demonstrated through volunteer activities).

Financial data The stipend is $2,000 per year. Recipients are required to teach 1 year in a Florida public school for each year they receive the scholarship. If they fail to teach in a public school, they are required to repay the total amount of support received at an annual interest rate of 8%.

Duration Up to 2 consecutive years, provided the recipient remains enrolled full time with a GPA of 2.5 or higher.

Additional information For a list of the 16 participating public institutions and the 18 participating private institutions, contact the Florida Fund for Minority Teachers (FFMT). Recipients are also required to attend the annual FFMT recruitment and retention conference.

Number awarded Varies each year.

Deadline July of each year for fall semester; November of each year for spring semester.

[99]
CREATIVE ARTS AWARD

Japanese American Citizens League
Attn: National Scholarship Awards
1765 Sutter Street
San Francisco, CA 94115
(415) 921-5225   Fax: (415) 931-4671
E-mail: jacl@jacl.org
Web: www.jacl.org/edu/scholar.htm

Summary To provide financial assistance to student members of the Japanese American Citizens League (JACL) interested in working on an undergraduate or graduate degree in the creative arts.

Eligibility This program is open to JACL members who are interested in working on an undergraduate or graduate degree in the creative arts. Professional artists are not eligible. Applicants must submit a detailed proposal on the nature of their project, including a time plan, anticipated date of completion, and itemized budget. They must also submit information on their involvement in JACL and a 2-page essay on a topic that changes annually but relates to Japanese Americans. Selection is based on that essay, academic history, extracurricular activities, JACL involvement, scholastic honors, and a letter of recommendation. Preference is given to students who are interested in creative projects that reflect the Japanese American experience and culture.

Financial data Stipends generally average approximately $2,000.

Duration 1 year; nonrenewable.

Number awarded At least 1 each year.

Deadline March of each year.

[100]
CSLA LEADERSHIP FOR DIVERSITY SCHOLARSHIP

California School Library Association
Attn: Executive Director
950 Glenn Drive, Suite 150
Folsom, CA 95630
(916) 447-2684   Fax: (916) 447-2695
E-mail: info@csla.net
Web: www.csla.net/awa/scholarships.htm

Summary To provide financial assistance to Asian Americans and other students who reflect the diversity of California's population and are interested in earning a credential as a library media teacher in the state.

Eligibility This program is open to students who are members of a traditionally underrepresented group enrolled in a college or university library media teacher credential program in California. Applicants must intend to work as a library media teacher in a California school library media center for a minimum of 3 years. Along with their application, they must submit a 250-word statement on their school library media career interests and goals, why they should be considered, what they can contribute, their commitment to serving the needs of multicultural and multilingual students, and their financial situation.

Financial data The stipend is $1,500.

Duration 1 year.

Number awarded 1 each year.

Deadline April of each year.

[101]
CSPI PUBLIC INTEREST INTERNSHIP PROGRAM

Center for Science in the Public Interest
Attn: Internships
1875 Connecticut Avenue, N.W., Suite 300
Washington, DC 20009-5728
(202) 332-9110   Fax: (202) 265-4954
E-mail: hr@cspinet.org
Web: www.cspinet.org/about/jobs/200801042.html

Summary To provide summer work experience to students (especially Asian Americans, other minorities, women, and those with disabilities) who are interested in working on health and nutritional issues at the Center for Science in the Public Interest (CSPI).

Eligibility This program is open to undergraduate, graduate, law, and medical students who are interested in working at the center, which is concerned with evaluating the effects of science and technology on society and promoting national policies responsive to consumers' interests. CSPI focuses primarily on health and nutritional issues, disclosing deceptive marketing practices, dangerous food additives or contaminants, and flawed science propagated by profits. Applicants must submit a cover letter indicating issues of interest, future plans, and dates of availability; a resume; writing samples; 2 letters of recommendation from instructors or employers; and an official transcript of courses and grades. Minorities, women, and persons with disabilities are especially encouraged to apply.

Financial data Undergraduate interns earn $8.25 per hour; graduate student interns earn $9.25 per hour.

Duration 10 weeks during the summer.

Number awarded A small number each year.

Deadline January of each year.

[102]
CULTURAL RESOURCES DIVERSITY INTERNSHIP PROGRAM

Student Conservation Association, Inc.
Attn: Diversity Internships
1800 North Kent Street, Suite 102
Arlington, VA 22209
(703) 524-2441   Fax: (703) 524-2451
E-mail: jchow@thesca.org
Web: www.thesca.org/partners/special-initiatives

Summary To offer an opportunity for Asian Americans, other ethnically diverse undergraduate and graduate students, and students with disabilities to intern at facilities of the U.S. National Park Service (NPS) during the summer.

Eligibility This program is open to currently-enrolled students at the sophomore or higher level. Applicants must be U.S. citizens or permanent residents with a GPA of 3.0 or higher. Although all students may apply, the program is designed to give ethnically diverse students and students with disabilities the opportunity to experience the diversity of careers in the federal sector. Applicants are assigned to a position within the NPS. Possible projects include editing publications, planning exhibits, participating in archaeological excavations, preparing research reports, cataloguing park and museum collections, providing interpretive programs on historical topics, developing community outreach, and writing lesson plans based on historical themes.

Financial data Interns receive a salary of $225 per week, basic medical insurance coverage, a housing stipend of up to $800 per month, a $100 uniform allowance, travel expenses up to $630, and eligibility for an Americorps Educational Award of $1,000.

Duration 10 weeks in the summer (beginning in June).

Additional information While participating in the internship, students engage in tri-weekly evening career and professional development events, ongoing career counseling, mentoring, and personal and career development services.

Number awarded Approximately 15 each year.

Deadline February of each year.

[103]
DAMON P. MOORE SCHOLARSHIP

Indiana State Teachers Association
Attn: Scholarships
150 West Market Street, Suite 900
Indianapolis, IN 46204-2875
(317) 263-3400   Toll Free: (800) 382-4037
Fax: (317) 655-3700   E-mail: mshoup@ista-in.org
Web: www.ista-in.org/dynamic.aspx?id=1212

Summary To provide financial assistance to Asian American and other minority high school seniors in Indiana who are interested in studying education in college.

Eligibility This program is open to ethnic minority public high school seniors in Indiana who are interested in studying education in college. Selection is based on academic achievement, leadership ability as expressed through co-curricular activities and community involvement, recommendations, and a 300-word essay on their educational goals and how they plan to use this scholarship.

Financial data The stipend is $1,000.

Duration 1 year; may be renewed for 2 additional years if the recipient maintains at least a "C+" GPA.

Additional information This program was established in 1987.

Number awarded 1 each year.

Deadline February of each year.

[104]
DAVID SANKEY MINORITY SCHOLARSHIP IN METEOROLOGY

National Weather Association
Attn: Executive Director
228 West Millbrook Road
Raleigh, NC 27609-4304
(919) 845-1546   Fax: (919) 845-2956
E-mail: exdir@nwas.org
Web: www.nwas.org

Summary To provide financial assistance to Asian Americans and other minorities working on an undergraduate or graduate degree in meteorology.

Eligibility This program is open to members of minority groups who are either entering their sophomore or higher year of undergraduate study or enrolled as graduate students. Applicants must be working on a degree in meteorology. Along with their application, they must submit a 1-page statement explaining why they are applying for this scholarship. Selection is based on that statement, academic achievement, and 2 letters of recommendation.

Financial data The stipend is $1,000.

Duration 1 year.

Additional information This program was established in 2002.

Number awarded 1 each year.

Deadline April of each year.

[105]
DEFENSE INTELLIGENCE AGENCY UNDERGRADUATE TRAINING ASSISTANCE PROGRAM

Defense Intelligence Agency
Attn: Human Resources, HCH-4
200 MacDill Boulevard, Building 6000
Bolling AFB, DC 20340-5100
(202) 231-8228   Fax: (202) 231-4889
TDD: (202) 231-5002   E-mail: staffing@dia.mil
Web: www.dia.mil/employment/student/index.htm

Summary To provide funding and work experience to high school seniors and lower-division students (particularly Asian Americans, other minorities, women, and those with disabilities) who are interested in majoring in specified fields and working for the U.S. Defense Intelligence Agency (DIA).

Eligibility This program is open to graduating high school seniors and college freshmen and sophomores interested in working full time on a baccalaureate degree in 1 of the following fields in college: biology, chemistry, computer science, engineering, foreign area studies, intelligence analysis, international relations, microbiology, pharmacology, physics, political science, or toxicology. High school seniors must have a GPA of 2.75 or higher and either 1) an SAT combined critical reading and mathematics score of 1000 or higher plus 500 or higher on the writing portion or 2) an ACT score of 21 or higher. College freshmen and sophomores must have a GPA of 3.0 or higher. All applicants must be able to demonstrate financial need (household income ceiling of $70,000 for a family of 4 or $80,000 for a family of 5 or more) and leadership abilities through extracurricular activities, civic involvement, volunteer work, or part-time employment. Students and all members of their immediate family must be U.S. citizens.

Minorities, women, and persons with disabilities are strongly encouraged to apply.

Financial data Students accepted into this program receive tuition (up to $18,000 per year) at an accredited college or university selected by the student and endorsed by the sponsor; reimbursement for books and needed supplies; an annual salary to cover college room and board expenses and for summer employment; and a position at the sponsoring agency after graduation. Recipients must work for DIA after college graduation for at least 1 and a half times the length of study. For participants who leave DIA earlier than scheduled, the agency arranges for payments to reimburse DIA for the total cost of education (including the employee's pay and allowances).

Duration 4 years, provided the recipient maintains a GPA of 2.75 during the freshman year and 3.0 or higher in subsequent semesters.

Additional information Recipients are provided a challenging summer internship and guaranteed a job at the agency in their field of study upon graduation.

Number awarded Only a few are awarded each year.

Deadline November of each year.

[106]
DELL THURMOND WOODARD FELLOWSHIP

The Fund for American Studies
Attn: Fellowships
1706 New Hampshire Avenue, N.W.
Washington, DC 20009
(202) 986-0384   Toll Free: (800) 741-6964
Fax: (202) 986-8930   E-mail: jtilley@tfas.org
Web: www.tfas.org/Page.aspx?pid=1511

Summary To provide an opportunity for Asian American and other upper-division or graduate students (especially those with an interest in diversity and ethics issues) to learn about high technology public policy issues during a summer internship in Washington, D.C.

Eligibility This program is open to juniors, seniors, and graduate students who have an interest and background in issues regarding diversity and ethics and are currently enrolled at a 4-year college or university in the United States. Applicants must be interested in working in the government relations office of a high technology company or association in Washington while they also attend weekly issues seminar lunches hosted by the program's sponsors. They must have an interest in public policy and the high technology industry; a background in computer science or other high technology fields is helpful but not required. International students are eligible. Selection is based on evidence of a strong interest in a career in high technology public policy, civic mindedness and participation in community activities or organizations, academic achievements, and recommendations.

Financial data Fellows receive a grant of $5,000.

Duration 8 weeks during the summer.

Additional information This program was established in 2007 with support from the Congressional Black Caucus Foundation (CBCF), the Congressional Hispanic Caucus Institute (CHCI), and the Asian Pacific Institute for Congressional Studies (APAICS). Those 3 sponsors select the fellow on a rotational basis.

Number awarded 1 each year.

Deadline February of each year.

[107]
DELOITTE ASCEND SCHOLARSHIP

Ascend: Pan-Asian Leaders
Attn: Director of Programs
120 Wall Street, Third Floor
New York, NY 10005
(212) 248-4888   Fax: (212) 344-5636
E-mail: info@ascendleadership.org
Web: www.ascendleadership.org

Summary To provide financial assistance to undergraduate members of Ascend: Pan-Asian Leaders who are working on a degree in accounting.

Eligibility This program is open to members of Ascend who are enrolled as full-time sophomores, juniors, or seniors (in 5-year programs) at 4-year colleges and universities in the United States. Applicants must have a GPA of 3.3 or higher overall and in their major. Along with their application, they must submit a 500-word personal essay on how they have demonstrated leadership and teamwork in their academic studies, professional career, and/or extracurricular activities and community volunteer work; why they believe those qualities are important to be competitive in a borderless world; their career goals after graduation; and the role Ascend has played in the achievement of their academic and career goals. They must also answer questions on whether they have an academic and career interest in professional services at Deloitte LLP in accounting, consulting, and advisory fields. Financial need is not considered in the selection process.

Financial data The stipend is $3,000.

Duration 1 year.

Additional information Ascend was formed in 2004 as the National Asian American Society of Accountants. This program is sponsored by Deloitte LLP.

Number awarded 1 each year.

Deadline July of each year.

[108]
DENI AND JUNE UEJIMA MEMORIAL SCHOLARSHIP

Japanese American Citizens League
Attn: National Scholarship Awards
1765 Sutter Street
San Francisco, CA 94115
(415) 921-5225   Fax: (415) 931-4671
E-mail: jacl@jacl.org
Web: www.jacl.org/edu/scholar.htm

Summary To provide financial assistance for college to student members of the Japanese American Citizens League (JACL) who are high school seniors.

Eligibility This program is open to JACL members who are high school seniors interested in attending a college, university, trade school, business college, or other institution of higher learning. Applicants must submit information on their involvement in JACL and a 2-page essay on a topic that changes annually but relates to Japanese Americans. Selection is based on that essay, academic history, extracurricular activities, JACL involvement, scholastic honors, and a letter of recommendation.

Financial data Stipends generally average approximately $2,000.

Duration 1 year; nonrenewable.

Number awarded At least 1 each year.

Deadline February of each year.

[109]
DENVER BUDDHIST TEMPLE DOJO SENSEI MEMORIAL SCHOLARSHIP

Japanese American Community Graduation Program
P.O. Box 13665
Denver, CO 80201-3665
(303) 288-6083
Web: www.jacgp.com/student-scholarships

Summary To provide financial assistance to high school seniors of Japanese descent in the Rocky Mountain region who have participated in judo or another martial art and plan to attend college in any state.

Eligibility This program is open to graduating high school seniors 1) residing in the Rocky Mountain region who are either an American citizen of Japanese ancestry or an American citizen whose legal parents are of Japanese ancestry; or 2) of Japanese ancestry residing in the Rocky Mountain region and have permanent residence status (green card) in the United States; or 3) who have a parent who is an active member of: Mile Hi Chapter of Japanese American Citizens League (JACL), Japanese Association of Colorado, Nisei Veterans' Heritage Foundation, Simpson United Method Church, Tri-State/Denver Buddhist Temples, Denver Nisei Bowling Association, Brighton Japanese American Association, Japanese Firms Association of Colorado, Longmont Buddhist Temple, or Fort Lupton JACL. Applicants must be planning to attend a college or university in any state. They must have been associated with a recognized martial arts program. Along with their application, they must submit a 1-page essay on how the philosophy taught in martial arts guides them in the way they intend to live their life. Selection is based on that essay; longevity of enrollment, participation, and volunteerism in a martial art; school records; and school and community activities and awards.

Financial data Stipends up to $4,000 are available.

Duration 1 year.

Additional information This program is sponsored by the Denver Buddhist Temple in honor of the Senseis who have taught or promoted the sport of judo in the community and the Rocky Mountain region.

Number awarded 1 each year.

Deadline April of each year.

[110]
DEPARTMENT OF STATE STUDENT INTERN PROGRAM

Department of State
Attn: HR/REE
2401 E Street, N.W., Suite 518 H
Washington, DC 20522-0108
(202) 261-8888   Toll Free: (800) JOB-OVERSEAS
Fax: (301) 562-8968   E-mail: Careers@state.gov
Web: www.careers.state.gov/students/programs

Summary To provide a work/study opportunity to undergraduate and graduate students (especially Asian Americans, other minorities, and women) who are interested in foreign service.

Eligibility This program is open to full- and part-time continuing college and university juniors, seniors, and graduate students. Applications are encouraged from students with a broad range of majors, such as business or public administration, social work, economics, information management, journalism, and the biological, engineering, and physical sciences, as well as those majors more traditionally identified with international affairs. U.S. citizenship is required. The State Department particularly encourages eligible women and minority students with an interest in foreign affairs to apply.

Financial data Most internships are unpaid. A few paid internships are granted to applicants who can demonstrate financial need. If they qualify for a paid internship, they are placed at the GS-4 step 5 level (currently with an annual rate of $27,786). Interns placed abroad may also receive housing, medical insurance, a travel allowance, and a dependents' allowance.

Duration Paid internships are available only for 10 weeks during the summer. Unpaid internships are available for 1 semester or quarter during the academic year, or for 10 weeks during the summer.

Additional information About half of all internships are in Washington, D.C., or occasionally in other large cities in the United States. The remaining internships are at embassies and consulates abroad. Depending upon the needs of the department, interns are assigned junior-level professional duties, which may include research, preparing reports, drafting replies to correspondence, working in computer science, analyzing international issues, financial management, intelligence, security, or assisting in cases related to domestic and international law. Interns must agree to return to their schooling immediately upon completion of their internship.

Number awarded Approximately 800 internships are offered each year, but only about 5% of those are paid positions.

Deadline February of each year for fall internships; June of each year for spring internships; October of each year for summer internships.

[111]
DIVERSITY COMMITTEE SCHOLARSHIP

American Society of Safety Engineers
Attn: ASSE Foundation
1800 East Oakton Street
Des Plaines, IL 60018
(847) 768-3435   Fax: (847) 768-3434
E-mail: agabanski@asse.org
Web: www.asse.org

Summary To provide financial assistance to Asian American and other upper-division and graduate student members of the American Society of Safety Engineers (ASSE) who come from diverse groups.

Eligibility This program is open to ASSE student members who are working on an undergraduate or graduate degree in occupational safety, health, and environment or a closely-related field (e.g., industrial or environmental engineering, environmental science, industrial hygiene, occupational health nursing). Applicants must be full-time students who have completed at least 60 semester hours with a GPA of 3.0 or higher as undergraduates or at least 9 semester hours with a GPA of 3.5 or higher as graduate students. Along with their application, they must submit 2 essays of 300 words or less: 1) why they are seeking a degree in occupational safety and health or a closely-related field, a brief description of their current activities, and how those relate to their career goals and objectives; and 2) why they should be awarded this scholarship (including career goals and financial need). A goal of this program is to support individuals regardless of race, ethnicity, gender, religion, personal beliefs, age, sexual orientation, physical challenges, geographic location, university, or specific area of study. U.S. citizenship is not required.

Financial data The stipend is $1,000 per year.

Duration 1 year; recipients may reapply.

Number awarded 1 each year.

Deadline November of each year.

[112]
DIVERSITY SUMMER HEALTH-RELATED RESEARCH EDUCATION PROGRAM

Medical College of Wisconsin
Attn: Student Affairs/Diversity Program Coordinator
8701 Watertown Plank Road
Milwaukee, WI 53226
(414) 955-8735   Fax: (414) 955-0129
Web: www.mcw.edu/display/router.asp?docid=619

Summary To provide an opportunity for Asian Americans and other undergraduate residents of any state who come from diverse backgrounds to participate in a summer research training experience at the Medical College of Wisconsin.

Eligibility This program is open to U.S. citizens and permanent residents who come from diverse and economically and/or educationally disadvantaged backgrounds. Applicants must be interested in participating in a summer research training program at the Medical College of Wisconsin. They must have completed at least 1 year of undergraduate study at an accredited college or university (or be a community college student enrolled in at least 3 courses per academic term) and have a GPA of 3.0 or higher.

Financial data The stipend is $10 per hour for a 40-hour week. Housing is provided for students who live outside the Milwaukee area and travel expenses are paid for those who live outside Wisconsin.

Duration 10 weeks during the summer.

Additional information Students are "matched" with a full-time faculty investigator to participate in a research project addressing the causes, prevention, and treatment of cardiovascular, pulmonary, or hematological diseases. This program is funded by the National Heart, Lung, and Blood Institute (NHLBI) of the National Institutes of Health (NIH). Participants are required to prepare an abstract of their research and make a brief oral presentation of their project at the conclusion of the summer.

Number awarded Approximately 12 each year.

Deadline February of each year.

[113]
DOLLARS FOR SCHOLARS PROGRAM

United Methodist Higher Education Foundation
Attn: Scholarships Administrator
1001 19th Avenue South
P.O. Box 340005
Nashville, TN 37203-0005
(615) 340-7385   Toll Free: (800) 811-8110
Fax: (615) 340-7330
E-mail: umhefscholarships@gbhem.org
Web: www.umhef.org/receive.php?id=dollars_for_scholars

Summary To provide financial assistance to students (especially Asian American and other minority students) who are at Methodist colleges, universities, and seminaries and whose home churches agree to contribute to their support.

Eligibility The Double Your Dollars for Scholars program is open to students attending or planning to attend a United Methodist-related college, university, or seminary as a full-time student. Applicants must have been an active, full member of a United Methodist Church for at least 1 year prior to applying. Their home church must nominate them and agree to contribute to their support. Many of the United Methodist colleges and universities have also agreed to contribute matching funds for a Triple Your Dollars for Scholars Program, and a few United Methodist conference foundations have agreed to contribute additional matching funds for a Quadruple Your Dollars for Scholars Program. Awards are granted on a first-come, first-served basis. Some of the awards are designated for Hispanic, Asian, and Native American (HANA) students funded by the General Board of Higher Education and Ministry.

Financial data The sponsoring church contributes $1,000 and the United Methodist Higher Education Foundation (UMHEF) contributes a matching $1,000. Students who attend a participating United Methodist college or university receive an additional $1,000 for the Triple Your Dollars for Scholars Program, and those from a participating conference receive a fourth $1,000 increment for the Quadruple Your Dollars for Scholars Program.

Duration 1 year; may be renewed as long as the recipients maintain satisfactory academic progress as defined by their institution.

Additional information Currently, participants in the Double Your Dollars for Scholars program include 2 United Methodist seminaries and theological schools, 1 professional school, 19 senior colleges and universities, and 1 2-year college. The Triple Your Dollars for Scholars program includes an additional 11 United Methodist seminaries and theological schools, 73 senior colleges and universities, and 5 2-year colleges (for a complete list, consult the UMHEF). The conference foundations participating in the Quadruple Your Dollars for Scholars Program are limited to the Alabama-West Florida United Methodist Foundation, the Mississippi United Methodist Foundation (for students at Millsaps College or Rust College), the Missouri United Methodist Foundation (for students at Saint Paul School of Theology or Central Methodist University), the Nashville Area United Methodist Foundation, the North Carolina United Methodist Foundation (for students at Louisburg College, Methodist University, or North Carolina Wesleyan College), the North Georgia United Methodist Foundation, the Oklahoma United Methodist Foundation (for students at Oklahoma City University) the United Methodist

Foundation of Arkansas (for students at Hendrix College or Philander Smith College), the United Methodist Foundation of South Indiana, and the United Methodist Foundation of Western North Carolina.

Number awarded 350 each year, including 25 designated for HANA students.

Deadline Local churches must submit applications in March of each year for senior colleges and universities and seminaries or May of each year for 2-year colleges.

[114]
DON SAHLI–KATHY WOODALL MINORITY STUDENT SCHOLARSHIP

Tennessee Education Association
801 Second Avenue North
Nashville, TN 37201-1099
(615) 242-8392 Toll Free: (800) 342-8367
Fax: (615) 259-4581 E-mail: wdickens@tea.nea.org
Web: www.teateachers.org

Summary To provide financial assistance to Asian American and other minority high school seniors in Tennessee who are interested in majoring in education at a college or university in the state.

Eligibility This program is open to minority high school seniors in Tennessee who are planning to attend a college or university in the state and major in education. Application must be made either by a Future Teachers of America chapter affiliated with the Tennessee Education Association (TEA) or by the student with the recommendation of an active TEA member. Selection is based on academic record, leadership ability, financial need, and demonstrated interest in becoming a teacher.

Financial data The stipend is $1,000.

Duration 1 year.

Number awarded 1 each year.

Deadline February of each year.

[115]
DORA AMES LEE LEADERSHIP DEVELOPMENT FUND

United Methodist Church
General Board of Global Ministries
Attn: United Methodist Committee on Relief
475 Riverside Drive, Room 1522
New York, NY 10115
(212) 870-3871 Toll Free: (800) UMC-GBGM
E-mail: jyoung@gbgm-umc.org
Web: gbgm-umc.org/health/doralee.cfm

Summary To provide financial assistance to Methodists and other Christians of Asian or Native American descent who are preparing for a career in a health-related field.

Eligibility This program is open to undergraduate and graduate students along with college graduates who are U.S. citizens of Asian American or Native American descent. Applicants must be professed Christians, preferably United Methodists. They must be attending a college or university to enter or continue in a health-related field. Financial need is considered in the selection process.

Financial data The stipend is $2,000.

Duration 1 year.

Additional information This program was established in 1980.

Number awarded 5 each year.

Deadline June of each year.

[116]
DOUVAS MEMORIAL SCHOLARSHIP

Wyoming Department of Education
Attn: Consultant
2300 Capitol Avenue, First Floor
Cheyenne, WY 82002-0050
(307) 777-6198 Fax: (307) 777-6234
E-mail: bhayes@educ.state.wy.us
Web: edu.wyoming.gov

Summary To provide financial assistance to Asian American and other high school seniors or students in Wyoming who are first-generation Americans.

Eligibility This program is open to first-generation youth in Wyoming who demonstrate need and are motivated to attend college. First-generation Americans are those born in the United States but whose parents were not born here. Applicants must be high school seniors or between the ages of 18 and 22. They must be Wyoming residents and be willing to use the scholarship at Wyoming's community colleges or the University of Wyoming.

Financial data The stipend is $500, payable in 2 equal installments. Funds are paid directly to the recipient's school.

Duration 1 year.

Additional information This scholarship was first awarded in 1995.

Number awarded 1 each year.

Deadline May of each year.

[117]
DR. JO ANN OTA FUJIOKA SCHOLARSHIP

Phi Delta Kappa International
Attn: PDK Educational Foundation
408 North Union Street
P.O. Box 7888
Bloomington, IN 47407-7888
(812) 339-1156 Toll Free: (800) 766-1156
Fax: (812) 339-0018 E-mail: scholarships@pdkintl.org
Web: www.pdkintl.org/awards/prospective.htm

Summary To provide financial assistance to Asian Americans and other high school seniors of color who plan to study education at a college in any state and have a connection to Phi Delta Kappa (PDK).

Eligibility This program is open to high school seniors of color who are planning to major in education and can meet 1 of the following criteria: 1) is a member of a Future Educators Association (FEA) chapter; 2) is the child or grandchild of a PDK member; 3) has a reference letter written by a PDK member; or 4) is selected to represent the local PDK chapter. Applicants must submit a 500-word essay on a topic related to education that changes annually; recently, they were invited to explain what caused them to choose a career in education, what they hope to accomplish during their career as an educator, and how they will measure their success. Selection is based on the essay, academic standing, letters of recommendation, service activities, educational activities, and leadership activities; financial need is not considered.

Financial data The stipend depends on the availability of funds; recently, it was $2,000.

Duration 1 year.

Additional information This program was established in 2006.

Number awarded 1 each year.

Deadline January of each year.

[118]
DR. THOMAS T. YATABE MEMORIAL SCHOLARSHIP

Japanese American Citizens League
Attn: National Scholarship Awards
1765 Sutter Street
San Francisco, CA 94115
(415) 921-5225   Fax: (415) 931-4671
E-mail: jacl@jacl.org
Web: www.jacl.org/edu/scholar.htm

Summary To provide financial assistance for college to student members of the Japanese American Citizens League (JACL).

Eligibility This program is open to JACL members who are currently enrolled at a college, university, trade school, business college, or other institution of higher learning. Applicants must submit information on their involvement in JACL and a 2-page essay on a topic that changes annually but relates to Japanese Americans. Selection is based on that essay, academic history, extracurricular activities, JACL involvement, scholastic honors, and a letter of recommendation.

Financial data Stipends generally average approximately $2,000.

Duration 1 year; nonrenewable.

Number awarded At least 1 each year.

Deadline March of each year.

[119]
DRS. POH SHIEN AND JUDY YOUNG SCHOLARSHIP

US Pan Asian American Chamber of Commerce
Attn: Scholarship Coordinator
1329 18th Street, N.W.
Washington, DC 20036
(202) 296-5221   Toll Free: (800) 696-7818
Fax: (202) 296-5225   E-mail: info@uspaacc.com
Web: www.uspaacc.com

Summary To provide financial assistance for college to Asian Pacific American high school seniors who demonstrate financial need.

Eligibility This program is open to high school seniors of Asian or Pacific Islander heritage who are U.S. citizens or permanent residents. Applicants must be planning to enroll full time at an accredited postsecondary educational institution in the United States. Along with their application, they must submit a 500-word essay on their background, achievements, and personal goals. Selection is based on academic excellence (GPA of 3.3 or higher), leadership in extracurricular activities, community service involvement, and financial need.

Financial data The maximum stipend is $5,000. Funds are paid directly to the recipient's college or university.

Duration 1 year.

Additional information Funding is not provided for correspondence courses, Internet courses, or study in a country other than the United States.

Number awarded 1 each year.

Deadline March of each year.

[120]
DWIGHT MOSLEY SCHOLARSHIPS

United States Tennis Association
Attn: USTA Serves
70 West Red Oak Lane
White Plains, NY 10604
(914) 696-7223   E-mail: foundation@usta.com
Web: www.usta.com

Summary To provide financial assistance for college to Asian Americans and other high school seniors from diverse ethnic backgrounds who have participated in an organized community tennis program.

Eligibility This program is open to high school seniors from diverse ethnic backgrounds who have excelled academically, demonstrated achievements in leadership, and participated extensively in an organized community tennis program. Applicants must be planning to enroll as a full-time undergraduate student at a 4-year college or university. They must have a GPA of 3.0 or higher and be able to demonstrate financial need and sportsmanship. Along with their application, they must submit an essay of 1 to 2 pages about how their participation in a tennis and education program has influenced their life, including examples of special mentors, volunteer service, and future goals. Males and females are considered separately.

Financial data The stipend is $2,500 per year. Funds are paid directly to the recipient's college or university.

Duration 4 years.

Number awarded 2 each year: 1 male and 1 female.

Deadline February of each year.

[121]
EAST AMERICA CHAPTER UNDERGRADUATE SCHOLARSHIP AWARDS

Phi Tau Phi Scholastic Honor Society-East America
  Chapter
c/o Dr. Yung-Ching Shen, Scholarship Selection
  Committee
Siena College
515 Loudon Road
Loudonville, NY 12211
(518) 783-2960   E-mail: yshen@siena.edu
Web: phitauphi.org

Summary To provide financial assistance to college juniors and seniors of Chinese heritage at colleges and universities in eastern states.

Eligibility This program is open to juniors and seniors enrolled at an accredited institution of higher education east of a line along Ohio, Kentucky, and Alabama. Applicants must be of Chinese heritage or interested in and committed to Chinese heritage and culture, have a GPA of 3.4 or higher, and be sponsored by a member of Phi Tau Phi. Along with their application, they must submit a 1-page essay on their professional goals, achievements, financial need, and Chinese cultural interests.

Financial data The stipend is $1,000.

Duration 1 year.

Additional information Phi Tau Phi, first organized in 1921 in China and reestablished in 1964 in the United States, is a relatively small honor society of scholars, mainly of Chinese heritage, in various disciplines of science, technology, art, and humanities. Students who have difficulty in locating a sponsor should contact the Scholarship Selection Committee.

Number awarded 1 or 2 each year.

Deadline September of each year.

[122]
EASTERN REGION KOREAN AMERICAN SCHOLARSHIPS

Korean American Scholarship Foundation
Eastern Region
1952 Gallows Road, Suite 204
Vienna, VA 22182
(703) 748-5935   Fax: (703) 748-1874
E-mail: eastern@kasf.org
Web: www.kasf.org/application_set.html

Summary To provide financial assistance to Korean American students from any state who are working on an undergraduate or graduate degree in any field at a school in eastern states.

Eligibility This program is open to Korean American students who are currently enrolled or planning to enroll at a college or university in an eastern state as a full-time undergraduate or graduate student. Applicants may reside anywhere in the United States as long as they attend school in the eastern region: Delaware, District of Columbia, Kentucky, Maryland, North Carolina, Pennsylvania, Virginia, and West Virginia. They must have a GPA of 3.0 or higher. Selection is based on academic achievement, school activities, community service, and financial need.

Financial data Stipends range from $350 to $5,000.

Duration 1 year; renewable.

Number awarded Varies each year; recently, 54 of these scholarships were awarded.

Deadline May of each year.

[123]
ED BRADLEY SCHOLARSHIP

Radio Television Digital News Foundation
Attn: RTDNF Fellowship Program
4121 Plank Road, Suite 512
Fredericksburg, VA 22407
(202) 467-5214   Fax: (202) 223-4007
E-mail: staceys@rtdna.org
Web: www.rtdna.org/pages/education/undergraduates.php

Summary To provide financial assistance to Asian American and other minority undergraduate students who are preparing for a career in electronic journalism.

Eligibility This program is open to sophomore or more advanced minority undergraduate students enrolled in an electronic journalism sequence at an accredited or nationally-recognized college or university. Applicants must submit 1 to 3 examples of their journalistic skills on audio CD or DVD (no more than 15 minutes total, accompanied by scripts); a description of their role on each story and a list of who worked on each story and what they did; a 1-page statement explaining why they are preparing for a career in electronic journalism with reference to their specific career preference (radio, television, online, reporting, producing, or newsroom management); a resume; and a letter of reference from their dean or faculty sponsor explaining why they are a good candidate for the award and certifying that they have at least 1 year of school remaining.

Financial data The stipend is $10,000, paid in semiannual installments of $5,000 each.

Duration 1 year.

Additional information The Radio Television Digital News Foundation (RTDNF) also provides an all-expense paid trip to the Radio Television Digital News Association (RTDNA) annual international conference. The RTDNF was formerly the Radio and Television News Directors Foundation (RTNDF). Previous winners of any RTDNF scholarship or internship are not eligible.

Number awarded 1 each year.

Deadline May of each year.

[124]
EDSA MINORITY SCHOLARSHIP

Landscape Architecture Foundation
Attn: Scholarship Program
818 18th Street, N.W., Suite 810
Washington, DC 20006-3520
(202) 331-7070   Fax: (202) 331-7079
E-mail: scholarships@lafoundation.org
Web: www.laprofession.org/financial/scholarships.htm

Summary To provide financial assistance to Asian American and other minority college students who are interested in studying landscape architecture.

Eligibility This program is open to African American, Hispanic, Native American, and minority college students of other cultural and ethnic backgrounds. Applicants must be entering their final 2 years of undergraduate study in landscape architecture. Along with their application, they must submit a 500-word essay on a design or research effort they plan to pursue (explaining how it will contribute to the advancement of the profession and to their ethnic heritage), work samples, and 2 letters of recommendation. Selection is based on professional experience, community involvement, extracurricular activities, and financial need.

Financial data The stipend is $3,500.

Additional information This scholarship was formerly designated the Edward D. Stone, Jr. and Associates Minority Scholarship.

Number awarded 1 each year.

Deadline February of each year.

[125]
EDWARD S. ROTH MANUFACTURING ENGINEERING SCHOLARSHIP

Society of Manufacturing Engineers
Attn: SME Education Foundation
One SME Drive
P.O. Box 930
Dearborn, MI 48121-0930
(313) 425-3300   Toll Free: (800) 733-4763, ext. 3300
Fax: (313) 425-3411   E-mail: foundation@sme.org
Web: www.smeef.org

Summary To provide financial assistance to Asian Americans and other students enrolled or planning to work on a bachelor's or master's degree in manufacturing engineering at selected universities.

Eligibility This program is open to U.S. citizens who are graduating high school seniors or currently-enrolled undergraduate or graduate students. Applicants must be enrolled or planning to enroll as a full-time student at 1 of 13 selected 4-year universities to work on a bachelor's or master's degree in manufacturing engineering. They must have a GPA of 3.0 or higher. Preference is given to 1) students demonstrating financial need, 2) minority students, and 3) students participating in a co-op program. Some preference may also be given to graduating high school seniors and graduate students. Along with their application, they must submit a 300-word essay that covers their career and educational objectives, how this scholarship will help them attain those objectives, and why they want to enter this field.

Financial data Stipend amounts vary; recently, the value of all scholarships provided by this foundation annually averages approximately $2,700.

Duration 1 year; may be renewed.

Additional information The eligible institutions are California Polytechnic State University at San Luis Obispo, California State Polytechnic State University at Pomona, University of Miami (Florida), Bradley University (Illinois), Central State University (Ohio), Miami University (Ohio), Boston University, Worcester Polytechnic Institute (Massachusetts), University of Massachusetts, St. Cloud State University (Minnesota), University of Texas-Pan American, Brigham Young University (Utah), and Utah State University.

Number awarded 2 each year.

Deadline January of each year.

[126]
EIRO YAMADA MEMORIAL SCHOLARSHIP

Go For Broke Memorial Education Center
P.O. Box 2590
Gardena, CA 90247
(310) 222-5710   Fax: (310) 222-5700
E-mail: Cayleen@goforbroke.org
Web: www.goforbroke.org

Summary To provide financial assistance for college or graduate school to residents of any state who are descendants of World War II Japanese American veterans.

Eligibility This program is open to residents of any state who are attending or planning to attend a trade school, community college, or 4-year college or university on the undergraduate or graduate school level. Applicants must be 1) a direct descendant of a Japanese American World War II vet-

eran, or 2) a descendant once-removed (such as a grand-niece or a grand-nephew) of a Japanese American serviceman or servicewoman killed in action during World War II. Along with their application, they must submit a short essay on "The Values I Have Learned from My Japanese American Forefathers" or their personal reflections on the Japanese American experience during World War II.

Financial data Stipends range from $500 to $1,000.

Duration 1 year.

Number awarded Varies each year; recently, 12 of these scholarships were awarded.

Deadline April of each year.

[127]
ELI LILLY AND COMPANY/BLACK DATA PROCESSING ASSOCIATES SCHOLARSHIP

Black Data Processing Associates
Attn: BDPA Education Technology Foundation
4423 Lehigh Road, Number 277
College Park, MD 20740
(513) 284-4968   Fax: (202) 318-2194
E-mail: scholarships@betf.org
Web: www.betf.org/scholarships/eli-lilly.shtml

Summary To provide financial assistance to Asian American and other minority high school seniors and current college students who are interested in studying information technology at a college in any state.

Eligibility This program is open to graduating high school seniors and current college undergraduates who are members of minority groups (African American, Hispanic, Asian, or Native American). Applicants must be enrolled or planning to enroll at an accredited 4-year college or university and work on a degree in information technology. They must have a GPA of 3.0 or higher. Along with their application, they must submit a 500-word essay on why information technology is important. Selection is based on that essay, academic achievement, leadership ability through academic or civic involvement, and participation in community service activities. U.S. citizenship or permanent resident status is required.

Financial data The stipend is $2,500. Funds may be used to pay for tuition, fees, books, room and board, or other college-related expenses.

Duration 1 year; nonrenewable.

Additional information The BDPA established its Education and Technology Foundation (BETF) in 1992 to advance the skill sets needed by African American and other minority adults and young people to compete in the information technology industry. This program is sponsored by Eli Lilly and Company.

Number awarded 1 or more each year.

Deadline July of each year.

[128]
EMERGING DIVERSITY EDUCATION FUND SCHOLARSHIPS

Decisive Magazine
Attn: Emerging Diversity Education Fund
8201 Corporate Drive, Suite 500
Landover, MD 20785
(301) 850-2858
Web: www.decisivemagazine.com

Summary To provide financial assistance to Asian American and other minority students interested in preparing for a career in an automotive-related profession.

Eligibility This program is open to minority (African American, Asian Indian American, Asian Pacific American, Hispanic American, or Native American) high school seniors or students who are currently enrolled full time at a college, university, or technical school. Applicants must be interested in preparing for a career in the automotive industry. They must have a GPA of 2.7 or higher. Along with their application, they must submit 250-word essays on 1) what diversity in the automotive industry means to them, and 2) how their automotive profession or endeavors will have an impact on diversity. Financial need is not considered in the selection process. U.S. citizenship is required.

Financial data Stipends range from $1,000 to $2,500.

Duration 1 year.

Additional information This scholarship, established in 1998, was previously named the Edward Davis Scholarship Fund in honor of the first African American to own a new car dealership.

Deadline December of each year.

[129]
ENCOURAGE MINORITY PARTICIPATION IN OCCUPATIONS WITH EMPHASIS ON REHABILITATION

Courage Center
Attn: EMPOWER Scholarship Program
3915 Golden Valley Road
Minneapolis, MN 55422
(763) 520-0214   Toll Free: (888) 8-INTAKE
Fax: (763) 520-0562   TDD: (763) 520-0245
E-mail: empower@couragecenter.org
Web: www.couragecenter.org

Summary To provide financial assistance to Asian Americans and other students of color from Minnesota and western Wisconsin who are interested in attending college in any state to prepare for a career in the medical rehabilitation field.

Eligibility This program is open to ethnically diverse students accepted at or enrolled in an institution of higher learning in any state. Applicants must be residents of Minnesota or western Wisconsin (Burnett, Pierce, Polk, and St. Croix counties). They must be able to demonstrate a career interest in the medical rehabilitation field by a record of volunteer involvement related to health care and must have a GPA of 2.0 or higher. Along with their application, they must submit a 1-page essay that covers their experiences and interactions to date with the area of volunteering, what they have accomplished and gained from those experiences, how those experiences will assist them in their future endeavors, why education is important to them, how this scholarship will help them with their financial need and their future career goals.

Financial data The stipend is $1,500.

Duration 1 year.

Additional information This program, established in 1995, is also identified by its acronym as the EMPOWER Scholarship Award.

Number awarded 2 each year.

Deadline May of each year.

[130]
ENGENDERED SCHOLARSHIPS

South Asian Journalists Association
c/o Aseem Chhabra, Awards Committee Chair
4315 46th Street, Apartment E10
Sunnyside, NY 11104-2015
E-mail: chhabs@aol.com
Web: www.saja.org/programs/scholarships

Summary To provide financial assistance for undergraduate and graduate study to journalism students of south Asian descent who write on issues related to gender and sexuality.

Eligibility This program is open to students of south Asian descent (including Bangladesh, Bhutan, India, Maldives, Nepal, Pakistan, and Sri Lanka; Indo-Caribbeans are also eligible). Applicants must be enrolled at a college or university in the United States or Canada and working on an undergraduate or graduate degree in journalism with an interest in writing on issues related to gender and sexuality. Students with financial hardship are given special consideration. Selection is based on interest in journalism, writing skills, participation in the sponsoring organization, reasons for entering journalism, and financial need.

Financial data The stipend is $1,000.

Duration 1 year.

Additional information Recipients are expected to give back to the South Asian Journalists Association (SAJA) by volunteering at the annual convention or at other events during the year.

Number awarded 2 each year: 1 to an undergraduate and 1 to a graduate student.

Deadline March of each year.

[131]
ENVIRONMENTAL PROTECTION AGENCY STUDENT DIVERSITY INTERNSHIP PROGRAM

United Negro College Fund Special Programs
  Corporation
Attn: NASA Science and Technology Institute
6402 Arlington Boulevard, Suite 600
Falls Church, VA 22042
(703) 677-3400   Toll Free: (800) 530-6232
Fax: (703) 205-7645   E-mail: portal@uncfsp.org
Web: www.uncfsp.org

Summary To provide an opportunity for Asian American and other underrepresented undergraduate and graduate students to work on a summer research project at research sites of the U.S. Environmental Protection Agency (EPA).

Eligibility This program is open to rising college sophomores, juniors, and seniors and to full-time graduate students at accredited institutions who are members of underrepresented groups, including ethnic minorities (African Americans, Hispanic/Latinos, Native Americans, Asians, Alaskan Natives, and Native Hawaiians/Pacific Islanders) and persons with disabilities. Applicants must have a GPA of 2.8 or higher and be working on a degree in business, communications, economics, engineering, environmental science/management, finance, information technology, law, marketing, or science. They must be interested in working on a research project during the summer at their choice of 23 EPA research sites (for a list, contact EPA). U.S. citizenship is required.

Financial data The stipend is $5,000 for undergraduates or $6,000 for graduate students. Interns also receive a travel and housing allowance, but they are responsible for covering their local transportation, meals, and miscellaneous expenses.

Duration 10 weeks during the summer.

Additional information This program is funded by EPA and administered by the United Negro College Fund Special Programs Corporation.

Number awarded Varies each year.

Deadline May of each year.

[132]
ERNST & YOUNG ASCEND SCHOLARSHIPS

Ascend: Pan-Asian Leaders
Attn: Director of Programs
120 Wall Street, Third Floor
New York, NY 10005
(212) 248-4888   Fax: (212) 344-5636
E-mail: info@ascendleadership.org
Web: www.ascendleadership.org

Summary To provide financial assistance to members of Ascend: Pan-Asian Leaders who are undergraduates working on a degree in accounting.

Eligibility This program is open to members of Ascend who are enrolled as full-time rising sophomores or juniors at colleges and universities in the United States. Applicants must have a GPA of 3.5 or higher and a major in accounting. They may not have received a grade lower than a "B" in any accounting class. Along with their application, they must submit a 500-word personal essay on how they have demonstrated leadership and teamwork in their academic studies, professional career, and/or extracurricular activities and community volunteer work; why they believe those qualities are important to be competitive in a borderless world; their career goals after graduation; and the role Ascend has played in the achievement of their academic and career goals. They must also answer questions about their leadership experience. Financial need is not considered in the selection process.

Financial data The stipend is $5,000.

Duration 1 year.

Additional information Ascend was formed in 2004 as the National Asian American Society of Accountants. This program is sponsored by Ernst & Young LLP.

Number awarded 4 each year.

Deadline July of each year.

[133]
ESTER BOONE MEMORIAL SCHOLARSHIPS

National Naval Officers Association-Washington, D.C.
    Chapter
Attn: Scholarship Program
2701 Park Center Drive, A1108
Alexandria, VA 22302
(703) 566-3840   Fax: (703) 566-3813
E-mail: Stephen.Williams@Navy.mil
Web: dcnnoa.memberlodge.com

Summary To provide financial assistance to Asian American and other minority high school seniors from the Washington, D.C. area.

Eligibility This program is open to minority seniors at high schools in the Washington, D.C. metropolitan area who plan to enroll full time at an accredited 2- or 4-year college or university. Applicants must have a GPA of 2.5 or higher. Selection is based on academic achievement, community involvement, and financial need.

Financial data The stipend is $1,000.

Duration 1 year; nonrenewable.

Additional information Recipients are not required to join or affiliate with the military in any way.

Number awarded 1 or more each year.

Deadline March of each year.

[134]
EXCELLENCE IN CARDIOVASCULAR SCIENCES SUMMER RESEARCH PROGRAM

Wake Forest University School of Medicine
Attn: Hypertension and Vascular Research Center
Medical Center Boulevard
Winston-Salem, NC 27157-1032
(336) 716-1080   Fax: (336) 716-2456
E-mail: nsarver@wfubmc.edu
Web: www.wfubmc.edu

Summary To provide Asian Americans and other underrepresented students with an internship opportunity to engage in a summer research project in cardiovascular science at Wake Forest University in Winston-Salem, North Carolina.

Eligibility This program is open to undergraduates and master's degree students who are members of underrepresented minority groups (African Americans, Alaskan Natives, Asian Americans, Native Americans, Pacific Islanders, and Hispanics) or who come from disadvantaged backgrounds (e.g., rural areas, first generation college students). Applicants must be interested in participating in a program of summer research in the cardiovascular sciences that includes "hands-on" laboratory research, a lecture series by faculty and guest speakers, and a research symposium at which students present their research findings. U.S. citizenship or permanent resident status is required.

Financial data The stipend is $1,731 per month, housing in a university dormitory, and round-trip transportation expense.

Duration 2 months during the summer.

Additional information This program is sponsored by the National Heart, Lung, and Blood Institute (NHLBI) of the National Institutes of Health (NIH).

Number awarded Approximately 10 each year.

Deadline February of each year.

[135]
FACES OF DIVERSITY SCHOLARSHIPS

National Restaurant Association Educational Foundation
Attn: Scholarships Program
175 West Jackson Boulevard, Suite 1500
Chicago, IL 60604-2702
(312) 715-1010, ext. 738
Toll Free: (800) 765-2122, ext. 6738
Fax: (312) 566-9733   E-mail: scholars@nraef.org
Web: www.nraef.org/media/releases/20110425.aspx

Summary To provide financial assistance to Asian American and other minority undergraduate students who are interested in preparing for a career in the restaurant and food service industry.

Eligibility This program is open to Asian, Hispanic, African, and Native American students preparing for a career in the restaurant and food service industry. Applicants must be U.S. citizens or permanent residents who have completed at least 1 term of their college program. They must be enrolled full time or substantial part time and have a GPA of 2.75 or higher or a GED score of 470 or higher. Along with their application, they must submit 1) an essay of 200 to 250 words that provides a description of their current educational and work experience and their goals in the industry; and 2) an essay of 300 to 400 words on what diversity and inclusion mean to them, why they are important for a successful business, and how they plan to give back to the industry or community once they have reached their career goals. Selection is based on the essay, presentation of the application, GPA or GED scores, industry-related experience, and strength of letters of recommendation.

Financial data The stipend is $2,500.

Duration 1 year.

Additional information This program is jointly supported by the National Restaurant Association Educational Foundation (NRAEF) and PepsiCo Foodservice.

Number awarded 4 each year.

Deadline March of each year.

[136]
FALEA SCHOLARSHIP PROGRAM

Filipino American League of Engineers and Architects
Attn: FALEA Foundation
P.O. Box 4135
Honolulu, HI 96812-4135
E-mail: falea@falea.org
Web: www.falea.org

Summary To provide financial assistance to Hawaii residents who are of Filipino descent and are interested in attending college in any state to prepare for a career in engineering, architecture, or a related field.

Eligibility This program is open to high school seniors and currently-enrolled college students who are Hawaii residents and of Filipino descent. Applicants must be enrolled or planning to enroll full time at a college or university in any state to work on a degree in engineering, architecture, surveying, or a related field. They must have a GPA of 3.0 or higher. Along with their application, they must submit an essay on why they are seeking the scholarship, the extracurricular activities in which they have been involved, the positions they have held in organizations or clubs, their community service, and other information they feel might be helpful.

Financial data The stipend is $1,000.

Duration 1 year.

Additional information This program was started in 1994.

Number awarded Varies each year; recently, 5 of these scholarships were awarded.

Deadline August of each year.

[137]
FAPAC SCHOLARSHIPS

Federal Asian Pacific American Council
P.O. Box 23184
Washington, DC 20026-3184
(202) 422-6913   E-mail: fapac@fapac.org
Web: www.fapac.org

Summary To provide financial assistance for college to Asian Pacific Americans.

Eligibility This program is open to Asian Pacific Americans, including (but not restricted to) children, grandchildren, nieces, nephews, brothers, and sisters of members of the Federal Asian Pacific American Council (FAPAC). Applicants must be high school seniors or current college students. Along with their application, they must submit an essay of 500 to 750 words on the topic "Leadership, Diversity, and Harmony: Gateway to Success." Selection is based on academic and special achievement, skills and abilities, leadership in school, and leadership in civic and other extracurricular volunteer activities.

Financial data The stipend is $2,000.

Duration 1 year.

Additional information FAPAC is an organization of Asian Pacific Americans employed by the federal government and the District of Columbia.

Number awarded Varies each year; recently, 5 of these scholarships were awarded.

Deadline May of each year.

[138]
FARM CREDIT EAST SCHOLARSHIPS

Farm Credit East
Attn: Scholarship Program
240 South Road
Enfield, CT 06082
(860) 741-4380   Toll Free: (800) 562-2235
Fax: (860) 741-4389
Web: www.farmcrediteast.com

Summary To provide financial assistance to residents of designated northeastern states (particularly Asian Americans and other minorities) who plan to attend school in any state to work on an undergraduate or graduate degree in a field related to agriculture, forestry, or fishing.

Eligibility This program is open to residents of Massachusetts, Connecticut, Rhode Island, New Jersey, and portions of New York and New Hampshire. Applicants must be working on or planning to work on an associate, bachelor's, or graduate degree in production agriculture, agribusiness, the forest products industry, or commercial fishing at a college or university in any state. They must submit a 200-word essay on why they wish to prepare for a career in agriculture, forestry, or fishing. Selection is based on the essay, extracurricular activities (especially farm work experience and activities indicative of an interest in preparing for a career in agriculture or agribusiness), and interest in agriculture. The program includes scholarships reserved for members of minority (Black or African American, American Indian or Alaska Native, Asian, Native Hawaiian or other Pacific Islander, or Hispanic or Latino) groups.

Financial data The stipend is $1,500. Funds are paid directly to the student to be used for tuition, room and board, books, and other academic charges.

Duration 1 year; nonrenewable.

Additional information Recipients are given priority for an internship with the sponsor in the summer following their junior year. Farm Credit East was formerly named First Pioneer Farm Credit.

Number awarded Up to 28 each year, including several reserved for members of minority groups.

Deadline April of each year.

[139]
FEDERAL ASIAN PACIFIC AMERICAN COUNCIL INTERNSHIPS

Federal Asian Pacific American Council
P.O. Box 23184
Washington, DC 20026-3184
(202) 422-6913   E-mail: fapac@fapac.org
Web: www.fapac.org

Summary To provide work experience to Asian Pacific American upper-division students at the offices of the Federal Asian Pacific American Council (FAPAC).

Eligibility This program is open to college juniors and seniors from the Asian Pacific American communities who are interested in public service. Applicants may be relatives of FAPAC members or non-FAPAC members. They must be interested in working at the FAPAC offices to help plan, organize, and coordinate the Congressional Seminars and Training Conference. Selection is based on academic and special achievement, skills and abilities, leadership in school, and leadership in civic and other extracurricular volunteer activities.

Financial data The stipend is $2,000.

Duration 10 weeks, beginning in April.

Additional information FAPAC is an organization of Asian Pacific Americans employed by the federal government and the District of Columbia.

Number awarded Varies each year; recently, 2 of these internships were awarded.

Deadline May of each year.

[140]
FEDERAL INTERNSHIP PROGRAM

Conference on Asian Pacific American Leadership
Attn: Scholarship Committee
P.O. Box 65073
Washington, DC 20035-5073
(202) 628-1307   Fax: (877) 892-5427
E-mail: scholarships@capal.org
Web: www.capal.org/programs/federal-internship-program

Summary To provide funding for summer internships with designated federal agencies to Asian Pacific American undergraduate and graduate students.

Eligibility This program is open to Asian Pacific American (APA) undergraduate and graduate students who are working on a degree in any field. Applicants must be interested in a summer internship at a federal agency; recently, those included the Office of Personnel Management (OPM) and several agencies within the U.S. Department of Agriculture (Rural Development, Forest Service, Agricultural Research Service, and Food Safety and Inspection Service). Along with their application, they must submit a 750-word essay on 2 of the following topics: 1) their long-term career goals and how the summer internship experience will advance those; 2) their previous educational, community work, and internship experiences and how those experiences have influenced their long-term career goals; or 3) how they will use the experiences and knowledge that they gain during their summer in Washington to better the APA community and their local community. Selection is based on demonstrated commitment to public service, including service to the APA community; potential to benefit from the internship; demonstrated leadership and potential for continued growth in leadership skills; relevance of the proposed internship to overall public sector goals; academic achievement; and financial need. U.S. citizenship is required.

Financial data Interns receive a stipend of $2,000 to help pay expenses during their assignment.

Duration At least 6 weeks during the summer.

Additional information Assignments are available in Washington, D.C. or at sites nationwide.

Number awarded At least 10 each year.

Deadline January of each year.

[141]
FILIPINO CHAMBER OF COMMERCE OF HAWAII SCHOLARSHIPS

Filipino Chamber of Commerce of Hawaii
Attn: Foundation
1125 North King Street, Suite 302
Honolulu, HI 96817-3356
(808) 843-8838   Fax: (808) 843-8868
E-mail: info@filipinochamber.org
Web: www.filipinochamber.org

Summary To provide financial assistance to Filipino and other high school seniors in Hawaii who have an interest in business and are planning to attend college in any state.

Eligibility This program is open to seniors graduating from high schools in Hawaii who have a GPA of 3.5 or higher and have been accepted at a 4-year college or university in any state. Applicants must submit a 1-page essay describing how they expect to promote Hawaii's business community, broaden opportunities for Filipino entrepreneurs and other businesses, strengthen business links between Hawaii and the Philippines, and support the well-being of the community. Selection is based on that essay, academic record (including SAT and/or ACT scores), awards and honors, and activities.

Financial data Stipends are $4,000 or $3,000.

Duration 1 year.

Additional information The highest-ranked applicant receives the Renato and Maria A.F. Etrata Foundation/Filipino Chamber Foundation Scholarship.

Number awarded Varies each year; recently, 5 of these scholarships were awarded: 1 at $4,000 and 4 at $3,000.

Deadline March of each year.

[142]
FILIPINO NURSES' ORGANIZATION OF HAWAII SCHOLARSHIP

Hawai'i Community Foundation
Attn: Scholarship Department
827 Fort Street Mall
Honolulu, HI 96813
(808) 537-6333   Toll Free: (888) 731-3863
Fax: (808) 521-6286
E-mail: scholarships@hcf-hawaii.org
Web: www.hawaiicommunityfoundation.org/scholarships

Summary To provide financial assistance to Hawaii residents of Filipino ancestry who are interested in attending college in any state to prepare for a career as a nurse.

Eligibility This program is open to Hawaii residents of Filipino ancestry who are enrolled or planning to enroll full time at a college or university in any state and work on an undergraduate or graduate degree in nursing. Applicants must be able to demonstrate academic achievement (GPA of 2.7 or higher), good moral character, and financial need. Along with their application, they must submit a short statement indicating their reasons for attending college, their planned course of study, their career goals, and what community service means to them.

Financial data The amounts of the awards depend on the availability of funds and the need of the recipient. Recently, the average value of all scholarships awarded by the foundation was $2,041.

Duration 1 year.

Number awarded Varies each year; recently, 2 of these scholarships were awarded.

Deadline February of each year.

[143]
FINANCIAL NEED SCHOLARSHIPS

India American Cultural Association
Attn: Indian American Scholarship Fund
1281 Cooper Lake Road, S.E.
Smyrna, GA 30082
(770) 436-3719   Fax: (770) 436-4272
E-mail: iasf@imlogical.com
Web: www.iasf.org/IASF/Scholarships.html

Summary To provide need-based financial assistance to high school seniors in Georgia who are of Indian descent and plan to attend college in any state.

Eligibility This program is open to seniors graduating from high schools in Georgia who are of Indian descent (at least 1 grandparent was born in India). Applicants must be planning to attend a 4-year college or university in any state as a full-time student. Along with their application, they must submit an official school transcript, resume, SAT or ACT score report, the best essay they submitted to a college when they applied, and documentation of financial need. Selection is based primarily on financial need.

Financial data Stipends range from $1,000 to $2,500 per year.

Duration 1 year; may be renewed up to 3 additional years.

Additional information This program, established in 1993, includes the following named scholarships: the Paras Shah Memorial Award, the N.M. Kelkar Memorial Award, the Darshan S. Bhatia Memorial Award, the P.V. Jagannatha Rao

Memorial Award, the Raghavan Award, the Aman Daftari Memorial Award, the Boyapally Reddy Award, the Sadashiv Bhargave Memorial Award, and the Ishwarlal Shroff Memorial Award.

Number awarded Varies each year; recently, the sponsor awarded a total of 14 scholarships: 4 for 4 years, 1 for 2 years, and 9 for 1 year.

Deadline March of each year.

[144]
FISHER COMMUNICATIONS SCHOLARSHIPS FOR MINORITIES

Fisher Communications
Attn: Minority Scholarship
100 Fourth Avenue North, Suite 510
Seattle, WA 98109
(206) 404-7000   Fax: (206) 404-6037
E-mail: Info@fsci.com
Web: www.fsci.com/scholarship.html

Summary To provide financial assistance to Asian Americans and other minority college students in selected states who are interested in preparing for a career in broadcasting.

Eligibility This program is open to U.S. citizens of non-white origin who have a GPA of 2.5 or higher and are at least sophomores enrolled in 1) a broadcasting curriculum (radio, television, marketing, or broadcast technology) leading to a bachelor's degree at an accredited 4-year college or university; 2) a broadcast curriculum at an accredited community college, transferable to a 4-year baccalaureate degree program; or 3) a broadcast curriculum at an accredited vocational/technical school. Applicants must be either 1) residents of California, Washington, Oregon, Idaho, or Montana; or 2) attending a school in those states. They must submit an essay that explains their financial need, educational and career goals, any experience or interest they have in broadcast communications that they feel qualifies them for this scholarship, and involvement in school activities. Selection is based on need, academic achievement, and personal qualities.

Financial data A stipend is awarded (amount not specified).

Duration 1 year; recipients may reapply.

Additional information This program began in 1987.

Number awarded Varies; a total of $10,000 is available for this program each year.

Deadline May of each year.

[145]
FLORIDA BOARD OF ACCOUNTANCY MINORITY SCHOLARSHIPS

Florida Board of Accountancy
240 N.W. 76th Drive, Suite A
Gainesville, FL 32607-6656
(850) 487-1395   Fax: (352) 333-2508
Web: www.myflorida.com/dbpr/cpa

Summary To provide financial assistance to Asian Americans, other minorities, and women residents of Florida who are entering the fifth year of an accounting program.

Eligibility This program is open to Florida residents who have completed at least 120 credit hours at a college or university in the state and have a GPA of 2.5 or higher. Applicants must be planning to remain in school for the fifth year required to sit for the C.P.A. examination. They must be members of a minority group, defined to include African Americans, Hispanic Americans, Asian Americans, Native Americans, and women. Selection is based on scholastic ability and performance and financial need.

Financial data The stipend is $3,000 per semester.

Duration 1 semester; may be renewed 1 additional semester.

Number awarded Varies each year; a total of $100,000 is available for this program annually.

Deadline May of each year.

[146]
FLORIDA FUND FOR MINORITY TEACHERS SCHOLARSHIPS

Florida Fund for Minority Teachers, Inc.
Attn: Executive Director
G415 Norman Hall
P.O. Box 117045
Gainesville, FL 32611-7045
(352) 392-9196, ext. 21   Fax: (352) 846-3011
E-mail: info@ffmt.org
Web: www.ffmt.org

Summary To provide funding to Asian Americans and other minorities in Florida who are preparing for a career as a teacher.

Eligibility This program is open to Florida residents who are African American/Black, Hispanic/Latino, Asian American/Pacific Islander, or American Indian/Alaskan Native. Applicants must be entering their junior year in a teacher education program at a participating college or university in Florida. Special consideration is given to community college graduates. Selection is based on writing ability, communication skills, overall academic performance, and evidence of commitment to the youth of America (preferably demonstrated through volunteer activities).

Financial data The stipend is $4,000 per year. Recipients are required to teach 1 year in a Florida public school for each year they receive the scholarship. If they fail to teach in a public school, they are required to repay the total amount of support received at an annual interest rate of 8%.

Duration Up to 2 consecutive years, provided the recipient remains enrolled full time with a GPA of 2.5 or higher.

Additional information For a list of the 16 participating public institutions and the 18 participating private institutions, contact the Florida Fund for Minority Teachers (FFMT). Recipients are also required to attend the annual FFMT recruitment and retention conference.

Number awarded Varies each year.

Deadline July of each year for fall semester; November of each year for spring semester.

[147]
FORUM FOR CONCERNS OF MINORITIES SCHOLARSHIPS

American Society for Clinical Laboratory Science
Attn: Forum for Concerns of Minorities
2025 M Street, N.W., Suite 800
Washington, DC 20036
(202) 367-1174   E-mail: ascls@ascls.org
Web: www.ascls.org/?page=Awards_FCM

Summary To provide financial assistance to Asian American and other minority students in clinical laboratory scientist and clinical laboratory technician programs.

Eligibility This program is open to minority students who are enrolled in a program in clinical laboratory science, including clinical laboratory science/medical technology (CLS/MT) and clinical laboratory technician/medical laboratory technician (CLT/MLT). Applicants must be able to demonstrate financial need. Membership in the American Society for Clinical Laboratory Science is encouraged but not required.

Financial data Stipends depend on the need of the recipients and the availability of funds.

Duration 1 year.

Number awarded 2 each year: 1 to a CLS/MT student and 1 to a CLT/MLT student.

Deadline March of each year.

[148]
FRANCES SONN NAM MEMORIAL SCHOLARSHIP

Asian & Pacific Islander American Scholarship Fund
1900 L Street, N.W., Suite 210
Washington, DC 20036-5002
(202) 986-6892   Toll Free: (877) 808-7032
Fax: (202) 530-0643   E-mail: info@apiasf.org
Web: www.apiasf.org

Summary To provide financial assistance to Asian and Pacific Islander Americans who are entering their junior year of college and majoring in specified fields.

Eligibility This program is open to U.S. citizens, nationals, permanent residents, or citizens of the Freely Associated States who are of Asian or Pacific Islander heritage. Applicants must be entering their junior year of full-time study at an accredited 4-year college or university in the United States and preparing for a career in law, public service, or government affairs. They must have a GPA of 3.0 or higher. In addition, they must complete the FAFSA and apply for federal financial aid.

Financial data The stipend is $4,000 per year.

Duration 2 years.

Additional information This scholarship is sponsored by Sodexo.

Number awarded 1 or more each year.

Deadline January of each year.

[149]
FRANKLIN WILLIAMS INTERNSHIP

Council on Foreign Relations
Attn: Human Resources Office
58 East 68th Street
New York, NY 10021
(212) 434-9489   Fax: (212) 434-9893
E-mail: humanresources@cfr.org
Web: www.cfr.org

Summary To provide undergraduate and graduate students (particularly Asian Americans and other minorities) with an opportunity to gain work experience in international affairs at the Council on Foreign Relations in New York.

Eligibility Applicants should be currently enrolled in either their senior year of an undergraduate program or in a graduate program in the area of international relations or a related field. They should have a record of high academic achievement, proven leadership ability, and previous related internship or work experience. Minority students are strongly encouraged to apply.

Financial data The stipend is $10 per hour.

Duration 1 academic term (fall, spring, or summer). Fall and spring interns are required to make a commitment of at least 12 hours per week. Summer interns may choose to make a full-time commitment.

Additional information Interns work closely with a program director or fellow in either the studies or meetings program and are involved with program coordination, substantive and business writing, research, and budget management. In addition, they are encouraged to attend the council's programs and participate in informal training designed to enhance management and leadership skills.

Number awarded 3 each year: 1 each academic term.

Deadline Applications may be submitted at any time.

[150]
FRED G. LEE MEMORIAL SCHOLARSHIPS

Chinese American Citizens Alliance-Portland Lodge
11453 S.E. Hazel Hill Road
Clackamas, OR 97015
(503) 925-5226   Fax: (503) 719-8204
E-mail: scholarship@cacaportland.org
Web: www.cacaportland.org/scholarship.html

Summary To provide financial assistance to high school seniors of Chinese descent in Oregon or in Clark County, Washington who plan to attend college in any state.

Eligibility This program is open to seniors graduating from high schools in Oregon or in Clark County, Washington and planning to attend an accredited 2- or 4-year college or university in any state (although 1 scholarship is reserved for a student planning to attend college in Oregon or Washington). Applicants must be a U.S. citizen or permanent resident, have at least 1 parent who is a member of the Portland Lodge of the Chinese American Citizens Alliance, be active in school and community affairs, and have a GPA of 3.5 or higher. Along with their application, they must submit 2 essays of approximately 250 words: the relationship of their educational plans or goals to their Chinese heritage, and their personal philosophy and how their Chinese heritage has affected their perspective. Selection is based on scholarship, leadership in school, community activities, and financial need.

Financial data The stipend is $1,000 per year.

Duration Either 4 years or 1 year.

Number awarded 3 each year: 1 for 4 years and 2 for 1 year.

Deadline March of each year.

[151]
GATES MILLENNIUM SCHOLARS PROGRAM

Bill and Melinda Gates Foundation
P.O. Box 10500
Fairfax, VA 22031-8044
Toll Free: (877) 690-GMSP   Fax: (703) 205-2079
Web: www.gmsp.org

Summary To provide financial assistance to Asian Pacific Americans and other outstanding low-income minority students, particularly those interested in majoring in specific fields in college.

Eligibility This program is open to African Americans, Alaska Natives, American Indians, Hispanic Americans, and Asian Pacific Islander Americans who are graduating high school seniors with a GPA of 3.3 or higher. Principals, teachers, guidance counselors, tribal higher education representatives, and other professional educators are invited to nominate students with outstanding academic qualifications, particularly those likely to succeed in the fields of computer science, education, engineering, library science, mathematics, public health, or science. Nominees should have significant financial need and have demonstrated leadership abilities through participation in community service, extracurricular, or other activities. U.S. citizenship, nationality, or permanent resident status is required. Nominees must be planning to enter an accredited college or university as a full-time, degree-seeking freshman in the following fall.

Financial data The program covers the cost of tuition, fees, books, and living expenses not paid for by grants and scholarships already committed as part of the recipient's financial aid package.

Duration 4 years or the completion of the undergraduate degree, if the recipient maintains at least a 3.0 GPA.

Additional information This program, established in 1999, is funded by the Bill and Melinda Gates Foundation and administered by the United Negro College Fund with support from the American Indian Graduate Center, the Hispanic Scholarship Fund, and the Asian & Pacific Islander American Scholarship Fund.

Number awarded 1,000 new scholarships are awarded each year.

Deadline January of each year.

[152]
GEORGE GENG ON LEE MINORITIES IN LEADERSHIP SCHOLARSHIP

Capture the Dream, Inc.
Attn: Scholarship Program
484 Lake Park Avenue, Suite 15
Oakland, CA 94610
(510) 343-3635   E-mail: info@capturethedream.org
Web: www.capturethedream.org/programs/scholarship.php

Summary To provide financial assistance for college to Asian American and other minorities who can demonstrate leadership.

Eligibility This program is open to members of minority groups who are graduating high school seniors or current full-time undergraduates at 4-year colleges and universities. Applicants must submit a 1,000-word essay on why they should be selected to receive this scholarship, using their experiences within school, work, and home to display the challenges they have faced as a minority and how they overcame adversity to assume a leadership role. They should also explain how their career goals and future aspirations will build them as a future minority leader. Financial need is considered in the selection process. U.S. citizenship or permanent resident status is required.

Financial data The stipend is $1,000.

Duration 1 year.

Number awarded 1 or more each year.

Deadline July of each year.

[153]
GLOBAL CHANGE SUMMER UNDERGRADUATE RESEARCH EXPERIENCE (SURE)

Oak Ridge Institute for Science and Education
Attn: Global Change Education Program
120 Badger Avenue, M.S. 36
P.O. Box 117
Oak Ridge, TN 37831-0117
(865) 576-7009   Fax: (865) 241-9445
E-mail: gcep@orau.gov
Web: www.atmos.anl.gov/GCEP/SURE/index.html

Summary To provide undergraduate students (particularly Asian Americans, other minorities, and women) with an opportunity to conduct research during the summer on global change.

Eligibility This program is open to undergraduates in their sophomore and junior years, although outstanding freshman and seniors are also considered. Applicants must be proposing to conduct research in a program area within the Department of Energy's Office of Biological and Environmental Research (DOE-BER): the atmospheric science program, the environmental meteorology program, the atmospheric radiation measurement program, the terrestrial carbon processes effort, the program for ecosystem research, and studies carried out under the direction of the National Institute for Global Environmental Change. They must have a GPA of 3.0 or higher overall and in their major. Minority and female students are particularly encouraged to apply. U.S. citizenship is required.

Financial data Participants receive a weekly stipend of $475 and support for travel and housing.

Duration 10 weeks during the summer. Successful participants are expected to reapply for a second year of research with their mentors.

Additional information This program, funded by DOE-BER, began in summer 1999. The first week is spent in an orientation and focus session at a participating university. For the remaining 9 weeks, students conduct mentored research at 1 of the national laboratories or universities conducting BER-supported global change research.

Number awarded Approximately 20 each year.

Deadline December of each year.

[154]
GORDON STAFFORD SCHOLARSHIP IN ARCHITECTURE

Gordon Stafford Scholarship
Attn: Scholarship Selection Committee
622 20th Street
Sacramento, CA 95814
(916) 930-5900   Fax: (916) 930-5800
E-mail: scholarship@gsscholarship.com
Web: www.gsscholarship.com

Summary To provide financial assistance to Asian Americans and members of other minority groups from California interested in studying architecture at a college in any state.

Eligibility This program is open to California residents accepted by an accredited school of architecture in any state as first-year or transfer students. Applicants must be U.S. citizens or permanent residents who are persons of color (defined as Black, Hispanic, Native American, Pacific-Asian, or Asian-Indian). They must submit a 500-word statement expressing their desire to study architecture. Finalists are interviewed and must travel to Sacramento, California at their own expense for the interview.

Financial data The stipend is $2,000 per year. That includes $1,000 deposited in the recipient's school account and $1,000 paid to the recipient directly.

Duration 1 year; may be renewed up to 4 additional years.

Additional information This program was established in 1995 to celebrate the 50th anniversary of the architectural firm that sponsors it, Stafford King Wiese Architects.

Number awarded Up to 5 of these scholarships may be active at a time.

Deadline June of each year.

[155]
GREATER LOS ANGELES CHAPTER OCA INTERNSHIP

Organization of Chinese Americans-Greater Los Angeles
   Chapter
Attn: Jen Ju
1145 Wilshire Boulevard, First Floor
Los Angeles, CA 90017
(213) 250-9888   Fax: (213) 250-9898
E-mail: jennifer.je@oca-gla.org
Web: www.oca-gla.org

Summary To provide an opportunity for undergraduate students from any state to gain work experience at the offices of the Greater Los Angeles Chapter of the Organization of Chinese Americans (OCA).

Eligibility This program is open to undergraduate students from any state who are interested in working at the offices of the OCA Greater Los Angeles Chapter. Applicants must be able to demonstrate strong project management and organizational skills, strong research and writing skills, interest in civil rights, familiarity with the Asian Pacific American community, proficiency with Microsoft Office applications, and ability to organize and coordinate a project with maturity, initiative, and timeliness.

Financial data The intern receives a stipend of $500 at the completion of the internship.

Duration The intern works 2 to 3 days per week (maximum of 15 hours per week) during the spring semester.

Additional information The intern's assignments include, but are not limited to, national convention attendance and preparation, youth and community service days, political educational forums, voter education events, citizenship workshops, and social activities.

Number awarded 1 each year.

Deadline The position is open until filled.

[156]
HANA SCHOLARSHIPS

United Methodist Church
Attn: General Board of Higher Education and Ministry
Office of Loans and Scholarships
1001 19th Avenue South
P.O. Box 340007
Nashville, TN 37203-0007
(615) 340-7344 Fax: (615) 340-7367
E-mail: umscholar@gbhem.org
Web: www.gbhem.org/loansandscholarships

Summary To provide financial assistance to upper-division and graduate Methodist students who are of Asian, Native American, Pacific Islander, or Hispanic ancestry.

Eligibility This program is open to full-time juniors, seniors, and graduate students at accredited colleges and universities in the United States who have been active, full members of a United Methodist Church (UMC) for at least 1 year prior to applying. Applicants must have at least 1 parent who is Asian, Hispanic, Native American, or Pacific Islander. They must be able to demonstrate involvement in their Hispanic, Asian, or Native American (HANA) community in the UMC. Selection is based on that involvement, academic ability (GPA of at least 2.85), and financial need. U.S. citizenship or permanent resident status is required.

Financial data The maximum stipend is $3,000 for undergraduates or $5,000 for graduate students.

Duration 1 year; recipients may reapply.

Number awarded 50 each year.

Deadline March of each year.

[157]
HANAYAGI ROKUMIE MEMORIAL JAPANESE CULTURAL SCHOLARSHIP

Japanese American Citizens League
Attn: National Scholarship Awards
1765 Sutter Street
San Francisco, CA 94115
(415) 921-5225 Fax: (415) 931-4671
E-mail: jacl@jacl.org
Web: www.jacl.org/edu/scholar.htm

Summary To provide financial assistance for college to student members of the Japanese American Citizens League (JACL) who are high school seniors and excel in Japanese cultural activity.

Eligibility This program is open to JACL members who are high school seniors interested in attending a college, university, trade school, business college, or other institution of higher learning. Applicants must excel in Japanese cultural activity, including nihon buyo (classical dance); ikebana (flower arrangement); classical instruments (e.g., shamisen, koto, shakuhachi, taiko); martial arts (e.g., aikido, karate, judo kendo); or chado (tea ceremony). They may study any field in

college. Along with their application, they must submit information on their involvement in JACL and a 2-page essay on a topic that changes annually but relates to Japanese Americans. Selection is based on that essay, academic history, extracurricular activities, JACL involvement, scholastic honors, and a letter of recommendation.

Financial data Stipends generally average approximately $2,000.

Duration 1 year; nonrenewable.

Additional information This program was established in 2006.

Number awarded 1 each year.

Deadline February of each year.

[158]
HANNAH GRISWOLD GRANT

Delta Kappa Gamma Society International-Alpha Kappa
State Organization
c/o Cynthia C. Huppert, Professional Affairs Committee
Chair
63 Turn of the River Road
Stamford, CT 06905
E-mail: cchup3@sbcglobal.net
Web: www.deltakappagamma.org

Summary To provide financial assistance to Asian Americans and other minority high school seniors in Connecticut who are interested in working on a degree in education at a school in the state.

Eligibility This program is open to Asian American and other minority seniors graduating from high schools in Connecticut who plan to enroll at a college or university in the state to work on a degree in education. Applicants must be able to demonstrate qualities consistent with the promise of leadership in education, including scholarship and community service. Along with their application, they must submit a 500-word statement on their reasons for becoming a teacher. Financial need is not considered in the selection process.

Financial data The stipend is $750.

Duration 1 semester.

Number awarded 1 each year.

Deadline March of each year.

[159]
HAWAII KOREAN CHAMBER OF COMMERCE SCHOLARSHIPS

Hawaii Korean Chamber of Commerce
c/o Daniel J.Y. Pyun, Scholarship Committee
1188 Bishop Street, Suite 811
Honolulu, HI 96813
(808) 526-0999 Fax: (808) 599-8622
Web: www.hkccweb.org/en/scholarships.html

Summary To provide financial assistance to Hawaii residents who are of Korean ancestry and interested in attending college in any state.

Eligibility This program is open to residents of Hawaii who are of at least 50% Korean ancestry. Applicants must be graduating high school seniors or current undergraduates who are enrolled or planning to enroll full time at an accredited 4-year college or university in any state. Along with their application, they must submit an essay of 250 to 500 words that covers why they feel they are qualified to receive this scholarship, how they will participate in and contribute to their community after completing their program of study, whether or not their goal includes service to the Korean American community, and how their education will enable them to contribute to the Korean American community. Financial need is also considered in the selection process.

Financial data The stipend is $2,000.

Duration 1 year.

Number awarded 3 each year.

Deadline April of each year.

[160]
HDR ENGINEERING SCHOLARSHIP FOR DIVERSITY IN ENGINEERING

Association of Independent Colleges and Universities of Pennsylvania
101 North Front Street
Harrisburg, PA 17101-1405
(717) 232-8649   Fax: (717) 233-8574
E-mail: info@aicup.org
Web: www.aicup.org

Summary To provide financial assistance to Asian Americans, other minority students, and women from any state who are enrolled at member institutions of the Association of Independent Colleges and Universities of Pennsylvania (AICUP) and majoring in designated fields of engineering.

Eligibility This program is open to undergraduate students from any state enrolled full time at AICUP colleges and universities. Applicants must be women and/or members of the following minority groups: American Indians, Alaska Natives, Asians, Blacks/African Americans, Hispanics/Latinos, Native Hawaiians, or Pacific Islanders. They must be juniors majoring in civil, geotechnical, or structural engineering with a GPA of 3.0 or higher. Along with their application, they must submit a 2-page essay on their characteristics, accomplishments, primary interests, plans, and goals.

Financial data The stipend is $5,000 per year.

Duration 1 year; may be renewed 1 additional year if the recipient maintains appropriate academic standards.

Additional information This program, sponsored by HDR Engineering, Inc., is available at the 83 private colleges and universities in Pennsylvania that comprise the AICUP.

Number awarded 1 each year.

Deadline April of each year.

[161]
HEALTH RESEARCH AND EDUCATIONAL TRUST SCHOLARSHIPS

New Jersey Hospital Association
Attn: Health Research and Educational Trust
760 Alexander Road
P.O. Box 1
Princeton, NJ 08543-0001
(609) 275-4224   Fax: (609) 452-8097
Web: www.njha.com/hret/scholarship.aspx

Summary To provide financial assistance to New Jersey residents (particularly Asian Americans, other minorities, and women) who are working on an undergraduate or graduate degree in a field related to health care administration at a school in any state.

Eligibility This program is open to residents of New Jersey enrolled in an upper-division or graduate program in hospital or health care administration, public administration, nursing, or other allied health profession at a school in any state. Graduate students working on an advanced degree to prepare to teach nursing are also eligible. Applicants must have a GPA of 3.0 or higher and be able to demonstrate financial need. Along with their application, they must submit a 2-page essay (on which 50% of the selection is based) describing their academic plans for the future. Minorities and women are especially encouraged to apply.

Financial data The stipend is $2,000.

Duration 1 year.

Additional information This program began in 1983.

Number awarded Varies each year; recently, 3 of these scholarships were awarded.

Deadline July of each year.

[162]
HELEN LEE SCHOLARSHIP

Philip Jaisohn Memorial Foundation
Attn: Education and Scholarship Committee
6705 Old York Road
Philadelphia, PA 19126
(215) 224-2000   Fax: (215) 224-9164
E-mail: jaisohnhouse@gmail.com
Web: jaisohn.org

Summary To provide financial assistance to Korean American undergraduate and graduate students who demonstrate significant financial need.

Eligibility This program is open to Korean American undergraduate and graduate students who are currently enrolled at a college or university in the United States. Applicants must be able to demonstrate academic excellence, leadership and service to their school and community, and financial need. Along with their application, they must submit an essay on either "Who is Dr. Jaisohn to Me," or "The Significance of Dr. Jaisohn's Ideal to Korean Americans." They must also submit a brief statement on how they can contribute to and be involved in the activities of the Philip Jaisohn Memorial Foundation. Selection is based primarily on financial need.

Financial data The stipend is $1,500.

Duration 1 year.

Number awarded 2 each year.

Deadline November of each year.

[163]
HENRY AND CHIYO KUWAHARA MEMORIAL SCHOLARSHIPS

Japanese American Citizens League
Attn: National Scholarship Awards
1765 Sutter Street
San Francisco, CA 94115
(415) 921-5225   Fax: (415) 931-4671
E-mail: jacl@jacl.org
Web: www.jacl.org/edu/scholar.htm

Summary To provide financial assistance for undergraduate or graduate study to members of the Japanese American Citizens League (JACL).

Eligibility This program is open to JACL members who are high school seniors, undergraduates, or graduate students. Applicants must be attending or planning to attend a college, university, trade school, or business college. They must submit information on their involvement in JACL and a 2-page essay on a topic that changes annually but relates to Japanese Americans. Selection is based on that essay, academic history, extracurricular activities, JACL involvement, scholastic honors, and a letter of recommendation.

Financial data Stipends generally average approximately $2,000.

Duration 1 year; nonrenewable.

Number awarded 6 each year: 2 each to entering freshmen, continuing undergraduates, and entering or currently-enrolled graduate students.

Deadline February of each year for graduating high school seniors; March of each year for current undergraduate or graduate students.

[164]
HERBERT JENSEN SCHOLARSHIP

Japanese American Citizens League-Arizona Chapter
5414 West Glenn Drive
Glendale, AZ 85304
Glendale, AZ 85301-2628
E-mail: arizonajacl@gmail.com

Summary To provide financial assistance to graduating high school seniors in Arizona who are of Japanese American or other ethnic background and whose parents are affiliated with the Japanese American Citizens League (JACL).

Eligibility This program is open to graduating high school seniors in Arizona who are U.S. citizens, have at least a 3.0 GPA, and have a parent who has been a member of the Arizona Chapter of the JACL for at least 3 consecutive years prior to the application deadline. Applicants may be of Japanese American or other ethnic background. Financial need is not considered in the selection process.

Financial data A stipend is awarded (amount not specified).

Duration 1 year.

Additional information Recipients must attend the association's scholarship awards banquet and accept the award in person; failure to do so results in forfeiture of the award.

Number awarded 1 each year.

Deadline February of each year.

[165]
HIDEKO AND ZENZO MATSUYAMA SCHOLARSHIPS

Hawai'i Community Foundation
Attn: Scholarship Department
827 Fort Street Mall
Honolulu, HI 96813
(808) 537-6333   Toll Free: (888) 731-3863
Fax: (808) 521-6286
E-mail: scholarships@hcf-hawaii.org
Web: www.hawaiicommunityfoundation.org/scholarships

Summary To provide financial assistance to Hawaii residents, especially those of Japanese ancestry, who are interested in attending college or graduate school in any state.

Eligibility This program is open to graduates of high schools or recipients of GED certificates in Hawaii. Applicants must be enrolled or planning to enroll in an accredited college or university in any state as an undergraduate or graduate student. They must be able to demonstrate academic achievement (GPA of 3.0 or higher), good moral character, and financial need. Along with their application, they must submit a short statement indicating their reasons for attending college, their planned course of study, their career goals, and what community service means to them. Preference is given to students of Japanese ancestry born in Hawaii.

Financial data The amounts of the awards depend on the availability of funds and the need of the recipient. Recently, the average value of all scholarships awarded by the foundation was $2,041.

Duration 1 year.

Number awarded Varies each year; recently, 13 of these scholarships were awarded.

Deadline February of each year.

[166]
H-MART LEADERSHIP SCHOLARSHIP

Philip Jaisohn Memorial Foundation
Attn: Education and Scholarship Committee
6705 Old York Road
Philadelphia, PA 19126
(215) 224-2000   Fax: (215) 224-9164
E-mail: jaisohnhouse@gmail.com
Web: jaisohn.org

Summary To provide financial assistance to Korean American undergraduate and graduate students who demonstrate involvement in extracurricular, athletic, and community activities.

Eligibility This program is open to Korean American undergraduate and graduate students who are currently enrolled at a college or university in the United States. Applicants must be able to demonstrate academic excellence, leadership and service to their school and community, and financial need. Along with their application, they must submit an essay on either "Who is Dr. Jaisohn to Me," or "The Significance of Dr. Jaisohn's Ideal to Korean Americans." They must also submit a brief statement on how they can contribute to and be involved in the activities of the Philip Jaisohn Memorial Foundation. Selection is based primarily on leadership in extracurricular activities, varsity sports, or community activities.

Financial data The stipend is $1,500.

Duration 1 year.

Additional information This program is sponsored by H-Mart.

Number awarded 2 each year.

Deadline November of each year.

[167]
HOLY FAMILY MEMORIAL SCHOLARSHIP PROGRAM

Holy Family Memorial
Attn: Human Resources
2300 Western Avenue
P.O. Box 1450
Manitowoc, WI 54221-1450
(920) 320-4031   Toll Free: (800) 994-3662, ext. 4031
Fax: (920) 320-8522   E-mail: recruiter@hfmhealth.org
Web: www.hfmhealth.org/?id=118&sid=1

Summary To provide funding to students (particularly Asian Americans and other minorities) who are working on a degree in a health-related area and willing to work at a designated hospital in Wisconsin following completion of their degree.

Eligibility This program is open to students working on a degree in health-related areas that include, but are not limited to, nursing, pharmacy, sonography, occupational therapy, physical therapy, speech/language pathology, respiratory therapy, or radiology. Applicants must have a GPA of 3.0 or higher. Selection is based on a personal interview, likelihood for professional success, customer service orientation, work ethic, enthusiasm, and professionalism. Minorities are especially encouraged to apply.

Financial data Stipends are $800 per semester ($1,600 per year) for students at technical colleges, $2,000 per semester ($4,000 per year) for students at public universities, or $2,500 per semester ($5,000 per year) for students at private universities. Recipients must commit to working 6 months for each semester of support received at Holy Family Memorial in Manitowoc, Wisconsin following completion of their degree.

Duration 1 semester; renewable.

Deadline Deadline not specified.

[168]
HORACE AND SUSIE REVELS CAYTON SCHOLARSHIP

Public Relations Society of America-Puget Sound
  Chapter
c/o Diane Bevins
1006 Industry Drive
Seattle, WA 98188-4801
(206) 623-8632   E-mail: prsascholarship@asi-seattle.net
Web: www.prsapugetsound.org/scholars.html

Summary To provide financial assistance to Asian American and other minority upper-classmen from Washington who are interested in preparing for a career in public relations.

Eligibility This program is open to U.S. citizens who are members of minority groups, defined as African Americans, Asian Americans, Hispanic/Latino Americans, Native Americans, and Pacific Islanders. Applicants must be full-time juniors or seniors attending a college in Washington or Washington students (who graduated from a Washington high school or whose parents live in the state year-round) attending college elsewhere. They must be able to demonstrate aptitude in public relations and related courses, activities, and/or internships. Along with their application, they must submit a description of their career goals and the skills that are most important in general to a public relations career (15

points in the selection process); a description of their activities in communications in class, on campus, in the community, or during internships, including 3 samples of their work (15 points); a statement on the value of public relations to an organization (10 points); a description of any barriers, financial or otherwise, they have encountered in pursuing their academic or personal goals and how they have addressed them (15 points); a discussion of their heritage, and how their cultural background and/or the discrimination they may have experienced has impacted them (15 points); a certified transcript (15 points); and 2 or more letters of recommendation (15 points).

Financial data The stipend is $2,500.

Duration 1 year.

Additional information This program was established in 1992.

Number awarded 1 each year.

Deadline April of each year.

[169]
HORIZON PHARMA STUDENT ABSTRACT PRIZES

American Gastroenterological Association
Attn: AGA Research Foundation
Research Awards Manager
4930 Del Ray Avenue
Bethesda, MD 20814-2512
(301) 222-4012   Fax: (301) 654-5920
E-mail: awards@gastro.org
Web: www.gastro.org/aga-foundation/grants

Summary To recognize and reward Asian American and other students at any level who submit outstanding abstracts for presentation during Digestive Disease Week (DDW).

Eligibility This program is open to high school, undergraduate, premedical, predoctoral, and medical students and medical residents (up to and including postgraduate year 3) who have performed original research related to gastroenterology and hepatology. Postdoctoral fellows, technicians, visiting scientists, and M.D. research fellows are not eligible. Applicants must submit an abstract on their research and must be the designated presenter or first author of the abstract. They must be sponsored by a member of the American Gastroenterological Association (AGA). Travel awards are presented to authors of outstanding abstracts to enable them to attend DDW. After presentation of the papers at DDW, the most outstanding abstracts receive prizes. Selection is based on novelty, significance of the proposal, clarity of the abstract, and contribution of the student. Women and minority students are strongly encouraged to apply.

Financial data The prizes are $1,000; the travel awards are $500.

Duration Awards and prizes are presented annually.

Additional information This award is sponsored by Horizon Pharma.

Number awarded 8 travel awards are presented each year. Of the 8 awardees, 3 receive additional prizes of $1,000.

Deadline February of each year.

[170]
HYATT HOTELS FUND FOR MINORITY LODGING MANAGEMENT STUDENTS

American Hotel & Lodging Educational Foundation
Attn: Manager of Foundation Programs
1201 New York Avenue, N.W., Suite 600
Washington, DC 20005-3931
(202) 289-3181   Fax: (202) 289-3199
E-mail: ahlef@ahlef.org
Web: www.ahlef.org/content.aspx?id=19828

Summary   To provide financial assistance to Asian American and other minority college students working on a degree in hotel management.

Eligibility   This program is open to students majoring in hospitality management at a 4-year college or university as at least a sophomore. Applicants must be members of a minority group (African American, Hispanic, American Indian, Alaskan Native, Asian, or Pacific Islander). They must be enrolled full time. Along with their application, they must submit a 500-word essay on their personal background, including when they became interested in the hospitality field, what traits they possess or will need to succeed in the industry, and their plans as related to their educational and career objectives and future goals. Selection is based on industry-related work experience; financial need; academic record and educational qualifications; professional, community, and extracurricular activities; personal attributes, including career goals; the essay; and neatness and completeness of the application. U.S. citizenship or permanent resident status is required.

Financial data   The stipend is $2,000.

Duration   1 year.

Additional information   Funding for this program, established in 1988, is provided by Hyatt Hotels & Resorts.

Number awarded   Varies each year; recently, 10 of these scholarships were awarded. Since this program was established, it has awarded scholarships worth $508,000 to approximately 255 minority students.

Deadline   April of each year.

[171]
IDAHO STATE BROADCASTERS ASSOCIATION SCHOLARSHIPS

Idaho State Broadcasters Association
270 North 27th Street, Suite B
Boise, ID 83702-4741
(208) 345-3072   Fax: (208) 343-8946
E-mail: isba@qwestoffice.net
Web: www.idahobroadcasters.org/scholarships.aspx

Summary   To provide financial assistance to students at Idaho colleges and universities (particularly Asian Americans and other diverse students) who are preparing for a career in the broadcasting field.

Eligibility   This program is open to full-time students at Idaho schools who are preparing for a career in broadcasting, including business administration, sales, journalism, or engineering. Applicants must have a GPA of at least 2.0 for the first 2 years of school or 2.5 for the last 2 years. Along with their application, they must submit a letter of recommendation from the general manager of a broadcasting station that is a member of the Idaho State Broadcasters Association and a 1-page essay describing their career plans and why they

want the scholarship. Applications are encouraged from a wide and diverse student population. Financial need is not considered in the selection process.

Financial data   The stipend is $1,000.

Duration   1 year.

Number awarded   2 each year.

Deadline   March of each year.

[172]
ILLINOIS BROADCASTERS ASSOCIATION MULTICULTURAL INTERNSHIPS

Illinois Broadcasters Association
Attn: MIP Coordinator
200 Missouri Avenue
Carterville, IL 62918
(618) 985-5555   Fax: (618) 985-6070
E-mail: iba@ilba.org
Web: www.ilba.org

Summary   To provide funding to Asian American and other minority college students in Illinois who are majoring in broadcasting and interested in interning at a radio or television station in the state.

Eligibility   This program is open to currently-enrolled minority students majoring in broadcasting at a college or university in Illinois. Applicants must be interested in a fall, spring, or summer internship at a radio or television station that is a member of the Illinois Broadcasters Association. Along with their application, they must submit 1) a 250-word essay on how they expect to benefit from a grant through this program, and 2) at least 2 letters of recommendation from a broadcasting faculty member or professional familiar with their career potential and 1 other letter. The president of the sponsoring organization selects those students nominated by their schools who have the best opportunity to make it in the world of broadcasting and matches them with internship opportunities that would otherwise be unpaid.

Financial data   This program provides a grant to pay the living expenses for the interns in the Illinois communities where they are assigned. The amount of the grant depends on the length of the internship.

Duration   16 weeks in the fall and spring terms or 12 weeks in the summer.

Number awarded   12 each year: 4 in each of the 3 terms.

Deadline   Deadline not specified.

[173]
ILLINOIS FUTURE TEACHER CORPS PROGRAM

Illinois Student Assistance Commission
Attn: Scholarship and Grant Services
1755 Lake Cook Road
Deerfield, IL 60015-5209
(847) 948-8550   Toll Free: (800) 899-ISAC
Fax: (847) 831-8549   TDD: (800) 526-0844
E-mail: collegezone@isac.org
Web: www.collegezone.com/studentzone/407_660.htm

Summary   To provide funding to college students in Illinois (especially Asian Americans and other minorities) who are interested in training or retraining for a teaching career in academic shortage areas.

Eligibility   This program is open to Illinois residents who are enrolled at the junior level or higher at an institution of higher education in the state. Applicants must be planning to prepare for a career as a preschool, elementary, or secondary school teacher. They must have a cumulative GPA of 2.5 or higher. Priority is given to 1) minority students; 2) students with financial need; and 3) applicants working on a degree in designated teacher shortage disciplines or making a commitment to teach at a hard-to-staff school. Recently, the teacher shortage disciplines included early childhood education, special education (speech and language impaired, learning behavior specialist), and regular education (bilingual education, mathematics, physical education (K-8), reading, and science). U.S. citizenship or eligible noncitizen status is required.

Financial data Stipends are $5,000 per year for students who agree to teach in a teacher shortage discipline, $5,000 per year for students who agree to teach at a hard-to-staff school, or $10,000 for students who agree to teach in a teacher shortage discipline at a hard-to-staff school. Funds are paid directly to the school. This is a scholarship/loan program. Recipients must agree to teach in an Illinois public, private, or parochial preschool, elementary school, or secondary school for 1 year for each full year of assistance received. The teaching obligation must be completed within 5 years of completion of the degree or certificate program for which the scholarship was awarded. That time period may be extended if the recipient serves in the U.S. armed forces, enrolls full time in a graduate program related to teaching, becomes temporarily disabled, is unable to find employment as a teacher, or takes additional courses on at least a half-time basis to teach in a specialized teacher shortage discipline. Recipients who fail to honor this work obligation must repay the award with interest.

Duration 1 year; may be renewed.

Additional information This program was formerly known as the David A. DeBolt Teacher Shortage Scholarship Program.

Number awarded Varies each year, depending on the availability of funds.

Deadline Priority consideration is given to applications submitted by February of each year.

[174]
ILLINOIS MINORITY REAL ESTATE SCHOLARSHIP

Illinois Association of Realtors
Attn: Illinois Real Estate Educational Foundation
522 South Fifth Street
P.O. Box 2607
Springfield, IL 62708
Toll Free: (866) 854-REEF   Fax: (217) 241-9935
E-mail: lclayton@iar.org
Web: www.ilreef.org/Scholarships.htm

Summary To provide financial assistance to Illinois residents who Asian or members of other minority groups and preparing for a career in real estate.

Eligibility This program is open to residents of Illinois who are African American, Hispanic or Latino, Native American, or Asian. Applicants must be interested in preparing for a career in real estate by pursuing: 1) courses to meet Illinois salesperson license requirements; 2) course work to meet Illinois broker license requirement; 3) course work required for Illinois appraisal licensing/certification; 4) professional develop-

ment unrelated to obtaining license/certification; or 5) an undergraduate or graduate program of study. Along with their application, they must submit information on their employment history, transcripts, evidence of financial need, and an essay that describes their career goals and explains why they believe they should receive scholarship assistance through this program.

Financial data The maximum stipend is $500.

Duration Funds must be used within 24 months of the award date.

Deadline Applications may be submitted at any time, but they must be received at least 12 weeks prior to the beginning of the school term for which financial assistance is requested.

[175]
ILLINOIS NURSES ASSOCIATION CENTENNIAL SCHOLARSHIP

Illinois Nurses Association
Attn: Illinois Nurses Foundation
105 West Adams Street, Suite 2101
Chicago, IL 60603
(312) 419-2900   Fax: (312) 419-2920
E-mail: info@illinoisnurses.com
Web: www.illinoisnurses.com

Summary To provide financial assistance to Asian Americans and other underrepresented undergraduate and graduate students working on a nursing degree.

Eligibility This program is open to students working on an associate, bachelor's, or master's degree at an accredited NLNAC or CCNE school of nursing. Applicants must be members of a group underrepresented in nursing (African Americans, Hispanics, American Indians, Asians, and males). Undergraduates must have earned a passing grade in all nursing courses taken to date and have a GPA of 2.85 or higher. Graduate students must have completed at least 12 semester hours of graduate work and have a GPA of 3.0 or higher. All applicants must be willing to 1) act as a spokesperson to other student groups on the value of the scholarship to continuing their nursing education, and 2) be profiled in any media or marketing materials developed by the Illinois Nurses Foundation. Along with their application, they must submit a narrative of 250 to 500 words on how they, nurses, plan to affect policy at either the state or national level that impacts on nursing or health care generally, or how they believe they will impact the nursing profession in general.

Financial data A stipend is awarded (amount not specified).

Duration 1 year.

Number awarded 1 or more each year.

Deadline March of each year.

[176]
INDIAN AMERICAN SCHOLARSHIP FUND MERIT SCHOLARSHIPS

India American Cultural Association
Attn: Indian American Scholarship Fund
1281 Cooper Lake Road, S.E.
Smyrna, GA 30082
(770) 436-3719   Fax: (770) 436-4272
E-mail: iasf@imlogical.com
Web: www.iasf.org/IASF/Scholarships.html

Summary To provide merit-based financial assistance to high school seniors in Georgia who are of Indian descent and plan to attend college in any state.

Eligibility This program is open to seniors graduating from high schools in Georgia who are of Indian descent (at least 1 grandparent was born in India). Applicants must be planning to attend a 4-year college or university in any state as a full-time student. Along with their application, they must submit an official school transcript, resume, and SAT or ACT score report. Financial need is not considered in the selection process.

Financial data Stipends range from $500 to $1,000.

Duration 1 year; nonrenewable.

Additional information This program, established in 1993, includes the following named scholarships: the Paras Shah Memorial Award, the N.M. Kelkar Memorial Award, the Darshan S. Bhatia Memorial Award, the P.V. Jagannatha Rao Memorial Award, the Raghavan Award, the Aman Daftari Memorial Award, the Boyapally Reddy Award, the Sadashiv Bhargave Memorial Award, and the Ishwarlal Shroff Memorial Award.

Number awarded Varies each year; recently, the sponsor awarded a total of 9 1-year scholarships.

Deadline March of each year.

[177]
INDIANA INDUSTRY LIAISON GROUP SCHOLARSHIP

Indiana Industry Liaison Group
c/o Tony Pickell, Vice Chair
AAP Precision Planning, LLC
6215 Meridian Street West Drive
Indianapolis, IN 46260
(317) 590-4797
E-mail: tony.pickell@precisionplanningaap.com
Web: www.indianailg.org/scholardetails.html

Summary To provide financial assistance to Asian Americans and other students from any state enrolled at colleges and universities in Indiana who have been involved in activities to promote diversity.

Eligibility This program is open to residents of any state currently enrolled at an accredited college or university in Indiana. Applicants must either 1) be studying programs or classes related to diversity/Affirmative Action (AA)/Equal Employment Opportunity (EEO), or 2) have work or volunteer experience for diversity/AA/EEO organizations. Along with their application, they must submit an essay of 400 to 500 words on 1 of the following topics: 1) their personal commitment to diversity/AA/EEO within their community or business; 2) a time or situation in which they were able to establish and/or sustain a commitment to diversity; 3) a time when they have taken a position in favor of affirmative action and/or diversity; or 4) activities in which they have participated within their community that demonstrate their personal commitment to moving the community's diversity agenda forward. Financial need is not considered in the selection process.

Financial data The stipend is $1,000.

Duration 1 year.

Number awarded 1 each year.

Deadline March of each year.

[178]
ING SCHOLARSHIPS

Ascend: Pan-Asian Leaders
Attn: Director of Programs
120 Wall Street, Third Floor
New York, NY 10005
(212) 248-4888   Fax: (212) 344-5636
E-mail: info@ascendleadership.org
Web: www.ascendleadership.org

Summary To provide financial assistance to members of Ascend: Pan-Asian Leaders who are upper-division or graduate students working on a degree in a field related to accounting.

Eligibility This program is open to members of Ascend who are enrolled as junior or senior undergraduates or M.B.A. graduate students at colleges and universities in the United States. Applicants must have a GPA of 3.2 or higher and a major in accounting, finance, taxation, management information systems, or a business-related program. Along with their application, they must submit a 500-word personal essay on how they have demonstrated leadership and teamwork in their academic studies, professional career, and/or extracurricular activities and community volunteer work; why they believe those qualities are important to be competitive in a borderless world; their career goals after graduation; and the role Ascend has played in the achievement of their academic and career goals. They must also provide examples of their involvement in local community activities. Financial need is not considered in the selection process.

Financial data The stipend is $2,500.

Duration 1 year.

Additional information Ascend was formed in 2004 as the National Asian American Society of Accountants. This program is sponsored by ING North America Insurance Corporation.

Number awarded 2 each year.

Deadline July of each year.

[179]
INSTITUTE FOR INTERNATIONAL PUBLIC POLICY FELLOWSHIPS

United Negro College Fund Special Programs
  Corporation
Attn: Institute for International Public Policy
6402 Arlington Boulevard, Suite 600
Falls Church, VA 22042
(703) 677-3400   Toll Free: (800) 530-6232
Fax: (703) 205-7645   E-mail: iippl@uncfsp.org
Web: www.uncfsp.org

Summary To provide financial assistance and work experience to Asian Americans and other minority students who are interested in preparing for a career in international affairs.

Eligibility This program is open to full-time sophomores at 4-year institutions who have a GPA of 3.2 or higher and are nominated by the president of their institution. Applicants must be African American, Hispanic/Latino American, Asian American, American Indian, Alaskan Native, Native Hawaiian, or Pacific Islander. They must be interested in participating in policy institutes, study abroad, language training, internships, and graduate education that will prepare them for a career in international service. U.S. citizenship or permanent resident status is required.

Financial data For the sophomore summer policy institute, fellows receive student housing and meals in a university facility, books and materials, all field trips and excursions, and a $1,050 stipend. For the junior year study abroad component, half the expenses for 1 semester, to a maximum of $8,000, is provided. For the junior summer policy institute, fellows receive student housing and meals in a university facility, books and materials, travel to and from the institute, and a $1,000 stipend. For the summer language institute, fellows receive tuition and fees, books and materials, room and board, travel to and from the institute, and a $1,000 stipend. During the internship, a stipend of up to $3,500 is paid. During the graduate school period, fellowships are funded jointly by this program and the participating graduate school. The program provides $15,000 toward a master's degree in international affairs with the expectation that the graduate school will provide $15,000 in matching funds.

Duration 2 years of undergraduate work and 2 years of graduate work, as well as the intervening summers.

Additional information This program consists of 6 components: 1) a sophomore year summer policy institute based at Howard University that introduces fellows to international policy development, foreign affairs, cultural competence, careers in those fields, and options for graduate study; 2) a junior year study abroad program at an accredited overseas institution; 3) a 7-week junior year summer institute at the University of Maryland's School of Public Policy; 4) for students without established foreign language competency, a summer language institute at Middlebury College Language Schools in Middlebury, Vermont following the senior year; 5) fellows with previously established foreign language competence participate in a post-baccalaureate internship to provide the practical experience needed for successful graduate studies in international affairs; and 6) a master's degree in international affairs (for students who are admitted to such a program). This program is administered by the United Negro College Fund Special Programs Corporation with funding provided by a grant from the U.S. Department of Education.

Number awarded 30 each year.

Deadline February of each year.

[180]
INTERMOUNTAIN SECTION AWWA DIVERSITY SCHOLARSHIP

American Water Works Association-Intermountain
  Section
3430 East Danish Road
Sandy, UT 94093
(801) 712-1619   Fax: (801) 487-6699
E-mail: nicoleb@ims-awwa.org
Web: www.ims-awwa.org

Summary To provide financial assistance to Asian Americans, other minorities, and female undergraduate and graduate students working on a degree in the field of water quality, supply, and treatment at a university in Idaho or Utah.

Eligibility This program is open to women and students who identify as Hispanic or Latino, Black or African American, Native Hawaiian or other Pacific Islander, Asian, or American Indian or Alaska Native. Applicants must be entering or enrolled in an undergraduate or graduate program at a college or university in Idaho or Utah that relates to water quality, supply, or treatment. Along with their application, they must submit a 2-page essay on their academic interests and career goals and how those relate to water quality, supply, or treatment. Selection is based on that essay, letters of recommendation, and potential to contribute to the field of water quality, supply, and treatment in the Intermountain West.

Financial data The stipend is $1,000. The winner also receives a 1-year student membership in the Intermountain Section of the American Water Works Association (AWWA) and a 1-year subscription to *Journal AWWA*.

Duration 1 year; nonrenewable.

Number awarded 1 each year.

Deadline October of each year.

[181]
INTERNATIONAL COMMUNICATIONS INDUSTRIES FOUNDATION AV SCHOLARSHIPS

InfoComm International
International Communications Industries Foundation
11242 Waples Mill Road, Suite 200
Fairfax, VA 22030
(703) 273-7200   Toll Free: (800) 659-7469
Fax: (703) 278-8082   E-mail: srieger@infocomm.org
Web: www.infocomm.org

Summary To provide financial assistance to Asian Americans and other high school seniors and college students who are interested in preparing for a career in the audiovisual (AV) industry.

Eligibility This program is open to high school seniors, undergraduates, and graduate students already enrolled in college. Applicants must have a GPA of 2.75 or higher and be majoring or planning to major in audiovisual subjects or related fields, including audio, video, electronics, telecommunications, technical aspects of the theater, data networking, software development, or information technology. Students in other programs, such as journalism, may be eligible if they can demonstrate a relationship to career goals in the AV industry. Along with their application, they must submit 1) an essay of 150 to 200 words on the career path they plan to pursue in the audiovisual industry in the next 5 years, and 2) an essay of 250 to 300 words on the experience or person influencing them the most in selecting the audiovisual industry as their career of choice. Minority and women candidates are especially encouraged to apply. Selection is based on the essays, presentation of the application, GPA, AV-related experience, work experience, and letters of recommendation.

Financial data The stipend is $1,200 per year. Funds are sent directly to the school.

Duration 1 year; recipients may reapply.

Additional information InfoComm International, formerly the International Communications Industries Association, established the International Communications Industries Foundation (ICIF) to manage its charitable and educational activities.

Number awarded Varies each year; recently, 29 of these scholarships were awarded.

Deadline May of each year.

[182]
INTERNATIONAL RADIO AND TELEVISION SOCIETY SUMMER FELLOWSHIP PROGRAM

International Radio and Television Society Foundation
Attn: Director, Special Projects
420 Lexington Avenue, Suite 1601
New York, NY 10170-0101
(212) 867-6650   Toll Free: (888) 627-1266
Fax: (212) 867-6653   E-mail: apply@irts.org
Web: irts.org/summerfellowshipprogram.html

Summary   To provide summer work experience to upper-division and graduate students (especially Asian/Pacific Islanders and other minorities) who are interested in working during the summer in broadcasting and related fields in the New York City area.

Eligibility   This program is open to juniors, seniors, and graduate students at 4-year colleges and universities. Applicants must either be a communications major or have demonstrated a strong interest in the field through extracurricular activities or other practical experience. Minority (Black, Hispanic, Asian/Pacific Islander, American Indian/Alaskan Native) students are especially encouraged to apply.

Financial data   Travel, housing, and a living allowance are provided.

Duration   9 weeks during the summer.

Additional information   The first week consists of a comprehensive orientation to broadcasting, cable, advertising, and new media. Then, the participants are assigned an 8-week fellowship. This full-time "real world" experience in a New York-based corporation allows them to reinforce or redefine specific career goals before settling into a permanent job. Fellows have worked at all 4 major networks, at local New York City radio and television stations, and at national rep firms, advertising agencies, and cable operations. This program includes fellowships reserved for students at designated universities (Notre Dame, Pennsylvania State University, Boston College, Holy Cross College) and the following named awards: the Thomas S. Murphy Fellowship (sponsored by ABC National Television Sales), the Helen Karas Memorial Fellowship, the Leslie Moonves Fellowship (sponsored by CBS Television Station Sales), and the Sumner Redstone Fellowship (sponsored by CBS Television Station Sales).

Number awarded   Varies; recently, 23 of these fellowships were awarded.

Deadline   November of each year.

[183]
INTERPUBLIC GROUP SCHOLARSHIP AND INTERNSHIP

New York Women in Communications, Inc.
Attn: NYWICI Foundation
355 Lexington Avenue, 15th Floor
New York, NY 10017-6603
(212) 297-2133   Fax: (212) 370-9047
E-mail: nywicipr@nywici.org
Web: www.nywici.org/foundation/scholarships

Summary   To provide financial assistance and work experience to Asian American and other minority women who are residents of designated eastern states and enrolled as juniors at a college in any state to prepare for a career in advertising or public relations.

Eligibility   This program is open to female residents of New York, New Jersey, Connecticut, or Pennsylvania who are from ethnically diverse groups and currently enrolled as juniors at a college or university in any state. Also eligible are women who reside outside the 4 states but are currently enrolled at a college or university within 1 of the 5 boroughs of New York City. Applicants must be preparing for a career in advertising or public relations and have a GPA of 3.2 or higher. They must be available for a summer internship with Interpublic Group (IPG) in New York City. Along with their application, they must submit a 2-page resume that includes school and extracurricular activities, significant achievements, academic honors and awards, and community service work; a personal essay of 300 to 500 words on their choice of an assigned topic that changes annually; 2 letters of recommendation; and an official transcript. Selection is based on academic record, need, demonstrated leadership, participation in school and community activities, honors, work experience, goals and aspirations, and unusual personal and/or family circumstances. U.S. citizenship is required.

Financial data   The scholarship stipend ranges up to $10,000; the internship is paid (amount not specified).

Duration   1 year.

Additional information   This program is sponsored by IPG, a holding company for a large number of firms in the advertising industry.

Number awarded   1 each year.

Deadline   January of each year.

[184]
JACKIE ROBINSON SCHOLARSHIPS

Jackie Robinson Foundation
Attn: Education and Leadership Development Program
75 Varick Street, Second Floor
New York, NY 10013-1917
(212) 290-8600   Fax: (212) 290-8081
E-mail: general@jackierobinson.org
Web: www.jackierobinson.org

Summary   To provide financial assistance for college to Asian American and other minority high school seniors.

Eligibility   This program is open to members of an ethnic minority group who are high school seniors accepted at a 4-year college or university. Applicants must have a mathematics and critical reading SAT score of 1000 or higher or ACT score of 21 or higher. Selection is based on academic achievement, financial need, dedication towards community service, and leadership potential. U.S. citizenship is required.

Financial data   The maximum stipend is $7,500 per year.

Duration   4 years.

Additional information   The program also offers personal and career counseling on a year-round basis, a week of interaction with other scholarship students from around the country, and assistance in obtaining summer jobs and permanent employment after graduation. It was established in 1973 by a grant from Chesebrough-Pond.

Number awarded   100 or more each year.

Deadline   March of each year.

[185]
JACL/KENJI KASAI MEMORIAL SCHOLARSHIP

Japanese American Citizens League
Attn: National Scholarship Awards
1765 Sutter Street
San Francisco, CA 94115
(415) 921-5225   Fax: (415) 931-4671
E-mail: jacl@jacl.org
Web: www.jacl.org/edu/scholar.htm

Summary   To provide financial assistance for college to student members of the Japanese American Citizens League (JACL) who are high school seniors.

Eligibility   This program is open to JACL members who are high school seniors interested in attending a college, university, trade school, business college, or other institution of higher learning. Applicants must submit information on their involvement in JACL and a 2-page essay on a topic that changes annually but relates to Japanese Americans. Selection is based on that essay, academic history, extracurricular activities, JACL involvement, scholastic honors, and a letter of recommendation.

Financial data   Stipends generally average approximately $2,000.

Duration   1 year; nonrenewable.

Number awarded   At least 1 each year.

Deadline   February of each year.

[186]
JACOBS ENGINEERING SCHOLARSHIP

Conference of Minority Transportation Officials
Attn: National Scholarship Program
818 18th Street, N.W., Suite 850
Washington, DC 20006
(202) 530-0551   Fax: (202) 530-0617
Web: www.comto.org/news-youth.php

Summary   To provide financial assistance to Asian American and other minority upper-division and graduate students in a field related to transportation.

Eligibility   This program is open to minority juniors, seniors, and graduate students in fields related to transportation (e.g., civil engineering, construction engineering, environmental engineering, safety, transportation, urban planning). Undergraduates must have a GPA of 3.0 or higher; graduate students must have a GPA of at least 3.5. Applicants must submit a cover letter with a 500-word statement of career goals. Financial need is not considered in the selection process. U.S. citizenship is required.

Financial data   The stipend is $4,000. Funds are paid directly to the recipient's college or university.

Duration   1 year.

Additional information   The Conference of Minority Transportation Officials (COMTO) was established in 1971 to promote, strengthen, and expand the roles of minorities in all aspects of transportation. This program is sponsored by Jacobs Engineering Group Inc. Recipients are required to become members of COMTO and attend the COMTO National Scholarship Luncheon.

Number awarded   1 or more each year.

Deadline   April of each year.

[187]
JAMES B. MORRIS SCHOLARSHIP

James B. Morris Scholarship Fund
Attn: Scholarship Selection Committee
525 S.W. Fifth Street, Suite A
Des Moines, IA 50309-4501
(515) 282-8192   Fax: (515) 282-9117
E-mail: morris@assoc-mgmt.com
Web: www.morrisscholarship.org

Summary   To provide financial assistance to Asian American and other minority undergraduate, graduate, and law students in Iowa.

Eligibility   This program is open to minority students (African Americans, Asian/Pacific Islanders, Hispanics, or Native Americans) who are interested in studying at a college, graduate school, or law school. Applicants must be either Iowa residents and high school graduates who are attending a college or university anywhere in the United States or non-Iowa residents who are attending a college or university in Iowa; preference is given to native Iowans who are attending an Iowa college or university. Along with their application, they must submit an essay of 250 to 500 words on why they are applying for this scholarship, activities or organizations in which they are involved, and their future plans. Selection is based on the essay, academic achievement (GPA of 2.5 or higher), community service, and financial need. U.S. citizenship is required.

Financial data   The stipend is $2,300 per year.

Duration   1 year; may be renewed.

Additional information   This fund was established in 1978 in honor of the J.B. Morris family, who founded the Iowa branch of the National Association for the Advancement of Colored People and published the *Iowa Bystander* newspaper.

Number awarded   Varies each year; recently, 24 of these scholarships were awarded.

Deadline   March of each year.

[188]
JAMES CARLSON MEMORIAL SCHOLARSHIP

Oregon Student Assistance Commission
Attn: Grants and Scholarships Division
1500 Valley River Drive, Suite 100
Eugene, OR 97401-2146
(541) 687-7395   Toll Free: (800) 452-8807, ext. 7395
Fax: (541) 687-7414   TDD: (800) 735-2900
E-mail: awardinfo@osac.state.or.us
Web: www.osac.state.or.us/osac_programs.html

Summary   To provide financial assistance to Oregon residents (priority is given to Asian Americans and other minorities) who are majoring in education on the undergraduate or graduate school level at a school in any state.

Eligibility   This program is open to residents of Oregon who are U.S. citizens or permanent residents and enrolled at a college or university in any state. Applicants must be either 1) college seniors or fifth-year students majoring in elementary or secondary education or 2) graduate students working on an elementary or secondary certificate. Full-time enrollment and financial need are required. Priority is given to 1) students who come from diverse environments and submit an essay of 250 to 350 words on their experience living or working in diverse environments; 2) dependents of members of the Oregon Education Association; and 3) applicants committed to teaching autistic children.

Financial data   Stipend amounts vary; recently, they were at least $1,300.

Duration   1 year.

Additional information   This program is administered by the Oregon Student Assistance Commission (OSAC) with funds provided by the Oregon Community Foundation.

Number awarded   Varies each year; recently, 3 of these scholarships were awarded.

Deadline   February of each year.

[189]
JAMES E. WEBB INTERNSHIPS

Smithsonian Institution
Attn: Office of Fellowships
470 L'Enfant Plaza, Suite 7102
P.O. Box 37012, MRC 902
Washington, DC 20013-7012
(202) 633-7070   Fax: (202) 633-7069
E-mail: siofg@si.edu
Web: www.si.edu/ofg/Applications/WEBB/WEBBapp.htm

Summary   To provide internship opportunities throughout the Smithsonian Institution to Asian American and other minority upper-division and graduate students in business or public administration.

Eligibility   This program is open to minorities who are juniors, seniors, or graduate students majoring in areas of business or public administration (finance, human resource management, accounting, or general business administration). Applicants must have a GPA of 3.0 or higher. They must seek placement in offices, museums, and research institutes within the Smithsonian Institution.

Financial data   Interns receive a stipend of $550 per week and a travel allowance.

Duration   10 weeks during the summer, fall, or spring.

Number awarded   Varies each year; recently, 8 of these internships were awarded.

Deadline   January of each year for summer or fall; September of each year for spring.

[190]
JAMES ECHOLS SCHOLARSHIP

California Association for Health, Physical Education,
   Recreation and Dance
Attn: Chair, Scholarship Committee
1501 El Camino Avenue, Suite 3
Sacramento, CA 95815-2748
(916) 922-3596   Toll Free: (800) 499-3596 (within CA)
Fax: (916) 922-0133   E-mail: cahperd@cahperd.org
Web: www.cahperd.org/scholarships.html

Summary   To provide financial assistance to Asian American and other minority student members of the California Association for Health, Physical Education, Recreation and Dance.

Eligibility   This program is open to California residents who have been members of the association for at least 60 days and are attending a 2- or 4-year college or university in California. Applicants must be undergraduate or graduate students majoring in health, physical education, recreation, or

dance and have completed at least 60 semester hours of college work. Selection is based on scholastic proficiency (a GPA of 3.0 or higher); leadership ability in school, community, and professional activities; and personal qualities of enthusiasm, cooperativeness, responsibility, initiative, and ability to work with others. This scholarship is awarded to the highest-ranked minority (Asian, African American, Latino, or Native American) applicant.

Financial data   The stipend is $750.

Duration   1 year.

Number awarded   1 each year.

Deadline   November of each year.

[191]
JAMES J. WYCHOR SCHOLARSHIPS

Minnesota Broadcasters Association
Attn: Scholarship Program
3033 Excelsior Boulevard, Suite 440
Minneapolis, MN 55416
(612) 926-8123   Toll Free: (800) 245-5838
Fax: (612) 926-9761
E-mail: llasere@minnesotabroadcasters.com
Web: www.minnesotabroadcasters.com

Summary   To provide financial assistance to Minnesota residents (particularly Asian Americans, other minorities, and women) who are interested in studying broadcasting at a college in any state.

Eligibility   This program is open to residents of Minnesota who are accepted or enrolled at an accredited postsecondary institution in any state offering a broadcast-related curriculum. Applicants must have a high school or college GPA of 3.0 or higher and must submit a 500-word essay on why they wish to prepare for a career in broadcasting or electronic media. Employment in the broadcasting industry is not required, but students who are employed must include a letter from their general manager describing the duties they have performed as a radio or television station employee and evaluating their potential for success in the industry. Financial need is not considered in the selection process. Some of the scholarships are awarded only to minority and women candidates.

Financial data   The stipend is $1,500.

Duration   1 year; recipients who are college seniors may reapply for an additional 1-year renewal as a graduate student.

Number awarded   10 each year, distributed as follows: 3 within the 7-county metro area, 5 allocated geographically throughout the state (northeast, northwest, central, southeast, southwest), and 2 reserved specifically for women and minority applicants.

Deadline   June of each year.

[192]
JAVA MEMORIAL SCHOLARSHIPS

Japanese American Veterans Association
c/o Dave Buto
4226 Holborn Avenue
Annandale, VA 22003
(703) 503-3431   E-mail: admin@javadc.org
Web: www.javadc.org

Summary To provide financial assistance for college or graduate school to relatives of Japanese American veterans and military personnel.

Eligibility This program is open to graduating high school seniors and students currently working on an undergraduate or graduate degree at a college, university, or school of specialized study. Applicants must be related, by blood or marriage, to 1) a person who served with the 442nd Regimental Combat Team, the 100th Infantry Battalion, or other unit associated with those; 2) a person who served in the U.S. Military Intelligence Service during or after World War II; 3) a person of Japanese ancestry who is serving or has served in the U.S. armed forces and been honorable discharged; or 4) a member of the Japanese American Veterans Association (JAVA) whose membership extends back at least 1 year.

Financial data The stipend is $1,500.

Duration 1 year; recipients may reapply.

Additional information These scholarships, first awarded in 2008, include the following named awards: the Orville C. Shirey Memorial Scholarship, the Joseph Ichiuji Memorial Scholarship, the Sunao Phil Ishio Memorial Scholarship, the Kiyoko Tsuboi-Taubkin Memorial Scholarship, the Grant Hirabayashi Memorial Scholarship, the Teru Kamikawa Memorial Scholarship, the Mary Kozono Memorial Scholarship, and the Douglas Ishio Memorial Scholarship.

Number awarded 8 each year.

Deadline April of each year.

[193]
J.K. FUKUSHIMA SCHOLARSHIP FOR SEMINARIANS

Montebello Plymouth Congregational Church
144 South Greenwood Avenue
Montebello, CA 90640
(323) 721-5568 Fax: (323) 721-7955
E-mail: mpccucc@yahoo.com
Web: www.montebelloucc.org

Summary To provide financial assistance to undergraduate and graduate students who are preparing for a career in Christian ministry and can demonstrate a commitment to the Asian American community.

Eligibility This program is open to students who have completed at least 2 years of undergraduate study and are enrolled or accepted at an accredited school of theology. Applicants may not have completed a master's degree. They must be working on a degree that will provide them with the skills and understanding necessary to further the development of Christian ministries. Along with their application, they must submit an essay on their commitment to the Asian American community.

Financial data The stipend is $500.

Duration 1 year.

Number awarded 1 or more each year.

Deadline May of each year.

[194]
JOE ALLMAN SCHOLARSHIP

Japanese American Citizens League-Arizona Chapter
5414 West Glenn Drive
Glendale, AZ 85301-2628
E-mail: arizonajacl@gmail.com
Web: www.jaclaz.org

Summary To provide financial assistance to graduating high school seniors in Arizona who are of Japanese heritage.

Eligibility This program is open to graduating high school seniors in Arizona. Applicants or their parents must have been members of 1 of the following organizations for at least the preceding 3 years: Arizona Chapter of the Japanese American Citizens League (JACLA), the Phoenix Japanese Free Methodist Church, the Arizona Buddhist Church, a youth group of JACLA, a youth group of the Phoenix Free Methodist Church, or a youth group of the Arizona Buddhist Church. Financial need is not considered in the selection process. Special consideration is given to students currently involved in Scouting.

Financial data A stipend is awarded (amount not specified).

Duration 1 year.

Additional information Recipients must attend the association's scholarship awards banquet and accept the award in person; failure to do so results in forfeiture of the award.

Number awarded 1 each year.

Deadline February of each year.

[195]
JOHN AND MURIEL LANDIS SCHOLARSHIPS

American Nuclear Society
Attn: Scholarship Coordinator
555 North Kensington Avenue
La Grange Park, IL 60526-5592
(708) 352-6611 Toll Free: (800) 323-3044
Fax: (708) 352-0499 E-mail: outreach@ans.org
Web: www.ans.org/honors/scholarships

Summary To provide financial assistance to undergraduate or graduate students (especially Asian Americans, other minorities, and women) who are interested in preparing for a career in nuclear-related fields.

Eligibility This program is open to undergraduate and graduate students at colleges or universities located in the United States who are preparing for, or planning to prepare for, a career in nuclear science, nuclear engineering, or a nuclear-related field. Qualified high school seniors are also eligible. Applicants must have greater than average financial need and have experienced circumstances that render them disadvantaged. They must be sponsored by an organization (e.g., plant branch, local section, student section) within the American Nuclear Society (ANS). Along with their application, they must submit an essay on their academic and professional goals, experiences that have affected those goals, etc. Selection is based on that essay, academic achievement, letters of recommendation, and financial need. Women and members of minority groups are especially urged to apply. U.S. citizenship is not required.

Financial data The stipend is $5,000, to be used to cover tuition, books, fees, room, and board.

Duration 1 year; nonrenewable.

Number awarded　Up to 8 each year.
Deadline　January of each year.

[196]
JUSTINE E. GRANNER MEMORIAL SCHOLARSHIP

Iowa United Methodist Foundation
2301 Rittenhouse Street
Des Moines, IA 50321
(515) 974-8927
Web: www.iumf.org/otherscholarships.html

Summary　To provide financial assistance to Asian Americans and other ethnic minorities in Iowa interested in majoring in a health-related field.

Eligibility　This program is open to ethnic minority students preparing for a career in nursing, public health, or a related field at a college or school of nursing in Iowa. Applicants must have a GPA of 3.0 or higher. Preference is given to graduates of Iowa high schools. Financial need is considered in the selection process.

Financial data　The stipend is $1,000.
Duration　1 year.
Number awarded　1 each year.
Deadline　March of each year.

[197]
KAISER PERMANENTE COLORADO DIVERSITY SCHOLARSHIP PROGRAM

Kaiser Permanente
Attn: Multicultural Associations/Employee Resource
　Groups
P.O. Box 378066
Denver, CO 80247-8066
E-mail: co-diversitydevelopment@kp.org
Web: physiciancareers.kp.org

Summary　To provide financial assistance to Asian American and other Colorado residents from diverse backgrounds who are interested in working on an undergraduate or graduate degree in a health care field at a school in any state.

Eligibility　This program is open to all residents of Colorado, including those who identify as 1 or more of the following: African American, Asian Pacific, Latino, lesbian, gay, bisexual, transgender, intersex, Native American, and/or a person with a disability. Applicants must be 1) a graduating high school senior with a GPA of 2.7 or higher and planning to enroll full time at a college or technical school in any state; 2) a GED recipient with a GED score of 520 or higher and planning to enroll full time at a college or technical school in any state; 3) a full-time undergraduate student at a college or technical school in any state; or 4) a full-time graduate or doctoral student at a school in any state. They must be preparing for a career in health care (e.g., doctor, nurse, surgeon, physician assistant, dentist), mental health, public health, or health policy. Along with their application, they must submit 300-word essays on 1) a personal setback in their life and how they responded and learned from it; 2) how they give back to their community; and 3) why they have chosen health care and/or public health for their educational and career path. Selection is based on academic achievement, character qualities, community outreach and volunteering, and financial need.

Financial data　Stipends range from $1,400 to $2,600.
Duration　1 year.
Number awarded　Varies each year; recently, 17 of these scholarships were awarded.
Deadline　January of each year.

[198]
KANSAS ESOL/BILINGUAL EDUCATION SCHOLARSHIP

Kansas Association of Migrant Directors
c/o Cynthia Adcock
USD 305
P.O. Box 797
Salina, KS 67402
(785) 309-4718　　　E-mail: Cynthia.Adcock@usd305.com

Summary　To provide financial assistance for college to seniors graduating from high schools in Kansas who have been enrolled in a bilingual or English for Speakers of Other Languages (ESOL) program.

Eligibility　This program is open to seniors graduating from high schools in Kansas who are currently in a bilingual or ESOL program. Applicants must be planning to attend a college or university in Kansas as a full-time student. Along with their application, they must submit a paragraph about their educational goals, explaining why they want to go to college and describing their plans after graduation. Selection is based on the essay, GPA, school performance, and financial need.

Financial data　The stipend is $250 per semester.
Duration　4 semesters (2 years).
Number awarded　Varies each year; recently, 3 of these scholarships were awarded.
Deadline　March of each year.

[199]
KANSAS ETHNIC MINORITY SCHOLARSHIP PROGRAM

Kansas Board of Regents
Attn: Student Financial Assistance
1000 S.W. Jackson Street, Suite 520
Topeka, KS 66612-1368
(785) 296-3517　　　　　　　　Fax: (785) 296-0983
E-mail: dlindeman@ksbor.org
Web: www.kansasregents.org/scholarships_and_grants

Summary　To provide financial assistance to Asian Americans and other minority students in Kansas who are interested in attending college in the state.

Eligibility　Eligible to apply are Kansas residents who fall into 1 of these minority groups: American Indian, Alaskan Native, African American, Asian, Pacific Islander, or Hispanic. Applicants may be current college students (enrolled in community colleges, colleges, or universities in Kansas), but high school seniors graduating in the current year receive priority consideration. Minimum academic requirements include 1 of the following: 1) ACT score of 21 or higher or combined mathematics and critical reading SAT score of 990 or higher; 2) cumulative GPA of 3.0 or higher; 3) high school rank in upper 33%; 4) completion of the Kansas Scholars Curriculum (4 years of English, 3 years of mathematics, 3 years of science, 3 years of social studies, and 2 years of foreign language); 5) selection by the National Merit Corporation in any category;

or 6) selection by the College Board as a Hispanic Scholar. Selection is based primarily on financial need.

Financial data A stipend of up to $1,850 is provided, depending on financial need and availability of state funds.

Duration 1 year; may be renewed for up to 3 additional years (4 additional years for designated 5-year programs) if the recipient maintains a 2.0 cumulative GPA and has financial need.

Additional information There is a $10 application fee.

Number awarded Approximately 200 each year.

Deadline April of each year.

[200]
KANSAS SPJ MINORITY STUDENT SCHOLARSHIP

Society of Professional Journalists-Kansas Professional
  Chapter
c/o Denise Neil, Scholarship Committee
Wichita Eagle
825 East Douglas Avenue
P.O. Box 820
Wichita, KS 67201-0820
(316) 268-6327   E-mail: dneil@wichitaeagle.com
Web: www.spjchapters.org/kansas/gridiron.html

Summary To provide financial assistance to Asian American or other minority residents of any state enrolled at colleges and universities in Kansas who are interested in a career in journalism.

Eligibility This program is open to residents of any state who are members of a racial or ethnic minority group and entering their junior or senior year at colleges and universities in Kansas. Applicants do not have to be journalism or communication majors, but they must demonstrate a strong and sincere interest in print journalism, broadcast journalism, online journalism, or photojournalism. They must have a GPA of 2.5 or higher. Along with their application, they must submit a professional resume, 4 to 6 examples of their best work (clips or stories, copies of photographs, tapes or transcripts of broadcasts, printouts of web pages) and a 1-page cover letter about themselves, how they came to be interested in journalism, their professional goals, and (if appropriate) their financial need for this scholarship.

Financial data The stipend is $1,000.

Duration 1 year.

Number awarded 1 each year.

Deadline April of each year.

[201]
KATHY MANN MEMORIAL SCHOLARSHIP

Wisconsin Education Association Council
Attn: Scholarship Committee
33 Nob Hill Drive
P.O. Box 8003
Madison, WI 53708-8003
(608) 276-7711   Toll Free: (800) 362-8034, ext. 278
Fax: (608) 276-8203   E-mail: BrisackM@weac.org
Web: www.weac.org

Summary To provide financial assistance to Asian American and other minority high school seniors whose parent is a member of the Wisconsin Education Association Council

(WEAC) and who plan to study education at a college in any state.

Eligibility This program is open to high school seniors whose parent is an active WEAC member, an active retired member, or a person who died while holding a WEAC membership. Applicants must be members of a minority group (American Indian, Eskimo or Aleut, Hispanic, Asian or Pacific Islander, or Black). They must rank in the top 25% of their graduating class or have a GPA of 3.0 or higher, plan to major or minor in education at a college in any state, and intend to teach in Wisconsin. Along with their application, they must submit a 300-word essay on why they want to enter the education profession and what they hope to accomplish. Selection is based primarily on that essay, GPA, letters of recommendation, and school and community activities. Secondary consideration may be given to other factors, including financial need.

Financial data The stipend is $1,450 per year.

Duration 4 years, provided the recipient maintains a GPA of 3.0 or higher.

Additional information If no minority student applies for this scholarship, it may be awarded to a non-minority applicant.

Number awarded 1 each year.

Deadline February of each year.

[202]
KAYTE M. FEARN COUNCIL FOR EXCEPTIONAL CHILDREN ETHNIC DIVERSITY SCHOLARSHIP

Council for Exceptional Children
Attn: Student Awards
1110 North Glebe Road, Suite 300
Arlington, VA 22201-5704
(703) 264-9435   Toll Free: (888) CEC-SPED
Fax: (703) 264-9494   TDD: (866) 915-5000
E-mail: students@cec.sped.org
Web: www.cec.sped.org

Summary To provide financial assistance to Asian American and other ethnic minority student members of the Council for Exceptional Children (CEC).

Eligibility This program is open to student members of the council who are citizens of the United States or Canada, members of an ethnically diverse group (African American, American Indian, Alaska Native, Native Canadian, Hispanic, Asian, or Pacific Islander), and juniors, seniors, or graduate students enrolled in an accredited college or university. Applicants must be working on a degree in special education and have a GPA of 3.0 or higher. Along with their application, they must submit 2 letters of recommendation, a summary of Student CEC and/or other activities relating to individuals with disabilities, and a brief biography explaining why they chose special education as a career, how they view the role of special educators, and what they hope to accomplish as a special educator. Financial need is not considered.

Financial data The stipend is $500.

Duration 1 year; nonrenewable.

Number awarded 1 each year.

Deadline October of each year.

[203]
KEN KASHIWAHARA SCHOLARSHIP

Radio Television Digital News Foundation
Attn: RTDNF Fellowship Program
4121 Plank Road, Suite 512
Fredericksburg, VA 22407
(202) 467-5214   Fax: (202) 223-4007
E-mail: staceys@rtdna.org
Web: www.rtdna.org/pages/education/undergraduates.php

Summary To provide financial assistance to Asian Americans and other minority undergraduate students who are interested in preparing for a career in electronic journalism.

Eligibility This program is open to sophomores or more advanced minority undergraduate students enrolled in an electronic journalism sequence at an accredited or nationally-recognized college or university. Applicants must submit 1 to 3 examples of their journalistic skills on audio CD or DVD (no more than 15 minutes total, accompanied by scripts); a description of their role on each story and a list of who worked on each story and what they did; a 1-page statement explaining why they are preparing for a career in electronic journalism with reference to their specific career preference (radio, television, online, reporting, producing, or newsroom management); a resume; and a letter of reference from their dean or faculty sponsor explaining why they are a good candidate for the award and certifying that they have at least 1 year of school remaining.

Financial data The stipend is $2,500, paid in semiannual installments of $1,250 each.

Duration 1 year.

Additional information The Radio Television Digital News Foundation (RTDNF) was formerly the Radio and Television News Directors Foundation (RTNDF). Previous winners of any RTDNF scholarship or internship are not eligible to apply for this program.

Number awarded 1 each year.

Deadline May of each year.

[204]
KENJI KAJIWARA MEMORIAL SCHOLARSHIP

Japanese American Citizens League
Attn: National Scholarship Awards
1765 Sutter Street
San Francisco, CA 94115
(415) 921-5225   Fax: (415) 931-4671
E-mail: jacl@jacl.org
Web: www.jacl.org/edu/scholar.htm

Summary To provide financial assistance for college to student members of the Japanese American Citizens League (JACL).

Eligibility This program is open to JACL members who are currently enrolled at a college, university, trade school, business college, or other institution of higher learning. Applicants must submit information on their involvement in JACL and a 2-page essay on a topic that changes annually but relates to Japanese Americans. Selection is based on that essay, academic history, extracurricular activities, JACL involvement, scholastic honors, and a letter of recommendation.

Financial data Stipends generally average approximately $2,000.

Duration 1 year; nonrenewable.

Number awarded At least 1 each year.

Deadline March of each year.

[205]
KENTUCKY LIBRARY ASSOCIATION SCHOLARSHIP FOR MINORITY STUDENTS

Kentucky Library Association
c/o Executive Secretary
1501 Twilight Trail
Frankfort, KY 40601
(502) 223-5322   Fax: (502) 223-4937
E-mail: info@kylibasn.org
Web: www.kylibasn.org/scholarships965.cfm

Summary To provide financial assistance to Asian Americans and members of other minority groups who are residents of Kentucky or attending school there and are working on an undergraduate or graduate degree in library science.

Eligibility This program is open to members of minority groups (defined as American Indian, Alaskan Native, Black, Hispanic, Pacific Islander, or other ethnic group) who are entering or continuing at a graduate library school accredited by the American Library Association (ALA) or an undergraduate library program accredited by the National Council of Teacher Education (NCATE). Applicants must be residents of Kentucky or a student in a library program in the state. Along with their application, they must submit a statement of their career objectives, why they have chosen librarianship as a career, and their reasons for applying for this scholarship. U.S. citizenship or permanent resident status is required. Financial need is not considered in the selection process.

Financial data The stipend is $1,000.

Duration 1 year; nonrenewable.

Number awarded 1 or more each year.

Deadline June of each year.

[206]
KOREAN HONOR SCHOLARSHIP

Embassy of the Republic of Korea in the USA
2320 Massachusetts Avenue, N.W.
Washington, DC 20008
(202) 939-5663   Fax: (202) 342-1597
Web: www.dynamic-korea.com/education/scholarship.php

Summary To provide financial assistance to undergraduate and graduate students of Korean or Korean American heritage.

Eligibility This program is open to students of Korean or Korean American heritage. Applicants must be entering or enrolled full time in an undergraduate or graduate degree program at a college or university in the United States or Canada. They must have a GPA of 3.5 or higher. Along with their application, they must submit a 600-word essay (in English) on what their Korean heritage means to them. Selection is based on that essay, academic achievement, awards, honors, performances, extracurricular activities, and a letter of recommendation.

Financial data The stipend is $1,000.

Duration 1 year.

Additional information This program was established in 1981 when the government of the Republic of Korea donated $1 million to commemorate the 100th anniversary of the establishment of diplomatic relations between Korea and the United States. Subsequent donations have added to the fund.

Number awarded Approximately 140 each year.

Deadline June of each year.

[207]
KOREAN UNIVERSITY CLUB SCHOLARSHIP

Hawai'i Community Foundation
Attn: Scholarship Department
827 Fort Street Mall
Honolulu, HI 96813
(808) 537-6333   Toll Free: (888) 731-3863
Fax: (808) 521-6286
E-mail: scholarships@hcf-hawaii.org
Web: www.hawaiicommunityfoundation.org/scholarships

Summary To provide financial assistance to residents of Hawaii who are of Korean ancestry and interested in attending college in any state.

Eligibility This program is open to residents of Hawaii who are attending or planning to attend a 2- or 4-year college or university in any state. Applicants must be or Korean ancestry. They must be able to demonstrate academic achievement (GPA of 2.7 or higher), good moral character, and financial need. Along with their application, they must submit a short statement indicating their reasons for attending college, their planned course of study, their career goals, and what community service means to them.

Financial data The amounts of the awards depend on the availability of funds and the need of the recipient. Recently, the average value of all scholarships awarded by the foundation was $2,041.

Duration 1 year.

Additional information The Korean University Club of Hawaii was established in 1936 and began awarding scholarships to students of Korean ancestry in 1950.

Number awarded 1 or more each year.

Deadline February of each year.

[208]
KOREAN-AMERICAN SCIENTISTS AND ENGINEERS ASSOCIATION UNDERGRADUATE SCHOLARSHIPS

Korean-American Scientists and Engineers Association
Attn: Scholarship Committee
1952 Gallows Drive, Suite 300
Vienna, VA 22182
(703) 748-1221   Fax: (703) 748-1331
E-mail: admin@ksea.org
Web: scholarship.ksea.org/InfoUndergraduate.aspx

Summary To provide financial assistance to undergraduate student members of the Korean-American Scientists and Engineers Association (KSEA).

Eligibility This program is open to Korean American undergraduate students who are KSEA members, have completed at least 40 credits as a college student, and are majoring in science, engineering, or a related field. Along with their application, they must submit an essay on a topic that changes annually but relates to science or engineering; recently, students were asked to discuss the pros and cons of development vs. the environment. Selection is based on the essay (20%), KSEA activities and community service (30%),

recommendation letters (20%), and academic performance (30%).

Financial data The stipend is $1,000.

Duration 1 year.

Additional information This program includes the following named scholarships: the Inyong Ham Scholarship, the Wan-Kyoo Cho Scholarship, the Shoon Kyung Kim Scholarship, the Nam Sook and Je Hyun Kim Scholarship, the SeAh-Haiam Scholarship, the Yohan and Rumie Cho Scholarship, the Changkiu Riew and Hyunsoo Kim Scholarship, the Yoon Soo Park Scholarship, the Jae S. and Kyuho Lim Scholarship, and the Hyundai Scholarships.

Number awarded 15 to 20 each year.

Deadline February of each year.

[209]
KYUTARO AND YASUO ABIKO MEMORIAL SCHOLARSHIP

Japanese American Citizens League
Attn: National Scholarship Awards
1765 Sutter Street
San Francisco, CA 94115
(415) 921-5225   Fax: (415) 931-4671
E-mail: jacl@jacl.org
Web: www.jacl.org/edu/scholar.htm

Summary To provide financial assistance for college to student members of the Japanese American Citizens League (JACL), especially those majoring in journalism or agriculture.

Eligibility This program is open to JACL members who are currently enrolled at a college, university, trade school, business college, or other institution of higher learning. Applicants must submit information on their involvement in JACL and a 2-page essay on a topic that changes annually but relates to Japanese Americans. Selection is based on that essay, academic history, extracurricular activities, JACL involvement, scholastic honors, and a letter of recommendation. Preference is given to students majoring in journalism or agriculture.

Financial data Stipends generally average approximately $2,000.

Duration 1 year; nonrenewable.

Number awarded At least 1 each year.

Deadline March of each year.

[210]
LAGRANT FOUNDATION UNDERGRADUATE SCHOLARSHIPS

Lagrant Foundation
Attn: Programs Manager
626 Wilshire Boulevard, Suite 700
Los Angeles, CA 90071-2920
(323) 469-8680   Fax: (323) 469-8683
E-mail: erickaavila@lagrant.com
Web: www.lagrantfoundation.org/site/?page_id=3

Summary To provide financial assistance to Asian Pacific Americans and other minority college students who are interested in majoring in advertising, public relations, or marketing.

Eligibility This program is open to African Americans, Asian Pacific Americans, Hispanics/Latinos, and Native Americans/Alaska Natives who are full-time students at a 4-

year accredited institution. Applicants must have a GPA of 2.75 or higher and be either majoring in advertising, marketing, or public relations or minoring in communications with plans to prepare for a career in advertising, marketing, or public relations. Along with their application, they must submit 1) a 1- to 2-page essay outlining their career goals; what steps they will take to increase ethnic representation in the fields of advertising, marketing, and public relations; and the role of an advertising, marketing, or public relations practitioner; 2) a paragraph describing the college and/or community activities in which they are involved; 3) a brief paragraph describing any honors and awards they have received; 4) a letter of reference; 5) a resume; and 6) an official transcript. U.S. citizenship or permanent resident status is required.

Financial data   The stipend is $5,000.

Duration   1 year.

Number awarded   10 each year.

Deadline   February of each year.

[211]
LANDMARK SCHOLARS PROGRAM

Landmark Media Enterprises LLC
c/o Ann Morris, Managing Editor
Greensboro News & Record
200 East Market Street
Greensboro, NC 27401
(540) 981-3211   Toll Free: (800) 346-1234
E-mail: amorris@news-record.com
Web: company.news-record.com/intern.htm

Summary   To provide work experience and financial aid to Asian Americans and other minority undergraduates who are interested in preparing for a career in journalism.

Eligibility   This program is open to minority (Asian, Hispanic, African American, Native American) college sophomores, preferably those with ties to the mid-Atlantic states (Delaware, Maryland, North Carolina, South Carolina, Virginia, and Washington, D.C.). Applicants must be full-time students with a GPA of 2.5 or higher in a 4-year degree program. They must be interested in preparing for a career in print journalism and participating in an internship in news, features, sports, copy editing, photography, or graphics/illustration. U.S. citizenship or permanent resident status is required. Selection is based on grades, work samples, recommendations, targeted selection interview skills, and financial need.

Financial data   The stipend is $5,000 per year. During the summers following their sophomore and junior years, recipients are provided with paid internships. Following graduation, they are offered a 1-year internship with full benefits and the possibility of continued employment.

Duration   2 years (the junior and senior years of college).

Additional information   The internships are offered at the *News & Record* in Greensboro, North Carolina, the *Virginian-Pilot* in Norfolk, Virginia, or the *Roanoke Times* in Roanoke, Virginia.

Number awarded   1 or more each year.

Deadline   December of each year.

[212]
LAO AMERICAN WOMEN ASSOCIATION OF WASHINGTON D.C. METROPOLITAN AREA COLLEGE SCHOLARSHIP FUND

Lao American Women Association
Attn: Scholarship Fund
1628 16th Street, N.W.
Washington, DC 20009
(703) 913-1768   E-mail: info@lawadc.org
Web: www.lawadc.org

Summary   To provide financial assistance to high school seniors of Lao ancestry in the Washington, D.C. area who plan to attend college in any state.

Eligibility   This program is open to seniors graduating from high schools in Maryland, Virginia, and the District of Columbia who are of Lao parentage. Applicants must have a GPA of 2.8 or higher and be planning to attend college in any state in the following fall. Along with their application, they must submit a 150-word personal statement on their purpose or motivations for going to college. Financial need is considered in the selection process (must have family income less than $75,000 per year). U.S. citizenship or permanent resident status is required.

Financial data   The stipend is $1,000.

Duration   1 year.

Additional information   This scholarship was first awarded in 2004.

Number awarded   1 each year.

Deadline   April of each year.

[213]
LAO AMERICAN WOMEN ASSOCIATION OF WASHINGTON D.C. METROPOLITAN AREA VOCATIONAL TRAINING/GED SCHOLARSHIP FUND

Lao American Women Association
Attn: Scholarship Fund
1628 16th Street, N.W.
Washington, DC 20009
E-mail: info@lawadc.org
Web: www.lawadc.org

Summary   To provide financial assistance to women of Lao ancestry in the Washington, D.C. area who need additional training to find a job.

Eligibility   This program is open to women in Maryland, Virginia, and the District of Columbia who are of Lao parentage. Applicants must be in need of additional training to find a job, to obtain work at a higher level, or to completed a GED certificate. They must provide information on their personal situation, proposed training program, work experience, family and community activities, and financial situation. They must also submit a 150-word personal statement on their motivation for enrolling in a program of vocational training or GED completion.

Financial data   The stipend is $1,000.

Duration   1 year.

Number awarded   1 or more each year.

Deadline   April of each year.

[214]
LAPIZ FAMILY SCHOLARSHIP

Asian Pacific Fund
Attn: Scholarship Coordinator
225 Bush Street, Suite 590
San Francisco, CA 94104
(415) 433-6859   Toll Free: (800) 286-1688
Fax: (415) 433-2425
E-mail: scholarship@asianpacificfund.org
Web: www.asianpacificfund.org

Summary   To provide financial assistance to Asian American and other students enrolled at campuses of the University of California (UC) who are children of farm workers.

Eligibility   This program is open to residents of California who will be enrolled as a full time undergraduate at a UC campus in the following fall. Preference is given to students at UC Davis and UC Santa Cruz. Applicants must be a farm worker or the child of farm or migrant workers. They must have a GPA of 3.0 or higher and be able to demonstrate financial need. Along with their application, they must submit essays of 250 to 500 words each on 1) their experience as a farm worker or child of a farm worker and how that experience relates to their educational and career goals; 2) a project, experience, or person related to their academic and career goals that inspired them; and 3) any unusual family or personal circumstances that have affected their achievement in school, work experience, or participation in school activities. U.S. citizenship or permanent resident status is required.

Financial data   The stipend is $1,000.

Duration   1 year.

Number awarded   2 each year.

Deadline   March of each year.

[215]
LARRY W. MCCORMICK COMMUNICATIONS SCHOLARSHIP FOR UNDERREPRESENTED STUDENTS

The Lullaby Guild, Inc.
Attn: Scholarship Committee
6709 La Tijera, Suite 116
Los Angeles, CA 90045
(310) 335-5655   E-mail: mail@lullabyguild.org
Web: www.lullabyguild.org

Summary   To provide financial assistance to Asian Pacific Americans and other underrepresented upper-division students who are working on a degree in a field related to mass communications.

Eligibility   This program is open to underrepresented (e.g., African American, Hispanic American, Native American, Alaskan American, Pacific Islander, Asian) students entering their junior or senior year at an accredited college or university. Applicants must be working on a degree in a field related to mass communications, including audiovisual and electronic and print journalism. Along with their application, they must submit a personal statement regarding their volunteer services, official transcripts, 3 letters of recommendation, 3 samples of their journalistic work, and a 500-word personal statement about their interest in journalism or mass communication. Selection is based on academic achievement, letters of recommendation, journalistic experience and/or evidence of journalistic talent, clarity of purpose in plans and goals for a future in journalism or mass communications, and involvement in volunteer community service.

Financial data   The stipend is $2,500.

Duration   1 year.

Number awarded   1 each year.

Deadline   February of each year.

[216]
LAURENCE R. FOSTER MEMORIAL UNDERGRADUATE SCHOLARSHIPS

Oregon Student Assistance Commission
Attn: Grants and Scholarships Division
1500 Valley River Drive, Suite 100
Eugene, OR 97401-2146
(541) 687-7395   Toll Free: (800) 452-8807, ext. 7395
Fax: (541) 687-7414   TDD: (800) 735-2900
E-mail: awardinfo@osac.state.or.us
Web: www.osac.state.or.us/osac_programs.html

Summary   To provide financial assistance to minority and other undergraduate students from Oregon who are interested in enrolling at a school in any state to prepare for a public health career.

Eligibility   This program is open to residents of Oregon who are enrolled at least half time at a 4-year college or university in any state to prepare for a career in public health (not private practice). Applicants must be entering the junior or senior year of a health program, including nursing, medical technology, and physician assistant. Preference is given to applicants from diverse environments. Along with their application, they must submit brief essays on 1) what public health means to them; 2) the public health aspect they intend to practice and the health and population issues impacted by that aspect; and 3) their experience living or working in diverse environments.

Financial data   Stipend amounts vary; recently, they were at least $4,167.

Duration   1 year.

Additional information   This program is administered by the Oregon Student Assistance Commission (OSAC) with funds provided by the Oregon Community Foundation.

Number awarded   Varies each year; recently, 6 undergraduate and graduate scholarships were awarded.

Deadline   February of each year.

[217]
LE HOANG NGUYEN COLLEGE SCHOLARSHIP

Vietnamese American Scholarship Foundation
P.O. Box 429
Stafford, TX 77497
E-mail: scholarships@vietscholarships.org
Web: www.vietscholarships.org/scholarships.html

Summary   To provide financial assistance to high school seniors of Vietnamese descent in Texas who plan to attend college in any state.

Eligibility   This program is open to seniors graduating from high schools in Texas who are of Vietnamese descent. Applicants must be planning to enroll at an accredited college or university in any state. They must have a GPA of 3.0 or higher and rank in their class in the top 10%. Along with their application, they must submit a 750-word essay on either 1) accomplishments that illustrate their aptitude for leadership, or 2) where they see themselves in 5 years. An interview may be required. Financial need is not considered in the selection process.

Financial data   The stipend is $500.

Duration   1 year; nonrenewable.

Number awarded   1 each year.

Deadline   April of each year.

[218]
LEADERSHIP IN ACTION INTERNSHIP

Leadership Education for Asian Pacifics, Inc.
Attn: Executive Assistant
327 East Second Street, Suite 226
Los Angeles, CA 90012
(213) 485-1422, ext. 4119   Fax: (213) 485-0050
E-mail: nyap@leap.org
Web: leap.org/empower_lia.html

Summary   To provide college students and recent graduates from any state with an opportunity to gain leadership experience through a summer internship at a community based organization (CBO) within the Asian and Pacific Islander nonprofit sector in southern California.

Eligibility   This program is open to residents of any state who have completed at least 2 years of college or are recent graduates. Applicants must be able to demonstrate prior experience in Asian or Pacific Islander communities, a passion for learning and growing their leadership skills, and an interest in gaining work experience at an Asian and Pacific Islander nonprofit CBO. Along with their application, they must submit a 1-page statement on the types of experience they have had in leadership and community involvement, how their experience has contributed to their role in the Asian and Pacific Islander community, and what they hope to gain from this internship experience. Selection is based on demonstrated leadership, community service, interpersonal skills, written and verbal communication skills, maturity and professional demeanor, and GPA.

Financial data   Interns receive a stipend of $2,000 upon completion of the program.

Duration   8 weeks during the summer. During each week, interns spend 4 days at their assigned CBO and 1 day at LEAP headquarters.

Additional information   This program began in 1998.

Number awarded   Varies each year; since the program began, it has placed 109 interns with 38 CBOs in southern California.

Deadline   March of each year.

[219]
LEONARD M. PERRYMAN COMMUNICATIONS SCHOLARSHIP FOR ETHNIC MINORITY STUDENTS

United Methodist Communications
Attn: Communications Resourcing Team
810 12th Avenue South
P.O. Box 320
Nashville, TN 37202-0320
(615) 742-5481   Toll Free: (888) CRT-4UMC
Fax: (615) 742-5485   E-mail: scholarships@umcom.org
Web: crt.umc.org/interior.asp?ptid=44&mid=10270

Summary   To provide financial assistance to Asian Americans and other minorities who are United Methodist college students and interested in careers in religious communications.

Eligibility   This program is open to United Methodist ethnic minority students enrolled in accredited institutions of higher education as juniors or seniors. Applicants must be interested in preparing for a career in religious communications. For the purposes of this program, "communications" is meant to cover audiovisual, electronic, and print journalism. Selection is based on Christian commitment and involvement in the life of the United Methodist church, academic achievement, journalistic experience, clarity of purpose, and professional potential as a religion communicator.

Financial data   The stipend is $2,500 per year.

Duration   1 year.

Additional information   The scholarship may be used at any accredited institution of higher education.

Number awarded   1 each year.

Deadline   March of each year.

[220]
LIBRARY OF CONGRESS JUNIOR FELLOWS PROGRAM

Library of Congress
Library Services
Attn: Junior Fellows Program Coordinator
101 Independence Avenue, S.E., Room LM-642
Washington, DC 20540-4600
(202) 707-0901   Fax: (202) 707-6269
E-mail: jrfell@loc.gov
Web: www.loc.gov/hr/jrfellows/index.html

Summary   To provide summer work experience at the Library of Congress (LC) to upper-division students, graduate students, and recent graduates (particularly those who are Asian Americans, other minorities, women, and individuals with disabilities).

Eligibility   This program is open to U.S. citizens with subject expertise in the following areas: American history, including veterans and military history; American popular culture; area studies (African, Asian, European, Hispanic, Middle Eastern); bibliographic description and access; film, television, and radio; folklife; geography and maps; history of photography; history of popular and applied graphic arts, architecture, and design; manuscript collections processing; music; preservation and conservation; rare books and manuscripts; science, technology, and business; serials and government publications and newspapers; or sound recordings. Applicants must 1) be juniors or seniors at an accredited college or university, 2) be graduate students, or 3) have completed their degree in the past year. Applications from women, minorities, and persons with disabilities are particularly encouraged. Selection is based on academic achievement, letters of recommendation, and an interview.

Financial data   Fellows are paid a taxable stipend of $300 per week.

Duration   3 months, beginning in either May or June. Fellows work a 40-hour week.

Additional information   Fellows work with primary source materials and assist selected divisions at LC in the organization and documentation of archival collections, production of finding aids and bibliographic records, preparation of materials for preservation and service, completion of bibliographical research, and digitization of LC's historical collections.

Number awarded Varies each year; recently, 6 of these internships were awarded.

Deadline March of each year.

[221]
LIN MEDIA MINORITY SCHOLARSHIP AND TRAINING PROGRAM

LIN Television Corporation
Attn: Vice President, Human Resources
One West Exchange Street, Suite 5A
Providence, RI 02903-1064
(401) 454-2880   Fax: (401) 454-6990
Web: www.linmedia.com/contact-us/careers.php

Summary To provide funding to Asian American and other minority undergraduates interested in earning a degree in a field related to broadcast journalism and working at a station owned by LIN Television Corporation.

Eligibility This program is open to U.S. citizens of non-white origin who are enrolled as a sophomore or higher at a college or university. Applicants must have a declared major in broadcast journalism, mass communication, television production, or marketing and a GPA of 3.0 or higher. Along with their application, they must submit a list of organizations and activities in which they have held leadership positions, 3 references, a 50-word description of their career goals, a list of personal achievements and honors, and a 500-word essay about themselves. Financial need is not considered in the selection process.

Financial data The program pays for tuition and fees, books, and room and board, to a maximum of $20,000 per year. Recipients must sign an employment agreement that guarantees them part-time employment as an intern during school and a 2-year regular position at a television station owned by LIN Television Corporation following graduation. If they fail to honor the employment agreement, they must repay all scholarship funds received.

Duration 2 years.

Additional information LIN Television Corporation owns 28 television stations in 17 media markets in the United States. Recipients of these scholarships must work at a station selected by LIN management.

Number awarded 1 or more each year.

Deadline March of each year.

[222]
LINCOLN CULTURAL DIVERSITY SCHOLARSHIP

American Advertising Federation-Lincoln
Attn: Scholarship Chair
P.O. Box 80093
Lincoln, NE 68501-0093
Web: www.aaflincoln.org/resources/scholarships.htm

Summary To provide financial assistance to Asian American and other minority residents of any state preparing for a career in a field related to advertising at a college in Nebraska.

Eligibility This program is open to minority residents of any state currently enrolled full time at an accredited college or university in Nebraska. Applicants must be working on a

degree in advertising, marketing, public relations, communications, or commercial art. Along with their application, they must submit an essay describing their interest in receiving this scholarship and why they should be selected. They may also submit up to 3 samples of their work, although this is not required. Finalists are interviewed. Selection is based on ability, commitment and enthusiasm for the advertising profession, academic performance, participation in extracurricular activities, and career goals. U.S. citizenship is required.

Financial data The stipend is $1,000. Awards are provided in the form of a credit at the recipient's institution.

Duration 1 year.

Number awarded 1 each year.

Deadline October of each year.

[223]
LLOYD LACUESTA BROADCAST NEWS GRANT

Asian American Journalists Association
Attn: Student Programs Coordinator
5 Third Street, Suite 1108
San Francisco, CA 94103
(415) 346-2051, ext. 102   Fax: (415) 346-6343
E-mail: programs@aaja.org
Web: www.aaja.org/programs/internships

Summary To provide a supplemental grant to male members of the Asian American Journalists Association (AAJA) working as a summer intern at a television broadcasting company.

Eligibility This program is open to male AAJA members who are full-time college students or recent college graduates. Applicants must have secured a summer internship at a television broadcasting company before they apply. Along with their application, they must submit a 200-word essay on why they want to prepare for a career in broadcast journalism, what they want to gain from the experience, and why AAJA's mission is important to them; a letter of recommendation; a resume; proof of age (at least 18 years); verification of an internship; and statement of financial need.

Financial data The grant is $1,000. Funds are to be used for living expenses or transportation.

Duration Summer months.

Number awarded 1 each year.

Deadline May of each year.

[224]
LOUIS B. RUSSELL, JR. MEMORIAL SCHOLARSHIP

Indiana State Teachers Association
Attn: Scholarships
150 West Market Street, Suite 900
Indianapolis, IN 46204-2875
(317) 263-3400   Toll Free: (800) 382-4037
Fax: (317) 655-3700   E-mail: mshoup@ista-in.org
Web: www.ista-in.org/dynamic.aspx?id=1038

Summary To provide financial assistance to Asian American and other minority high school seniors in Indiana who are interested in attending vocational school in any state.

Eligibility This program is open to ethnic minority high school seniors in Indiana who are interested in continuing their education in the area of industrial arts, vocational education, or technical preparation at an accredited postsecondary institution in any state. Selection is based on academic achievement, leadership ability as expressed through co-curricular activities and community involvement, recommendations, and a 300-word essay on their educational goals and how they plan to use this scholarship.

Financial data The stipend is $1,000.

Duration 1 year; may be renewed for 1 additional year, provided the recipient maintains a GPA of "C+" or higher.

Number awarded 1 each year.

Deadline February of each year.

[225]
LTK SCHOLARSHIP

Conference of Minority Transportation Officials
Attn: National Scholarship Program
818 18th Street, N.W., Suite 850
Washington, DC 20006
(202) 530-0551   Fax: (202) 530-0617
Web: www.comto.org/news-youth.php

Summary To provide financial assistance to Asian American and other minority upper-division and graduate students majoring in engineering or fields related to transportation.

Eligibility This program is open to full-time minority juniors, seniors, and graduate students in engineering of other technical transportation-related disciplines. Applicants must have a GPA of 3.0 or higher. Along with their application, they must submit a cover letter with a 500-word statement of career goals. Financial need is not considered in the selection process. U.S. citizenship is required.

Financial data The stipend is $6,000. Funds are paid directly to the recipient's college or university.

Duration 1 year.

Additional information The Conference of Minority Transportation Officials (COMTO) was established in 1971 to promote, strengthen, and expand the roles of minorities in all aspects of transportation. This program is sponsored by LTK Engineering Services. Recipients are required to become members of COMTO if they are not already members and attend the COMTO National Scholarship Luncheon.

Number awarded 1 or more each year.

Deadline April of each year.

[226]
MABEL SMITH MEMORIAL SCHOLARSHIP

Wisconsin Women of Color Network, Inc.
Attn: MSMS Committee
P.O. Box 2337
Madison, WI 53701-2337
E-mail: contact@womenofcolornetwork-wis.org
Web: www.womenofcolornetwork-wis.org/scholarship.html

Summary To provide financial assistance for vocational/technical school or community college to Asian American and other minority residents of Wisconsin.

Eligibility This program is open to residents of Wisconsin who are high school or GED-equivalent graduating seniors planning to continue their education at a vocational/technical school or community college in any state. Applicants must be a member of 1 of the following groups: African American, Asian, American Indian, Hispanic, or biracial. They must have a GPA of 2.0 or higher and be able to demonstrate financial need. Along with their application, they must submit a 1-page

essay on how this scholarship will help them accomplish their educational goal. U.S. citizenship is required.

Financial data A stipend is awarded (amount not specified).

Duration 1 year.

Additional information This program was established in 1990.

Number awarded 1 each year.

Deadline May of each year.

[227]
MACY'S HALLMARK SCHOLARSHIP

US Pan Asian American Chamber of Commerce
Attn: Scholarship Coordinator
1329 18th Street, N.W.
Washington, DC 20036
(202) 296-5221   Toll Free: (800) 696-7818
Fax: (202) 296-5225   E-mail: info@uspaacc.com
Web: celebrasianconference.com

Summary To provide financial assistance for college to Asian Pacific American high school seniors who demonstrate academic achievement and financial need.

Eligibility This program is open to high school seniors of Asian or Pacific Islander heritage who are U.S. citizens or permanent residents. Applicants must be planning to enroll full time at an accredited postsecondary educational institution in the United States. Along with their application, they must submit a 500-word essay on their background, achievements, and personal goals. Selection is based on academic excellence (GPA of 3.3 or higher), leadership in extracurricular activities, community service involvement, and financial need.

Financial data The maximum stipend is $5,000. Funds are paid directly to the recipient's college or university.

Duration 1 year.

Additional information This program is sponsored by Macy's. Funding is not provided for correspondence courses, Internet courses, or study in a country other than the United States.

Number awarded 1 each year.

Deadline March of each year.

[228]
MADISON/KALATHAS/DAVIS SCHOLARSHIP AWARD

National Naval Officers Association-Washington, D.C.
   Chapter
Attn: Scholarship Program
2701 Park Center Drive, A1108
Alexandria, VA 22302
(703) 566-3840   Fax: (703) 566-3813
E-mail: Stephen.Williams@Navy.mil
Web: dcnnoa.memberlodge.com

Summary To provide financial assistance to Asian American and other minority high school seniors from the Washington, D.C. area who plan to attend college in any state.

Eligibility This program is open to minority seniors graduating from high schools in the Washington, D.C. metropolitan area who plan to enroll full time at an accredited 2- or 4-year college or university in any state. Applicants must be U.S. citizens or permanent residents and have a GPA of 3.0 or higher. Selection is based on academic achievement, community involvement, and financial need.

Financial data   The stipend is $1,500.

Duration   1 year; nonrenewable.

Additional information   Recipients are not required to join or affiliate with the military in any way.

Number awarded   1 each year.

Deadline   March of each year.

[229]
MAINE SECTION SCHOLARSHIP

American Society of Civil Engineers-Maine Section
c/o Leslie L. Corrow, Scholarship Chair
Kleinschmidt Associates
75 Main Street
P.O. Box 576
Pittsfield, ME 04967
(207) 487-3328   Fax: (207) 487-3124
E-mail: scholarships@maineasce.org
Web: www.maineasce.org

Summary   To provide financial assistance to minority and other high school seniors in Maine who are interested in studying civil engineering in college.

Eligibility   This program is open to graduating high school seniors who are Maine residents and who intend to study civil engineering in college. Women and minorities are especially encouraged to apply. Applicants must submit a 200-word statement describing why they have chosen civil engineering as a career and what they hope to accomplish by being a civil engineer. Selection is based on the statement, academic performance, extracurricular activities, and letters of recommendation.

Financial data   The stipend is $2,000.

Duration   1 year; nonrenewable.

Number awarded   1 each year.

Deadline   January of each year.

[230]
MARATHON OIL CORPORATION COLLEGE SCHOLARSHIP PROGRAM OF THE HISPANIC SCHOLARSHIP FUND

Hispanic Scholarship Fund
Attn: Selection Committee
55 Second Street, Suite 1500
San Francisco, CA 94105
(415) 808-2365   Toll Free: (877) HSF-INFO
Fax: (415) 808-2302   E-mail: scholar1@hsf.net
Web: www.hsf.net/Scholarships.aspx?id=464

Summary   To provide financial assistance to Asian American and other minority upper-division and graduate students working on a degree in a field related to the oil and gas industry.

Eligibility   This program is open to U.S. citizens and permanent residents (must have a permanent resident card or a passport stamped I-551) who are of Hispanic American, African American, Asian Pacific Islander American, or American Indian/Alaskan Native heritage. Applicants must be currently enrolled full time at an accredited 4-year college or university in the United States, Puerto Rico, Guam, or the U.S. Virgin Islands with a GPA of 3.0 or higher. They must be 1) sophomores majoring in accounting, chemical engineering, civil

engineering, computer engineering, computer science, electrical engineering, energy management or petroleum land management, environmental engineering, environmental health and safety, finance, geology, geophysics, geotechnical engineering, global procurement or supply chain management, information technology/management information systems, marketing, mechanical engineering, petroleum engineering, or transportation and logistics,; or 2) seniors planning to work on a master's degree in geology or geophysics. Selection is based on academic achievement, personal strengths, interest and commitment to a career in the oil and gas industry, leadership, and financial need.

Financial data   The stipend is $15,000 per year.

Duration   2 years (the junior and senior undergraduate years or the first 2 years of a master's degree program).

Additional information   This program is jointly sponsored by Marathon Oil Corporation and the Hispanic Scholarship Fund (HSF). Recipients may be offered a paid 8- to 10-week summer internship at various Marathon Oil Corporation locations.

Number awarded   1 or more each year.

Deadline   November of each year.

[231]
MARTIN LUTHER KING, JR. MEMORIAL SCHOLARSHIP FUND

California Teachers Association
Attn: Human Rights Department
1705 Murchison Drive
P.O. Box 921
Burlingame, CA 94011-0921
(650) 552-5446   Fax: (650) 552-5002
E-mail: scholarships@cta.org
Web: www.cta.org

Summary   To provide financial assistance for college or graduate school to Asian Americans and other minorities who are members of the California Teachers Association (CTA), children of members, or members of the Student CTA.

Eligibility   This program is open to members of racial or ethnic minority groups (African Americans, American Indians/Alaska Natives, Asians/Pacific Islanders, and Hispanics) who are 1) active CTA members; 2) dependent children of active, retired, or deceased CTA members; or 3) members of Student CTA. Applicants must be interested in preparing for a teaching career in public education or already engaged in such a career.

Financial data   Stipends vary each year; recently, they ranged from $1,000 to $4,000.

Duration   1 year.

Number awarded   Varies each year; recently, 12 of these scholarships were awarded: 4 to CTA members, 6 to children of CTA members, and 2 to Student CTA members.

Deadline   March of each year.

[232]
MARTIN LUTHER KING, JR. SCHOLARSHIP

North Carolina Association of Educators, Inc.
Attn: Minority Affairs Commission
700 South Salisbury Street
P.O. Box 27347
Raleigh, NC 27611-7347
(919) 832-3000, ext. 205
Toll Free: (800) 662-7924, ext. 205
Fax: (919) 839-8229
Web: www.ncae.org

Summary To provide financial assistance to high school seniors in North Carolina (especially Asian Americans and other minorities) who plan to attend college in any state.

Eligibility This program is open to seniors graduating from high schools in North Carolina who plan to attend a college or university in any state. They must have a GPA of 2.5 or higher. Applications are considered and judged by members of the association's Minority Affairs Commission. Selection is based on character, personality, and scholastic achievement.

Financial data A stipend is awarded (amount not specified).

Duration 1 year.

Number awarded 1 or more each year.

Deadline January of each year.

[233]
MARY HILL DAVIS ETHNIC/MINORITY STUDENT SCHOLARSHIP PROGRAM

Baptist General Convention of Texas
Attn: Institutional Ministries Department
333 North Washington
Dallas, TX 75246-1798
(214) 828-5252   Toll Free: (888) 244-9400
Fax: (214) 828-5261   E-mail: institutions@bgct.org
Web: texasbaptists.org

Summary To provide financial assistance for college to Asian Americans and other minority residents of Texas who are members of Texas Baptist congregations.

Eligibility This program is open to members of Texas Baptist congregations who are of African American, Hispanic, Native American, Asian, or other intercultural heritage. Applicants must be attending or planning to attend a university affiliated with the Baptist General Convention of Texas to work on a bachelor's degree as preparation for service as a future lay or vocational ministry leader in a Texas Baptist ethnic/minority church. They must have been active in their respective ethnic/minority community. Along with their application, they must submit a letter of recommendation from their pastor and transcripts. Students still in high school must have a GPA of at least 3.0; students previously enrolled in a college must have at least a 2.0 GPA. U.S. citizenship or permanent resident status is required.

Financial data Stipends are $800 per semester ($1,600 per year) for full-time students or $400 per semester ($800 per year) for part-time students.

Duration 1 semester; may be renewed up to 7 additional semesters.

Additional information The scholarships are funded through the Week of Prayer and the Mary Hill Davis Offering for state missions sponsored annually by Women's Mission-

ary Union of Texas. The eligible institutions are Baptist University of The Americas, Baylor University, Dallas Baptist University, East Texas Baptist University, Hardin Simmons University, Houston Baptist University, Howard Payne University, University of Mary Hardin Baylor, and Wayland Baptist University.

Number awarded Varies each year.

Deadline April of each year.

[234]
MARY MOY QUON ING MEMORIAL SCHOLARSHIP

Asian American Journalists Association
Attn: Student Programs Coordinator
5 Third Street, Suite 1108
San Francisco, CA 94103
(415) 346-2051, ext. 102   Fax: (415) 346-6343
E-mail: programs@aaja.org
Web: www.aaja.org/programs/scholarships

Summary To provide financial assistance to student members of the Asian American Journalists Association (AAJA) entering their sophomore year of college and interested in majoring in journalism.

Eligibility This program is open to AAJA members planning to enroll full time as college sophomores and study journalism. Applicants must submit a 500-word essay on their involvement or interest in the Asian American community and how, if they are awarded this scholarship, they would contribute to the field of journalism and/or media issues involving the Asian Pacific American and Pacific Islander community. Print applicants must submit up to 4 photocopied or printed articles; broadcast applicants must submit up to 3 stories (total length less than 10 minutes) copied onto CDs; photojournalism applicants must submit a portfolio with no more than 10 entries. Selection is based on academic achievement, commitment to journalism, sensitivity to Asian American and Pacific Islander issues, demonstrated journalistic ability, and financial need.

Financial data The stipend is $2,000.

Duration 1 year.

Number awarded 1 each year.

Deadline April of each year.

[235]
MARY WOLFSKILL TRUST FUND INTERNSHIP

Library of Congress
Library Services
Attn: Junior Fellows Program Coordinator
101 Independence Avenue, S.E., Room LM-642
Washington, DC 20540-4600
(202) 707-3301   Fax: (202) 707-6269
E-mail: jrfell@loc.gov
Web: www.loc.gov/hr/jrfellows/index.html

Summary To provide summer work experience in the Manuscript Division of the Library of Congress (LC) to upper-division and graduate students (especially Asian Americans and other minorities).

Eligibility This program is open to undergraduate and graduate students who have expertise in library science or collections conservation and preservation. Applicants must be interested in gaining an introductory knowledge of the principles, concepts, and techniques of archival management through a summer internship in the LC Manuscript Division. They should be able to demonstrate an ability to communicate effectively in writing and have knowledge of integrated library systems, basic library applications, and other information technologies. Knowledge of American history is beneficial. Applications from minorities and students at smaller and lesser-known schools are particularly encouraged. U.S. citizenship is required.

Financial data The stipend is $3,000.

Duration 10 weeks during the summer. Fellows work a 40-hour week.

Number awarded 1 each year.

Deadline March of each year.

[236]
MAS AND MAJIU UYESUGI MEMORIAL SCHOLARSHIP

Japanese American Citizens League
Attn: National Scholarship Awards
1765 Sutter Street
San Francisco, CA 94115
(415) 921-5225   Fax: (415) 931-4671
E-mail: jacl@jacl.org
Web: www.jacl.org/edu/scholar.htm

Summary To provide financial assistance for college to student members of the Japanese American Citizens League (JACL) who are high school seniors.

Eligibility This program is open to JACL members who are high school seniors interested in attending a college, university, trade school, business college, or other institution of higher learning. Applicants must submit information on their involvement in JACL and a 2-page essay on a topic that changes annually but relates to Japanese Americans. Selection is based on that essay, academic history, extracurricular activities, JACL involvement, scholastic honors, and a letter of recommendation.

Financial data Stipends generally average approximately $2,000.

Duration 1 year; nonrenewable.

Number awarded At least 1 each year.

Deadline February of each year.

[237]
MASAO AND SUMAKO ITANO MEMORIAL SCHOLARSHIP

Japanese American Citizens League
Attn: National Scholarship Awards
1765 Sutter Street
San Francisco, CA 94115
(415) 921-5225   Fax: (415) 931-4671
E-mail: jacl@jacl.org
Web: www.jacl.org/edu/scholar.htm

Summary To provide financial assistance for college to student members of the Japanese American Citizens League (JACL) who are high school seniors.

Eligibility This program is open to JACL members who are high school seniors interested in attending a college, university, trade school, business college, or other institution of higher learning. Applicants must submit information on their involvement in JACL and a 2-page essay a topic that changes

annually but relates to Japanese Americans. Selection is based on that essay, academic history, extracurricular activities, JACL involvement, scholastic honors, and a letter of recommendation.

Financial data Stipends generally average approximately $2,000.

Duration 1 year; nonrenewable.

Number awarded At least 1 each year.

Deadline February of each year.

[238]
MCGUIREWOODS/NLF INTERNSHIP PROGRAM

National Asian Pacific American Bar Association
Attn: NAPABA Law Foundation
1612 K Street, N.W., Suite 1400
Washington, DC 20006
(202) 775-9555   Fax: (202) 775-9333
E-mail: foundation@napaba.org
Web: www.napaba.org

Summary To provide funding to undergraduate and law students interested in a summer internship at the National Asian Pacific American Bar Association (NAPABA) and its Law Foundation (NLF).

Eligibility This program is open to 1) undergraduates interested in working as a fundraising and policy intern, and 2) law students interested in working as a clerk. Assignments for undergraduates require working 50% of their time on NAPABA projects and 50% on NLF projects. Assignments for law students require full-time work for NAPABA. Tasks involve promoting justice, equity, and opportunity for Asian Pacific Americans; fostering professional development, legal scholarship, advocacy, and community involvement; and developing and supporting programs to educate the legal profession and Asian Pacific American communities about legal issues affecting those communities.

Financial data The stipend for the law clerk is $3,000. The stipend for the fundraising and policy intern is $2,000.

Duration 10 weeks during the summer.

Additional information These internships were first awarded in 2010 with support from McGuireWoods LLP.

Number awarded 2 each year: 1 law clerk and 1 fundraising and policy intern.

Deadline Deadline not specified.

[239]
MEDIA ACTION NETWORK FOR ASIAN AMERICANS SCHOLARSHIPS

Media Action Network for Asian Americans
P.O. Box 11105
Burbank, CA 91510
(213) 486-4433   Toll Free: (888) 90-MANAA
E-mail: scholarship@manaa.org
Web: www.manaa.org

Summary To provide financial assistance to Asian Pacific Islander undergraduate and graduate students interested in advancing a positive image of Asian Americans in the mainstream media.

Eligibility This program is open to Asian Pacific Islander undergraduate and graduate students interested in preparing for careers in filmmaking or in television production (but not in broadcast journalism). Applicants must be interested in advancing a positive and enlightened understanding of the Asian American experience in the mainstream media. Along with their application, they must submit a 1,000-word essay on their involvement in the Asian Pacific Islander community, how that involvement influences their creative work, how their creative work will influence the Asian Pacific Islanders community and how it is perceived in the next 5 to 10 years. Selection is based on academic and personal merit, a desire to uplift the image of Asian Americans in film and television (as demonstrated in the essay), potential, and financial need.

Financial data The stipend is $1,000.

Duration 1 year.

Additional information This program began in 2001.

Number awarded 1 each year.

Deadline October of each year.

[240]
MICHAEL BAKER CORPORATION SCHOLARSHIP PROGRAM FOR DIVERSITY IN ENGINEERING

Association of Independent Colleges and Universities of
  Pennsylvania
101 North Front Street
Harrisburg, PA 17101-1405
(717) 232-8649   Fax: (717) 233-8574
E-mail: info@aicup.org
Web: www.aicup.org/fundraising

Summary To provide financial assistance to Asian Americans, other minorities, and women from any state who are enrolled at member institutions of the Association of Independent Colleges and Universities of Pennsylvania (AICUP) and majoring in designated fields of engineering.

Eligibility This program is open to full-time undergraduate students from any state enrolled at designated AICUP colleges and universities who are women and/or members of the following minority groups: American Indians, Alaska Natives, Asians, Blacks/African Americans, Hispanics/Latinos, Native Hawaiians, or Pacific Islanders. Applicants must be juniors majoring in architectural, civil, or environmental engineering with a GPA of 3.0 or higher. Along with their application, they must submit a 2-page essay on what they believe will be the greatest challenge facing the engineering profession over the next decade, and why.

Financial data The stipend is $2,500 per year.

Duration 1 year; may be renewed 1 additional year if the recipient maintains appropriate academic standards.

Additional information This program, sponsored by the Michael Baker Corporation, is available at the 83 private colleges and universities in Pennsylvania that comprise the AICUP.

Number awarded 1 each year.

Deadline April of each year.

[241]
MID-AMERICA CHAPTER SCHOLARSHIPS

Phi Tau Phi Scholastic Honor Society-Mid-America
  Chapter
c/o Dorothy Li, President
Library, John Marshall Law School
315 South Plymouth Court, Sixth Floor
Chicago, IL 60604
(312) 427-2737   E-mail: 8li@jmls.edu
Web: phitauphi.org

Summary To provide financial assistance to undergraduate and graduate students of Chinese heritage at colleges and universities in selected midwestern states.

Eligibility This program is open to undergraduate and graduate students enrolled at colleges and universities in Illinois, Indiana, Iowa, Kansas, Michigan, Ohio, Texas, and Wisconsin. Applicants must be Chinese Americans or students from China, including Taiwan, Macao, Hong Kong, and China. They must submit an autobiography that includes GPA, records of awards, volunteer experiences, and other relevant information.

Financial data The stipend is $1,000.

Duration 1 year.

Additional information Phi Tau Phi, first organized in 1921 in China and reestablished in 1964 in the United States, is a relatively small honor society of scholars, mainly of Chinese heritage, in various disciplines of science, technology, art, and the humanities.

Number awarded 4 each year: 2 for undergraduates and 2 for graduate students.

Deadline April of each year.

[242]
MIDEASTERN REGION KOREAN AMERICAN SCHOLARSHIPS

Korean American Scholarship Foundation
Mideastern Region
c/o Jong Dae Kim, Scholarship Committee Chair
24666 Northwestern Highway Service Drive
Southfield, MI 48075
(313) 963-3299   E-mail: mideastern@kasf.org
Web: www.kasf.org/application_set.html

Summary To provide financial assistance to Korean American students from any state who are working on an undergraduate or graduate degree in any field at a school in Indiana, Michigan, or Ohio.

Eligibility This program is open to Korean American students who are currently enrolled in a college or university as full-time undergraduate or graduate students. Applicants may reside anywhere in the United States, as long as they attend school in Indiana, Michigan, or Ohio. Selection is based on academic achievement, school activities, community service, and financial need.

Financial data Stipends range from $1,000 to $2,000.

Duration 1 year; renewable.

Number awarded Varies each year.

Deadline March of each year.

[243]
MIDWESTERN REGION KOREAN AMERICAN SCHOLARSHIPS

Korean American Scholarship Foundation
Midwestern Region
c/o Augie Lee, Scholarship Committee Chair
1760 South Braymore Drive
Inverness, IL 60010
E-mail: midwestern@kasf.org
Web: www.kasf.org/application_set.html

Summary To provide financial assistance to Korean American students from any state who are working on or planning to work on an undergraduate or graduate degree in any field at a school in the Midwest.

Eligibility This program is open to Korean American students who are currently enrolled or planning to enroll at a college or university in the midwestern states as full-time undergraduate or graduate students. Applicants may reside anywhere in the United States, as long as they attend school in the midwestern region: Illinois, Iowa, Kansas, Minnesota, Missouri, Nebraska, North Dakota, South Dakota, and Wisconsin. Selection is based on academic achievement, school activities, community service, and financial need.

Financial data Stipends range from $1,000 to $2,000.

Duration 1 year; renewable.

Number awarded Varies each year; recently, 48 of these scholarships were awarded.

Deadline May of each year.

[244]
MINE AND GONSAKULTO SCHOLARSHIP

Far West Athletic Trainers' Association
c/o Jason Bennett, Scholarship Chair
Chapman University
1 University Drive
Orange, CA 92866
(714) 997-6567   Fax: (714) 997-6991
E-mail: jbennett@chapman.edu
Web: www.fwata.org/com_scholarships.html

Summary To provide financial assistance to members of the National Athletic Trainers Association (NATA) from any state who are of Asian descent and working on an undergraduate or graduate degree in its District 8.

Eligibility This program is open to students of Asian descent from any state who are enrolled as undergraduate or graduate students at colleges and universities in California, Guam, Hawaii, or Nevada and preparing for a career as an athletic trainer. Applicants must be student members of NATA and a District 8 member of NATA working on a bachelor's, master's, or doctoral degree in athletic training. They must have a GPA of 3.0 or higher and a record of distinction in their athletic training program, academic major, institution, intercollegiate athletics, and higher education. Along with their application, they must submit a statement on their athletic training background, experience, philosophy, and goals. Financial need is not considered in the selection process.

Financial data The stipend is $1,500.

Duration 1 year.

Additional information FWATA serves as District 8 of NATA.

Number awarded 1 each year.

Deadline February of each year.

[245]
MINNESOTA ASSOCIATION FOR KOREAN AMERICANS SCHOLARSHIPS

Minnesota Association for Korean Americans
Attn: Scholarship Committee
P.O. Box 390553
Edina, MN 55439-0553
E-mail: info@makaweb.org
Web: www.makaweb.org/scholarships.html

Summary To provide financial assistance to Korean American high school seniors in Minnesota who are planning to attend college in any state.

Eligibility This program is open to seniors graduating from high schools in Minnesota who are of Korean origin or heritage. Applicants must be planning to attend college in any state. They must be U.S. citizens and have a GPA of 2.5 or higher. Along with their application, they must submit grade transcripts, SAT and/or ACT scores, 2 letters of recommendation, and a 2- or 3-page essay on a topic that changes annually; recently, students were asked to identify a person who has had a significant influence on them and explain the impact. Selection is based on the essay, academic achievement, honors, extracurricular activities, and letters of recommendation.

Financial data Stipends range from $500 to $2,000 per year.

Duration 1 year; nonrenewable.

Number awarded Approximately 15 to 20 each year.

Deadline September of each year.

[246]
MINORITIES IN HOSPITALITY SCHOLARS PROGRAM

International Franchise Association
Attn: IFA Educational Foundation
1501 K Street, N.W., Suite 350
Washington, DC 20005
(202) 662-0784   Fax: (202) 628-0812
E-mail: mbrewer@franchise.org
Web: www.franchise.org/Scholarships.aspx

Summary To provide financial assistance to Asian Americans and other minority students working on an undergraduate degree related to hospitality.

Eligibility This program is open to college sophomores, juniors, and seniors who are U.S. citizens and members of a minority group (defined as African Americans, American Indians, Hispanic Americans, and Asian Americans). Applicants must be working on a degree in a field related to the hospitality industry. Along with their application, they must submit a 500-word essay on why they should be selected to receive this scholarship. Financial need is not considered in the selection process.

Financial data The stipend is $2,000.

Duration 1 year.

Additional information This program is cosponsored by the IFA Educational Foundation and Choice Hotels International.

Number awarded 1 or more each year.

Deadline January of each year.

[247]
MINORITY ACCESS INTERNSHIP

Minority Access, Inc.
Attn: Directory of Internship Program
5214 Baltimore Avenue
Hyattsville, MD 20781
(301) 779-7100   Fax: (301) 779-9812
Web: www.minorityaccess.org

Summary To provide work experience to Asian American and other minority undergraduate and graduate students interested in internships at participating entities in Washington, D.C. and throughout the United States.

Eligibility This program is open to full-time undergraduate and graduate students who have a GPA of 3.0 or higher. Applicants must be U.S. citizens for most positions. All academic majors are eligible. Interns are selected by participating federal government and other agencies. Most of these are located in Washington, D.C., but placements may be made anywhere in the United States.

Financial data The weekly stipend is $450 for sophomores and juniors, $500 for seniors, or $550 for graduate and professional students. In addition, most internships include paid round-trip travel between home and the internship location.

Duration Spring internships are 5 months, starting in January; summer internships are 3 months, starting in August; fall internships are 4 months, starting in September.

Additional information Minority Access, Inc. is committed to the diversification of institutions, federal agencies, and corporations of all kinds and to improving their recruitment, retention, and enhancement of minorities. The majority of interns are placed in the Washington, D.C. metropolitan area. Both full-time and part-time internships are awarded. Students may receive academic credit for full-time internships. Students are expected to pay all housing costs. They are required to attend a pre-employment session in Washington, D.C., all seminars and workshops hosted by Minority Access, and any mandatory activities sponsored by the host agency.

Number awarded Varies each year.

Deadline February of each year for summer internships; June of each year for fall internships; and November of each year for spring internships.

[248]
MINORITY ENTREPRENEURS SCHOLARSHIP PROGRAM

International Franchise Association
Attn: IFA Educational Foundation
1501 K Street, N.W., Suite 350
Washington, DC 20005
(202) 662-0784   Fax: (202) 628-0812
E-mail: mbrewer@franchise.org
Web: www.franchise.org/Scholarships.aspx

Summary To provide financial assistance to Asian Americans, other minorities, and adult entrepreneurs enrolled in academic or professional development programs related to franchising.

Eligibility This program is open to 1) college students enrolled at an accredited college or university, and 2) adult entrepreneurs who have at least 5 years of business ownership or managerial experience. Applicants must be U.S. citizens and members of a minority group (defined as African Americans, American Indians, Hispanic Americans, and Asian Americans). Students should be enrolled in courses or programs relating to business, finance, marketing, hospitality, franchising, or entrepreneurship. Adult entrepreneurs should be enrolled in professional development courses related to franchising, such as those recognized by the Institute of Certified Franchise Executives (ICFE). All applicants must submit a 500-word essay on why they want the scholarship and their career goals. Financial need is not considered in the selection process.

Financial data The stipend is $3,000.

Duration 1 year.

Additional information This program is cosponsored by the IFA Educational Foundation and Marriott International.

Number awarded 5 each year.

Deadline June of each year.

[249]
MINORITY SCHOLARSHIP AWARD FOR ACADEMIC EXCELLENCE IN PHYSICAL THERAPY

American Physical Therapy Association
Attn: Honors and Awards Program
1111 North Fairfax Street
Alexandria, VA 22314-1488
(703) 684-APTA   Toll Free: (800) 999-APTA
Fax: (703) 684-7343   TDD: (703) 683-6748
E-mail: executivedept@apta.org
Web: www.apta.org

Summary To provide financial assistance to Asian American and other minority students who are interested in becoming a physical therapist or physical therapy assistant.

Eligibility This program is open to U.S. citizens and permanent residents who are members of the following minority groups: African American or Black, Asian, Native Hawaiian or other Pacific Islander, American Indian or Alaska Native, or Hispanic/Latino. Applicants must be in the final year of a professional physical therapy or physical therapy assistant education program. They must submit a personal essay outlining their professional goals and minority service. U.S. citizenship or permanent resident status is required. Selection is based on 1) demonstrated evidence of contributions in the area of minority affairs and services with an emphasis on contributions made while enrolled in a physical therapy program; 2) potential to contribute to the profession of physical therapy; and 3) scholastic achievement.

Financial data The stipend varies; recently, minimum awards were $6,000 for physical therapy students or $2,500 for physical therapy assistant students.

Duration 1 year.

Number awarded Varies each year; recently, 8 of these awards were granted: 7 to professional physical therapy students and 1 to a physical therapy assistant student.

Deadline November of each year.

[250]
MINORITY SCIENCE WRITERS INTERNSHIP

American Association for the Advancement of Science
Directorate for Education and Human Resources
Attn: Minority Science Writers Internship
1200 New York Avenue, N.W., Room 639
Washington, DC 20005-3920
(202) 326-6441   Fax: (202) 371-9849
E-mail: raculver@aaas.org
Web: www.aaas.org

Summary To provide summer work experience at *Science* magazine to Asian American and other minority undergraduate students.

Eligibility This program is open to minority undergraduates with a serious interest in science writing. Preference is given to students majoring in journalism. Applicants must be interested in a summer internship at *Science* magazine, the journal of the American Association for the Advancement of Science (AAAS). Along with their application, they must submit an 800-word essay on their commitment to journalism, their career goals, their thoughts about science and science writing, and what they hope to get out of this opportunity. A telephone interview is conducted of semifinalists.

Financial data Interns receive a salary and reimbursement of travel expenses to the work site in Washington, D.C.

Duration 10 weeks during the summer.

Number awarded Varies each year.

Deadline February of each year.

[251]
MINORITY TEACHERS OF ILLINOIS SCHOLARSHIP PROGRAM

Illinois Student Assistance Commission
Attn: Scholarship and Grant Services
1755 Lake Cook Road
Deerfield, IL 60015-5209
(847) 948-8550   Toll Free: (800) 899-ISAC
Fax: (847) 831-8549   TDD: (800) 526-0844
E-mail: collegezone@isac.org
Web: www.collegezone.com/studentzone/407_655.htm

Summary To provide funding to Asian American and other minority students in Illinois who plan to become teachers at the preschool, elementary, or secondary level.

Eligibility Applicants must be Illinois residents, U.S. citizens or eligible noncitizens, members of a minority group (African American/Black, Hispanic American, Asian American, or Native American), and high school graduates or holders of a General Educational Development (GED) certificate. They must be enrolled in college full time at the sophomore level or above, have a GPA of 2.5 or higher, not be in default on any student loan, and be enrolled or accepted for enrollment in a teacher education program. U.S. citizenship or eligible noncitizenship status is required.

Financial data Grants up to $5,000 per year are awarded. This is a scholarship/loan program. Recipients must agree to teach full time 1 year for each year of support received. The teaching agreement may be fulfilled at a public, private, or parochial preschool, elementary school, or secondary school in Illinois; at least 30% of the student body at those schools must be minority. It must be fulfilled within the 5-year period following the completion of the undergraduate program for which the scholarship was awarded. The time period may be extended if the recipient serves in the U.S. armed forces, enrolls full time in a graduate program related to teaching, becomes temporarily disabled, is unable to find employment as a teacher at a qualifying school, or takes additional courses on at least a half-time basis to obtain certification as a teacher in Illinois. Recipients who fail to honor this work obligation must repay the award with 5% interest.

Duration 1 year; may be renewed for a total of 8 semesters or 12 quarters.

Number awarded Varies each year.

Deadline Priority consideration is given to applications received by February of each year.

[252]
MIRIAM WEINSTEIN PEACE AND JUSTICE EDUCATION AWARD

Philanthrofund Foundation
Attn: Scholarship Committee
1409 Willow Street, Suite 210
Minneapolis, MN 55403-3251
(612) 870-1806   Toll Free: (800) 435-1402
Fax: (612) 871-6587   E-mail: info@PfundOnline.org
Web: www.pfundonline.org/scholarships.html

Summary To provide financial assistance to Asian American and other minority students from Minnesota who are associated with gay, lesbian, bisexual, and transgender (GLBT) activities and interested in working on a degree in education.

Eligibility This program is open to residents of Minnesota and students attending a Minnesota educational institution who are members of a religious, racial, or ethnic minority. Applicants must be self-identified as GLBT or from a GLBT family and have demonstrated a commitment to peace and justice issues. They may be attending or planning to attend trade school, technical college, college, or university (as an undergraduate or graduate student). Preference is given to students who have completed at least 2 years of college and are working on a degree in education. Selection is based on the applicant's 1) affirmation of GLBT identity or commitment to GLBT communities; 2) participation and leadership in community and/or GLBT activities; and 3) service as role model, mentor, and/or adviser for the GLBT community.

Financial data The stipend is $3,000. Funds must be used for tuition, books, fees, or dissertation expenses.

Duration 1 year.

Number awarded 1 each year.

Deadline January of each year.

[253]
MISSOURI MINORITY TEACHER EDUCATION SCHOLARSHIP PROGRAM

Missouri Department of Higher Education
Attn: Student Financial Assistance
3515 Amazonas Drive
Jefferson City, MO 65109-5717
(573) 751-2361   Toll Free: (800) 473-6757
Fax: (573) 751-6635   E-mail: info@dhe.mo.gov
Web: www.dhe.mo.gov/minorityteaching.html

Summary To provide funding to Asian American and other minority high school seniors, high school graduates, and college students in Missouri who are interested in preparing for a teaching career in mathematics or science.

Eligibility This program is open to Missouri residents who are African American, Asian American, Hispanic American, or Native American. Applicants must be 1) high school seniors, college students, or returning adults (without a degree) who rank in the top 25% of their high school class and scored at or above the 75th percentile on the ACT or SAT examination; 2) individuals who have completed 30 college hours and have a cumulative GPA of 3.0 or better; or 3) baccalaureate degree-holders who are returning to an approved mathematics or science teacher education program. They must be a U.S. citizen or permanent resident or otherwise lawfully present in the United States. All applicants must be enrolled full time in an approved teacher education program at a community college, 4-year college, or university in Missouri. Selection is based on academic performance, the quantity and quality of school and community activities, range of interests and activities, leadership abilities, interpersonal skills, and desire to enter the field of education.

Financial data The stipend is $3,000 per year, of which $2,000 is provided by the state as a forgivable loan and $1,000 is provided by the school as a scholarship. Recipients must commit to teaching in a Missouri public elementary or secondary school for 5 years following graduation. If they fail to fulfill that obligation, they must repay the state portion of the scholarship with interest at 9.5%.

Duration Up to 4 years.

Number awarded Up to 100 each year.

Deadline February of each year.

[254]
MITSUYUKI YONEMURA MEMORIAL SCHOLARSHIP

Japanese American Citizens League
Attn: National Scholarship Awards
1765 Sutter Street
San Francisco, CA 94115
(415) 921-5225   Fax: (415) 931-4671
E-mail: jacl@jacl.org
Web: www.jacl.org/edu/scholar.htm

Summary To provide financial assistance for college to student members of the Japanese American Citizens League (JACL) who are high school seniors.

Eligibility This program is open to JACL members who are high school seniors interested in attending a college, university, trade school, business college, or other institution of higher learning. Applicants must submit information on their involvement in JACL and a 2-page essay on a topic that changes annually but relates to Japanese Americans. Selection is based on that essay, academic history, extracurricular activities, JACL involvement, scholastic honors, and a letter of recommendation.

Financial data Stipends generally average approximately $2,000.

Duration 1 year; nonrenewable.

Number awarded At least 1 each year.

Deadline February of each year.

[255]
MR. AND MRS. TAKASHI MORIUCHI SCHOLARSHIP

Japanese American Citizens League
Attn: National Scholarship Awards
1765 Sutter Street
San Francisco, CA 94115
(415) 921-5225   Fax: (415) 931-4671
E-mail: jacl@jacl.org
Web: www.jacl.org/edu/scholar.htm

Summary To provide financial assistance for college to student members of the Japanese American Citizens League (JACL) who are high school seniors.

Eligibility This program is open to JACL members who are high school seniors interested in attending a college, university, trade school, business college, or other institution of higher learning. Applicants must submit information on their involvement in JACL and a 2-page essay on a topic that changes annually but relates to Japanese Americans. Selection is based on that essay, academic history, extracurricular activities, JACL involvement, scholastic honors, and a letter of recommendation.

Financial data Stipends generally average approximately $2,000.

Duration 1 year; nonrenewable.

Number awarded At least 1 each year.

Deadline February of each year.

[256]
MULTICULTURAL ADVERTISING INTERN PROGRAM

American Association of Advertising Agencies
Attn: Manager of Diversity Programs
405 Lexington Avenue, 18th Floor
New York, NY 10174-1801
(212) 850-0732   Toll Free: (800) 676-9333
Fax: (212) 682-2028   E-mail: maip@aaaa.org
Web: www2.aaaa.org

Summary To provide Asian American and other minority students with summer work experience in advertising agencies and to present them with an overview of the agency business.

Eligibility This program is open to U.S. citizens and permanent residents who are Black/African American, Asian/ Asian American, Pacific Islander, Hispanic, North American Indian/Native American, or multiracial and either 1) college juniors, seniors, or graduate students at an accredited college or university, or 2) students at any academic level attending a portfolio school of the sponsor. Applicants may be majoring in any field, but they must be able to demonstrate a serious commitment to preparing for a career in advertising. They must have a GPA of 3.0 or higher. Students with a cumulative GPA of 2.7 to 2.9 are encouraged to apply, but they must complete an additional essay question.

Financial data Interns are paid a salary of at least $70 per day. If they do not live in the area of their host agencies, they may stay in housing arranged by the sponsor. They are responsible for a percentage of the cost of housing and materials.

Duration 10 weeks during the summer.

Additional information Interns may be assigned duties in the following departments: account management, broadcast production, media buying/planning, creative (art direction or copywriting), digital/interactive technologies, print production, strategic/account planning, or traffic. The portfolio schools are the AdCenter at Virginia Commonwealth University, the Creative Circus and the Portfolio Center in Atlanta, the Miami Ad School, the University of Texas at Austin, Pratt Institute, the Minneapolis College of Art and Design, and the Art Center College of Design in Pasadena, California.

Number awarded 70 to 100 each year.

Deadline December of each year.

[257]
MULTICULTURAL UNDERGRADUATE INTERNSHIPS AT THE GETTY CENTER

Getty Foundation
Attn: Multicultural Undergraduate Internships
1200 Getty Center Drive, Suite 800
Los Angeles, CA 90049-1685
(310) 440-7320   Fax: (310) 440-7703
E-mail: summerinterns@getty.edu
Web: www.getty.edu

Summary To provide summer work experience at facilities of the Getty Center to Asian American and other minority undergraduates with ties to Los Angeles County, California.

Eligibility This program is open to currently-enrolled undergraduates who either reside or attend college in Los Angeles County, California. Applicants must be members of groups currently underrepresented in museum professions and fields related to the visual arts and humanities: individuals of African American, Asian, Latino/Hispanic, Native American, or Pacific Islander descent. They may be majoring in any field, including the sciences and technology, and are not required to have demonstrated a previous commitment to the visual arts. Along with their application, they must submit a personal statement of up to 500 words on why they are interested in this internship, including what they hope to gain from the program, their interest or involvement in issues of multiculturalism, aspects of their past experience that they feel are most relevant to the application, and any specific career or educational avenues they are interested in exploring. U.S. citizenship or permanent resident status is required.

Financial data The stipend is $3,500.

Duration 10 weeks during the summer.

Additional information Internships provide training and work experience in such areas as conservation, curatorship, education, publications, and related programmatic activities.

Number awarded 15 to 20 each year.

Deadline February of each year.

[258]
MUTUAL OF OMAHA ACTUARIAL SCHOLARSHIP FOR MINORITY STUDENTS

Mutual of Omaha
Attn: Strategic Staffing-Actuarial Recruitment
Mutual of Omaha Plaza
Omaha, NE 68175
(402) 351-3300   E-mail: diversity@mutualofomaha.com
Web: www.mutualofomaha.com

Summary To provide financial assistance and work experience to Asian American and other minority undergraduate students who are preparing for an actuarial career.

Eligibility This program is open to members of minority groups (African American, Hispanic, Native American, Asian or Pacific Islander, or Alaskan Eskimo) who have completed at least 24 semester hours of full-time study. Applicants must be working on an actuarial or mathematics-related degree with the goal of preparing for an actuarial career. They must have a GPA of 3.0 or higher and have passed at least 1 actuarial examination. Prior to accepting the award, they must be available to complete a summer internship at the sponsor's home office in Omaha, Nebraska. Along with their application, they must submit a 1-page personal statement on why they are interested in becoming an actuary and how they are preparing themselves for an actuarial career. Status as a U.S. citizen, permanent resident, or asylee or refugee must be established.

Financial data The scholarship stipend is $5,000 per year. Funds are paid directly to the student. For the internship, students receive an hourly rate of pay, subsidized housing, and financial incentives for successful examination results received during the internship period.

Duration 1 year. Recipients may reapply if they maintain a cumulative GPA of 3.0 or higher.

Number awarded Varies each year.

Deadline October of each year.

[259]
NANCY WONG YEE SCHOLARSHIP

Associated Chinese University Women, Inc.
c/o Sybil Kyi, Special Scholarships
5930 Haleola Street
Honolulu, HI 96821
(808) 373-1129   E-mail: kyis@hawaii.rr.com
Web: www.acuwhawaii.org/main

Summary To provide financial assistance to residents of Hawaii who are of Chinese ancestry and interested in majoring in Chinese studies at a college in any state.

Eligibility This program is open to residents of Hawaii who are of Chinese or part Chinese ancestry. Applicants must be attending or planning to attend an accredited 4-year U.S. college or university as a full-time student with the objective of earning a baccalaureate degree. They must have a GPA of 3.8 or higher and be planning to major in Chinese studies, including Chinese language, music, art, dance, and/or theater. Along with their application, they must submit a personal statement on why they should be awarded this scholarship, including their plans for serving their community after graduation. Selection is based on academic achievement (including GPA and SAT score), character, extracurricular activities, school and/or community service, and financial need. U.S. citizenship or permanent resident status is required.

Financial data The stipend is $1,000.

Duration 1 year.

Number awarded 1 each year.

Deadline April of each year.

[260]
NASPA UNDERGRADUATE FELLOWSHIP PROGRAM

National Association of Student Personnel Administrators
Attn: NUFP
111 K Street, N.E., Tenth Floor
Washington, DC 20002
(202) 204-6079   Fax: (202) 893-5737
E-mail: nvictoria@naspa.org
Web: www.naspa.org/programs/nufp/index.cfm

Summary To provide summer work experience and leadership training to minorities, students with disabilities, and persons who identify as lesbian, gay, bisexual, or transgender (LGBT) and are completing their second year in college.

Eligibility Eligible to be nominated for this program are 1) ethnic minority students (Indigenous, African, Asian, or Hispanic Americans), 2) students with disabilities; or 3) students who identify as LGBT. Applicants must be completing their sophomore year in a 4-year institution or their second year in a 2-year transfer program. They must have a GPA of 2.5 or higher and be able to demonstrate academic promise and an interest in a future in higher education.

Financial data Participants are offered a paid summer internship, and all expenses are paid to attend the leadership institutes.

Duration The internship lasts 8 weeks during the summer. Leadership institutes last 4 days.

Additional information The program was initiated in the 1989-90 academic year as the Minority Undergraduate Fellows Program (MUFP). In 2000-01 it was broadened to include students with disabilities and in 2005 was renamed and expanded again to include LGBT students. It offers 3 main components: 1) participation in a 1- or 2-year internship or field experience under the guidance of a mentor; 2) participation in a summer leadership institute designed to enhance skill building and career development; and 3) participation in an 8-week paid summer internship designed to encourage the development of future student affairs and higher education administrators.

Number awarded Varies each year; recently, 65 undergraduates were participating in the program.

Deadline September of each year.

[261]
NATIONAL PRESS CLUB SCHOLARSHIP FOR JOURNALISM DIVERSITY

National Press Club
Attn: General Manager's Office
529 14th Street, N.W.
Washington, DC 20045
(202) 662-7599
Web: www.press.org/activities/aboutscholarship.cfm

Summary To provide funding to Asian American and other high school seniors who are planning to major in journalism in college and will bring diversity to the field.

Eligibility This program is open to high school seniors who have been accepted to college and plan to prepare for a career in journalism. Applicants must submit 1) a 500-word essay explaining how they would add diversity to U.S. journalism; 2) up to 5 work samples demonstrating an ongoing interest in journalism through work on a high school newspaper or other media; 3) letters of recommendation from 3 people; 4) a copy of their high school transcript; 5) documentation of financial need; 6) a letter of acceptance from the college or university of their choice; and 7) a brief description of how they have pursued journalism in high school.

Financial data The stipend is $2,000 for the first year and $2,500 for each subsequent year. The program also provides an additional $500 book stipend, designated the Ellen Masin Persina Scholarship, for the first year.

Duration 4 years.

Additional information The program began in 1990.

Number awarded 1 each year.

Deadline February of each year.

[262]
NAVY/MARINE CORPS JROTC SCHOLARSHIP

National Naval Officers Association-Washington, D.C.
   Chapter
Attn: Scholarship Program
2701 Park Center Drive, A1108
Alexandria, VA 22302
(703) 566-3840   Fax: (703) 566-3813
E-mail: Stephen.Williams@Navy.mil
Web: dcnnoa.memberlodge.com

Summary To provide financial assistance to Asian American and other minority high school seniors from the Washington, D.C. area who have participated in Navy or Marine Corps Junior Reserve Officers Training Corps (JROTC) and are planning to attend college in any state.

Eligibility This program is open to minority seniors graduating from high schools in the Washington, D.C. metropolitan area who have participated in Navy or Marine Corps JROTC. Applicants must be planning to enroll full time at an accredited 2- or 4-year college or university in any state. They must have a GPA of 2.5 or higher. Selection is based on academic achievement, community involvement, and financial need.

Financial data The stipend is $1,000.

Duration 1 year; nonrenewable.

Additional information Recipients are not required to join or affiliate with the military in any way after college.

Number awarded 1 each year.

Deadline March of each year.

[263]
NEED-BASED KSEA SCHOLARSHIPS

Korean-American Scientists and Engineers Association
Attn: Scholarship Committee
1952 Gallows Drive, Suite 300
Vienna, VA 22182
(703) 748-1221   Fax: (703) 748-1331
E-mail: admin@ksea.org
Web: scholarship.ksea.org/InfoUndergraduate.aspx

Summary To provide financial assistance to undergraduate student members of the Korean-American Scientists and Engineers Association (KSEA) who can demonstrate financial need.

Eligibility This program is open to Korean American undergraduate students who are KSEA members, have completed at least 40 credits as a college student, and are majoring in science, engineering, or a related field. Applicants must be able to demonstrate financial need. Along with their application, they must submit an essay on why they should receive a need-based scholarship. Selection is based on the essay (20%), KSEA activities and community service (30%), recommendation letters (20%), and academic performance (30%).

Financial data The stipend is $1,000.

Duration 1 year.

Number awarded Up to 5 each year.

Deadline February of each year.

[264]
NEW JERSEY CHAPTER INTERNSHIP PROGRAM

Organization of Chinese Americans-New Jersey Chapter
22 West Grand Avenue
P.O. Box 268
Montvale, NJ 07645-0268
(973) 873-8315
Web: www.oca-nj.com

Summary To provide Asian American college students from New Jersey with an opportunity to work in the office of an elected official in the state during the summer.

Eligibility This program is open to college students who are of Asian American descent and reside in New Jersey. Applicants must be interested in working during the summer in the New Jersey office of their choice of 7 elected officials. They must be able to demonstrate an interest in public affairs and have good oral and written communication skills. Along with their application, they must submit a 2-page essay discussing why they want to participate in this internship program.

Financial data Interns receive a stipend of $1,000 after completing the internship.

Duration 4 weeks during the summer.

Additional information Recipients must attend the sponsor's Asian American Heritage Month luncheon in May.

Number awarded Varies each year.

Deadline April of each year.

[265]
NEW JERSEY UTILITIES ASSOCIATION EQUAL EMPLOYMENT OPPORTUNITY SCHOLARSHIPS

New Jersey Utilities Association
50 West State Street, Suite 1117
Trenton, NJ 08608
(609) 392-1000   Fax: (609) 396-4231
Web: www.njua.org/html/njua_eeo_scholarship.cfm

Summary To provide financial assistance to Asian Americans, other minorities, women, and disabled high school seniors in New Jersey who are interested in attending college in any state.

Eligibility This program is open to seniors graduating from high schools in New Jersey who are women, minorities (Black or African American, Hispanic or Latino, American Indian or Alaska Native, Asian, Native Hawaiian or Pacific Islander, or 2 or more races), and persons with disabilities. Applicants must be planning to work on a bachelor's degree at a college or university in any state. They must be able to demonstrate financial need. Children of employees of any New Jersey Utilities Association-member company are ineligible. Selection is based on overall academic excellence and demonstrated financial need. U.S. citizenship or permanent resident status is required.

Financial data The stipend is $1,500 per year.

Duration 4 years.

Number awarded 2 each year.

Deadline March of each year.

[266]
NICK AND TERRY NI SCHOLARSHIP

Organization of Chinese Americans-Wisconsin Chapter
Attn: Scholarship Committee
P.O. Box 301
Dousman, WI 53118
(414) 258-2410   E-mail: ocawischolarship@yahoo.com
Web: www.ocawi.org

Summary To provide financial assistance to high school seniors who are 1) children of members or business affiliates of the Wisconsin Chapter of the Organization of Chinese Americans (OCA-WI) and 2) interested in studying engineering or natural science at a college in any state.

Eligibility This program is open to graduating high school seniors whose parent has been an OCA-WI member or business affiliate for at least 2 years. Applicants must be planning to enroll full time at an accredited college or university in any state and major in engineering or natural science. They must have a GPA of 3.0 or higher. Along with their application, they must submit a personal statement that includes information on their future college and career plans; a list of scholastic awards, honors, extracurricular activities, and honor societies and offices; and a description of their volunteer service to OCA-WI and their community. Financial need is not considered in the selection process.

Financial data A stipend is awarded (amount not specified).

Duration 1 year.

Number awarded 1 each year.

Deadline March of each year.

[267]
NISEI STUDENT RELOCATION COMMEMORATIVE FUND SCHOLARSHIPS

Nisei Student Relocation Commemorative Fund, Inc.
19 Scenic Drive
Portland, CT 06480
E-mail: info@nsrcfund.org
Web: www.nsrcfund.org

Summary To provide financial assistance for college to high school seniors in selected locations who are of southeast Asian descent.

Eligibility Each year, this program operates in a different city or state (recently, Washington D.C., Maryland, and northern Virginia). Within the selected area, graduating high school seniors and recent GED recipients are eligible to apply if they are first- or second-generation students from Cambodia, Laos, or Vietnam. Applicants must be planning to attend an accredited 2- or 4-year college or university or a vocational program in any state. Selection is based on academic achievement; 2 letters of reference; extracurricular activities and/or work experience; financial need; and a personal essay on educational, career, and personal goals. Finalists may be interviewed.

Financial data Stipends for named scholarships are $2,000; other stipends range up to $1,000.

Duration 1 year.

Additional information This program was established in 1983. The named scholarships currently available include the Nobu Kumekawa Hibino Scholarship, the Koh, Mitsu, and Dr. Kotaro Murai Scholarship, the Gladys Ishida Stone Scholarship, the Kay Yamashita Scholarship, and the Lafayette and Mayme Noda Scholarship.

Number awarded Varies each year; recently, a total of $45,000 was available for this program, including 10 scholarships at $2,000 each and a varying number totaling another $25,000. Since the program was established, it has awarded nearly $540,000 to 570 students.

Deadline March of each year.

[268]
NOBUKO R. KODAMA FONG MEMORIAL SCHOLARSHIP

Japanese American Citizens League
Attn: National Scholarship Awards
1765 Sutter Street
San Francisco, CA 94115
(415) 921-5225   Fax: (415) 931-4671
E-mail: jacl@jacl.org
Web: www.jacl.org/edu/scholar.htm

Summary To provide financial assistance for college to student members of the Japanese American Citizens League (JACL), particularly those in the Pacific Northwest and children of single parents.

Eligibility This program is open to JACL members who are currently enrolled at a college, university, trade school, business college, or other institution of higher learning. Applicants must submit information on their involvement in JACL and a 2-page essay on a topic that changes annually but relates to Japanese Americans. Selection is based on that essay, academic history, extracurricular activities, JACL involvement, scholastic honors, and a letter of recommendation. Preference is given to residents of the Pacific Northwest District and children of single parents.

Financial data Stipends generally average approximately $2,000.

Duration 1 year; nonrenewable.

Number awarded 1 each year.

Deadline March of each year.

[269]
NORTH CAROLINA TEACHING FELLOWS SCHOLARSHIP PROGRAM

North Carolina Teaching Fellows Commission
Koger Center, Cumberland Building
3739 National Drive, Suite 100
Raleigh, NC 27612
(919) 781-6833   Fax: (919) 781-6527
E-mail: tfellows@ncforum.org
Web: www.teachingfellows.org

Summary To provide funding to high school seniors in North Carolina (especially Asian Americans, other minorities, and males) who wish to prepare for a career in teaching.

Eligibility This program is open to seniors at high schools in North Carolina who are interested in preparing for a career as a teacher and have been accepted for enrollment at a participating school in the state. Applicants must demonstrate superior achievement on the basis of high school grades, class standing, SAT scores, writing samples, community service, extracurricular activities, and references from teachers and members of the community. U.S. citizenship is required. A particular goal of the program is to recruit and retain greater numbers of male and minority teacher education candidates in North Carolina. Financial need is not considered in the selection process.

Financial data The maximum stipend is $6,500 per year. This is a scholarship/loan program; recipients must teach in a North Carolina public school 1 year for each year of support received. If they cannot fulfill the service requirement, they must repay the loan with 10% interest.

Duration 1 year; renewable for up to 3 additional years if the recipient maintains full-time enrollment and a GPA of 2.25 or higher for the freshman year and 2.50 or higher in the sophomore year.

Additional information The participating schools are Appalachian State University, Campbell University, Catawba College, East Carolina University, Elon College, Lenoir-Rhyne College, Meredith College, North Carolina A&T State University, North Carolina Central University, North Carolina State University, Queens University of Charlotte, University of North Carolina at Asheville, University of North Carolina at Chapel Hill, University of North Carolina at Charlotte, University of North Carolina at Greensboro, University of North Carolina at Pembroke, University of North Carolina at Wilmington, and Western Carolina University. This program was established in 1986 and the first fellows were named in 1987.

Number awarded Up to 500 each year. Approximately 20% of the program's recipients are minority and 30% are male.

Deadline October of each year.

[270]
NORTHEASTERN REGION KOREAN AMERICAN SCHOLARSHIPS

Korean American Scholarship Foundation
Northeastern Region
c/o James Lee, Scholarship Committee Chair
472 11th Street, Room 202
Palisades Park, NJ 07650
E-mail: Jae.h.shin@us.hsbc.com
Web: www.kasf.org/application_set.html

Summary To provide financial assistance to Korean American students from any state who are working on an undergraduate or graduate degree in any field at a school in northeastern states.

Eligibility This program is open to Korean American students who are currently enrolled in a college or university in a northeastern state as a full-time undergraduate or graduate student. Applicants may reside anywhere in the United States, as long as they attend school in the northeastern region: Connecticut, Maine, Massachusetts, New Hampshire, New Jersey, New York, Rhode Island, and Vermont. Selection is based on academic achievement, school activities, community service, and financial need.

Financial data Stipends range from $1,000 to $2,000.

Duration 1 year; renewable.

Number awarded Varies each year; recently, 54 of these scholarships were awarded.

Deadline June of each year.

[271]
NORTHWEST JOURNALISTS OF COLOR SCHOLARSHIP AWARDS

Northwest Journalists of Color
c/o Caroline Li
14601 Ninth Avenue N.E.
Shoreline, WA 98155
E-mail: editor@earthwalkersmag.com
Web: www.aajaseattle.org

Summary To provide financial assistance to Asian Americans and other minority students from Washington state who are interested in careers in journalism.

Eligibility This program is open to members of minority groups (Asian American, African American, Native American, and Latino) who are 1) residents of Washington attending an accredited college or university in any state; 2) residents of any state attending a Washington college or university; or 3) seniors graduating from Washington high schools. Applicants must be planning a career in broadcast, photo, or print journalism. Along with their application, they must submit 1) a brief essay about themselves, including why they want to be a journalist, challenges they foresee, how they think they can contribute to the profession, and the influence their ethnic heritage might have on their perspective as a working journalist; 2) a current resume; 3) up to 3 work samples; 4) reference letters; and 5) documentation of financial need.

Financial data Stipends range up to $2,500 per year.

Duration 1 year; may be renewed.

Additional information This program, established in 1986, is sponsored by the Seattle chapters of the Asian American Journalists Association, the Native American Journalists Association, the National Association of Black Journalists, and the Latino Media Association. It includes the Walt and Milly Woodward Memorial Scholarship donated by the Western Washington Chapter of the Society of Professional Journalists.

Number awarded Varies each year.

Deadline April of each year.

[272]
OHIO NEWSPAPERS FOUNDATION MINORITY SCHOLARSHIPS

Ohio Newspapers Foundation
1335 Dublin Road, Suite 216-B
Columbus, OH 43215-7038
(614) 486-6677   Fax: (614) 486-4940
E-mail: ariggs@ohionews.org
Web: www.ohionews.org/students/scholarships

Summary To provide financial assistance to Asian American and other minority high school seniors in Ohio planning to attend college in the state to prepare for a career in journalism.

Eligibility This program is open to high school seniors in Ohio who are members of minority groups (African American, Hispanic, Asian American, or American Indian) and planning to prepare for a career in newspaper journalism. Applicants must have a high school GPA of 2.5 or higher and demonstrate writing ability in an autobiography of 750 to 1,000 words that describes their academic and career interests, awards, extracurricular activities, and journalism-related activities. They must be planning to attend a college or university in Ohio.

Financial data The stipend is $1,500.

Duration 1 year; nonrenewable.

Additional information This program was established in 1990.

Number awarded 1 each year.

Deadline March of each year.

[273]
ONE PUKA PUKA ACHIEVEMENT SCHOLARSHIP

Club 100 Veterans
Attn: Scholarship Committee
520 Kamoku Street
Honolulu, HI 96826-5120
(808) 946-0272   E-mail: daisyy@hgea.net

Summary To provide financial assistance for college to family members of veterans who served in the 100th Infantry Battalion of World War II.

Eligibility This program is open to direct family members and descendants of 100th Infantry Battalion World War II veterans. Applicants must be high school seniors planning to attend an institution of higher learning or full-time undergraduate students at community colleges, vocational/trade schools, 4-year colleges, and universities. Along with their application, they must submit an essay on a topic that changes annually but relates to the experience of the Nisei men who fought in the racially-segregated 100th Infantry Battalion during World War II. Selection is based on that essay, academic achievement, extracurricular activities, and community service. Financial need is not considered.

Financial data The stipend is $3,000.

Duration 1 year; nonrenewable.

Number awarded 1 each year.

Deadline April of each year.

[274]
OPERATION JUMP START III SCHOLARSHIPS

American Association of Advertising Agencies
Attn: AAAA Foundation
405 Lexington Avenue, 18th Floor
New York, NY 10174-1801
(212) 682-2500   Toll Free: (800) 676-9333
Fax: (212) 682-2028   E-mail: ameadows@aaaa.org
Web: www2.aaaa.org

Summary To provide financial assistance to Asian American and other multicultural art directors or copywriters interested in working on an undergraduate or graduate degree in advertising.

Eligibility This program is open to African Americans, Asian Americans, Hispanic Americans, and Native Americans who are U.S. citizens or permanent residents. Applicants must be incoming graduate students at 1 of 6 designated portfolio schools or full-time juniors at 1 of 2 designated colleges. They must be able to demonstrate extreme financial need, creative talent, and promise. Along with their application, they must submit 10 samples of creative work in their respective field of expertise.

Financial data The stipend is $5,000 per year.

Duration Most awards are for 2 years.

Additional information Operation Jump Start began in 1997 and was followed by Operation Jump Start II in 2002. The current program began in 2006. The 6 designated portfolio schools are the AdCenter at Virginia Commonwealth University, the Creative Circus in Atlanta, the Portfolio Center in Atlanta, the Miami Ad School, the University of Texas at Austin, and Pratt Institute. The 2 designated colleges are the Minneapolis College of Art and Design and the Art Center College of Design at Pasadena, California.

Number awarded 20 each year.

Deadline Deadline not specified.

[275]
OREGON-IDAHO CONFERENCE UMC ETHNIC MINORITY LEADERSHIP AWARDS

United Methodist Church-Oregon-Idaho Conference
Attn: Campus Ministries and Higher Education Ministry
 Team
1505 S.W. 18th Avenue
Portland, OR 97201-2524
(503) 226-7031   Toll Free: (800) J-WESLEY
Web: www.umoi.org/pages/detail/45

Summary To provide financial assistance to Asian Americans and other minorities who are Methodists from Oregon and Idaho and interested in attending a college or graduate school in any state.

Eligibility This program is open to members of ethnic minority groups (African American, Native American, Asian, Pacific Islander, or Hispanic) who have belonged to a congregation affiliated with the Oregon-Idaho Conference of the United Methodist Church (UMC) for at least 1 year. Applicants must be enrolled or planning to enroll full time as an undergraduate or graduate student at a 2- or 4-year college or university in any state. Along with their application, they must submit personal statements on 1) their faith development; and 2) where they sense God is calling the church in the present and future. Selection is based primarily on demonstrated leadership excellence and/or the potential for leadership excellence in the UMC and in community projects or activities, but other factors, including financial need, are also considered.

Financial data The stipend is $750.

Duration 1 year.

Number awarded 1 each year.

Deadline April of each year.

[276]
ORGANIZATION OF CHINESE AMERICANS INTERNSHIP PROGRAM

Organization of Chinese Americans, Inc.
1322 18th Street, N.W.
Washington, DC 20036-1803
(202) 223-5500   Fax: (202) 296-0540
E-mail: oca@ocanational.org
Web: www.ocanational.org

Summary To provide an opportunity for Asian Pacific American college and graduate students to gain summer work experience through the Organization of Chinese Americans (OCA).

Eligibility This program is open to college and graduate students who have a demonstrated interest in civil rights, Asian Pacific American issues, and public affairs. Applicants must be interested in working at the OCA national office, in a Congressional office, or in a federal agency. Along with their application, they must submit a resume, an academic transcript, an essay on why they want to participate in the internship, and 2 letters of reference. Selection criteria emphasize oral and written communication skills.

Financial data A stipend is paid (amount not specified).

Duration 10 weeks in the summer, at the OCA national office, at a Congressional office, or at a federal agency; 10 weeks in the fall, winter, or spring at the OCA national office.

Additional information At the OCA national office, general internships and development internships are available year round. Public policy, technical, communications and public relations, and scholarship services internships are available only in the summer.

Number awarded Varies each year.

Deadline March of each year for summer; July of each year for fall; November of each year for winter or spring.

[277]
PAGE EDUCATION FOUNDATION GRANTS

Page Education Foundation
P.O. Box 581254
Minneapolis, MN 55458-1254
(612) 332-0406   E-mail: info@page-ed.org
Web: www.page-ed.org

Summary To provide funding to Asian American and other high school seniors of color in Minnesota who plan to attend college in the state.

Eligibility This program is open to students of color who are graduating from high schools in Minnesota and planning to enroll full time at a postsecondary school in the state. Applicants must submit a 500-word essay that deals with why they believe education is important, their plans for the future, and the service-to-children project they would like to complete in the coming school year. Selection is based on the essay, 3 letters of recommendation, and financial need.

Financial data Stipends range from $1,000 to $2,500 per year.

Duration 1 year; may be renewed up to 3 additional years.

Additional information This program was founded in 1988 by Alan Page, a former football player for the Minnesota Vikings. While attending college, the Page Scholars fulfill a 50-hour service-to-children contract that brings them into contact with K-8 students of color.

Number awarded Varies each year; recently, 560 Page Scholars (218 new recipients and 342 renewals) were enrolled, of whom 337 were African American, 114 Asian American, 63 Chicano/Latino, and 16 American Indian.

Deadline April of each year.

[278]
PARSONS BRINCKERHOFF ENGINEERING SCHOLARSHIP

Conference of Minority Transportation Officials
Attn: National Scholarship Program
818 18th Street, N.W., Suite 850
Washington, DC 20006
(202) 530-0551 Fax: (202) 530-0617
Web: www.comto.org/news-youth.php

Summary To provide financial assistance to Asian American and other members of the Conference of Minority Transportation Officials (COMTO) who are working on an undergraduate degree in engineering.

Eligibility This program is open to undergraduate students who have been members of COMTO for at least 1 year. Applicants must be working on a degree in engineering with a GPA of 3.0 or higher. Along with their application, they must submit a cover letter with a 500-word statement of career goals. Financial need is not considered in the selection process. U.S. citizenship is required.

Financial data The stipend is $5,000. Funds are paid directly to the recipient's college or university.

Duration 1 year.

Additional information COMTO was established in 1971 to promote, strengthen, and expand the roles of minorities in all aspects of transportation. This program is sponsored by Parsons Brinckerhoff, Inc. Recipients are expected to attend the COMTO National Scholarship Luncheon.

Number awarded 1 or more each year.

Deadline April of each year.

[279]
PARSONS BRINCKERHOFF GOLDEN APPLE SCHOLARSHIP

Conference of Minority Transportation Officials
Attn: National Scholarship Program
818 18th Street, N.W., Suite 850
Washington, DC 20006
(202) 530-0551 Fax: (202) 530-0617
Web: www.comto.org/news-youth.php

Summary To provide financial assistance to Asian Americans and other members of the Conference of Minority Transportation Officials (COMTO) who are high school seniors planning to attend college to prepare for a career in the business aspects of the transportation industry.

Eligibility This program is open to graduating high school seniors who have been members of COMTO for at least 1 year. Applicants must be planning to attend an accredited college, university, or vocational/technical institution to prepare for a career in transportation in the fields of communications, finance, or marketing. They must have a GPA of 2.0 or higher. Along with their application, they must submit a cover letter with a 500-word statement of career goals. Financial need is not considered in the selection process. U.S. citizenship is required.

Financial data The stipend is $2,500. Funds are paid directly to the recipient's college or university.

Duration 1 year.

Additional information COMTO was established in 1971 to promote, strengthen, and expand the roles of minorities in all aspects of transportation. This program is sponsored by

Parsons Brinckerhoff, Inc. Recipients are expected to attend the COMTO National Scholarship Luncheon.

Number awarded 1 or more each year.

Deadline April of each year.

[280]
PATRICIA AND GAIL ISHIMOTO MEMORIAL SCHOLARSHIP

Japanese American Citizens League
Attn: National Scholarship Awards
1765 Sutter Street
San Francisco, CA 94115
(415) 921-5225 Fax: (415) 931-4671
E-mail: jacl@jacl.org
Web: www.jacl.org/edu/scholar.htm

Summary To provide financial assistance for college to student members of the Japanese American Citizens League (JACL) who are high school seniors.

Eligibility This program is open to JACL members who are high school seniors interested in attending a college, university, trade school, business college, or other institution of higher learning. Applicants must submit information on their involvement in JACL and a 2-page essay on a topic that changes annually but relates to Japanese Americans. Selection is based on that essay, academic history, extracurricular activities, JACL involvement, scholastic honors, and a letter of recommendation.

Financial data Stipends generally average approximately $2,000.

Duration 1 year; nonrenewable.

Number awarded At least 1 each year.

Deadline February of each year.

[281]
PAUL SHEARMAN ALLEN & ASSOCIATES SCHOLARSHIP

US Pan Asian American Chamber of Commerce
Attn: Scholarship Coordinator
1329 18th Street, N.W.
Washington, DC 20036
(202) 296-5221 Toll Free: (800) 696-7818
Fax: (202) 296-5225 E-mail: info@uspaacc.com
Web: celebrasianconference.com

Summary To provide financial assistance for college to Asian Pacific American high school seniors who can demonstrate financial need.

Eligibility This program is open to high school seniors of Asian or Pacific Islander heritage who are U.S. citizens or permanent residents. Applicants must be planning to enroll full time at an accredited postsecondary educational institution in the United States. Along with their application, they must submit a 500-word essay on their background, achievements, and personal goals. Selection is based on academic excellence (GPA of 3.3 or higher), leadership in extracurricular activities, community service involvement, and financial need.

Financial data The maximum stipend is $5,000. Funds are paid directly to the recipient's college or university.

Duration 1 year.

Additional information This program is sponsored by Paul Shearman Allen & Associates. Funding is not provided for correspondence courses, Internet courses, or study in a country other than the United States.

Number awarded 1 each year.

Deadline March of each year.

[282]
PBS&J ACHIEVEMENT SCHOLARSHIP

Conference of Minority Transportation Officials
Attn: National Scholarship Program
818 18th Street, N.W., Suite 850
Washington, DC 20006
(202) 530-0551　　　　　　Fax: (202) 530-0617
Web: www.comto.org/news-youth.php

Summary To provide financial assistance to Asian American and other minority high school seniors, undergraduates, and graduate students interested in studying the field of transportation.

Eligibility This program is open to minority graduating high school seniors, current undergraduates, and graduate students interested in the field of transportation. Applicants must be enrolled or planning to enroll full time at an accredited college, university, or vocational/technical institution. They must have a GPA of 2.0 or higher. Along with their application, they must submit a cover letter with a 500-word statement of career goals. Financial need is not considered in the selection process. U.S. citizenship is required.

Financial data The stipend is $4,000. Funds are paid directly to the recipient's college or university.

Duration 1 year.

Additional information The Conference of Minority Transportation Officials (COMTO) was established in 1971 to promote, strengthen, and expand the roles of minorities in all aspects of transportation. This program is sponsored by the engineering, architecture, and sciences company PBS&J. Recipients are expected to attend the COMTO National Scholarship Luncheon.

Number awarded 1 or more each year.

Deadline April of each year.

[283]
PENNSYLVANIA DIETETIC ASSOCIATION FOUNDATION DIVERSITY SCHOLARSHIP

Pennsylvania Dietetic Association
Attn: Foundation
96 Northwoods Boulevard, Suite B2
Columbus, OH 43235
(614) 436-6136
Web: www.eatrightpa.org/scholarships/applications.htm

Summary To provide financial assistance to members of the Pennsylvania Dietetic Association (PDA) who are Asian Americans or other minorities and working on an associate or bachelor's degree in dietetics.

Eligibility This program is open to PDA members who are Black, Hispanic, Asian or Pacific Islander, or Native American (Alaskan Native, American Indian, or Hawaiian Native). Applicants must be 1) enrolled in the first year of study in an accredited dietetic technology program; or 2) enrolled in the third year of study in an accredited undergraduate or coordinated program in dietetics. They must have a GPA of 2.5 or higher. Along with their application, they must submit a letter indicating their intent and the reason they are applying for the

scholarship, including a description of their personal financial situation. Selection is based on academic achievement (20%), commitment to the dietetic profession (30%), leadership ability (30%), and financial need (20%).

Financial data The stipend is $1,000.

Duration 1 year.

Number awarded 1 or more each year.

Deadline March of each year.

[284]
PEPSICO HALLMARK SCHOLARSHIPS

US Pan Asian American Chamber of Commerce
Attn: Scholarship Coordinator
1329 18th Street, N.W.
Washington, DC 20036
(202) 296-5221　　　　Toll Free: (800) 696-7818
Fax: (202) 296-5225　　　E-mail: info@uspaacc.com
Web: celebrasianconference.com

Summary To provide financial assistance for college to Asian Pacific American high school seniors who can demonstrate financial need.

Eligibility This program is open to high school seniors of Asian or Pacific Islander heritage who are U.S. citizens or permanent residents. Applicants must be planning to enroll full time at an accredited postsecondary educational institution in the United States. Along with their application, they must submit a 500-word essay on their background, achievements, and personal goals. Selection is based on academic excellence (GPA of 3.3 or higher), leadership in extracurricular activities, community service involvement, and financial need.

Financial data The maximum stipend is $5,000. Funds are paid directly to the recipient's college or university.

Duration 1 year.

Additional information This program, established in 2005, is sponsored by PepsiCo. Funding is not provided for correspondence courses, Internet courses, or study in a country other than the United States.

Number awarded 2 each year.

Deadline March of each year.

[285]
PGA TOUR DIVERSITY INTERNSHIP PROGRAM

PGA Tour, Inc.
Attn: Minority Internship Program
100 PGA Tour Boulevard
Ponte Vedra Beach, FL 32082
(904) 285-3700
Web: www.pgatour.com/company/internships.html

Summary To provide summer work experience to Asian American and other undergraduate and graduate students who are interested in learning about the business side of golf and will contribute to diversity in the profession.

Eligibility This program is open to students who either have completed at least their sophomore year at an accredited 4-year college or university or are enrolled in graduate school. Applicants should be able to enrich the PGA Tour and its partnering organizations through diversity. They must have a GPA of 2.8 or higher. International students are eligible if they are legally permitted to work in the United States. Although all interns work in the business side of golf, the ability to play golf or knowledge of the game is not required for many positions.

Financial data Interns receive competitive wages and up to $500 for travel expenses to orientation in Ponte Vedra Beach, Florida or their initial work location. Depending on position and location, other benefits include subsidized housing, discounts on company merchandise, access to company training seminars, and possible golf privileges.

Duration Most assignments are for 10 to 12 weeks during the summer.

Additional information This program was established in 1992. Positions are available in accounting, corporate marketing, business development, international TV, information systems, event management, tournament services, tournament operations, retail licensing, sales, human resources, new media, and other areas within the PGA Tour. Most assignments are in Ponte Vedra Beach, Florida.

Number awarded Approximately 30 each year.

Deadline February of each year.

[286]
PHILIPPINE AMERICAN CHAMBER OF COMMERCE OF OREGON COLLEGE SCHOLARSHIP

Philippine American Chamber of Commerce of Oregon
5424 North Michigan Street
Portland, OR 97217
(503) 285-1994   E-mail: junpioquinto@yahoo.com
Web: www.pacco.org

Summary To provide financial assistance to Filipino residents of Oregon and Washington who are interested in attending college in any state.

Eligibility This program is open to residents of Oregon and Washington who are high school seniors or current college students of Filipino descent. Applicant must be enrolled or planning to enroll full time at an accredited 2- or 4-year college, university, or vocational/technical school in any state. They must have a GPA of 3.0 or higher and be able to demonstrate financial need. Along with their application, they must submit a 500-word essay on the significance of college education.

Financial data The stipend is $500.

Duration 1 year.

Number awarded 4 each year.

Deadline March of each year.

[287]
PHYSICAL AND LIFE SCIENCES DIRECTORATE INTERNSHIPS

Lawrence Livermore National Laboratory
Physical and Life Sciences Directorate
Attn: Education Coordinator
7000 East Avenue, L-418
Livermore, CA 94550
(925) 422-0455   E-mail: hutcheon3@llnl.gov
Web: www-pls.llnl.gov

Summary To provide an opportunity for undergraduate and graduate students (particularly Asian Americans, other minorities, and women) to work on summer research projects within the Physical and Life Sciences Directorate (PLS) of Lawrence Livermore National Laboratory (LLNL).

Eligibility This program is open to full-time undergraduate and graduate students who are interested in working on research projects within the PLS Directorate of LLNL. Openings are currently available in chemistry (organic, inorganic, synthetic, analytical, computational, nuclear, and environmental) and materials science (theory, simulation and modeling, synthesis and processing, materials under extreme conditions, dynamic materials science, metallurgy, nuclear fuels, optical materials, and surface science). Applicants must have a GPA of 3.0 or higher. Selection is based on academic record, aptitude, research interests, and recommendations of instructors. Women and minorities are encouraged to apply.

Financial data The stipend is $14 to $20 per hour for undergraduates or $4,100 to $4,900 per month for graduate students. Living accommodations and arrangements are the responsibility of the intern.

Duration 2 or 3 months, during the summer.

Number awarded Varies each year.

Deadline February of each year.

[288]
PLANNED SYSTEMS INTERNATIONAL SCHOLARSHIP

US Pan Asian American Chamber of Commerce
Attn: Scholarship Coordinator
1329 18th Street, N.W.
Washington, DC 20036
(202) 296-5221   Toll Free: (800) 696-7818
Fax: (202) 296-5225   E-mail: info@uspaacc.com
Web: celebrasianconference.com

Summary To provide financial assistance for college to Asian Pacific American high school seniors who demonstrate academic achievement and financial need.

Eligibility This program is open to high school seniors of Asian or Pacific Islander heritage who are U.S. citizens or permanent residents. Applicants must be planning to enroll full time at an accredited postsecondary educational institution in the United States. Along with their application, they must submit a 500-word essay on their background, achievements, and personal goals. Selection is based on academic excellence (GPA of 3.3 or higher), leadership in extracurricular activities, community service involvement, and financial need.

Financial data The maximum stipend is $5,000. Funds are paid directly to the recipient's college or university.

Duration 1 year.

Additional information This program is sponsored by Planned Systems International, Inc. Funding is not provided for correspondence courses, Internet courses, or study in a country other than the United States.

Number awarded 1 each year.

Deadline March of each year.

[289]
PNANC UNDERGRADUATE NURSING STUDENT SCHOLARSHIP

Philippine Nurses Association of Northern California, Inc.
c/o Teresita Baluyut, Scholarship Chair
845 Mt. Vernon Avenue
San Francisco, CA 94112
E-mail: pnanorthcal@gmail.com
Web: www.pnanorthcal.org

Summary To provide financial assistance to Filipino Americans from any state enrolled in an undergraduate nursing program at a school in northern California.

Eligibility This program is open to Filipino American residents of any state who are currently enrolled in at least the third year of an accredited undergraduate nursing program in northern California. Applicants must have a GPA of 3.0 or higher and a record of participation in extracurricular or community activities. They must have demonstrated leadership ability or potential both within and outside the clinical setting. Along with their application, they must submit brief statements on their strengths and opportunities for improvement, their career goals, why they need a financial scholarship, and how they can contribute to the goals of the Philippine Nurses Association of Northern California (PNANC). They must also submit a 1-page essay on either 1) why they chose the field of nursing, or 2) an accomplishment or activity as a nursing student that has impacted their life or the life of another person.

Financial data The stipend is $1,000.

Duration 1 year.

Additional information The recipient must commit to serve on a committee of the PNANC for at least 2 years.

Number awarded 1 each year.

Deadline June of each year.

[290]
PNAO SCHOLARSHIP AWARD

Philippine Nurses Association of Ohio
c/o Audrey T. Godoy, President
15227 Scarlet Oak Trail
Strongsville, OH 44149
(216) 312-0510   E-mail: atgrn@roadrunner.com
Web: www.pnao.org/awards_scholarships.html

Summary To provide financial assistance to students who have a tie to the Philippine Nurses Association of Ohio (PNAO) and are working on an undergraduate or graduate degree at a school of nursing in any state.

Eligibility This program is open to residents of Ohio and the Philippines who are of at least 50% Filipino ethnicity and an associate member of PNAO, a relative of a member, or recommended by a member. Applicants must be enrolled in an undergraduate or graduate nursing program at a school in any state. They must have a GPA of 3.0 or higher and be able to demonstrate financial need. Along with their application, they must submit a 1-page essay on their vision of nursing.

Financial data The stipend is $500.

Duration 1 year.

Number awarded 2 each year.

Deadline July of each year.

[291]
PORTLAND CHAPTER AAJA SCHOLARSHIPS

Asian American Journalists Association-Portland Chapter
c/o Amy Hsuan, Co-President
The Oregonian
1320 S.W. Broadway
Portland, OR 97201
(503) 997-4909   Fax: (503) 294-4193
E-mail: amyhsuan@news.oregonian.com
Web: chapters.aaja.org/Portland/scholar.html

Summary To provide financial assistance to undergraduate and graduate journalism students in Oregon and southwestern Washington who have been involved in the Asian American community.

Eligibility This program is open to high school seniors, undergraduates, and graduate students who live or attend school in Oregon or southwestern Washington. Applicants must be enrolled or planning to enroll full time in a journalism program and be able to demonstrate involvement in the Asian American community. Along with their application, they must submit an essay (up to 750 words) on how they became interested in journalism or how they see themselves contributing to the Asian American community. They must also submit work samples (print: up to 3 articles; radio: up to 3 different stories on standard audio tapes; television: up to 3 different stories on a VHS tape; photojournalism: a portfolio of up to 15 entries). Selection is based on scholastic ability, commitment to journalism, sensitivity to Asian American issues as demonstrated by community involvement, journalistic ability, and financial need.

Financial data Stipends up to $2,000 are available.

Duration 1 year.

Number awarded 1 each year.

Deadline April of each year.

[292]
PROFESSIONAL GOLF MANAGEMENT DIVERSITY SCHOLARSHIP

Professional Golfers' Association of America
Attn: PGA Foundation
100 Avenue of the Champions
Palm Beach Gardens, FL 33418
Toll Free: (888) 532-6661
Web: www.pgafoundation.com

Summary To provide financial assistance to Asian Americans, other minorities, and women who are interested in attending a designated college or university to prepare for a career as a golf professional.

Eligibility This program is open to women and minorities interested in becoming a licensed PGA Professional. Applicants must be interested in attending 1 of 20 colleges and universities that offer the Professional Golf Management (PGM) curriculum sanctioned by the PGA.

Financial data The stipend is $3,000 per year.

Duration 1 year; may be renewed.

Additional information This program began in 1993. Programs are offered at Arizona State University (Mesa, Arizona), Campbell University (Buies Creek, North Carolina), Clemson University (Clemson, South Carolina), Coastal Carolina University (Conway, South Carolina), Eastern Kentucky University (Richmond, Kentucky), Ferris State University (Big

Rapids, Michigan), Florida Gulf Coast University (Fort Myers, Florida), Florida State University (Tallahassee, Florida), Methodist College (Fayetteville, North Carolina), Mississippi State University (Mississippi State, Mississippi), New Mexico State University (Las Cruces, New Mexico), North Carolina State University (Raleigh, North Carolina), Pennsylvania State University (University Park, Pennsylvania), Sam Houston State University (Huntsville, Texas), University of Central Oklahoma (Edmond, Oklahoma), University of Colorado (Colorado Springs, Colorado), University of Idaho (Moscow, Idaho), University of Maryland Eastern Shore (Princess Anne, Maryland), University of Nebraska (Lincoln, Nebraska), and University of Nevada (Las Vegas, Nevada).

Number awarded Varies each year; recently, 20 of these scholarships were awarded.

Deadline Deadline not specified.

[293]
PROFESSOR CHEN WEN-CHEN SCHOLARSHIPS

Professor Chen Wen-Chen Memorial Foundation
Attn: Scholarship Committee
P.O. Box 136
Kingston, NJ 08528
(609) 936-1352   E-mail: cwcmfusa@gmail.com
Web: cwcmf.net

Summary To provide financial assistance to students at North American colleges and universities who have been involved in the Taiwanese community.

Eligibility This program is open to students who have participated in Taiwanese social-political movements or have made significant contributions to the Taiwanese community in North America. Applicants must be currently enrolled at a college or university in North America. Selection is based on character, academic ability, financial need, and participation in Taiwanese American community affairs.

Financial data The stipend ranges from $1,000 to $1,500.

Duration 1 year.

Number awarded 4 to 6 each year.

Deadline July of each year.

[294]
PUBLIC RELATIONS SOCIETY OF AMERICA MULTICULTURAL AFFAIRS SCHOLARSHIPS

Public Relations Student Society of America
Attn: Vice President of Member Services
33 Maiden Lane, 11th Floor
New York, NY 10038-5150
(212) 460-1474   Fax: (212) 995-0757
E-mail: prssa@prsa.org
Web: www.prssa.org/awards/awardMulticultural.aspx

Summary To provide financial assistance to Asian American and other minority college students who are interested in preparing for a career in public relations.

Eligibility This program is open to minority (African American/Black, Hispanic/Latino, Asian, Native American, Alaskan Native, or Pacific Islander) students who are at least juniors at an accredited 4-year college or university. Applicants must be enrolled full time, be able to demonstrate financial need, and have earned a GPA of 3.0 or higher. Membership in the Public Relations Student Society of America is preferred but not required. A major or minor in public relations is preferred; stu-

dents who attend a school that does not offer a public relations degree or program must be enrolled in a communications degree program (e.g., journalism, mass communications).

Financial data The stipend is $1,500.

Duration 1 year.

Additional information This program was established in 1989.

Number awarded 2 each year.

Deadline April of each year.

[295]
PWC ASCEND SCHOLARSHIPS

Ascend: Pan-Asian Leaders
Attn: Director of Programs
120 Wall Street, Third Floor
New York, NY 10005
(212) 248-4888   Fax: (212) 344-5636
E-mail: info@ascendleadership.org
Web: www.ascendleadership.org

Summary To provide financial assistance to members of Ascend: Pan-Asian Leaders who are college undergraduates with a career interest in accounting.

Eligibility This program is open to members of Ascend who are enrolled as freshmen, sophomores, or juniors (in 5-year programs) at colleges and universities in the United States. Applicants must have a GPA of 3.5 or higher and a major in accounting. Along with their application, they must submit a 500-word personal essay on how they have demonstrated leadership and teamwork in their academic studies, professional career, and/or extracurricular activities and community volunteer work; why they believe those qualities are important to be competitive in a borderless world; their career goals after graduation; and the role Ascend has played in the achievement of their academic and career goals. They must also answer questions on whether they are authorized to work in the United States without employer sponsorship, if they are willing to be interviewed for an internship with PricewaterhouseCoopers (PwC), if they have worked for other Big 4 accounting firms, and if they completed a PwC talent profile at the firm's web site. Financial need is not considered in the selection process.

Financial data The stipend is $3,000.

Duration 1 year.

Additional information Ascend was formed in 2004 as the National Asian American Society of Accountants. This program, sponsored by PwC, began in 2008.

Number awarded 4 each year.

Deadline July of each year.

[296]
RACE RELATIONS MULTIRACIAL STUDENT SCHOLARSHIP

Christian Reformed Church
Attn: Office of Race Relations
2850 Kalamazoo Avenue, S.E.
Grand Rapids, MI 49560-0200
(616) 241-1691   Toll Free: (877) 279-9994
Fax: (616) 224-0803   E-mail: crcna@crcna.org
Web: www.crcna.org/pages/racerelations_scholar.cfm

Summary   To provide financial assistance to Asian American and other undergraduate and graduate minority students interested in attending colleges related to the Christian Reformed Church in North America (CRCNA).
Eligibility   Students of color in the United States and Canada are eligible to apply. Normally, applicants are expected to be members of CRCNA congregations who plan to pursue their educational goals at Calvin Theological Seminary or any of the colleges affiliated with the CRCNA. Students who have no prior history with the CRCNA must attend a CRCNA-related college or seminary for a full academic year before they are eligible to apply for this program. Students entering their sophomore year must have earned a GPA of 2.0 or higher as freshmen; students entering their junior year must have earned a GPA of 2.3 or higher as sophomores; students entering their senior year must have earned a GPA of 2.6 or higher as juniors.
Financial data   First-year students receive $500 per semester. Other levels of students may receive up to $2,000 per academic year.
Duration   1 year.
Additional information   This program was first established in 1971 and revised in 1991. Recipients are expected to train to engage actively in the ministry of racial reconciliation in church and in society. They must be able to work in the United States or Canada upon graduating and must consider working for 1 of the agencies of the CRCNA.
Number awarded   Varies each year; recently, 31 students received a total of $21,000 in support.
Deadline   March of each year.

[297]
RACIAL ETHNIC EDUCATIONAL SCHOLARSHIPS

Synod of the Trinity
Attn: Scholarships
3040 Market Street
Camp Hill, PA 17011-4599
(717) 737-0421, ext. 233
Toll Free: (800) 242-0534, ext. 233
Fax: (717) 737-8211   E-mail: mhumer@syntrinity.org
Web: www.syntrinity.org
Summary   To provide financial assistance to Asian American and other minority students in Pennsylvania, West Virginia, and designated counties in Ohio who are interested in attending college in any state.
Eligibility   This program is open to members of a racial minority group (African American, Asian, Hispanic, Latino, Middle Eastern, or Native American) who are enrolled or planning to enroll full time at an accredited college or vocational school in any state. Applicants may be of any religious denomination, but they must be residents of the area served by the Presbyterian Church (USA) Synod of the Trinity, which covers all of Pennsylvania; West Virginia except for the counties of Berkeley, Grant, Hampshire, Hardy, Jefferson, Mineral, Morgan, and Pendleton; and the Ohio counties of Belmont, Harrison, Jefferson, Monroe, and the southern sector of Columbiana. They must have total income of less than $85,000 for a family of 4. U.S. citizenship or permanent resident status is required.
Financial data   Awards range from $100 to $1,000 per year, depending on the need of the recipient.
Duration   1 year; recipients may reapply.

Number awarded   Varies each year.
Deadline   April of each year.

[298]
RAMA SCHOLARSHIP FOR THE AMERICAN DREAM

American Hotel & Lodging Educational Foundation
Attn: Manager of Foundation Programs
1201 New York Avenue, N.W., Suite 600
Washington, DC 20005-3931
(202) 289-3181   Fax: (202) 289-3199
E-mail: ahlef@ahlef.org
Web: www.ahlef.org/content.aspx?id=19820
Summary   To provide financial assistance to Asian American and other minority undergraduate and graduate students working on a degree in hotel management at designated schools.
Eligibility   This program is open to U.S. citizens and permanent residents enrolled as full-time undergraduate or graduate students with a GPA of 2.5 or higher. Applicants must be attending 1 of 13 designated hospitality management schools, which select the recipients. Preference is given to students of Asian-Indian descent and other minority groups and to JHM Hotel employees and their dependents.
Financial data   The stipend varies at each of the participating schools, but ranges from $1,000 to $3,000.
Duration   1 year.
Additional information   This program was established by JHM Hotels, Inc. in 1998. The participating institutions are Bethune-Cookman College, California State Polytechnic University at Pomona, Cornell University, Florida International University, Georgia State University, Greenville Technical College, Howard University, Johnson & Wales University (Providence, Rhode Island), New York University, University of Central Florida, University of Houston, University of South Carolina, and Virginia Polytechnic Institute and State University.
Number awarded   Varies each year; recently, 20 of these scholarships were awarded. Since the program was established, it has awarded more than $491,000 to 287 recipients.
Deadline   April of each year.

[299]
RDW GROUP, INC. MINORITY SCHOLARSHIP FOR COMMUNICATIONS

Rhode Island Foundation
Attn: Funds Administrator
One Union Station
Providence, RI 02903
(401) 427-4017   Fax: (401) 331-8085
E-mail: lmonahan@rifoundation.org
Web: www.rifoundation.org
Summary   To provide financial assistance to Asian Americans and other undergraduate and graduate students of color in Rhode Island who are interested in preparing for a career in communications at a school in any state.
Eligibility   This program is open to undergraduate and graduate students at colleges and universities in any state who are Asian Americans or other Rhode Island residents of color. Applicants must intend to work on a degree in communications (including computer graphics, art, cinematography, or other fields that would prepare them for a career in adver-

tising). They must be able to demonstrate financial need and a commitment to a career in communications. Along with their application, they must submit an essay (up to 300 words) on the impact they would like to have on the communications field.

Financial data The stipend ranges from $1,000 to $2,500 per year.

Duration 1 year; recipients may reapply.

Additional information This program is sponsored by the RDW Group, Inc.

Number awarded 1 each year.

Deadline April of each year.

[300]
REFORMED CHURCH IN AMERICA ETHNIC SCHOLARSHIP FUND

Reformed Church in America
Attn: Director of Operations and Support
475 Riverside Drive, Room 1814
New York, NY 10115
(212) 870-3071   Toll Free: (800) 722-9977, ext. 3017
Fax: (212) 870-2499   E-mail: mrich@rca.org
Web: www.rca.org/sslpage.aspx?&pid=2177

Summary To provide assistance to Pacific/Asian American and other minority student members of the Reformed Church in America (RCA) who are interested in working on an undergraduate degree.

Eligibility This program is open to members of minority groups (American Indian, African American/Caribbean American, Hispanic, or Pacific/Asian American) who are attending or planning to attend a college or other institution of higher learning. Applicants must be member of the RCA congregation or attending an RCA institution. Priority is given to applicants who will be entering undergraduate colleges or universities and students currently enrolled in occupational training programs. Selection is based primarily on financial need.

Financial data Stipends range up to $500.

Duration 1 academic year; may be renewed until completion of an academic program.

Number awarded Several each year.

Deadline April of each year.

[301]
RESOURCES FOR THE FUTURE SUMMER INTERNSHIPS

Resources for the Future
Attn: Internship Coordinator
1616 P Street, N.W., Suite 600
Washington, DC 20036-1400
(202) 328-5008   Fax: (202) 939-3460
E-mail: IC@rff.org
Web: www.rff.org

Summary To provide internships to undergraduate and graduate students (particularly Asian Americans, other minorities, and women) who are interested in working on research projects in public policy during the summer.

Eligibility This program is open to undergraduate and graduate students (with priority to graduate students) interested in an internship at Resources for the Future (RFF). Applicants must be working on a degree in the social and natural sciences and have training in economics and quantitative

methods or an interest in public policy. They should display strong writing skills and a desire to analyze complex environmental policy problems amenable to interdisciplinary methods. The ability to work without supervision in a careful and conscientious manner is essential. Women and minority candidates are strongly encouraged to apply. Both U.S. and non-U.S. citizens are eligible, if the latter have proper work and residency documentation.

Financial data The stipend is $375 per week for graduate students or $350 per week for undergraduates. Housing assistance is not provided.

Duration 10 weeks during the summer; beginning and ending dates can be adjusted to meet particular student needs.

Deadline March of each year.

[302]
RICHARD LOUIE MEMORIAL INTERNSHIP FOR HIGH SCHOOL STUDENTS OF ASIAN DESCENT

Freer and Sackler Galleries
Attn: Education Department
1050 Independence Avenue, S.W.
P.O. Box 37012, MRC 707
Washington, DC 20013-7012
(202) 633-0466   TDD: (202) 786-2374
E-mail: asiainternship@si.edu
Web: www.asia.si.edu/research/richardlouie.asp

Summary To enable Asian American high school students in the Washington, D.C. area to gain practical experience in a museum setting.

Eligibility This program is students at high schools in the Washington, D.C. area who are 16 years of age or older and of Asian descent. High school graduates are also eligible for the term immediately following their graduation. Applicants must be seeking an internship at the Smithsonian's Freer and Sackler Galleries, with their renowned collection of Asian art. They need not be planning a career in museum work or Asian studies, but they should be interested in learning about museum work and Asian art.

Financial data The stipend is $1,500. No housing or transportation is provided.

Duration Interns who complete 200 internship hours within the span of 1 year receive the stipend.

Number awarded Varies each year.

Deadline November of each year for winter or spring terms; March of each year for summer term; July of each year for fall term.

[303]
RICHARD S. SMITH SCHOLARSHIP

United Methodist Church
Attn: General Board of Discipleship
Division on Ministries with Young People
P.O. Box 340003
Nashville, TN 37203-0003
(615) 340-7184   Toll Free: (877) 899-2780, ext. 7184
Fax: (615) 340-7063   E-mail: youngpeople@gbod.org
Web: www.gbod.org

Summary To provide financial assistance to Asian American and other minority high school seniors who wish to prepare for a Methodist church-related career.

Eligibility This program is open to graduating high school seniors who are members of racial/ethnic minority groups and have been active members of a United Methodist Church for at least 1 year. Applicants must have been admitted to an accredited college or university to prepare for a church-related career. They must have maintained at least a "C" average throughout high school and be able to demonstrate financial need. Along with their application, they must submit brief essays on their participation in church projects and activities, a leadership experience, the role their faith plays in their life, the church-related vocation to which God is calling them, and their extracurricular interests and activities. U.S. citizenship or permanent resident status is required.

Financial data The stipend is $1,000.

Duration 1 year; nonrenewable.

Additional information This scholarship was first awarded in 1997. Recipients must enroll full time in their first year of undergraduate study.

Number awarded 2 each year.

Deadline May of each year.

[304]
ROBERT HALF INTERNATIONAL ASCEND SCHOLARSHIPS

Ascend: Pan-Asian Leaders
Attn: Director of Programs
120 Wall Street, Third Floor
New York, NY 10005
(212) 248-4888   Fax: (212) 344-5636
E-mail: info@ascendleadership.org
Web: www.ascendleadership.org

Summary To provide financial assistance to members of Ascend: Pan-Asian Leaders who are upper-division students working on a degree in accounting or finance.

Eligibility This program is open to members of Ascend who are enrolled as juniors or seniors at colleges and universities in the United States. Applicants must have a GPA of 3.5 or higher and a major in accounting or finance. Along with their application, they must submit a 500-word personal essay on how they have demonstrated leadership and teamwork in their academic studies, professional career, and/or extracurricular activities and community volunteer work; why they believe those qualities are important to be competitive in a borderless world; their career goals after graduation; and the role Ascend has played in the achievement of their academic and career goals. Financial need is not considered in the selection process.

Financial data The stipend is $5,000.

Duration 1 year.

Additional information Ascend was formed in 2004 as the National Asian American Society of Accountants. This program is sponsored by Robert Half International Inc.

Number awarded 2 each year.

Deadline July of each year.

[305]
RYU FAMILY FOUNDATION SCHOLARSHIP GRANTS

Ryu Family Foundation, Inc.
186 Parish Drive
Wayne, NJ 07470
(973) 692-9696   Fax: (973) 692-0999
Web: www.seolbong.org

Summary To provide financial assistance to Korean and Korean American students in the Northeast who are working on an undergraduate or graduate degree in any field.

Eligibility This program is open to Korean Americans (U.S. citizens) and Koreans (with or without permanent resident status). Applicants must be enrolled full time and working on an undergraduate or graduate degree; have a GPA of 3.5 or higher; be able to document financial need; and be either residing or attending college in 1 of the following 10 northeastern states: Connecticut, Delaware, Maine, Massachusetts, New Hampshire, New Jersey, New York, Pennsylvania, Rhode Island, or Vermont. Along with their application, they must submit a 500-word essay on a subject that changes annually; recently, students were asked to present their opinion of the future of the United States.

Financial data A stipend is awarded (amount not specified). Checks are made out jointly to the recipient and the recipient's school.

Duration 1 year; may be renewed.

Deadline November of each year.

[306]
SABURO KIDO MEMORIAL SCHOLARSHIP

Japanese American Citizens League
Attn: National Scholarship Awards
1765 Sutter Street
San Francisco, CA 94115
(415) 921-5225   Fax: (415) 931-4671
E-mail: jacl@jacl.org
Web: www.jacl.org/edu/scholar.htm

Summary To provide financial assistance for college to student members of the Japanese American Citizens League (JACL).

Eligibility This program is open to JACL members who are currently enrolled at a college, university, trade school, business college, or other institution of higher learning. Applicants must submit information on their involvement in JACL and a 2-page essay on a topic that changes annually but relates to Japanese Americans. Selection is based on that essay, academic history, extracurricular activities, JACL involvement, scholastic honors, and a letter of recommendation.

Financial data Stipends generally average approximately $2,000.

Duration 1 year; nonrenewable.

Number awarded At least 1 each year.

Deadline March of each year.

[307]
SAJA SCHOLARSHIPS

South Asian Journalists Association
c/o Aseem Chhabra, Awards Committee Chair
4315 46th Street, Apartment E10
Sunnyside, NY 11104-2015
E-mail: chhabs@aol.com
Web: www.saja.org/programs/scholarships

Summary To provide financial assistance for undergraduate and graduate study to journalism students of south Asian descent.

Eligibility This program is open to students of south Asian descent (including Bangladesh, Bhutan, India, Maldives, Nepal, Pakistan, and Sri Lanka; Indo-Caribbeans are also eligible). Applicants must be serious about preparing for a journalism career and must provide evidence they plan to do so through courses, internships, or freelancing. They may be 1) high school seniors about to enroll in an accredited college or university; 2) current students in an accredited college or university in the United States or Canada; or 3) students enrolled or about to enter a graduate program in the United States or Canada. Applicants with financial hardship are given special consideration. Selection is based on interest in journalism, writing skills, participation in the sponsoring organization, reasons for entering journalism, and financial need.

Financial data The stipends are $1,000 for high school seniors, $1,500 for current college students, or $2,000 for graduate students.

Duration 1 year.

Additional information Recipients are expected to give back to the South Asian Journalists Association (SAJA) by volunteering at the annual convention or at other events during the year.

Number awarded 4 each year: 1 to a high school senior entering college, 1 to a current college student, and 2 to graduate students.

Deadline March of each year.

[308]
SAKAE TAKAHASHI SCHOLARSHIP

Club 100 Veterans
Attn: Scholarship Committee
520 Kamoku Street
Honolulu, HI 96826-5120
(808) 946-0272   E-mail: daisyy@hgea.net

Summary To provide financial assistance to Asian American and other high school seniors and college students who major in business, political science, or law and exemplify the sponsor's motto of "For Continuing Service."

Eligibility This program is open to high school seniors planning to attend an institution of higher learning and full-time undergraduate students at community colleges, vocational/trade schools, 4-year colleges, and universities. Applicants must have a GPA of 2.5 or higher and be able to demonstrate civic responsibility and community service. They must be majoring or planning to major in business, political science, or law. Along with their application, they must submit an essay on a topic that changes annually but relates to Asian Americans who served in the military. Selection is based on that essay and the applicant's promotion of the legacy of the

100th Infantry Battalion and its motto of "For Continuing Service." Financial need is not considered.

Financial data The stipend is $1,000.

Duration 1 year; nonrenewable.

Number awarded 1 each year.

Deadline April of each year.

[309]
SAM CHU LIN BROADCAST NEWS GRANT

Asian American Journalists Association
Attn: Student Programs Coordinator
5 Third Street, Suite 1108
San Francisco, CA 94103
(415) 346-2051, ext. 102   Fax: (415) 346-6343
E-mail: programs@aaja.org
Web: www.aaja.org/programs/internships

Summary To provide a supplemental grant to student and other members of the Asian American Journalists Association (AAJA) working as a summer intern at a radio or television broadcasting company.

Eligibility This program is open to AAJA members who are full-time college students or recent college graduates. Applicants must have secured a summer internship at a television or radio broadcasting company before they apply. Along with their application, they must submit a 200-word essay on why they want to prepare for a career in broadcast journalism, what they want to gain from the experience, and why AAJA's mission is important to them; a letter of recommendation; a resume; proof of age (at least 18 years); verification of an internship; and statement of financial need.

Financial data The grant is $2,500. Funds are to be used for living expenses or transportation.

Duration Summer months.

Number awarded 1 each year.

Deadline May of each year.

[310]
SANDRA R. SPAULDING MEMORIAL SCHOLARSHIPS

California Nurses Association
Attn: Scholarship Fund
2000 Franklin Street, Suite 300
Oakland, CA 94612
(510) 273-2200, ext. 344   Fax: (510) 663-1625
E-mail: membershipbenefits@calnurses.org
Web: www.calnurses.org/membership

Summary To provide financial assistance to Asian Americans and other students from diverse ethnic backgrounds who are enrolled in an associate degree in nursing (A.D.N.) program in California.

Eligibility This program is open to students who have been admitted to a second-year accredited A.D.N. program in California and plan to complete the degree within 2 years. Along with their application, they must submit a 1-page essay describing their personal and professional goals. Selection is based on that essay, commitment and active participation in nursing and health-related organizations, professional vision and direction, and financial need. A goal of this scholarship program is to encourage ethnic and socioeconomic diversity in nursing.

Financial data A stipend is awarded (amount not specified).

Duration 1 year; nonrenewable.

Additional information This program was established in 1985.

Number awarded 1 or more each year.

Deadline June of each year.

[311]
SARA HUTCHINGS CLARDY SCHOLARSHIP AWARDS

Japanese American Citizens League-Arizona Chapter
5414 West Glenn Drive
Glendale, AZ 85301-2628
E-mail: arizonajacl@gmail.com
Web: www.jaclaz.org

Summary To provide financial assistance to graduating high school seniors in Arizona who are of Japanese heritage.

Eligibility This program is open to graduating high school seniors in Arizona who have a GPA of 3.0 or higher. Applicants or their parents must have been members of 1 of the following organizations for at least the preceding 3 years: Arizona Chapter of the Japanese American Citizens League (JACLA), the Phoenix Japanese Free Methodist Church, the Arizona Buddhist Church, a youth group of JACLA, a youth group of the Phoenix Free Methodist Church, or a youth group of the Arizona Buddhist Church. Financial need is not considered in the selection process.

Financial data A stipend is awarded (amount not specified).

Duration 1 year.

Additional information Recipients must attend the association's scholarship awards banquet and accept the award in person; failure to do so results in forfeiture of the award.

Number awarded 4 each year.

Deadline February of each year.

[312]
SARA LEE FOUNDATION SCHOLARSHIP

Asian & Pacific Islander American Scholarship Fund
1900 L Street, N.W., Suite 210
Washington, DC 20036-5002
(202) 986-6892   Toll Free: (877) 808-7032
Fax: (202) 530-0643   E-mail: info@apiasf.org
Web: www.apiasf.org/scholarship_apiasf_saralee.html

Summary To provide financial assistance to female Asian and Pacific Islander Americans who are entering college for the first time.

Eligibility This program is open to women who are U.S. citizens, nationals, permanent residents, or citizens of the Freely Associated States and of Asian or Pacific Islander heritage. Applicants must be enrolling full time at an accredited 2- or 4-year college or university in the United States as a first-year student. They must have a GPA of 2.7 or higher or the GED equivalent. In addition, they must complete the FAFSA and apply for federal financial aid.

Financial data The stipend is $2,500.

Duration 1 year; nonrenewable.

Additional information This scholarship is sponsored by the Sara Lee Foundation.

Number awarded 1 each year.

Deadline January of each year.

[313]
SCHOLARSHIP FOR DIVERSITY IN TEACHING

Mid-Atlantic Association for Employment in Education
c/o Kerri G. Gardi
Kutztown University
Director, Career Development Center
P.O. Box 730
Kutztown, PA 19530
(610) 683-4647   E-mail: gardi@kutztown.edu
Web: www.maeeonline.org/pages/scholarships_jump.aspx

Summary To provide financial assistance to Asian American and other minority upper-division students at universities in the Mid-Atlantic region who are preparing for a career as a teacher.

Eligibility This program is open to members of racial and ethnic minority groups who have completed between 48 and 90 credits at a college or university in Delaware, Maryland, New Jersey, New York, Pennsylvania, Virginia, Washington, D.C., or West Virginia. Applicants must be enrolled full time majoring in a field to prepare for a career in teaching. Along with their application, they must submit a 1-page essay on why they have chosen to become a teacher and what they hope to accomplish as an educator. Selection is based on academic success, service to college and/or community, and potential to achieve excellence as a teacher. U.S. citizenship is required.

Financial data The stipend is $1,000.

Duration 1 year; nonrenewable.

Number awarded 1 each year.

Deadline November of each year.

[314]
SCHOLARSHIPS FOR MINORITY ACCOUNTING STUDENTS

American Institute of Certified Public Accountants
Attn: Academic and Career Development Division
220 Leigh Farm Road
Durham, NC 27707-8110
(919) 402-4931   Fax: (919) 419-4705
E-mail: MIC_Programs@aicpa.org
Web: www.aicpa.org/members/div/career/mini/smas.htm

Summary To provide financial assistance to Asian Americans and other minorities interested in studying accounting at the undergraduate or graduate school level.

Eligibility This program is open to minority undergraduate and graduate students, enrolled full time, who have a GPA of 3.3 or higher (both cumulatively and in their major) and intend to pursue a C.P.A. credential. Undergraduates must have completed at least 30 semester hours, including at least 6 semester hours of a major in accounting. Graduate students must be working on a master's degree in accounting, finance, taxation, or a related program. Applicants must be U.S. citizens or permanent residents and student affiliate members of the American Institute of Certified Public Accountants (AICPA). The program defines minority students as those whose heritage is Black or African American, Hispanic or Latino, Native American, or Asian American.

Financial data Stipends range from $1,500 to $3,000 per year. Funds are disbursed directly to the recipient's school.

Duration 1 year; may be renewed up to 3 additional years or until completion of a bachelor's or master's degree, whichever is earlier.

Additional information This program is administered by The Center for Scholarship Administration, E-mail: allison-lee@bellsouth.net. The most outstanding applicant for this program is awarded the Stuart A. Kessler Scholarship for Minority Students.

Number awarded Varies each year; recently, 94 students received funding through this program.

Deadline March of each year.

[315]
SCHOLARSHIPS FOR SOCIAL JUSTICE

Higher Education Consortium for Urban Affairs
Attn: Student Services
2233 University Avenue West, Suite 210
St. Paul, MN 55114-1698
(651) 646-8831   Toll Free: (800) 554-1089
Fax: (651) 659-9421   E-mail: hecua@hecua.org
Web: www.hecua.org/scholarships.php

Summary To provide financial assistance to students from Asian American and other targeted groups who are enrolled in programs of the Higher Education Consortium for Urban Affairs (HECUA) at participating colleges and universities.

Eligibility This program is open to students at member colleges and universities who are participating in HECUA programs. Applicants must be a first-generation college student, from a low-income family, or a student of color. Along with their application, they must submit a reflective essay, drawing on their life experiences and their personal and academic goals, on what they believe they can contribute to the mission of HECUA to equip students with the knowledge, experiences, tools, and passion to address issues of social justice and social change. The essay should also explain how the HECUA program will benefit them and the people, issues, and communities they care about.

Financial data The stipend is $1,500. Funds are applied as a credit to the student's HECUA program fees for the semester.

Duration 1 semester.

Additional information This program was established in 2006. Consortium members include Augsburg College (Minneapolis, Minnesota), Augustana College (Sioux Falls, South Dakota), Carleton College (Northfield, Minnesota), College of Saint Scholastica (Duluth, Minnesota), Colorado College (Colorado Springs, Colorado), Denison University (Granville, Ohio), Gustavus Adolphus College (St. Peter, Minnesota), Hamline University (St. Paul, Minnesota), Macalester College (St. Paul, Minnesota), Saint Mary's University (Winona, Minnesota), Saint Catherine University (St. Paul, Minnesota), Saint Olaf College (Northfield, Minnesota), Swarthmore College (Swarthmore, Pennsylvania), University of Minnesota (Minneapolis, Minnesota), University of Saint Thomas (St. Paul, Minnesota), and Viterbo University (La Crosse, Wisconsin).

Number awarded 2 each year.

Deadline April of each year for summer and fall programs; November of each year for January and spring programs.

[316]
SCIENCE APPLICATIONS INTERNATIONAL CORPORATION ENGINEERING SCHOLARSHIP

National Naval Officers Association-Washington, D.C.
   Chapter
Attn: Scholarship Program
2701 Park Center Drive, A1108
Alexandria, VA 22302
(703) 566-3840   Fax: (703) 566-3813
E-mail: Stephen.Williams@Navy.mil
Web: dcnnoa.memberlodge.com

Summary To provide financial assistance to Asian American and other minority high school seniors from the Washington, D.C. area who are interested in majoring in engineering at a college in any state.

Eligibility This program is open to minority seniors graduating from high schools in the Washington, D.C. metropolitan area who plan to enroll full time in an engineering program at an accredited 2- or 4-year college or university in any state. Applicants must have a GPA of 2.5 or higher and be U.S. citizens or permanent residents. Selection is based on academic achievement, community involvement, and financial need.

Financial data The stipend is $4,500.

Duration 1 year; nonrenewable.

Additional information Recipients are not required to join or affiliate with the military in any way. This program is sponsored by Science Applications International Corporation.

Number awarded 1 each year.

Deadline March of each year.

[317]
SCIENCE APPLICATIONS INTERNATIONAL CORPORATION SCIENCE AND MATHEMATICS SCHOLARSHIP

National Naval Officers Association-Washington, D.C.
   Chapter
Attn: Scholarship Program
2701 Park Center Drive, A1108
Alexandria, VA 22302
(703) 566-3840   Fax: (703) 566-3813
E-mail: Stephen.Williams@Navy.mil
Web: dcnnoa.memberlodge.com

Summary To provide financial assistance to Asian American and other minority high school seniors from the Washington, D.C. area who are interested in majoring in science or mathematics at a college in any state.

Eligibility This program is open to minority seniors graduating from high schools in the Washington, D.C. metropolitan area who plan to enroll full time at an accredited 2- or 4-year college or university in any state and major in science or mathematics. Applicants must have a GPA of 2.5 or higher and be U.S. citizens or permanent residents. Selection is based on academic achievement, community involvement, and financial need.

Financial data The stipend is $4,500.

Duration 1 year; nonrenewable.

Additional information Recipients are not required to join or affiliate with the military in any way. This program is sponsored by Science Applications International Corporation.

Number awarded   1 each year.

Deadline   March of each year.

[318]
SCOTTS COMPANY SCHOLARS PROGRAM

Golf Course Superintendents Association of America
Attn: Environmental Institute for Golf
1421 Research Park Drive
Lawrence, KS 66049-3859
(785) 832-4445   Toll Free: (800) 472-7878, ext. 4445
Fax: (785) 832-4448   E-mail: mwright@gcsaa.org
Web: www.gcsaa.org/students/Scholarships.aspx

Summary   To provide financial assistance and summer work experience to high school seniors and college students, particularly those from diverse backgrounds, who are preparing for a career in golf management.

Eligibility   This program is open to high school seniors and college students (freshmen, sophomores, and juniors) who are interested in preparing for a career in golf management (the "green industry"). Applicants should come from diverse ethnic, cultural, or socioeconomic backgrounds, defined to include women, minorities, and people with disabilities. Selection is based on cultural diversity, academic achievement, extracurricular activities, leadership, employment potential, essay responses, and letters of recommendation. Financial need is not considered. Finalists are selected for summer internships and then compete for scholarships.

Financial data   The finalists receive a $500 award to supplement their summer internship income. Scholarship stipends are $2,500.

Duration   1 year.

Additional information   The program is funded from a permanent endowment established by Scotts Company. Finalists are responsible for securing their own internships.

Number awarded   5 finalists, of whom 2 receive scholarships, are selected each year.

Deadline   February of each year.

[319]
SEO CAREER PROGRAM

Sponsors for Educational Opportunity
Attn: Career Program
55 Exchange Place
New York, NY 10005
(212) 979-2040   Toll Free: (800) 462-2332
Fax: (646) 706-7113
E-mail: careerprogram@seo-usa.org
Web: www.seo-usa.org/Career/Career_Program_Overview

Summary   To provide Asian Americans and other undergraduate students of color with an opportunity to gain summer work experience in selected fields.

Eligibility   This program is open to sophomores, juniors, and seniors of color at colleges and universities in the United States. Applicants must be interested in a summer internship in 1 of the following fields: corporate financial leadership, banking and asset management (including accounting/finance, asset management, information technology, investment banking, investment research, sales and trading, or transaction services), or nonprofit sector. They should be able to demonstrate analytical and quantitative skills, interpersonal and community skills, maturity, and a cumulative

GPA of 3.0 or higher. Along with their application, they must submit 1) information on their extracurricular and employment experience; 2) an essay of 75 to 100 words on how the program area to which they are applying relates to their professional goals; and 3) an essay of 250 to 400 words on either an example of a time when they had to operate outside their "comfort zone" or their definition of success. Personal interviews are required.

Financial data   Interns receive a competitive stipend.

Duration   10 weeks during the summer.

Additional information   This program was established in 1980. Most banking and asset management internships are available in the New York City metropolitan area (including Connecticut and New Jersey), but corporate financial leadership and nonprofit sector placements are nationwide.

Number awarded   Varies each year; recently, more than 300 internships were available at more than 40 firms.

Deadline   October of each year for most programs; December of each year for sales and trading or nonprofit sector.

[320]
SHIGEKI "SHAKE" USHIO MEMORIAL LEADERSHIP SCHOLARSHIP

Japanese American Citizens League
Attn: National Scholarship Awards
1765 Sutter Street
San Francisco, CA 94115
(415) 921-5225   Fax: (415) 931-4671
E-mail: jacl@jacl.org
Web: www.jacl.org/edu/scholar.htm

Summary   To provide financial assistance for college to student members of the Japanese American Citizens League (JACL) who are high school seniors and have demonstrated outstanding leadership qualities.

Eligibility   This program is open to JACL members who are high school seniors interested in attending a college, university, trade school, business college, or other institution of higher learning. Applicants must submit information on their involvement in JACL and a 2-page essay on a topic that changes annually but relates to Japanese Americans. They must be able to demonstrate outstanding leadership qualities. Selection is based on their essay, academic history, extracurricular activities, JACL involvement, scholastic honors, and a letter of recommendation.

Financial data   Stipends generally average approximately $2,000.

Duration   1 year; nonrenewable.

Additional information   This program was established in 2003.

Number awarded   1 each year.

Deadline   February of each year.

[321]
SHIGERU "SHIG" NAKAHIRA MEMORIAL SCHOLARSHIP

Japanese American Citizens League
Attn: National Scholarship Awards
1765 Sutter Street
San Francisco, CA 94115
(415) 921-5225   Fax: (415) 931-4671
E-mail: jacl@jacl.org
Web: www.jacl.org/edu/scholar.htm

Summary To provide financial assistance for college to student members of the Japanese American Citizens League (JACL).

Eligibility This program is open to JACL members who are currently enrolled at a college, university, trade school, business college, or other institution of higher learning. Applicants must submit information on their involvement in JACL and a 2-page essay on a topic that changes annually but relates to Japanese Americans. Selection is based on that essay, academic history, extracurricular activities, JACL involvement, scholastic honors, and a letter of recommendation.

Financial data Stipends generally average approximately $2,000.

Duration 1 year; nonrenewable.

Additional information This program was established in 2009.

Number awarded At least 1 each year.

Deadline March of each year.

[322]
SHUI KUEN AND ALLEN CHIN SCHOLARSHIP

Asian Pacific Fund
Attn: Scholarship Coordinator
225 Bush Street, Suite 590
San Francisco, CA 94104
(415) 433-6859   Toll Free: (800) 286-1688
Fax: (415) 433-2425
E-mail: scholarship@asianpacificfund.org
Web: www.asianpacificfund.org

Summary To provide financial assistance for college to students who have worked or whose parent has worked in an Asian restaurant.

Eligibility This program is open to students who are entering or currently enrolled full time in an undergraduate degree program at an accredited college or university in any state. Applicants or their parents must have worked at an Asian restaurant (Asian-owned or Asian cuisine). They must have a GPA of 3.0 or higher and be able to demonstrate financial need. Along with their application, they must submit essays of 250 to 500 words each on 1) their experience as a restaurant worker or child of a restaurant worker and how that experience has affected their values, ethics, or world view; 2) any community service or school studies or projects that have shaped their ideas about Asian Americans and the Asian American community; and 3) any unusual family or personal circumstances that have affected their achievement in school, work, or school activities. Preference is given to students who have been involved in community advocacy and social justice work on behalf of Asian American, immigrant, gay and lesbian, or other progressive causes. U.S. citizenship or permanent resident status is required.

Financial data The stipend is $1,000 per year.

Duration 1 year; recipients may reapply.

Additional information This scholarship was first awarded in 2007.

Number awarded Up to 2 each year.

Deadline March of each year.

[323]
SMITHSONIAN MINORITY STUDENT INTERNSHIP

Smithsonian Institution
Attn: Office of Fellowships
Victor Building, Suite 9300, MRC 902
P.O. Box 37012
Washington, DC 20013-7012
(202) 633-7070   Fax: (202) 633-7069
E-mail: siofg@si.edu
Web: www.si.edu/ofg/Applications/MIP/MIPapp.htm

Summary To provide Asian American and other minority undergraduate or graduate students with the opportunity to work on research or museum procedure projects in specific areas of history, art, or science at the Smithsonian Institution.

Eligibility Internships are offered to minority students who are actively engaged in graduate study at any level or in upper-division undergraduate study. An overall GPA of 3.0 or higher is generally expected. Applicants must be interested in conducting research in specified fields of interest to the Smithsonian.

Financial data The program provides a stipend of $550 per week; travel allowances may also be offered.

Duration 10 weeks during the summer or academic year.

Additional information Eligible fields of study currently include animal behavior, ecology, and environmental science (including an emphasis on the tropics); anthropology (including archaeology); astrophysics and astronomy; earth sciences and paleobiology; evolutionary and systematic biology; history of science and technology; history of art (especially American, contemporary, African, Asian, and 20th-century art); American crafts and decorative arts; social and cultural history of the United States; and folklife.

Number awarded Varies each year.

Deadline January of each year for summer or fall; September of each year for spring.

[324]
SOO YUEN BENEVOLENT ASSOCIATION SCHOLARSHIPS

Soo Yuen Benevolent Association
806 Clay Street
San Francisco, CA 94108
(415) 421-0602   Fax: (415) 421-0606
Web: sooyuen.org/scholarship

Summary To provide financial assistance for college to children of members of the Soo Yuen Benevolent Association.

Eligibility This program is open to high school seniors whose parents have been members of the association for at least 1 year. Membership in the association is limited to members of the following clans: Louie (including Loui, Lui, Lei), Fong (including Fang), and Kwong (including Kwang, Kuang, and Kong). Applicants must have a GPA of 3.0 or higher and be planning to attend college in any state. As part of the selection process, a personal interview may be required.

Financial data A stipend is awarded (amount not specified).

Duration 1 year.

Number awarded 1 or more each year.

Deadline January of each year.

[325]
SOUTHERN REGION KOREAN AMERICAN SCHOLARSHIPS

Korean American Scholarship Foundation
Southern Region
c/o Professor Myung Hoon Kim, Scholarship Committee Chair
1500 Chipping Court
Rosewell, GA 30076
(770) 274-5059   Fax: (770) 551-7097
E-mail: southern@kasf.org
Web: www.kasf.org/application_set.html

Summary To provide financial assistance to Korean American students from any state who are working on or planning to work on an undergraduate or graduate degree in any field at a school in southern states.

Eligibility This program is open to Korean American students who are currently enrolled in a college or university in the southern states as full-time undergraduate or graduate students. Applicants may reside anywhere in the United States as long as they attend school in the southern region: Alabama, Arkansas, Florida, Georgia, Louisiana, Mississippi, Oklahoma, South Carolina, Tennessee, and Texas. Selection is based on academic achievement, school activities, community service, and financial need.

Financial data Stipends are $1,000 for undergraduate, graduate, or professional students or $500 for high school seniors.

Duration 1 year; renewable.

Number awarded Varies each year; recently, 39 of these scholarships were awarded.

Deadline May of each year.

[326]
STANFORD CHEN INTERNSHIP GRANTS

Asian American Journalists Association
Attn: Student Programs Coordinator
5 Third Street, Suite 1108
San Francisco, CA 94103
(415) 346-2051, ext. 102   Fax: (415) 346-6343
E-mail: programs@aaja.org
Web: www.aaja.org/programs/internships

Summary To provide supplemental grants to student members of the Asian American Journalists Association (AAJA) working as interns at small or medium-size news organizations.

Eligibility This program is open to AAJA members who are college juniors, seniors, or graduate students with a serious intent to prepare for a career in journalism (print, online, broadcast, or photography). Applicants must have already secured an internship with a print company (daily circulation less than 100,000) or broadcast company (market smaller than the top 50). Along with their application, they must sub-

mit a 200-word essay on the kind of experience they expect as an intern at a small to medium-size media company, their career goals, and why AAJA's mission is important to them; a resume; verification of the internship; a letter of recommendation; and a statement of financial need.

Financial data The grant is $1,750. Funds are to be used for living expenses or transportation.

Duration Summer months.

Additional information This program was established in 1998.

Number awarded 1 each year.

Deadline April of each year.

[327]
STATE COUNCIL ON ADAPTED PHYSICAL EDUCATION CULTURAL DIVERSITY STUDENT SCHOLARSHIP

California Association for Health, Physical Education, Recreation and Dance
Attn: State Council on Adapted Physical Education
1501 El Camino Avenue, Suite 3
Sacramento, CA 95815-2748
(916) 922-3596   Toll Free: (800) 499-3596 (within CA)
Fax: (916) 922-0133   E-mail: cahperd@cahperd.org
Web: www.napeconference.org/Awards.htm

Summary To provide financial assistance to Asian American and other culturally diverse members of the California Association for Health, Physical Education, Recreation and Dance (CAHPERD) who are preparing to become a student teacher in the field of adapted physical education.

Eligibility This program is open to CAHPERD members who are attending a California college or university and specializing in the field of adapted physical education. Applicants must be members of an ethnic or cultural minority group (e.g., Asian American, African American, American Indian/Native American, Mexican American, other Latino, Pacific Islander). They must be planning to become a student teacher during the following academic year. Along with their application, they must submit a 300-word statement of their professional goals and philosophy of physical education for individuals with disabilities. Selection is based on academic proficiency; leadership ability; personal qualities; school, community, and professional activities; and experience and interest in working with individuals with disabilities.

Financial data The stipend is $500.

Duration 1 year.

Number awarded 1 each year.

Deadline January of each year.

[328]
STRAIGHTFORWARD MEDIA MINORITY SCHOLARSHIPS

StraightForward Media
508 Seventh Street, Suite 202
Rapid City, SD 57701
(605) 348-3042   Fax: (605) 348-3043
E-mail: info@straightforwardmedia.com
Web: www.straightforwardmedia.com/minority

Summary To provide financial assistance for college to Asian Americans and members of other minority groups who submit essays on why they chose their field of study.

Eligibility This program is open to members of ethnic or racial minority groups. Applicants must be attending or planning to attend a community college, university, vocational/technical school, or continuing education program. Along with their application, they must submit online essays (no minimum or maximum word limit) on 1) why they chose their field of study over other educational opportunities and what contribution they will make to the world, and 2) how this scholarship will help them meet their educational and professional goals. Financial need is not considered in the selection process.

Financial data The stipend is $500. Funds are paid directly to the student.

Duration 1 year.

Number awarded 4 each year: 1 for each award cycle.

Deadline February, May, August, or November of each year.

[329]
STUDENT JOURNALISM AWARDS

South Asian Journalists Association
c/o Aseem Chhabra, Awards Committee Chair
4315 46th Street, Apartment E10
Sunnyside, NY 11104-2015
E-mail: chhabs@aol.com
Web: www.saja.org/programs/awards

Summary To recognize and reward outstanding reporting on any subject by undergraduate and graduate students of south Asian origin.

Eligibility Eligible to be considered for these awards are print, broadcast, new media, and photographic works submitted by south Asian students in the United States or Canada (on any subject). Entries must have been completed as part of a class assignment.

Financial data Prizes are $500 for the winner and $250 for the finalists.

Duration The competition is held annually.

Number awarded 3 each year.

Deadline March of each year.

[330]
STUDENT OPPORTUNITY SCHOLARSHIPS FOR ETHNIC MINORITY GROUPS

Presbyterian Church (USA)
Attn: Office of Financial Aid for Studies
100 Witherspoon Street, Room M-052
Louisville, KY 40202-1396
(502) 569-5224   Toll Free: (888) 728-7228, ext. 5224
Fax: (502) 569-8766   E-mail: finaid@pcusa.org
Web: www.pcusa.org

Summary To provide financial assistance to upper-division college students who are Presbyterians, especially those of Asian American and other racial/ethnic minority heritages majoring in designated fields.

Eligibility This program is open to members of the Presbyterian Church (USA), especially those from racial/ethnic minority groups (Asian American, African American, Hispanic American, Native American, Alaska Native). Applicants must be able to demonstrate financial need, be entering their junior or senior year of college as full-time students, and have a GPA of 2.5 or higher. Preference is given to applicants who are majoring in the following fields of interest to missions of

the church: education, health services and sciences, religious studies, sacred music, social services, and social sciences.

Financial data Stipends range up to $3,000 per year, depending upon the financial need of the recipient.

Duration 1 year; may be renewed for up to 3 additional years if the recipient continues to need financial assistance and demonstrates satisfactory academic progress.

Number awarded Varies each year.

Deadline June of each year.

[331]
SUMMER TRANSPORTATION INTERNSHIP PROGRAM FOR DIVERSE GROUPS

Department of Transportation
Attn: Summer Transportation Internship Program for Diverse Groups
HAHR-40, Room E63-433
1200 New Jersey Avenue, S.E.
Washington, DC 20590
(202) 366-2907   E-mail: lafayette.melton@dot.gov
Web: www.fhwa.dot.gov/education/stipdg.htm

Summary To enable Asian American undergraduate, graduate, and law students, as well as those from other diverse groups, to gain work experience during the summer at facilities of the U.S. Department of Transportation (DOT).

Eligibility This program is open to all qualified applicants, but it is designed to provide women, persons with disabilities, and members of diverse social and ethnic groups with summer opportunities in transportation. Applicants must be U.S. citizens currently enrolled in a degree-granting program of study at an accredited institution of higher learning at the undergraduate (community or junior college, university, college, or Tribal College or University) or graduate level. Undergraduates must be entering their junior or senior year; students attending a Tribal or community college must have completed their first year of school; law students must be entering their second or third year of school. Students who will graduate during the spring or summer are not eligible unless they have been accepted for enrollment in graduate school. The program accepts applications from students in all majors who are interested in working on transportation-related topics and issues. Preference is given to students with a GPA of 3.0 or higher. Undergraduates must submit a 1-page essay on their transportation interests and how participation in this program will enhance their educational and career plans and goals. Graduate students must submit a writing sample representing their educational and career plans and goals. Law students must submit a legal writing sample.

Financial data The stipend is $4,000 for undergraduates or $5,000 for graduate and law students. The program also provides housing and reimbursement of travel expenses from interns' homes to their assignment location.

Duration 10 weeks during the summer.

Additional information Assignments are at the DOT headquarters in Washington, D.C., a selected modal administration, or selected field offices around the country.

Number awarded 80 to 100 each year.

Deadline January of each year.

[332]
SUMMER UNDERGRADUATE RESEARCH FELLOWSHIPS IN ORGANIC CHEMISTRY

American Chemical Society
Division of Organic Chemistry
1155 16th Street, N.W.
Washington, DC 20036
(202) 872-4401   Toll Free: (800) 227-5558, ext. 4401
E-mail: division@acs.org
Web: www.organicdivision.org/?nd=p_surf_program

Summary To provide an opportunity for college juniors (especially Asian American and other minority students) to work on a research project in organic chemistry during the summer.

Eligibility This program is open to students who are currently enrolled as juniors at a college or university in the United States and are nominated by their school. Nominees must be interested in conducting a mentored research project in organic chemistry at the home institution during the following summer. Along with their application, they must submit brief statements on the project they propose to undertake, their background that has prepared them to do this work, their proposed methodology, and how a summer research project fits into their long-range plans. U.S. citizenship or permanent resident status is required. Selection is based on demonstrated interest and talent in organic chemistry, merit and feasibility of the research project, commitment of a faculty mentor to support the student, academic record (particularly in organic chemistry and related sciences), and importance of the award in facilitating the personal and career plans of the student. Applications from minorities are especially encouraged.

Financial data Grants range up to $5,000. Funding includes the costs of a trip by all participants to an industrial campus in the fall for a dinner, award session, scientific talks, a tour of the campus, and a poster session where the results of the summer research investigations are presented.

Duration Summer months.

Additional information Current corporate sponsors of this program include Pfizer, Roche, Cubist, Novartis, and Amgen.

Number awarded 16 each year.

Deadline January of each year.

[333]
SYNOD OF THE COVENANT ETHNIC STUDENT SCHOLARSHIPS

Synod of the Covenant
Attn: Ministries in Higher Education
1911 Indianwood Circle, Suite B
Maumee, OH 43537-4063
(419) 754-4050
Toll Free: (800) 848-1030 (within MI and OH)
Fax: (419) 754-4051
Web: www.synodofthecovenant.org

Summary To provide financial assistance to Asian Americans and other minorities working on an undergraduate degree (with priority given to Presbyterian applicants from Ohio and Michigan).

Eligibility This program is open to ethnic minority students working full or part time on a baccalaureate degree or certifi-

cation at a college, university, or vocational school in any state. Applicants must have a GPA of 3.0 or higher and be able to demonstrate participation in a Presbyterian church. Priority is given to Presbyterian applicants from the states of Michigan and Ohio. Financial need is considered in the selection process.

Financial data The maximum amount allowed within a calendar year is $600 (for full-time students in their first year), $800 (for renewals to full-time students), or $400 (for part-time students). Funds are made payable to the session for distribution.

Duration Students are eligible to receive scholarships 1 time per year, up to a maximum of 5 years. Renewals are granted provided 1) the completed application is received before the deadline date, 2) the recipient earned at least a 2.0 GPA last year, and 3) the application contains evidence of Presbyterian church participation and continued spiritual development.

Number awarded Varies each year.

Deadline August of each year for fall semester; January of each year for spring semester.

[334]
TAIWON SUHR JOURNALISM SCHOLARSHIP

Philip Jaisohn Memorial Foundation
Attn: Education and Scholarship Committee
6705 Old York Road
Philadelphia, PA 19126
(215) 224-2000   Fax: (215) 224-9164
E-mail: jaisohnhouse@gmail.com
Web: jaisohn.org

Summary To provide financial assistance to Korean American undergraduate and graduate students who are working on a degree in journalism.

Eligibility This program is open to Korean American undergraduate and graduate students who are currently enrolled at a college or university in the United States. Applicants must be working on a degree in journalism. They must be able to demonstrate academic excellence, leadership and service to their school and community, and financial need. Along with their application, they must submit an essay on either "Who is Dr. Jaisohn to Me," or "The Significance of Dr. Jaisohn's Ideal to Korean Americans." They must also submit a brief statement on how they can contribute to and be involved in the activities of the Philip Jaisohn Memorial Foundation.

Financial data The stipend is $1,000.

Duration 1 year.

Number awarded 1 each year.

Deadline November of each year.

[335]
TARGETED OPPORTUNITY PROGRAM (TOPJOBS)

Wisconsin Office of State Employment Relations
Attn: Division of Affirmative Action Workforce Planning
101 East Wilson Street, Fourth Floor
P.O. Box 7855
Madison, WI 53707-7855
(608) 267-1005 Fax: (608) 267-1020
E-mail: Claire.Dehnert@wisconsin.gov
Web: oser.state.wi.us/category.asp?linkcatid=342

Summary To provide an opportunity for Asian Americans, other minorities, women, and persons with disabilities to gain summer work experience with agencies of the state of Wisconsin.

Eligibility This program is open to women, ethnic/racial minorities (Black or African American, Asian, Native Hawaiian or other Pacific Islander, American Indian or Alaska Native, or Hispanic or Latino), and persons with disabilities. Applicants must be juniors, seniors, or graduate students at an accredited 4-year college or university or second-year students in the second year of a 2-year technical or vocational school program. They must be 1) Wisconsin residents enrolled full time at a school in Wisconsin or any other state, or 2) residents of other states who are enrolled full time at a school in Wisconsin.

Financial data Most internships provide a competitive stipend.

Duration Summer months.

Additional information This program was established in 1974. Relevant fields of study include, but are not limited to, the liberal arts and sciences (e.g., history, mathematics, library science, political science, philosophy, physics, psychology, social services, social work, sociology, women's studies); agriculture and natural resources (e.g., animal and dairy science, biology, botany, chemistry, geography, entomology, environmental studies, horticulture, landscape architecture, microbiology, plant pathology, soil science, urban planning, water resources management, wildlife ecology); business (e.g., accounting, business management, economics, finance, human resources, marketing, public administration, real estate); criminal justice; education; health care (including nursing); engineering; information systems and computers; journalism and communications; and law.

Number awarded Varies each year. Since the program was established, it has placed more than 2,500 students with more than 30 different agencies and universities throughout the state.

Deadline February of each year.

[336]
TEACHER QUEST SCHOLARSHIP

Brown Foundation for Educational Equity, Excellence and Research
Attn: Scholarship Committee
1515 S.E. Monroe
Topeka, KS 66615
(785) 235-3939 Fax: (785) 235-1001
E-mail: brownfound@juno.com
Web: brownvboard.org

Summary To provide financial assistance to Asian American and other undergraduate or graduate students of color who are interested in preparing for a teaching career.

Eligibility This program is open to members of minority groups who are enrolled at least half time at an institution of higher education with an accredited teacher education program. Applicants must be enrolled at the undergraduate, graduate, or post-baccalaureate level and have a GPA of 3.0 or higher. Along with their application, they must submit brief essays on 1) their involvement in school, community, and/or other activities and how those activities have prepared them to be an educator; 2) why they aspire to a career in education, their goals, and the level at which they plan to teach; and 3) how they think *Brown v. Board of Education* has influenced their own life experiences. Selection is based on the essays; GPA; school, community, and leisure activities; career plans and goals in education; and recommendations.

Financial data The stipend is $1,000 per year.

Duration 2 years.

Additional information The first Brown Foundation Scholarships were awarded in 1989. The current program replaced the Brown Foundation Academic Scholarships in 2009.

Number awarded Varies each year; recently, 5 of these scholarships were awarded.

Deadline March of each year.

[337]
TENNESSEE MINORITY TEACHING FELLOWS PROGRAM

Tennessee Student Assistance Corporation
Parkway Towers
404 James Robertson Parkway, Suite 1510
Nashville, TN 37243-0820
(615) 741-1346 Toll Free: (800) 342-1663
Fax: (615) 741-6101 E-mail: TSAC.Aidinfo@tn.gov
Web: www.tn.gov

Summary To provide funding to Asian American and other minority residents of Tennessee who wish to attend college in the state to prepare for a career in the teaching field.

Eligibility This program is open to minority residents of Tennessee who are either high school seniors planning to enroll full time at a college or university in the state or continuing college students at a Tennessee college or university. High school seniors must have a GPA of 2.75 or higher and an ACT score of at least 18, a combined mathematics and critical reading SAT score of at least 860, or a rank in the top 25% of their high school class. Continuing college students must have a college GPA of 2.5 or higher. All applicants must agree to teach at the K-12 level in a Tennessee public school following graduation from college. Along with their application, they must submit a 250-word essay on why they chose teaching as a profession. U.S. citizenship is required.

Financial data The funding is $5,000 per year. Recipients incur an obligation to teach at the preK-12 level in a Tennessee public school 1 year for each year the award is received.

Duration 1 year; may be renewed for up to 3 additional years, provided the recipient maintains full-time enrollment and a cumulative GPA of 2.5 or higher.

Additional information This program was established in 1989.

Number awarded   20 new awards are granted each year.

Deadline   April of each year.

[338]
TEXAS CHAPTER SCHOLARSHIPS

Asian American Journalists Association-Texas Chapter
c/o Scott Nishimura, Scholarship Committee Chair
Fort Worth Star-Telegram
P.O. Box 1870
Fort Worth, TX 76115
(817) 390-7808   E-mail: snishimura@star-telegram.com
Web: www.aajatexas.org/programs/student-programs

Summary   To provide financial assistance to students from designated southwestern states who are working on an undergraduate or graduate degree in journalism and can demonstrate an awareness of Asian American issues.

Eligibility   This program is open to graduating high school seniors, undergraduates, and graduate students who are either 1) residents of Arkansas, Louisiana, New Mexico, Oklahoma, or Texas; or 2) attending or planning to attend an accredited college or university in those states. Applicants are not required to be members of the Asian American Journalists Association (AAJA) when they apply. Along with their application, they must submit a 250-word autobiography that explains why they are interested in a career in journalism, a 500-word essay on the role of ethnic diversity in news coverage (both for the subjects of the news events and also the journalists involved), their most recent official transcript, 2 letters of recommendation, and a resume. Work samples to be submitted are 3 legible clips from print journalism students; 3 to 5 prints or slides with captions or descriptions from print photojournalism students; 2 taped VHS or DVD excerpts with corresponding scripts from television broadcast students; 2 edited VHS or DVD excepts from television photojournalism students; 3 taped cassette excerpts with corresponding scripts from radio broadcast students; or 3 legible online articles from web journalism students. Selection is based on commitment to the field of journalism, awareness of Asian American issues, journalistic ability, and scholastic ability.

Financial data   The stipend is $1,000.

Duration   1 year.

Additional information   Scholarship winners are also given a 1-year free membership in the AAJA Texas chapter.

Number awarded   2 each year.

Deadline   May of each year.

[339]
THAI ALLIANCE IN AMERICA SCHOLARSHIPS

Asian & Pacific Islander American Scholarship Fund
1900 L Street, N.W., Suite 210
Washington, DC 20036-5002
(202) 986-6892   Toll Free: (877) 808-7032
Fax: (202) 530-0643   E-mail: info@apiasf.org
Web: www.apiasf.org/scholarship_apiasf_thai.html

Summary   To provide financial assistance to high school seniors of Thai heritage who are entering college for the first time.

Eligibility   This program is open to graduating high school seniors who are Thai Americans, Thai nationals studying in the United States, or descendants of Thai heritage. Applicants must be enrolling full time at an accredited 2- or 4-year

college or university in the United States as a first-year student. They must be U.S. citizens, nationals, permanent residents, or citizens of the Freely Associated States. In addition, they must complete the FAFSA and apply for federal financial aid. In the selection process, consideration is given to their record of helping the local Thai community. The program includes 1 scholarship reserved for a resident of Maryland, Virginia, or Washington, D.C.

Financial data   The stipend is $2,500.

Duration   1 year; nonrenewable.

Additional information   This scholarship is sponsored by the Thai Alliance in America.

Number awarded   2 each year: 1 to a resident of Maryland, Virginia, or Washington, D.C. and 1 to a resident of other states.

Deadline   January of each year.

[340]
THOMAS G. NEUSOM SCHOLARSHIPS

Conference of Minority Transportation Officials
Attn: National Scholarship Program
818 18th Street, N.W., Suite 850
Washington, DC 20006
(202) 530-0551   Fax: (202) 530-0617
Web: www.comto.org/news-youth.php

Summary   To provide financial assistance for college or graduate school to Asian American and other members of the Conference of Minority Transportation Officials (COMTO).

Eligibility   This program is open to undergraduate and graduate students who have been members of COMTO for at least 1 year. Applicants must be working on a degree in a field related to transportation with a GPA of 2.5 or higher. Along with their application, they must submit a cover letter with a 500-word statement of career goals. Financial need is not considered in the selection process. U.S. citizenship is required.

Financial data   The stipend is $5,500. Funds are paid directly to the recipient's college or university.

Duration   1 year.

Additional information   COMTO was established in 1971 to promote, strengthen, and expand the roles of minorities in all aspects of transportation. Recipients are expected to attend the COMTO National Scholarship Luncheon.

Number awarded   2 each year.

Deadline   April of each year.

[341]
THOMAS R. DARGAN SCHOLARSHIP

KATU-TV
Attn: Human Resources
2153 N.E. Sandy Boulevard
P.O. Box 2
Portland, OR 97207-0002
(503) 231-4222
Web: www.katu.com/about/scholarship

Summary   To provide financial assistance and work experience to Asian Americans and other minority students from Oregon and Washington who are studying broadcasting or communications in college.

Eligibility   This program is open to minority (Asian, Black/African American, Hispanic or Latino, Native Hawaiian or

Pacific Islander, American Indian or Alaska Native) U.S. citizens currently enrolled as a sophomore or higher at a 4-year college or university or an accredited community college in Oregon or Washington. Residents of Oregon or Washington enrolled at a school in any state are also eligible. Applicants must be majoring in broadcasting or communications and have a GPA of 3.0 or higher. Community college students must be enrolled in a broadcast curriculum that is transferable to a 4-year accredited university. Finalists will be interviewed. Selection is based on financial need, academic achievement, and an essay on personal and professional goals.

Financial data The stipend is $6,000. Funds are sent directly to the recipient's school.

Duration 1 year; recipients may reapply if they have maintained a GPA of 3.0 or higher.

Additional information Winners are also eligible for a paid internship in selected departments at Fisher Broadcasting/KATU in Portland, Oregon.

Number awarded 1 each year.

Deadline April of each year.

[342]
THZ FO FARM SCHOLARSHIP

Hawai'i Community Foundation
Attn: Scholarship Department
827 Fort Street Mall
Honolulu, HI 96813
(808) 537-6333   Toll Free: (888) 731-3863
Fax: (808) 521-6286
E-mail: scholarships@hcf-hawaii.org
Web: www.hawaiicommunityfoundation.org/scholarships

Summary To provide financial assistance to Hawaii residents of Chinese descent who are interested in working on an undergraduate or graduate degree in gerontology at a school in any state.

Eligibility This program is open to high school seniors, high school graduates, and college students in Hawaii who are of Chinese ancestry and interested in studying gerontology as full-time undergraduate or graduate students at a college or university in any state. Applicants must be able to demonstrate academic achievement (GPA of 2.7 or higher), good moral character, and financial need. Along with their application, they must submit a short statement indicating their reasons for attending college, their planned course of study, their career goals, and what community service means to them.

Financial data The amounts of the awards depend on the availability of funds and the need of the recipient. Recently, the average value of all scholarships awarded by the foundation was $2,041.

Duration 1 year.

Number awarded Varies each year; recently, 6 of these scholarships were awarded.

Deadline February of each year.

[343]
TONGAN CULTURAL SOCIETY SCHOLARSHIPS

Hawai'i Community Foundation
Attn: Scholarship Department
827 Fort Street Mall
Honolulu, HI 96813
(808) 537-6333   Toll Free: (888) 731-3863
Fax: (808) 521-6286
E-mail: scholarships@hcf-hawaii.org
Web: www.hawaiicommunityfoundation.org/scholarships

Summary To provide financial assistance to Hawaii residents of Tongan ancestry who are interested in attending college or graduate school in the state.

Eligibility This program is open to Hawaii residents of Tongan ancestry who are enrolled in or planning to enroll in an accredited college or university in Hawaii. Applicants must be full-time undergraduate or graduate students and able to demonstrate academic achievement (GPA of 2.7 or higher), good moral character, and financial need. Along with their application, they must submit a short statement indicating their reasons for attending college, their planned course of study, their career goals, and what community service means to them.

Financial data The amounts of the awards depend on the availability of funds and the need of the recipient. Recently, the average value of all scholarships awarded by the foundation was $2,041.

Duration 1 year.

Number awarded Varies each year; recently, 3 of these scholarships were awarded.

Deadline February of each year.

[344]
TRAILBLAZER SCHOLARSHIPS

Conference of Minority Transportation Officials
Attn: National Scholarship Program
818 18th Street, N.W., Suite 850
Washington, DC 20006
(202) 530-0551   Fax: (202) 530-0617
Web: www.comto.org/news-youth.php

Summary To provide financial assistance to Asian Americans and other minority undergraduate and graduate students working on a degree in a field related to transportation.

Eligibility This program is open to undergraduate and graduate students who are working on a degree in a field related to transportation with a GPA of 2.5 or higher. Along with their application, they must submit a cover letter with a 500-word statement of career goals. Financial need is not considered in the selection process. U.S. citizenship is required.

Financial data The stipend is $2,500. Funds are paid directly to the recipient's college or university.

Duration 1 year.

Additional information The Conference of Minority Transportation Officials (COMTO) was established in 1971 to promote, strengthen, and expand the roles of minorities in all aspects of transportation. Recipients are expected to attend the COMTO National Scholarship Luncheon.

Number awarded 2 each year.

Deadline April of each year.

[345]
UNITED HEALTH FOUNDATION APIASF SCHOLARSHIP

Asian & Pacific Islander American Scholarship Fund
1900 L Street, N.W., Suite 210
Washington, DC 20036-5002
(202) 986-6892   Toll Free: (877) 808-7032
Fax: (202) 530-0643   E-mail: info@apiasf.org
Web: www.apiasf.org/scholarship_apiasf_uhf.html

Summary To provide financial assistance to Asian and Pacific Islander Americans who are entering college for the first time to prepare for a career in the health field.

Eligibility This program is open to U.S. citizens, nationals, permanent residents, or citizens of the Freely Associated States who are of Asian or Pacific Islander heritage. Applicants must be enrolling full time at an accredited 2- or 4-year college or university in the United States as a first-year student; preference is given to students entering a 2-year institution and planning to transfer to a 4-year school. They must have a GPA of 2.7 or higher or the GED equivalent and be preparing for a career in the health field. In addition, they must complete the FAFSA and apply for federal financial aid. Preference is given to students who 1) demonstrate the intent to work in an underserved community; 2) are fluent in an Asian or Pacific Islander languages; or 3) reside in or attend college in the sponsor's priority states of California, Illinois, New Jersey, New York, or Texas.

Financial data The stipend is $2,500 per year.

Duration 2 years.

Additional information This scholarship is sponsored by the United Health Foundation and administered by the Asian & Pacific Islander American Scholarship Fund (APIASF).

Number awarded 1 each year.

Deadline January of each year.

[346]
UNITED METHODIST ETHNIC MINORITY SCHOLARSHIPS

United Methodist Church
Attn: General Board of Higher Education and Ministry
Office of Loans and Scholarships
1001 19th Avenue South
P.O. Box 340007
Nashville, TN 37203-0007
(615) 340-7344   Fax: (615) 340-7367
E-mail: umscholar@gbhem.org
Web: www.gbhem.org/loansandscholarships

Summary To provide financial assistance to Asian American and other undergraduate Methodist students of minority ancestry.

Eligibility This program is open to full-time undergraduate students at accredited colleges and universities in the United States who have been active, full members of a United Methodist Church for at least 1 year prior to applying. Applicants must have at least 1 parent who is African American, Hispanic, Asian, Native American, or Pacific Islander. They must have a GPA of 2.5 or higher and be able to demonstrate financial need. U.S. citizenship, permanent resident status, or membership in a central conference of the United Methodist Church is required. Selection is based on church member-

ship, involvement in church and community activities, GPA, and financial need.

Financial data A stipend is awarded (amount not specified).

Duration 1 year; recipients may reapply.

Number awarded Varies each year.

Deadline March of each year.

[347]
UNITED PARCEL SERVICE SCHOLARSHIP FOR MINORITY STUDENTS

Institute of Industrial Engineers
Attn: Scholarship Coordinator
3577 Parkway Lane, Suite 200
Norcross, GA 30092
(770) 449-0461, ext. 105   Toll Free: (800) 494-0460
Fax: (770) 441-3295   E-mail: bcameron@iienet.org
Web: www.iienet2.org/Details.aspx?id=857

Summary To provide financial assistance to Asian American and other minority undergraduates who are studying industrial engineering at a school in the United States, Canada, or Mexico.

Eligibility Eligible to be nominated are minority undergraduate students enrolled at any school in the United States and its territories, Canada, or Mexico, provided the school's engineering program is accredited by an agency recognized by the Institute of Industrial Engineers (IIE) and the student is pursuing a full-time course of study in industrial engineering with a GPA of at least 3.4. Nominees must have at least 5 full quarters or 3 full semesters remaining until graduation. Students may not apply directly for these awards; they must be nominated by the head of their industrial engineering department. Nominees must be IIE members. Selection is based on scholastic ability, character, leadership, potential service to the industrial engineering profession, and need for financial assistance.

Financial data The stipend is $4,000.

Duration 1 year.

Additional information Funding for this program is provided by the UPS Foundation.

Number awarded 1 each year.

Deadline Schools must submit nominations by November of each year.

[348]
UNITEDHEALTHCARE ASIAN INITIATIVE SUMMER INTERNSHIP PROGRAM

UnitedHealthcare
Attn: Summer Internship Program
202 Canal Street, Sixth Floor
New York, NY 10013
(646) 571-8268   E-mail: info@UnitedHealthcareSIP.com
Web: unitedhealthcaresip.com/students

Summary To provide summer work experience to high school students of Chinese, Korean, and south Asian heritage.

Eligibility This program is open to Chinese, Korean, and south Asian high school juniors and seniors who have a GPA of "B" or higher. Applicants may live in any state, but they must be eligible to work legally in the United States and available for a summer assignment with a hiring firm in New York

City. They must be fluent in English and able to converse in Mandarin, Cantonese, Korean, or a south Asian language. Selection is based on academic achievement, extracurricular and personal activities, ability to work will with others, willingness to learn, and computer literacy (especially using Asian language software).

Financial data Each company sets its own wage, but the sponsor recommends a stipend of $7.25 per hour.

Duration 7 weeks during the summer.

Additional information This program began in 1996.

Number awarded Varies each year.

Deadline May of each year.

[349]
UNIVERSITY SCHOLARSHIP PROGRAM

Filipino Women's League
Attn: Community Scholarship Committee
P.O. Box 419
Pearl City, HI 96782

Summary To provide financial assistance to Hawaii high school seniors who are of Filipino descent and are interested in attending a university in Hawaii.

Eligibility This program is open to Hawaii residents who are graduating high school seniors, of Filipino ancestry, and enrolling full time at a 4-year college or university in the state. Applicants must have a high school GPA of 3.5 or higher. Selection is based primarily on financial need; other selection criteria include scholastic achievement (measured by transcripts and SAT or ACT scores), educational goals, and extracurricular interests.

Financial data Stipends provide full or partial payment of tuition (to a maximum of $1,000 per year). Funds are paid directly to the financial aid office of the recipient's university.

Duration 1 year; nonrenewable.

Number awarded 1 or more each year.

Deadline March of each year.

[350]
UPS GOLD MOUNTAIN SCHOLARSHIP

Organization of Chinese Americans, Inc.
1322 18th Street, N.W.
Washington, DC 20036-1803
(202) 223-5500   Fax: (202) 296-0540
E-mail: oca@ocanational.org
Web: ocanational.org

Summary To provide financial assistance for college to Asian Pacific Americans who are the first person in their family to attend an institution of higher education.

Eligibility This program is open to graduating high school seniors of Asian and/or Pacific Islander ethnicity who are entering their first year at a college, university, or community college in the following fall. Applicants must be the first person in their immediate family to attend college, have a cumulative GPA of 3.0 or higher, be able to demonstrate financial need, and be a U.S. citizen, national, or permanent resident.

Financial data The stipend is $2,000.

Duration 1 year.

Additional information This program, established in 1999, is funded by the UPS Foundation and administered by the Organization of Chinese Americans (OCA).

Number awarded 12 each year.

Deadline April of each year.

[351]
UPS HALLMARK SCHOLARSHIPS

US Pan Asian American Chamber of Commerce
Attn: Scholarship Coordinator
1329 18th Street, N.W.
Washington, DC 20036
(202) 296-5221   Toll Free: (800) 696-7818
Fax: (202) 296-5225   E-mail: info@uspaacc.com
Web: celebrasianconference.com

Summary To provide financial assistance for college to Asian Pacific American high school seniors who demonstrate financial need.

Eligibility This program is open to high school seniors of Asian or Pacific Islander heritage who are U.S. citizens or permanent residents. Applicants must be planning to enroll full time at an accredited postsecondary educational institution in the United States. Along with their application, they must submit a 500-word essay on their background, achievements, and personal goals. Selection is based on academic excellence (GPA of 3.3 or higher), leadership in extracurricular activities, community service involvement, and financial need.

Financial data The maximum stipend is $5,000. Funds are paid directly to the recipient's college or university.

Duration 1 year.

Additional information This program, established in 2005, is sponsored by UPS. Funding is not provided for correspondence courses, Internet courses, or study in a country other than the United States.

Number awarded 2 each year.

Deadline March of each year.

[352]
USA FUNDS ACCESS TO EDUCATION SCHOLARSHIPS

Scholarship America
Attn: Scholarship Management Services
One Scholarship Way
P.O. Box 297
St. Peter, MN 56082
(507) 931-1682   Toll Free: (800) 537-4180
Fax: (507) 931-9168   E-mail: scholarship@usafunds.org
Web: www.usafunds.org

Summary To provide financial assistance to undergraduate and graduate students, especially Asian Americans, other minorities, and students with physical disabilities.

Eligibility This program is open to high school seniors and graduates who plan to enroll or are already enrolled in full- or half-time undergraduate or full-time graduate course work at an accredited 2- or 4-year college, university, or vocational/technical school. GED recipients are also eligible. Up to 50% of the awards are targeted at students who have a documented physical disability or are a member of an ethnic minority group, including but not limited to Native Hawaiian, Alaskan Native, Black/African American, Asian, Pacific Islander, American Indian, Hispanic/Latino, or multiracial. Residents of all 50 states, the District of Columbia, Puerto Rico, Guam, the U.S. Virgin Islands, and all U.S. territories and commonwealths are eligible. Applicants must also be U.S. citizens or eligible noncitizens and come from a family with an annual adjusted gross income of $35,000 or less. In addition to financial need, selection is based on past academic performance and future potential, leadership and participation in school and community activities, work experience, career and educational aspirations and goals, and unusual personal or family circumstances.

Financial data The stipend is $1,500 per year for full-time undergraduate or graduate students or $750 per year for half-time undergraduate students. Funds are paid jointly to the student and the school.

Duration 1 year; may be renewed until the student receives a final degree or certificate or until the total award to a student reaches $6,000, whichever comes first. Renewal requires the recipient to maintain a GPA of 2.5 or higher.

Additional information This program, established in 2000, is sponsored by USA Funds.

Number awarded Varies each year; recently, a total of $3.2 million was available for this program.

Deadline February of each year.

[353]
VAID FELLOWSHIPS

National Gay and Lesbian Task Force
Attn: The Task Force Policy Institute
80 Maiden Lane, Suite 1504
New York, NY 10038
(212) 604-9830   Fax: (212) 604-9831
E-mail: ngltf@ngltf.org
Web: www.thetaskforce.org

Summary To provide work experience to undergraduate and graduate students or professionals (especially Asian Americans and other minorities) who are interested in participating in the leadership of people of color in the progressive movement for gay, lesbian, bisexual, and transgender (GLBT) equality.

Eligibility Applicants must be enrolled in a degree program at least half time as a law, graduate, or undergraduate student or have successfully completed a law, graduate, or undergraduate degree within the preceding 12 months. They should have 1) a desire to work in a multicultural environment where commitment to diversity based on race, ethnic origin, gender, age, sexual orientation, and physical ability is an important institutional value; 2) demonstrated leadership in progressive and/or GLBT communities; 3) extensive research, writing, and critical thinking skills; 4) knowledge of, and commitment to, GLBT issues; and 5) computer proficiency in word processing, database work, e-mail, and Internet research. The program supports and recognizes the leadership of people of color and other emerging leaders in public policy, legal, and social science research.

Financial data The stipend ranges from $200 to $400 per week ($10 per hour). Fellows are responsible for their own housing and living expenses.

Duration Summer fellowships are 40 hours per week and spring/fall fellowships are 20 hours per week.

Additional information The Policy Institute of the National Gay and Lesbian Task Force (NGLTF), founded in 1995, is the largest think tank in the United States engaged in research, policy analysis, and strategic action to advance equality and understanding of GLBT people. Its primary pro-

grams are the racial and economic justice initiative, the family policy program, and the aging initiative. In addition to their primary roles of providing research and analysis, all 3 programs work closely with NGLTF colleagues in Washington, D.C. and other allies on advocacy and legislative efforts to actively change laws and policies affecting GLBT people.

Number awarded 3 fellows are selected each session.

Deadline April for the summer, July for the fall, and November for the spring.

[354]
VANGUARD MINORITY SCHOLARSHIP PROGRAM

Scholarship America
Attn: Scholarship Management Services
One Scholarship Way
P.O. Box 297
St. Peter, MN 56082
(507) 931-1682   Toll Free: (800) 537-4180
Fax: (507) 931-9168
Web: sms.scholarshipamerica.org/vanguard

Summary To provide financial assistance to Asian American and other minority students working on an undergraduate degree in specified fields.

Eligibility This program is open to U.S. citizens and permanent residents who are members of racial or ethnic minorities. Applicants must be entering their junior or senior year as a full-time student at an accredited 4-year college or university in the United States and have a GPA of 3.0 or higher. They must be working on a degree in accounting, business, economics, or finance. Selection is based on academic record, demonstrated leadership and participation in school and community activities, honors, work experience, a statement of goals and aspirations, unusual personal or family circumstances, recommendations, and a resume; financial need is not considered. Students who attended a 2-year college while working on a bachelor's degree are not eligible.

Financial data The stipend ranges up to $10,000.

Duration 1 year; nonrenewable.

Additional information This program, established in 2004, is sponsored by Vanguard Group, Inc.

Number awarded Up to 10 each year.

Deadline November of each year.

[355]
VERA TRAN MEMORIAL SCHOLARSHIP

Vietnamese American Scholarship Foundation
P.O. Box 429
Stafford, TX 77497
E-mail: scholarships@vietscholarships.org
Web: www.vietscholarships.org/scholarships.html

Summary To provide financial assistance to high school seniors of Vietnamese descent who plan to attend college in any state.

Eligibility This program is open to seniors graduating from high schools in any state who are of Vietnamese descent. Applicants must be planning to enroll at an accredited 4-year college or university in any state. Along with their application, they must submit a 2,000-word essay on the most valuable lesson they have learned about the world or about themselves through community service. Selection is based on dedication to academic excellence, commitment to community service, passion for learning, and compassion and desire to help others.

Financial data The stipend is $2,000.

Duration 1 year; nonrenewable.

Number awarded 1 each year.

Deadline April of each year.

[356]
VERIZON APIASF SCHOLARSHIP

Asian & Pacific Islander American Scholarship Fund
1900 L Street, N.W., Suite 210
Washington, DC 20036-5002
(202) 986-6892   Toll Free: (877) 808-7032
Fax: (202) 530-0643   E-mail: info@apiasf.org
Web: www.apiasf.org/scholarship_apiasf_verizon.html

Summary To provide financial assistance to Asian and Pacific Islander Americans who are enrolled at or entering college.

Eligibility This program is open to U.S. citizens, nationals, permanent residents, or citizens of the Freely Associated States who are of Asian or Pacific Islander heritage. Applicants must be enrolling full time at an accredited 2- or 4-year college or university in the United States; preference is given to students entering their sophomore, junior, or senior year, but incoming freshmen are also eligible. They must have a GPA of 3.0 or higher or the GED equivalent. In addition, they must complete the FAFSA and apply for federal financial aid. Preference is given to residents of Maine, New Hampshire, New Jersey, Washington, and Washington, D.C. and of selected cities and counties within California, Florida, Massachusetts, New York, Pennsylvania, Texas, and Virginia.

Financial data The stipend is $3,000.

Duration 1 year.

Additional information This scholarship is sponsored by Verizon.

Number awarded 1 or more each year.

Deadline January of each year.

[357]
VERIZON SCHOLARSHIPS

Organization of Chinese Americans, Inc.
1322 18th Street, N.W.
Washington, DC 20036-1803
(202) 223-5500   Fax: (202) 296-0540
E-mail: oca@ocanational.org
Web: ocanational.org

Summary To provide financial assistance to upper-division Asian Pacific American students who are majoring in fields related to business or engineering.

Eligibility This program is open to students of Asian and/or Pacific Islander ethnicity entering their junior or senior year at a college or university in the following fall. Applicants must be majoring in accounting, business administration, computer electronics, computer engineering, computer information systems, computer programming, computer science, economics, electrical engineering, finance, human resources management, industrial engineering, information technology, international business, management information systems, marketing, mechanical engineering, or network administration. They must have a cumulative GPA of 3.0 or higher and be able to

demonstrate financial need, academic achievement, leadership, and commitment to community service. U.S. citizenship or permanent resident status is required. Students with disabilities are also highly encouraged to apply.

Financial data The stipend is $2,000.

Duration 1 year.

Additional information This program, established in 2002, is funded by the Verizon Foundation and administered by the Organization of Chinese Americans (OCA).

Number awarded 10 each year.

Deadline April of each year.

[358]
VINCENT CHIN SCHOLARSHIP

Asian American Journalists Association
Attn: Student Programs Coordinator
5 Third Street, Suite 1108
San Francisco, CA 94103
(415) 346-2051, ext. 102   Fax: (415) 346-6343
E-mail: programs@aaja.org
Web: www.aaja.org/programs/scholarships

Summary To provide financial assistance to student members of the Asian American Journalists Association (AAJA) who are high school seniors, undergraduates, or graduate students and interested in preparing for a career in journalism.

Eligibility This program is open to AAJA members who are working or planning to work full time on an undergraduate or graduate degree in journalism. Applicants must submit a 500-word essay on their involvement or interest in the Asian American community and how, if they are awarded this scholarship, they would keep Vincent Chin's memory alive through their journalism work. Print applicants must submit up to 4 photocopied or printed articles; broadcast applicants must submit up to 3 stories (total length less than 10 minutes) copied on CDs; photojournalism applicants must submit a portfolio with no more than 10 entries. Selection is based on academic achievement, commitment to journalism, sensitivity to Asian American and Pacific Islander issues, demonstrated journalistic ability, and financial need.

Financial data The stipend is $500.

Duration 1 year.

Number awarded 1 each year.

Deadline May of each year.

[359]
VIRGINIA TEACHING SCHOLARSHIP LOAN PROGRAM

Virginia Department of Education
Division of Teacher Education and Licensure
Attn: Director of Teacher Education
P.O. Box 2120
Richmond, VA 23218-2120
(804) 371-2475   Toll Free: (800) 292-3820
Fax: (804) 786-6759
E-mail: JoAnne.Carver@doe.virginia.gov
Web: www.doe.virginia.gov

Summary To provide funding to upper-division and graduate students in Virginia (particularly Asian Americans and other minorities) who are interested in a career in teaching.

Eligibility This program is open to Virginia residents who are enrolled full or part time as a sophomore, junior, senior, or graduate student in a state-approved teacher preparation program in Virginia with a GPA of 2.7 or higher. Applicants must agree to engage in full-time teaching following graduation in 1) designated teacher shortage areas within Virginia; 2) a school with a high concentration of students eligible for free or reduced lunch; 3) within a school division with a shortage of teachers; 4) in a rural or urban region of the state with a teacher shortage; or 5) in a career and technical education discipline. Males interested in teaching in the elementary grades and people of color in all teaching areas also qualify.

Financial data The scholarship/loan is $3,720 per year. Loans are forgiven at the rate of $1,000 for each semester the recipient teaches in designated teacher shortage areas. If the recipient fails to fulfill the teaching service requirement, the loan must be repaid with interest.

Duration 1 year; may be renewed 1 additional year.

Additional information Critical shortage teaching areas in Virginia are currently identified as all areas of special education (severe disturbances, hearing impairment, learning disabilities, mental retardation, severe disabilities, visual impairment, early childhood special education, emotional disturbance, and speech and language disorders), career and technical education (including technology education, trade and industrial education, business education, and family and consumer sciences), mathematics (6-12), foreign language (preK-12), English (6-12), middle school (6-8), elementary education (preK-6), science (6-12), health and physical education (preK-12), and school counselor (preK-12).

Number awarded Varies each year; recently, 265 of these scholarship/loans were granted, including 111 in elementary education, 14 in English, 8 in foreign languages, 2 in history and social science, 18 in mathematics, 22 in middle grades, 2 in science, 30 in special education, 20 for males in elementary grades, 4 for males in middle grades, and 34 for people of color.

Deadline Deadline not specified.

[360]
WAL-MART FOUNDATION APIASF SCHOLARSHIP

Asian & Pacific Islander American Scholarship Fund
1900 L Street, N.W., Suite 210
Washington, DC 20036-5002
(202) 986-6892　　　　　Toll Free: (877) 808-7032
Fax: (202) 530-0643　　　　E-mail: info@apiasf.org
Web: www.apiasf.org/scholarship_apiasf_walmart.html

Summary To provide financial assistance to Asian and Pacific Islander Americans who are planning to attend designated community colleges and study specified subjects.

Eligibility This program is open to U.S. citizens, nationals, permanent residents, or citizens of the Freely Associated States who are of Asian or Pacific Islander heritage. Applicants must be enrolling full time at City College of San Francisco, De Anza College, or South Seattle Community College as first-year students. They must have a GPA of 2.7 or higher or the GED equivalent and be planning to major in business, engineering, information systems, logistics, or supply chain management. In addition, they must complete the FAFSA and apply for federal financial aid.

Financial data The stipend is $2,500.

Duration 1 year; nonrenewable.

Additional information This scholarship is sponsored by the Wal-Mart Foundation.

Number awarded 21 each year.

Deadline January of each year.

[361]
WALTER U. LUM HIGH SCHOOL SCHOLARSHIPS

Chinese American Citizens Alliance
1044 Stockton Street
San Francisco, CA 94108
(415) 434-2222　　　　E-mail: info@cacanational.org
Web: www.cacanational.org

Summary To provide financial assistance for college to Chinese American high school students.

Eligibility This program is open to students of Chinese descent who are high school seniors or recent graduates planning to attend college. Preference is given to U.S. citizens. Applicants must submit a copy of their high school transcripts, starting with grades 9 or 10; an essay (up to 500 words) that describes their community activities, college scholastic goals, career goals, and personal outlook; and 2 reference letters. Selection is based on academic achievement, campus and community extracurricular activities, career goals and personal outlook, and the quality of the essay.

Financial data The stipend is $500.

Duration 1 year; nonrenewable.

Additional information Students must submit their applications and supporting information to their local lodge of the Chinese American Citizens Alliance; applications directly submitted by students are not accepted.

Number awarded 2 each odd-numbered year.

Deadline April of each odd-numbered year.

[362]
WALTER U. LUM UNDERGRADUATE SCHOLARSHIP

Chinese American Citizens Alliance
1044 Stockton Street
San Francisco, CA 94108
(415) 434-2222　　　　E-mail: info@cacanational.org
Web: www.cacanational.org

Summary To provide financial assistance to Chinese American undergraduate students.

Eligibility This program is open to students of Chinese descent who have completed the sophomore year of college. Preference is given to U.S. citizens. Applicants must submit a copy of their college transcripts; copies of their and their parents' latest income tax returns; copies of successful applications for financial aid; an essay (up to 500 words) that describes their community activities, career goals, and personal outlook; and 2 reference letters. Selection is based on academic achievement and campus and community extracurricular activities, career goals and personal outlook, quality of the essay, and financial need.

Financial data The stipend is $1,000.

Duration 1 year; nonrenewable.

Additional information Students must submit their applications and supporting information to their local lodge of the

Chinese American Citizens Alliance; applications directly submitted by students are not accepted.

Number awarded 2 each odd-numbered year.

Deadline April of each odd-numbered year.

[363]
WARNER NORCROSS & JUDD PARALEGAL ASSISTANT SCHOLARSHIP

Grand Rapids Community Foundation
Attn: Education Program Officer
185 Oakes Street S.W.
Grand Rapids, MI 49503-4008
(616) 454-1751, ext. 103   Fax: (616) 454-6455
E-mail: rbishop@grfoundation.org
Web: www.grfoundation.org/scholarships

Summary To provide financial assistance to Asian American and other minority residents of Michigan who are interested in working on a paralegal studies degree at an institution in the state.

Eligibility This program is open to residents of Michigan who are students of color attending or planning to attend an accredited public or private 2- or 4-year college or university in the state. Applicants must have a declared major in paralegal/legal assistant studies. They must be U.S. citizens or permanent residents and have a GPA of 2.5 or higher. Financial need is considered in the selection process.

Financial data The stipend is $2,000. Funds are paid directly to the recipient's institution.

Duration 1 year.

Additional information Funding for this program is provided by the law firm Warner Norcross & Judd LLP.

Number awarded 1 each year.

Deadline March of each year.

[364]
WARREN FENCL SCHOLARSHIP

Club 100 Veterans
Attn: Scholarship Committee
520 Kamoku Street
Honolulu, HI 96826-5120
(808) 946-0272   E-mail: daisyy@hgea.net

Summary To provide financial assistance to Japanese American high school seniors and college students who exemplify the sponsor's motto of "For Continuing Service."

Eligibility This program is open to high school seniors planning to attend an institution of higher learning and full-time undergraduate students at community colleges, vocational/trade schools, 4-year colleges, and universities. Applicants must have a GPA of 2.5 or higher and be able to demonstrate civic responsibility and community service. Along with their application, they must submit an essay on a topic that changes annually but relates to challenges faced by Japanese Americans. Selection is based on that essay and the applicant's promotion of the legacy of the 100th Infantry Battalion and its motto of "For Continuing Service." Financial need is not considered.

Financial data The stipend is $2,000.

Duration 1 year; nonrenewable.

Additional information This scholarship is named in honor of a World War II veteran of the 34th Infantry Division who fought alongside the Japanese American soldiers of the 100th Infantry Battalion and subsequently campaigned to correct the injustices committed against Japanese Americans during the war.

Number awarded 1 each year.

Deadline April of each year.

[365]
WASHINGTON ADMIRAL'S FUND SCHOLARSHIP

National Naval Officers Association-Washington, D.C.
  Chapter
Attn: Scholarship Program
2701 Park Center Drive, A1108
Alexandria, VA 22302
(703) 566-3840   Fax: (703) 566-3813
E-mail: Stephen.Williams@Navy.mil
Web: dcnnoa.memberlodge.com

Summary To provide financial assistance to Asian American and other minority high school seniors from the Washington, D.C. area who are interested in attending a college or university in any state and enrolling in the Navy Reserve Officers Training Corps (NROTC) program.

Eligibility This program is open to minority seniors graduating from high schools in the Washington, D.C. metropolitan area who plan to enroll full time at an accredited 2- or 4-year college or university in any state. Applicants must be planning to enroll in the NROTC program. They must have a GPA of 2.5 or higher and be U.S. citizens or permanent residents. Selection is based on academic achievement, community involvement, and financial need.

Financial data The stipend is $1,000.

Duration 1 year; nonrenewable.

Additional information If the recipient fails to enroll in the NROTC unit, all scholarship funds must be returned.

Number awarded 1 each year.

Deadline March of each year.

[366]
WASHINGTON POST HIGH SCHOOL WRITING SEMINAR AND SCHOLARSHIP PROGRAM

Washington Post
Attn: Young Journalists Development Program
1150 15th Street, N.W.
Washington, DC 20071
(202) 334-7132   Fax: (202) 496-3516
E-mail: knighta@washpost.com
Web: washpost.com

Summary To provide financial assistance to minority and other high school seniors in the Washington, D.C. area who are interested in preparing for a career in newspaper journalism.

Eligibility This program is open to high school seniors in 19 designated public school systems in the Washington, D.C. area. Applicants must have an interest in a print journalism career and a command of the English language. All students are eligible, but special emphasis is placed on participation by minority students. They must submit a 1-page autobiography and an essay of 250 to 500 words on why they want to be a journalist. From the original applicants, a group is selected to participate in a program of 4 Saturday seminars at *The Washington Post*. During those seminars, conducted by the newspaper's reporters and editors, students produce a newspaper or magazine story. Scholarship winners are selected on the basis of those stories, attendance and participation in the seminars, and financial need.

Financial data The stipend is $2,500.

Duration 1 year; nonrenewable.

Additional information The eligible public school systems are those in Washington, D.C.; the counties of Anne Arundel, Calvert, Charles, Frederick, Howard, Montgomery, Prince George's, and St. Mary's in Maryland; the cities of Alexandria, Falls Church, Manassas, and Manassas Park in Virginia; and the counties of Arlington, Fairfax, Fauquier, Loudoun, Prince William, and Stafford in Virginia. This program, which began in 1997, is offered in collaboration with the National Association of Hispanic Journalists and the Asian American Journalists Association.

Number awarded Recently, 19 students were selected to participate in the seminar. >From those, 2 were chosen to receive scholarships.

Deadline February of each year.

[367]
WATSON MIDWIVES OF COLOR SCHOLARSHIP

American College of Nurse-Midwives
Attn: ACNM Foundation, Inc.
8403 Colesville Road, Suite 1550
Silver Spring, MD 20910-6374
(240) 485-1850   Fax: (240) 485-1818
Web: www.midwife.org/foundation_award.cfm

Summary To provide financial assistance for midwifery education to Asian Americans and other students of color who belong to the American College of Nurse-Midwives (ACNM).

Eligibility This program is open to ACNM members of color who are currently enrolled in an accredited basic midwife education program and have successfully completed 1 academic or clinical semester/quarter or clinical module. Applicants must submit a 150-word essay on their 5-year midwifery career plans and a 100-word essay on their intended future participation in the local, regional, and/or national activities of the ACNM. Selection is based on leadership potential, financial need, academic history, and potential for future professional contribution to the organization.

Financial data The stipend is $3,000.

Duration 1 year.

Number awarded Varies each year; recently, 3 of these scholarships were awarded.

Deadline March of each year.

[368]
WAYNE D. CORNILS SCHOLARSHIP

Idaho State Broadcasters Association
270 North 27th Street, Suite B
Boise, ID 83702-4741
(208) 345-3072   Fax: (208) 343-8946
E-mail: isba@qwestoffice.net
Web: www.idahobroadcasters.org/scholarships.aspx

Summary To provide financial assistance to students at Idaho colleges and universities (especially Asian Americans and other diverse students) who are preparing for a career in the broadcasting field and can demonstrate financial need.

Eligibility This program is open to full-time students at Idaho schools who are preparing for a career in broadcasting, including business administration, sales, journalism, or engineering. Applicants must have a GPA of at least 2.0 for the first 2 years of school or 2.5 for the last 2 years. Along with their application, they must submit a letter of recommendation from the general manager of a broadcasting station that is a member of the Idaho State Broadcasters Association and a 1-page essay describing their career plans and why they want the scholarship. Applications are encouraged from a wide and diverse student population. This scholarship is reserved for a less advantaged applicant.

Financial data The stipend depends on the need of the recipient.

Duration 1 year.

Number awarded 1 each year.

Deadline March of each year.

[369]
WEISMAN SCHOLARSHIPS

Connecticut Department of Higher Education
Attn: Office of Student Financial Aid
61 Woodland Street
Hartford, CT 06105-2326
(860) 947-1857   Fax: (860) 947-1838
E-mail: mtip@ctdhe.org
Web: www.ctdhe.org/SFA/default.htm

Summary To provide financial assistance to Asian American and other minority upper-division college students from any state who are enrolled at a college in Connecticut and interested in teaching mathematics or science at public middle and high schools in the state.

Eligibility This program is open to residents of any state who are enrolled full time as juniors or seniors at Connecticut colleges and universities and preparing to become a mathematics or science teacher at the middle or high school level. Applicants must be members of a minority group, defined as African American, Hispanic/Latino, Asian American, or Native American. They must be nominated by the education dean at their institution.

Financial data The maximum stipend is $5,000 per year. In addition, if recipients complete a credential and begin teaching at a public school in Connecticut within 16 months of graduation, they may receive up to $2,500 per year, for up to 4 years, to help pay off college loans.

Number awarded Varies each year.

Deadline September of each year.

[370]
WEST AMERICA CHAPTER SCHOLARSHIP AWARDS

Phi Tau Phi Scholastic Honor Society-West America
   Chapter
c/o Nai-Chang Yeh, President
California Institute of Technology
Kavli Nanoscience Institute
128 Sloan Annex, Mail Code 114-36
1200 East California Boulevard
Pasadena, CA 91125
(626) 395-4313   E-mail: ncyeh@caltech.edu
Web: phitauphi.org

Summary To provide financial assistance to upper-division and graduate students of Chinese heritage from any state at colleges and universities in southern California.

Eligibility This program is open to juniors, seniors, and graduate students from any state enrolled at accredited institutions of higher education in southern California. Applicants must be of Chinese heritage or have a demonstrated interest in Chinese and culture. They must have a GPA of 3.4 or higher. Along with their application, they must submit a 1-page essay on their professional goals, achievements, and interest in Chinese culture. Financial need is not considered in the selection process.

Financial data The stipend is $1,000.

Duration 1 year.

Additional information Phi Tau Phi, first organized in 1921 in China and reestablished in 1964 in the United States, is a relatively small honor society of scholars, mainly of Chinese heritage, in various disciplines of science, technology, art, and the humanities.

Number awarded 4 or more each year.

Deadline August of each year.

[371]
WESTERN REGION KOREAN AMERICAN SCHOLARSHIPS

Korean American Scholarship Foundation
Western Region
Attn: Scholarship Committee
3540 Wilshire Boulevard, Suite 920
Los Angeles, CA 90010
(213) 380-KASF   Fax: (213) 380-KASF
E-mail: western@kasf.org
Web: www.kasf.org/application_set.html

Summary To provide financial assistance to Korean American students from any state who are working on or planning to work on an undergraduate or graduate degree in any field at a school in western states.

Eligibility This program is open to Korean American students who are high school seniors, undergraduates, or graduate students. Applicants may be residents of any state as long as they are attending or planning to attend school full time in the western region (Alaska, Arizona, California, Colorado, Hawaii, Idaho, Montana, Nevada, New Mexico, Oregon, Utah, Washington, or Wyoming). They must have a GPA of 3.0 or higher. Selection is based on academic achievement, community service, school activities, and financial need.

Financial data Stipends are at least $2,000.

Duration 1 year; renewable.

Number awarded Varies each year; recently, 37 of these scholarships were awarded.

Deadline May of each year.

[372]
WESTERN STATES AHA AFFILIATE UNDERGRADUATE STUDENT RESEARCH PROGRAM

American Heart Association-Western States Affiliate
Attn: Research Department
1710 Gilbreth Road
Burlingame, CA 94010-1317
(650) 259-6700   Fax: (650) 259-6891
E-mail: research@heart.org
Web: www.americanheart.org

Summary To provide students (particularly Asian Americans, other minorities, and women) from California, Nevada, and Utah with an opportunity to work on a cardiovascular research project during the summer.

Eligibility This program is open to college students who are enrolled full time at an accredited academic institution at the junior or senior level and are interested in a career in heart or stroke research. Applicants must be residents of California, Nevada, or Utah (or attending a college or university in 1 of those states) and interested in a summer internship at a cardiovascular research laboratory in those states. They must be U.S. citizens or foreign nationals holding a student, exchange, or permanent resident visa. They must have completed the following (or equivalent) courses: 4 semesters (or 6 quarters) of biological sciences, physics, or chemistry; and 1 quarter of calculus, statistics, computational methods, or computer science. Selection is based on an assessment of the student's application, academic record (preference is given to students with superior academic standing), and faculty recommendations. Women and minorities are particularly encouraged to apply.

Financial data Participants receive a $4,000 stipend.

Duration 10 weeks during the summer.

Additional information Participants are assigned to laboratories in California, Nevada, or Utah to work under the direction and supervision of experienced scientists.

Deadline December of each year.

[373]
WILLIAM K. SCHUBERT M.D. MINORITY NURSING SCHOLARSHIP PROGRAM

Cincinnati Children's Hospital Medical Center
Attn: Office of Diversity and Inclusion, MLC 9008
3333 Burnet Avenue
Cincinnati, OH 45229-3039
(513) 803-6416   Toll Free: (800) 344-2462
Fax: (513) 636-5643   TDD: (513) 636-4900
E-mail: owen.burke@cchmc.org
Web: www.cincinnatichildrens.org

Summary To provide financial assistance to Asian Americans and members of other underrepresented groups interested in working on a bachelor's or master's degree in nursing to prepare for licensure in Ohio.

Eligibility This program is open to members of groups underrepresented in the nursing profession (males, American Indians or Alaska Natives, Blacks or African Americans, Hawaiian Natives or other Pacific Islanders, Hispanics or Latinos, or Asians). Applicants must be enrolled or accepted in a professional bachelor's or master's registered nurse program at an accredited school of nursing to prepare for initial licensure in Ohio. They must have a GPA of 2.75 or higher. Along with their application, they must submit a 750-word essay that covers 1) their long-range personal, educational, and professional goals and why they chose nursing as a profession; 2) any unique qualifications, experiences, or special talents that demonstrate their creativity; and 3) if they are able to pay any college expenses through work and how their work experience has contributed to their personal development.

Financial data The stipend is $2,750 per year.

Duration 1 year. May be renewed up to 3 additional years for students working on a bachelor's degree or 1 additional year for students working on a master's degree; renewal requires that students maintain a GPA of 2.75 or higher.

Number awarded 1 or more each year.

Deadline April of each year.

[374]
WILLIAM ORR DINGWALL FOUNDATION KOREAN ANCESTRY GRANTS

William Orr Dingwall Foundation
2201 N Street, N.W., Suite 117
Washington, DC 20037
E-mail: apply@dingwallfoundation.org
Web: www.dingwallfoundation.org/KAG.html

Summary To provide financial assistance to undergraduates of Asian (preferably Korean) ancestry.

Eligibility This program is open to graduating high school seniors and undergraduates currently enrolled at a college or university in the United States. Applicants should be of Korean ancestry, although exceptional students of other Asian ancestry may also be considered. They must have a GPA of 3.5 or higher but they may be majoring in any field. Selection is based on academic record, written statements, and letters of recommendation.

Financial data The stipend is $20,000 per year.

Duration 1 year; may be renewed up to 3 additional years, provided the recipient maintains a GPA of 3.5 or higher.

Number awarded Varies each year; recently, 26 of these grants were awarded.

Deadline January of each year.

[375]
WILLIAM RUCKER GREENWOOD SCHOLARSHIP

Association for Women Geoscientists
Attn: AWG Foundation
12000 North Washington Street, Suite 285
Thornton, CO 80241
(303) 412-6219   Fax: (303) 253-9220
E-mail: office@awg.org
Web: www.awg.org/EAS/scholarships.html

Summary To provide financial assistance to Asian American and other minority women from any state working on an undergraduate or graduate degree in the geosciences at a college in the Potomac Bay region.

Eligibility This program is open to minority women who are residents of any state and currently enrolled as full-time undergraduate or graduate geoscience majors at an accredited, degree-granting college or university in Delaware, the District of Columbia, Maryland, Virginia, or West Virginia. Selection is based on the applicant's 1) participation in geoscience or earth science educational activities, and 2) potential for leadership as a future geoscience professional.

Financial data The stipend is $1,000. The recipient also is granted a 1-year membership in the Association for Women Geoscientists (AWG).

Duration 1 year.

Additional information This program is sponsored by the AWG Potomac Area Chapter.

Number awarded 1 each year.

Deadline April of each year.

[376]
WILLIAM WOO INTERNSHIP FUND

Asian American Journalists Association
Attn: Student Programs Coordinator
5 Third Street, Suite 1108
San Francisco, CA 94103
(415) 346-2051, ext. 102   Fax: (415) 346-6343
E-mail: programs@aaja.org
Web: www.aaja.org/programs/internships

Summary To provide a supplemental grant to student and other members of the Asian American Journalists Association (AAJA) working as a summer intern at a print or online journalism company.

Eligibility This program is open to AAJA members who are full-time college students or recent college graduates. Applicants must have secured a summer internship at a print or online company before they apply. Along with their application, they must submit a 200-word essay on why they want to prepare for a career in print or online journalism, what they want to gain from the experience, and why AAJA's mission is important to them; a letter of recommendation; a resume; proof of age (at least 18 years); verification of an internship; and statement of financial need.

Financial data The grant is $1,000. Funds are to be used for living expenses or transportation.

Duration Summer months.

Additional information This program began in 2006.

Number awarded 1 each year.

Deadline May of each year.

[377]
WISCONSIN CHAPTER GENERAL SCHOLARSHIPS

Organization of Chinese Americans-Wisconsin Chapter
Attn: Scholarship Committee
P.O. Box 301
Dousman, WI 53118
(414) 258-2410   E-mail: ocawischolarship@yahoo.com
Web: www.ocawi.org

Summary To provide financial assistance to high school seniors who are 1) children of members or business affiliates of the Wisconsin Chapter of the Organization of Chinese Americans (OCA-WI) and 2) interested in attending college in any state.

Eligibility This program is open to graduating high school seniors whose parent has been an OCA-WI member or business affiliate for at least 2 years and who are planning to enroll full time at an accredited college or university in any state. Applicants must have a GPA of 3.0 or higher. Along with their application, they must submit a personal statement that includes information on their future college and career plans; a list of scholastic awards, honors, extracurricular activities, and honor societies and offices; and a description of their volunteer service to OCA-WI and their community. Financial need is not considered in the selection process.

Financial data A stipend is awarded (amount not specified).

Duration 1 year.

Additional information This program was established in 1988. It includes the following named scholarships (awarded on a rotating basis): the Professor Kwang Yu Memorial Scholarship, the Dr. Benjamin P.C. Ho and Mrs. Lien-Haw (T'ao) Ho Memorial Scholarship, the Benjamin Tsong-Wei Wu Memorial Scholarship, the Professor Shien-Ming (Samuel) Wu Memorial Scholarship, the Yulin and King Ying His Memorial Scholarship, and the Maryanne Yu Tsao Memorial Scholarship.

Number awarded Varies each year; recently, 5 of these scholarships were awarded.

Deadline March of each year.

[378]
WISCONSIN MINORITY TEACHER LOANS

Wisconsin Higher Educational Aids Board
131 West Wilson Street, Suite 902
P.O. Box 7885
Madison, WI 53707-7885
(608) 267-2212   Fax: (608) 267-2808
E-mail: Mary.Kuzdas@wisconsin.gov
Web: heab.state.wi.us/programs.html

Summary To provide funding to Asian Americans and other minorities in Wisconsin who are interested in teaching in Wisconsin school districts with large minority enrollments.

Eligibility This program is open to residents of Wisconsin who are African Americans, Hispanic Americans, American Indians, or southeast Asians (students who were admitted to the United States after December 31, 1975 and who are a former citizen of Laos, Vietnam, or Cambodia or whose ancestor was a citizen of 1 of those countries). Applicants must be enrolled at least half time as juniors, seniors, or graduate students at an independent or public institution in the state in a program leading to teaching licensure and have a GPA of 2.5 or higher. They must agree to teach in a Wisconsin school district in which minority students constitute at least 29% of total enrollment or in a school district participating in the interdistrict pupil transfer program. Financial need is not considered in the selection process.

Financial data forgivable loans are provided up to $2,500 per year. For each year the student teaches in an eligible school district, 25% of the loan is forgiven; if the student does not teach in an eligible district, the loan must be repaid at an interest rate of 5%.

Duration 1 year; may be renewed 1 additional year.

Additional information Eligible students should apply through their school's financial aid office.

Number awarded Varies each year.

Deadline Deadline dates vary by institution; check with your school's financial aid office.

[379]
WISCONSIN MINORITY UNDERGRADUATE RETENTION GRANTS

Wisconsin Higher Educational Aids Board
131 West Wilson Street, Suite 902
P.O. Box 7885
Madison, WI 53707-7885
(608) 267-2212   Fax: (608) 267-2808
E-mail: Mary.Kuzdas@wisconsin.gov
Web: heab.state.wi.us/programs.html

Summary To provide financial assistance to Asian Americans and other minorities in Wisconsin who are currently enrolled at a college in the state.

Eligibility This program is open to residents of Wisconsin who are African Americans, Hispanic Americans, American Indians, or southeast Asians (students who were admitted to the United States after December 31, 1975 and who are a former citizen of Laos, Vietnam, or Cambodia or whose ancestor was a citizen of 1 of those countries). Applicants must be enrolled at least half time as sophomores, juniors, seniors, or fifth-year undergraduates at a Wisconsin technical college, tribal college, or independent college or university in the state. They must be nominated by their institution and be able to demonstrate financial need.

Financial data Stipends range from $250 to $2,500 per year, depending on the need of the recipient.

Duration Up to 4 years.

Additional information The Wisconsin Higher Educational Aids Board administers this program for students at private nonprofit institutions, technical colleges, and tribal colleges. The University of Wisconsin has a similar program for students attending any of the branches of that system. Eligible students should apply through their school's financial aid office.

Number awarded Varies each year.

Deadline Deadline dates vary by institution; check with your school's financial aid office.

[380]
WISCONSIN PUBLIC SERVICE FOUNDATION BUSINESS AND TECHNOLOGY SCHOLARSHIPS

Wisconsin Public Service Corporation
Attn: Wisconsin Public Service Foundation
c/o Scholarship Assessment Service
P.O. Box 997
Appleton, WI 54912-0997
(920) 832-8322
Web: www.wisconsinpublicservice.com

Summary To provide financial assistance to Asian Americans, other minorities, and female upper-division students who are majoring in business or engineering at universities in selected states.

Eligibility This program is open to women and African American, Native American, Asian American, and Hispanic students from any state who are enrolled full time as a junior or senior with a GPA of 2.8 or higher. Applicants must be attending a college or university in Illinois, Indiana, Iowa, Michigan, Minnesota, or Wisconsin. They must be majoring in business or engineering (chemical, civil, computer, electrical, environmental, industrial, or mechanical). Along with their application, they must submit 250-word essays on 1) their educational goals and why they have chosen their major; and 2) how they have demonstrated their leadership skills.

Financial data The stipend is $1,500 per year.

Duration 1 year; may be renewed if the recipient remains in good academic standing.

Number awarded Varies each year; recently, 15 of these scholarships were awarded.

Deadline February of each year.

[381]
WISCONSIN TALENT INCENTIVE PROGRAM (TIP) GRANTS

Wisconsin Higher Educational Aids Board
131 West Wilson Street, Suite 902
P.O. Box 7885
Madison, WI 53707-7885
(608) 266-1665   Fax: (608) 267-2808
E-mail: colettem1.brown@wi.gov
Web: heab.state.wi.us/programs.html

Summary To provide financial assistance for college to Asian Americans and other needy or educationally disadvantaged students in Wisconsin.

Eligibility This program is open to residents of Wisconsin entering a college or university in the state who meet the requirements of both financial need and educational disadvantage. Financial need qualifications include 1) family contribution (a dependent student whose expected parent contribution is $200 or less, an independent student with dependents whose academic year contribution is $200 or less, or an independent student with no dependents whose maximum contribution is $200 or less); 2) Temporary Assistance to Needy Families (TANF) or Wisconsin Works (W2) benefits (a dependent student whose family is receiving TANF or W2 benefits or an independent student who is receiving TANF or W2 benefits); or 3) unemployment (a dependent student whose parents are ineligible for unemployment compensation and have no current income from employment, or an independent student and spouse, if married, who are ineligible for unemployment compensation and have no current income from employment). Educational disadvantage qualifications include students who are 1) minorities (African American, Native American, Hispanic, or southeast Asian); 2) enrolled in a special academic support program due to insufficient academic preparation; 3) a first-generation college student (neither parent graduated from a 4-year college or university); 4) disabled according to the Department of Workforce Development, the Division of Vocational Rehabilitation, or a Wisconsin college or university that uses the Americans with Disabilities Act definition; 5) currently or formerly incarcerated in a correctional institution; or 6) from an environmental and academic background that deters the pursuit of educational plans. Students already in college are not eligible.

Financial data Stipends range up to $1,800 per year.

Duration 1 year; may be renewed up to 4 additional years, provided the recipient continues to be a Wisconsin resident enrolled at least half time in a degree or certificate program, makes satisfactory academic progress, demonstrates financial need, and remains enrolled continuously from semester to semester and from year to year. If recipients withdraw from school or cease to attend classes for any reason (other than medical necessity), they may not reapply.

Number awarded Varies each year.

Deadline Deadline not specified.

[382]
WOODS HOLE OCEANOGRAPHIC INSTITUTION MINORITY FELLOWSHIPS

Woods Hole Oceanographic Institution
Attn: Academic Programs Office
Clark Laboratory 223, MS 31
360 Woods Hole Road
Woods Hole, MA 02543-1541
(508) 289-2219   Fax: (508) 457-2188
E-mail: education@whoi.edu
Web: www.whoi.edu/page.do?pid=36375

Summary To provide work experience to Asian American and other minority undergraduates who are interested in preparing for careers in the marine sciences, oceanographic engineering, or marine policy.

Eligibility This program is open to ethnic minority undergraduates enrolled in U.S. colleges or universities who have completed at least 2 semesters of study and who are interested in the physical or natural sciences, mathematics, engineering, or marine policy. Applicants must be U.S. citizens or permanent residents and African American or Black; Asian American; Chicano, Mexican American, Puerto Rican or other Hispanic; or Native American, Alaska Native, or Native Hawaiian. They must be interested in participating in a program of study and research at Woods Hole Oceanographic Institution.

Financial data The stipend is $488 per week; trainees may also receive additional support for travel to Woods Hole.

Duration 10 to 12 weeks during the summer or 1 semester during the academic year; renewable.

Additional information Trainees are assigned advisers who supervise their research programs and supplementary study activities. Some traineeships involve field work or research cruises. This program is conducted with support from and in cooperation with the Center for Marine and Coastal Geology of the U.S. Geological Survey.

Number awarded 4 to 5 each year.

Deadline For a summer appointment, applications must be submitted in February of each year. For the remaining portion of the year, applications may be submitted at any time, but they must be received at least 2 months before the anticipated starting date.

[383]
XEROX TECHNICAL MINORITY SCHOLARSHIP PROGRAM

Xerox Corporation
Attn: Technical Minority Scholarship Program
150 State Street, Fourth Floor
Rochester, NY 14614
(585) 422-7689   E-mail: xtmsp@rballiance.com
Web: www.xeroxstudentcareers.com

Summary To provide financial assistance to Asian Americans and other minorities interested in undergraduate or graduate education in the sciences and/or engineering.

Eligibility This program is open to minorities (people of African American, Asian, Pacific Islander, Native American, Native Alaskan, or Hispanic descent) working full time on a bachelor's, master's, or doctoral degree in chemistry, computing and software systems, engineering (chemical, computer, electrical, imaging, manufacturing, mechanical, optical, or software), information management, laser optics, materials science, physics, or printing management science. Applicants must be U.S. citizens or permanent residents with a GPA of 3.0 or higher and attending a 4-year college or university.

Financial data Stipends range from $1,000 to $10,000.

Duration 1 year.

Number awarded Varies each year, recently, 125 of these scholarships were awarded.

Deadline September of each year.

Graduate Students

Listed alphabetically by program title and described in detail here are 422 fellowships, grants, awards, internships, and other sources of "free money" set aside for incoming, continuing, or returning graduate students of Asian origins (including those of subcontinent Asian and Pacific Islander descent) who are working on a master's. doctoral, or professional degree. This funding is available to support study, training, research, and/or creative activities in the United States.

[384]
100TH INFANTRY BATTALION MEMORIAL SCHOLARSHIP FUND

Hawai'i Community Foundation
Attn: Scholarship Department
827 Fort Street Mall
Honolulu, HI 96813
(808) 537-6333   Toll Free: (888) 731-3863
Fax: (808) 521-6286
E-mail: scholarships@hcf-hawaii.org
Web: www.hawaiicommunityfoundation.org/scholarships

Summary To provide financial assistance for college or graduate school to Japanese American descendants of 100th Infantry Battalion World War II veterans.

Eligibility This program is open to entering and continuing full-time undergraduate and graduate students at 2- and 4-year colleges and universities. Applicants must be a direct descendant of a World War II veteran of the 100th Infantry Battalion (which was comprised of Americans of Japanese descent). They must be able to demonstrate academic achievement (GPA of 3.5 or higher), an active record of extra-curricular activities and community service, a willingness to promote the legacy of the 100th Infantry Battalion of World War II, and financial need. Along with their application, they must submit a short statement indicating their reasons for attending college, their planned course of study, their career goals, and what community service means to them. They must also submit a separate essay on the legacy of the 100th Infantry Battalion and how they will contribute to forwarding that legacy. Current residency in Hawaii is not required.

Financial data The amounts of the awards depend on the availability of funds and the need of the recipient. Recently, the average value of all scholarships awarded by the foundation was $2,041.

Duration 1 year.

Number awarded Varies each year; recently, 2 of these scholarships were awarded.

Deadline February of each year.

[385]
AABA LAW FOUNDATION SCHOLARSHIPS

Asian American Bar Association of the Greater Bay Area
Attn: Law Foundation
P.O. Box 190517
San Francisco, CA 94119-0517
E-mail: info@aaba-bay.com
Web: aaba-bay.com

Summary To provide financial assistance to Asian American residents of any state who are enrolled at law schools in the San Francisco Bay area and planning to serve the Asian American community after graduation.

Eligibility This program is open to Asian American students from any state who are attending law schools in the Bay area and have demonstrated a strong commitment to serving the needs of the Asian American community. Applicants must submit a 3-page personal statement that covers 1) what they see as a pressing issue or concern facing the Asian American community and the role they see themselves playing in advocating for engaging in such an issue; 2) their experiences in overcoming economic and other discriminatory barriers; and 3) who they see as a successful leader within the Asian American community. An interview may be required.

Financial data The amount awarded varies but is usually around $1,000.

Duration 1 year.

Additional information This program includes the Asian American Judges Scholarship, the Joe Morozumi Scholarship and the Raymond L. Ocampo Jr. President's Scholarship.

Number awarded Varies each year; recently, 4 of these scholarships were awarded.

Deadline January of each year.

[386]
AAPI CREATIVE WRITING COMPETITION

American Association of Physicians of Indian Origin
Attn: Medical Students, Residents and Fellows Section
600 Enterprise Drive, Suite 108
Oak Brook, IL 60523
(630) 990-2277   Fax: (630) 990-2281
E-mail: preselect@aapimsr.org
Web: www.aapimsr.org

Summary To recognize and reward members of the American Association of Physicians of Indian Origin (AAPI) who submit outstanding samples of creative writing, poetry, or photography.

Eligibility This competition is open to members of the Medical Students, Residents and Fellows (MSRF) section and the Young Physician's Section (YPS) of the AAPI. Applicants must submit 1) original writings, up to 1,000 words in length, on a medically-related topic, including stories based on real life experiences, travel-related stories, personal experiences on campus, or innovative management of patients; 2) poems, up to 50 lines, related to the medical experience, whether from the point of view of a health care worker, a patient, or simply an observer; or 3) photographs, not necessarily medically-related, that may capture an interesting scene, mood, or moment in life.

Financial data Prizes in each category are $500 for first, $400 for second, and $300 for third.

Duration The competition is held annually.

Additional information This competition was first held in 2011.

Number awarded 9 each year: 3 in each category.

Deadline April of each year.

[387]
ABE AND ESTHER HAGIWARA STUDENT AID AWARD

Japanese American Citizens League
Attn: National Scholarship Awards
1765 Sutter Street
San Francisco, CA 94115
(415) 921-5225   Fax: (415) 931-4671
E-mail: jacl@jacl.org
Web: www.jacl.org/edu/scholar.htm

Summary To provide financial assistance for college or graduate school to student members of the Japanese American Citizens League (JACL) who can demonstrate severe financial need.

Eligibility This program is open to JACL members who are enrolled or planning to enroll at a college, university, trade school, or business college. Applicants must be undergraduate or graduate students who are able to demonstrate that, without this aid, they will have to delay or terminate their education. They must submit information on their involvement in JACL and a 2-page essay on a topic that changes annually but relates to Japanese Americans. Selection is based on that essay, financial need, academic record, extracurricular activities, and community involvement.

Financial data   Stipends generally average approximately $2,000.

Duration   1 year; nonrenewable.

Number awarded   At least 1 each year.

Deadline   March of each year.

[388]
ACADEMIC LIBRARY ASSOCIATION OF OHIO DIVERSITY SCHOLARSHIP

Academic Library Association of Ohio
c/o Ken Burhanna, Diversity Committee Chair
Kent State University, Instructional Services
P.O. Box 5190
Kent, OH 44242-0001
(330) 672-1660   E-mail: kburhann@kent.edu
Web: www.alaoweb.org

Summary   To provide financial assistance to Asian Americans and other residents of Ohio who are working on a master's degree in library science at a school in any state and will contribute to diversity in the profession.

Eligibility   This program is open to residents of Ohio who are enrolled or entering an ALA-accredited program for a master's degree in library science, either on campus or via distance education. Applicants must be able to demonstrate how they will contribute to diversity in the profession, including (but not limited to) race or ethnicity, sexual orientation, life experience, physical ability, and a sense of commitment to those and other diversity issues. Along with their application, they must submit 1) a list of participation in honor societies or professional organizations, awards, scholarships, prizes, honors, or class offices; 2) a list of community, civic, organizational, or volunteer experiences; and 3) an essay on their understanding of and commitment to diversity in libraries, including how they, as library school students and future professionals, might address the issue.

Financial data   The stipend is $1,500.

Duration   1 year.

Number awarded   1 each year.

Deadline   March of each year.

[389]
ADLER POLLOCK & SHEEHAN DIVERSITY SCHOLARSHIP

Adler Pollock & Sheehan P.C.
Attn: Diversity Committee Chair
175 Federal Street
Boston, MA 02110-2210
(617) 482-0600   Fax: (617) 482-0604
E-mail: Diversitycomm@apslaw.com
Web: www.apslaw.com/firm-diversity.html

Summary   To provide financial assistance to Asian American and other residents of Massachusetts and Rhode Island who are members of diverse groups and plan to attend law school in any state.

Eligibility   This program is open to residents of Massachusetts and Rhode Island who are members of a diverse group, including African American, American Indian, Hispanic, Asian/Pacific Islander, gay/lesbian, or other minority group. Applicants must be entering their first year at an ABA-accredited law school anywhere in the United States. They must be able to demonstrate academic achievement, a desire to work and reside in Massachusetts or Rhode Island after graduation, a demonstrated commitment to the community, a vision of contributions to the profession and community after graduation, and financial need.

Financial data   The stipend is $10,000.

Duration   1 year.

Number awarded   1 each year.

Deadline   May of each year.

[390]
ADRIENNE M. AND CHARLES SHELBY ROOKS FELLOWSHIP FOR RACIAL AND ETHNIC THEOLOGICAL STUDENTS

United Church of Christ
Attn: Local Church Ministries
700 Prospect Avenue East
Cleveland, OH 44115-1100
(216) 736-3865   Toll Free: (866) 822-8224, ext. 3848
Fax: (216) 736-3783   E-mail: lcm@ucc.org
Web: www.ucc.org/seminarians/ucc-scholarships-for.html

Summary   To provide financial assistance to Asian American and other minority students who are either enrolled at an accredited seminary preparing for a career of service in the United Church of Christ (UCC) or working on a doctoral degree in the field of religion.

Eligibility   This program is open to members of underrepresented ethnic groups (African American, Hispanic American, Asian American, Native American Indian, or Pacific Islander) who have been a member of a UCC congregation for at least 1 year. Applicants must be either 1) enrolled in an accredited school of theology in the United States or Canada and working on an M.Div. degree with the intent of becoming a pastor or teacher within the UCC, or 2) doctoral (Ph.D., Th.D., or Ed.D.) students within a field related to religious studies. Seminary students must have a GPA in all postsecondary work of 3.0 or higher and must have begun the in-care process; preference is given to students who have demonstrated leadership (through a history of service to the church) and scholarship (through exceptional academic performance). For doctoral students, preference is given to applicants who have demonstrated academic excellence, teaching effectiveness, and commitment to the UCC and who intend to become professors in colleges, seminaries, or graduate schools.

Financial data   Grants range from $500 to $5,000 per year.

Duration   1 year; may be renewed.

Number awarded   Varies each year; recently, 11 of these scholarships, including 8 for M.Div. students and 3 for doctoral students, were awarded.

Deadline   February of each year.

[391]
AEF FELLOWSHIPS

Asian Pacific American Bar Association Educational Fund
P.O. Box 2209
Washington, DC 20013-2209
Fax: (202) 408-4400   E-mail: aefboard@gmail.com
Web: www.aefdc.com/?page_id=6

Summary To provide funding to Asian American and other law students from any state who are interested in interning during the summer with a public interest organization that benefits either the Asian Pacific American community or the metropolitan Washington, D.C. community at large.

Eligibility This program is open to law students who have obtained an unpaid internship with a public interest organization (e.g., government organizations and other nonprofits serving the public interest). The organization must be based in the greater Washington, D.C. area and serve either the Asian Pacific American community or the community at large. Applicants must submit an essay, up to 750 words, on the internship, how it will benefit the Asian Pacific American community or the community at large in the metropolitan Washington, D.C. area, and how their activities show past and/or present commitment to public interest and/or Asian Pacific American issues. Preference is given to applicants interning at direct service organizations. Selection is based primarily on the essay, but the applicant's maturity and responsibility are also considered. An effort is made to place fellows in diverse employment settings.

Financial data Grant amounts vary; recently, they averaged more than $4,000.

Duration At least 10 weeks or a total of 400 hours during the summer.

Additional information This program includes the Anheuser-Busch Norman Y. Mineta Fellowship, funded by Anheuser-Busch Companies, Inc., and the Robert E. Wone Fellowship, established in 2007.

Number awarded Varies each year; recently, 6 of these fellowships were funded.

Deadline April of each year.

[392]
AGI/AAPG SEMESTER INTERNSHIPS IN GEOSCIENCE PUBLIC POLICY

American Geological Institute
Attn: Government Affairs Program
4220 King Street
Alexandria, VA 22302-1502
(703) 379-2480   Fax: (703) 379-7563
E-mail: govt@agiweb.org
Web: www.agiweb.org/gap/interns/index.html

Summary To provide work experience to geoscience students (particularly Asian Americans, other minorities, and women) who have a strong interest in federal science policy.

Eligibility This program is open to geoscience students who are interested in working with Congress and federal agencies to promote sound public policy in areas that affect geoscientists, including water, energy, and mineral resources; geologic hazards; environmental protection, and federal funding for geoscience research and education. Applicants must submit official copies of college transcripts, a resume with the names and contact information for 2 refer-

ences, and a statement of their science and policy interests and what they feel they can contribute to the program. Women and minorities are especially encouraged to apply.

Financial data The stipend is $5,000.

Duration 14 weeks, during the fall or spring semester.

Additional information This program is jointly funded by the American Geological Institute (AGI) and the American Association of Petroleum Geologists (AAPG). Activities for the interns include monitoring and analyzing geoscience-related legislation in Congress, updating legislative and policy information on AGI's web site, attending House and Senate hearings and preparing summaries, responding to information requests from AGI's member societies, and attending meetings with policy-level staff members in Congress, federal agencies, and non-governmental organizations.

Number awarded 1 each semester.

Deadline April of each year for fall internships; October of each year for spring internships.

[393]
AGI/AIPG SUMMER INTERNSHIPS IN GEOSCIENCE PUBLIC POLICY

American Geological Institute
Attn: Government Affairs Program
4220 King Street
Alexandria, VA 22302-1502
(703) 379-2480, ext. 212   Fax: (703) 379-7563
E-mail: govt@agiweb.org
Web: www.agiweb.org/gap/interns/internsu.html

Summary To provide summer work experience to geoscience students (especially Asian Americans, other minorities, and women) who have a strong interest in federal science policy.

Eligibility This program is open to geoscience students who are interested in working with Congress and federal agencies to promote sound public policy in areas that affect geoscientists, including water, energy, and mineral resources; geologic hazards; environmental protection, and federal funding for geoscience research and education. Applicants must submit official copies of college transcripts, a resume with the names and contact information for 2 references, and a statement of their science and policy interests and what they feel they can contribute to the program. Minorities and women are especially encouraged to apply.

Financial data The stipend is $5,000.

Duration 12 weeks during the summer.

Additional information This program is jointly funded by the American Geological Institute (AGI) and the American Institute of Professional Geologists (AIPG). Activities for the interns include monitoring and analyzing geoscience-related legislation in Congress, updating legislative and policy information on AGI's web site, attending House and Senate hearings and preparing summaries, responding to information requests from AGI's member societies, and attending meetings with policy-level staff members in Congress, federal agencies, and non-governmental organizations.

Number awarded 3 each summer.

Deadline March of each year.

[394]
AMERICAN ADVERTISING FEDERATION FOURTH DISTRICT MOSAIC SCHOLARSHIP

American Advertising Federation-District 4
c/o Tami L. Grimes, Education Chair
4712 Southwood Lane
Lakeland, FL 33813
(863) 648-5392   E-mail: tamilgrimes@yahoo.com
Web: www.4aaf.com/scholarships.cfm

Summary To provide financial assistance to Asian American and other minority undergraduate and graduate students from any state who are enrolled at colleges and universities in Florida and interested in entering the field of advertising.

Eligibility This program is open to undergraduate and graduate students from any state enrolled at accredited colleges and universities in Florida who are U.S. citizens or permanent residents of African, African American, Hispanic, Hispanic American, Indian, Native American, Asian, Asian American, or Pacific Islander descent. Applicants must be working on a bachelor's or master's degree in advertising, marketing, communications, public relations, art, graphic arts, or a related field. They must have an overall GPA of 3.0 or higher. Along with their application, they must submit a 250-word essay on why multiculturalism, diversity, and inclusion are important in the advertising, marketing, and communications industry today. Preference is given to members of the American Advertising Federation.

Financial data The stipend is $1,000.

Duration 1 year.

Number awarded 1 or more each year.

Deadline May of each year.

[395]
AMERICAN ASSOCIATION OF CHINESE IN TOXICOLOGY AND CHARLES RIVER BEST ABSTRACT AWARD

Society of Toxicology
Attn: American Association of Chinese in Toxicology
  Special Interest Group
1821 Michael Faraday Drive, Suite 300
Reston, VA 20190-5348
(703) 438-3115   Fax: (703) 438-3113
E-mail: sothq@toxicology.org
Web: www.toxicology.org/ai/af/awards.aspx

Summary To recognize and reward graduate student and postdoctoral members of the Society of Toxicology (SOT) who are of Chinese ethnic origin and present outstanding papers at the annual meeting.

Eligibility This award is available to SOT members who are graduate students or postdoctoral fellows of Chinese descent (having 1 or more parents of Chinese descent). Candidates must have an accepted abstract for the SOT annual meeting. Along with the abstract, they must submit a cover letter outlining the significance of the work to the field of toxicology.

Financial data The prizes are $500 for first, $300 for second, and $200 for third.

Duration The prizes are presented annually.

Number awarded 3 each year.

Deadline December of each year.

[396]
AMERICAN ASSOCIATION OF JAPANESE UNIVERSITY WOMEN SCHOLARSHIP PROGRAM

American Association of Japanese University Women
c/o Scholarship Committee
3543 West Boulevard
Los Angeles, CA 90016
E-mail: scholarship@aajuw.org
Web: www.aajuw.org/Scholarship.htm

Summary To provide financial assistance to Japanese and other female students currently enrolled in upper-division or graduate classes in California.

Eligibility This program is open to women enrolled at accredited colleges or universities in California as juniors, seniors, or graduate students. Applicants must be involved in U.S.-Japan relations, cultural exchanges, and leadership development in the areas of their designated field of study. Along with their application, they must submit a current resume, an official transcript of the past 2 years of college work, 2 letters of recommendation, and an essay (up to 2 pages in English or 1,200 characters in Japanese) on what they hope to accomplish in their field of study and how that will contribute to better U.S.-Japan relations.

Financial data The stipend is $2,000.

Duration 1 year.

Additional information The association was founded in 1970 to promote the education of women as well as to contribute to U.S.-Japan relations, cultural exchanges, and leadership development.

Number awarded 2 or 3 each year. Since this program was established, it has awarded nearly $100,000 worth of scholarships to more than 90 women.

Deadline Deadline not specified.

[397]
AMERICAN ASSOCIATION OF PHYSICIANS OF INDIAN ORIGIN NATIONAL RESEARCH COMPETITION

American Association of Physicians of Indian Origin
Attn: Medical Students, Residents and Fellows Section
600 Enterprise Drive, Suite 108
Oak Brook, IL 60523
(630) 990-2277   Fax: (630) 990-2281
E-mail: preselect@aapimsr.org
Web: www.aapimsr.org

Summary To recognize and reward members of the American Association of Physicians of Indian Origin (AAPI) who submit outstanding research abstracts for presentation at the annual conference.

Eligibility This competition is open to members of the Medical Students, Residents and Fellows (MSRF) section and the Young Physician's Section (YPS) of the AAPI. Applicants must submit abstracts of research for presentation at the AAPI annual conference. Abstracts should be limited to 500 words with sections on background, methods, results, conclusions, and (for basic science articles) clinical relevance. Applicants must attend the conference where finalists are chosen for a poster and an 8-minute oral presentation.

Financial data Prizes are $1,000 for first and $750 for second.

Duration The competition is held annually.

Number awarded   2 each year.

Deadline   April of each year.

[398]
AMERICAN ASSOCIATION OF UNIVERSITY WOMEN FOCUS PROFESSIONS GROUP FELLOWSHIPS

American Association of University Women
Attn: AAUW Educational Foundation
301 ACT Drive, Department 60
P.O. Box 4030
Iowa City, IA 52243-4030
(319) 337-1716, ext. 60   Fax: (319) 337-1204
E-mail: aauw@act.org
Web: www.aauw.org/learn/fellowships_grants/selected.cfm

Summary   To aid Asian American women, and other women of color, who are in their final year of graduate training in the fields of business administration, law, or medicine.

Eligibility   This program is open to women who are working full time on a degree in fields in which women of color have been historically underrepresented: business administration (M.B.A.), law (J.D.), or medicine (M.D., D.O.). They must be African Americans, Mexican Americans, Puerto Ricans and other Hispanics, Native Americans, Alaska Natives, Asian Americans, or Pacific Islanders. U.S. citizenship or permanent resident status is required. Applicants in business administration must be entering their second year of study; applicants in law must be entering their third year of study; applicants in medicine may be entering their third or fourth year of study. Special consideration is given to applicants who 1) demonstrate their intent to enter professional practice in disciplines in which women are underrepresented, to serve underserved populations and communities, or to pursue public interest areas; and 2) are nontraditional students. Selection is based on professional promise and personal attributes (50%), academic excellence and related academic success indicators (40%), and financial need (10%).

Financial data   Stipends range from $5,000 to $18,000.

Duration   1 academic year, beginning in September.

Additional information   The filing fee is $35.

Number awarded   Varies each year.

Deadline   January of each year.

[399]
AMERICAN BAR ASSOCIATION LEGAL OPPORTUNITY SCHOLARSHIP

American Bar Association
Attn: Fund for Justice and Education
321 North Clark Street
Chicago, IL 60654-7598
(312) 988-5415   Fax: (312) 988-6392
E-mail: legalosf@staff.abanet.org
Web: www.abanet.org/fje/losfpage.html

Summary   To provide financial assistance to Asian American and other minority students who are interested in attending law school.

Eligibility   This program is open to racial and ethnic minority college graduates who are interested in attending an ABA-accredited law school. Only students beginning law school may apply; students who have completed 1 or more semesters of law school are not eligible. Applicants must have a cumulative GPA of 2.5 or higher and be citizens or permanent residents of the United States. Along with their application, they must submit a 1,000-word statement describing their personal and family background, community service activities, and other connections to their racial and ethnic minority community. Financial need is also considered in the selection process.

Financial data   The stipend is $5,000 per year.

Duration   1 year; may be renewed for 2 additional years if satisfactory performance in law school has been achieved.

Additional information   This program began in the 2000-01 academic year.

Number awarded   Approximately 20 each year.

Deadline   February of each year.

[400]
AMERICAN POLITICAL SCIENCE ASSOCIATION MINORITY FELLOWS PROGRAM

American Political Science Association
Attn: APSA Minority Fellows Program
1527 New Hampshire Avenue, N.W.
Washington, DC 20036-1206
(202) 483-2512, ext. 123   Fax: (202) 483-2657
E-mail: apsa@apsanet.org
Web: www.apsanet.org/content_3284.cfm

Summary   To provide financial assistance to Asian Pacific Islanders and other minorities interested in working on a doctoral degree in political science.

Eligibility   This program is open to African Americans, Asian Pacific Americans, Latino(a)s, and Native Americans who are in their senior year at a college or university or currently enrolled in a master's degree program. Applicants must be planning to enroll in a doctoral program in political science to prepare for a career in teaching and research. They must be U.S. citizens and able to demonstrate financial need. Along with their application, they must submit a 500-word personal statement that includes why they are interested in attending graduate school in political science, what specific fields within the discipline they plan to study, and how they intend to contribute to research within the discipline. Selection is based on interest in teaching and potential for research in political science.

Financial data   The stipend is $2,000 per year.

Duration   2 years.

Additional information   In addition to the fellows who receive stipends from this program, students who are selected as fellows without stipend are recommended for admission and financial support to every doctoral political science program in the country. This program was established in 1969.

Number awarded   Up to 12 fellows receive stipends each year.

Deadline   October of each year.

[401]
AMERICAN SPEECH-LANGUAGE-HEARING FOUNDATION SCHOLARSHIP FOR MINORITY STUDENTS

American Speech-Language-Hearing Foundation
Attn: Program Assistant
2200 Research Boulevard
Rockville, MD 20850-3289
(301) 296-8703   Toll Free: (800) 498-2071, ext. 8703
E-mail: foundationprograms@asha.org
Web: www.ashfoundation.org/grants/GraduateScholarships

Summary   To provide financial assistance to Asian American and other minority graduate students in communication sciences and disorders programs.

Eligibility   This program is open to minorities and others who are full-time graduate students and enrolled in communication sciences and disorders programs. They should be U.S. citizens. Applicants must submit an essay, up to 5 pages in length, on a topic that relates to the future of leadership in the discipline. Selection is based on academic promise and outstanding academic achievement.

Financial data   The stipend ranges from $2,000 to $4,000. Funds must be used for educational support (e.g., tuition, books, school living expenses), not for personal or conference travel.

Duration   1 year.

Number awarded   1 each year.

Deadline   June of each year.

[402]
ANAPATA DIVERSITY SCHOLARSHIP CONTEST

Ms. JD
Attn: Executive Director
1659 Lyman Place
Los Angeles, CA 90027
(917) 446-8991   E-mail: kornberg@ms-jd.org
Web: ms-jd.org/anapata-student-scholarship

Summary   To provide financial assistance to Asian Americans and other law students who are members of groups traditionally underrepresented in the legal profession.

Eligibility   This program is open to students currently enrolled at ABA-approved law schools in the United States. Members of groups traditionally underrepresented in the legal profession are especially encouraged to apply. They must submit a resume, transcript, personal introduction paragraph, 2 recommendations, and a 750-word essay demonstrating their personal philosophy regarding diversity in the legal profession. Selection is based on academic achievement, leadership ability, writing and interpersonal skills, and interest in promoting diversity in the legal profession.

Financial data   The stipend is $1,000.

Duration   1 year.

Additional information   This program is offered by Ms. JD in partnership with Anapata, Inc.

Number awarded   1 or more each year.

Deadline   February of each year.

[403]
ANDREW W. MELLON FOUNDATION/ACLS DISSERTATION COMPLETION FELLOWSHIPS

American Council of Learned Societies
Attn: Office of Fellowships and Grants
633 Third Avenue
New York, NY 10017-6795
(212) 697-1505   Fax: (212) 949-8058
E-mail: fellowships@acls.org
Web: www.acls.org/programs/dcf

Summary   To provide research funding to doctoral candidates in all disciplines of the humanities and the humanities-related social sciences (particularly Asian Americans, other minorities, and women) who are ready to complete their dissertations.

Eligibility   This program is open to doctoral candidates in a humanities or humanities-related social science discipline at a U.S. institution. Applicants must have completed all requirements for the Ph.D. except the dissertation. They may have completed no more than 6 years in the degree program. Research may be conducted at the home institution, abroad, or another appropriate site. Appropriate fields of specialization include, but are not limited to, American studies; anthropology; archaeology; art and architectural history; classics; economics; film; geography; history; languages and literatures; legal studies; linguistics; musicology; philosophy; political science; psychology; religious studies; rhetoric, communication, and media studies; sociology; and theater, dance, and performance studies. Proposals in the social sciences are eligible only if they employ predominantly humanistic approaches (e.g., economic history, law and literature, political philosophy). Proposals in interdisciplinary and cross-disciplinary studies are welcome, as are proposals focused on a geographic region or on a cultural or linguistic group. Applications are particularly invited from women and members of minority groups.

Financial data   Grants provide a stipend of $25,000, funds for research costs up to $3,000, and payment of university fees up to $5,000.

Duration   1 academic year. Grantees may accept this fellowship no later than their seventh year.

Additional information   This program, which began in 2006, is supported by funding from the Andrew W. Mellon Foundation and administered by the American Council of Learned Societies (ACLS).

Number awarded   65 each year.

Deadline   November of each year.

[404]
ANGELFIRE SCHOLARSHIP

Datatel Scholars Foundation
4375 Fair Lakes Court
Fairfax, VA 22033
(703) 968-9000, ext. 4549   Toll Free: (800) 486-4332
Fax: (703) 968-4625   E-mail: scholars@datatel.com
Web: www.datatelscholars.org

Summary   To provide financial assistance to graduating high school seniors, continuing college students, and graduate students who will be studying at a Datatel client school and are veterans, veterans' dependents, or refugees from southeast Asia.

Eligibility This program is open to 1) veterans who served in the Asian theater (Vietnam, Cambodia, or Laos) between 1964 and 1975; 2) their spouses and children; 3) refugees from Vietnam, Cambodia, or Laos; and 4) veterans who served in Operation Desert Storm, Operation Enduring Freedom, and/or Operation Iraqi Freedom. Applicants must attend a Datatel client college or university during the upcoming school year as a full- or part-time undergraduate or graduate student. They must first apply to their institution, which selects 2 semifinalists and forwards their applications to the sponsor. Along with their application, they must include a 1,000-word personal statement that discusses how the conflict has affected them personally, summarizes how the conflict has impacted their educational goals, and describes how being awarded this scholarship will help them achieve their goals. Selection is based on the quality of the personal statement (60%) and academic merit (40%).

Financial data The stipend is $1,700. Funds are paid directly to the institution.

Duration 1 year.

Additional information Datatel, Inc. produces advanced information technology solutions for higher education. It has more than 750 client sites in the United States and Canada. This scholarship was created to commemorate those who lost their lives in Vietnam or Iraq and is named after a memorial administered by the Disabled American Veterans Association in Angelfire, New Mexico.

Number awarded 10 each year.

Deadline Students must submit online applications to their institution or organization by January of each year.

[405]
ANHEUSER-BUSCH NAPABA LAW FOUNDATION PRESIDENTIAL SCHOLARSHIPS

National Asian Pacific American Bar Association
Attn: NAPABA Law Foundation
1612 K Street, N.W., Suite 1400
Washington, DC 20006
(202) 775-9555   Fax: (202) 775-9333
E-mail: foundation@napaba.org
Web: www.napaba.org

Summary To provide financial assistance to law students interested in serving the Asian Pacific American community.

Eligibility This program is open to students at ABA-accredited law schools in the United States. Applicants must demonstrate leadership potential to serve the Asian Pacific American community upon graduation. Along with their application, they must submit a 500-word essay that covers 1) the most significant experiences in their background that have shaped and demonstrated their commitment to serving the needs of Asian Pacific Americans; and 2) how they intend to serve the needs of the Asian Pacific American community in their future legal career. Selection is based on demonstrated commitment to and interest in pro bono, public interest, and/or public service legal work; financial need; leadership potential; maturity and responsibility; and commitment to serving the needs of the Asian Pacific American community.

Financial data The stipend is $7,500.

Duration 1 year.

Additional information This program is supported by Anheuser-Busch Companies, Inc.

Number awarded 2 each year.

Deadline September of each year.

[406]
AOS/NORMAN'S ORCHIDS MASTERS SCHOLARSHIP

American Orchid Society
16700 AOS Lane
Delray Beach, FL 33446-4351
(561) 404-2000   Fax: (561) 404-2045
E-mail: TheAOS@aos.org
Web: www.aos.org

Summary To provide funding for research to students (especially Asian American and other diverse students) who are working on a master's degree in a field related to orchids.

Eligibility This program is open to students working on a master's degree at an accredited institution. Applicants must have a thesis project that deals with an aspect of orchid education, applied science, or orchid biology in the disciplines of physiology, molecular biology, structure, systematics, cytology, ecology, or evolution. They must submit a current curriculum vitae, transcripts of all college course work, a synopsis of the proposed project or research, a 1-page statement of the value of their project and importance to the future of orchid education or orchidology, and a letter of recommendation from their chairperson. Women, minorities, and persons with disabilities are especially encouraged to apply.

Financial data The grant is $5,000 per year. Funds are paid through the recipient's college or university, but institutional overhead is not allowed.

Duration 2 years.

Additional information This program, established in 2005, is supported by Norman's Orchids of Montclair, California.

Number awarded 1 each year.

Deadline February of each year.

[407]
APA MINORITY MEDICAL STUDENT SUMMER MENTORING PROGRAM

American Psychiatric Association
Attn: Department of Minority and National Affairs
1000 Wilson Boulevard, Suite 1825
Arlington, VA 22209-3901
(703) 907-8653   Toll Free: (888) 35-PSYCH
Fax: (703) 907-7852   E-mail: mking@psych.org
Web: www.psych.org/Resources/OMNA/MFP.aspx

Summary To provide funding to Asian American and other minority medical students who are interested in working on a summer project with a psychiatrist mentor.

Eligibility This program is open to minority medical students who are interested in psychiatric issues. Minorities include American Indians, Alaska Natives, Native Hawaiians, Asian Americans, Hispanic/Latinos, and African Americans. Applicants must be interested in working with a psychiatrist mentor, primarily on clinical work with underserved minority populations and mental health care disparities. Work settings may be in a research, academic, or clinical environment. Most of them are inner-city or rural and dealing with psychiatric subspecialties, particularly substance abuse and geriatrics. Selection is based on interest of the medical student and specialty of the mentor, practice setting, and geographic proximity of the mentor to the student. U.S. citizenship or permanent resident status is required.

Financial data　Fellowships provide $1,500 for living and out-of-pocket expenses directly related to the conduct of the fellowship.

Duration　Summer months.

Additional information　This program is funded by the Substance Abuse and Mental Health Services Administration.

Number awarded　Varies each year.

Deadline　February of each year.

[408]
APABA SUMMER FELLOWSHIP

Asian Pacific American Bar Association of South Florida
c/o Jane F. Bolin
PeytonBolin, PL
4792 West Commercial Boulevard
Fort Lauderdale, FL 33319
(954) 316-1339　　　　　　　Fax: (954) 727-5776
Web: www.apabasfla.org/scholarship/scholarship.htm

Summary　To provide an opportunity for summer employment in public interest law in south Florida to law students who are members of their school's chapter of the Asian Pacific American Law Student Association (APASLA).

Eligibility　This program is open to APASLA members at law schools in any state. Applicants must have secured a summer placement with a nonprofit or governmental agency in south Florida that serves the public interest. Selection is based on demonstrated commitment to public service and public interest law and/or pro bono service; participation in and commitment to their APALSA chapter as well as any involvement with the Asian Pacific American Bar Association (APABA) of South Florida; the extent to which the proposed placement organization, and the applicant's summer service within it, serve the interests of an unmet legal need; the extent to which the proposed placement organization, and the applicant's summer service within it, serve the Asian Pacific American community; the quality of the proposed placement and agency; the quality of legal supervision; and the capabilities of the applicant. Financial need is not considered.

Financial data　The stipend is $2,000.

Duration　Fellows are expected to work 300 hours during the course of the summer.

Number awarded　1 each year.

Deadline　March of each year.

[409]
APALA SCHOLARSHIP

Asian Pacific American Librarians Association
Attn: Executive Director
University of California at Santa Barbara
Davidson Library
Santa Barbara, CA 93106
(805) 893-8067　　　　E-mail: colmenar@library.ucsb.edu
Web: www.apalaweb.org/awards/scholarship.htm

Summary　To provide financial assistance to students of Asian or Pacific Islander descent who are working on a graduate library degree.

Eligibility　This program is open to students of Asian or Pacific Islander background who are enrolled or have been accepted into a master's program or doctoral degree program in library or information science at a library school accredited by the American Library Association (ALA). Applicants must be citizens or permanent residents of the United States or Canada. Along with their application, they must submit a 1-page essay on either their vision of a librarian's role in the 21st century or the contributions they can make as an Asian or Pacific Islander librarian.

Financial data　The stipend is $1,000.

Duration　1 year.

Number awarded　1 each year.

Deadline　March of each year.

[410]
ARCHIE MOTLEY MEMORIAL SCHOLARSHIP FOR MINORITY STUDENTS

Midwest Archives Conference
c/o Kimberly Neuenschwander
Marianist Archives
310 Roesch Library, University of Dayton
300 College Park
Dayton, OH 45469-1360
(937) 229-5538　　　　　　　Fax: (937) 229-5142
E-mail: neuenskm@notes.udayton.edu
Web: www.midwestarchives.org

Summary　To provide financial assistance to Asian American and other minority graduate students preparing for a career in archival administration.

Eligibility　This program is open to graduate students of African, American Indian, Asian, Pacific Islander, or Latino descent who are enrolled or accepted for enrollment in a graduate, multi-course program in archival administration at a college or university in any state. The graduate program must offer at least 3 courses in archival administration or be listed in the current Directory of Archival Education of the Society of American Archivists (SAA). Applicants must have a GPA of 3.0 or higher. They may be residents of any state and attending school in any state. Along with their application, they must submit a 500-word essay on their interests and future goals in archival administration.

Financial data　The stipend is $750.

Duration　1 year.

Additional information　These scholarships were first awarded in 2004.

Number awarded　2 each year.

Deadline　March of each year.

[411]
ARENT FOX DIVERSITY SCHOLARSHIPS

Arent Fox LLP
Attn: Attorney Recruitment and Professional Development
　Coordinator
1050 Connecticut Avenue, N.W.
Washington, DC 20036-5339
(202) 715-8503　　　　　　　Fax: (202) 857-6395
E-mail: lawrecruit@arentfox.com
Web: www.arentfox.com

Summary　To provide financial assistance and work experience to Asian Americans and other minority law students.

Eligibility This program is open to first-year law students who are members of a diverse population that historically has been underrepresented in the legal profession. Applicants must be U.S. citizens or otherwise authorized to work in the United States. They must also be willing to work as a summer intern at the sponsoring law firm's offices in Los Angeles, New York City, or Washington, D.C. Along with their application, they must submit a resume, an undergraduate transcript and law school grades when available, a 5- to 10-page legal writing sample, 3 letters of recommendation, and an essay on how their background, skills, experience, and interest equip them to meet the sponsor's goal of commitment to diversity. Selection is based on academic performance during college and law school, oral and writing communication skills, leadership qualities, and community involvement.

Financial data The scholarship stipend is $15,000. The summer salary is $2,500 per week.

Duration 1 year.

Additional information These scholarships were first offered in 2006. Recipients are also offered summer internships with Arent Fox: 1 in Los Angeles, 1 in New York City, and 1 in Washington, D.C.

Number awarded 3 each year.

Deadline January of each year.

[412]
ARKANSAS CONFERENCE ETHNIC LOCAL CHURCH CONCERNS SCHOLARSHIPS

United Methodist Church-Arkansas Conference
Attn: Committee on Ethnic Local Church Concerns
800 Daisy Bates Drive
Little Rock, AR 72202
(501) 324-8045   Toll Free: (877) 646-1816
Fax: (501) 324-8018   E-mail: mallen@arumc.org
Web: www.arumc.org

Summary To provide financial assistance to Asian American and other minority Methodist students from Arkansas who are interested in attending college or graduate school in any state.

Eligibility This program is open to ethnic minority undergraduate and graduate students who are active members of local congregations affiliated with the Arkansas Conference of the United Methodist Church (UMC). Applicants must be currently enrolled in an accredited institution of higher education in any state. Along with their application, they must submit a transcript (GPA of 2.0 or higher) and documentation of participation in local church activities. Preference is given to students attending a UMC-affiliated college or university.

Financial data The stipend is $500 per semester ($1,000 per year) for undergraduates or $1,000 per semester ($2,000 per year) for graduate students.

Duration 1 year; may be renewed.

Number awarded 1 or more each year.

Deadline September of each year.

[413]
ARKANSAS MINORITY MASTERS FELLOWS PROGRAM

Arkansas Department of Higher Education
Attn: Financial Aid Division
114 East Capitol Avenue
Little Rock, AR 72201-3818
(501) 371-2050   Toll Free: (800) 54-STUDY
Fax: (501) 371-2001   E-mail: finaid@adhe.edu
Web: www.adhe.edu

Summary To provide funding to Asian American and other minority graduate students in Arkansas who want to become teachers in the state.

Eligibility This program is open to minority (African American, Hispanic, Native American, or Asian American) residents of Arkansas who are U.S. citizens or permanent residents and enrolled in a master's degree program in education (other than administration) at an Arkansas public or independent institution. Applicants must have a cumulative GPA of 2.75 or higher. They must be willing to teach in an Arkansas public school or public institution of higher education for at least 2 years after completion of their education. Preference is given to applicants who completed their baccalaureate degrees within the previous 2 years.

Financial data The loan is $1,250 per 3-credit course, to a maximum of $3,750 per semester or $7,500 over a lifetime. The loan will be forgiven if the recipient teaches full time in an Arkansas public school or public institution of higher education for 2 years. If the recipient withdraws from an approved teacher education program or does not fulfill the required teaching obligation, the loan must be repaid in full with 10% interest.

Duration 1 semester; may be renewed until the recipient completes 3 years of study, earns a master's degree, or reaches the maximum lifetime loan limit, whichever comes first. Renewal requires the recipient to maintain a GPA of 3.0 or higher.

Number awarded Varies each year; recently, 25 of these forgivable loans were approved.

Deadline May of each year.

[414]
ARMONICA LAW STUDENT GRANT PROGRAM

Oregon Women Lawyers Foundation
P.O. Box 82522
Portland, OR 97282
(503) 775-4396   E-mail: orwomenlaw@aol.com
Web: www.owlsfoundation.org/grants.htm

Summary To provide financial assistance to law students in Oregon, especially Asian Americans, other minorities, and women.

Eligibility This program is open to residents of any state entering their third year at a law school in Oregon. Applicants must be able to demonstrate, through their personal, volunteer, or education experience, a commitment to the goals of the sponsoring foundation: increasing diversity in the legal profession through grants and scholarships, promoting pro bono legal work, encouraging child care in Oregon's courthouses, promoting access to justice for low-income Oregonians, and providing education about domestic violence and abuse. Ethnic minorities and women are especially encouraged to apply.

Financial data The stipend is $500.

Duration 1 year.

Additional information This program was established in 2007 to honor Armonica Gilford, the first African American female assistant attorney general for the Oregon Department of Justice. Each recipient is matched with an ethnic minority female judge or attorney to serve as the student's mentor for the year.

Number awarded 3 each year: 1 at each law school in Oregon.

Deadline September of each year.

[415]
ARMY JUDGE ADVOCATE GENERAL CORPS SUMMER INTERN PROGRAM

U.S. Army
Attn: Judge Advocate Recruiting Office
1777 North Kent Street, Suite 5200
Rosslyn, VA 22209-2194
(703) 696-2822   Toll Free: (866) ARMY-JAG
Fax: (703) 588-0100
Web: www.goarmy.com/jag/summer_intern_program.jsp

Summary To provide law students (especially Asian Americans, other minorities, and women) with an opportunity to gain work experience during the summer in Army legal offices throughout the United States and overseas.

Eligibility This program is open to full-time students enrolled in law schools accredited by the American Bar Association. Applications are accepted both from students who are completing the first year of law school and those completing the second year. Students must be interested in a summer internship with the Army Judge Advocate General's Corps (JAGC). U.S. citizenship is required. The program actively seeks applications from women and minority group members. Selection is based on academic ability and demonstrated leadership potential.

Financial data Interns who have completed the first year of law school are paid at the GS-5 scale, starting at $474 per week. Interns who have completed the second year of law school are paid at the GS-7 scale, starting at $588 per week.

Duration Approximately 60 days, beginning in May or June.

Additional information Interns work under the supervision of an attorney and perform legal research, write briefs and opinions, conduct investigations, interview witnesses, and otherwise assist in preparing civil or criminal cases. Positions are available at Department of the Army legal offices in Washington, D.C. and at Army installations throughout the United States and overseas. These are not military positions. No military obligation is incurred by participating in the summer intern program.

Number awarded 100 per year: 25 first-year students and 75 second-year students.

Deadline February of each year for first-year students; October of each year for second-year students.

[416]
ASA MINORITY FELLOWSHIP PROGRAM GENERAL FELLOWSHIP

American Sociological Association
Attn: Minority Affairs Program
1430 K Street, N.W., Suite 600
Washington, DC 20005-2504
(202) 383-9005, ext. 322   Fax: (202) 638-0882
TDD: (202) 638-0981 E-mail: minority.affairs@asanet.org
Web: www.asanet.org/funding/mfp.cfm

Summary To provide financial assistance to Asian American and other minority doctoral students in sociology.

Eligibility This program is open to U.S. citizens, permanent residents, and non-citizen nationals who are Blacks/African Americans, Latinos (e.g., Mexican Americans, Puerto Ricans, Cubans), American Indians or Alaskan Natives, Asian Americans (e.g., southeast Asians, Japanese, Chinese, Koreans), or Pacific Islanders (e.g., Filipinos, Samoans, Hawaiians, Guamanians). Applicants must be entering or continuing students in sociology at the doctoral level. Along with their application, they must submit 3-page essays on 1) the reasons why they decided to undertake graduate study in sociology, their primary research interests, and why they hope to do with a Ph.D. in sociology; and 2) what led them to select the doctoral program they attend or hope to attend and how they see that doctoral program preparing them for a professional career in sociology. Selection is based on commitment to research, focus of research experience, academic achievement, writing ability, research potential, and financial need.

Financial data The stipend is $18,000 per year.

Duration 1 year; may be renewed up to 2 additional years.

Additional information This program, which began in 1974, is supported by individual members of the American Sociological Association (ASA) and by several affiliated organizations (Alpha Kappa Delta, Sociologists for Women in Society, the Association of Black Sociologists, and the Southwestern Sociological Association).

Number awarded Varies each year; since the program began, approximately 500 of these fellowships have been awarded.

Deadline January of each year.

[417]
ASCA FOUNDATION SCHOLARSHIPS

American School Counselor Association
Attn: ASCA Foundation
1101 King Street, Suite 625
Alexandria, VA 22314
(703) 683-ASCA   Toll Free: (800) 306-4722
Fax: (703) 683-1619 E-mail: asca@schoolcounselor.org
Web: www.schoolcounselor.org

Summary To provide financial assistance for graduate school to members of the American School Counselor Association (ASCA), especially Asian Americans, other minorities, and males.

Eligibility This program is open to ASCA members working full time on a master's degree in school counseling. Applicants must submit a 2-page essay on a topic that changes annually but relates to the role of counselors in schools. Males and minorities are especially encouraged to apply.

Financial data The stipend is $1,000.

Duration 1 year.

Additional information Support for this program is provided by Anheuser-Busch.

Number awarded Up to 10 each year.

Deadline October of each year.

[418]
ASEI GRADUATE SCHOLARSHIPS

American Society of Engineers of Indian Origin
Attn: Southern California Chapter
P.O. Box 466
Cypress, CA 90630
E-mail: scholarships@aseisocal.net
Web: www.aseisocal.net/12.html

Summary To provide financial assistance to graduate students of Indian origin (from India) who are working on a degree in engineering, computer science, or related areas.

Eligibility This program is open to graduate students of Indian origin (by birth, ancestry, or relation). Applicants must be enrolled full time at an ABET-accredited college or university in the United States and working on a degree in engineering, computer science, or an allied science and have a GPA of 3.5 or higher. They must be members of the American Society of Engineers of Indian Origin (ASEI). Selection is based on demonstrated ability, academic achievement (including GPA, honors, and awards), career objectives, faculty recommendations, involvement in science fair and campus activities, financial hardship, industrial exposure (including part-time work and internships), and involvement in ASEI and other community activities.

Financial data Stipends range from $500 to $1,000.

Duration 1 year.

Number awarded Several each year.

Deadline August of each year.

[419]
ASIAN AMERICAN ARCHITECTS AND
ENGINEERS FOUNDATION SCHOLARSHIPS

Asian American Architects/Engineers Association
Attn: Foundation
11301 West Olympic Boulevard, Suite 387
Los Angeles, CA 90064
(213) 896-9270   Fax: (866) 276-1712
E-mail: info@aaaesc.org
Web: www.aaaesc.org

Summary To provide financial assistance to members of the Asian American Architects/Engineers Association (AAa/e) who are interested in working on an undergraduate or graduate degree at a school in southern California.

Eligibility This program is open to student members of AAa/e who are U.S. citizens, permanent residents, or noncitizens enrolled full time at a college or university in southern California. Applicants must be graduating seniors, undergraduates, or graduate students working on or planning to work on a degree in architecture, civil engineering (environmental, geotechnical, structural, transportation), electrical engineering, mechanical engineering, landscape architecture or planning and urban design, or construction and construction management. Along with their application, they must submit 1) a 1-page personal statement on their involvement and service

to the Asian Pacific Islander community; 2) letters of recommendation from 2 faculty members or employers; and 3) a sample of their work, which may be a design or research project, a completed project, or a proposed project, including an assignment from a class, a senior project, or an assignment from work. Financial need is not considered in the selection process.

Financial data Stipends are $2,500 or $1,500.

Duration 1 year.

Number awarded At least 3 each year: 1 at $2,500 and at least 2 at $1,500.

Deadline July of each year.

[420]
ASIAN AMERICAN LAW FUND OF NEW YORK
COMMUNITY SERVICE SCHOLARSHIPS

Asian American Bar Association of New York
Attn: Asian American Law Fund of New York, Inc.
c/o Sylvia Fung Chin
White & Case LLP
1155 Avenue of the Americas
New York, NY 10036-2787
(212) 819-8200   Fax: (212) 354-8113
E-mail: schin@whitecase.com
Web: www.aabany.org/displaycommon.cfm?an=5

Summary To provide an opportunity for law students from any state to conduct a project that will benefit the Asian American community of New York.

Eligibility This program is open to students enrolled at least half time at ABA- or AALS-accredited law schools in the United States. Applicants must be interested in conducting a community service project as a volunteer for a nonprofit organization that serves the Asian American community of New York. The project should involve legal work and have a supervising attorney. Along with their application, they must submit a 750-word essay that covers 1) the most significant experiences in their background that have shaped and demonstrated their commitment to serving the needs of Asian Pacific Americans; 2) what they hope to learn, accomplish, or change through their project; 3) how they will use the experience that they will gain from their project; and 4) how they will serve the needs of the Asian American community in their future legal career. Selection is based on commitment to and interest in pro bono and/or public interest legal work to the Asian American community, leadership potential, maturity and responsibility, and financial need. U.S. citizenship or permanent resident status is required.

Financial data The grant is $5,000. Funds are to be used to assist the students with their tuition while encouraging them to use their legal knowledge and training to benefit the Asian American community in New York.

Duration Recipients are expected to volunteer for at least 6 weeks during the summer.

Number awarded Up to 3 each year.

Deadline April of each year.

[421]
ASIAN AMERICAN LAWYERS ASSOCIATION OF MASSACHUSETTS SCHOLARSHIP

Asian American Lawyers Association of Massachusetts
c/o Emily K. Yu, Scholarship Committee
Edwards Angell Palmer & Dodge LLP
111 Huntington Avenue
Boston, MA 02199-7613
(617) 239-0835   Fax: (617) 227-4420
E-mail: eyu@eapdlaw.com
Web: www.aalam.org/membership_lawstudents.shtml

Summary To provide financial assistance to Asian American students from any state enrolled at law schools in Massachusetts.

Eligibility This program is open to students currently enrolled at law schools in Massachusetts who can demonstrate leadership potential, maturity and responsibility, and a commitment to making a contribution to the Asian Pacific American community. Applicants must submit a 500-word essay on how they, as a future Asian Pacific American lawyer, think they can best contribute to the Asian Pacific American community. Financial need is not considered in the selection process.

Financial data The stipend is $2,500.

Duration 1 year.

Number awarded 1 each year.

Deadline April of each year.

[422]
ASIAN AMERICAN SUMMER INTERN GRANTS

American Baptist Churches USA
National Ministries
Attn: Office of Financial Aid for Studies
P.O. Box 851
Valley Forge, PA 19482-0851
(610) 768-2067   Toll Free: (800) ABC-3USA, ext. 2067
Fax: (610) 768-2453
E-mail: Financialaid.Web@abc-usa.org
Web: www.nationalministries.org

Summary To provide ministerial experience during the summer to Asian American Baptist seminarians.

Eligibility This program is open to Asian American seminarians who are interested in gaining local church experience in the summer months. Applicants must be U.S. citizens who have been a member of a church affiliated with American Baptist Churches USA for at least 1 year.

Financial data The grant is $500; the employing church is expected to match the grant.

Duration Summer months.

Number awarded Varies each year.

Deadline May of each year.

[423]
ASIAN AND PACIFIC AMERICAN LAWYERS ASSOCIATION OF NEW JERSEY SCHOLARSHIPS

Asian and Pacific American Lawyers Association of New Jersey
c/o Eugene Huang, Scholarship Committee Chair
Wiley Malehorn Sirota & Raynes
250 Madison Avenue
Morristown, NJ 07960
(973) 539-1313   Fax: (973) 539-0573
E-mail: ehuang@wmands.com
Web: www.apalanj.com

Summary To provide financial assistance to students who are enrolled at law schools in New Jersey and who have demonstrated an interest in the Asian American community.

Eligibility This program is open to students currently enrolled at a law school in New Jersey either as a full-time first- or second-year student or as a part-time first-, second-, or third-year student. Applicants must submit 400-word essays on 1) the most pressing issue or concern they believe the Asian American community is facing today and they role they see themselves playing in advocating for that issue or concern; 2) their suggestions on how Asians and Pacific Islander Americans can stand up and be counted in the legal community and the community at large; and 3) who they see as a successful leader within the Asian American community and the characteristics that make the leader so successful. Selection is based on the essays' content, clarity, ability to follow directions, and professionalism.

Financial data The stipend is at least $1,000.

Duration 1 year.

Number awarded 3 each year: 1 at each law school in New Jersey.

Deadline April of each year.

[424]
ASIAN BAR ASSOCIATION OF WASHINGTON STUDENT SCHOLARSHIPS

Asian Bar Association of Washington
Attn: Student Scholarship Foundation
c/o Jeff Liang, Student Liaison
Paramount Law Group, PLLC
601 Union Street, Suite 4200
Seattle, WA 98101
(206) 395-6448   E-mail: jliang@paramountcounsel.com
Web: www.abaw.org/scholarships.html

Summary To provide financial assistance to students from any state who are attending law school in Washington and who have been involved in the Asian community.

Eligibility This program is open to students from any state currently attending law school in the state of Washington. Applicants must be a member of the Asian Pacific Islander (API) student organization at their school. Along with their application, they must submit a 1,000-word personal statement describing their contributions to the API community and their plans to contribute to that community following graduation from law school, a resume, a copy of their most recent law school transcript, and 2 letters of reference.

Financial data Stipends range from $500 to $6,000.

Duration 1 year.

Additional information This program includes the Yamashita Scholarship, the Sharon A. Sakamoto President's Scholarship, and the Northwest Minority Job Fair Scholarship.

Number awarded Varies each year; recently, 5 of these scholarships were awarded: 1 at $6,000, 1 at $4,000, 2 at $2,000, and 1 at $500.

Deadline October of each year.

[425]
ASIAN PACIFIC AMERICAN BAR ASSOCIATION OF COLORADO SCHOLARSHIPS

Asian Pacific American Bar Association of Colorado
c/o Elisa Chen
Stettner Miller, P.C.
1050 17th Street, Suite 700
Denver, CO 80265
(303) 534-0273   Fax: (303) 534-5036
E-mail: echen@stetmil.com
Web: www.apaba-co.org/foundation.php

Summary To provide financial assistance to Asian American law students in Colorado.

Eligibility This program is open to students from any state currently enrolled at law schools in Colorado. Applicants must demonstrate a record of public service to the Asian community in the state.

Financial data The stipend is $1,000. The recipients' law schools must match the award, so the total is $2,000.

Duration 1 year.

Additional information This program began in 1996.

Number awarded 2 each year.

Deadline Deadline not specified.

[426]
ASIAN PACIFIC AMERICAN BAR ASSOCIATION OF MARYLAND SCHOLARSHIPS

Asian Pacific American Bar Association of Maryland
c/o Linette F. Golden
Robert A. Ades and Associates, P.C.
4301 Garden City Drive, Suite 300
Landover, MD 20785
(301) 459-3333   Fax: (301) 306-0728
E-mail: linettegolden@yahoo.com
Web: www.apaba-md.org

Summary To provide financial assistance to students from any state who are enrolled at law schools in Maryland and are committed to serving the needs of Asian Pacific Americans.

Eligibility This program is open to residents of any state who are currently enrolled at law schools in Maryland. Applicants must submit a 2-page essay on 1) the most significant experiences in their background that have shaped and demonstrated their commitment to serving the needs of Asian Pacific Americans, and 2) how they will best serve the needs of the Asian Pacific American community in their future legal career. Financial need is not considered in the selection process.

Financial data The stipend is $750.

Duration 1 year.

Number awarded 2 each year.

Deadline April of each year.

[427]
ASIAN PACIFIC BAR ASSOCIATION OF THE SILICON VALLEY SCHOLARSHIP

Asian Pacific Bar Association of the Silicon Valley
c/o Steve Chariyasatit, Scholarship Committee Co-Chair
Orrick, Herrington & Sutcliffe LLP
1000 Marsh Road
Menlo Park, CA 94025-1015
(650) 614-7400   Fax: (650) 614-7401
E-mail: schariyasatit@orrick.com
Web: www.apabasv.org/scholarship.html

Summary To provide financial assistance to students from any state who are enrolled at law schools in the San Francisco Bay area and have been involved in the Asian Pacific Islander community.

Eligibility This program is open to law students in the San Francisco Bay area who have demonstrated leadership in or service to the Asian Pacific Islander community in the United States. Applicants must submit an essay on their personal history in overcoming hardships or challenges, involvement in the Asian Pacific Islander community in the United States, and financial need. Finalists are interviewed.

Financial data The stipend is $3,000.

Duration 1 year.

Number awarded Varies each year; recently, 3 of these scholarships were awarded.

Deadline September of each year.

[428]
ASIAN PACIFIC ISLANDER AMERICAN PUBLIC AFFAIRS ASSOCIATION SCHOLARSHIPS

Asian Pacific Islander American Public Affairs Association
Attn: Community Education Foundation
185 Butcher Road
Vacaville, CA 95687
(707) 451-0130   Fax: (707) 451-0131
E-mail: info@apapa.org
Web: www.apapa.org

Summary To provide financial assistance to residents of California, especially those of Asian or Pacific Islander ancestry, who are attending college or graduate school in any state.

Eligibility This program is open to residents of California who are currently enrolled as an undergraduate or graduate student at an accredited 2- or 4-year college or university in any state. All students are eligible, but applications are especially encouraged from those who have Asian or Pacific Islander ancestry. They must have a GPA of 2.75 or higher. Along with their application, they must submit a personal statement demonstrating their commitment to the Asian Pacific Islander community. Selection is based on academic achievement, abilities, career goals, civic activities, leadership skills, and demonstrated commitment to the Asian Pacific Islander community. U.S. citizenship or permanent resident status is required.

Financial data The stipend is $1,000.

Duration 1 year; nonrenewable.

Number awarded 1 or more each year.

Deadline March of each year.

[429]
ASSOCIATION OF CHINESE AMERICAN PHYSICIANS-MID-ATLANTIC CHAPTER SCHOLARSHIP

Association of Chinese American Physicians-Mid-Atlantic Chapter
c/o Richard Chang, Scholarship Committee
13216 Maplecrest Drive
Potomac, MD 20845
(301) 424-0136   E-mail: orthochang@hotmail.com
Web: www.camsdc.org/scholarship.html

Summary To provide financial assistance to medical and dental students of Chinese descent who reside or attend school in the greater Washington, D.C. metropolitan area.

Eligibility This program is open to Chinese American medical and dental students who reside or attend school in Washington, D.C., Virginia, or Maryland. Applicants must submit their curriculum vitae, a description of their community service experiences, and an essay of 1 to 2 pages identifying a health issue that they think Asian Americans face and what they would propose to resolve it.

Financial data Stipends range up to $5,000.

Duration 1 year.

Additional information Until 2011, this sponsor was named the Mid-Atlantic Chapter of the Chinese American Medical Society.

Number awarded 1 or more each year.

Deadline December of each year.

[430]
ASSOCIATION OF RESEARCH LIBRARIES CAREER ENHANCEMENT PROGRAM

Association of Research Libraries
Attn: Director of Diversity Programs
21 Dupont Circle, N.W., Suite 800
Washington, DC 20036
(202) 296-2296   Fax: (202) 872-0884
E-mail: mpuente@arl.org
Web: www.arl.org/diversity/cep/index.shtml

Summary To provide financial assistance for further study and an opportunity for Asian Americans or other minorities to gain work experience at a library that is a member of the Association of Research Libraries (ARL).

Eligibility This program is open to members of racial and ethnic minority groups that are underrepresented as professionals in academic and research libraries (American Indian or Alaska Native, Asian, Black or African American, Native Hawaiian or other Pacific Islander, or Hispanic or Latino). Applicants must have completed at least 12 credit hours of an M.L.I.S. degree program at an ALA-accredited institution. They must be interested in an internship at 1 of 7 ARL member institutions. Along with their application, they must submit a 400-word essay on what attracts them to an internship opportunity in an ARL library, their professional interests as related to the internship, and their goals for the internship.

Financial data Fellows receive a stipend of $4,800 for the internship, an academic stipend of up to $2,500, a housing stipend of up to $2,000, a travel stipend of up to $1,000 for transportation expenses to and from the internship site, and financial support (approximately $1,000) to attend the annual ARL Leadership Institute.

Duration The internship lasts 6 to 12 weeks (or 240 hours). The academic stipend is for 1 year.

Additional information This program is funded by the Institute of Museum and Library Services. Recently, the 7 participating ARL institutions were the University of Arizona, University of California at San Diego, Columbia University, University of Kentucky, National Library of Medicine, North Carolina State University, and University of Washington.

Number awarded Varies each year; recently, 18 of these fellows were selected.

Deadline October of each year.

[431]
BAKER & DANIELS DIVERSITY SCHOLARSHIPS

Baker & Daniels LLP
Attn: Diversity and Pro Bono Coordinator
300 North Meridian Street, Suite 2700
Indianapolis, IN 46204
(317) 237-8298   Fax: (317) 237-1000
E-mail: brita.horvath@bakerd.com
Web: www.bakerdaniels.com/AboutUs/recruitment.aspx

Summary To provide financial assistance and summer work experience to Asian Americans and other students from diverse backgrounds entering the second year of law school in Indiana.

Eligibility This program is open to residents of any state who are entering their second year at selected law schools in Indiana. Applicants must reflect diversity, defined to mean that they come from varied ethnic, racial, cultural, and lifestyle backgrounds, as well as those with disabilities or unique viewpoints. They must also be interested in a place in the sponsor's summer associate program. Along with their application, they must submit a personal statement that includes an explanation of how this scholarship would benefit them, an overview of their background and interests, an explanation of what diversity they would bring to the firm, and any other financial assistance they are receiving. Selection is based primarily on academic excellence.

Financial data The stipend is $10,000.

Duration 1 year.

Additional information The eligible law schools are those at Indiana University at Bloomington, Indiana University at Indianapolis, and the University of Notre Dame.

Number awarded 2 each year.

Deadline June of each year.

[432]
BAKER DONELSON DIVERSITY SCHOLARSHIPS

Baker, Donelson, Bearman, Caldwell & Berkowitz, P.C.
Attn: Director of Attorney Recruiting
3414 Peachtree Road N.E.
Atlanta, GA 30326
(404) 577-6000   Fax: (404) 221-6501
E-mail: lklein@bakerdonelson.com
Web: www.bakerdonelson.com

Summary To provide financial assistance to Asian American and other law students who are members of groups underrepresented at large law firms.

Eligibility This program is open to students who have completed the first year at an ABA-accredited law school. Applicants must be members of a group traditionally underrepresented at large law firms (American Indian or Alaskan Native, Native Hawaiian or Pacific Islander, Hispanic or Latino, Black, or Asian). Along with their application, they must submit a 10-page legal writing sample and a 1-page personal statement on challenges they have faced in pursuit of their legal career that have helped them to understand the value of diversity and its inclusion in the legal profession. Finalists are interviewed.

Financial data The stipend is $10,000.

Duration 1 year.

Additional information Recipients are also offered summer internships at Baker Donelson offices in Atlanta (Georgia), Baton Rouge (Louisiana), Birmingham (Alabama), Chattanooga (Tennessee), Jackson (Mississippi), Johnson City (Tennessee), Knoxville (Tennessee), Memphis (Tennessee), Nashville (Tennessee), and New Orleans (Louisiana).

Number awarded 3 each year.

Deadline June of each year.

[433]
BAKER HOSTETLER DIVERSITY FELLOWSHIP PROGRAM

Baker Hostetler LLP
Attn: Attorney Recruitment and Development Manager
PNC Center
1900 East Ninth Street, Suite 3200
Cleveland, OH 44114-3482
(216) 621-0200   Fax: (216) 696-0740
E-mail: ddriscole@bakerlaw.com
Web: www.bakerlaw.com/diversity/fellowshipprogram

Summary To provide summer work experience to Asian American and other minority law school students.

Eligibility This program is open to full-time second-year students at ABA-accredited law schools who are members of underrepresented groups (Asian American/Pacific Islander, Black/African American, Hispanic, American Indian/Alaskan Native, 2 or more races, or gay, lesbian, bisexual, transgender). Applicants must be interested in a summer associate position with Baker Hostetler and possible full-time employment following graduation. They must be U.S. citizens or otherwise authorized to work in the United States. Along with their application, they must submit a 500-word personal statement presenting their views of or experience with diversity, including why they are interested in Baker Hostetler and how they will be able to contribute to the diversity objectives of the firm. Selection is based on academic performance in college and law school, personal achievements, community involvement, oral and written communication skills, demonstrated leadership achievements, and a sincere interest and commitment to join Baker Hostetler.

Financial data The stipend is $25,000, of which $10,000 is paid within the first 30 days of starting a summer associate position with the firm and the remaining $15,000 is contingent upon receiving and accepting a full-time offer with the firm.

Duration Summer associate positions are for 8 weeks.

Additional information Summer associate positions may be performed at any of the firm's offices in Chicago, Cincinnati, Cleveland, Columbus, Costa Mesa, Denver, Houston, Los Angeles, New York, Orlando, or Washington, D.C.

Number awarded 1 or more each year.

Deadline October of each year.

[434]
BEHAVIORAL SCIENCES STUDENT FELLOWSHIPS IN EPILEPSY

Epilepsy Foundation
Attn: Research Department
8301 Professional Place
Landover, MD 20785-2237
(301) 459-3700   Toll Free: (800) EFA-1000
Fax: (301) 577-2684   TDD: (800) 332-2070
E-mail: grants@efa.org
Web: www.epilepsyfoundation.org

Summary To provide funding to undergraduate and graduate students (especially Asian Americans, other minorities, women, and individuals with disabilities) who are interested in working on a summer research training project in a behavioral science field relevant to epilepsy.

Eligibility This program is open to undergraduate and graduate students in a behavioral science program relevant to epilepsy research or clinical care, including, but not limited to, sociology, social work, psychology, anthropology, nursing, economics, vocational rehabilitation, counseling, or political science. Applicants must be interested in working on an epilepsy research project under the supervision of a qualified mentor. Because the program is designed as a training opportunity, the quality of the training plans and environment are considered in the selection process. Other selection criteria include the quality of the proposed project, the relevance of the proposed work to epilepsy, the applicant's interest in the field of epilepsy, the applicant's qualifications, and the mentor's qualifications (including his or her commitment to the student and the project), and the quality of the training environment for research related to epilepsy. U.S. citizenship is not required, but the project must be conducted in the United States. Applications from women, members of minority groups, and people with disabilities are especially encouraged. The program is not intended for students working on a dissertation research project.

Financial data The grant is $3,000.

Duration 3 months during the summer.

Additional information This program is supported by the American Epilepsy Society, Abbott Laboratories, Ortho-McNeil Pharmaceutical Corporation, and Pfizer Inc.

Number awarded Varies each year.

Deadline March of each year.

[435]
BILL BERNBACH DIVERSITY SCHOLARSHIPS

American Association of Advertising Agencies
Attn: AAAA Foundation
405 Lexington Avenue, 18th Floor
New York, NY 10174-1801
(212) 682-2500   Toll Free: (800) 676-9333
Fax: (212) 682-2028   E-mail: ameadows@aaaa.org
Web: www2.aaaa.org

Summary To provide financial assistance to Asian American and other multicultural students interested in working on a graduate degree in advertising at designated schools.

Eligibility This program is open to Asian Americans, African Americans, Hispanic Americans, and Native Americans who are interested in studying the advertising creative arts at designated institutions. Applicants must have already received an undergraduate degree and be able to demonstrate creative talent and promise. Along with their application, they must submit 10 samples of creative work in their respective field of expertise. U.S. citizenship or permanent resident status is required.

Financial data   The stipend is $5,000.

Duration   1 year.

Additional information   This program, which began in 1998, is currently sponsored by DDB Worldwide. The participating schools are the AdCenter at Virginia Commonwealth University, the Creative Circus and the Portfolio Center in Atlanta, the Miami Ad School, the University of Texas at Austin, and the Art Center College of Design in Pasadena, California.

Number awarded   5 each year.

Deadline   Deadline not specified.

[436]
BISHOP THOMAS HOYT, JR. FELLOWSHIP

St. John's University
Attn: Collegeville Institute for Ecumenical and Cultural
   Research
14027 Fruit Farm Road
Box 2000
Collegeville, MN 56321-2000
(320) 363-3366   Fax: (320) 363-3313
E-mail: staff@CollegevilleInstitute.org
Web: collegevilleinstitute.org/res-fellowships

Summary   To provide funding to Asian Americans and other students of color who wish to complete their doctoral dissertation while in residence at the Collegeville Institute for Ecumenical and Cultural Research of St. John's University in Collegeville, Minnesota.

Eligibility   This program is open to people of color completing a doctoral dissertation in ecumenical and cultural research. Applicants must be interested in a residency at the Collegeville Institute for Ecumenical and Cultural Research of St. John's University. Along with their application, they must submit a 1,000-word description of the research project they plan to complete while in residence at the Institute.

Financial data   The stipend covers the residency fee of $2,000, which includes housing and utilities.

Duration   1 year.

Additional information   Residents at the Institute engage in study, research, and publication on the important intersections between faith and culture. They seek to discern and communicate the meaning of Christian identity and unity in a religiously and culturally diverse world.

Number awarded   1 each year.

Deadline   October of each year.

[437]
BOB CHIN SCHOLARSHIP

National Asian Pacific American Bar Association
Attn: NAPABA Law Foundation
1612 K Street, N.W., Suite 1400
Washington, DC 20006
(202) 775-9555   Fax: (202) 775-9333
E-mail: foundation@napaba.org
Web: www.napaba.org

Summary   To provide financial assistance to students at law schools in the New York City tri-state area who have had

a diagnosis of cancer within their family and are interested in serving the Asian Pacific American community.

Eligibility   This program is open to students from any state enrolled at ABA-accredited law schools in the New York City tri-state area. Applicants must demonstrate leadership potential to serve the Asian Pacific American community upon graduation. Their lives must have been impacted by a diagnosis of cancer within their immediate family. Along with their application, they must submit a 500-word essay that covers 1) the most significant experiences in their background that have shaped and demonstrated their commitment to serving the needs of Asian Pacific Americans; and 2) how they intend to serve the needs of the Asian Pacific American community in their future legal career. Selection is based on demonstrated commitment to pro bono service; leadership potential; financial need; commitment to serving the needs of the Asian Pacific American community; and commitment to attend a scholarship award ceremony in the New York City tri-state area. U.S. citizenship or permanent resident status is required.

Financial data   The stipend is $2,500.

Duration   1 year.

Number awarded   1 each year.

Deadline   September of each year.

[438]
BONG HAK HYUN MEMORIAL SCHOLARSHIP

Philip Jaisohn Memorial Foundation
Attn: Education and Scholarship Committee
6705 Old York Road
Philadelphia, PA 19126
(215) 224-2000   Fax: (215) 224-9164
E-mail: jaisohnhouse@gmail.com
Web: jaisohn.org

Summary   To provide financial assistance to Korean American medical students.

Eligibility   This program is open to Korean American students who are currently enrolled at a medical school in the United States. Applicants must be able to demonstrate excellence in community activities and financial need. Along with their application, they must submit an essay on either "Who is Dr. Jaisohn to Me," or "The Significance of Dr. Jaisohn's Ideal to Korean Americans." They must also submit a brief statement on how they can contribute to and be involved in the activities of the Philip Jaisohn Memorial Foundation.

Financial data   The stipend is $1,500.

Duration   1 year.

Number awarded   1 each year.

Deadline   November of each year.

[439]
BOR-UEI CHEN SCHOLARSHIPS

Photonics Society of Chinese-Americans
c/o Chun-Ching Shih
1517 Via Fernandez
Palos Verdes Estates, CA 90274
(310) 814-0318   E-mail: admin@psc-a.org
Web: www.psc-a.org

Summary   To provide financial assistance to Chinese American graduate students in the field of optical communications and photonic devices.

Eligibility This program is open to Chinese American graduate students at universities in the United States who are nominated by a member of the Photonics Society of Chinese-Americans. Nominees must be working on a degree in a field related to optical communications and photonic devices. Selection is based on the merits of the candidate's research work as documented by publications in technical journals, conference presentations, and recommendations from the candidate's sponsor or adviser.

Financial data The stipend is $1,000.

Duration 1 year.

Additional information These scholarships were first awarded in 1995.

Number awarded Varies each year; recently, 4 of these scholarships were awarded.

Deadline February of each year.

[440]
BREAKTHROUGH TO NURSING SCHOLARSHIPS

National Student Nurses' Association
Attn: Foundation
45 Main Street, Suite 606
Brooklyn, NY 11201
(718) 210-0705   Fax: (718) 797-1186
E-mail: nsna@nsna.org
Web: www.nsna.org

Summary To provide financial assistance to Asian American and other minority undergraduate and graduate students who wish to prepare for careers in nursing.

Eligibility This program is open to students currently enrolled in state-approved schools of nursing or pre-nursing associate degree, baccalaureate, diploma, generic master's, generic doctoral, R.N. to B.S.N., R.N. to M.S.N., or L.P.N./L.V.N. to R.N. programs. Graduating high school seniors are not eligible. Support for graduate education is provided only for a first degree in nursing. Applicants must be members of a racial or ethnic minority underrepresented among registered nurses (American Indian or Alaska Native, Hispanic or Latino, Native Hawaiian or other Pacific Islander, Black or African American, or Asian). They must be committed to providing quality health care services to underserved populations. Along with their application, they must submit a 200-word description of their professional and educational goals and how this scholarship will help them achieve those goals. Selection is based on academic achievement, financial need, and involvement in student nursing organizations and community health activities. U.S. citizenship or permanent resident status is required.

Financial data Stipends range from $1,000 to $2,500. A total of approximately $155,000 is awarded each year by the foundation for all its scholarship programs.

Duration 1 year.

Additional information Applications must be accompanied by a $10 processing fee.

Number awarded Varies each year; recently, 5 of these scholarships were awarded: 2 sponsored by the American Association of Critical-Care Nurses and 3 sponsored by the Mayo Clinic.

Deadline January of each year.

[441]
BROADCAST SALES ASSOCIATE PROGRAM

International Radio and Television Society Foundation
Attn: Director, Special Projects
420 Lexington Avenue, Suite 1601
New York, NY 10170-0101
(212) 867-6650   Toll Free: (888) 627-1266
Fax: (212) 867-6653   E-mail: apply@irts.org
Web: irts.org/broadcast-sales-associate-program.html

Summary To provide summer work experience to Asian American and other minority graduate students interested in working in broadcast sales in the New York City area.

Eligibility This program is open to graduate students at 4-year colleges and universities who are members of a minority (Black, Hispanic, Asian/Pacific Islander, American Indian/Alaskan Native) group. Applicants must be interested in working during the summer in a sales training program traditionally reserved for actual station group employees. They must be a communications major or have demonstrated a strong interest in the field through extracurricular activities or other practical experience, but they are not required to have experience in broadcast sales.

Financial data Travel, housing, and a living allowance are provided.

Duration 9 weeks during the summer.

Additional information The program consists of a 1-week orientation to the media and entertainment business, followed by an 8-week internship experience in the sales division of a network stations group.

Number awarded Varies each year.

Deadline February of each year.

[442]
BUCKINGHAM, DOOLITTLE & BURROUGHS DIVERSITY SCHOLARSHIP PROGRAM

Buckingham, Doolittle & Burroughs, LLP
Attn: Benefits and Employment Coordinator
3800 Embassy Parkway, Suite 300
Akron, OH 44333
(330) 376-5300   Toll Free: (800) 686-2825
E-mail: bdb@bdblaw.com
Web: www.bdblaw.com/diversity-program.asp

Summary To provide financial assistance and summer work experience to Asian American and other minority students from any state who are enrolled at designated law schools in Ohio and Florida.

Eligibility This program is open to first-year students at law schools in Ohio and Florida who are of minority (African American, Hispanic, Asian, or Native American) descent. Applicants must submit a 1,000-word personal statement about themselves that includes a discussion of the life influences that have contributed to the person they are today. Selection is based on academic excellence, demonstrated leadership skills, service to the community, and commitment to excellence.

Financial data As summer associates, students receive a salary of $1,538.46 per week at offices in Akron and Canton, $1,586.54 per week at offices in Cleveland and Columbus, or $1,730.77 per week at offices in Boca Raton and West Palm Beach. The stipend for the academic year following completion of the associateship is $5,000.

Duration 1 year.

Additional information This program, which began in 2005, is available at the following Ohio law schools: Capital University Law School, Case Western Reserve University School of Law, Cleveland-Marshall College of Law, Ohio Northern University Pettit College of Law, Ohio State University Moritz College of Law, University of Akron School of Law, University of Cincinnati College of Law, University of Dayton School of Law, and University of Toledo College of Law. It is also available to students at the following Florida law schools: University of Florida Levin College of Law, Florida State University College of Law, University of Miami School of Law, Nova Southeastern University Shepard Broad Law Center, Stetson University College of Law, Barry University School of Law, Florida Coastal School of Law, and St. Thomas University School of Law. Summer associateships are available at the firm's offices in Ohio (Akron, Canton, Cleveland, and Columbus) and in Florida (Boca Raton and West Palm Beach).

Number awarded 1 each year.

Deadline January of each year.

[443]
BUILDING ACADEMIC GERIATRIC NURSING CAPACITY PROGRAM PREDOCTORAL SCHOLARSHIP PROGRAM

American Academy of Nursing
Attn: Building Academic Geriatric Nursing Capacity
  Program
888 17th Street, N.W., Suite 800
Washington, DC 20006
(202) 777-1170   Fax: (202) 777-0107
E-mail: bagnc@aannet.org
Web: www.geriatricnursing.org

Summary To provide funding to nurses (especially Asian Americans and members of other underrepresented groups) who are interested in working on a doctoral degree in gerontological nursing.

Eligibility This program is open to registered nurses who hold a degree in nursing and have been admitted to a doctoral program as a full-time student. Applicants must plan an academic career in geriatric nursing. They must identify a mentor/adviser with whom they will work and whose program of research in geriatric nursing is a good match with their own research interest area. Selection is based on potential for substantial long-term contributions to the knowledge base in geriatric nursing; leadership potential; evidence of commitment to a career in academic geriatric nursing; and evidence of involvement in educational, research, and professional activities. Members of underrepresented minority groups (Asians, American Indians, Alaska Natives, Blacks or African Americans, Hispanics or Latinos/Latinas, Native Hawaiians or other Pacific Islanders) are especially encouraged to apply. U.S. citizenship or permanent resident status is required.

Financial data The stipend is $50,000 per year. An additional stipend of $5,000 is available to fellows whose research includes the study of pain in the elderly.

Duration 2 years.

Additional information This program began in 2001 with funding from the John A. Hartford Foundation. In 2004, the Mayday Fund added support to scholars who focus on the study of pain in the elderly.

Number awarded Varies each year; recently, 12 of these scholarships were awarded.

Deadline January of each year.

[444]
BULLIVANT HOUSER BAILEY LAW STUDENT DIVERSITY FELLOWSHIP PROGRAM

Bullivant Houser Bailey PC
Attn: Recruitment and Diversity Manager
888 S.W. Fifth Avenue, Suite 300
Portland, OR 97204-2089
(503) 499-4558   Toll Free: (800) 654-8972
Fax: (503) 295-0915   E-mail: jill.valentine@bullivant.com
Web: www.bullivant.com/diversity

Summary To provide financial assistance and work experience to Asian American and other law students who come from a minority or disadvantaged background.

Eligibility This program is open to first-year law students who are members of a minority group (including any group underrepresented in the legal profession) and/or students coming from a disadvantaged educational or economic background. Applicants must have 1) a record of academic achievement and leadership in college and law school; 2) a willingness to complete a 12-week summer associateship at an office of the firm; and 3) a record of contributions to the community that promote diversity within society, the legal community, and/or law school.

Financial data The program provides a salaried associate position at an office of the firm during the summer following the first year of law school and a stipend of $7,500 for the second year.

Duration 1 year.

Number awarded 2 each year: 1 assigned to an associateship in the Sacramento office and 1 assigned to an associateship in the Portland office.

Deadline January of each year.

[445]
BUTLER RUBIN DIVERSITY SCHOLARSHIP

Butler Rubin Saltarelli & Boyd LLP
Attn: Diversity Partner
70 West Madison Street, Suite 1800
Chicago, IL 60602
(312) 242-4120   Fax: (312) 444-9843
E-mail: kborg@butlerrubin.com
Web: www.butlerrubin.com/web/br.nsf/diversity

Summary To provide financial assistance and summer work experience to Asian American and other minority law students who are interested in the area of business litigation.

Eligibility This program is open to law students of racial and ethnic backgrounds that will contribute to diversity in the legal profession. Applicants must be interested in the private practice of law in the area of business litigation and in a summer associateship in that field with Butler Rubin Saltarelli & Boyd in Chicago. Selection is based on academic performance and achievement, intention to remain in the Chicago area following graduation, and interpersonal and communication skills.

Financial data The stipend is $10,000 per year; funds are to be used for tuition and other expenses associated with law school. For the summer associateship, a stipend is paid.

Duration 1 year; may be renewed.
Additional information This program was established in 2006.
Number awarded 1 each year.
Deadline Deadline not specified.

[446]
C. CLYDE FERGUSON LAW SCHOLARSHIP

New Jersey Commission on Higher Education
Attn: Educational Opportunity Fund
20 West State Street, Fourth Floor
P.O. Box 542
Trenton, NJ 08625-0542
(609) 984-2709 Fax: (609) 292-7225
E-mail: nj_che@che.state.nj.us
Web: www.nj.gov

Summary To provide financial assistance to Asian American and other disadvantaged or minority students from New Jersey who want to study law in the state.

Eligibility This program is open to students who 1) fall within specified income guidelines (currently, less than $21,660 for a family of 1 rising to $74,020 for a family of 8); 2) minority or disadvantaged students with financial need; or 3) former or current recipients of a New Jersey Educational Opportunity Fund undergraduate or graduate grant, or who would have been eligible to receive the grant as an undergraduate. Applicants must have been New Jersey residents for at least 12 months before receiving the award and must plan to enroll full time in the Minority Student Program at law schools in New Jersey (Rutgers University School of Law at Newark, Rutgers University School of Law at Camden, or Seton Hall Law School).

Financial data Awards are based on financial need. In no case, however, can awards exceed the maximum amount of tuition, fees, room, and board charged at Rutgers University School of Law at Newark.

Duration 1 year; may be renewed.
Deadline Deadline not specified.

[447]
CALA SCHOLARSHIP

Chinese American Librarians Association
c/o Ying Xu, Scholarship Committee Chair
California State University at Los Angeles
University Library 2014
Los Angeles, CA 90032-8300
(323) 343-3959 E-mail: yxu1@calstatela.edu
Web: www.cala-web.org/node/204

Summary To provide financial assistance to Chinese American students interested in working on a graduate degree in library or information science.

Eligibility This program is open to students enrolled full time in an accredited library school in North America and working on a master's or doctoral degree. Applicants must be of Chinese nationality or Chinese descent. They must submit a resume and a personal statement of 300 to 500 words on their past experiences, career interests, and commitment to library and information science.

Financial data The stipend is $1,000.
Duration 1 year.

Additional information This program was established in 2004.
Number awarded 1 each year.
Deadline March of each year.

[448]
CALIFORNIA BAR FOUNDATION DIVERSITY SCHOLARSHIPS

State Bar of California
Attn: California Bar Foundation
180 Howard Street
San Francisco, CA 94105-1639
(415) 856-0780, ext. 302 Fax: (415) 856-0788
E-mail: jguillory@calbarfoundation.org
Web: www.calbarfoundation.org

Summary To provide financial assistance to Asian American and other law students from any state who are members of racial or ethnic groups historically underrepresented in the legal profession and entering law school in California.

Eligibility This program to open to residents of any state who are entering their first year at a law school in California. Applicants must self-identify as being from a racial or ethnic group that historically has been underrepresented in the legal profession (Latino, African American, Asian and Pacific Islander, and Native American). They must be committed to making an impact in the community through leadership. Along with their application, they must submit a 500-word essay describing their commitment to serving the community and, if applicable, any significant obstacles or hurdles they have overcome to attend law school. Financial need is considered in the selection process.

Financial data Stipends for named awards are $7,500. Other stipends are $5,000 or $2,500.
Duration 1 year.
Additional information These scholarships were first awarded in 2008. Each year, the foundation grants awards named after sponsors that donate funding for the scholarships. Recipients are required to attend a reception in their honor in October of the year of their award and to submit a report on their progress at the end of that year.
Number awarded Varies each year; recently, the foundation awarded 28 of these scholarships: 20 named awards at $7,500, 4 awards at $5,000, and 4 awards at $2,500.
Deadline June of each year.

[449]
CALIFORNIA CAPITOL SUMMER INTERNSHIP PROGRAM

Asian Pacific Islander American Public Affairs Association
Attn: Community Education Foundation
185 Butcher Road
Vacaville, CA 95687
(707) 451-0130 Fax: (707) 451-0131
E-mail: info@apapa.org
Web: www.apapa.org

Summary To provide summer work experience at an office of state government in Sacramento to undergraduate and graduate student residents of California who are of Asian or Pacific Islander descent.

Eligibility This program is open to undergraduate and graduate students who are of Asian or Pacific Islander background and residents of California attending college in the state. Applicants must be interested in a summer internship in Sacramento at an office of state government. They must have a GPA of 2.75 or higher. Along with their application, they must submit a 2-page statement on their Asian or Pacific Islander background, community and public service involvement, academic and career goals, and future plans for public services and/or politics and government involvement. Selection is based on GPA, demonstrated leadership, interpersonal skills, written and verbal communication skills, and community service.

Financial data   Interns receive a stipend of $1,000 upon successful completion of the program.

Duration   8 weeks, beginning in June.

Additional information   Interns must also complete 20 community service hours for the sponsor's Sacramento chapter.

Number awarded   1 or more each year.

Deadline   February of each year.

[450]
CALIFORNIA DIVERSITY FELLOWSHIPS IN ENVIRONMENTAL LAW

American Bar Association
Attn: Section of Environment, Energy, and Resources
321 North Clark Street
Chicago, IL 60654-7598
(312) 988-5602   Fax: (312) 988-5572
E-mail: jonusaid@staff.abanet.org
Web: www.abanet.org

Summary   To provide funding to Asian American and other law students from underrepresented and underserved groups who are interested in working on a summer project in environmental, energy, or resources law in California.

Eligibility   This program is open to first- and second-year law students and third-year night students who are members of underrepresented and underserved groups, such as minority or low-income populations. Students may be residents of any state and attending school in any state; preference is given to residents of California and to students who are enrolled at law schools in California or who have a strong interest in the state. Applicants must be interested in working during the summer at a government agency or public interest organization on a project in California, with an emphasis on air quality issues in the Los Angeles basin and the Central Valley. Selection is based on interest in environmental issues, academic record, personal qualities, and leadership abilities.

Financial data   The stipend is $5,000.

Duration   8 to 10 weeks during the summer.

Additional information   This program is cosponsored by the State Bar of California's Environmental Law Section and the William and Flora Hewlett Foundation.

Number awarded   Varies each year; recently, 13 of these fellowships were awarded.

Deadline   April of each year.

[451]
CALIFORNIA PLANNING FOUNDATION OUTSTANDING DIVERSITY AWARD

American Planning Association-California Chapter
Attn: California Planning Foundation
c/o Paul Wack
P.O. Box 1086
Morro Bay, CA 93443-1086
(805) 756-6331   Fax: (805) 756-1340
E-mail: pwack@calpoly.edu
Web: www.californiaplanningfoundation.org

Summary   To provide financial assistance to Asian American and other undergraduate and graduate students in accredited planning programs at California universities who will increase diversity in the profession.

Eligibility   This program is open to students entering their final year for an undergraduate or master's degree in an accredited planning program at a university in California. Applicants must be students who will increase diversity in the planning profession. Selection is based on academic performance, professional promise, and financial need.

Financial data   The stipend is $3,000. The award includes a 1-year student membership in the American Planning Association (APA) and payment of registration for the APA California Conference.

Duration   1 year.

Additional information   The accredited planning programs are at 3 campuses of the California State University system (California State Polytechnic University at Pomona, California Polytechnic State University at San Luis Obispo, and San Jose State University), 3 campuses of the University of California (Berkeley, Irvine, and Los Angeles), and the University of Southern California.

Number awarded   1 each year.

Deadline   March of each year.

[452]
CAMS SCHOLARSHIP PROGRAM

Chinese American Medical Society
Attn: Jerry Huo, Scholarship Committee
41 Elizabeth Street, Suite 403
New York, NY 10013
(212) 334-4760   Fax: (212) 965-1876
E-mail: jerryhuomd@gmail.com
Web: www.camsociety.org/scholarshipprogram.html

Summary   To provide financial assistance to Chinese and Chinese American students who are working on a degree in medicine or dentistry.

Eligibility   This program is open to Chinese or Chinese American students who are currently enrolled in the first, second, or third year at an approved medical or dental school in the United States. Applicants must submit a personal statement that includes their career goals, a current vitae, 2 letters of recommendation, and documentation of financial need. Special consideration is given to applicants with research projects relating to health care of the Chinese.

Financial data   The scholarships range from $1,000 to $1,500.

Duration   1 year; recipients may reapply.

Additional information   This program includes the Esther Lim Memorial Scholarship established in 1989, the Ruth Liu

Memorial Scholarship established in 1996, and the American Center for Chinese Medical Sciences Scholarship established in 2004 upon the dissolution of that organization. Recipients who do not complete their planned study, research, or teaching must make a prorated refund to the society.

Number awarded Varies; recently, 3 to 5 scholarships have been awarded each year.

Deadline April of each year.

[453]
CAMS SUMMER RESEARCH FELLOWSHIP

Chinese American Medical Society
Attn: Jerry Huo, Scholarship Committee
41 Elizabeth Street, Suite 403
New York, NY 10013
(212) 334-4760   Fax: (212) 965-1876
E-mail: jerryhuomd@gmail.com
Web: www.camsociety.org/summerprogram.html

Summary To provide funding to Chinese American medical and dental students who are interested in conducting a summer research project.

Eligibility This program is open to Chinese or Chinese Americans who are enrolled in a medical or dental school in the United States and are interested in conducting a research project. The research can be basic science or clinical. A physician or dentist must sponsor and supervise the project. Special consideration is given to proposals involving Chinese American health issues.

Financial data The stipend is $400 per week.

Duration 8 to 10 weeks during the summer.

Additional information A written report is expected at the conclusion of the project.

Number awarded Varies each year.

Deadline April of each year.

[454]
CANFIT PROGRAM GRADUATE SCHOLARSHIPS

California Adolescent Nutrition and Fitness Program
Attn: Scholarship Program
2140 Shattuck Avenue, Suite 610
Berkeley, CA 94704
(510) 644-1533   Toll Free: (800) 200-3131
Fax: (510) 644-1535   E-mail: info@canfit.org
Web: canfit.org/scholarships

Summary To provide financial assistance to Asian American and other minority students who are working on a graduate degree in nutrition, physical education, or public health in California.

Eligibility This program is open to American Indians, Alaska Natives, African Americans, Asian Americans, Pacific Islanders, and Latinos/Hispanics from California who are enrolled in 1) an approved master's or doctoral program in nutrition, public health, or physical education in the state, or 2) a preprofessional practice program approved by the American Dietetic Association at an accredited university in the state. Applicants must have completed 12 to 15 units of graduate course work and have a cumulative GPA of 3.0 or higher. Along with their application, they must submit 1) documentation of financial need; 2) letters of recommendation from 2 individuals; 3) a 1-to 2-page letter describing their academic

goals and involvement in community nutrition and/or physical education activities; and 4) an essay of 500 to 1,000 words on a topic related to healthy foods for youth from low-income communities of color.

Financial data A stipend is awarded (amount not specified).

Number awarded 1 or more each year.

Deadline March of each year.

[455]
CAREER DEVELOPMENT GRANTS

American Association of University Women
Attn: AAUW Educational Foundation
301 ACT Drive, Department 60
P.O. Box 4030
Iowa City, IA 52243-4030
(319) 337-1716, ext. 60   Fax: (319) 337-1204
E-mail: aauw@act.org
Web: www.aauw.org

Summary To provide financial assistance to women (particularly Asian American and other minority women) who are seeking career advancement, career change, or reentry into the workforce.

Eligibility This program is open to women who are U.S. citizens or permanent residents, have earned a bachelor's degree, received their most recent degree more than 4 years ago, and are making career changes, seeking to advance in current careers, or reentering the work force. Applicants must be interested in working toward a master's degree, second bachelor's or associate degree, professional degree (e.g., M.D., J.D.), certification program, or technical school certificate. They must be planning to undertake course work at an accredited 2- or 4-year college or university (or a technical school that is licensed, accredited, or approved by the U.S. Department of Education). Special consideration is given to women of color and women pursuing credentials in nontraditional fields. Support is not provided for prerequisite course work or for Ph.D. course work or dissertations. Selection is based on demonstrated commitment to education and equity for women and girls, reason for seeking higher education or technical training, degree to which study plan is consistent with career objectives, potential for success in chosen field, documentation of opportunities in chosen field, feasibility of study plans and proposed time schedule, validity of proposed budget and budget narrative (including sufficient outside support), and quality of written proposal.

Financial data Grants range from $2,000 to $12,000. Funds may be used for tuition, fees, books, supplies, local transportation, dependent child care, or purchase of a computer required for the study program.

Duration 1 year, beginning in July; nonrenewable.

Additional information The filing fee is $35.

Number awarded Varies each year; recently, 47 of these grants, with a value of $500,000, were awarded.

Deadline December of each year.

[456]
CARL A. SCOTT BOOK FELLOWSHIPS

Council on Social Work Education
Attn: Chair, Carl A. Scott Memorial Fund
1701 Duke Street, Suite 200
Alexandria, VA 22314-3429
(703) 683-8080   Fax: (703) 683-8099
E-mail: info@cswe.org
Web: www.cswe.org

Summary To provide financial assistance to Asian Americans and other minorities who are working on an undergraduate or master's degree in social work and are in their last year of study.

Eligibility This program is open to students from ethnic groups of color (African American, Asian American, Hispanic/Latino, or American Indian) who are in the last year of study for a social work degree in an accredited baccalaureate or master's degree program. Applicants must have a cumulative GPA of 3.0 or higher and be enrolled full time. They must demonstrate a commitment to work for equity and social justice in social work.

Financial data The stipend is $500.

Duration This is a 1-time award.

Number awarded 2 each year.

Deadline May of each year.

[457]
CARMEN E. TURNER SCHOLARSHIPS

Conference of Minority Transportation Officials
Attn: National Scholarship Program
818 18th Street, N.W., Suite 850
Washington, DC 20006
(202) 530-0551   Fax: (202) 530-0617
Web: www.comto.org/news-youth.php

Summary To provide financial assistance for college or graduate school to Asian American and other members of the Conference of Minority Transportation Officials (COMTO).

Eligibility This program is open to undergraduate and graduate students who have been members of COMTO for at least 1 year. Applicants must be working on a degree in a field related to transportation with a GPA of 2.5 or higher. Along with their application, they must submit a cover letter with a 500-word statement of career goals. Financial need is not considered in the selection process. U.S. citizenship is required.

Financial data The stipend is $3,500. Funds are paid directly to the recipient's college or university.

Duration 1 year.

Additional information COMTO was established in 1971 to promote, strengthen, and expand the roles of minorities in all aspects of transportation. Recipients are expected to attend the COMTO National Scholarship Luncheon.

Number awarded 2 each year.

Deadline April of each year.

[458]
CATHY L. BROCK MEMORIAL SCHOLARSHIP

Institute for Diversity in Health Management
Attn: Executive Assistant
One North Franklin Street, 30th Floor
Chicago, IL 60606
(312) 422-2630   Toll Free: (800) 233-0996
Fax: (312) 895-4511   E-mail: ejohnson@aha.org
Web: www.applicantsoft.com

Summary To provide financial assistance to Asian Americans and other minority graduate students in health care management, especially financial operations.

Eligibility This program is open to members of ethnic minority groups who are accepted or enrolled in an accredited graduate program in health care administration. Applicants must have a GPA of 3.0 or higher. They must demonstrate commitment to a career in health care administration. Along with their application, they must submit a personal statement of 300 to 500 words on their interest in health care management and their career goals. Selection is based on academic achievement, leadership potential, financial need, community involvement, commitment to health care administration, and overall professional maturity. Preference is given to applicants studying financial operations. U.S. citizenship is required.

Financial data The stipend ranges from $500 to $1,000.

Duration 1 year.

Number awarded 1 or more each year, depending on the availability of funds.

Deadline December of each year.

[459]
CDC/PRC MINORITY FELLOWSHIPS

Association of Schools of Public Health
Attn: Senior Manager, Graduate Training Programs
1101 15th Street, N.W., Suite 910
Washington, DC 20005
(202) 296-1099   Fax: (202) 296-1252
E-mail: TrainingPrograms@asph.org
Web: www.asph.org

Summary To provide an opportunity for Asian American and other minority doctoral students to conduct research at Prevention Research Centers (PRCs) funded by the U.S. Centers for Disease Control and Prevention (CDC).

Eligibility This program is open to minority (African American/Black American, Hispanic/Latino, American Indian/Alaska Native, and Asian/Pacific Islander) students working on a doctoral degree at a school of public health with a CDC-funded PRC. Applicants must be proposing to conduct a research project that is related to the PRC activities and is endorsed by the PRC director. Along with their application, they must submit a personal statement (2 pages or less) on why they are interested in this fellowship, including specifics regarding their interest in the opportunity, benefits they expect to receive from the fellowship experience, how the experience will shape their future career plans, and how the proposed project will advance the field of public health prevention research. Selection is based on the personal statement (30 points), curriculum vitae and transcripts (20 points), and project proposal (50 points). U.S. citizenship or permanent resident status is required.

Financial data The stipend is $22,500 per year. Fellows are also reimbursed up to $3,000 per year for health-related expenses, project-related travel, tuition, journal subscriptions, and association dues.

Duration 2 years.

Number awarded Varies each year; recently, 11 of these fellowships were awarded.

Deadline March of each year.

[460]
CENTER ON BUDGET AND POLICY PRIORITIES INTERNSHIPS

Center on Budget and Policy Priorities
Attn: Internship Coordinator
820 First Street, N.E., Suite 510
Washington, DC 20002
(202) 408-1080   Fax: (202) 408-1056
E-mail: internship@cbpp.org
Web: www.cbpp.org/jobs/index.cfm?fa=internships

Summary To provide work experience at the Center on Budget and Policy Priorities (CBPP) in Washington, D.C. to undergraduates, graduate students, and recent college graduates, especially Asian Americans or other minorities, women, and international students.

Eligibility This program is open to undergraduates, graduate students, and recent college graduates who are interested in public policy issues affecting low-income families and individuals. Applicants must be interested in working at CBPP in the following areas: media, federal legislation, health policy, housing policy, international budget project, Food Stamps, national budget and tax policy, outreach campaigns, state budget and tax policy, welfare reform, and income support. They should have research, fact-gathering, writing, analytic, and computer skills and a willingness to do administrative as well as substantive tasks. Women, international students, and minorities are encouraged to apply.

Financial data Hourly stipends are $8.50 for undergraduates, $9.50 for interns with a bachelor's degree, $10.50 for graduate students, $12.50 for interns with a master's or law degree, and $12.50 to $15.50 for doctoral students (depending on progress towards completion of degree requirements, relevant course work, and research).

Duration 1 semester; may be renewed.

Additional information The center specializes in research and analysis oriented toward practical policy decisions and produces analytic reports that are accessible to public officials at national, state, and local levels, to nonprofit organizations, and to the media.

Number awarded Varies each semester; recently, 5 interns were appointed for a fall semester.

Deadline February of each year for summer internships; June of each year for fall internships; October of each year for spring internships.

[461]
CHINESE AMERICAN ASSOCIATION OF MINNESOTA SCHOLARSHIPS

Chinese American Association of Minnesota
Attn: Scholarship Program
P.O. Box 582584
Minneapolis, MN 55458-2584
E-mail: office@caam.org
Web: www.caam.org

Summary To provide financial assistance to Minnesota residents of Chinese descent who are interested in attending college or graduate school in any state.

Eligibility This program is open to Minnesota residents of Chinese descent who are enrolled or planning to enroll full time at a postsecondary school, college, or graduate school in any state. Applicants must submit an essay on the role their Chinese heritage has played in their work, study, and accomplishments. Selection is based on academic record, leadership qualities, and community service; financial need is also considered for some awards. Membership in the Chinese American Association of Minnesota (CAAM) is not required. Priority is given to applicants who have not previously received a CAAM scholarship.

Financial data The stipend ranges from $1,000 to $1,500.

Duration 1 year.

Additional information Recipients who are not CAAM members are expected to become members for at least 2 years.

Number awarded 1 or more each year.

Deadline November of each year.

[462]
CHINESE AMERICAN PHYSICIANS SOCIETY SCHOLARSHIP PROGRAM FOR U.S. MEDICAL STUDENTS

Chinese American Physicians Society
c/o Lawrence Ng, M.D., Executive Director
345 Ninth Street, Suite 204
Oakland, CA 94607-4206
(510) 839-1072   Fax: (510) 839-0988
E-mail: admin@caps-ca.org
Web: www.caps-ca.org

Summary To provide financial assistance to medical students in the United States, especially those willing to serve Chinese communities after graduation.

Eligibility This program is open to students attending or planning to attend a U.S. medical school. Applicants may be from any location. Preference is given to those willing to serve Chinese communities after graduation. Along with their application, they must submit a 500-word essay on a topic that changes annually; recently, students who asked to write on how they use their time wisely. Selection is based on the essay, academic achievement, financial need, and service.

Financial data Stipends range from $2,500 to $4,500 per year.

Duration 1 year; may be renewed.

Number awarded Varies each year; recently, 6 of these fellowships were awarded.

Deadline February of each year.

[463]
CHIYOKO AND THOMAS SHIMAZAKI SCHOLARSHIP

Japanese American Citizens League
Attn: National Scholarship Awards
1765 Sutter Street
San Francisco, CA 94115
(415) 921-5225   Fax: (415) 931-4671
E-mail: jacl@jacl.org
Web: www.jacl.org/edu/scholar.htm

Summary   To provide financial assistance to student members of the Japanese American Citizens League (JACL) who are interested in preparing for a career in medicine.

Eligibility   This program is open to JACL members who are interested in preparing for a career in the medical field. Applicants must submit information on their involvement in JACL and a 2-page essay on a topic that changes annually but relates to Japanese Americans. Selection is based on that essay, academic history, extracurricular activities, JACL involvement, scholastic honors, and a letter of recommendation.

Financial data   Stipends generally average approximately $2,000.

Duration   1 year; nonrenewable.

Number awarded   At least 1 each year.

Deadline   March of each year.

[464]
CJAAA SCHOLARSHIP PROGRAM

California Japanese American Alumni Association
Attn: Katherine Yoshii
P.O. Box 15235
San Francisco, CA 94115-0235
(510) 559-9277   E-mail: scholarships@cjaaa.org
Web: www.cjaaa.org/scholarship.html

Summary   To provide financial assistance to undergraduate or graduate students of Japanese American descent who are currently enrolled at campuses of the University of California.

Eligibility   This program is open to continuing or returning undergraduate or graduate students of Japanese American descent from California who are attending 1 of the 10 UC campuses. They must be U.S. citizens and may be studying in any field or discipline. A GPA of 3.0 or higher is strongly recommended but not required. Applicants interested in participating in the University of California Education Abroad Program in Japan must have a GPA of 3.5 or higher. Selection is based on academic achievement, contribution to the community, personal attributes, and financial need (in that order).

Financial data   Stipends range from $1,000 to $5,000. The Moriaki "Mo" Noguchi Memorial Scholarship of $3,000 is given to the top overall candidate. The George Kondo Award is at least $1,000 and is awarded to the applicant with the best community service record. The Yori Wada Award is $2,000 and is awarded to the applicant with the most outstanding record of public service. The stipend for a student accepted to the University of California Education Abroad Program ranges from $2,500 to $5,000.

Duration   1 year; nonrenewable.

Number awarded   8 to 10 each year.

Deadline   April of each year.

[465]
CLA SCHOLARSHIP FOR MINORITY STUDENTS IN MEMORY OF EDNA YELLAND

California Library Association
2471 Flores Street
San Mateo, CA 94403
(650) 376-0886   Fax: (650) 539-2341
E-mail: info@cla-net.org
Web: www.cla-net.org

Summary   To provide financial assistance to Asian American and other minority students in California who are interested in preparing for a career in library or information science.

Eligibility   This program is open to California residents who are members of ethnic minority groups (American Indian, African American/Black, Mexican American/Chicano, Latino/Hispanic, Asian American, Pacific Islander, or Filipino). Applicants must be enrolled or accepted for enrollment in a master's program at an accredited graduate library school in California. Evidence of financial need and U.S. citizenship or permanent resident status must be submitted. Finalists are interviewed.

Financial data   The stipend is $2,500.

Duration   1 academic year.

Additional information   This fellowship is named for the executive secretary of the California Library Association from 1947 to 1963 who worked to promote the goals of the California Library Association and the profession. Until 1985, it was named the Edna Yelland Memorial Scholarship.

Number awarded   3 each year.

Deadline   July of each year.

[466]
CNN-SAJA SCHOLARSHIP FOR BROADCAST JOURNALISM

South Asian Journalists Association
c/o Aseem Chhabra, Awards Committee Chair
4315 46th Street, Apartment E10
Sunnyside, NY 11104-2015
E-mail: chhabs@aol.com
Web: www.saja.org/programs/scholarships

Summary   To provide financial assistance to undergraduate and graduate broadcast journalism students of south Asian descent.

Eligibility   This program is open to students of south Asian descent (including Bangladesh, Bhutan, India, Maldives, Nepal, Pakistan, and Sri Lanka; Indo-Caribbeans are also eligible). Applicants must be currently enrolled in an undergraduate or graduate program in broadcast journalism at a college or university in North America. Selection is based on interest in broadcast journalism, participation in the sponsoring organization, reasons for entering journalism, and financial need.

Financial data   The stipend is $2,000.

Duration   1 year.

Additional information   This program, sponsored by CNN, began in 2007. Recipients are expected to give back to the South Asian Journalists Association (SAJA) by volunteering at the annual convention or at other events during the year.

Number awarded   1 each year.

Deadline   March of each year.

[467]
COMMERCIAL AND FEDERAL LITIGATION SECTION MINORITY FELLOWSHIP

The New York Bar Foundation
One Elk Street
Albany, NY 12207
(518) 487-5651   Fax: (518) 487-5699
E-mail: foundation@tnybf.org
Web: www.tnybf.org/restrictedfunds.htm

Summary To provide an opportunity for Asian American and other minority residents of any state attending law school in New York to gain summer work experience in a litigation position in the public sector in the state.

Eligibility This program is open to minority students from any state who are enrolled in the first year at a law school in New York state. Applicants must have demonstrated an interest in commercial and federal litigation. They must be interested in working in a litigation position during the summer in the public sector in New York.

Financial data The stipend is $5,000.

Duration 10 weeks during the summer.

Additional information This program was established in 2007 by the Commercial and Federal Litigation Section of the New York State Bar Association. It is administered by The New York Bar Foundation.

Number awarded 1 each year.

Deadline January of each year.

[468]
COMMITTEE ON ETHNIC MINORITY RECRUITMENT SCHOLARSHIP

United Methodist Church-California-Pacific Annual
  Conference
Attn: Board of Ordained Ministry
1720 East Linfield Street
Glendora, CA 91740
(626) 335-6629   Fax: (626) 335-5750
E-mail: cathy.adminbom@gmail.com
Web: www.calpacordainedministry.org/523451

Summary To provide financial assistance to Asian Americans and other minorities in the California-Pacific Annual Conference of the United Methodist Church (UMC) who are attending a seminary in any state to qualify for ordination as an elder or deacon.

Eligibility This program is open to members of ethnic minority groups in the UMC California-Pacific Annual Conference who are enrolled at a seminary in any state approved by the UMC University Senate. Applicants must have been approved as certified candidates by their district committee and be seeking Probationary Deacon or Elder's Orders. They may apply for 1 or more types of assistance: tuition scholarships, grants for books and school supplies (including computers), or emergency living expense grants.

Financial data Tuition stipends are $1,000 per year; books and supplies grants range up to $1,000 per year; emergency living expense grants depend on need and the availability of funds.

Duration 1 year; may be renewed up to 2 additional years.

Additional information The California-Pacific Annual Conference includes churches in southern California, Hawaii, Guam, and Saipan.

Number awarded Varies each year.

Deadline August of each year for fall term; December of each year for spring term.

[469]
COMTO ROSA L. PARKS SCHOLARSHIPS

Conference of Minority Transportation Officials
Attn: National Scholarship Program
818 18th Street, N.W., Suite 850
Washington, DC 20006
(202) 530-0551   Fax: (202) 530-0617
Web: www.comto.org/news-youth.php

Summary To provide financial assistance for college to children of Asian American and other members of the Conference of Minority Transportation Officials (COMTO) and to other students working on a bachelor's or master's degree in transportation.

Eligibility This program is open to 1) college-bound high school seniors whose parent has been a COMTO member for at least 1 year; 2) undergraduates who have completed at least 60 semester credit hours in a transportation discipline; and 3) students working on a master's degree in transportation who have completed at least 15 credits. Applicants must have a GPA of 3.0 or higher. Along with their application, they must submit a cover letter with a 500-word statement of career goals. Financial need is not considered in the selection process. U.S. citizenship is required.

Financial data The stipend is $4,500. Funds are paid directly to the recipient's college or university.

Duration 1 year.

Additional information COMTO was established in 1971 to promote, strengthen, and expand the roles of minorities in all aspects of transportation. Recipients are expected to attend the COMTO National Scholarship Luncheon.

Number awarded 2 each year.

Deadline April of each year.

[470]
CONFERENCE ON ASIAN PACIFIC AMERICAN LEADERSHIP SCHOLARSHIPS

Conference on Asian Pacific American Leadership
Attn: Scholarship Committee
P.O. Box 65073
Washington, DC 20035-5073
(202) 628-1307   Fax: (877) 892-5427
E-mail: scholarships@capal.org
Web: www.capal.org/programs/scholarship-program

Summary To provide funding for summer internships in Washington, D.C. to Asian Pacific American undergraduate and graduate students.

Eligibility This program is open to Asian Pacific American (APA) undergraduate and graduate students who have secured a public sector internship within the Washington, D.C. metropolitan area at a federal government agency, a Capitol Hill legislative office, or a nonprofit organization. Applicants must demonstrate a desire to build skills and develop their commitment to public service and the APA community. Along with their application, they must submit a 750-word essay on 2 of the following topics: 1) their long-term career goals and how the summer internship experience will advance those; 2) their previous educational, community work, and internship experiences and how those experiences have influenced their long-term career goals; or 3) how they will use the experiences and knowledge that they gain during their summer in Washington to better the APA community and their local community. Selection is based on demonstrated commitment to public service, including service to the APA community; potential to benefit from the internship; demonstrated leadership and potential for continued growth in leadership skills; relevance of the proposed internship to overall public sector goals; academic achievement; and financial need.

Financial data Awardees receive a stipend of $2,000 to help pay expenses during their internship.

Duration At least 6 weeks during the summer.

Additional information This program began in 1992 with separate scholarships named for distinguished leaders of the APA community: the Asha Jaini Emerging Leader Scholarship, the Attapong P. Mellenthin Memorial Scholarship, and the Senator Paul Simon Scholarship. Recipients must agree to have a Community Action Plan (CAP) proposed, approved, and presented before their departure from Washington, D.C. at the end of the summer.

Number awarded 2 or 3 each year.

Deadline February of each year.

[471]
CONNECTICUT COMMUNITY COLLEGE MINORITY FELLOWSHIP PROGRAM

Connecticut Community College System
Attn: System Officer for Diversity Awareness
61 Woodland Street
Hartford, CT 06105-9949
(860) 244-7606   Fax: (860) 566-6624
E-mail: karmstrong@commnet.edu
Web: www.commnet.edu/minority_fellowship.asp

Summary To provide financial assistance and work experience to graduate students in Connecticut (especially Asian Americans and other minorities) who are interested in preparing for a career in community college teaching or administration.

Eligibility This program is open to graduate students who have completed at least 6 credits of graduate work and have indicated an interest in a career in community colleges. Current employees of the Connecticut Community Colleges are also eligible. Applicants must be willing to commit to at least 1 year of employment in the Connecticut Community College System. Although all qualified graduate students are eligible, the program encourages applicants to register who strengthen the racial and cultural diversity of the minority fellow registry. That includes, in particular, making all possible efforts to recruit from historically underrepresented groups.

Financial data Non-employee fellows receive a stipend of $3,500 per semester. Fellows who are current employees are reassigned time from their responsibilities.

Duration 1 year; may be renewed.

Additional information Teaching fellows are expected to spend 6 hours per week in teaching-related activities under the supervision of the mentor; those activities may include assisting the mentor. Administrative fellows spend at least 6 hours per week in structured administrative activity. In addition, all fellows are expected to spend at least 3 hours per week in additional assigned activities, including (but not limited to) attendance at Minority Fellowship Program and campus orientation activities, attendance at relevant faculty and staff meetings, participation in other system and college meetings or professional development activities, and evaluation of the fellowship experience at the end of the academic year.

Number awarded Up to 13 each year: 1 at each of the 12 colleges in the system and 1 in the chancellor's office.

Deadline July of each year.

[472]
CONSTANGY, BROOKS & SMITH DIVERSITY SCHOLARS AWARD

Constangy, Brooks & Smith LLC
Attn: Chair, Diversity Council
200 West Forsyth Street, Suite 1700
Jacksonville, FL 32202-4317
(904) 356-8900   Fax: (904) 356-8200
E-mail: mzabijaka@constangy.com
Web: www.constangy.com/f-4.html

Summary To provide financial assistance to students enrolled in law schools in selected states, especially those who are Asian Americans of members of other minority groups).

Eligibility This program is open to second-year students enrolled in accredited law schools located in 1 of 3 regions: South (Alabama, Florida, Georgia, Tennessee), Midwest/West Coast (California, Illinois, Missouri, Texas, Wisconsin), or East (Massachusetts, New Jersey, North Carolina, South Carolina, Virginia/Washington, D.C.). Applicants must submit a personal statement on why diversity is important to them personally and in the legal profession. They must have a GPA of 2.7 or higher. Selection is based on academic achievement, commitment to diversity, and personal achievement in overcoming obstacles.

Financial data The stipend is $3,000.

Duration 1 year.

Number awarded 3 each year: 1 in each region.

Deadline November of each year.

[473]
CORA AGUDA MANAYAN FUND

Hawai'i Community Foundation
Attn: Scholarship Department
827 Fort Street Mall
Honolulu, HI 96813
(808) 537-6333   Toll Free: (888) 731-3863
Fax: (808) 521-6286
E-mail: scholarships@hcf-hawaii.org
Web: www.hawaiicommunityfoundation.org/scholarships

Summary To provide financial assistance to Hawaii residents of Filipino ancestry who are interested in attending college or graduate school to prepare for a career in the health field.

Eligibility This program is open to Hawaii residents of Filipino ancestry who are interested in enrolling full time in a health-related field (on the undergraduate or graduate school level). Applicants must be able to demonstrate academic achievement (GPA of 2.7 or higher), good moral character, and financial need. Along with their application, they must submit a short statement indicating their reasons for attending college, their planned course of study, their career goals, and what community service means to them. Preference may be given to applicants studying at a college or university in Hawaii.

Financial data The amounts of the awards depend on the availability of funds and the need of the recipient. Recently, the average value of all scholarships awarded by the foundation was $2,041.

Duration 1 year.

Number awarded Varies each year; recently, 10 of these scholarships were awarded.

Deadline February of each year.

[474]
CREATIVE ARTS AWARD

Japanese American Citizens League
Attn: National Scholarship Awards
1765 Sutter Street
San Francisco, CA 94115
(415) 921-5225   Fax: (415) 931-4671
E-mail: jacl@jacl.org
Web: www.jacl.org/edu/scholar.htm

Summary To provide financial assistance to student members of the Japanese American Citizens League (JACL) interested in working on an undergraduate or graduate degree in the creative arts.

Eligibility This program is open to JACL members who are interested in working on an undergraduate or graduate degree in the creative arts. Professional artists are not eligible. Applicants must submit a detailed proposal on the nature of their project, including a time plan, anticipated date of completion, and itemized budget. They must also submit information on their involvement in JACL and a 2-page essay on a topic that changes annually but relates to Japanese Americans. Selection is based on that essay, academic history, extracurricular activities, JACL involvement, scholastic honors, and a letter of recommendation. Preference is given to students who are interested in creative projects that reflect the Japanese American experience and culture.

Financial data Stipends generally average approximately $2,000.

Duration 1 year; nonrenewable.

Number awarded At least 1 each year.

Deadline March of each year.

[475]
CROWELL & MORING DIVERSITY IN THE LEGAL PROFESSION SCHOLARSHIP

Crowell & Moring LLP
Attn: Diversity in the Legal Profession Scholarship
1001 Pennsylvania Avenue, N.W.
Washington, DC 20004-2595
(202) 624-2500   Fax: (202) 628-5116
E-mail: scholarship@crowell.com
Web: www.crowell.com/Careers/DiversityScholarship.aspx

Summary To provide financial assistance to Asian Americans and members of other racial and ethnic groups from any state who are underrepresented in the legal profession and attending law school in the District of Columbia.

Eligibility This program is open to underrepresented racial and ethnic minorities (American Indians/Alaskan Natives, Blacks/African Americans or Africans, Hispanics/Latinos, or Asians/Pacific Islanders) from any state currently working on a J.D. degree and enrolled in their second year at an accredited law school in the District of Columbia. Applicants must have overcome significant obstacles, disadvantages, or challenges in their pursuit of a legal education. Selection is based on academic performance, demonstrated leadership skills, relevant work experience, community service, special accomplishments and honors, and financial need. Finalists are interviewed.

Financial data Stipends are $10,000 or $7,500.

Duration 1 year; nonrenewable.

Number awarded 3 each year: 1 at $10,000 and 2 at $7,500.

Deadline December of each year.

[476]
CSLA LEADERSHIP FOR DIVERSITY SCHOLARSHIP

California School Library Association
Attn: Executive Director
950 Glenn Drive, Suite 150
Folsom, CA 95630
(916) 447-2684   Fax: (916) 447-2695
E-mail: info@csla.net
Web: www.csla.net/awa/scholarships.htm

Summary To provide financial assistance to Asian Americans and other students who reflect the diversity of California's population and are interested in earning a credential as a library media teacher in the state.

Eligibility This program is open to students who are members of a traditionally underrepresented group enrolled in a college or university library media teacher credential program in California. Applicants must intend to work as a library media teacher in a California school library media center for a minimum of 3 years. Along with their application, they must submit a 250-word statement on their school library media career interests and goals, why they should be considered, what they can contribute, their commitment to serving the needs of multicultural and multilingual students, and their financial situation.

Financial data The stipend is $1,500.

Duration 1 year.

Number awarded 1 each year.

Deadline April of each year.

[477]
CSPI PUBLIC INTEREST INTERNSHIP PROGRAM

Center for Science in the Public Interest
Attn: Internships
1875 Connecticut Avenue, N.W., Suite 300
Washington, DC 20009-5728
(202) 332-9110   Fax: (202) 265-4954
E-mail: hr@cspinet.org
Web: www.cspinet.org/about/jobs/200801042.html

Summary To provide summer work experience to students (especially Asian Americans, other minorities, women, and those with disabilities) who are interested in working on health and nutritional issues at the Center for Science in the Public Interest (CSPI).

Eligibility This program is open to undergraduate, graduate, law, and medical students who are interested in working at the center, which is concerned with evaluating the effects of science and technology on society and promoting national policies responsive to consumers' interests. CSPI focuses primarily on health and nutritional issues, disclosing deceptive marketing practices, dangerous food additives or contaminants, and flawed science propagated by profits. Applicants must submit a cover letter indicating issues of interest, future plans, and dates of availability; a resume; writing samples; 2 letters of recommendation from instructors or employers; and an official transcript of courses and grades. Minorities, women, and persons with disabilities are especially encouraged to apply.

Financial data Undergraduate interns earn $8.25 per hour; graduate student interns earn $9.25 per hour.

Duration 10 weeks during the summer.

Number awarded A small number each year.

Deadline January of each year.

[478]
CULTURAL RESOURCES DIVERSITY INTERNSHIP PROGRAM

Student Conservation Association, Inc.
Attn: Diversity Internships
1800 North Kent Street, Suite 102
Arlington, VA 22209
(703) 524-2441   Fax: (703) 524-2451
E-mail: jchow@thesca.org
Web: www.thesca.org/partners/special-initiatives

Summary To offer an opportunity for Asian Americans, other ethnically diverse undergraduate and graduate students, and students with disabilities to intern at facilities of the U.S. National Park Service (NPS) during the summer.

Eligibility This program is open to currently-enrolled students at the sophomore or higher level. Applicants must be U.S. citizens or permanent residents with a GPA of 3.0 or higher. Although all students may apply, the program is designed to give ethnically diverse students and students with disabilities the opportunity to experience the diversity of careers in the federal sector. Applicants are assigned to a position within the NPS. Possible projects include editing publications, planning exhibits, participating in archaeological excavations, preparing research reports, cataloguing park and museum collections, providing interpretive programs on historical topics, developing community outreach, and writing lesson plans based on historical themes.

Financial data Interns receive a salary of $225 per week, basic medical insurance coverage, a housing stipend of up to $800 per month, a $100 uniform allowance, travel expenses up to $630, and eligibility for an Americorps Educational Award of $1,000.

Duration 10 weeks in the summer (beginning in June).

Additional information While participating in the internship, students engage in tri-weekly evening career and professional development events, ongoing career counseling, mentoring, and personal and career development services.

Number awarded Approximately 15 each year.

Deadline February of each year.

[479]
DAN BRADLEY FELLOWSHIP PROGRAM

Legal Aid Association of California
c/o Public Interest Clearinghouse
433 California Street, Suite 815
San Francisco, CA 94104
(415) 834-0100, ext. 306   Fax: (415) 834-0202
E-mail: scopeland@pic.org
Web: www.calegaladvocates.org/search/item.339371

Summary To provide funding to law students from any state (particularly Asian Americans, other minorities, and women) who are interested in a summer internship with legal services programs that are members of the Legal Aid Association of California (LAAC).

Eligibility This program is open to law students who have a strong interest in working to defend and expand the legal rights of the poor and the disadvantaged. Applicants must be interested in a summer internship with a legal aid services agency that is an LAAC member and that agrees to supervise the student on a major litigation or "impact" advocacy project. Applications must be submitted jointly by the student and a representative of an eligible legal services program. Students must include a personal statement describing how their experience relates to the goals of the program, the nature of the work they will perform if awarded a fellowship, their current career objectives, and how they envision their project playing a role in moving toward their objectives. People of color and students from low-income or working class backgrounds are particularly encouraged to apply. At least 1 fellowship is reserved for a student who works in a rural program or on a rural issue.

Financial data The stipend is up to $3,500. The LAAC contributes $3,000 and the program selected to receive the fellow is expected to provide up to an additional $500.

Duration 10 weeks during the summer.

Additional information This program began in 1991.

Number awarded Varies each year; recently, 3 of these fellowships were awarded.

Deadline April of each year.

[480]
DAVID HILLIARD EATON SCHOLARSHIP

Unitarian Universalist Association
Attn: Ministerial Credentialing Office
25 Beacon Street
Boston, MA 02108-2800
(617) 948-6403   Fax: (617) 742-2875
E-mail: mco@uua.org
Web: www.uua.org

Summary To provide financial assistance to Asian American and other minority women preparing for the Unitarian Universalist (UU) ministry.

Eligibility This program is open to women from historically marginalized groups who are currently enrolled or planning to enroll full or at least half time in a UU ministerial training program with aspirant or candidate status. Applicants must be citizens of the United States or Canada. Priority is given first to those who have demonstrated outstanding ministerial ability and secondarily to students with the greatest financial need (especially persons of color).

Financial data The stipend ranges from $1,000 to $11,000 per year.

Duration 1 year.

Number awarded Varies each year; recently, 2 of these scholarships were awarded.

Deadline April of each year.

[481]
DAVID POHL SCHOLARSHIP

Unitarian Universalist Association
Attn: Ministerial Credentialing Office
25 Beacon Street
Boston, MA 02108-2800
(617) 948-6403   Fax: (617) 742-2875
E-mail: mco@uua.org
Web: www.uua.org

Summary To provide financial assistance to seminary students (especially Asian Americans and other minorities) who are preparing for the Unitarian Universalist (UU) ministry.

Eligibility This program is open to seminary students who are enrolled full or at least half time in a UU ministerial training program with aspirant or candidate status. Applicants must be citizens of the United States or Canada. Priority is given first to those who have demonstrated outstanding ministerial ability and secondarily to students with the greatest financial need (especially persons of color).

Financial data The stipend ranges from $1,000 to $11,000 per year.

Duration 1 year.

Number awarded 1 each year.

Deadline April of each year.

[482]
DAVID SANKEY MINORITY SCHOLARSHIP IN METEOROLOGY

National Weather Association
Attn: Executive Director
228 West Millbrook Road
Raleigh, NC 27609-4304
(919) 845-1546   Fax: (919) 845-2956
E-mail: exdir@nwas.org
Web: www.nwas.org

Summary To provide financial assistance to Asian Americans and other minorities working on an undergraduate or graduate degree in meteorology.

Eligibility This program is open to members of minority groups who are either entering their sophomore or higher year of undergraduate study or enrolled as graduate students. Applicants must be working on a degree in meteorology. Along with their application, they must submit a 1-page statement explaining why they are applying for this scholarship. Selection is based on that statement, academic achievement, and 2 letters of recommendation.

Financial data The stipend is $1,000.

Duration 1 year.

Additional information This program was established in 2002.

Number awarded 1 each year.

Deadline April of each year.

[483]
DAVIS WRIGHT TREMAINE 1L DIVERSITY SCHOLARSHIP PROGRAM

Davis Wright Tremaine LLP
Attn: Diversity Scholarship Program
1201 Third Avenue, Suite 2200
Seattle, WA 98101-3045
(206) 622-3150   Toll Free: (877) 398-8416
Fax: (206) 757-7700   E-mail: carolyuly@dwt.com
Web: www.dwt.com

Summary To provide financial assistance and summer work experience to Asian American and other law students of color.

Eligibility This program is open to first-year law students of color and others of diverse backgrounds. Applicants must have a record of academic achievement as an undergraduate and in the first year of law school that demonstrates promise for a successful career in law, a commitment to civic involvement that promotes diversity and will continue after entering the legal profession, and a willingness to become an associate in the sponsor's Seattle or Portland office during the summer between their first and second year of law school. They must submit a current resume, a complete undergraduate transcript, grades from the first semester of law school, a 1-page essay describing their eligibility for and interest in the scholarship, a legal writing sample, and 2 or 3 references. Although demonstrated need may be taken into account, applicants need not disclose their financial circumstances.

Financial data The award consists of a $7,500 stipend for second-year tuition and expenses and a paid summer clerkship.

Duration 1 academic year and summer.

Number awarded 2 each year: 1 in the Seattle office and 1 in the Portland office.

Deadline January of each year.

[484]
DELL THURMOND WOODARD FELLOWSHIP

The Fund for American Studies
Attn: Fellowships
1706 New Hampshire Avenue, N.W.
Washington, DC 20009
(202) 986-0384   Toll Free: (800) 741-6964
Fax: (202) 986-8930   E-mail: jtilley@tfas.org
Web: www.tfas.org/Page.aspx?pid=1511

Summary To provide an opportunity for Asian American and other upper-division or graduate students (especially those with an interest in diversity and ethics issues) to learn about high technology public policy issues during a summer internship in Washington, D.C.

Eligibility This program is open to juniors, seniors, and graduate students who have an interest and background in issues regarding diversity and ethics and are currently enrolled at a 4-year college or university in the United States. Applicants must be interested in working in the government relations office of a high technology company or association in Washington while they also attend weekly issues seminar lunches hosted by the program's sponsors. They must have an interest in public policy and the high technology industry; a background in computer science or other high technology fields is helpful but not required. International students are eligible. Selection is based on evidence of a strong interest in a career in high technology public policy, civic mindedness and participation in community activities or organizations, academic achievements, and recommendations.

Financial data   Fellows receive a grant of $5,000.

Duration   8 weeks during the summer.

Additional information   This program was established in 2007 with support from the Congressional Black Caucus Foundation (CBCF), the Congressional Hispanic Caucus Institute (CHCI), and the Asian Pacific Institute for Congressional Studies (APAICS). Those 3 sponsors select the fellow on a rotational basis.

Number awarded   1 each year.

Deadline   February of each year.

[485]
DEPARTMENT OF STATE STUDENT INTERN PROGRAM

Department of State
Attn: HR/REE
2401 E Street, N.W., Suite 518 H
Washington, DC 20522-0108
(202) 261-8888   Toll Free: (800) JOB-OVERSEAS
Fax: (301) 562-8968   E-mail: Careers@state.gov
Web: www.careers.state.gov/students/programs

Summary   To provide a work/study opportunity to undergraduate and graduate students (especially Asian Americans, other minorities, and women) who are interested in foreign service.

Eligibility   This program is open to full- and part-time continuing college and university juniors, seniors, and graduate students. Applications are encouraged from students with a broad range of majors, such as business or public administration, social work, economics, information management, journalism, and the biological, engineering, and physical sciences, as well as those majors more traditionally identified with international affairs. U.S. citizenship is required. The State Department particularly encourages eligible women and minority students with an interest in foreign affairs to apply.

Financial data   Most internships are unpaid. A few paid internships are granted to applicants who can demonstrate financial need. If they qualify for a paid internship, they are placed at the GS-4 step 5 level (currently with an annual rate of $27,786). Interns placed abroad may also receive housing, medical insurance, a travel allowance, and a dependents' allowance.

Duration   Paid internships are available only for 10 weeks during the summer. Unpaid internships are available for 1 semester or quarter during the academic year, or for 10 weeks during the summer.

Additional information   About half of all internships are in Washington, D.C., or occasionally in other large cities in the United States. The remaining internships are at embassies and consulates abroad. Depending upon the needs of the department, interns are assigned junior-level professional duties, which may include research, preparing reports, drafting replies to correspondence, working in computer science, analyzing international issues, financial management, intelligence, security, or assisting in cases related to domestic and international law. Interns must agree to return to their schooling immediately upon completion of their internship.

Number awarded   Approximately 800 internships are offered each year, but only about 5% of those are paid positions.

Deadline   February of each year for fall internships; June of each year for spring internships; October of each year for summer internships.

[486]
DICKSTEIN SHAPIRO DIVERSITY SCHOLARSHIP

Dickstein Shapiro LLP
Attn: Director of Professional Development and Attorney Recruiting
1825 Eye Street, N.W.
Washington, DC 20006-5403
(202) 420-4880   Fax: (202) 420-2201
E-mail: careers@dicksteinshapiro.com
Web: www.dicksteinshapiro.com/careers/diversity

Summary   To provide financial assistance and summer work experience at Dickstein Shapiro in Washington, D.C. or New York City to Asian American and other diverse law students from any state.

Eligibility   This program is open to second-year diverse law students, including 1) members of the lesbian, gay, bisexual, and transgender (LGBT) community; 2) members of minority ethnic and racial groups (Blacks, Hispanics and Latinos, Asians, American Indians and Native Alaskans, and Native Hawaiians and Pacific Islanders); and 3) students with disabilities. Applicants must be interested in a summer associateship with Dickstein Shapiro in Washington, D.C. or New York City. Selection is based on academic and professional experience as well as the extent to which they reflect the core values of the firm: excellence, loyalty, respect, initiative, and integrity.

Financial data   The stipend is $25,000, including $15,000 upon completion of the summer associate program and $10,000 upon acceptance of a full-time offer of employment following graduation.

Duration   The associateship takes place during the summer following the second year of law school and the stipend covers the third year of law school.

Additional information   This program was established in 2006.

Number awarded   1 or more each year.

Deadline   September of each year.

[487]
DINSMORE & SHOHL LLP DIVERSITY SCHOLARSHIP PROGRAM

Dinsmore & Shohl LLP
Attn: Manager of Legal Recruiting
255 East Fifth Street, Suite 1900
Cincinnati, OH 45202
(513) 977-8488   Fax: (513) 977-8141
E-mail: dinsmore.legalrecuiting@dinslaw.com
Web: www.dinslaw.com/careers/diversityscholarship

Summary   To provide financial assistance and summer work experience to Asian Americans and other law students traditionally underrepresented in the legal profession.

Eligibility   This program is open to first- and second-year law students who are members of groups traditionally underrepresented in the legal profession. Applicants must have a demonstrated record of academic or professional achievement and leadership qualities. They must also be interested in a summer associateship with Dinsmore & Shohl LLP. Along with their application, they must submit a 500-word personal statement explaining their interest in the scholarship program and how diversity has impacted their life.

Financial data The program provides an academic scholarship of $10,000 and a paid associateship at the firm.

Duration The academic scholarship is for 1 year. The summer associateship is for 12 weeks.

Additional information Associateships are available at firm offices in Charleston (West Virginia), Cincinnati (Ohio), Columbus (Ohio), Lexington (Kentucky), or Louisville (Kentucky). The program includes 1 associateship in which the student spends 6 weeks as a clerk in the legal department of the Procter & Gamble Company's worldwide headquarters in Cincinnati and 6 weeks at Dinsmore & Shohl's Cincinnati office. All associates are assigned to an attorney with the firm who serves as a mentor.

Number awarded Varies each year.

Deadline September of each year for second-year students; December of each year for first-year students.

[488]
DISSERTATION FELLOWSHIPS IN EAST EUROPEAN STUDIES

American Council of Learned Societies
Attn: Office of Fellowships and Grants
633 Third Avenue
New York, NY 10017-6795
(212) 697-1505 Fax: (212) 949-8058
E-mail: fellowships@acls.org
Web: www.acls.org/grants/Default.aspx?id=532

Summary To provide funding to doctoral candidates (particularly Asian Americans, minorities, and women) who are interested in conducting dissertation research in the social sciences and humanities relating to eastern Europe.

Eligibility This program is open to U.S. citizens or permanent residents who are working on a dissertation in the humanities or social sciences as related to eastern Europe, including Albania, Bosnia and Herzegovina, Bulgaria, Croatia, Czech Republic, Estonia, Hungary, Latvia, Lithuania, Former Yugoslav Republic of Macedonia, Kosovo, Montenegro, Poland, Romania, Serbia, Slovakia, and Slovenia. Applicants may be proposing projects comparing more than 1 country of eastern Europe or relating eastern European societies to those of other parts of the world. They may be seeking support for research fellowships (for use in eastern Europe to conduct fieldwork or archival investigations) or writing fellowships (for use in the United States, after all research is complete, to write the dissertation). Selection is based on the scholarly potential of the applicant, the quality and scholarly importance of the proposed work, and its importance to the development of scholarship on eastern Europe. Applications are particularly invited from women and members of minority groups.

Financial data The maximum stipend is $18,000. Recipients' home universities are required (consistent with their policies and regulations) to provide or to waive normal academic year tuition payments or to provide alternative cost-sharing support.

Duration 1 year. Students may apply for 1-year research and writing fellowships in sequence, but they may not apply for a second year of funding in either category.

Additional information This program is sponsored jointly by the American Council of Learned Societies, (ACLS) and the Social Science Research Council, funded by the U.S. Department of State under the Research and Training for Eastern Europe and the Independent States of the Former Soviet Union Act of 1983 (Title VIII) but administered by ACLS.

Number awarded Varies each year; recently, 8 of these fellowships were awarded.

Deadline November of each year.

[489]
DISSERTATION FELLOWSHIPS OF THE MINORITY SCHOLAR-IN-RESIDENCE PROGRAM

Consortium for Faculty Diversity at Liberal Arts Colleges
c/o DePauw University
Academic Affairs Office
305 Harrison Hall
7 East Larabee Street
Greencastle, IN 46135
(765) 658-6595 E-mail: jgriswold@depauw.edu
Web: www.depauw.edu

Summary To provide an opportunity for Asian American and other minority students to work on their dissertation while in residence at selected liberal arts colleges.

Eligibility This program is open to African American, Asian American, Hispanic American, and Native American doctoral candidates who have completed all the requirements for the Ph.D. or M.F.A. except the dissertation. Applicants must be interested in a residency at a member institution of the Consortium for Faculty Diversity at Liberal Arts Colleges during which they will complete their dissertation. They must be U.S. citizens or permanent residents.

Financial data Dissertation fellows receive a stipend based on the average salary paid to instructors at the participating college. Modest funds are made available to finance the fellow's proposed research, subject to the usual institutional procedures.

Duration 1 year.

Additional information The following schools are participating in the program: Agnes Scott College, Bard College at Simon's Rock, Bowdoin College, Bryn Mawr College, Carleton College, Centre College, College of Wooster, Colorado College, Denison University, DePauw University, Dickinson College, Gettysburg College, Goucher College, Grinnell College, Hamilton College, Harvey Mudd College, Haverford College, Hobart and William Smith Colleges, Kalamazoo College, Lafayette College, Lawrence University, Luther College, Macalester College, Mount Holyoke College, Muhlenberg College, New College of Florida, Oberlin College, Pomona College, Reed College, Rhodes College, University of Richmond, Scripps College, St. Olaf College, Sewanee: The University of the South, Skidmore College, Smith College, Southwestern University, Swarthmore College, Trinity College, Vassar College, Wellesley College, Whitman College, and Willamette University. Fellows are expected to teach at least 1 course, participate in departmental seminars, and interact with students.

Number awarded Varies each year.

Deadline October of each year.

[490]
DISSERTATION PROPOSAL DEVELOPMENT FELLOWSHIP PROGRAM

Social Science Research Council
Attn: DPDF Program
One Pierrepont Plaza, 15th Floor
Brooklyn, NY 11201
(212) 377-2700   Fax: (212) 377-2727
E-mail: dpdf@ssrc.org
Web: www.ssrc.org/fellowships/dpdf-fellowship

Summary To provide an opportunity for doctoral students in the social sciences and humanities (particularly Asian Americans, other minorities and women) to formulate their dissertation proposals and conduct predissertation research.

Eligibility This program is open to full-time graduate students in the second or third year of a doctoral program who have not yet had their dissertation proposals accepted by their thesis directors and their home institutions. Each year, the program selects 6 subdisciplinary and interdisciplinary fields within the social sciences and humanities, and students apply to participate in 1 of those fields. They must be able to attend a workshop in the spring to prepare to undertake predissertation research, spend the summer conducting that research, and then attend another workshop in the fall to synthesize their summer research and draft proposals for dissertation funding. Workshop participants are selected on the basis of the originality and appropriateness of their dissertation topic, the preparation of the student, and the quality of the summer predissertation research plan. Minorities and women are particularly encouraged to apply.

Financial data For all fellows, expenses to attend the workshops (airfare, hotel, meals, ground transport) are paid. Those fellows who are selected for summer predissertation research receive $5,000 grants.

Duration The program extends over 1 calendar year.

Additional information Funding for this program is provided by the Andrew W. Mellon Foundation. Recently, the designated research fields were: new approaches to religion and modernity; discrimination studies; interdisciplinary approaches to the study of contentious politics; multiculturalism, immigration, and identity in western Europe and the United States; spaces of inquiry; and virtual worlds.

Number awarded Each research field accepts 10 to 12 graduate students.

Deadline January of each year.

[491]
DISTRICT OF COLUMBIA-ELI DIVERSITY FELLOWSHIPS IN ENVIRONMENTAL LAW

American Bar Association
Attn: Section of Environment, Energy, and Resources
321 North Clark Street
Chicago, IL 60654-7598
(312) 988-5602   Fax: (312) 988-5572
E-mail: jonusaid@staff.abanet.org
Web: www.abanet.org

Summary To provide funding to Asian American and other law students from traditionally underrepresented groups who are interested in working on a summer project at the Environmental Law Institute (ELI) in Washington, D.C.

Eligibility This program is open to first- and second-year law students and third-year night students who come from minority or other disadvantaged households. Students may be residents of any state and attending school in any state; preference is given to residents of the District of Columbia and to students who are enrolled at law schools in the District or who have a strong interest in the District. Applicants must be interested in a summer internship at ELI, where they work on projects involving domestic and international environmental law. Subject areas include wetlands and watershed policy, sustainable land use, biodiversity, environmental enforcement, long-term management of hazardous sites, public participation, and international environmental policy. Selection is based on research and writing skills, academic performance, and communication skills.

Financial data The stipend is $5,000.

Duration 8 to 10 weeks during the summer.

Additional information This program is cosponsored by ELI, Additional support is provided by Pfizer Inc. and Beveridge & Diamond PC.

Number awarded 2 each year.

Deadline November of each year.

[492]
DIVERSIFIED INVESTMENT ADVISORS LEADERS IN HEALTHCARE SCHOLARSHIP

Institute for Diversity in Health Management
Attn: Executive Assistant
One North Franklin Street, 30th Floor
Chicago, IL 60606
(312) 422-2630   Toll Free: (800) 233-0996
Fax: (312) 895-4511   E-mail: ejohnson@aha.org
Web: www.applicantsoft.com

Summary To provide financial assistance to Asian American and other minority graduate students in health services management.

Eligibility This program is open to members of ethnic minority groups who are accepted or enrolled in a graduate program in health care administration. Applicants must have a GPA of 3.0 or higher. They must demonstrate commitment to a career in health care administration. Along with their application, they must submit a personal statement of 300 to 500 words on their interest in health care management and their career goals. Selection is based on academic achievement, leadership potential, financial need, community involvement, commitment to health care administration, and overall professional maturity. U.S. citizenship is required.

Financial data The stipend is $5,000.

Duration 1 year.

Additional information This program was established in 2007 by Diversified Investment Advisors.

Number awarded 2 each year.

Deadline December of each year.

[493]
DIVERSITY COMMITTEE SCHOLARSHIP

American Society of Safety Engineers
Attn: ASSE Foundation
1800 East Oakton Street
Des Plaines, IL 60018
(847) 768-3435   Fax: (847) 768-3434
E-mail: agabanski@asse.org
Web: www.asse.org

Summary To provide financial assistance to Asian American and other upper-division and graduate student members of the American Society of Safety Engineers (ASSE) who come from diverse groups.

Eligibility This program is open to ASSE student members who are working on an undergraduate or graduate degree in occupational safety, health, and environment or a closely-related field (e.g., industrial or environmental engineering, environmental science, industrial hygiene, occupational health nursing). Applicants must be full-time students who have completed at least 60 semester hours with a GPA of 3.0 or higher as undergraduates or at least 9 semester hours with a GPA of 3.5 or higher as graduate students. Along with their application, they must submit 2 essays of 300 words or less: 1) why they are seeking a degree in occupational safety and health or a closely-related field, a brief description of their current activities, and how those relate to their career goals and objectives; and 2) why they should be awarded this scholarship (including career goals and financial need). A goal of this program is to support individuals regardless of race, ethnicity, gender, religion, personal beliefs, age, sexual orientation, physical challenges, geographic location, university, or specific area of study. U.S. citizenship is not required.

Financial data The stipend is $1,000 per year.

Duration 1 year; recipients may reapply.

Number awarded 1 each year.

Deadline November of each year.

[494]
DOCTORAL FELLOWSHIPS IN ARCHIVAL STUDIES

UCLA Center for Information as Evidence
c/o Department of Information Studies
GSEIS Building 208A
P.O. Box 951520
Los Angeles, CA 90095-1520
(310) 825-7310   Fax: (310) 206-4460
E-mail: aeri@gseis.ucla.edu
Web: aeri.gseis.ucla.edu/fellowships.htm

Summary To provide financial assistance to students (especially Asian American and other minority students) who are entering a doctoral program in archival studies at designated universities.

Eligibility This program is open to students entering a doctoral program in archival studies at the University of California at Los Angeles, University of Michigan, University of Pittsburgh, University of North Carolina at Chapel Hill, Simmons College, University of Maryland, University of Texas at Austin, or University of Wisconsin at Madison. Applicants are not required to have received a master's degree in archival studies, library and information studies, or a related field, but they must be able to exhibit evidence of the ability to excel as a scholar and educator in the field. Selection is based on commitment to archival studies education, potential to make a strong scholarly contribution to the field of archival studies, and commitment to diversity within archival studies education and scholarship. Applications are particularly encouraged from students of Asian, American Indian/Alaska Native, Black/African American, Hispanic/Latino, or Native Hawaiian/other Pacific Islander heritage. U.S. citizenship or permanent resident status is required.

Financial data The program provides payment of full tuition and a stipend of $20,000 per year.

Duration 2 years; the partner universities provide full tuition and stipends to their fellows for 2 additional years of study.

Additional information These fellowships were first awarded in 2010. Funding for the program is provided by a grant from the Laura Bush 21st Century Librarian Program of the Institute of Museum and Library Services.

Number awarded At least 2 each year.

Deadline January of each year.

[495]
DOCTORAL FELLOWSHIPS IN LAW AND SOCIAL SCIENCE

American Bar Foundation
Attn: Administrative Assistant for Academic Affairs and
    Research Administration
750 North Lake Shore Drive
Chicago, IL 60611-4403
(312) 988-6548   Fax: (312) 988-6579
E-mail: alynch@abfn.org
Web: www.americanbarfoundation.org

Summary To provide research funding to scholars (particularly Asian American and other minority scholars) who are completing or have completed doctoral degrees in fields related to law, the legal profession, and legal institutions.

Eligibility This program is open to Ph.D. candidates in the social sciences who have completed all doctoral requirements except the dissertation. Applicants who have completed the dissertation are also eligible. Doctoral and proposed research must be in the general area of sociolegal studies or in social scientific approaches to law, the legal profession, or legal institutions and legal processes. Applications must include 1) a dissertation abstract or proposal with an outline of the substance and methods of the research; 2) 2 letters of recommendation; and 3) a curriculum vitae. Minority candidates are especially encouraged to apply.

Financial data The stipend is $27,000. Fellows may request up to $1,500 to reimburse expenses associated with research, travel to meet with advisers, or travel to conferences at which papers are presented. Relocation expenses of up to $2,500 may be reimbursed on application.

Duration 12 months, beginning in September.

Additional information Fellows are offered access to the computing and word processing facilities of the American Bar Foundation and the libraries of Northwestern University and the University of Chicago. This program was established in 1996. Fellowships must be held in residence at the American Bar Foundation. Appointments to the fellowship are full time; fellows are not permitted to undertake other work.

Number awarded 1 or more each year.

Deadline December of each year.

[496]
DOLLARS FOR SCHOLARS PROGRAM

United Methodist Higher Education Foundation
Attn: Scholarships Administrator
1001 19th Avenue South
P.O. Box 340005
Nashville, TN 37203-0005
(615) 340-7385   Toll Free: (800) 811-8110
Fax: (615) 340-7330
E-mail: umhefscholarships@gbhem.org
Web: www.umhef.org/receive.php?id=dollars_for_scholars

Summary To provide financial assistance to students (especially Asian American and other minority students) who are at Methodist colleges, universities, and seminaries and whose home churches agree to contribute to their support.

Eligibility The Double Your Dollars for Scholars program is open to students attending or planning to attend a United Methodist-related college, university, or seminary as a full-time student. Applicants must have been an active, full member of a United Methodist Church for at least 1 year prior to applying. Their home church must nominate them and agree to contribute to their support. Many of the United Methodist colleges and universities have also agreed to contribute matching funds for a Triple Your Dollars for Scholars Program, and a few United Methodist conference foundations have agreed to contribute additional matching funds for a Quadruple Your Dollars for Scholars Program. Awards are granted on a first-come, first-served basis. Some of the awards are designated for Hispanic, Asian, and Native American (HANA) students funded by the General Board of Higher Education and Ministry.

Financial data The sponsoring church contributes $1,000 and the United Methodist Higher Education Foundation (UMHEF) contributes a matching $1,000. Students who attend a participating United Methodist college or university receive an additional $1,000 for the Triple Your Dollars for Scholars Program, and those from a participating conference receive a fourth $1,000 increment for the Quadruple Your Dollars for Scholars Program.

Duration 1 year; may be renewed as long as the recipients maintain satisfactory academic progress as defined by their institution.

Additional information Currently, participants in the Double Your Dollars for Scholars program include 2 United Methodist seminaries and theological schools, 1 professional school, 19 senior colleges and universities, and 1 2-year college. The Triple Your Dollars for Scholars program includes an additional 11 United Methodist seminaries and theological schools, 73 senior colleges and universities, and 5 2-year colleges (for a complete list, consult the UMHEF). The conference foundations participating in the Quadruple Your Dollars for Scholars Program are limited to the Alabama-West Florida United Methodist Foundation, the Mississippi United Methodist Foundation (for students at Millsaps College or Rust College), the Missouri United Methodist Foundation (for students at Saint Paul School of Theology or Central Methodist University), the Nashville Area United Methodist Foundation, the North Carolina United Methodist Foundation (for students at Louisburg College, Methodist University, or North Carolina Wesleyan College), the North Georgia United Methodist Foundation, the Oklahoma United Methodist Foundation (for students at Oklahoma City University) the United Methodist

Foundation of Arkansas (for students at Hendrix College or Philander Smith College), the United Methodist Foundation of South Indiana, and the United Methodist Foundation of Western North Carolina.

Number awarded 350 each year, including 25 designated for HANA students.

Deadline Local churches must submit applications in March of each year for senior colleges and universities and seminaries or May of each year for 2-year colleges.

[497]
DOLORES NYHUS GRADUATE FELLOWSHIP

California Dietetic Association
Attn: CDA Foundation
7740 Manchester Avenue, Suite 102
Playa del Rey, CA 90293-8499
(310) 822-0177   Fax: (310) 823-0264
E-mail: patsmith@dietitian.org
Web: www.dietitian.org/cdaf_scholarships.htm

Summary To provide financial assistance to members of the American Dietetic Association (particularly Asian Americans, other minorities, males, and individuals with disabilities) who live in California and are interested in working on a graduate degree in dietetics or a related field at a school in any state.

Eligibility This program is open to California residents who are association members and have a bachelor's degree with 3 to 5 years of professional experience. Applicants must be a registered dietitian (R.D.), be a registered dietetic technician (D.T.R.), or have a credential earned at least 6 months previously. They must be enrolled in or admitted to a graduate school in any state in the areas of public health, gerontology, or a community-related program with the intention of practicing in the field of dietetics. Along with their application, they must submit a letter of application that includes a discussion of their career goals. Selection is based on that letter (15%), academic ability (25%), work or volunteer experience (15%), letters of recommendation (15%), extracurricular activities (5%), and financial need (25%). Applications are especially encouraged from ethnic minorities, men, and people with physical disabilities.

Financial data The stipend is normally $1,000.

Duration 1 year.

Number awarded 1 each year.

Deadline February of each year.

[498]
DONALD W. BANNER DIVERSITY SCHOLARSHIP

Banner & Witcoff, Ltd.
Attn: Christopher Hummel
1100 13th Street, N.W., Suite 1200
Washington, DC 20005-4051
(202) 824-3000   Fax: (202) 824-3001
E-mail: chummel@bannerwitcoff.com
Web: www.bannerwitcoff.com

Summary To provide financial assistance to Asian American and other law students who come from groups historically underrepresented in intellectual property law.

Eligibility This program is open to students enrolled in the first or second year of a J.D. program at an ABA-accredited law school in the United States. Applicants must come from a group historically underrepresented in intellectual property law; that underrepresentation may be the result of race, sex, ethnicity, sexual orientation, or disability. Selection is based on academic merit, commitment to the pursuit of a career in intellectual property law, written communication skills, oral communication skills (determined through an interview), leadership qualities, and community involvement.

Financial data The stipend is $5,000 per year.

Duration 1 year (the second or third year of law school); students who accept and successfully complete the firm's summer associate program may receive an additional $5,000 for a subsequent semester of law school.

Number awarded 2 each year.

Deadline October of each year.

[499]
DORA AMES LEE LEADERSHIP DEVELOPMENT FUND

United Methodist Church
General Board of Global Ministries
Attn: United Methodist Committee on Relief
475 Riverside Drive, Room 1522
New York, NY 10115
(212) 870-3871   Toll Free: (800) UMC-GBGM
E-mail: jyoung@gbgm-umc.org
Web: gbgm-umc.org/health/doralee.cfm

Summary To provide financial assistance to Methodists and other Christians of Asian or Native American descent who are preparing for a career in a health-related field.

Eligibility This program is open to undergraduate and graduate students along with college graduates who are U.S. citizens of Asian American or Native American descent. Applicants must be professed Christians, preferably United Methodists. They must be attending a college or university to enter or continue in a health-related field. Financial need is considered in the selection process.

Financial data The stipend is $2,000.

Duration 1 year.

Additional information This program was established in 1980.

Number awarded 5 each year.

Deadline June of each year.

[500]
DORSEY & WHITNEY DIVERSITY FELLOWSHIPS

Dorsey & Whitney LLP
Attn: Recruiting Manager
50 South Sixth Street, Suite 1500
Minneapolis, MN 55402-1498
(612) 340-2600   Toll Free: (800) 759-4929
Fax: (612) 340-2868 E-mail: forsmark.claire@dorsey.com
Web: www.dorsey.com/diversity_fellowship_12111

Summary To provide financial assistance for law school to Asian Americans and other students from diverse backgrounds who are interested in working during the summer at offices of the sponsoring law firm.

Eligibility This program is open to first-year students at ABA-accredited law schools who have accepted a summer associate position at an office of the sponsor in Denver, Minneapolis, or Seattle. Applicants must be able to demonstrate academic achievement and a commitment to promoting diversity in the legal community. Along with their application, they must submit a personal statement on the ways in which they have promoted and will continue to promote diversity in the legal community, what diversity means to them, and why they are interested in the sponsoring law firm.

Financial data Fellows receive a stipend of $7,500 for the second year of law school and, if they complete a summer associate position in the following summer, another stipend of $7,500 for the third year of law school. If they join the firm following graduation, they receive an additional $5,000.

Duration 1 year; may be renewed for 1 additional year.

Additional information This program was established in 2006.

Number awarded 1 or more each year.

Deadline January of each year.

[501]
DR. HARIHARA MEHENDALE GRADUATE STUDENT BEST ABSTRACT AWARD

Society of Toxicology
Attn: Association of Scientists of Indian Origin Special
    Interest Group
1821 Michael Faraday Drive, Suite 300
Reston, VA 20190-5348
(703) 438-3115   Fax: (703) 438-3113
E-mail: sothq@toxicology.org
Web: www.toxicology.org/ai/af/awards.aspx

Summary To recognize and reward graduate student members of the Society of Toxicology (SOT) who are of Indian origin and present outstanding papers at the annual meeting.

Eligibility This award is available to graduate students of Indian origin who are members of SOT and its Association of Scientists of Indian Origin (ASIO). Candidates must have an accepted abstract of a research poster or platform presentation for the SOT annual meeting. Along with the abstract, they must submit a short curriculum vitae and a recommendation letter by their academic adviser outlining their role in the research.

Financial data A plaque and a cash award (amount not specified) are presented.

Duration The award is presented annually.

Additional information This award was established in 2008.

Number awarded 1 each year.

Deadline January of each year.

[502]
DR. KIYOSHI SONODA MEMORIAL SCHOLARSHIP

Japanese American Citizens League
Attn: National Scholarship Awards
1765 Sutter Street
San Francisco, CA 94115
(415) 921-5225   Fax: (415) 931-4671
E-mail: jacl@jacl.org
Web: www.jacl.org/edu/scholar.htm

Summary To provide financial assistance to student members of the Japanese American Citizens League (JACL) who are interested in preparing for a career in dentistry.

Eligibility This program is open to JACL members who are enrolled or planning to enroll at a school of dentistry. Applicants must submit information on their involvement in JACL and a 2-page essay on a topic that changes annually but relates to Japanese Americans. Selection is based on that essay, academic history, extracurricular activities, JACL involvement, scholastic honors, and a letter of recommendation.

Financial data Stipends generally average approximately $2,000.

Duration 1 year; nonrenewable.

Number awarded At least 1 each year.

Deadline March of each year.

[503]
DRI LAW STUDENT DIVERSITY SCHOLARSHIP

DRI-The Voice of the Defense Bar
Attn: Deputy Executive Director
55 West Monroe Street, Suite 2000
Chicago, IL 60603
(312) 795-1101   Fax: (312) 795-0747
E-mail: dri@dri.org
Web: www.dri.org/open/About.aspx

Summary To provide financial assistance to Asian Americans, other minorities, and women law students.

Eligibility This program is open to students entering their second or third year of law school who are African American, Hispanic, Asian, Pan Asian, Native American, or female. Applicants must submit an essay, up to 1,000 words, on a topic that changes annually but relates to the work of defense attorneys. Selection is based on that essay, demonstrated academic excellence, service to the profession, service to the community, and service to the cause of diversity. Students affiliated with the American Association for Justice as members, student members, or employees are not eligible. Finalists are invited to participate in personal interviews.

Financial data The stipend is $10,000.

Duration 1 year.

Additional information This program was established in 2004.

Number awarded 2 each year.

Deadline May of each year.

[504]
EAST EUROPEAN LANGUAGE GRANTS TO INDIVIDUALS FOR SUMMER STUDY

American Council of Learned Societies
Attn: Office of Fellowships and Grants
633 Third Avenue
New York, NY 10017-6795
(212) 697-1505   Fax: (212) 949-8058
E-mail: fellowships@acls.org
Web: www.acls.org/grants/Default.aspx?id=540

Summary To provide financial support to graduate students, professionals, and postdoctorates (particularly Asian Americans, other minorities, and women) who are interested in studying eastern European languages during the summer.

Eligibility Applicants must have completed at least a 4-year college degree. They must be interested in a program of training in the languages of eastern Europe, including Albanian, Bosnian-Croatian-Serbian, Bulgarian, Czech, Estonian, Hungarian, Latvian, Lithuanian, Macedonian, Polish, Romanian, Slovak, or Slovene. The language course may be at the beginning, intermediate, or advanced level. Normally, requests for beginning and intermediate level training should be for attendance at intensive courses offered by institutions in the United States; proposals for study at the advanced level are ordinarily for courses in eastern Europe. Applications are particularly encouraged from women and members of minority groups.

Financial data Grants up to $2,500 are available.

Duration Summer months.

Additional information This program, reinstituted in 2002, is supported by the U.S. Department of State under the Research and Training for Eastern Europe and the Independent States of the Former Soviet Union Act of 1983 (Title VIII).

Number awarded Approximately 15 each year.

Deadline January of each year.

[505]
EASTERN REGION KOREAN AMERICAN SCHOLARSHIPS

Korean American Scholarship Foundation
Eastern Region
1952 Gallows Road, Suite 204
Vienna, VA 22182
(703) 748-5935   Fax: (703) 748-1874
E-mail: eastern@kasf.org
Web: www.kasf.org/application_set.html

Summary To provide financial assistance to Korean American students from any state who are working on an undergraduate or graduate degree in any field at a school in eastern states.

Eligibility This program is open to Korean American students who are currently enrolled or planning to enroll at a college or university in an eastern state as a full-time undergraduate or graduate student. Applicants may reside anywhere in the United States as long as they attend school in the eastern region: Delaware, District of Columbia, Kentucky, Maryland, North Carolina, Pennsylvania, Virginia, and West Virginia. They must have a GPA of 3.0 or higher. Selection is based on academic achievement, school activities, community service, and financial need.

Financial data Stipends range from $350 to $5,000.

Duration 1 year; renewable.

Number awarded Varies each year; recently, 54 of these scholarships were awarded.

Deadline May of each year.

[506]
EDWARD S. ROTH MANUFACTURING ENGINEERING SCHOLARSHIP

Society of Manufacturing Engineers
Attn: SME Education Foundation
One SME Drive
P.O. Box 930
Dearborn, MI 48121-0930
(313) 425-3300   Toll Free: (800) 733-4763, ext. 3300
Fax: (313) 425-3411   E-mail: foundation@sme.org
Web: www.smeef.org

Summary To provide financial assistance to Asian Americans and other students enrolled or planning to work on a bachelor's or master's degree in manufacturing engineering at selected universities.

Eligibility This program is open to U.S. citizens who are graduating high school seniors or currently-enrolled undergraduate or graduate students. Applicants must be enrolled or planning to enroll as a full-time student at 1 of 13 selected 4-year universities to work on a bachelor's or master's degree in manufacturing engineering. They must have a GPA of 3.0 or higher. Preference is given to 1) students demonstrating financial need, 2) minority students, and 3) students participating in a co-op program. Some preference may also be given to graduating high school seniors and graduate students. Along with their application, they must submit a 300-word essay that covers their career and educational objectives, how this scholarship will help them attain those objectives, and why they want to enter this field.

Financial data Stipend amounts vary; recently, the value of all scholarships provided by this foundation annually averages approximately $2,700.

Duration 1 year; may be renewed.

Additional information The eligible institutions are California Polytechnic State University at San Luis Obispo, California State Polytechnic State University at Pomona, University of Miami (Florida), Bradley University (Illinois), Central State University (Ohio), Miami University (Ohio), Boston University, Worcester Polytechnic Institute (Massachusetts), University of Massachusetts, St. Cloud State University (Minnesota), University of Texas-Pan American, Brigham Young University (Utah), and Utah State University.

Number awarded 2 each year.

Deadline January of each year.

[507]
EIICHI MATSUSHITA MEMORIAL SCHOLARSHIP FUND

Evangelical Lutheran Church in America
Association of Asians and Pacific Islanders
8765 West Higgins Road
Chicago, IL 60631
(630) 380-2700   Toll Free: (800) 638-3522
Fax: (773) 380-1465   E-mail: jykmoy@wavecable.com
Web: archive.elca.org/asian/fund.html

Summary To provide financial assistance to Asian/Pacific Islanders who wish to receive seminary training to become ordained Lutheran pastors or certified lay teachers.

Eligibility This program is open to students who are of Asian or Pacific Islander background and are attending a Lutheran seminary, have been endorsed by the appropriate synodical or district commissions, have demonstrated financial need, and have received partial financial support from their home congregations. Applicants must include a 250-word statement on their commitment to Asian/Pacific Islander ministry.

Financial data The stipend is $750.

Duration 1 year; may be renewed.

Additional information The scholarship was established by Asian Lutherans in North America. It is administered by Tierrasanta Lutheran Church on behalf of all the seminaries of the 3 Lutheran churches that united in 1988 to form the Evangelical Lutheran Church in America: the Association of Evangelical Lutheran Churches, the American Lutheran Church, and the Lutheran Church in America.

Number awarded 2 each year.

Deadline September of each year.

[508]
EIRO YAMADA MEMORIAL SCHOLARSHIP

Go For Broke Memorial Education Center
P.O. Box 2590
Gardena, CA 90247
(310) 222-5710   Fax: (310) 222-5700
E-mail: Cayleen@goforbroke.org
Web: www.goforbroke.org

Summary To provide financial assistance for college or graduate school to residents of any state who are descendants of World War II Japanese American veterans.

Eligibility This program is open to residents of any state who are attending or planning to attend a trade school, community college, or 4-year college or university on the undergraduate or graduate school level. Applicants must be 1) a direct descendant of a Japanese American World War II veteran, or 2) a descendant once-removed (such as a grand-niece or a grand-nephew) of a Japanese American serviceman or servicewoman killed in action during World War II. Along with their application, they must submit a short essay on "The Values I Have Learned from My Japanese American Forefathers" or their personal reflections on the Japanese American experience during World War II.

Financial data Stipends range from $500 to $1,000.

Duration 1 year.

Number awarded Varies each year; recently, 12 of these scholarships were awarded.

Deadline April of each year.

[509]
EIZO AND TOYO SAKUMOTO TRUST SCHOLARSHIPS

Hawai'i Community Foundation
Attn: Scholarship Department
827 Fort Street Mall
Honolulu, HI 96813
(808) 537-6333   Toll Free: (888) 731-3863
Fax: (808) 521-6286
E-mail: scholarships@hcf-hawaii.org
Web: www.hawaiicommunityfoundation.org/scholarships

Summary To provide financial assistance to Hawaii residents of Japanese ancestry who are interested in attending graduate school in the state.

Eligibility This program is open to Hawaiian residents of Japanese ancestry who are enrolled or planning to enroll at an accredited college or university in the state. Applicants must be full-time graduate students and able to demonstrate academic achievement (GPA of 3.5 or higher), good moral character, and financial need. They must have been born in Hawaii. Along with their application, they must submit a short statement indicating their reasons for attending college, their planned course of study, their career goals, and what community service means to them.

Financial data The amounts of the awards depend on the availability of funds and the need of the recipient. Recently, the average value of all scholarships awarded by the foundation was $2,041.

Duration 1 year.

Number awarded Varies each year; recently, 30 of these scholarships were awarded.

Deadline February of each year.

[510]
ELLIOTT C. ROBERTS, SR. SCHOLARSHIP

Institute for Diversity in Health Management
Attn: Executive Assistant
One North Franklin Street, 30th Floor
Chicago, IL 60606
(312) 422-2630   Toll Free: (800) 233-0996
Fax: (312) 895-4511   E-mail: ejohnson@aha.org
Web: www.applicantsoft.com

Summary To provide financial assistance to Asian American and other minority graduate students in health services management.

Eligibility This program is open to members of ethnic minority groups who are accepted or enrolled in a graduate program in health care administration. Applicants must have a GPA of 3.0 or higher. They must demonstrate commitment to a career in health care administration. Along with their application, they must submit a personal statement of 300 to 500 words on their interest in health care management and their career goals. Selection is based on academic achievement, leadership potential, financial need, community involvement, commitment to health care administration, and overall professional maturity. U.S. citizenship is required.

Financial data The stipend ranges from $500 to $1,000.

Duration 1 year.

Number awarded 1 or more each year, depending on the availability of funds.

Deadline December of each year.

[511]
ENDOWMENT FOR SOUTH ASIAN STUDENTS OF INDIAN DESCENT

Pennsylvania Medical Society
Attn: Foundation
777 East Park Drive
P.O. Box 8820
Harrisburg, PA 17105-8820
(717) 558-7854
Toll Free: (800) 228-7823, ext. 7854 (within PA)
Fax: (717) 558-7818
E-mail: studentservices-foundation@pamedsoc.org
Web: www.foundationpamedsoc.org

Summary To provide financial assistance to south Asian Indian residents of Pennsylvania who are enrolled at a medical school in the state.

Eligibility This program is open to South Asian Indians or descendants of South Asian Indian immigrants to the United States who have been Pennsylvania residents for at least 12 months. Applicants must be entering the second, third, or fourth year of full-time study at an accredited allopathic or osteopathic medical school in Pennsylvania. They must submit a 1-page essay explaining why they chose to become a physician and what contributions they expect to make to the

health profession. Financial need is considered in the selection process.

Financial data The stipend is $2,000. Funds are paid directly to the recipient's medical school through the appropriate channels.

Duration 1 year.

Additional information These scholarships were first awarded in 2003.

Number awarded 1 each year.

Deadline September of each year.

[512]
ENGENDERED SCHOLARSHIPS

South Asian Journalists Association
c/o Aseem Chhabra, Awards Committee Chair
4315 46th Street, Apartment E10
Sunnyside, NY 11104-2015
E-mail: chhabs@aol.com
Web: www.saja.org/programs/scholarships

Summary To provide financial assistance for undergraduate and graduate study to journalism students of south Asian descent who write on issues related to gender and sexuality.

Eligibility This program is open to students of south Asian descent (including Bangladesh, Bhutan, India, Maldives, Nepal, Pakistan, and Sri Lanka; Indo-Caribbeans are also eligible). Applicants must be enrolled at a college or university in the United States or Canada and working on an undergraduate or graduate degree in journalism with an interest in writing on issues related to gender and sexuality. Students with financial hardship are given special consideration. Selection is based on interest in journalism, writing skills, participation in the sponsoring organization, reasons for entering journalism, and financial need.

Financial data The stipend is $1,000.

Duration 1 year.

Additional information Recipients are expected to give back to the South Asian Journalists Association (SAJA) by volunteering at the annual convention or at other events during the year.

Number awarded 2 each year: 1 to an undergraduate and 1 to a graduate student.

Deadline March of each year.

[513]
ENVIRONMENTAL PROTECTION AGENCY STUDENT DIVERSITY INTERNSHIP PROGRAM

United Negro College Fund Special Programs
  Corporation
Attn: NASA Science and Technology Institute
6402 Arlington Boulevard, Suite 600
Falls Church, VA 22042
(703) 677-3400   Toll Free: (800) 530-6232
Fax: (703) 205-7645   E-mail: portal@uncfsp.org
Web: www.uncfsp.org

Summary To provide an opportunity for Asian American and other underrepresented undergraduate and graduate students to work on a summer research project at research sites of the U.S. Environmental Protection Agency (EPA).

Eligibility This program is open to rising college sophomores, juniors, and seniors and to full-time graduate students at accredited institutions who are members of underrepresented groups, including ethnic minorities (African Americans, Hispanic/Latinos, Native Americans, Asians, Alaskan Natives, and Native Hawaiians/Pacific Islanders) and persons with disabilities. Applicants must have a GPA of 2.8 or higher and be working on a degree in business, communications, economics, engineering, environmental science/management, finance, information technology, law, marketing, or science. They must be interested in working on a research project during the summer at their choice of 23 EPA research sites (for a list, contact EPA). U.S. citizenship is required.

Financial data The stipend is $5,000 for undergraduates or $6,000 for graduate students. Interns also receive a travel and housing allowance, but they are responsible for covering their local transportation, meals, and miscellaneous expenses.

Duration 10 weeks during the summer.

Additional information This program is funded by EPA and administered by the United Negro College Fund Special Programs Corporation.

Number awarded Varies each year.

Deadline May of each year.

[514]
EPISCOPAL ASIAMERICA MINISTRY COMMISSION CONTINUING EDUCATION SCHOLARSHIPS AND FELLOWSHIPS

Episcopal Church Center
Attn: Office of Asian American Ministries
815 Second Avenue
New York, NY 10017-4594
(212) 922-5344   Toll Free: (800) 334-7626
Fax: (212) 867-7652
E-mail: wvergara@episcopalchurch.org
Web: www.episcopalchurch.org/asian.htm

Summary To provide financial assistance to Asian Americans interested in seeking ordination and serving in a ministry involving Asians in the Episcopal Church.

Eligibility This program is open to Asian students pursuing theological education, including diocesan programs as well as seminary education. Applicants must be a member of an Asian constituency in the Episcopal Church and have begun the process of seeking ordination through a local Episcopal diocese. Scholarships are presented only for full-time study.

Financial data The maximum scholarship is $4,000 per semester for seminary study and $2,500 per semester for diocesan theological study programs.

Duration 1 semester; renewable.

Additional information This program was established in 1991 as part of the Episcopal Legacy Fund for Scholarships Honoring the Memory of the Rev. Dr. Martin Luther King, Jr. Applications must include an essay indicating an understanding of the life and ministry of Dr. King.

Number awarded Varies each year.

Deadline April of each year for the fall semester; August of each year for the spring semester.

[515]
EPISCOPAL ASIAMERICA MINISTRY THEOLOGICAL EDUCATION SCHOLARSHIPS FOR ASIAN AND PACIFIC ISLAND AMERICANS

Episcopal Church Center
Attn: Office of Asian American Ministries
815 Second Avenue
New York, NY 10017-4594
(212) 922-5344   Toll Free: (800) 334-7626
Fax: (212) 867-7652
E-mail: wvergara@episcopalchurch.org
Web: www.episcopalchurch.org/asian.htm

Summary To provide financial assistance to Asian and Pacific Island Americans interested in seeking ordination and serving in a ministry involving Asians and Pacific Islanders in the Episcopal Church.

Eligibility This program is open to Asian and Pacific Island students pursuing theological education, including diocesan programs as well as seminary education. Applicants must be a member of an Asian or Pacific Island constituency in the Episcopal Church and have begun the process of seeking ordination through a local Episcopal diocese. Scholarships are presented only for full-time study.

Financial data The maximum scholarship is $4,000 per semester for seminary study or $2,500 per semester for diocesan theological study programs.

Duration 1 semester; renewable.

Additional information This program was established in 1983 with a grant from undesignated funds received through the Venture in Mission Project. Additional funding was received from the Diocese of Southern Virginia.

Number awarded Varies each year.

Deadline April of each year for the fall semester; August of each year for the spring semester.

[516]
ESTHER NGAN-LING CHOW AND MAREYJOYCE GREEN SCHOLARSHIP

Sociologists for Women in Society
Attn: Executive Officer
University of Rhode Island
Department of Sociology
10 Chafee Road
Kingston, RI 02881
(401) 874-9510   Fax: (401) 874-2588
E-mail: swseo@socwomen.org
Web: www.socwomen.org/page.php?sss=115

Summary To provide funding to Asian American and other women of color who are conducting dissertation research in sociology.

Eligibility This program is open to women from a racial/ethnic group that faces racial discrimination in the United States. Applicants must be in the early stages of writing a doctoral dissertation in sociology on a topic relating to the concerns that women of color face domestically and/or internationally. They must be able to demonstrate financial need. Both domestic and international students are eligible to apply. Along with their application, they must submit a personal statement that details their short- and long-term career and research goals; a resume or curriculum vitae; 2 letters of recommendation; and a 5-page dissertation proposal that includes the purpose of the research, the work to be accomplished through support from this scholarship, and a time line for completion.

Financial data The stipend is $15,000. An additional grant of $500 is provided to enable the recipient to attend the winter meeting of Sociologists for Women in Society (SWS), and travel expenses to attend the summer meeting are reimbursed.

Duration 1 year.

Additional information This program was established in 2007 and originally named the Women of Color Dissertation Scholarship.

Number awarded 1 each year.

Deadline March of each year.

[517]
ETHEL BOLDEN MINORITY SCHOLARSHIP

Richland County Public Library Foundation
Attn: Development Manager
1431 Assembly Street
Columbia, SC 29201
(803) 929-3424   E-mail: tgills@myrcpl.com
Web: www.myrcpl.com/foundation/bolden

Summary To provide financial assistance to Asian American and other minority residents of South Carolina who are interested in working on a master's degree in library and information science at a school in any state.

Eligibility This program is open to residents of South Carolina who are members of ethnic and racial groups underrepresented in the field of library and information science (American Indians, African Americans, Asian Americans, or Hispanic Americans). Applicants must have been admitted to an ALA-accredited school of library and information science in any state. Along with their application, they must submit a 300-word essay describing their interest and any work in the field of librarianship and the specific competencies or characteristics they believe they can contribute to the library profession. Selection is based on academic performance and demonstrated leadership abilities through participation in community service or other activities.

Financial data The stipend is $2,500.

Duration 1 year.

Additional information This program was established in 2010.

Number awarded 1 each year.

Deadline March of each year.

[518]
ETHNIC MINORITY ADMINISTRATOR IN TRAINING INTERNSHIP

Indiana Health Care Association
Attn: Executive Director
One North Capitol, Suite 100
Indianapolis, IN 46204
(317) 636-6406   Toll Free: (800) 466-IHCA
Fax: (877) 298-3749   E-mail: dhenry@ihca.org
Web: www.ihca.org

Summary To provide work experience to Asian American and other minority residents of Indiana interested in gaining work experience at the Indiana Health Care Association (IHCA).

Eligibility This program is open to residents of Indiana who are members of ethnic minority groups (African Americans, Hispanics, American Indians, Asian Americans). Applicants must have a bachelor's degree or higher and an employment history that reflects management or leadership skills. They must be interested in preparing for a career in long-term care as a health facility administrator by working under a preceptor at IHCA. Preference is given to applicants interested in working with elderly or disabled populations. An interview at IHCA headquarters is required.

Financial data This is a paid internship (stipend not specified).

Duration 6 months.

Number awarded 1 each year.

Deadline July of each year.

[519]
ETHNIC MINORITY POSTGRADUATE SCHOLARSHIP FOR CAREERS IN ATHLETICS

Black Coaches Association
Attn: Director of Operations and Administration
Pan American Plaza
201 South Capitol Avenue, Suite 495
Indianapolis, IN 46225-1089
(317) 829-5619   Toll Free: (877) 789-1222
Fax: (317) 829-5601
Web: bcasports.cstv.com

Summary To provide financial assistance to Asian Americans and other minorities who participated in college athletics and are interested in working on a graduate degree in athletic administration.

Eligibility This program is open to former student-athletes on the college level who are of ethnic minority origin. Applicants must be entering or enrolled full time in a graduate program in sports administration or a related field to prepare for a career in athletics. They must have performed with distinction as student body members at their undergraduate institution and have a GPA of 2.5 or higher. U.S. citizenship is required. Selection is based on academic course work, extracurricular activities, commitment to preparing for a career in athletics, and promise of success in their career.

Financial data The stipend is $2,500. Funds are paid to the college or university of the recipient's choice.

Duration 1 year; nonrenewable.

Additional information This program was established in 1995.

Number awarded Varies each year; recently, 6 of these scholarships were awarded.

Deadline April of each year.

[520]
EURASIA DISSERTATION SUPPORT FELLOWSHIPS

Social Science Research Council
Attn: Eurasia Program
One Pierrepont Plaza, 15th Floor
Brooklyn, NY 11201
(212) 377-2700   Fax: (212) 377-2727
E-mail: eurasia@ssrc.org
Web: www.ssrc.org/fellowships/Eurasia-fellowship

Summary To provide funding to graduate students (particularly Asian Americans, other minorities, and women) who are completing a dissertation dealing with Eurasia.

Eligibility This program is open to students who have completed field research for their doctoral dissertation and who plan to work on writing it during the next academic year. Applicants must have been conducting research in a discipline of the social sciences or humanities that deals with the Russian Empire, the Soviet Union, or the New States of Eurasia. Research related to the non-Russian states, regions, and peoples is particularly encouraged. Regions and countries currently supported by the program include Armenia, Azerbaijan, Belarus, Georgia, Kazakhstan, Kyrgyzstan, Moldova, Russian Federation, Tajikistan, Turkmenistan, Ukraine, and Uzbekistan; funding is not presently available for research on the Baltic states. U.S. citizenship or permanent resident status is required. Minorities and women are particularly encouraged to apply.

Financial data Grants up to $25,000 are available.

Duration Up to 1 year.

Additional information Funding for this program is provided by the U.S. Department of State under the Program for Research and Training on Eastern Europe and the Independent States of the Former Soviet Union (Title VIII).

Number awarded Varies each year; recently, 7 of these fellowships were awarded.

Deadline December of each year.

[521]
EXCELLENCE IN CARDIOVASCULAR SCIENCES SUMMER RESEARCH PROGRAM

Wake Forest University School of Medicine
Attn: Hypertension and Vascular Research Center
Medical Center Boulevard
Winston-Salem, NC 27157-1032
(336) 716-1080   Fax: (336) 716-2456
E-mail: nsarver@wfubmc.edu
Web: www.wfubmc.edu

Summary To provide Asian Americans and other underrepresented students with an internship opportunity to engage in a summer research project in cardiovascular science at Wake Forest University in Winston-Salem, North Carolina.

Eligibility This program is open to undergraduates and master's degree students who are members of underrepresented minority groups (African Americans, Alaskan Natives, Asian Americans, Native Americans, Pacific Islanders, and Hispanics) or who come from disadvantaged backgrounds (e.g., rural areas, first generation college students). Applicants must be interested in participating in a program of summer research in the cardiovascular sciences that includes "hands-on" laboratory research, a lecture series by faculty and guest speakers, and a research symposium at which students present their research findings. U.S. citizenship or permanent resident status is required.

Financial data The stipend is $1,731 per month, housing in a university dormitory, and round-trip transportation expense.

Duration 2 months during the summer.

Additional information This program is sponsored by the National Heart, Lung, and Blood Institute (NHLBI) of the National Institutes of Health (NIH).

Number awarded Approximately 10 each year.

Deadline February of each year.

[522]
FACSE GRADUATE FELLOWSHIPS

National Association of Teacher Educators for Family and Consumer Sciences
c/o Lela G. Goar, Fellowship Committee Chair
225 CR 207A
Burnet, TX 78611
(512) 715-8249   Fax: (512) 585-7606
E-mail: lkgoar@earthlink.net
Web: www.natefacs.org/scholarship.html

Summary To provide financial assistance to graduate students (particularly Asian Americans and other minorities) in family and consumer science education.

Eligibility This program is open to graduate students working on a master's or doctoral degree in family and consumer sciences education. Applicants must submit an autobiographical sketch (up to 3 pages in length) presenting their professional goals, including information on the institution where they are studying or planning to study, areas or emphases of study, possible research topic, and other pertinent information regarding their plans. Selection is based on likelihood of completing the degree, likelihood of contribution to family and consumer sciences education, previous academic work, professional association involvement, professional experience (including scholarly work), and references. At least 1 fellowship is reserved for a minority (African American, Hispanic American, Native American, or Asian American) candidate.

Financial data Stipends range from $2,000 to $4,000.

Duration 1 year.

Additional information The sponsor is an affiliate of the Family and Consumer Sciences (FACS) Division of the Association for Career and Technical Education.

Number awarded Varies each year.

Deadline November of each year.

[523]
FAEGRE & BENSON DIVERSITY SCHOLARSHIP

Faegre & Benson LLP
Attn: Manager of Junior Legal Talent Recruitment
2200 Wells Fargo Center
90 South Seventh Street
Minneapolis, MN 55402-3901
(612) 766-8952   Toll Free: (800) 328-4393
Fax: (612) 766-1600   E-mail: tselden@faegre.com
Web: www.faegre.com/12399

Summary To provide financial assistance and work experience to Asian American and other law students who will contribute to diversity in the legal profession.

Eligibility This program is open to students enrolled in the first year at an accredited law school in the United States. Applicants must submit a 500-word personal statement explaining their interest in the scholarship program, how diversity has influenced their life, and how it impacts the legal profession. Selection is based on that statement, a resume, undergraduate transcripts, a legal writing sample, and 2 professional recommendations.

Financial data The stipend is $6,000 per year.

Duration 2 years: the second and third year of law school.

Additional information Recipients are also offered an associateship during the summer between the first and second year at an office of the firm in Minneapolis, Denver, Boulder, or Des Moines. An attorney from the firm is assigned as a mentor to help them adjust to the firm and to the legal profession.

Number awarded 2 each year.

Deadline January of each year.

[524]
FARM CREDIT EAST SCHOLARSHIPS

Farm Credit East
Attn: Scholarship Program
240 South Road
Enfield, CT 06082
(860) 741-4380   Toll Free: (800) 562-2235
Fax: (860) 741-4389
Web: www.farmcrediteast.com

Summary To provide financial assistance to residents of designated northeastern states (particularly Asian Americans and other minorities) who plan to attend school in any state to work on an undergraduate or graduate degree in a field related to agriculture, forestry, or fishing.

Eligibility This program is open to residents of Massachusetts, Connecticut, Rhode Island, New Jersey, and portions of New York and New Hampshire. Applicants must be working on or planning to work on an associate, bachelor's, or graduate degree in production agriculture, agribusiness, the forest products industry, or commercial fishing at a college or university in any state. They must submit a 200-word essay on why they wish to prepare for a career in agriculture, forestry, or fishing. Selection is based on the essay, extracurricular activities (especially farm work experience and activities indicative of an interest in preparing for a career in agriculture or agribusiness), and interest in agriculture. The program includes scholarships reserved for members of minority (Black or African American, American Indian or Alaska Native, Asian, Native Hawaiian or other Pacific Islander, or Hispanic or Latino) groups.

Financial data The stipend is $1,500. Funds are paid directly to the student to be used for tuition, room and board, books, and other academic charges.

Duration 1 year; nonrenewable.

Additional information Recipients are given priority for an internship with the sponsor in the summer following their junior year. Farm Credit East was formerly named First Pioneer Farm Credit.

Number awarded Up to 28 each year, including several reserved for members of minority groups.

Deadline April of each year.

[525]
FASSE/CUFA INQUIRY GRANT

National Council for the Social Studies
Attn: Program Manager, External Relations
8555 16th Street, Suite 500
Silver Spring, MD 20910-2844
(301) 588-1800, ext. 106   Fax: (301) 588-2049
E-mail: excellence@ncss.org
Web: www.socialstudies.org/getinvolved/awards/fasse-cufa

Summary To provide funding to faculty and graduate student members of the National Council for the Social Studies (NCSS), particularly Asian Americans and other minorities who are interested in conducting research projects in "citizenship education."

Eligibility This program is open to members of the council who are assistant, associate, or full professors or graduate students with the demonstrated support of a university mentor/adviser. Graduate student applicants must have a mentor/adviser who is also an NCSS member. Researchers from all groups, including underrepresented groups, are encouraged to apply. They must be interested in a project in "citizenship education" that affirms social, cultural, and racial diversity and that addresses issues of equality, equity, and social justice. Proposals that address aims for citizen action are preferred. All proposals should be relevant to school, university, or community-based educational settings. They should either 1) serve student bodies that are socially, culturally, and racially diverse; or 2) involve teachers or prospective teachers who work or will work with diverse student populations. They can address a range of educational levels and settings, from K-12 to collegiate levels, and from school to community settings.

Financial data Grants up to $10,000 are available.

Duration Funded projects must be completed within 1 academic year.

Additional information This program is sponsored by the College and University Faculty Assembly (CUFA) and the Fund for the Advancement of Social Studies Education (FASSE), established by the NCAA in 1984.

Number awarded 1 every 2 or 3 years.

Deadline June of the years in which grants are offered.

[526]
FBANC SCHOLARSHIP

Filipino Bar Association of Northern California
268 Bush Street, Suite 2928
San Francisco, CA 94104
E-mail: fbancinfo@gmail.com
Web: www.fbanc.org/law-students

Summary To provide financial assistance to entering or continuing law students who are interested in serving the Filipino American community.

Eligibility This program is open to currently-enrolled and entering law students who have a tie to the Filipino American community and intend to provide legal services to that community after graduation from law school. Applicants must submit a current transcript or admit letter, a resume, and a 2-page essay on why they want to become a lawyer and what can the sponsor do to get Filipinos interested in a law career. An interview may be required.

Financial data The stipend is $2,500.

Duration 1 year.

Number awarded 1 each year.

Deadline March of each year.

[527]
FEDERAL INTERNSHIP PROGRAM

Conference on Asian Pacific American Leadership
Attn: Scholarship Committee
P.O. Box 65073
Washington, DC 20035-5073
(202) 628-1307   Fax: (877) 892-5427
E-mail: scholarships@capal.org
Web: www.capal.org/programs/federal-internship-program

Summary To provide funding for summer internships with designated federal agencies to Asian Pacific American undergraduate and graduate students.

Eligibility This program is open to Asian Pacific American (APA) undergraduate and graduate students who are working on a degree in any field. Applicants must be interested in a summer internship at a federal agency; recently, those included the Office of Personnel Management (OPM) and several agencies within the U.S. Department of Agriculture (Rural Development, Forest Service, Agricultural Research Service, and Food Safety and Inspection Service). Along with their application, they must submit a 750-word essay on 2 of the following topics: 1) their long-term career goals and how the summer internship experience will advance those; 2) their previous educational, community work, and internship experiences and how those experiences have influenced their long-term career goals; or 3) how they will use the experiences and knowledge that they gain during their summer in Washington to better the APA community and their local community. Selection is based on demonstrated commitment to public service, including service to the APA community; potential to benefit from the internship; demonstrated leadership and potential for continued growth in leadership skills; relevance of the proposed internship to overall public sector goals; academic achievement; and financial need. U.S. citizenship is required.

Financial data Interns receive a stipend of $2,000 to help pay expenses during their assignment.

Duration At least 6 weeks during the summer.

Additional information Assignments are available in Washington, D.C. or at sites nationwide.

Number awarded At least 10 each year.

Deadline January of each year.

[528]
FELLOWSHIPS IN SCIENCE AND INTERNATIONAL AFFAIRS

Harvard University
John F. Kennedy School of Government
Belfer Center for Science and International Affairs
Attn: Fellowship Coordinator
79 John F. Kennedy Street
Cambridge, MA 02138
(617) 495-8806   Fax: (617) 495-8963
E-mail: bcsia_fellowships@ksg.harvard.edu
Web: belfercenter.ksg.harvard.edu/fellowships

Summary To provide funding to professionals, postdoctorates, and doctoral students (especially Asian Americans, other minorities, and women) who are interested in conducting research in areas of concern to the Belfer Center for Science and International Affairs at Harvard University in Cambridge, Massachusetts.

Eligibility The postdoctoral fellowship is open to recent recipients of the Ph.D. or equivalent degree, university faculty members, and employees of government, military, international, humanitarian, and private research institutions who have appropriate professional experience. Applicants for predoctoral fellowships must have passed their general examinations. Lawyers, economists, political scientists, those in the natural sciences, and others of diverse disciplinary backgrounds are also welcome to apply. The program especially encourages applications from women, minorities, and citizens of all countries. All applicants must be interested in conducting research in 1 of the 3 major program areas of the center: 1) the International Security Program (ISP), including Religion in International Affairs; 2) the Science, Technology, and Public Policy Program (STPP), including information and communications technology, energy and water policy, managing the atom project, and the energy technology innovation policy research group; 3) and the Dubai initiative.

Financial data The stipend is $34,000 for postdoctoral research fellows or $20,000 for predoctoral research fellows. Health insurance is also provided.

Duration 10 months.

Number awarded A limited number each year.

Deadline January of each year.

[529]
FILIPINO NURSES' ORGANIZATION OF HAWAII SCHOLARSHIP

Hawai'i Community Foundation
Attn: Scholarship Department
827 Fort Street Mall
Honolulu, HI 96813
(808) 537-6333   Toll Free: (888) 731-3863
Fax: (808) 521-6286
E-mail: scholarships@hcf-hawaii.org
Web: www.hawaiicommunityfoundation.org/scholarships

Summary To provide financial assistance to Hawaii residents of Filipino ancestry who are interested in attending college in any state to prepare for a career as a nurse.

Eligibility This program is open to Hawaii residents of Filipino ancestry who are enrolled or planning to enroll full time at a college or university in any state and work on an undergraduate or graduate degree in nursing. Applicants must be able to demonstrate academic achievement (GPA of 2.7 or higher), good moral character, and financial need. Along with their application, they must submit a short statement indicating their reasons for attending college, their planned course of study, their career goals, and what community service means to them.

Financial data The amounts of the awards depend on the availability of funds and the need of the recipient. Recently, the average value of all scholarships awarded by the foundation was $2,041.

Duration 1 year.

Number awarded Varies each year; recently, 2 of these scholarships were awarded.

Deadline February of each year.

[530]
FINNEGAN HENDERSON DIVERSITY SCHOLARSHIP

Finnegan, Henderson, Farabow, Garrett & Dunner, LLP
Attn: Attorney Recruitment Manager
901 New York Avenue, N.W.
Washington, DC 20001-4413
(202) 408-4034   Fax: (202) 408-4400
E-mail: diversityscholarship@finnegan.com
Web: www.finnegan.com/careers/summerprogram/overview

Summary To provide financial assistance and work experience to Asian American and other minority law students interested in a career in intellectual property law.

Eligibility This program is open to law students from underrepresented minority groups who have demonstrated a commitment to a career in intellectual property law and are currently enrolled either as a first-year full-time student or second-year part-time student. The sponsor defines underrepresented minorities to include American Indians/Alaskan Natives, Blacks/African Americans, Asian Americans, Native Hawaiians or other Pacific Islanders, and Hispanics/Latinos. Applicants must have earned an undergraduate degree in life sciences, engineering, or computer science, or have substantial prior trademark experience. Selection is based on academic performance at the undergraduate, graduate (if applicable), and law school level; relevant work experience; community service; leadership skills; and special accomplishments.

Financial data The stipend is $15,000 per year.

Duration 1 year; may be renewed 1 additional year as long as the recipient completes a summer associateship with the sponsor and maintains of GPA of 3.0 or higher.

Additional information The sponsor, the world's largest intellectual property law firm, established this scholarship in 2003. Summer associateships are available at its offices in Washington, D.C.; Atlanta, Georgia; Cambridge, Massachusetts; Palo Alto, California; or Reston, Virginia.

Number awarded 1 each year.

Deadline February of each year.

[531]
FIRST-YEAR INTERNSHIP PROGRAM OF THE OREGON STATE BAR

Oregon State Bar
Attn: Affirmative Action Program
16037 S.W. Upper Boones Ferry Road
P.O. Box 231935
Tigard, OR 97281-1935
(503) 431-6338
Toll Free: (800) 452-8260, ext. 338 (within OR)
Fax: (503) 598-6938   E-mail: eyip@osbar.org
Web: www.osbar.org/aap

Summary To provide work experience to Asian American and other minority law students in Oregon.

Eligibility This program is open to ethnic minority students from any state who are completing the first year of law school in Oregon. Applicants must be interested in a summer internship at a law firm in the state. Along with their application, they must submit 1) a resume that includes their community activities; 2) up to 10 pages of a first-semester legal writing assignment; and 3) a 2-page personal statement that covers

their past and present ties to ethnic minority communities in Oregon and elsewhere, diversity issues that inspired them to become a lawyer, and their expectations of this internship experience. Participating employers receive a catalog with all application packets; they select students whom they wish to interview and make the final hiring decisions.

Financial data Employers who hire interns through this program pay competitive stipends.

Duration Summer months.

Number awarded Varies each year.

Deadline January of each year.

[532]
FISH & RICHARDSON DIVERSITY FELLOWSHIP PROGRAM

Fish & Richardson P.C.
Attn: Recruiting Department
One Marina Park Drive
Boston, MA 02110
(617) 542-5070   Fax: (617) 542-8906
E-mail: Kiley@fr.com
Web: www.fr.com/careers/diversity

Summary To provide financial assistance for law school to Asian Americans and other students who will contribute to diversity in the legal profession.

Eligibility This program is open to students enrolled in the first year at a law school anywhere in the country. Applicants must be African American/Black, American Indian/Alaskan, Hispanic/Latino, Native Hawaiian/Pacific Islander, Asian, 2 or more races, disabled, or openly homosexual, bisexual, and/or transgender. Along with their application, they must submit a 500-word essay describing their background, what led them to the legal field, their interest in the sponsoring law firm, and what they could contribute to its practice and the profession. They must also indicate their first 3 choices of an office of the firm where they are interested in a summer associate clerkship.

Financial data The stipend is $5,000.

Duration 1 year: the second year of law school.

Additional information Recipients are also offered a paid associate clerkship during the summer following their first year of law school at an office of the firm in the location of their choice in Atlanta, Boston, Dallas, Delaware, Houston, New York, San Diego, Silicon Valley, Twin Cities, or Washington, D.C. This program began in 2005.

Number awarded 1 or more each year.

Deadline January of each year.

[533]
FIVE COLLEGE FELLOWSHIP PROGRAM

Five Colleges, Incorporated
Attn: Five Colleges Fellowship Program Committee
97 Spring Street
Amherst, MA 01002-2324
(413) 256-8316   Fax: (413) 256-0249
E-mail: neckert@fivecolleges.edu
Web: www.fivecolleges.edu

Summary To provide funding to Asian American and other graduate students from underrepresented groups who have completed all the requirements for the Ph.D. except the dissertation and are interested in teaching at selected colleges in Massachusetts.

Eligibility Fellows are chosen by the host department in each of the 5 participating campuses (Amherst, Hampshire, Mount Holyoke, Smith, and the University of Massachusetts). Applicants must be graduate students at an accredited school who have completed all doctoral requirements except the dissertation and are interested in devoting full time to the completion of the dissertation. The chief goal of the program is to support scholars from underrepresented groups and/or scholars "with unique interests and histories whose engagement in the Academy will enrich scholarship and teaching."

Financial data The program provides a stipend of $30,000, a research grant, fringe benefits, office space, library privileges, and housing assistance.

Duration 1 academic year; nonrenewable.

Additional information Although the primary goal is completion of the dissertation, each fellow also has many opportunities to experience working with students and faculty colleagues on the host campus as well as with those at the other colleges. The fellows are also given an opportunity to teach (generally as a team teacher, in a section of a core course, or in a component within a course). Fellows meet monthly with each other to share their experiences. At Smith College, this program is named Mendenhall Fellowships.

Number awarded 4 each year.

Deadline January of each year.

[534]
FLORIDA BAR FOUNDATION LEGAL AID SUMMER FELLOWSHIP PROGRAM

Florida Bar Foundation
Attn: Grants Coordinator
250 South Orange Avenue, Suite 600P
P.O. Box 1553
Orlando, FL 32802-1553
(407) 843-0045, ext. 105
Toll Free: (800) 541-2195 (within FL)
Fax: (407) 839-0287   E-mail: cbevington@flabarfndn.org
Web: www.flabarfndn.org/grant-programs/lsa

Summary To provide summer work experience at Florida legal assistance providers to students (particularly Asian Americans and other minorities) from law schools in any state.

Eligibility This program is open to first- and second-year students at accredited law schools in any state. Applicants must be interested in working during the summer at a legal aid and legal services provider funded by Florida's Interest on Trust Accounts (IOTA) program. Minority students are specifically encouraged to apply. Selection is based on experience in working with the low-income community, academic achievement, writing skills, and previous contact with and long-term commitment and interest in public service/pro bono work.

Financial data The stipend is $5,500 for first-year students or $7,000 for second-year students.

Duration 11 weeks during the summer.

Additional information This program was initiated in 1995.

Number awarded Approximately 20 each year. Since the program began, more than 200 students have participated.

Deadline January of each year.

[535]
FLORIDA DIVERSITY FELLOWSHIPS IN ENVIRONMENTAL LAW

American Bar Association
Attn: Section of Environment, Energy, and Resources
321 North Clark Street
Chicago, IL 60654-7598
(312) 988-5602   Fax: (312) 988-5572
E-mail: jonusaid@staff.abanet.org
Web: www.abanet.org

Summary To provide funding to Asian American and other law students from underserved groups who are interested in working on a summer project in environmental, energy, or natural resources law in Florida.

Eligibility This program is open to first- and second-year law students and third-year night students who are members of underrepresented and underserved groups, such as minority or low-income populations. Students may be residents of any state and attending school in any state; preference is given to residents of Florida and to students who are enrolled at law schools in Florida or who have a strong interest in the state. Applicants must be interested in working during the summer at a government agency or public interest organization on a project in Florida in the areas of environmental, energy, or natural resources law. Selection is based on interest in environmental issues, academic record, personal qualities, and leadership abilities.

Financial data The stipend is $5,000.

Duration 8 to 10 weeks during the summer.

Additional information This program is cosponsored by the Florida Department of Environmental Protection and the Florida Bar Association's Environmental and Land Use Law Section.

Number awarded 2 each year.

Deadline March of each year.

[536]
FLORIDA LIBRARY ASSOCIATION MINORITY SCHOLARSHIPS

Florida Library Association
164 N.W. Madison Street, Suite 104
P.O. Box 1571
Lake City, FL 32056-1571
(336) 438-5795   Fax: (336) 438-5796
Web: www.flalib.org/scholarships.php

Summary To provide financial assistance to Asian American and other minority students working on a graduate degree in library and information science in Florida.

Eligibility This program is open to residents of Florida who are working on a graduate degree in library and information science at schools in the state. Applicants must be members of a minority group: Black/African American, American Indian/Alaska Native, Asian/Pacific Islander, or Hispanic/Latino. They must have some experience in a Florida library, must be a member of the Florida Library Association, and must commit to working in a Florida library for at least 1 year after graduation. Along with their application, they must submit 1) a list of activities, honors, awards, and/or offices held during college and outside college; and 2) a statement of their reasons for entering librarianship and their career goals with respect to Florida libraries. Financial need is considered in the selection process.

Financial data   The stipend is $2,000.

Duration   1 year.

Number awarded   1 each year.

Deadline   February of each year.

[537]
FOLEY & LARDNER DIVERSITY SCHOLARSHIP

Foley & Lardner LLP
Attn: Diversity Outreach Coordinator
777 East Wisconsin Avenue
Milwaukee, WI 53202-5367
(414) 297-5452   Fax: (414) 297-4900
E-mail: alois@foley.com
Web: apps.foley.com

Summary   To provide scholarships to Asian American and other first-year students who are attending selected law schools and will contribute to diversity in the legal profession.

Eligibility   This program is open to students in the first year at the following law schools: Berkeley, Duke, Florida, Georgetown, Michigan, Northwestern, UCLA, or Wisconsin. Applicants must 1) be a member of a racial or ethnic group defined as minority (American Indian/Alaska Native, Asian/Pacific Islander, Black, or Hispanic); or 2) self-identify as lesbian, gay, bisexual, or transgender. Selection is based on involvement in diversity-related student organizations, involvement in community activities, undergraduate and law school academic achievement, and work or personal achievements. Financial need is not a consideration.

Financial data   The stipend is $5,000; funds are paid at the beginning of the recipient's second semester in law school and must be applied to tuition, books, fees, and other expenses incidental to law school attendance.

Duration   1 semester (the second semester of the first year in law school).

Additional information   This program was established in 1998.

Number awarded   8 each year (1 at each of the participating schools).

Deadline   February of each year.

[538]
FOSTER PEPPER DIVERSITY FELLOWSHIP

Foster Pepper PLLC
Attn: Manager, Attorney Recruitment and Professional
   Development
1111 Third Avenue, Suite 3400
Seattle, WA 98101-3299
(206) 447-4400   Toll Free: (800) 995-5902
Fax: (206) 447-9700   E-mail: browb@foster.com
Web: www.foster.com/about.aspx?pid=20

Summary   To provide financial assistance and work experience to Asian American and other law students of color who are interested in practicing law in Seattle, Washington following graduation.

Eligibility   This program is open to students of color or other diverse background who are enrolled in the first year at

an ABA-accredited law school. Applicants must be able to demonstrate 1) a record of academic achievement that offers great promise for a successful career during the remainder of law school and in the legal profession; 2) meaningful contributions to the diversity of the law school student body and, upon entering the legal profession, the legal community; and 3) a commitment to practice law in Seattle following graduation from law school. Along with their application, they must submit a 500-word personal statement describing their interest in practicing law in Seattle, their interest in the sponsoring firm and its summer program, and how they would contribute to the diversity of the firm and the Seattle legal community.

Financial data   The stipend is $7,500.

Duration   1 year.

Additional information   This program was established in 2008. The program also includes a paid summer associate position in the firm's Seattle office.

Number awarded   1 or more each year.

Deadline   January of each year.

[539]
FRANCHISE LAW DIVERSITY SCHOLARSHIP AWARD

International Franchise Association
Attn: President, Educational Foundation
1501 K Street, N.W., Suite 350
Washington, DC 20005
(202) 662-0764   Fax: (202) 628-0812
E-mail: jreynolds@franchise.org
Web: www.franchise.org/files/Scholarships.aspx

Summary   To provide financial assistance to Asian American and other law students from underrepresented groups who are interested in taking courses related to franchise law.

Eligibility   This program is open to second- and third-year students who are enrolled at ABA-accredited law schools and a member of a diverse group (defined as African Americans, American Indians, Hispanic Americans, Asian Americans, or gays/lesbians). Applicants must be enrolled in at least 1 course oriented toward franchise law (e.g., torts, unfair trade practices, trade secrets, antitrust, trademarks, contracts, agency, or securities). Along with their application, they must submit current transcript, an essay explaining their interest in franchise law, and 2 letters of recommendation.

Financial data   The stipend is $4,000. Funds are paid to the recipient's law school and are to be used for tuition.

Duration   1 year.

Additional information   This award is cosponsored by the IFA Educational Foundation and DLA Piper US LLP. It may not be used by the recipient's law school to reduce the amount of any institutionally-awarded financial aid.

Number awarded   1 or more each year.

Deadline   October of each year.

[540]
FRANKLIN WILLIAMS INTERNSHIP

Council on Foreign Relations
Attn: Human Resources Office
58 East 68th Street
New York, NY 10021
(212) 434-9489   Fax: (212) 434-9893
E-mail: humanresources@cfr.org
Web: www.cfr.org

Summary To provide undergraduate and graduate students (particularly Asian Americans and other minorities) with an opportunity to gain work experience in international affairs at the Council on Foreign Relations in New York.

Eligibility Applicants should be currently enrolled in either their senior year of an undergraduate program or in a graduate program in the area of international relations or a related field. They should have a record of high academic achievement, proven leadership ability, and previous related internship or work experience. Minority students are strongly encouraged to apply.

Financial data The stipend is $10 per hour.

Duration 1 academic term (fall, spring, or summer). Fall and spring interns are required to make a commitment of at least 12 hours per week. Summer interns may choose to make a full-time commitment.

Additional information Interns work closely with a program director or fellow in either the studies or meetings program and are involved with program coordination, substantive and business writing, research, and budget management. In addition, they are encouraged to attend the council's programs and participate in informal training designed to enhance management and leadership skills.

Number awarded 3 each year: 1 each academic term.

Deadline Applications may be submitted at any time.

[541]
FREDRIKSON & BYRON FOUNDATION MINORITY SCHOLARSHIP

Fredrikson & Byron Foundation
Attn: Attorney Recruiting Administrator
200 South Sixth Street, Suite 4000
Minneapolis, MN 55402-1425
(612) 492-7141   Fax: (612) 492-7077
E-mail: glarson@fredlaw.com
Web: www.fredlaw.com/firm/scholarship.htm

Summary To provide financial assistance and summer work experience to Asian American and other minority law students from any state who are interested in practicing in the Twin Cities area of Minnesota.

Eligibility This program is open to African American, Asian American, Pacific Islander, Hispanic, Native American, and Alaska Native students enrolled in their first year of law school. Applicants must be interested in practicing law in the Minneapolis-St. Paul area. Along with their application, they must submit brief statement on their expectations and objectives in applying for this scholarship; the factors they will use to measure success in their legal career; what they see as potential issues, obstacles, and opportunities facing new lawyers in a large private practice firm; and their interest in a summer associate position in private practice, including their interest in practicing law in the Minneapolis-St. Paul area. Financial need is not considered.

Financial data The fellowship stipend is $10,000. The internship portion of the program provides a $1,000 weekly stipend.

Duration 1 year.

Additional information Fellows are also eligible to participate in an internship at the firm's offices in Minneapolis.

Number awarded 1 each year.

Deadline March of each year.

[542]
FURNISS FOUNDATION/AOS GRADUATE FELLOWSHIP

American Orchid Society
16700 AOS Lane
Delray Beach, FL 33446-4351
(561) 404-2000   Fax: (561) 404-2045
E-mail: TheAOS@aos.org
Web: www.aos.org

Summary To provide funding to doctoral candidates (particularly Asian Americans, other minorities, and women) who are conducting dissertation research related to orchids.

Eligibility This program is open to graduate students whose doctoral dissertation relates to orchids within the disciplines of physiology, molecular biology, structure, systematics, cytology, ecology, and/or evolution. Applicants must submit an outline of their project, their college transcript, a letter of recommendation from their chair, and a 1-page statement on why their project should be considered and the impact it will have on the future of orchidology. Women, minorities, and persons with disabilities are especially encouraged to apply.

Financial data The grant is $9,000 per year. Funds are paid directly to the recipient's college or university, but indirect overhead is not allowed.

Duration Up to a maximum of 3 years.

Additional information This fellowship was first awarded in 1990.

Number awarded 1 each year.

Deadline February of each year.

[543]
GAIUS CHARLES BOLIN DISSERTATION AND POST-MFA FELLOWSHIPS

Williams College
Attn: Dean of the Faculty
Hopkins Hall, Third Floor
P.O. Box 141
Williamstown, MA 01267
(413) 597-4351   Fax: (413) 597-3553
E-mail: gburda@williams.edu
Web: dean-faculty.williams.edu/graduate-fellowships

Summary To provide financial assistance to Asian Americans and members of other underrepresented groups who are interested in teaching courses at Williams College while working on their doctoral dissertation or building their post-M.F.A. professional portfolio.

Eligibility This program is open to members of underrepresented groups, including ethnic minorities, first-generation college students, women in predominantly male fields, and scholars with disabilities. Applicants must be 1) doctoral candidates in any field who have completed all work for a Ph.D. except for the dissertation; or 2) artists who completed an M.F.A. degree within the past 2 years and are building their professional portfolio. They must be willing to teach a course at Williams College. Along with their application, they must submit a full curriculum vitae, a graduate school transcript, 3 letters of recommendation, a copy of their dissertation prospectus or samples of their artistic work, and a description of their teaching interests within a department or program at Williams College. U.S. citizenship or permanent resident status is required.

Financial data Fellows receive $33,000 for the academic year, plus housing assistance, office space, computer and library privileges, and a research allowance of up to $4,000.

Duration 2 years.

Additional information Bolin fellows are assigned a faculty advisor in the appropriate department. This program was established in 1985. Fellows are expected to teach a 1-semester course each year. They must be in residence at Williams College for the duration of the fellowship.

Number awarded 3 each year.

Deadline November of each year.

[544]
GEORGE A. STRAIT MINORITY SCHOLARSHIP ENDOWMENT

American Association of Law Libraries
Attn: Chair, Scholarships Committee
105 West Adams Street, Suite 3300
Chicago, IL 60603
(312) 939-4764   Fax: (312) 431-1097
E-mail: scholarships@aall.org
Web: www.aallnet.org/services/sch_strait.asp

Summary To provide financial assistance to Asian American and other minority college seniors or college graduates who are interested in becoming law librarians.

Eligibility This program is open to college graduates with meaningful law library experience who are members of minority groups and intend to have a career in law librarianship. Applicants must be degree candidates at an ALA-accredited library school or an ABA-accredited law school. Along with their application, they must submit a personal statement that discusses their interest in law librarianship, reason for applying for this scholarship, career goals as a law librarian, etc.

Financial data The stipend is $3,500.

Duration 1 year.

Additional information This program, established in 1990, is currently supported by Thomson West.

Number awarded Varies each year; recently, 5 of these scholarships were awarded.

Deadline March of each year.

[545]
GEORGE V. POWELL DIVERSITY SCHOLARSHIP

Lane Powell Spears Lubersky LLP
Attn: Manager of Attorney Recruiting
1420 Fifth Avenue, Suite 4100
Seattle, WA 98101-2338
(206) 223-6123   Fax: (206) 223-7107
E-mail: rodenl@lanepowell.com
Web: www.lanepowell.com/422/diversity-scholarship

Summary To provide financial assistance and work experience to Asian American and other law students who will contribute to the diversity of the legal community.

Eligibility This program is open to second-year students in good standing at an ABA-accredited law school. Applicants must be able to contribute meaningfully to the diversity of the legal community and have a demonstrated desire to work, live, and eventually practice law in Seattle or Portland. They must submit a cover letter that includes a statement indicating eligibility to participate in the program, a resume, a current copy of law school transcript, a legal writing sample, and a list of 2 or 3 professional or academic references. Selection is based on academic achievement and record of leadership abilities, community service, and involvement in community issues.

Financial data The program provides a stipend of $7,500 for the third year of law school and a paid summer associate clerkship.

Duration 1 year, including the summer.

Additional information This program was established in 2005. Clerkships are provided at the offices of the sponsor in Seattle or Portland.

Number awarded 1 each year.

Deadline September of each year.

[546]
GLOBAL CHANGE GRADUATE RESEARCH ENVIRONMENTAL FELLOWSHIPS (GREF)

Oak Ridge Institute for Science and Education
Attn: Global Change Education Program
120 Badger Avenue, M.S. 36
P.O. Box 117
Oak Ridge, TN 37831-0117
(865) 576-7009   Fax: (865) 241-9445
E-mail: gcep@orau.gov
Web: www.atmos.anl.gov/GCEP/GREF/index.html

Summary To provide doctoral students (particularly Asian Americans, other minorities, and women) with an opportunity to conduct research on global change.

Eligibility This program is open to students who have completed their first year of graduate school, unless they previously participated in the Global Change Summer Undergraduate Research Experience (SURE). Applicants must be proposing to conduct research at a national laboratory in a program area within the Department of Energy's Office of Biological and Environmental Research (DOE-BER): the atmospheric science program, the environmental meteorology program, the atmospheric radiation measurement program, the terrestrial carbon processes effort, the program for ecosystem research, and studies carried out under the direction of the National Institute for Global Environmental

Change. Minority and female students are particularly encouraged to apply. U.S. citizenship is required.

Financial data Participants receive an annual stipend of $19,500 ($1,500 per month plus a $600 research education supplement in March and October); reimbursement of tuition and fees at the college or university they attend; and transportation, per diem, and lodging for summer activities.

Duration Up to 3 years.

Additional information This program, funded by DOE-BER, began in 1999. Fellows are encouraged to participate in the Summer Undergraduate Research Experience (SURE) orientation and focus sessions at a participating university.

Number awarded 10 to 15 each year.

Deadline December of each year.

[547]
GOODWIN PUBLIC INTEREST FELLOWSHIPS FOR LAW STUDENTS OF COLOR

Goodwin Procter LLP
Attn: Recruiting Manager
53 State Street
Boston, MA 02109
(617) 570-8156 E-mail: fellowships@goodwinprocter.com
Web: www.goodwinprocter.com

Summary To provide financial assistance to Asian Americans and other minority students who are interested in public interest law.

Eligibility This program is open to students of color entering their second year at a law school in any state. Applicants must actively express an interest in working in the sponsoring firm's summer program in public interest law. If they are applying for the Goodwin MassMutual Diversity, they must express an interest in working with MassMutual's legal department in Springfield, Massachusetts for 2 weeks as part of the summer program and specializing in the investment or insurance business or in a legal focus to advance business objectives. Selection is based on academic performance, leadership abilities, involvement in minority student organizations, commitment to community service, interpersonal skills, other special achievements and honors, and interest in working with the firm during the summer.

Financial data The stipend is $7,500.

Duration 1 year; nonrenewable.

Additional information This program was established in 2005. In 2007, it added the Goodwin MassMutual Diversity Fellowship, created in conjunction with its long-standing client, Massachusetts Mutual Life Insurance Company (Mass-Mutual). Summer positions are available at the firm's offices in Boston, Los Angeles, New York, Palo Alto, San Diego, San Francisco, and Washington, D.C.

Number awarded 3 each year, including 1 Goodwin MassMutual Diversity Fellowship.

Deadline October of each year.

[548]
GRACE ANDOW MEMORIAL SCHOLARSHIP

Japanese American Citizens League
Attn: National Scholarship Awards
1765 Sutter Street
San Francisco, CA 94115
(415) 921-5225   Fax: (415) 931-4671
E-mail: jacl@jacl.org
Web: www.jacl.org/edu/scholar.htm

Summary To provide financial assistance to student members of the Japanese American Citizens League (JACL) who are interested in preparing for a career in law.

Eligibility This program is open to JACL members who are currently enrolled or planning to enroll at an accredited law school. Applicants must submit information on their involvement in JACL and a 2-page essay on a topic that changes annually but relates to Japanese Americans. Selection is based on that essay, academic history, extracurricular activities, JACL involvement, scholastic honors, and a letter of recommendation.

Financial data Stipends generally average approximately $2,000.

Duration 1 year; nonrenewable.

Number awarded 1 each year.

Deadline March of each year.

[549]
GRADUATE STUDENTS OF ASIAN/ASIAN-AMERICAN/PACIFIC-ISLANDER DESCENT STUDENT ESSAY AWARD

National Women's Studies Association
Attn: Women of Color Caucus
7100 Baltimore Avenue, Suite 203
College Park, MD 20740
(301) 403-0407   Fax: (301) 403-4137
E-mail: nwsaoffice@nwsa.org
Web: www.nwsa.org/students/scholarships/woccguide.php

Summary To recognize and reward Asian American/Pacific Islander graduate students and recent postdoctorates who are members of the National Women's Studies Association (NWSA) and submit outstanding essays on feminist issues.

Eligibility This competition is open to women of Asian, Asian American, or Pacific Islander descent who are currently enrolled in a graduate or professional program. Recipients of Ph.D.s who completed their degree requirements within the past year are also eligible. Applicants must submit a scholarly essay that provides critical theoretical discussions and/or analyses of issues and experiences of women and girls of Asian, Asian American, or Pacific Islander descent in the United States and throughout the Diaspora. They must be members of the NWSA.

Financial data The award is $500.

Duration The award is presented annually.

Number awarded 1 each year.

Deadline May of each year.

[550]
HANA SCHOLARSHIPS

United Methodist Church
Attn: General Board of Higher Education and Ministry
Office of Loans and Scholarships
1001 19th Avenue South
P.O. Box 340007
Nashville, TN 37203-0007
(615) 340-7344   Fax: (615) 340-7367
E-mail: umscholar@gbhem.org
Web: www.gbhem.org/loansandscholarships

Summary   To provide financial assistance to upper-division and graduate Methodist students who are of Asian, Native American, Pacific Islander, or Hispanic ancestry.

Eligibility   This program is open to full-time juniors, seniors, and graduate students at accredited colleges and universities in the United States who have been active, full members of a United Methodist Church (UMC) for at least 1 year prior to applying. Applicants must have at least 1 parent who is Asian, Hispanic, Native American, or Pacific Islander. They must be able to demonstrate involvement in their Hispanic, Asian, or Native American (HANA) community in the UMC. Selection is based on that involvement, academic ability (GPA of at least 2.85), and financial need. U.S. citizenship or permanent resident status is required.

Financial data   The maximum stipend is $3,000 for undergraduates or $5,000 for graduate students.

Duration   1 year; recipients may reapply.

Number awarded   50 each year.

Deadline   March of each year.

[551]
HAWAII DIVERSITY FELLOWSHIPS IN ENVIRONMENTAL LAW

American Bar Association
Attn: Section of Environment, Energy, and Resources
321 North Clark Street
Chicago, IL 60654-7598
(312) 988-5602   Fax: (312) 988-5572
E-mail: jonusaid@staff.abanet.org
Web: www.abanet.org

Summary   To provide funding to Asian American and law students from other underrepresented groups who are interested in working on a summer project in environmental, energy, or natural resources law in Hawaii.

Eligibility   This program is open to first- and second-year law students and third-year night students who 1) are either enrolled at a law school in Hawaii or residents of Hawaii enrolled at a law school in another state; and 2) will contribute to increasing diversity in the Hawaii environmental bar. Applicants must be interested in working during the summer at a government agency or public interest organization in Hawaii in the field of environmental, energy, or natural resources law. Selection is based on interest in environmental issues, academic record, personal qualities, leadership abilities, and ability to contribute to diversity in the Hawaii environmental bar.

Financial data   The stipend is $5,000.

Duration   8 to 10 weeks during the summer.

Additional information   This program is cosponsored by the Hawai'i State Bar Association's Natural Resources Section.

Number awarded   1 each year.

Deadline   April of each year.

[552]
HEALTH RESEARCH AND EDUCATIONAL TRUST SCHOLARSHIPS

New Jersey Hospital Association
Attn: Health Research and Educational Trust
760 Alexander Road
P.O. Box 1
Princeton, NJ 08543-0001
(609) 275-4224   Fax: (609) 452-8097
Web: www.njha.com/hret/scholarship.aspx

Summary   To provide financial assistance to New Jersey residents (particularly Asian Americans, other minorities, and women) who are working on an undergraduate or graduate degree in a field related to health care administration at a school in any state.

Eligibility   This program is open to residents of New Jersey enrolled in an upper-division or graduate program in hospital or health care administration, public administration, nursing, or other allied health profession at a school in any state. Graduate students working on an advanced degree to prepare to teach nursing are also eligible. Applicants must have a GPA of 3.0 or higher and be able to demonstrate financial need. Along with their application, they must submit a 2-page essay (on which 50% of the selection is based) describing their academic plans for the future. Minorities and women are especially encouraged to apply.

Financial data   The stipend is $2,000.

Duration   1 year.

Additional information   This program began in 1983.

Number awarded   Varies each year; recently, 3 of these scholarships were awarded.

Deadline   July of each year.

[553]
HEALTH SCIENCES STUDENT FELLOWSHIPS IN EPILEPSY

Epilepsy Foundation
Attn: Research Department
8301 Professional Place
Landover, MD 20785-2237
(301) 459-3700   Toll Free: (800) EFA-1000
Fax: (301) 577-2684   TDD: (800) 332-2070
E-mail: grants@efa.org
Web: www.epilepsyfoundation.org

Summary   To provide financial assistance to medical and health science graduate students (especially Asian Americans, other minorities, women, and individuals with disabilities) who are interested in working on an epilepsy project during the summer.

Eligibility   This program is open to students enrolled, or accepted for enrollment, in a medical school, a doctoral program, or other graduate program. Applicants must have a defined epilepsy-related study or research plan to be carried out under the supervision of a qualified mentor. Because the program is designed as a training opportunity, the quality of the training plans and environment are considered in the selection process. Other selection criteria include the quality of the proposed project, the relevance of the proposed work to epilepsy, the applicant's interest in the field of epilepsy, the applicant's qualifications, the mentor's qualifications (including his or her commitment to the student and the project), and the quality of the training environment for research related to epilepsy. U.S. citizenship is not required, but the project must be conducted in the United States. Applications from women, members of minority groups, and people with disabilities are especially encouraged. The program is not intended for students working on a dissertation research project.

Financial data Stipends are $3,000.

Duration 3 months during the summer.

Additional information Support for this program is provided by many individuals, families, and corporations, especially the American Epilepsy Society, Abbott Laboratories, Ortho-McNeil Pharmaceutical, and Pfizer Inc.

Number awarded Varies each year; recently, 3 of these fellowships were awarded.

Deadline March of each year.

[554]
HELEN LEE SCHOLARSHIP

Philip Jaisohn Memorial Foundation
Attn: Education and Scholarship Committee
6705 Old York Road
Philadelphia, PA 19126
(215) 224-2000   Fax: (215) 224-9164
E-mail: jaisohnhouse@gmail.com
Web: jaisohn.org

Summary To provide financial assistance to Korean American undergraduate and graduate students who demonstrate significant financial need.

Eligibility This program is open to Korean American undergraduate and graduate students who are currently enrolled at a college or university in the United States. Applicants must be able to demonstrate academic excellence, leadership and service to their school and community, and financial need. Along with their application, they must submit an essay on either "Who is Dr. Jaisohn to Me," or "The Significance of Dr. Jaisohn's Ideal to Korean Americans." They must also submit a brief statement on how they can contribute to and be involved in the activities of the Philip Jaisohn Memorial Foundation. Selection is based primarily on financial need.

Financial data The stipend is $1,500.

Duration 1 year.

Number awarded 2 each year.

Deadline November of each year.

[555]
HENRY AND CHIYO KUWAHARA MEMORIAL SCHOLARSHIPS

Japanese American Citizens League
Attn: National Scholarship Awards
1765 Sutter Street
San Francisco, CA 94115
(415) 921-5225   Fax: (415) 931-4671
E-mail: jacl@jacl.org
Web: www.jacl.org/edu/scholar.htm

Summary To provide financial assistance for undergraduate or graduate study to members of the Japanese American Citizens League (JACL).

Eligibility This program is open to JACL members who are high school seniors, undergraduates, or graduate students. Applicants must be attending or planning to attend a college, university, trade school, or business college. They must submit information on their involvement in JACL and a 2-page essay on a topic that changes annually but relates to Japanese Americans. Selection is based on that essay, academic history, extracurricular activities, JACL involvement, scholastic honors, and a letter of recommendation.

Financial data Stipends generally average approximately $2,000.

Duration 1 year; nonrenewable.

Number awarded 6 each year: 2 each to entering freshmen, continuing undergraduates, and entering or currently-enrolled graduate students.

Deadline February of each year for graduating high school seniors; March of each year for current undergraduate or graduate students.

[556]
HENRY LUCE FOUNDATION/ACLS DISSERTATION FELLOWSHIPS IN AMERICAN ART

American Council of Learned Societies
Attn: Office of Fellowships and Grants
633 Third Avenue
New York, NY 10017-6795
(212) 697-1505   Fax: (212) 949-8058
E-mail: fellowships@acls.org
Web: www.acls.org/programs/American-art

Summary To provide funding to doctoral students (especially Asian Americans, other minorities, and women) who are interested in conducting dissertation research anywhere in the world on the history of American art.

Eligibility This program is open to Ph.D. candidates in departments of art history whose dissertations are focused on the history of the visual arts in the United States and are object-oriented. Applicants may be proposing to conduct research at their home institution, abroad, or at another appropriate site. U.S. citizenship or permanent resident status is required. Students preparing theses for a Master of Fine Arts degree are not eligible. Applications are particularly invited from women and members of minority groups.

Financial data The grant is $25,000. Fellowship funds may not be used to pay tuition costs.

Duration 1 year; nonrenewable.

Additional information This program is funded by the Henry Luce Foundation and administered by the American Council of Learned Societies (ACLS).

Number awarded 10 each year.

Deadline November of each year.

[557]
HIDEKO AND ZENZO MATSUYAMA SCHOLARSHIPS

Hawai'i Community Foundation
Attn: Scholarship Department
827 Fort Street Mall
Honolulu, HI 96813
(808) 537-6333   Toll Free: (888) 731-3863
Fax: (808) 521-6286
E-mail: scholarships@hcf-hawaii.org
Web: www.hawaiicommunityfoundation.org/scholarships

Summary   To provide financial assistance to Hawaii residents, especially those of Japanese ancestry, who are interested in attending college or graduate school in any state.

Eligibility   This program is open to graduates of high schools or recipients of GED certificates in Hawaii. Applicants must be enrolled or planning to enroll in an accredited college or university in any state as an undergraduate or graduate student. They must be able to demonstrate academic achievement (GPA of 3.0 or higher), good moral character, and financial need. Along with their application, they must submit a short statement indicating their reasons for attending college, their planned course of study, their career goals, and what community service means to them. Preference is given to students of Japanese ancestry born in Hawaii.

Financial data   The amounts of the awards depend on the availability of funds and the need of the recipient. Recently, the average value of all scholarships awarded by the foundation was $2,041.

Duration   1 year.

Number awarded   Varies each year; recently, 13 of these scholarships were awarded.

Deadline   February of each year.

[558]
HILLIS CLARK MARTIN & PETERSON DIVERSITY FELLOWSHIP

Hillis Clark Martin & Peterson P.S.
Attn: Recruiting and Marketing Coordinator
1221 Second Avenue, Suite 500
Seattle, WA 98101-2925
(206) 623-1745   Fax: (206) 623-7789
E-mail: abt@hcmp.com
Web: www.hcmp.com

Summary   To provide financial assistance to Asian American and other law students who will bring diversity to the field.

Eligibility   This program is open to students enrolled in the first year at an ABA-accredited law school. Applicants must have a diverse background and life experiences and demonstrate the capacity to contribute meaningfully to the diversity of the legal community. Along with their application, they must submit a resume, transcripts, a personal statement of 1 to 2 pages describing their background and addressing the selection criteria, a legal writing sample, and a list of 3 references. Selection is based on distinction in academic performance, accomplishments and activities, commitment to community service, leadership ability, and financial need.

Financial data   The stipend is $7,500.

Duration   1 year.

Additional information   The program includes a salaried summer associate position following the first year of law school.

Number awarded   1 or more each year.

Deadline   January of each year.

[559]
H-MART LEADERSHIP SCHOLARSHIP

Philip Jaisohn Memorial Foundation
Attn: Education and Scholarship Committee
6705 Old York Road
Philadelphia, PA 19126
(215) 224-2000   Fax: (215) 224-9164
E-mail: jaisohnhouse@gmail.com
Web: jaisohn.org

Summary   To provide financial assistance to Korean American undergraduate and graduate students who demonstrate involvement in extracurricular, athletic, and community activities.

Eligibility   This program is open to Korean American undergraduate and graduate students who are currently enrolled at a college or university in the United States. Applicants must be able to demonstrate academic excellence, leadership and service to their school and community, and financial need. Along with their application, they must submit an essay on either "Who is Dr. Jaisohn to Me," or "The Significance of Dr. Jaisohn's Ideal to Korean Americans." They must also submit a brief statement on how they can contribute to and be involved in the activities of the Philip Jaisohn Memorial Foundation. Selection is based primarily on leadership in extracurricular activities, varsity sports, or community activities.

Financial data   The stipend is $1,500.

Duration   1 year.

Additional information   This program is sponsored by H-Mart.

Number awarded   2 each year.

Deadline   November of each year.

[560]
HONORABLE KENNETH B. CHANG MEMORIAL SCHOLARSHIPS

Korean American Bar Association of Southern California
c/o Lisa H. Kwon
TroyGould PC
1801 Century Park East, Suite 1600
Los Angeles, CA 90067-2367
(310) 789-1270   Fax: (310) 789-1470
E-mail: lkwon@troygould.com
Web: kabasocal.net

Summary   To provide financial assistance to students from any state who are enrolled at law schools in southern California and have been active in the Asian Pacific Islander and/or Korean American community.

Eligibility   This program is open to students from any state currently enrolled at law schools in southern California. Applicants must be able to demonstrate a commitment to the Korean American community and/or Asian Pacific Islander community through past, current, or future contributions. Students are evaluated on the basis of their written applications and an interview.

Financial data The stipend is $2,000.
Duration 1 year.
Number awarded Varies each year.
Deadline March of each year.

[561]
HONORABLE THOMAS TANG INTERNATIONAL MOOT COURT COMPETITION SCHOLARSHIPS

National Asian Pacific American Bar Association
Attn: NAPABA Law Foundation
1612 K Street, N.W., Suite 1400
Washington, DC 20006
(202) 775-9555   Fax: (202) 775-9333
E-mail: foundation@napaba.org
Web: www.napaba.org/napaba/showpage.asp?code=moot

Summary To recognize and reward law students who participate in a moot court competition sponsored by the National Asian Pacific American Bar Association (NAPABA).

Eligibility This competition is open to students at ABA-accredited law schools who have completed the first year of study. A goal of the program is to reach out to Asian Pacific American law students and provide them with an opportunity to showcase their writing and oral advocacy skills. Applicants must enter the competition as teams of 2 students each.

Financial data Awards include a $2,000 scholarship for each member of the championship team, $1,000 scholarship for each member of the runner-up team, $1,000 scholarship for the best brief, and $1,000 scholarship for the best oralist.

Duration The competition is held annually.

Additional information This competition was initiated in 1993 and has been supported since then by Anheuser-Busch. The entry fee is $200 per team.

Number awarded 6 each year: 2 for members of the first-place team, 2 for members of the second-place team, 1 for best brief, and 1 for best oralist.

Deadline September of each year.

[562]
HORIZON PHARMA STUDENT ABSTRACT PRIZES

American Gastroenterological Association
Attn: AGA Research Foundation
Research Awards Manager
4930 Del Ray Avenue
Bethesda, MD 20814-2512
(301) 222-4012   Fax: (301) 654-5920
E-mail: awards@gastro.org
Web: www.gastro.org/aga-foundation/grants

Summary To recognize and reward Asian American and other students at any level who submit outstanding abstracts for presentation during Digestive Disease Week (DDW).

Eligibility This program is open to high school, undergraduate, premedical, predoctoral, and medical students and medical residents (up to and including postgraduate year 3) who have performed original research related to gastroenterology and hepatology. Postdoctoral fellows, technicians, visiting scientists, and M.D. research fellows are not eligible. Applicants must submit an abstract on their research and must be the designated presenter or first author of the abstract. They must be sponsored by a member of the American Gastroenterological Association (AGA). Travel awards are presented to authors of outstanding abstracts to enable them to attend DDW. After presentation of the papers at DDW, the most outstanding abstracts receive prizes. Selection is based on novelty, significance of the proposal, clarity of the abstract, and contribution of the student. Women and minority students are strongly encouraged to apply.

Financial data The prizes are $1,000; the travel awards are $500.

Duration Awards and prizes are presented annually.

Additional information This award is sponsored by Horizon Pharma.

Number awarded 8 travel awards are presented each year. Of the 8 awardees, 3 receive additional prizes of $1,000.

Deadline February of each year.

[563]
HSIAO MEMORIAL ECONOMICS SCHOLARSHIP

Asian Pacific Fund
Attn: Scholarship Coordinator
225 Bush Street, Suite 590
San Francisco, CA 94104
(415) 433-6859   Toll Free: (800) 286-1688
Fax: (415) 433-2425
E-mail: scholarship@asianpacificfund.org
Web: www.asianpacificfund.org

Summary To provide financial assistance to Asian American graduate students from any state who are working on a Ph.D. degree in economics.

Eligibility This program is open to graduate students at colleges and universities in the United States who are working on a Ph.D. degree in economics. Preference is given to students preparing for a career in academia. Applicants must be of at least 50% Asian heritage; preference is given to students of Chinese descent. They must have a GPA of 3.0 or higher and be able to demonstrate financial need. Along with their application, they must submit essays of 250 to 500 words each on 1) how their undergraduate studies shaped their choice of major and graduate studies; 2) their area of specialization, theoretical focus, or research; and 3) their teaching experience to date and what they consider to be an ideal situation for them in academia after they complete graduate studies. U.S. citizens, permanent residents, and foreign nationals are all eligible. Preference is given to applicants whose research interests would benefit Asians, Asian Americans, or persons in social or economic need.

Financial data The stipend is $1,000.

Duration 1 year; nonrenewable.

Number awarded 1 each year.

Deadline March of each year.

[564]
HUD DOCTORAL DISSERTATION RESEARCH GRANT PROGRAM

Department of Housing and Urban Development
Attn: Office of University Partnerships
451 Seventh Street, S.W., Room 8226
Washington, DC 20410
(202) 708-3852   Fax: (202) 708-0309
E-mail: oup@oup.org
Web: www.oup.org/programs/aboutDDRG.asp

Summary To provide funding to doctoral candidates (especially Asian Americans and other minorities) who are interested in conducting dissertation research related to housing and urban development issues.

Eligibility This program is open to currently-enrolled doctoral candidates in an academic discipline that provides policy-relevant insight on issues in housing and urban development. Applicants must have fully-developed and approved dissertation proposals that can be completed within 2 years and must have completed all written and oral Ph.D. requirements. Examples of eligible topics include increasing homeownership opportunities; promoting decent affordable housing; strengthening communities; ensuring equal opportunity in housing; embracing high standards of ethics, management, and accountability; and promoting participation of faith-based and community organizations. U.S. citizenship or permanent resident status is required.

Financial data The grant is $25,000. Funds must be used to support direct costs incurred in completing the project, including stipends, computer software, purchase of data, travel expenses to collect data, transcription services, or compensation for interviews. Funds may not be used for tuition, computer hardware, or meals.

Duration Up to 24 months.

Additional information This program was established in 1994.

Number awarded Varies each year; recently, 12 of these grants were awarded.

Deadline June of each year.

[565]
HUGH J. ANDERSEN MEMORIAL SCHOLARSHIPS

National Medical Fellowships, Inc.
Attn: Scholarship Program
347 Fifth Avenue, Suite 510
New York, NY 10016
(212) 483-8880　　Toll Free: (877) NMF-1DOC
Fax: (212) 483-8897　　E-mail: info@nmfonline.org
Web: www.nmfonline.org

Summary To provide financial assistance to Vietnamese, Cambodian, and other underrepresented minority medical students who reside or attend school in Minnesota.

Eligibility This program is open to African Americans, Mexican Americans, Native Hawaiians, Alaska Natives, American Indians, Vietnamese, Cambodians, and mainland Puerto Ricans who have completed at least 1 year of medical school. Applicants must be Minnesota residents enrolled in an accredited U.S. medical school or residents of other states attending medical school in Minnesota. Selection is based on leadership, community service, and financial need. Direct applications are not accepted; candidates must be nominated by medical school deans.

Financial data The award is $2,500.

Duration 1 year.

Additional information This award was established in 1982.

Number awarded Up to 5 each year.

Deadline Nominations must be submitted by March of each year.

[566]
IBM PHD FELLOWSHIP PROGRAM

IBM Corporation
Attn: University Relations
1133 Westchester Avenue
White Plains, NY 10604
Toll Free: (800) IBM-4YOU　　TDD: (800) IBM-3383
E-mail: phdfellow@us.ibm.com
Web: www.ibm.com

Summary To provide funding and work experience to students (Asian Americans and others from diverse groups) who are working on a Ph.D. in a research area of broad interest to IBM.

Eligibility Students nominated for this fellowship should be enrolled full time at an accredited college or university in any country and should have completed at least 1 year of graduate study in the following fields: business sciences (including financial services, risk management, marketing, communication, and learning/knowledge management); computer science and engineering; electrical and mechanical engineering; management; mathematical sciences (including analytics, statistics, operations research, and optimization); physical sciences (including chemistry, materials sciences, and physics); or service science, management, and engineering (SSME). They should be planning a career in research. Nominations must be made by a faculty member and endorsed by the department head. The program values diversity, and encourages nominations of women, minorities, and others who contribute to that diversity. Selection is based on the applicants' potential for research excellence, the degree to which their technical interests align with those of IBM, and academic progress to date. Preference is given to students who have had an IBM internship or have closely collaborated with technical or services people from IBM.

Financial data Fellowships pay tuition, fees, and a stipend of $17,500 per year.

Duration 1 year; may be renewed up to 2 additional years, provided the recipient is renominated, interacts with IBM's technical community, and demonstrates continued progress and achievement.

Additional information Recipients are offered an internship at 1 of the IBM Research Division laboratories and are given an IBM computer.

Number awarded Varies each year; recently, 57 of these scholarships were awarded.

Deadline October of each year.

[567]
ILLINOIS MINORITY REAL ESTATE SCHOLARSHIP

Illinois Association of Realtors
Attn: Illinois Real Estate Educational Foundation
522 South Fifth Street
P.O. Box 2607
Springfield, IL 62708
Toll Free: (866) 854-REEF　　Fax: (217) 241-9935
E-mail: lclayton@iar.org
Web: www.ilreef.org/Scholarships.htm

Summary To provide financial assistance to Illinois residents who Asian or members of other minority groups and preparing for a career in real estate.

Eligibility This program is open to residents of Illinois who are African American, Hispanic or Latino, Native American, or Asian. Applicants must be interested in preparing for a career in real estate by pursuing: 1) courses to meet Illinois salesperson license requirements; 2) course work to meet Illinois broker license requirement; 3) course work required for Illinois appraisal licensing/certification; 4) professional development unrelated to obtaining license/certification; or 5) an undergraduate or graduate program of study. Along with their application, they must submit information on their employment history, transcripts, evidence of financial need, and an essay that describes their career goals and explains why they believe they should receive scholarship assistance through this program.

Financial data The maximum stipend is $500.

Duration Funds must be used within 24 months of the award date.

Deadline Applications may be submitted at any time, but they must be received at least 12 weeks prior to the beginning of the school term for which financial assistance is requested.

[568]
ILLINOIS NURSES ASSOCIATION CENTENNIAL SCHOLARSHIP

Illinois Nurses Association
Attn: Illinois Nurses Foundation
105 West Adams Street, Suite 2101
Chicago, IL 60603
(312) 419-2900   Fax: (312) 419-2920
E-mail: info@illinoisnurses.com
Web: www.illinoisnurses.com

Summary To provide financial assistance to Asian Americans and other underrepresented undergraduate and graduate students working on a nursing degree.

Eligibility This program is open to students working on an associate, bachelor's, or master's degree at an accredited NLNAC or CCNE school of nursing. Applicants must be members of a group underrepresented in nursing (African Americans, Hispanics, American Indians, Asians, and males). Undergraduates must have earned a passing grade in all nursing courses taken to date and have a GPA of 2.85 or higher. Graduate students must have completed at least 12 semester hours of graduate work and have a GPA of 3.0 or higher. All applicants must be willing to 1) act as a spokesperson to other student groups on the value of the scholarship to continuing their nursing education, and 2) be profiled in any media or marketing materials developed by the Illinois Nurses Foundation. Along with their application, they must submit a narrative of 250 to 500 words on how they, nurses, plan to affect policy at either the state or national level that impacts on nursing or health care generally, or how they believe they will impact the nursing profession in general.

Financial data A stipend is awarded (amount not specified).

Duration 1 year.

Number awarded 1 or more each year.

Deadline March of each year.

[569]
INDIANA CLEO FELLOWSHIPS

Indiana Supreme Court
Attn: Division of State Court Administration
115 West Washington Street, Suite 1080
Indianapolis, IN 46204-3417
(317) 232-2542   Toll Free: (800) 452-9963
Fax: (317) 233-6586
Web: www.in.gov/judiciary/cleo

Summary To provide financial assistance to Asian American and other minority college seniors from any state interested in attending law school in Indiana.

Eligibility This program is open to graduating college seniors who have applied to a law school in Indiana. Selected applicants are invited to participate in the Indiana Conference for Legal Education Opportunity (Indiana CLEO) Summer Institute, held at a law school in the state. Admission to that program is based on GPA, LSAT scores, 3 letters of recommendation, a resume, a personal statement, and financial need. Students who successfully complete the Institute and become certified graduates of the program may be eligible to receive a fellowship.

Financial data All expenses for the Indiana CLEO Summer Institute are paid. The fellowship stipend is $6,500 per year for students who attend a public law school or $9,000 per year for students who attend a private law school.

Duration The Indiana CLEO Summer Institute lasts 6 weeks. Fellowships are for 1 year and may be renewed up to 2 additional years.

Additional information The first Summer Institute was held in 1997.

Number awarded 30 students are invited to participate in the summer institute; the number of those selected to receive a fellowship varies each year.

Deadline March of each year.

[570]
ING SCHOLARSHIPS

Ascend: Pan-Asian Leaders
Attn: Director of Programs
120 Wall Street, Third Floor
New York, NY 10005
(212) 248-4888   Fax: (212) 344-5636
E-mail: info@ascendleadership.org
Web: www.ascendleadership.org

Summary To provide financial assistance to members of Ascend: Pan-Asian Leaders who are upper-division or graduate students working on a degree in a field related to accounting.

Eligibility This program is open to members of Ascend who are enrolled as junior or senior undergraduates or M.B.A. graduate students at colleges and universities in the United States. Applicants must have a GPA of 3.2 or higher and a major in accounting, finance, taxation, management information systems, or a business-related program. Along with their application, they must submit a 500-word personal essay on how they have demonstrated leadership and teamwork in their academic studies, professional career, and/or extracurricular activities and community volunteer work; why they believe those qualities are important to be competitive in a borderless world; their career goals after graduation; and the role Ascend has played in the achievement of their academic and career goals. They must also provide examples of their involvement in local community activities. Financial need is not considered in the selection process.

Financial data The stipend is $2,500.

Duration 1 year.

Additional information Ascend was formed in 2004 as the National Asian American Society of Accountants. This program is sponsored by ING North America Insurance Corporation.

Number awarded 2 each year.

Deadline July of each year.

[571]
INITIATIVE TO RECRUIT A DIVERSE WORKFORCE

Association of Research Libraries
Attn: Director of Diversity Programs
21 Dupont Circle, N.W., Suite 800
Washington, DC 20036
(202) 296-2296   Fax: (202) 872-0884
E-mail: mpuente@arl.org
Web: www.arl.org/diversity/init/index.shtml

Summary To provide financial assistance to Asian Americans and other minorities interested in preparing for a career as an academic or research librarian.

Eligibility This program is open to members of racial and ethnic minority groups that are underrepresented as professionals in academic and research libraries (American Indian or Alaska Native, Asian, Black or African American, Native Hawaiian or other Pacific Islander, or Hispanic or Latino). Applicants must be interested in working on an M.L.I.S. degree at an ALA-accredited program. Along with their application, they must submit a 350-word essay on what attracts them to a career in a research library. The essays are judged on clarity and content of form, clear goals and benefits, enthusiasm, potential growth perceived, and professional goals.

Financial data The stipend is $5,000 per year.

Duration 2 years.

Additional information This program began in 2000. Funding is currently provided by the Institute of Museum and Library Services and by the contributions of 52 libraries that are members of the Association of Research Libraries (ARL). Recipients must agree to work for at least 2 years in an ARL library after completing their degree.

Number awarded 20 each year.

Deadline August of each year.

[572]
INSTITUTE FOR INTERNATIONAL PUBLIC POLICY FELLOWSHIPS

United Negro College Fund Special Programs
  Corporation
Attn: Institute for International Public Policy
6402 Arlington Boulevard, Suite 600
Falls Church, VA 22042
(703) 677-3400   Toll Free: (800) 530-6232
Fax: (703) 205-7645   E-mail: iippl@uncfsp.org
Web: www.uncfsp.org

Summary To provide financial assistance and work experience to Asian Americans and other minority students who are interested in preparing for a career in international affairs.

Eligibility This program is open to full-time sophomores at 4-year institutions who have a GPA of 3.2 or higher and are nominated by the president of their institution. Applicants must be African American, Hispanic/Latino American, Asian American, American Indian, Alaskan Native, Native Hawaiian, or Pacific Islander. They must be interested in participating in policy institutes, study abroad, language training, internships, and graduate education that will prepare them for a career in international service. U.S. citizenship or permanent resident status is required.

Financial data For the sophomore summer policy institute, fellows receive student housing and meals in a university facility, books and materials, all field trips and excursions, and a $1,050 stipend. For the junior year study abroad component, half the expenses for 1 semester, to a maximum of $8,000, is provided. For the junior summer policy institute, fellows receive student housing and meals in a university facility, books and materials, travel to and from the institute, and a $1,000 stipend. For the summer language institute, fellows receive tuition and fees, books and materials, room and board, travel to and from the institute, and a $1,000 stipend. During the internship, a stipend of up to $3,500 is paid. During the graduate school period, fellowships are funded jointly by this program and the participating graduate school. The program provides $15,000 toward a master's degree in international affairs with the expectation that the graduate school will provide $15,000 in matching funds.

Duration 2 years of undergraduate work and 2 years of graduate work, as well as the intervening summers.

Additional information This program consists of 6 components: 1) a sophomore year summer policy institute based at Howard University that introduces fellows to international policy development, foreign affairs, cultural competence, careers in those fields, and options for graduate study; 2) a junior year study abroad program at an accredited overseas institution; 3) a 7-week junior year summer institute at the University of Maryland's School of Public Policy; 4) for students without established foreign language competency, a summer language institute at Middlebury College Language Schools in Middlebury, Vermont following the senior year; 5) fellows with previously established foreign language competence participate in a post-baccalaureate internship to provide the practical experience needed for successful graduate studies in international affairs; and 6) a master's degree in international affairs (for students who are admitted to such a program). This program is administered by the United Negro College Fund Special Programs Corporation with funding provided by a grant from the U.S. Department of Education.

Number awarded 30 each year.

Deadline February of each year.

To provide summer work experience to upper-
~nd graduate students (especially Asian/Pacific
~nd other minorities) who are interested in working
summer in broadcasting and related fields in the
City area.

This program is open to juniors, seniors, and
~tudents at 4-year colleges and universities. Appli-
~t either be a communications major or have dem-
~a strong interest in the field through extracurricular
~r other practical experience. Minority (Black, His-
~sian/Pacific Islander, American Indian/Alaskan
~dents are especially encouraged to apply.

~ data Travel, housing, and a living allowance are

9 weeks during the summer.

~al information The first week consists of a com-
~ve orientation to broadcasting, cable, advertising,
media. Then, the participants are assigned an 8-
~owship. This full-time "real world" experience in a
~-based corporation allows them to reinforce or rede-
~ific career goals before settling into a permanent job.
~nave worked at all 4 major networks, at local New
~ radio and television stations, and at national rep
~vertising agencies, and cable operations. This pro-
~cludes fellowships reserved for students at desig-
~iversities (Notre Dame, Pennsylvania State Univer-
~ton College, Holy Cross College) and the following
~awards: the Thomas S. Murphy Fellowship (spon-
~ ABC National Television Sales), the Helen Karas
~al Fellowship, the Leslie Moonves Fellowship (spon-
~ CBS Television Station Sales, and the Sumner Red-
~ellowship (sponsored by CBS Television Station

~r awarded Varies; recently, 23 of these fellowships
~varded.

~ne November of each year.

~ J. "IKE" CRUMBLY MINORITIES IN
~GY GRANT

~rican Association of Petroleum Geologists
~undation
~: Grants-in-Aid Program
~4 South Boulder Avenue
~ Box 979
~a, OK 74101-0979
~3) 560-2644   Toll Free: (888) 945-2274, ext. 644
~: (918) 560-2642   E-mail: tcampbell@aapg.org
~b: foundation.aapg.org/gia/crumbly.cfm

~nary To provide funding to Asian Americans, other
~ties, and female graduate students who are interested
~ducting research related to earth science aspects of the
~eum industry.

~ility This program is open to women and ethnic
~ities (Black, Hispanic, Asian, or Native American,
~ing American Indian, Eskimo, Hawaiian, or Samoan)
~re working on a master's or doctoral degree. Applicants
~ be interested in conducting research related to the
~h for and development of petroleum and energy-miner-
~sources and to related environmental geology issues.
~tion is based on merit and, in part, on financial need.
~rs weighed in selecting the successful applicants

include: the applicant's past academic performance, originality and imagination of the proposed project, departmental
support, and significance of the project to petroleum, energy
minerals, and related environmental geology.

Financial data Grants range from $500 to $3,000. Funds
are to be applied to research-related expenses (e.g., a summer of field work). They may not be used to purchase capital
equipment or to pay salaries, tuition, room, or board.

Duration 1 year. Doctoral candidates may receive a 1-year
renewal.

Number awarded 1 each year.

Deadline January of each year.

[578]
JACOBS ENGINEERING SCHOLARSHIP

Conference of Minority Transportation Officials
Attn: National Scholarship Program
818 18th Street, N.W., Suite 850
Washington, DC 20006
(202) 530-0551   Fax: (202) 530-0617
Web: www.comto.org/news-youth.php

Summary To provide financial assistance to Asian American and other minority upper-division and graduate students
in a field related to transportation.

Eligibility This program is open to minority juniors, seniors,
and graduate students in fields related to transportation (e.g.,
civil engineering, construction engineering, environmental
engineering, safety, transportation, urban planning). Undergraduates must have a GPA of 3.0 or higher; graduate students must have a GPA of at least 3.5. Applicants must submit a cover letter with a 500-word statement of career goals.
Financial need is not considered in the selection process.
U.S. citizenship is required.

Financial data The stipend is $4,000. Funds are paid
directly to the recipient's college or university.

Duration 1 year.

Additional information The Conference of Minority
Transportation Officials (COMTO) was established in 1971 to
promote, strengthen, and expand the roles of minorities in all
aspects of transportation. This program is sponsored by
Jacobs Engineering Group Inc. Recipients are required to
become members of COMTO and attend the COMTO
National Scholarship Luncheon.

Number awarded 1 or more each year.

Deadline April of each year.

[579]
JAMES B. MORRIS SCHOLARSHIP

James B. Morris Scholarship Fund
Attn: Scholarship Selection Committee
525 S.W. Fifth Street, Suite A
Des Moines, IA 50309-4501
(515) 282-8192   Fax: (515) 282-9117
E-mail: morris@assoc-mgmt.com
Web: www.morrisscholarship.org

Summary To provide financial assistance to Asian American and other minority undergraduate, graduate, and law students in Iowa.

Eligibility This program is open to minority students (African Americans, Asian/Pacific Islanders, Hispanics, or Native
Americans) who are interested in studying at a college, grad-

[573]
INTELLECTUAL PROPERTY LAW SECTION WOMEN AND MINORITY SCHOLARSHIP

State Bar of Texas
Attn: Intellectual Property Law Section
c/o Bhaveeni D. Parmar, Scholarship Selection
  Committee
Klemchuk Kubasta LLP
Campbell Centre II
9150 North Central Expressway, Suite 1150
Dallas, TX 75206
(214) 367-6000   E-mail: bhaveeni@kk-llp.com
Web: www.texasbariplaw.org/index.htm

Summary To provide financial assistance to Asian Americans, other minorities, and female students at law schools in Texas who plan to practice intellectual property law.

Eligibility This program is open to women and members of minority groups (African Americans, Hispanics, Asian Americans, and Native Americans) from any state who are currently enrolled at an ABA-accredited law school in Texas. Applicants must be planning to practice intellectual property law in Texas. Along with their application, they must submit a 2-page essay explaining why they plan to prepare for a career in intellectual property law in Texas, any qualifications they believe are relevant for their consideration for this scholarship, and (optionally) any issues of financial need they wish to have considered.

Financial data The stipend is $2,500.

Duration 1 year.

Number awarded 2 each year: 1 to a women and 1 to a minority.

Deadline April of each year.

[574]
INTERMOUNTAIN SECTION AWWA DIVERSITY SCHOLARSHIP

American Water Works Association-Intermountain
  Section
3430 East Danish Road
Sandy, UT 94093
(801) 712-1619   Fax: (801) 487-6699
E-mail: nicoleb@ims-awwa.org
Web: www.ims-awwa.org

Summary To provide financial assistance to Asian Americans, other minorities, and female undergraduate and graduate students working on a degree in the field of water quality, supply, and treatment at a university in Idaho or Utah.

Eligibility This program is open to women and students who identify as Hispanic or Latino, Black or African American, Native Hawaiian or other Pacific Islander, Asian, or American Indian or Alaska Native. Applicants must be entering or enrolled in an undergraduate or graduate program at a college or university in Idaho or Utah that relates to water quality, supply, or treatment. Along with their application, they must submit a 2-page essay on their academic interests and career goals and how those relate to water quality, supply, or treatment. Selection is based on that essay, letters of recommendation, and potential to contribute to the field of water quality, supply, and treatment in the Intermountain West.

Financial data The stipend is $1,000. The winner also receives a 1-year student membership in the Intermountain

Section of the American Wate
and a 1-year subscription to J
Duration 1 year; nonrenewa
Number awarded 1 each y
Deadline October of each ye

[575]
INTERNATIONAL COMMU
INDUSTRIES FOUNDATIO

InfoComm International
International Communication
11242 Waples Mill Road, Sui
Fairfax, VA 22030
(703) 273-7200
Fax: (703) 278-8082   E-
Web: www.infocomm.org

Summary To provide financial
cans and other high school senio
are interested in preparing for a ca
industry.

Eligibility This program is ope
undergraduates, and graduate st
college. Applicants must have a G
majoring or planning to major i
related fields, including audio, vide
nications, technical aspects of the
software development, or informati
other programs, such as journalis
can demonstrate a relationship to
industry. Along with their applicatio
essay of 150 to 200 words on the ca
sue in the audiovisual industry in th
essay of 250 to 300 words on the e
encing them the most in selecting th
their career of choice. Minority and
especially encouraged to apply. Se
essays, presentation of the applic
experience, work experience, and let

Financial data The stipend is $1,
sent directly to the school.

Duration 1 year; recipients may rea

Additional information InfoComm
the International Communications I
established the International Comm
Foundation (ICIF) to manage its char
activities.

Number awarded Varies each yea
scholarships were awarded.

Deadline May of each year.

[576]
INTERNATIONAL RADIO AND TE
SOCIETY SUMMER FELLOWSHI

International Radio and Television So
Attn: Director, Special Projects
420 Lexington Avenue, Suite 1601
New York, NY 10170-0101
(212) 867-6650   Toll F
Fax: (212) 867-6653   E-
Web: irts.org/summerfellowshipprogra

Summar
division
Islanders
during th
New York

Eligibilit
graduate
cants mu
onstrated
activities
panic,
Native) s

Financi
provided

Duratio

Additio
prehens
and new
week fe
New Yo
fine spe
Fellows
York Cit
firms, a
gram ir
nated u
sity, Bo
named
sored
Memor
sored b
stone
Sales)

Numb
were a

Deadl

[577
ISAA
ENEI

An
F
Att
14
P.C
Tu
(9
Fa
W

Sum
mino
in co
petro

Eligi
mino
inclu
who
mus
sea
als
Sele
Fac

uate school, or law school. Applicants must be either Iowa residents and high school graduates who are attending a college or university anywhere in the United States or non-Iowa residents who are attending a college or university in Iowa; preference is given to native Iowans who are attending an Iowa college or university. Along with their application, they must submit an essay of 250 to 500 words on why they are applying for this scholarship, activities or organizations in which they are involved, and their future plans. Selection is based on the essay, academic achievement (GPA of 2.5 or higher), community service, and financial need. U.S. citizenship is required.

Financial data The stipend is $2,300 per year.

Duration 1 year; may be renewed.

Additional information This fund was established in 1978 in honor of the J.B. Morris family, who founded the Iowa branch of the National Association for the Advancement of Colored People and published the *Iowa Bystander* newspaper.

Number awarded Varies each year; recently, 24 of these scholarships were awarded.

Deadline March of each year.

[580]
JAMES CARLSON MEMORIAL SCHOLARSHIP

Oregon Student Assistance Commission
Attn: Grants and Scholarships Division
1500 Valley River Drive, Suite 100
Eugene, OR 97401-2146
(541) 687-7395   Toll Free: (800) 452-8807, ext. 7395
Fax: (541) 687-7414   TDD: (800) 735-2900
E-mail: awardinfo@osac.state.or.us
Web: www.osac.state.or.us/osac_programs.html

Summary To provide financial assistance to Oregon residents (priority is given to Asian Americans and other minorities) who are majoring in education on the undergraduate or graduate school level at a school in any state.

Eligibility This program is open to residents of Oregon who are U.S. citizens or permanent residents and enrolled at a college or university in any state. Applicants must be either 1) college seniors or fifth-year students majoring in elementary or secondary education or 2) graduate students working on an elementary or secondary certificate. Full-time enrollment and financial need are required. Priority is given to 1) students who come from diverse environments and submit an essay of 250 to 350 words on their experience living or working in diverse environments; 2) dependents of members of the Oregon Education Association; and 3) applicants committed to teaching autistic children.

Financial data Stipend amounts vary; recently, they were at least $1,300.

Duration 1 year.

Additional information This program is administered by the Oregon Student Assistance Commission (OSAC) with funds provided by the Oregon Community Foundation.

Number awarded Varies each year; recently, 3 of these scholarships were awarded.

Deadline February of each year.

[581]
JAMES E. WEBB INTERNSHIPS

Smithsonian Institution
Attn: Office of Fellowships
470 L'Enfant Plaza, Suite 7102
P.O. Box 37012, MRC 902
Washington, DC 20013-7012
(202) 633-7070   Fax: (202) 633-7069
E-mail: siofg@si.edu
Web: www.si.edu/ofg/Applications/WEBB/WEBBapp.htm

Summary To provide internship opportunities throughout the Smithsonian Institution to Asian American and other minority upper-division and graduate students in business or public administration.

Eligibility This program is open to minorities who are juniors, seniors, or graduate students majoring in areas of business or public administration (finance, human resource management, accounting, or general business administration). Applicants must have a GPA of 3.0 or higher. They must seek placement in offices, museums, and research institutes within the Smithsonian Institution.

Financial data Interns receive a stipend of $550 per week and a travel allowance.

Duration 10 weeks during the summer, fall, or spring.

Number awarded Varies each year; recently, 8 of these internships were awarded.

Deadline January of each year for summer or fall; September of each year for spring.

[582]
JAMES ECHOLS SCHOLARSHIP

California Association for Health, Physical Education,
    Recreation and Dance
Attn: Chair, Scholarship Committee
1501 El Camino Avenue, Suite 3
Sacramento, CA 95815-2748
(916) 922-3596   Toll Free: (800) 499-3596 (within CA)
Fax: (916) 922-0133   E-mail: cahperd@cahperd.org
Web: www.cahperd.org/scholarships.html

Summary To provide financial assistance to Asian American and other minority student members of the California Association for Health, Physical Education, Recreation and Dance.

Eligibility This program is open to California residents who have been members of the association for at least 60 days and are attending a 2- or 4-year college or university in California. Applicants must be undergraduate or graduate students majoring in health, physical education, recreation, or dance and have completed at least 60 semester hours of college work. Selection is based on scholastic proficiency (a GPA of 3.0 or higher); leadership ability in school, community, and professional activities; and personal qualities of enthusiasm, cooperativeness, responsibility, initiative, and ability to work with others. This scholarship is awarded to the highest-ranked minority (Asian, African American, Latino, or Native American) applicant.

Financial data The stipend is $750.

Duration 1 year.

Number awarded 1 each year.

Deadline November of each year.

[583]
JAPANESE AMERICAN BAR ASSOCIATION EDUCATIONAL FOUNDATION SCHOLARSHIPS

Japanese American Bar Association
Attn: JABA Educational Foundation
P.O. Box 86063
Los Angeles, CA 90086
(310) 785-6881   E-mail: JEFscholarship@gmail.com
Web: www.jabaonline.org/scholarships.html

Summary To provide financial assistance to law students who have participated in the Asian Pacific American community.

Eligibility This program is open to students currently enrolled in law school. Applicants must demonstrate an intention to practice law in southern California. Selection is based on service to the Asian Pacific American community, academic achievement, adversities overcome, desire to practice law in the southern California area, and financial need.

Financial data The stipend is $2,000.

Duration 1 year.

Additional information This program, which began in 1984, includes the Justice John F. Aiso Scholarship, the Justice Stephen K. Tamura Scholarship, and the Lim, Ruger & Kim Foundation Scholarship (established in 2007).

Number awarded 3 each year.

Deadline January of each year.

[584]
JAPANESE MEDICAL SOCIETY OF AMERICA SCHOLARSHIPS

Japanese Medical Society of America, Inc.
100 Park Avenue, Suite 1600
New York, NY 10017
(212) 351-5038   Fax: (212) 351-5047
E-mail: info@jmsa.org
Web: www.jmsa.org

Summary To provide funding to Japanese American medical school students, residents, and fellows who are interested in working on a project.

Eligibility This program is open to Japanese Americans who are currently enrolled as medical students, residents, or fellows. Applicants must be proposing to conduct a project that will benefit the Japanese Medical Society of America (JMSA) and the Japanese community. Along with their application, they must submit a 1-page essay about themselves and what they will do to contribute to the JMSA. Selection is based on academic excellence and interest in JMSA.

Financial data Stipends depend on the availability of funds, but have ranged from $2,500 to $20,000. Support is provided primarily for tuition, but a portion of the funds may be used to carry out the proposed project.

Duration 1 year.

Additional information This program receives support from a number of sponsors, including the Honjo Foundation, Nishioka Foundation, Mitsui USA, and Toyota USA. Examples of past projects include a service to connect elderly Japanese American patients with health care, a medical blog in Japanese detailing the experiences of a medical student in America, and a collaborative web site to connect Japanese and American medical students.

Number awarded Varies each year; recently, 11 of these scholarships were awarded.

Deadline December of each year.

[585]
JAVA MEMORIAL SCHOLARSHIPS

Japanese American Veterans Association
c/o Dave Buto
4226 Holborn Avenue
Annandale, VA 22003
(703) 503-3431   E-mail: admin@javadc.org
Web: www.javadc.org

Summary To provide financial assistance for college or graduate school to relatives of Japanese American veterans and military personnel.

Eligibility This program is open to graduating high school seniors and students currently working on an undergraduate or graduate degree at a college, university, or school of specialized study. Applicants must be related, by blood or marriage, to 1) a person who served with the 442nd Regimental Combat Team, the 100th Infantry Battalion, or other unit associated with those; 2) a person who served in the U.S. Military Intelligence Service during or after World War II; 3) a person of Japanese ancestry who is serving or has served in the U.S. armed forces and been honorable discharged; or 4) a member of the Japanese American Veterans Association (JAVA) whose membership extends back at least 1 year.

Financial data The stipend is $1,500.

Duration 1 year; recipients may reapply.

Additional information These scholarships, first awarded in 2008, include the following named awards: the Orville C. Shirey Memorial Scholarship, the Joseph Ichiuji Memorial Scholarship, the Sunao Phil Ishio Memorial Scholarship, the Kiyoko Tsuboi-Taubkin Memorial Scholarship, the Grant Hirabayashi Memorial Scholarship, the Teru Kamikawa Memorial Scholarship, the Mary Kozono Memorial Scholarship, and the Douglas Ishio Memorial Scholarship.

Number awarded 8 each year.

Deadline April of each year.

[586]
JEAN LU STUDENT SCHOLARSHIP AWARD

Society of Toxicology
Attn: American Association of Chinese in Toxicology
  Special Interest Group
1821 Michael Faraday Drive, Suite 300
Reston, VA 20190-5348
(703) 438-3115   Fax: (703) 438-3113
E-mail: sothq@toxicology.org
Web: www.toxicology.org/ai/af/awards.aspx

Summary To provide funding for research to graduate student and postdoctoral members of the Society of Toxicology (SOT) who are of Chinese ethnic origin and working on a Ph.D. in the field.

Eligibility This program is open to Chinese students (born in China or, if born in the United States, having 1 or more parents of Chinese descent) who are SOT members. Applicants must be enrolled full time in a Ph.D. program in toxicology and have been advanced to candidacy. Selection is based on academic achievement, demonstration of leadership, relevance of thesis to toxicology, and letters of recommendation. Finalists are interviewed by telephone.

Financial data The stipend is $1,000. Funds may be used for payment of tuition and/or other educational and research-related expenses, including travel.

Duration 1 year.

Additional information This program was established in 2008.

Number awarded 1 each year.

Deadline December of each year.

[587]
JEANNE SPURLOCK MINORITY MEDICAL STUDENT CLINICAL FELLOWSHIP IN CHILD AND ADOLESCENT PSYCHIATRY

American Academy of Child and Adolescent Psychiatry
Attn: Department of Research, Training, and Education
3615 Wisconsin Avenue, N.W.
Washington, DC 20016-3007
(202) 966-7300, ext. 117   Fax: (202) 364-5925
E-mail: training@aacap.org
Web: www.aacap.org/cs/awards

Summary To provide funding to Asian American and other minority medical students who are interested in working with a child and adolescent psychiatrist during the summer.

Eligibility This program is open to African American, Asian American, Native American, Alaska Native, Mexican American, Hispanic, and Pacific Islander students in accredited U.S. medical schools. Applicants must present a plan for a clinical training experience that involves significant contact between the student and a mentor. The plan should include program planning discussions, instruction in treatment planning and implementation, regular meetings with the mentor and other treatment providers, and assigned readings. Clinical assignments may include responsibility for part of the observation or evaluation, conducting interviews or tests, using rating scales, and psychological or cognitive testing of patients. The training plan should also include discussion of ethical issues in treatment. U.S. citizenship or permanent resident status is required.

Financial data The stipend is $3,500. Fellows also receive reimbursement of travel expenses to attend the annual meeting of the American Academy of Child and Adolescent Psychiatry.

Duration 12 weeks during the summer.

Additional information Upon completion of the training program, the student is required to submit a brief paper summarizing the clinical experience. The fellowship pays expenses for the fellow to attend the academy's annual meeting and present this paper. This program is supported by the Center for Mental Health Services of the Substance Abuse and Mental Health Services Administration.

Number awarded Up to 14 each year.

Deadline February of each year.

[588]
JEANNE SPURLOCK RESEARCH FELLOWSHIP IN SUBSTANCE ABUSE AND ADDICTION FOR MINORITY MEDICAL STUDENTS

American Academy of Child and Adolescent Psychiatry
Attn: Department of Research, Training, and Education
3615 Wisconsin Avenue, N.W.
Washington, DC 20016-3007
(202) 966-7300, ext. 117   Fax: (202) 364-5925
E-mail: training@aacap.org
Web: www.aacap.org/cs/awards

Summary To provide funding to Asian American and other minority medical students who are interested in working on the topics of drug abuse and addiction with a child and adolescent psychiatrist researcher-mentor during the summer.

Eligibility This program is open to African American, Asian American, Native American, Alaska Native, Mexican American, Hispanic, and Pacific Islander students in accredited U.S. medical schools. Applicants must present a plan for a program of research training in drug abuse and addiction that involves significant contact with a mentor who is an experienced child and adolescent psychiatrist researcher. The plan should include program planning discussions; instruction in research planning and implementation; regular meetings with the mentor, laboratory director, and the research group; and assigned readings. The mentor must be a member of the American Academy of Child and Adolescent Psychiatry (AACAP). Research assignments may include responsibility for part of the observation or evaluation, developing specific aspects of the research mechanisms, conducting interviews or tests, using rating scales, and psychological or cognitive testing of subjects. The training plan also should include discussion of ethical issues in research, such as protocol development, informed consent, collection and storage of raw data, safeguarding data, bias in analyzing data, plagiarism, protection of patients, and ethical treatment of animals. U.S. citizenship or permanent resident status is required.

Financial data The stipend is $3,500. Fellows also receive reimbursement of travel expenses to attend the annual meeting of the American Academy of Child and Adolescent Psychiatry.

Duration 12 weeks during the summer.

Additional information Upon completion of the training program, the student is required to submit a brief paper summarizing the research experience. The fellowship pays expenses for the fellow to attend the academy's annual meeting and present this paper. This program is co-sponsored by the National Institute on Drug Abuse.

Number awarded Up to 5 each year.

Deadline February of each year.

[589]
JEFFREY CAMPBELL GRADUATE FELLOWS PROGRAM

St. Lawrence University
Attn: Human Resources/Office of Equity Programs
Jeffrey Campbell Graduate Fellowship Program
23 Romoda Drive
Canton, NY 13617
(315) 229-5509   E-mail: humanresources@stlawu.edu
Web: www.stlawu.edu

Summary To provide funding to Asian American and other minority graduate students who have completed their course work and are interested in conducting research at St. Lawrence University in New York.
Eligibility This program is open to graduate students who are members of racial or ethnic groups historically underrepresented at the university and in American higher education. Applicants must have completed their course work and preliminary examinations for the Ph.D. They must be interested in working on their dissertations or terminal degree projects while in residence at the University.
Financial data The stipend is $28,500 per academic year. Additional funds may be available to support travel to conferences and professional meetings. Office space and a personal computer are provided.
Duration 1 academic year.
Additional information This program is named for 1 of the university's early African American graduates. Recipients must teach 1 course a semester in a department or program at St. Lawrence University related to their research interests. In addition, they must present a research-based paper in the fellows' lecture series each semester.
Deadline January of each year.

[590]
J.K. FUKUSHIMA SCHOLARSHIP FOR SEMINARIANS

Montebello Plymouth Congregational Church
144 South Greenwood Avenue
Montebello, CA 90640
(323) 721-5568   Fax: (323) 721-7955
E-mail: mpccucc@yahoo.com
Web: www.montebelloucc.org

Summary To provide financial assistance to undergraduate and graduate students who are preparing for a career in Christian ministry and can demonstrate a commitment to the Asian American community.
Eligibility This program is open to students who have completed at least 2 years of undergraduate study and are enrolled or accepted at an accredited school of theology. Applicants may not have completed a master's degree. They must be working on a degree that will provide them with the skills and understanding necessary to further the development of Christian ministries. Along with their application, they must submit an essay on their commitment to the Asian American community.
Financial data The stipend is $500.
Duration 1 year.
Number awarded 1 or more each year.
Deadline May of each year.

[591]
J.K. SASAKI MEMORIAL SCHOLARSHIPS

West Los Angeles United Methodist Church
Attn: Scholarship Committee
1913 Purdue Avenue
Los Angeles, CA 90025
(310) 479-1379   Fax: (310) 478-7756
E-mail: wlaumc@aol.com
Web: www.wlaumc.org

Summary To provide financial assistance to Japanese American and other Asian American seminary students who are preparing for ordained ministry in the United Methodist Church.
Eligibility This program is open to Japanese American and other Asian American students at Protestant seminaries in the United States. Applicants must be planning to serve a Japanese American or Asian American congregation of the United Methodist Church as an ordained minister. They must have a GPA of 2.5 or higher. Along with their application, they must submit 2 essays (of 500 words each) on 1) their motivations for preparing for a career in the United Methodist Church, and 2) their concerns for the local church and the United Methodist Church with issues related to Asian Americans and/or Pacific Islanders.
Financial data Stipends range from $250 to $1,000.
Duration 1 year; recipients may reapply.
Additional information This program was established in 1972 and given its current name in 2006.
Number awarded 1 or more each year.
Deadline March of each year.

[592]
JOHN AND MURIEL LANDIS SCHOLARSHIPS

American Nuclear Society
Attn: Scholarship Coordinator
555 North Kensington Avenue
La Grange Park, IL 60526-5592
(708) 352-6611   Toll Free: (800) 323-3044
Fax: (708) 352-0499   E-mail: outreach@ans.org
Web: www.ans.org/honors/scholarships

Summary To provide financial assistance to undergraduate or graduate students (especially Asian Americans, other minorities, and women) who are interested in preparing for a career in nuclear-related fields.
Eligibility This program is open to undergraduate and graduate students at colleges or universities located in the United States who are preparing for, or planning to prepare for, a career in nuclear science, nuclear engineering, or a nuclear-related field. Qualified high school seniors are also eligible. Applicants must have greater than average financial need and have experienced circumstances that render them disadvantaged. They must be sponsored by an organization (e.g., plant branch, local section, student section) within the American Nuclear Society (ANS). Along with their application, they must submit an essay on their academic and professional goals, experiences that have affected those goals, etc. Selection is based on that essay, academic achievement, letters of recommendation, and financial need. Women and members of minority groups are especially urged to apply. U.S. citizenship is not required.
Financial data The stipend is $5,000, to be used to cover tuition, books, fees, room, and board.
Duration 1 year; nonrenewable.
Number awarded Up to 8 each year.
Deadline January of each year.

[593]
JOHN STANFORD MEMORIAL WLMA SCHOLARSHIP

Washington Library Media Association
c/o Jeanne Staley
711 Scenic Bluff
Yakima, WA 98908
(509) 972-5899   E-mail: scholarships@wlma.org
Web: www.wlma.org/scholarships

Summary   To provide financial assistance to Asian Americans and other minorities in Washington who are interested in preparing for a library media career.

Eligibility   This program is open to residents of Washington who are working toward a library media endorsement or graduate degree in the field. Applicants must be members of an ethnic minority group. They must be working or planning to work in a school library. Along with their application, they must submit a brief description of their reasons for applying, goals as a teacher librarian, plans for the future, interest in librarianship, plans for further education, and interest in this award. Financial need is considered in the selection process.

Financial data   The stipend is $1,000.

Duration   1 year.

Number awarded   1 each year.

Deadline   March of each year.

[594]
JOHNSON & JOHNSON CAMPAIGN FOR NURSING'S FUTURE-AMERICAN ASSOCIATION OF COLLEGES OF NURSING MINORITY NURSE FACULTY SCHOLARS PROGRAM

American Association of Colleges of Nursing
One Dupont Circle, N.W., Suite 530
Washington, DC 20036
(202) 463-6930   Fax: (202) 785-8320
E-mail: scholarship@aacn.nche.edu
Web: www.aacn.nche.edu/Education/financialaid.htm

Summary   To provide funding to Asian American and other minority students who are working on a graduate degree in nursing to prepare for a career as a faculty member.

Eligibility   This program is open to members of racial and ethnic minority groups (Alaska Native, American Indian, Black or African American, Native Hawaiian or other, Pacific Islander, Hispanic or Latino, or Asian American) who are enrolled full time at a school of nursing. Applicants must be working on 1) a doctoral nursing degree (e.g., Ph.D., D.N.P.), or 2) a clinically-focused master's degree in nursing (e.g., M.S.N., M.S.). They must commit to 1) serve in a teaching capacity at a nursing school for a minimum of 1 year for each year of support they receive; 2) provide 6-month progress reports to the American Association of Colleges of Nursing (AACN) throughout the entire funding process and during the payback period; 3) agree to work with an assigned mentor throughout the period of the scholarship grant; and 4) attend an annual leadership training conference to connect with their mentor, fellow scholars, and colleagues. Selection is based on ability to contribute to nursing education; leadership potential; development of goals reflecting education, research, and professional involvement; ability to work with a mentor/adviser throughout the award period; proposed research and/or practice projects that are significant and show commitment to improving nursing education and clinical nursing practice in the United States; and evidence of commitment to a career in nursing education and to recruiting, mentoring, and retaining future underrepresented minority nurses. Preference is given to students enrolled in doctoral nursing programs. Applicants must be U.S. citizens, permanent residents, refugees, or qualified immigrants.

Financial data   The stipend is $18,000 per year. The award includes $1,500 that is held in escrow to cover the costs for the recipient to attend the leadership training conference. Recipients are required to sign a letter of commitment that they will provide 1 year of service in a teaching capacity at a nursing school in the United States for each year of support received; if they fail to complete that service requirement, they must repay all funds received.

Duration   1 year; may be renewed 1 additional year.

Additional information   This program, established in 2007, is sponsored by the Johnson & Johnson Campaign for Nursing's Future.

Number awarded   5 each year.

Deadline   May of each year.

[595]
JOSEPH L. FISHER DOCTORAL DISSERTATION FELLOWSHIPS

Resources for the Future
Attn: Coordinator for Academic Programs
1616 P Street, N.W., Suite 600
Washington, DC 20036-1400
(202) 328-5008   Fax: (202) 939-3460
E-mail: fisher-award@rff.org
Web: www.rff.org/About_RFF/Pages/default.aspx

Summary   To provide funding to doctoral candidates in economics (especially Asian Americans, other minorities, and women) who are interested in conducting dissertation research on issues related to the environment, natural resources, or energy.

Eligibility   This program is open to graduate students in their final year of research on a dissertation related to the environment, natural resources, or energy. Applicants must submit a brief letter of application and a curriculum vitae, a graduate transcript, a 1-page abstract of the dissertation, a technical summary of the dissertation (up to 2,500 words), a letter from the student's department chair, and 2 letters of recommendation from faculty members on the student's dissertation committee. The technical summary should describe clearly the aim of the dissertation, its significance in relation to the existing literature, and the research methods to be used. Women and minority candidates are strongly encouraged to apply.

Financial data   The stipend is $18,000.

Duration   1 academic year.

Additional information   It is expected that recipients will not hold other employment during the fellowship period. Recipients must notify Resources for the Future of any financial assistance they receive from any other source for support of doctoral work.

Number awarded   2 or 3 each year.

Deadline   February of each year.

[596]
JOSEPHINE FORMAN SCHOLARSHIP

Society of American Archivists
Attn: Chair, Awards Committee
17 North State Street, Suite 1425
Chicago, IL 60602-3315
(312) 606-0722　　　　　Toll Free: (866) 722-7858
Fax: (312) 606-0728　　　　E-mail: info@archivists.org
Web: www2.archivists.org

Summary　To provide financial assistance to Asian American and other minority graduate students working on a degree in archival science.

Eligibility　This program is open to members of minority groups (American Indian/Alaska Native, Asian, Black/African American, Hispanic/Latino, or Native Hawaiian/other Pacific Islander) currently enrolled in or accepted to a graduate program or a multi-course program in archival administration. The program must offer at least 3 courses in archival science and students may have completed no more than half of the credit requirements toward their graduate degree. Selection is based on potential for scholastic and personal achievement and commitment both to the archives profession and to advancing diversity concerns within it. U.S. citizenship or permanent resident status is required.

Financial data　The stipend is $10,000.

Duration　1 year.

Additional information　Funding for this program, established in 2011, is provided by the General Commission on Archives and History of the United Methodist Church.

Number awarded　1 each year.

Deadline　February of each year.

[597]
JTBF JUDICIAL EXTERNSHIP PROGRAM

Just the Beginning Foundation
c/o Paula Lucas, Executive Director
Schiff Hardin LLP
233 South Wacker Drive, Suite 6600
Chicago, IL 60606
(312) 258-5930　　　　　E-mail: plucas@jtbf.org
Web: www.jtbf.org

Summary　To provide work experience to Asian American and other minority or economically disadvantaged law students who plan to seek judicial clerkships after graduation.

Eligibility　This program is open to students currently enrolled in their second or third year of law school who are members of minority or economically disadvantaged groups. Applicants must intend to work as a clerk in the federal or state judiciary upon graduation or within 5 years of graduation.

Financial data　Program externs receive a quarterly or summer stipend in an amount determined by the sponsor.

Duration　The academic year externships require a 1- or 2-year commitment, beginning each September and ending in May or June. During the academic year, participants are expected to work a minimum of 10 hours per week on externship assignments. The summer externships require students to perform at least 35 hours per week of work for at least 8 weeks during the summer.

Additional information　This program began in 2005. Law students are matched with federal and state judges across the country who provide assignments to the participants that will enhance their legal research, writing, and analytical skills (e.g., drafting memoranda). Students are expected to complete at least 1 memorandum of law or other key legal document each semester of the externship. Course credit may be offered, but students may not receive academic credit and a stipend simultaneously.

Number awarded　Varies each year.

Deadline　February of each year for summer and fall appointments.

[598]
JUDGE EDWARD Y. KAKITA SCHOLARSHIP

Japanese American Bar Association
Attn: JABA Educational Foundation
P.O. Box 86063
Los Angeles, CA 90086
(310) 785-6881　　　　E-mail: JEFscholarship@gmail.com
Web: www.jabaonline.org/scholarships.html

Summary　To provide financial assistance to law students who have participated in the Asian Pacific American community and are interested in international law, commercial litigation, and/or corporate law.

Eligibility　This program is open to students currently enrolled in law school. Applicants must demonstrate an intention to practice law in southern California. Along with their application, they must submit a 500-word personal statement discussing their interest in international law, commercial litigation, and/or corporate law. Selection is based on service to the Asian Pacific American community; academic achievement; overcoming adversity; desire to practice law in the southern California area; desire to practice in the areas of international law, commercial litigation, and/or corporate law; and financial need.

Financial data　The stipend is $2,000.

Duration　1 year.

Additional information　This program was established in 2006.

Number awarded　1 each year.

Deadline　January of each year.

[599]
JUDGE ROBERT M. TAKASUGI FELLOWSHIPS FOR PUBLIC INTEREST LAW

National Asian Pacific American Bar Association
Attn: NAPABA Law Foundation
1612 K Street, N.W., Suite 1400
Washington, DC 20006
(202) 775-9555　　　　　Fax: (202) 775-9333
E-mail: foundation@napaba.org
Web: www.takasugifellowship.com

Summary　To provide an opportunity for law students to gain work experience in public interest law at nonprofit organizations that serve the Asian Pacific American community in San Francisco or Los Angeles.

Eligibility　This program is open to students at ABA-accredited law schools in any state who have a demonstrated commitment to public interest law, especially as it affects the Asian Pacific American community. Applicants must be interested in a summer internship at a nonprofit public interest organization in the San Francisco Bay area or the Greater

Los Angeles Metropolitan area. They must submit a cover letter, a resume, 3 references, and a 3-page statement that answers such questions as the individuals they look to as role models, their career goals, how their background and upbringing have shaped their goals, how they and their work would further the mission and carry on the ideals of Judge Robert M. Takasugi, and their finances.

Financial data The stipend is $5,000.

Duration 10 weeks during the summer.

Number awarded 2 each year: 1 assigned to the San Francisco Bay area and 1 to the Greater Los Angeles Metropolitan area.

Deadline March of each year.

[600]
JUDGE WILLIAM M. MARUTANI FELLOWSHIP

Philadelphia Bar Association
Attn: Foundation
1101 Market Street, 11th Floor
Philadelphia, PA 19107-2911
(215) 238-6347   Fax: (215) 238-1159
E-mail: foundation@philabar.org
Web: www.philabarfoundation.org

Summary To provide financial assistance to Asian American residents of any state who are enrolled at law schools in the Philadelphia area and interested in taking a summer internship.

Eligibility This program is open to Asian American first-year law students at Dickinson School of Law, Rutgers-Camden University School of Law, Temple University James E. Beasley School of Law, University of Pennsylvania School of Law, Villanova University School of Law, Drexel University College of Law, and Widener University School of Law. Applicants must be interested in taking a summer internship position with federal, state, or municipal government offices or agencies (including the judiciary) or nonprofit public interest organizations in the Greater Philadelphia area. Along with their application, they must submit a 2-page essay describing a life experience they have had or a personal/professional aspiration that would reflect the spirit and professional legacy of Judge William M. Marutani. Selection is based on that essay, law school transcripts, past and present work and community service experience, prior accomplishments and awards, and character.

Financial data The stipend is $5,000.

Duration 10 weeks during the summer.

Additional information This program was established by the Asian Pacific American Bar Association of Pennsylvania in conjunction with the Philadelphia Bar Foundation.

Number awarded 1 each year.

Deadline February of each year.

[601]
JUDICIAL INTERN OPPORTUNITY PROGRAM

American Bar Association
Attn: Section of Litigation
321 North Clark Street
Chicago, IL 60654-7598
(312) 988-6348   Fax: (312) 988-6234
E-mail: howardg@staff.abanet.org
Web: www.abanet.org/litigation/jiop

Summary To provide an opportunity for Asian American and other minority or economically disadvantaged law students to gain experience as judicial interns in selected courts during the summer.

Eligibility This program is open to first- and second-year students at ABA-accredited law schools who are 1) members racial or ethnic groups that are traditionally underrepresented in the legal profession (African Americans, Asians, Hispanics/Latinos, Native Americans); 2) students with disabilities; 3) students who are economically disadvantaged; or 4) students who identify themselves as lesbian, gay, bisexual, or transgender. Applicants must be interested in a judicial internship at courts in selected areas and communities. They may indicate a preference for the area in which they wish to work, but they may not specify a court or a judge. Along with their application, they must submit a current resume, a 10-page legal writing sample, and a 2-page statement of interest that outlines their qualifications for the internship. Screening interviews are conducted by staff of the American Bar Association, either in person or by telephone. Final interviews are conducted by the judges with whom the interns will work. Some spots are reserved for students with an interest in intellectual property law.

Financial data The stipend is $1,500.

Duration 6 weeks during the summer.

Additional information Recently, internships were available in the following locations: Chicago and surrounding suburbs; central and southern Illinois; Houston, Dallas, southern, and eastern Texas; Miami, Florida; Phoenix, Arizona; Los Angeles, California; Philadelphia, Pennsylvania; San Francisco, California; and Washington, D.C. Some internships in Chicago, Los Angeles, Texas, and Washington, D.C. are reserved for students with an interest in intellectual property law.

Number awarded Varies each year; recently, 171 of these internships were awarded, including 9 at courts in Arizona, 36 in California, 12 in Florida, 51 in Illinois, 17 in Pennsylvania, 33 in Texas, and 13 in Washington, D.C.

Deadline January of each year.

[602]
JUSTIN HARUYAMA MINISTERIAL SCHOLARSHIP

Japanese American United Church
Attn: Haruyama Scholarship Committee
255 Seventh Avenue
New York, NY 10001
(212) 242-9444   Fax: (212) 242-5274
E-mail: infojauc@gmail.com
Web: www.jauc.org/haruyama_e.html

Summary To provide financial assistance to Protestant seminary students who are interested in serving in Japanese American congregations.

Eligibility This program is open to students of Japanese ancestry who are enrolled full time at an accredited Protestant seminary in the United States. Applicants must be working on a ministerial degree in order to serve Japanese American congregations. Along with their application, they must submit 2 letters of recommendation, a transcript, information on their financial situation, and a brief statement of their spiritual journey.

Financial data The stipend is $500.

Duration   1 year; may be renewed.

Number awarded   1 or more each year.

Deadline   May of each year.

[603]
KAISER PERMANENTE COLORADO DIVERSITY SCHOLARSHIP PROGRAM

Kaiser Permanente
Attn: Multicultural Associations/Employee Resource
 Groups
P.O. Box 378066
Denver, CO 80247-8066
E-mail: co-diversitydevelopment@kp.org
Web: physiciancareers.kp.org

Summary   To provide financial assistance to Asian American and other Colorado residents from diverse backgrounds who are interested in working on an undergraduate or graduate degree in a health care field at a school in any state.

Eligibility   This program is open to all residents of Colorado, including those who identify as 1 or more of the following: African American, Asian Pacific, Latino, lesbian, gay, bisexual, transgender, intersex, Native American, and/or a person with a disability. Applicants must be 1) a graduating high school senior with a GPA of 2.7 or higher and planning to enroll full time at a college or technical school in any state; 2) a GED recipient with a GED score of 520 or higher and planning to enroll full time at a college or technical school in any state; 3) a full-time undergraduate student at a college or technical school in any state; or 4) a full-time graduate or doctoral student at a school in any state. They must be preparing for a career in health care (e.g., doctor, nurse, surgeon, physician assistant, dentist), mental health, public health, or health policy. Along with their application, they must submit 300-word essays on 1) a personal setback in their life and how they responded and learned from it; 2) how they give back to their community; and 3) why they have chosen health care and/or public health for their educational and career path. Selection is based on academic achievement, character qualities, community outreach and volunteering, and financial need.

Financial data   Stipends range from $1,400 to $2,600.

Duration   1 year.

Number awarded   Varies each year; recently, 17 of these scholarships were awarded.

Deadline   January of each year.

[604]
KALPANA CHAWLA SCHOLARSHIP AWARD

American Society of Engineers of Indian Origin
Attn: Southern California Chapter
P.O. Box 466
Cypress, CA 90630
E-mail: scholarships@aseisocal.net
Web: www.aseisocal.net/12.html

Summary   To provide financial assistance to graduate students of Indian origin (from India) who are working on a degree in aerospace.

Eligibility   This program is open to graduate students of Indian origin (by birth, ancestry, or relation). Applicants must be enrolled full time at an accredited college or university in the United States and working on a degree in aerospace

engineering with a GPA of 3.7 or higher. They must be members of the American Society of Engineers of Indian Origin (ASEI) Selection is based on academic achievement, technical expertise, and leadership excellence.

Financial data   The stipend is $2,000.

Duration   1 year.

Additional information   This program was established in 2003 with support from Ford Motor Company.

Number awarded   1 each year.

Deadline   August of each year.

[605]
KATTEN MUCHIN ROSENMAN MINORITY SCHOLARSHIPS

Katten Muchin Rosenman LLP
Attn: Legal Recruiting Coordinator
525 West Monroe Street
Chicago, IL 60661-3693
(312) 577-8406   Fax: (312) 577-4572
E-mail: grace.johnson@kattenlaw.com
Web: www.kattenlaw.com

Summary   To provide financial assistance and summer work experience in Chicago or New York City to Asian American and other minority law students from any state.

Eligibility   This program is open to minority students from any state who have completed their first year of law school. Applicants must have applied for and been accepted as a summer associate at the sponsoring law firm's Chicago or New York office. Along with their application, they must submit 250-word statements on 1) their strongest qualifications for this award; 2) their reasons for preparing for law as a profession; and 3) their views on diversity and how their personal experience and philosophy will be an asset to the firm. Selection is based on academic achievement, leadership experience, and personal qualities that reflect the potential for outstanding contributions to the firm and the legal profession.

Financial data   Participants receive the standard salary for the summer internship and a stipend of $15,000 for the academic year.

Duration   1 year.

Number awarded   1 each year.

Deadline   October of each year.

[606]
KAY LONGCOPE SCHOLARSHIP AWARD

National Lesbian & Gay Journalists Association
2120 L Street, N.W., Suite 850
Washington, DC 20037
(202) 588-9888   Fax: (202) 588-1818
E-mail: info@nlgfa.org
Web: www.nlgja.org/students/longcope.htm

Summary   To provide financial assistance to 1) Asian American and other graduate students of color and 2) lesbian, gay, bisexual, and transgender (LGBT) undergraduate and graduate students who are interested in preparing for a career in journalism.

Eligibility   This program is open to LGBT students of color who are 1) high school seniors accepted to a U.S. community college or 4-year university and planning to enroll full time; 2) full-time undergraduate students at U.S. community colleges and 4-year universities; or 3) undergraduate students who have been accepted for their first year at a U.S. graduate school. Applicants must be planning a career in journalism and be committed to furthering the sponsoring organization's mission of fair and accurate coverage of the LGBT community. They must demonstrate an awareness of the issues facing the LGBT community and the importance of fair and accurate news coverage. For undergraduates, a declared major in journalism and/or communications is desirable but not required; non-journalism majors may demonstrate their commitment to a journalism career through work samples, internships, and work on a school news publication, online news service, or broadcast affiliate. Graduate students must be enrolled in a journalism program. Along with their application, they must submit a 1-page resume, 5 work samples, official transcripts, 3 letters of recommendation, and a 1,000-word autobiography written in the third person as a news story, describing the applicant's commitment and passion for journalism and career goals. U.S. citizenship or permanent resident status is required. Selection is based on journalistic and scholastic ability.

Financial data The stipend is $5,000.

Duration 1 year.

Additional information This program was established in 2008.

Number awarded 1 each year.

Deadline January of each year.

[607]
KAYTE M. FEARN COUNCIL FOR EXCEPTIONAL CHILDREN ETHNIC DIVERSITY SCHOLARSHIP

Council for Exceptional Children
Attn: Student Awards
1110 North Glebe Road, Suite 300
Arlington, VA 22201-5704
(703) 264-9435   Toll Free: (888) CEC-SPED
Fax: (703) 264-9494   TDD: (866) 915-5000
E-mail: students@cec.sped.org
Web: www.cec.sped.org

Summary To provide financial assistance to Asian American and other ethnic minority student members of the Council for Exceptional Children (CEC).

Eligibility This program is open to student members of the council who are citizens of the United States or Canada, members of an ethnically diverse group (African American, American Indian, Alaska Native, Native Canadian, Hispanic, Asian, or Pacific Islander), and juniors, seniors, or graduate students enrolled in an accredited college or university. Applicants must be working on a degree in special education and have a GPA of 3.0 or higher. Along with their application, they must submit 2 letters of recommendation, a summary of Student CEC and/or other activities relating to individuals with disabilities, and a brief biography explaining why they chose special education as a career, how they view the role of special educators, and what they hope to accomplish as a special educator. Financial need is not considered.

Financial data The stipend is $500.

Duration 1 year; nonrenewable.

Number awarded 1 each year.

Deadline October of each year.

[608]
KEGLER, BROWN, HILL & RITTER MINORITY MERIT SCHOLARSHIP

Kegler, Brown, Hill & Ritter
Attn: Human Resources Manager
Capitol Square, Suite 1800
65 East State Street
Columbus, OH 43215
(614) 462-5467   Fax: (614) 464-2634
E-mail: ctammaro@keglerbrown.com
Web: www.keglerbrown.com

Summary To provide financial assistance and summer work experience at Kegler, Brown, Hill & Ritter in Columbus, Ohio to Asian American and other minority students at law schools in any state.

Eligibility This program is open to first-year students of minority descent at law schools in any state. Applicants must be interested in a summer clerkship with the firm following their first year of law school. Along with their application, they must submit brief essays on 1) a major accomplishment that has shaped their life, how it influenced their decision to prepare for a career in law, and how it prepared them for a future as a lawyer; 2) what diversity means to them; 3) why they have applied for the scholarship; and 4) any training and/or experience they believe to be relevant to the clerkship. Selection is based on academic performance, accomplishments, activities, and potential contributions to the legal community.

Financial data The program provides a $5,000 stipend for law school tuition and a paid summer clerkship position.

Duration 1 year.

Additional information This program began in 2004.

Number awarded 1 each year.

Deadline January of each year.

[609]
KENTUCKY LIBRARY ASSOCIATION SCHOLARSHIP FOR MINORITY STUDENTS

Kentucky Library Association
c/o Executive Secretary
1501 Twilight Trail
Frankfort, KY 40601
(502) 223-5322   Fax: (502) 223-4937
E-mail: info@kylibasn.org
Web: www.kylibasn.org/scholarships965.cfm

Summary To provide financial assistance to Asian Americans and members of other minority groups who are residents of Kentucky or attending school there and are working on an undergraduate or graduate degree in library science.

Eligibility This program is open to members of minority groups (defined as American Indian, Alaskan Native, Black, Hispanic, Pacific Islander, or other ethnic group) who are entering or continuing at a graduate library school accredited by the American Library Association (ALA) or an undergraduate library program accredited by the National Council of Teacher Education (NCATE). Applicants must be residents of Kentucky or a student in a library program in the state. Along with their application, they must submit a statement of their career objectives, why they have chosen librarianship as a career, and their reasons for applying for this scholarship. U.S. citizenship or permanent resident status is required. Financial need is not considered in the selection process.

Financial data   The stipend is $1,000.
Duration   1 year; nonrenewable.
Number awarded   1 or more each year.
Deadline   June of each year.

[610]
KING & SPALDING DIVERSITY FELLOWSHIP PROGRAM

King & Spalding
Attn: Diversity Fellowship Program
1180 Peachtree Street
Atlanta, GA 30309
(404) 572-4643   Fax: (404) 572-5100
E-mail: fellowship@kslaw.com
Web: www.kslaw.com

Summary   To provide financial assistance and summer work experience at U.S. offices of the sponsoring law firm to Asian American and other law students who will contribute to the diversity of the legal community.

Eligibility   This program is open to second-year law students who 1) come from a minority ethnic or racial group (American Indian/Alaskan Native, Asian American/Pacific Islander, Black/African American, Hispanic, or multi-racial); 2) are a member of the gay, lesbian, bisexual, or transgender (GLBT) community; or 3) have a disability. Applicants must receive an offer of a clerkship at a U.S. office of King & Spalding during their second-year summer. Along with their application, they must submit a 500-word personal statement that describes their talents, qualities, and experiences and how they would contribute to the diversity of the firm.

Financial data   Fellows receive a stipend of $10,000 for their second year of law school and a paid summer associate clerkship at a U.S. office of the firm during the following summer.

Duration   1 year.

Additional information   The firm's U.S. offices are located in Atlanta, Charlotte, Houston, New York, San Francisco, Silicon Valley, and Washington.

Number awarded   Up to 4 each year.

Deadline   August of each year.

[611]
KIRKLAND & ELLIS LLP DIVERSITY FELLOWSHIP PROGRAM

Kirkland & Ellis LLP
Attn: Attorney Recruiting Manager
333 South Hope Street
Los Angeles, CA 90071
(213) 680-8436   Fax: (213) 680-8500
E-mail: cherie.conrad@kirkland.com
Web: www.kirkland.com

Summary   To provide financial assistance and summer work experience at an office of Kirkland & Ellis to Asian American and other minority law students from any state.

Eligibility   This program is open to second-year students at ABA-accredited law schools who meet the racial and ethnic categories established by the Equal Employment Opportunity Commission. Applicants must have been accepted as summer associates at a domestic office of the sponsoring law firm (Chicago, Los Angeles, New York, Palo Alto, San Francisco, Washington, D.C.) and be likely to practice at 1 of those

offices after graduation. Along with their application, they must submit a 1-page personal statement that describes ways in which they have promoted and will continue to promote diversity in the legal community, along with their interest in the firm. Selection is based on merit.

Financial data   Fellows receive a salary during their summer associateship and a $15,000 stipend at the conclusion of the summer. Stipend funds are to be used for payment of educational expenses during the third year of law school.

Duration   1 year.

Additional information   This program, which replaced the Kirkland & Ellis Minority Fellowship Program, was established at 14 law schools in 2004. In 2006, it began accepting a limited number of applications from students at all ABA-accredited law schools.

Number awarded   Varies each year; recently, 14 of these fellowships were awarded.

Deadline   September of each year.

[612]
K&L GATES DIVERSITY FELLOWSHIP

Kirkpatrick & Lockhart Preston Gates Ellis LLP
Attn: Regional Recruiting Manager
925 Fourth Avenue, Suite 2900
Seattle, WA 98104
(206) 370-5744   E-mail: dana.mills@klgates.com
Web: www.klgates.com/lawstudents/studentsdiversity

Summary   To provide financial assistance and summer work experience in Seattle to Asian American and other law students from any state who come from diverse racial and ethnic backgrounds.

Eligibility   This program is open to first-year students at ABA-accredited law schools in the United States. Applicants must be members of minority racial and ethnic groups. Along with their application, they must submit a 500-word personal statement describing the contribution they would make to the legal profession and the sponsoring firm in particular.

Financial data   Fellows receive a paid associateship with the Seattle office of the sponsoring firm during the summer following their first year of law school and an academic scholarship of $10,000 for their second year of law school.

Duration   1 year.

Number awarded   1 each year.

Deadline   January of each year.

[613]
KOREAN AMERICAN BAR ASSOCIATION OF WASHINGTON SCHOLARSHIP

Korean American Bar Association of Washington
c/o Peter Kim
Swedish Health Services
747 Broadway
Seattle, WA 98122-4307
(206) 386-6000   Fax: (206) 215-3242
TDD: (206) 386-2022   E-mail: peter.kim@swedish.org
Web: kaba-washington.org/for-students

Summary   To provide financial assistance to students from any state who are enrolled at law schools in Washington and have a record of service to the Korean community.

Eligibility   This program is open to residents of any state currently enrolled at law schools in Washington. Applicants must have a demonstrated significant commitment to community service, particularly service to the Korean or Korean American community. Along with their application, they must submit a 2-page essay on what they see as a challenge facing the Korean American community and what they feel they can do to help overcome that challenge as an attorney. Selection is based on the essay, academic achievement, work experience, activities, post-law school goals, and service to the Korean or Korean American community.

Financial data The stipend is $1,000.

Duration 1 year.

Number awarded 1 each year.

Deadline January of each year.

[614]
KOREAN AMERICAN BAR ASSOCIATION SUMMER FELLOWSHIP

Korean American Bar Association of Southern California
c/o Lisa H. Kwon
TroyGould PC
1801 Century Park East, Suite 1600
Los Angeles, CA 90067-2367
(310) 789-1270   Fax: (310) 789-1470
E-mail: lkwon@troygould.com
Web: kabasocal.net

Summary To provide funding for a summer internship to students from any state who are enrolled at law schools in southern California and have been active in the Asian Pacific Islander and/or Korean American community.

Eligibility This program is open to students from any state currently enrolled at law schools in southern California. Applicants must be able to demonstrate a commitment to the Korean American community and/or Asian Pacific Islander community through past, current, or future contributions. They must be planning to work at a public interest organization in southern California during the summer. Students are evaluated on the basis of their written applications and an interview.

Financial data The stipend is $5,000.

Duration Summer months.

Number awarded 1 each year.

Deadline March of each year.

[615]
KOREAN AMERICAN LIBRARIANS AND INFORMATION PROFESSIONALS ASSOCIATION SCHOLARSHIP

Korean American Librarians and Information
  Professionals Association
c/o Heawon Paick, Scholarship Committee Chair
Los Angeles Public Library
Junipero Serra Branch
4607 South Main Street
Los Angeles, CA 90037
(323) 846-5382   Fax: (323) 846-5389
E-mail: hpaick@lapl.org
Web: kalipa.apanet.org

Summary To provide funding to students of Korean descent who are interested in working on a graduate degree in library science.

Eligibility This program is open to students of Korean heritage who are enrolled in an ALA-accredited school of library and information science. Applicants must be working on a master's or doctoral degree. Along with their application, they must submit a 1-page essay on the contributions they can make as a Korean American librarian to the profession and the community. U.S. citizenship or permanent resident status is required.

Financial data A stipend is awarded (amount not specified).

Duration 1 year.

Number awarded 2 each year.

Deadline March of each year.

[616]
KOREAN HONOR SCHOLARSHIP

Embassy of the Republic of Korea in the USA
2320 Massachusetts Avenue, N.W.
Washington, DC 20008
(202) 939-5663   Fax: (202) 342-1597
Web: www.dynamic-korea.com/education/scholarship.php

Summary To provide financial assistance to undergraduate and graduate students of Korean or Korean American heritage.

Eligibility This program is open to students of Korean or Korean American heritage. Applicants must be entering or enrolled full time in an undergraduate or graduate degree program at a college or university in the United States or Canada. They must have a GPA of 3.5 or higher. Along with their application, they must submit a 600-word essay (in English) on what their Korean heritage means to them. Selection is based on that essay, academic achievement, awards, honors, performances, extracurricular activities, and a letter of recommendation.

Financial data The stipend is $1,000.

Duration 1 year.

Additional information This program was established in 1981 when the government of the Republic of Korea donated $1 million to commemorate the 100th anniversary of the establishment of diplomatic relations between Korea and the United States. Subsequent donations have added to the fund.

Number awarded Approximately 140 each year.

Deadline June of each year.

[617]
KOREAN TOXICOLOGISTS ASSOCIATION IN AMERICA BEST PRESENTATIONS BY GRADUATE STUDENT AND POSTDOCTORAL TRAINEE AWARD

Society of Toxicology
Attn: Korean Toxicologists Association in America Special
  Interest Group
1821 Michael Faraday Drive, Suite 300
Reston, VA 20190-5348
(703) 438-3115   Fax: (703) 438-3113
E-mail: sothq@toxicology.org
Web: www.toxicology.org/ai/af/awards.aspx

Summary To recognize and reward graduate students and postdoctoral trainees who present outstanding papers during a session of the Korean Toxicologists Association in America

(KTAA) at the annual meeting of the Society of Toxicology (SOT).

Eligibility This award is available to graduate students and postdoctoral trainees who have an accepted abstract of a research poster or platform presentation for a KTAA session at the SOT annual meeting. Along with the abstract, they must submit a letter of nomination from their major adviser.

Financial data A plaque and a cash award (amount not specified) are presented.

Duration The awards are presented annually.

Additional information These awards are presented jointly by KTAA and the Korean Institute of Toxicology (KIT).

Number awarded 2 each year.

Deadline January of each year.

[618]
KOREAN-AMERICAN MEDICAL ASSOCIATION SCHOLARSHIPS

Korean-American Medical Association
40 Bennett Road
Englewood, NJ 07631
(201) 541-1345   Fax: (201) 541-1344
E-mail: kamausa2001@yahoo.com
Web: www.koreanama.org/scholarship.html

Summary To provide financial assistance to medical students of Korean heritage.

Eligibility This program is open to medical school students who are Korean Americans. Applicants must be U.S. citizens or permanent residents. Along with their application, they must submit transcripts, 2 letters of recommendation, and 500-word essays on 1) that challenges that Korean-American physicians face; and 2) what they propose to do if awarded this scholarship.

Financial data The stipend is $1,000 per year.

Duration 1 year.

Additional information This program was established in 1993.

Number awarded Varies each year; recently, 7 of these scholarships were awarded.

Deadline May of each year.

[619]
KUSCO-KSEA SCHOLARSHIPS FOR GRADUATE STUDENTS

Korean-American Scientists and Engineers Association
Attn: Scholarship Committee
1952 Gallows Drive, Suite 300
Vienna, VA 22182
(703) 748-1221   Fax: (703) 748-1331
E-mail: admin@ksea.org
Web: scholarship.ksea.org/InfoGraduate.aspx

Summary To provide financial assistance to graduate student members of the Korean-American Scientists and Engineers Association (KSEA) studying Korea-U.S. science and technology cooperation.

Eligibility This program is open to graduate students at colleges and universities in the United States who are either 1) of Korean heritage, or 2) non-ethnic Korean students working on a degree related to Korea-U.S. science and technology cooperation. All applicants must be KSEA members working

on a degree in science, engineering, or a related field. Along with their application, they must submit an essay on a topic that changes annually but relates to cooperation in science; recently, students were asked to discuss the effectiveness of "Interdisciplinary Research." Selection is based on that essay (20%), KSEA activities and community service (30%), recommendation letters (20%), and academic performance (30%).

Financial data The stipend is $1,500.

Duration 1 year.

Additional information This program, established in 2005, is supported by the Korea-US Science Cooperation Center (KUSCO).

Number awarded Approximately 15 each year.

Deadline February of each year.

[620]
LAGRANT FOUNDATION GRADUATE SCHOLARSHIPS

Lagrant Foundation
Attn: Programs Manager
626 Wilshire Boulevard, Suite 700
Los Angeles, CA 90071-2920
(323) 469-8680   Fax: (323) 469-8683
E-mail: erickaavila@lagrant.com
Web: www.lagrantfoundation.org/site/?page_id=3

Summary To provide financial assistance to Asian Pacific Americans and other minority graduate students who are working on a degree in advertising, public relations, or marketing.

Eligibility This program is open to African Americans, Asian Pacific Americans, Hispanics/Latinos, and Native Americans/Alaska Natives who are full-time graduate students at an accredited institution. Applicants must have a GPA of 3.2 or higher and be working on a master's degree in advertising, marketing, or public relations. They must have at least 2 academic semesters remaining to complete their degree. Along with their application, they must submit 1) a 1- to 2-page essay outlining their career goals; why it is important to increase ethnic representation in the fields of advertising, marketing, and public relations; and the role of an advertising, marketing, or public relations practitioner; 2) a paragraph describing the graduate school and/or community activities in which they are involved; 3) a brief paragraph describing any honors and awards they have received; 4) a letter of reference; 5) a resume; and 6) an official transcript. U.S. citizenship or permanent resident status is required.

Financial data The stipend is $10,000 per year.

Duration 1 year.

Number awarded 5 each year.

Deadline February of each year.

[621]
LATHAM & WATKINS DIVERSITY SCHOLARS PROGRAM

Latham & Watkins LLP
Attn: Diversity Scholars Program Selection Panel
12636 High Bluff Drive, Suite 400
San Diego, CA 92130
(858) 523-5459   Fax: (858) 523-5450
E-mail: heather.sardinha@lw.com
Web: www.lw.com/AboutLatham.aspx?page=Diversity

Summary To provide financial assistance to Asian American and other minority law students interested in working for a global law firm.

Eligibility Applicants must be second-year law students at an ABA-accredited law school and plan to practice law in a major city in the United States. Students who have received a similar scholarship from another sponsor are not eligible to apply. Applicants must submit a 500-word personal statement that describes their ability to contribute to the diversity objects of global law firms; the life experiences that have shaped their values and that provide them with a unique perspective, including any obstacles or challenges they have overcome; their academic and/or leadership achievements; and their intent to practice in a global law firm environment.

Financial data The stipend is $10,000.

Duration 1 year; nonrenewable.

Additional information This program was established in 2005. Recipients are not required to work for Latham & Watkins after graduation.

Number awarded 4 each year.

Deadline September of each year.

[622]
LAURENCE R. FOSTER MEMORIAL GRADUATE SCHOLARSHIP

Oregon Student Assistance Commission
Attn: Grants and Scholarships Division
1500 Valley River Drive, Suite 100
Eugene, OR 97401-2146
(541) 687-7395   Toll Free: (800) 452-8807, ext. 7395
Fax: (541) 687-7414   TDD: (800) 735-2900
E-mail: awardinfo@osac.state.or.us
Web: www.osac.state.or.us/osac_programs.html

Summary To provide financial assistance to residents of Oregon (particularly Asian Americans and other minorities) who are interested in enrolling in graduate school in any state to prepare for a public health career.

Eligibility This program is open to residents of Oregon who are enrolled at least half time at a college or university in any state to prepare for a career in public health (not private practice). Applicants must be either a college graduate currently working in public health or enrolled as graduate students in that field. Preference is given to applicants from diverse environments. Along with their application, they must submit brief essays on 1) what public health means to them; 2) the public health aspect they intend to practice and the health and population issues impacted by that aspect; and 3) their experience living or working in diverse environments.

Financial data Stipend amounts vary; recently, they were at least $4,167.

Duration 1 year.

Additional information This program is administered by the Oregon Student Assistance Commission (OSAC) with funds provided by the Oregon Community Foundation.

Number awarded Varies each year; recently, 6 undergraduate and graduate scholarships were awarded.

Deadline February of each year.

[623]
LAW STUDENT SUMMER GRANT

Asian American Bar Association of the Greater Bay Area
Attn: Law Foundation
P.O. Box 190517
San Francisco, CA 94119-0517
E-mail: info@aaba-bay.com
Web: aaba-bay.com

Summary To provide funding to law students interested in working on a summer project that will provide legal assistance to the Asian American community in the service area of the Asian American Bar Association of the Greater Bay Area (AABA).

Eligibility This program is open to law students from any state who have obtained a summer position with a nonprofit legal service organization. Applicants must be planning to work on a project or projects that will provide legal assistance to the Asian American community in San Francisco, Alameda, Contra Costa, San Mateo, Marin, or Santa Clara counties in California. The organization must have agreed to supervise the applicant.

Financial data The stipend is $3,000.

Duration At least 10 weeks, during the summer.

Number awarded 1 or more each year.

Deadline April of each year.

[624]
LEIGH COOK FELLOWSHIP

New Jersey Department of Health and Senior Services
Attn: Office of Minority and Multicultural Health
P.O. Box 360 Suite 501
Trenton, NJ 08625-0360
(609) 292-6962   Fax: (609) 292-8713
E-mail: Jose.Gonzalez@doh.state.nj.us
Web: www.state.nj.us/health/omh/index.shtml

Summary To provide financial support for a summer research internship to law, public health, and medical students in New Jersey, especially Asian American and other minority students.

Eligibility This program is open to students in medical science, law, or master's of public health programs who are 1) residents of New Jersey attending school in the state or elsewhere, or 2) residents of other states attending a college or university in New Jersey. Applicants must be interested in working on a supervised project at the New Jersey Department of Health and Senior Services in Trenton in the areas of minority health, senior services, HIV/AIDS, substance abuse, health insurance, environmental or occupational health, public health, or family health. Minority students are encouraged to apply. Selection is based on commitment to minority and/or public health, as demonstrated by community-based service, volunteer work, public health service advocacy, coalition building, and involvement in student organizations that address minority and public health issues.

Financial data The stipend is $6,000.

Duration 10 to 12 weeks during the summer.

Number awarded 1 each year.

Deadline April of each year.

[625]
LIBRARY AND INFORMATION TECHNOLOGY ASSOCIATION/OCLC MINORITY SCHOLARSHIP

American Library Association
Attn: Library and Information Technology Association
50 East Huron Street
Chicago, IL 60611-2795
(312) 280-4270   Toll Free: (800) 545-2433, ext. 4270
Fax: (312) 280-3257   TDD: (888) 814-7692
E-mail: lita@ala.org
Web: www.ala.org/ala/mgrps/divs/lita/awards/oclc/index.cfm

Summary   To provide financial assistance to Asian American and other minority graduate students interested in preparing for a career in library automation.

Eligibility   This program is open to U.S. or Canadian citizens who are interested in working on a master's degree in library/information science and preparing for a career in the field of library and automated systems. Applicants must be a member of 1 of the following ethnic groups: American Indian, Alaskan Native, Asian, Pacific Islander, African American, or Hispanic. They may not have completed more than 12 credit hours of course work for their degree. Selection is based on academic excellence, leadership potential, evidence of a commitment to a career in library automation and information technology, and prior activity and experience in those fields. Financial need is considered when all other factors are equal.

Financial data   The stipend is $3,000.

Duration   1 year.

Additional information   This scholarship, first awarded in 1991, is funded by Online Computer Library Center (OCLC) and administered by the Library and Information Technology Association (LITA) of the American Library Association.

Number awarded   1 each year.

Deadline   February of each year.

[626]
LIBRARY OF CONGRESS JUNIOR FELLOWS PROGRAM

Library of Congress
Library Services
Attn: Junior Fellows Program Coordinator
101 Independence Avenue, S.E., Room LM-642
Washington, DC 20540-4600
(202) 707-0901   Fax: (202) 707-6269
E-mail: jrfell@loc.gov
Web: www.loc.gov/hr/jrfellows/index.html

Summary   To provide summer work experience at the Library of Congress (LC) to upper-division students, graduate students, and recent graduates (particularly those who are Asian Americans, other minorities, women, and individuals with disabilities).

Eligibility   This program is open to U.S. citizens with subject expertise in the following areas: American history, including veterans and military history; American popular culture; area studies (African, Asian, European, Hispanic, Middle Eastern); bibliographic description and access; film, television, and radio; folklife; geography and maps; history of photography; history of popular and applied graphic arts, architecture, and design; manuscript collections processing; music; preservation and conservation; rare books and manuscripts; science, technology, and business; serials and gov-

ernment publications and newspapers; or sound recordings. Applicants must 1) be juniors or seniors at an accredited college or university, 2) be graduate students, or 3) have completed their degree in the past year. Applications from women, minorities, and persons with disabilities are particularly encouraged. Selection is based on academic achievement, letters of recommendation, and an interview.

Financial data   Fellows are paid a taxable stipend of $300 per week.

Duration   3 months, beginning in either May or June. Fellows work a 40-hour week.

Additional information   Fellows work with primary source materials and assist selected divisions at LC in the organization and documentation of archival collections, production of finding aids and bibliographic records, preparation of materials for preservation and service, completion of bibliographical research, and digitization of LC's historical collections.

Number awarded   Varies each year; recently, 6 of these internships were awarded.

Deadline   March of each year.

[627]
LIM, RUGER & KIM SCHOLARSHIP

National Asian Pacific American Bar Association
Attn: NAPABA Law Foundation
1612 K Street, N.W., Suite 1400
Washington, DC 20006
(202) 775-9555   Fax: (202) 775-9333
E-mail: foundation@napaba.org
Web: www.napaba.org

Summary   To provide financial assistance to law students interested in serving the Asian Pacific American community.

Eligibility   This program is open to students at ABA-accredited law schools in the United States. Applicants must demonstrate leadership potential to serve the Asian Pacific American community upon graduation. Along with their application, they must submit a 500-word essay that covers 1) the most significant experiences in their background that have shaped and demonstrated their commitment to serving the needs of Asian Pacific Americans; and 2) how they intend to serve the needs of the Asian Pacific American community in their future legal career. Selection is based on demonstrated commitment to and interest in pro bono, public interest, and/or public service legal work; financial need; leadership potential; maturity and responsibility; and commitment to serving the needs of the Asian Pacific American community.

Financial data   The stipend is $2,500 per year.

Duration   1 year.

Additional information   This program was established in 2004 by the Los Angeles law firm of Lim, Ruger & Kim.

Number awarded   1 each year.

Deadline   September of each year.

[628]
LIONEL C. BARROW MINORITY DOCTORAL STUDENT SCHOLARSHIP

Association for Education in Journalism and Mass Communication
Attn: Communication Theory and Methodology Division
234 Outlet Pointe Boulevard, Suite A
Columbia, SC 29210-5667
(803) 798-0271　　　　　　　Fax: (803) 772-3509
E-mail: aejmc@aejmc.org
Web: aejmcctm.blogspot.com

Summary To provide financial assistance to Asian Americans and other minorities who are interested in working on a doctorate in mass communication.

Eligibility This program is open to minority students enrolled in a Ph.D. program in journalism and/or mass communication. Applicants must submit 2 letters of recommendation, a resume, and a brief letter outlining their research interests and career plans. Membership in the association is not required, but applicants must be U.S. citizens or permanent residents. Selection is based on the likelihood that the applicant's work will contribute to communication theory and/or methodology.

Financial data The stipend is $1,400.

Duration 1 year.

Additional information This program began in 1972.

Number awarded 1 each year.

Deadline May of each year.

[629]
LITA/LSSI MINORITY SCHOLARSHIP

American Library Association
Attn: Library and Information Technology Association
50 East Huron Street
Chicago, IL 60611-2795
(312) 280-4270　　　Toll Free: (800) 545-2433, ext. 4270
Fax: (312) 280-3257　　　　　TDD: (888) 814-7692
E-mail: lita@ala.org
Web: www.ala.org

Summary To provide financial assistance to Asian American and other minority graduate students interested in preparing for a career in library automation.

Eligibility This program is open to U.S. or Canadian citizens who are interested in working on a master's degree in library/information science and preparing for a career in the field of library and automated systems. Applicants must be a member of 1 of the following ethnic groups: American Indian, Alaskan Native, Asian, Pacific Islander, African American, or Hispanic. They may not have completed more than 12 credit hours of course work for their degree. Selection is based on academic excellence, leadership potential, evidence of a commitment to a career in library automation and information technology, and prior activity and experience in those fields. Financial need is considered when all other factors are equal.

Financial data The stipend is $2,500.

Duration 1 year.

Additional information This scholarship, first awarded in 1995, is funded by Library Systems & Services, Inc. (LSSI) and administered by the Library and Information Technology Association (LITA) of the American Library Association.

Number awarded 1 each year.

Deadline February of each year.

[630]
LLOYD M. JOHNSON, JR. SCHOLARSHIP PROGRAM

United Negro College Fund
Attn: Scholarships and Grants Department
8260 Willow Oaks Corporate Drive
P.O. Box 10444
Fairfax, VA 22031-8044
(703) 205-3466　　　　　　Toll Free: (800) 331-2244
Fax: (703) 205-3574
Web: www.uncf.org

Summary To provide financial assistance to Asian American and other law students who will contribute to diversity in the legal profession.

Eligibility Applicants must be U.S. citizens, have a strong academic record (at least a 3.2 GPA), have been accepted to an ABA-accredited law school, be able to demonstrate community service and leadership qualities, have an interest in diversity, be financially disadvantaged, plan to study on a full-time basis, and have an interest in corporate law, including working in a corporate law department and/or law firm. Applicants must submit a current transcript, a resume, 2 letters of recommendation, a personal statement, and a diversity essay (1 page). All students are eligible, but the sponsor expects that most recipients will be students of color.

Financial data The stipend is $10,000 per year.

Duration 1 year. Full scholarships may be renewed for up to 2 additional years, provided the recipient maintains a GPA of 3.2 or higher. Other scholarships are for 1 year only.

Additional information The Minority Corporate Counsel Association first began this program in 2005 and now cosponsors it with the United Negro College Fund. Mentoring and internship experiences are also offered to the winners.

Number awarded Varies each year; recently, 17 of these scholarships were awarded.

Deadline May of each year.

[631]
LTK SCHOLARSHIP

Conference of Minority Transportation Officials
Attn: National Scholarship Program
818 18th Street, N.W., Suite 850
Washington, DC 20006
(202) 530-0551　　　　　　Fax: (202) 530-0617
Web: www.comto.org/news-youth.php

Summary To provide financial assistance to Asian American and other minority upper-division and graduate students majoring in engineering or fields related to transportation.

Eligibility This program is open to full-time minority juniors, seniors, and graduate students in engineering of other technical transportation-related disciplines. Applicants must have a GPA of 3.0 or higher. Along with their application, they must submit a cover letter with a 500-word statement of career goals. Financial need is not considered in the selection process. U.S. citizenship is required.

Financial data The stipend is $6,000. Funds are paid directly to the recipient's college or university.

Duration 1 year.

Additional information The Conference of Minority Transportation Officials (COMTO) was established in 1971 to promote, strengthen, and expand the roles of minorities in all aspects of transportation. This program is sponsored by LTK Engineering Services. Recipients are required to become members of COMTO if they are not already members and attend the COMTO National Scholarship Luncheon.

Number awarded 1 or more each year.

Deadline April of each year.

[632]
MAGOICHI AND SHIZUKO KATO MEMORIAL SCHOLARSHIP

Japanese American Citizens League
Attn: National Scholarship Awards
1765 Sutter Street
San Francisco, CA 94115
(415) 921-5225   Fax: (415) 931-4671
E-mail: jacl@jacl.org
Web: www.jacl.org/edu/scholar.htm

Summary To provide financial assistance for graduate study, especially in medicine or the ministry, to members of the Japanese American Citizens League (JACL).

Eligibility This program is open to JACL members who are attending or planning to attend an accredited college or university as a graduate student. Applicants must submit information on their involvement in JACL and a 2-page essay on a topic that changes annually but relates to Japanese Americans. Selection is based on that essay, academic history, extracurricular activities, JACL involvement, scholastic honors, and a letter of recommendation. Preference is given to applicants planning a career in medicine or the ministry.

Financial data Stipends generally average approximately $2,000.

Duration 1 year; nonrenewable.

Number awarded 1 each year.

Deadline March of each year.

[633]
MARATHON OIL CORPORATION COLLEGE SCHOLARSHIP PROGRAM OF THE HISPANIC SCHOLARSHIP FUND

Hispanic Scholarship Fund
Attn: Selection Committee
55 Second Street, Suite 1500
San Francisco, CA 94105
(415) 808-2365   Toll Free: (877) HSF-INFO
Fax: (415) 808-2302   E-mail: scholar1@hsf.net
Web: www.hsf.net/Scholarships.aspx?id=464

Summary To provide financial assistance to Asian American and other minority upper-division and graduate students working on a degree in a field related to the oil and gas industry.

Eligibility This program is open to U.S. citizens and permanent residents (must have a permanent resident card or a passport stamped I-551) who are of Hispanic American, African American, Asian Pacific Islander American, or American Indian/Alaskan Native heritage. Applicants must be currently enrolled full time at an accredited 4-year college or university in the United States, Puerto Rico, Guam, or the U.S. Virgin Islands with a GPA of 3.0 or higher. They must be 1) sopho-

mores majoring in accounting, chemical engineering, civil engineering, computer engineering, computer science, electrical engineering, energy management or petroleum land management, environmental engineering, environmental health and safety, finance, geology, geophysics, geotechnical engineering, global procurement or supply chain management, information technology/management information systems, marketing, mechanical engineering, petroleum engineering, or transportation and logistics,; or 2) seniors planning to work on a master's degree in geology or geophysics. Selection is based on academic achievement, personal strengths, interest and commitment to a career in the oil and gas industry, leadership, and financial need.

Financial data The stipend is $15,000 per year.

Duration 2 years (the junior and senior undergraduate years or the first 2 years of a master's degree program).

Additional information This program is jointly sponsored by Marathon Oil Corporation and the Hispanic Scholarship Fund (HSF). Recipients may be offered a paid 8- to 10-week summer internship at various Marathon Oil Corporation locations.

Number awarded 1 or more each year.

Deadline November of each year.

[634]
MARK T. BANNER SCHOLARSHIP FOR LAW STUDENTS

Richard Linn American Inn of Court
c/o Cynthia M. Ho, Programs Chair
Loyola University School of Law
25 East Pearson Street, Room 1324
Chicago, IL 60611
(312) 915-7148
Web: www.linninn.org/marktbanner.htm

Summary To provide financial assistance to Asian American and other law students who are members of a group historically underrepresented in intellectual property law.

Eligibility This program is open to students at ABA-accredited law schools in the United States who are members of groups historically underrepresented (by race, sex, ethnicity, sexual orientation, or disability) in intellectual property law. Applicants must submit a 1-page statement on how they have focused on ethics, civility, and professionalism and how diversity has impacted them; transcripts; a writing sample; and contact information for 3 references. Selection is based on academic merit, written and oral communication skills (determined in part through a telephone interview), leadership qualities, community involvement, and commitment to the pursuit of a career in intellectual property law.

Financial data The stipend is $5,000.

Duration 1 year.

Number awarded 1 each year.

Deadline November of each year.

[635]
MARTHA AND ROBERT ATHERTON MINISTERIAL SCHOLARSHIP

Unitarian Universalist Association
Attn: Ministerial Credentialing Office
25 Beacon Street
Boston, MA 02108-2800
(617) 948-6403   Fax: (617) 742-2875
E-mail: mco@uua.org
Web: www.uua.org

Summary To provide financial assistance to seminary students (especially Asian Americans and other students of color) who are preparing for the Unitarian Universalist (UU) ministry.

Eligibility This program is open to second- or third-year seminary students currently enrolled full or at least half time in a UU ministerial training program with aspirant or candidate status. Applicants must respect hard work as a foundation of a full life and appreciate the freedom, political system, and philosophical underpinnings of our country. They should be citizens of the United States or Canada. Preference is given to applicants who have demonstrated outstanding ministerial ability and to those with the greatest financial need, especially persons of color.

Financial data The stipend ranges from $1,000 to $11,000 per year.

Duration 1 year.

Additional information This program was established in 1997.

Number awarded 1 or 2 each year.

Deadline April of each year.

[636]
MARTIN LUTHER KING, JR. MEMORIAL SCHOLARSHIP FUND

California Teachers Association
Attn: Human Rights Department
1705 Murchison Drive
P.O. Box 921
Burlingame, CA 94011-0921
(650) 552-5446   Fax: (650) 552-5002
E-mail: scholarships@cta.org
Web: www.cta.org

Summary To provide financial assistance for college or graduate school to Asian Americans and other minorities who are members of the California Teachers Association (CTA), children of members, or members of the Student CTA.

Eligibility This program is open to members of racial or ethnic minority groups (African Americans, American Indians/Alaska Natives, Asians/Pacific Islanders, and Hispanics) who are 1) active CTA members; 2) dependent children of active, retired, or deceased CTA members; or 3) members of Student CTA. Applicants must be interested in preparing for a teaching career in public education or already engaged in such a career.

Financial data Stipends vary each year; recently, they ranged from $1,000 to $4,000.

Duration 1 year.

Number awarded Varies each year; recently, 12 of these scholarships were awarded: 4 to CTA members, 6 to children of CTA members, and 2 to Student CTA members.

Deadline March of each year.

[637]
MARY REIKO OSAKA MEMORIAL SCHOLARSHIP

Japanese American Citizens League
Attn: National Scholarship Awards
1765 Sutter Street
San Francisco, CA 94115
(415) 921-5225   Fax: (415) 931-4671
E-mail: jacl@jacl.org
Web: www.jacl.org/edu/scholar.htm

Summary To provide financial assistance to student members of the Japanese American Citizens League (JACL) who are interested in preparing for a career in law.

Eligibility This program is open to JACL members who are currently enrolled or planning to enroll in an accredited law school. Applicants must submit information on their involvement in JACL and a 2-page essay on a topic that changes annually but relates to Japanese Americans. Selection is based on that essay, academic history, extracurricular activities, JACL involvement, scholastic honors, and a letter of recommendation.

Financial data Stipends generally average approximately $2,000.

Duration 1 year; nonrenewable.

Number awarded 1 each year.

Deadline March of each year.

[638]
MARY WOLFSKILL TRUST FUND INTERNSHIP

Library of Congress
Library Services
Attn: Junior Fellows Program Coordinator
101 Independence Avenue, S.E., Room LM-642
Washington, DC 20540-4600
(202) 707-3301   Fax: (202) 707-6269
E-mail: jrfell@loc.gov
Web: www.loc.gov/hr/jrfellows/index.html

Summary To provide summer work experience in the Manuscript Division of the Library of Congress (LC) to upper-division and graduate students (especially Asian Americans and other minorities).

Eligibility This program is open to undergraduate and graduate students who have expertise in library science or collections conservation and preservation. Applicants must be interested in gaining an introductory knowledge of the principles, concepts, and techniques of archival management through a summer internship in the LC Manuscript Division. They should be able to demonstrate an ability to communicate effectively in writing and have knowledge of integrated library systems, basic library applications, and other information technologies. Knowledge of American history is beneficial. Applications from minorities and students at smaller and lesser-known schools are particularly encouraged. U.S. citizenship is required.

Financial data The stipend is $3,000.

Duration 10 weeks during the summer. Fellows work a 40-hour week.

Number awarded 1 each year.

Deadline March of each year.

[639]
MCANDREWS DIVERSITY IN PATENT LAW FELLOWSHIP

McAndrews, Held & Malloy, Ltd.
Attn: Diversity Fellowship
500 West Madison Street, 34th Floor
Chicago, IL 60661
(312) 775-8000   Fax: (312) 775-8100
E-mail: info@mcandrews-ip.com
Web: www.mcandrews-ip.com/diversity_fellowship.html

Summary To provide financial assistance to Asian American and other law students who come from a diverse background and are interested in patent law.

Eligibility This program is open to first-year students at ABA-accredited law schools who come from a diverse background. Applicants must have a degree in science or engineering and be planning to practice patent law in the Chicago area. Along with their application, they must submit a 500-word personal statement on why they wish to prepare for a career in patent law, why they are interested in the sponsoring firm as a place to work, and how their background and/or life experiences would improved diversity in the field of intellectual property law. Selection is based on that statement, a resume (including their science or engineering educational credentials), a legal writing sample, undergraduate transcript, and at least 1 letter of recommendation.

Financial data The stipend is $5,000.

Duration 1 year (the second year of law school).

Additional information This fellowship was first awarded in 2008. It includes a paid clerkship position at McAndrews, Held & Malloy during the summer after the first year of law school and possibly another clerkship during the summer after the second year.

Number awarded 1 each year.

Deadline January of each year.

[640]
MCDERMOTT MINORITY SCHOLARSHIP

McDermott Will & Emery
Attn: Recruiting Coordinator
227 West Monroe Street
Chicago, IL 60606
(312) 984-6470   Fax: (312) 984-7700
E-mail: mcdermottscholarship@mwe.com
Web: www.mwe.com

Summary To provide financial assistance and work experience to Asian American and other minority law students.

Eligibility This program is open to second-year minority (African American, Asian, Hispanic, Middle Eastern, Native American) law students at ABA-accredited U.S. law schools. Applicants must be able to demonstrate leadership, community involvement, and a commitment to improving diversity in the legal community. They must be interested in participating in the sponsor's summer program and be able to meet its hiring criteria. Along with their application, they must submit an essay of 1 to 2 pages that provides ideas they have on how the number of minority students in law schools can be increased and how they have improved and intend to help improve diversity in the legal profession throughout their law school and legal career.

Financial data The stipend is $15,000.

Duration 1 year.

Additional information Recipients also participate in a summer program at the sponsor's offices in Boston, Chicago, Houston, Los Angeles, Miami, New York, Orange County, San Diego, Silicon Valley, or Washington, D.C.

Number awarded 2 each year.

Deadline October of each year.

[641]
MCGUIREWOODS/NLF INTERNSHIP PROGRAM

National Asian Pacific American Bar Association
Attn: NAPABA Law Foundation
1612 K Street, N.W., Suite 1400
Washington, DC 20006
(202) 775-9555   Fax: (202) 775-9333
E-mail: foundation@napaba.org
Web: www.napaba.org

Summary To provide funding to undergraduate and law students interested in a summer internship at the National Asian Pacific American Bar Association (NAPABA) and its Law Foundation (NLF).

Eligibility This program is open to 1) undergraduates interested in working as a fundraising and policy intern, and 2) law students interested in working as a clerk. Assignments for undergraduates require working 50% of their time on NAPABA projects and 50% on NLF projects. Assignments for law students require full-time work for NAPABA. Tasks involve promoting justice, equity, and opportunity for Asian Pacific Americans; fostering professional development, legal scholarship, advocacy, and community involvement; and developing and supporting programs to educate the legal profession and Asian Pacific American communities about legal issues affecting those communities.

Financial data The stipend for the law clerk is $3,000. The stipend for the fundraising and policy intern is $2,000.

Duration 10 weeks during the summer.

Additional information These internships were first awarded in 2010 with support from McGuireWoods LLP.

Number awarded 2 each year: 1 law clerk and 1 fundraising and policy intern.

Deadline Deadline not specified.

[642]
MEDIA ACTION NETWORK FOR ASIAN AMERICANS SCHOLARSHIPS

Media Action Network for Asian Americans
P.O. Box 11105
Burbank, CA 91510
(213) 486-4433   Toll Free: (888) 90-MANAA
E-mail: scholarship@manaa.org
Web: www.manaa.org

Summary To provide financial assistance to Asian Pacific Islander undergraduate and graduate students interested in advancing a positive image of Asian Americans in the mainstream media.

Eligibility This program is open to Asian Pacific Islander undergraduate and graduate students interested in preparing for careers in filmmaking or in television production (but not in broadcast journalism). Applicants must be interested in advancing a positive and enlightened understanding of the Asian American experience in the mainstream media. Along with their application, they must submit a 1,000-word essay on their involvement in the Asian Pacific Islander community, how that involvement influences their creative work, how their creative work will influence the Asian Pacific Islanders community and how it is perceived in the next 5 to 10 years. Selection is based on academic and personal merit, a desire to uplift the image of Asian Americans in film and television (as demonstrated in the essay), potential, and financial need.

Financial data The stipend is $1,000.

Duration 1 year.

Additional information This program began in 2001.

Number awarded 1 each year.

Deadline October of each year.

[643]
MENTAL HEALTH AND SUBSTANCE ABUSE FELLOWSHIP PROGRAM

Council on Social Work Education
Attn: Minority Fellowship Program
1701 Duke Street, Suite 200
Alexandria, VA 22314-3429
(703) 519-2050   Fax: (703) 683-8099
E-mail: mfp@cswe.org
Web: www.cswe.org

Summary To provide funding to Asian Americans and other minorities interested in preparing for a clinical career in the mental health fields.

Eligibility This program is open to U.S. citizens, non-citizen nationals, and permanent residents who have been underrepresented in the field of social work. These include but are not limited to the following groups: American Indians/ Alaskan Natives, Asian/Pacific Islanders (e.g., Chinese, East Indians, South Asians, Filipinos, Hawaiians, Japanese, Koreans, and Samoans), Blacks, and Hispanics (e.g., Mexicans/ Chicanos, Puerto Ricans, Cubans, Central or South Americans). Applicants must be interested in and committed to a career in mental health and/or substance abuse, with a specialization in the delivery of services of ethnic and racial minority groups. They must have a master's degree in social work and be accepted to or enrolled in a full-time doctoral degree program. Selection is based on potential for assuming leadership roles; potential for success in doctoral studies; and commitment to a career providing mental health and substance abuse services to ethnic, racial, social, and cultural minority individuals and communities.

Financial data Awards provide a stipend of $21,180 per year and tuition support to a maximum of $3,000.

Duration 1 academic year; renewable for 2 additional years if funds are available and the recipient makes satisfactory progress toward the degree objectives.

Additional information This program has been funded since 1978 by the Center for Mental Health Services (CMHS), the Center for Substance Abuse Prevention (CSAP), and the Center for Substance Abuse Treatment (CSAT) in the Substance Abuse and Mental Health Services Administration.

Number awarded Varies each year; recently, 9 new fellows and 16 returning fellows were appointed.

Deadline February of each year.

[644]
METROPOLITAN LIFE FOUNDATION AWARDS PROGRAM FOR ACADEMIC EXCELLENCE IN MEDICINE

National Medical Fellowships, Inc.
Attn: Scholarship Program
347 Fifth Avenue, Suite 510
New York, NY 10016
(212) 483-8880   Toll Free: (877) NMF-1DOC
Fax: (212) 483-8897   E-mail: info@nmfonline.org
Web: www.nmfonline.org

Summary To provide financial assistance to Vietnamese, Cambodians, and other minorities enrolled as medical students who reside or attend school in designated cities throughout the country.

Eligibility This program is open to African American, mainland Puerto Rican, Mexican American, Native Hawaiian, Alaska Native, Vietnamese, Cambodian, or American Indian medical students in their second through fourth year who are nominated by their dean. Nominees must be enrolled in medical schools located in (or be residents of) designated cities that change annually. Selection is based on demonstrated financial need, outstanding academic achievement, leadership, and potential for distinguished contributions to medicine.

Financial data The stipend is $4,000.

Duration 1 year; nonrenewable.

Additional information Funding for this program, established in 1987, is provided by the Metropolitan Life Foundation of New York, New York.

Number awarded 17 each year.

Deadline March of each year.

[645]
MID-AMERICA CHAPTER SCHOLARSHIPS

Phi Tau Phi Scholastic Honor Society-Mid-America
  Chapter
c/o Dorothy Li, President
Library, John Marshall Law School
315 South Plymouth Court, Sixth Floor
Chicago, IL 60604
(312) 427-2737   E-mail: 8li@jmls.edu
Web: phitauphi.org

Summary To provide financial assistance to undergraduate and graduate students of Chinese heritage at colleges and universities in selected midwestern states.

Eligibility This program is open to undergraduate and graduate students enrolled at colleges and universities in Illinois, Indiana, Iowa, Kansas, Michigan, Ohio, Texas, and Wisconsin. Applicants must be Chinese Americans or students from China, including Taiwan, Macao, Hong Kong, and China. They must submit an autobiography that includes GPA, records of awards, volunteer experiences, and other relevant information.

Financial data The stipend is $1,000.

Duration 1 year.

Additional information Phi Tau Phi, first organized in 1921 in China and reestablished in 1964 in the United States, is a relatively small honor society of scholars, mainly of Chinese heritage, in various disciplines of science, technology, art, and the humanities.

Number awarded 4 each year: 2 for undergraduates and 2 for graduate students.
Deadline April of each year.

[646]
MIDEASTERN REGION KOREAN AMERICAN SCHOLARSHIPS

Korean American Scholarship Foundation
Mideastern Region
c/o Jong Dae Kim, Scholarship Committee Chair
24666 Northwestern Highway Service Drive
Southfield, MI 48075
(313) 963-3299   E-mail: mideastern@kasf.org
Web: www.kasf.org/application_set.html

Summary To provide financial assistance to Korean American students from any state who are working on an undergraduate or graduate degree in any field at a school in Indiana, Michigan, or Ohio.

Eligibility This program is open to Korean American students who are currently enrolled in a college or university as full-time undergraduate or graduate students. Applicants may reside anywhere in the United States, as long as they attend school in Indiana, Michigan, or Ohio. Selection is based on academic achievement, school activities, community service, and financial need.

Financial data Stipends range from $1,000 to $2,000.
Duration 1 year; renewable.
Number awarded Varies each year.
Deadline March of each year.

[647]
MIDWESTERN REGION KOREAN AMERICAN SCHOLARSHIPS

Korean American Scholarship Foundation
Midwestern Region
c/o Augie Lee, Scholarship Committee Chair
1760 South Braymore Drive
Inverness, IL 60010
E-mail: midwestern@kasf.org
Web: www.kasf.org/application_set.html

Summary To provide financial assistance to Korean American students from any state who are working on or planning to work on an undergraduate or graduate degree in any field at a school in the Midwest.

Eligibility This program is open to Korean American students who are currently enrolled or planning to enroll at a college or university in the midwestern states as full-time undergraduate or graduate students. Applicants may reside anywhere in the United States, as long as they attend school in the midwestern region: Illinois, Iowa, Kansas, Minnesota, Missouri, Nebraska, North Dakota, South Dakota, and Wisconsin. Selection is based on academic achievement, school activities, community service, and financial need.

Financial data Stipends range from $1,000 to $2,000.
Duration 1 year; renewable.
Number awarded Varies each year; recently, 48 of these scholarships were awarded.
Deadline May of each year.

[648]
MIKE M. MASAOKA CONGRESSIONAL FELLOWSHIP

Japanese American Citizens League
Attn: Washington Office
1850 M Street, N.W., Suite 1100
Washington, DC 20036
(202) 223-1240   Fax: (202) 296-8082
E-mail: policy@jacl.org
Web: www.jacl.org/leadership/masaoka.htm

Summary To provide an opportunity for student members of the Japanese American Citizens League (JACL) to gain work experience on the staff of a member of Congress.

Eligibility This program is open to U.S. citizens who are graduating college seniors or students in a graduate or professional program. Applicants must be JACL members who are interested in working in Washington on the staff of a member of Congress. Preference is given to those having a demonstrated commitment to Asian American issues, particularly those affecting the Japanese American community. Along with their application, they must submit essays on their career goals and how this award would further those goals.

Financial data The stipend ranges from $2,200 to $2,500 per month.
Duration 6 to 8 months.
Number awarded 1 each year.
Deadline April of each year.

[649]
MILBANK DIVERSITY SCHOLARS PROGRAM

Milbank, Tweed, Hadley & McCloy LLP
Attn: Manager of Law School Recruiting
One Chase Manhattan Plaza
New York, NY 10005
(212) 530-5757   Fax: (212) 822-5757
E-mail: alevitt@milbank.com
Web: www.milbank.com/careers

Summary To provide financial assistance and work experience to law students, especially Asian Americans and members of other groups underrepresented at large law firms.

Eligibility This program is open to students who have completed their first year of a full-time J.D. program at an ABA-accredited law school. Joint degree candidates must have successfully completed 2 years of a J.D. program. Applications are particularly encouraged from members of groups traditionally underrepresented at large law firms. Applicants must submit a 500-word essay on 1) the challenges they have faced in pursuit of a legal career that have helped them understand the value of diversity and inclusion in the legal profession; and 2) the personal contributions they would make to furthering the diversity objectives of the sponsoring law firm. Selection is based on academic achievement, demonstrated leadership ability, writing and interpersonal skills, and interest in the firm's practice.

Financial data The stipend is $25,000. A paid associate position during the summer after the second year of law school is also provided. If the student is offered and accepts a permanent position with the firm after graduation, an additional $25,000 scholarship stipend is also awarded.
Duration 1 year (the third year of law school).

Additional information Scholars may be offered a permanent position with the firm, but there is no guarantee of such an offer.

Number awarded At least 2 each year.

Deadline August of each year.

[650]
MILLER JOHNSON WEST MICHIGAN DIVERSITY LAW SCHOOL SCHOLARSHIP

Grand Rapids Community Foundation
Attn: Education Program Officer
185 Oakes Street S.W.
Grand Rapids, MI 49503-4008
(616) 454-1751, ext. 103   Fax: (616) 454-6455
E-mail: rbishop@grfoundation.org
Web: www.grfoundation.org/scholarships

Summary To provide financial assistance to Asian Americans and other minorities from Michigan who are attending law school in any state.

Eligibility This program is open to U.S. citizens and permanent residents who are students of color and residents of Michigan. Preference is given to residents of western Michigan. Applicants must be attending an accredited law school in any state. They must have a GPA of 3.0 or higher and be able to demonstrate financial need.

Financial data The stipend is $5,000. Funds are paid directly to the recipient's institution.

Duration 1 year.

Number awarded 1 each year.

Deadline March of each year.

[651]
MILLER NASH LAW STUDENT DIVERSITY FELLOWSHIP PROGRAM

Miller Nash LLP
Attn: Director of Recruiting and Professional Development
3400 U.S. Bancorp Tower
111 S.W. Fifth Avenue
Portland, OR 97204-3699
(503) 224-5858   Fax: (503) 224-0155
E-mail: michelle.baird-johnson@millernash.com
Web: www.millernash.com/fellowship.aspx

Summary To provide financial assistance and work experience to Asian American and other law students who will contribute to diversity and are interested in living and working in the Pacific Northwest following graduation from law school.

Eligibility This program is open to first- and second-year students at ABA-accredited law schools in any state. Applicants must be able to demonstrate academic excellence, interpersonal skills, leadership qualities, contributions to diversity, and meaningful contributions to the community. They must intend to work, live, and practice law in the Pacific Northwest. Along with their application, they must submit a personal statement of 2 to 4 pages that includes a description of organizations or projects in which they currently participate or have participated that address diversity issues or support diversity in their legal, business, or local communities.

Financial data Fellows receive a paid summer clerk position and a stipend of $7,500 for law school.

Duration 1 year (including 12 weeks for the summer clerk position); nonrenewable.

Additional information Summer clerk positions may be offered (depending on availability) at the sponsoring law firm's offices in Portland (Oregon), Seattle (Washington), or Vancouver (Washington).

Number awarded Up to 2 each year.

Deadline September of each year for second-year students; January of each year for first-year students.

[652]
MINE AND GONSAKULTO SCHOLARSHIP

Far West Athletic Trainers' Association
c/o Jason Bennett, Scholarship Chair
Chapman University
1 University Drive
Orange, CA 92866
(714) 997-6567   Fax: (714) 997-6991
E-mail: jbennett@chapman.edu
Web: www.fwata.org/com_scholarships.html

Summary To provide financial assistance to members of the National Athletic Trainers Association (NATA) from any state who are of Asian descent and working on an undergraduate or graduate degree in its District 8.

Eligibility This program is open to students of Asian descent from any state who are enrolled as undergraduate or graduate students at colleges and universities in California, Guam, Hawaii, or Nevada and preparing for a career as an athletic trainer. Applicants must be student members of NATA and a District 8 member of NATA working on a bachelor's, master's, or doctoral degree in athletic training. They must have a GPA of 3.0 or higher and a record of distinction in their athletic training program, academic major, institution, intercollegiate athletics, and higher education. Along with their application, they must submit a statement on their athletic training background, experience, philosophy, and goals. Financial need is not considered in the selection process.

Financial data The stipend is $1,500.

Duration 1 year.

Additional information FWATA serves as District 8 of NATA.

Number awarded 1 each year.

Deadline February of each year.

[653]
MINORITY ACCESS INTERNSHIP

Minority Access, Inc.
Attn: Directory of Internship Program
5214 Baltimore Avenue
Hyattsville, MD 20781
(301) 779-7100   Fax: (301) 779-9812
Web: www.minorityaccess.org

Summary To provide work experience to Asian American and other minority undergraduate and graduate students interested in internships at participating entities in Washington, D.C. and throughout the United States.

Eligibility This program is open to full-time undergraduate and graduate students who have a GPA of 3.0 or higher. Applicants must be U.S. citizens for most positions. All academic majors are eligible. Interns are selected by participating federal government and other agencies. Most of these are located in Washington, D.C., but placements may be made anywhere in the United States.

Financial data The weekly stipend is $450 for sophomores and juniors, $500 for seniors, or $550 for graduate and professional students. In addition, most internships include paid round-trip travel between home and the internship location.

Duration Spring internships are 5 months, starting in January; summer internships are 3 months, starting in August; fall internships are 4 months, starting in September.

Additional information Minority Access, Inc. is committed to the diversification of institutions, federal agencies, and corporations of all kinds and to improving their recruitment, retention, and enhancement of minorities. The majority of interns are placed in the Washington, D.C. metropolitan area. Both full-time and part-time internships are awarded. Students may receive academic credit for full-time internships. Students are expected to pay all housing costs. They are required to attend a pre-employment session in Washington, D.C., all seminars and workshops hosted by Minority Access, and any mandatory activities sponsored by the host agency.

Number awarded Varies each year.

Deadline February of each year for summer internships; June of each year for fall internships; and November of each year for spring internships.

[654]
MINORITY FACULTY DEVELOPMENT SCHOLARSHIP AWARD IN PHYSICAL THERAPY

American Physical Therapy Association
Attn: Honors and Awards Program
1111 North Fairfax Street
Alexandria, VA 22314-1488
(703) 684-APTA   Toll Free: (800) 999-APTA
Fax: (703) 684-7343   TDD: (703) 683-6748
E-mail: executivedept@apta.org
Web: www.apta.org

Summary To provide financial assistance to Asian American and other minority faculty members in physical therapy who are interested in working on a doctoral degree.

Eligibility This program is open to U.S. citizens and permanent residents who are members of the following minority groups: African American or Black, Asian, Native Hawaiian or other Pacific Islander, American Indian or Alaska Native, or Hispanic/Latino. Applicants must be full-time faculty members, teaching in an accredited or developing professional physical therapist education program, who will have completed the equivalent of 2 full semesters of post-professional doctoral course work. They must possess a license to practice physical therapy in a U.S. jurisdiction and be enrolled as a student in an accredited post-professional doctoral program whose content has a demonstrated relationship to physical therapy. Along with their application, they must submit a personal essay on their professional goals, including their plans to contribute to the profession and minority services. Selection is based on 1) commitment to minority affairs and services; 2) commitment to further the physical therapy profession through teaching and research; and 3) scholastic achievement.

Financial data A stipend is awarded (amount not specified).

Duration 1 year.

Additional information This program was established in 1999.

Number awarded 1 or more each year.

Deadline November of each year.

[655]
MINORITY FELLOWSHIPS IN EDUCATION RESEARCH

American Educational Research Association
1430 K Street, N.W., Suite 1200
Washington, DC 20005
(202) 238-3200   Fax: (202) 238-3250
E-mail: fellowships@aera.net
Web: www.aera.net

Summary To provide funding to Asian American and other minority doctoral students writing their dissertation on educational research.

Eligibility This program is open to U.S. citizens and permanent residents who have advanced to candidacy and successfully defended their Ph.D./Ed.D. dissertation research proposal. Applicants must plan to work full time on their dissertation in educational research. This program is targeted for members of groups historically underrepresented in higher education (African Americans, American Indians, Alaskan Natives, Asian Americans, Native Hawaiian or Pacific Islanders, and Hispanics or Latinos). Selection is based on scholarly achievements and publications, letters of recommendation, quality and significance of the proposed research, and commitment of the applicant's faculty mentor to the goals of the program.

Financial data The grant is $12,000. Up to $1,000 is provided to pay for travel to the sponsor's annual conference.

Duration 1 year; nonrenewable.

Additional information This program was established in 1991.

Number awarded Up to 3 each year.

Deadline December of each year.

[656]
MINORITY MEDICAL STUDENT ELECTIVE IN HIV PSYCHIATRY

American Psychiatric Association
Attn: Office of HIV Psychiatry
1000 Wilson Boulevard, Suite 1825
Arlington, VA 22209-3901
(703) 907-8668   Toll Free: (888) 357-7849
Fax: (703) 907-1089   E-mail: dpennessi@psych.org
Web: www.psych.org/Resources/OMNA/MFP.aspx

Summary To provide an opportunity for Asian Americans and other minority medical students to spend an elective residency learning about HIV psychiatry.

Eligibility This program is open to medical students entering their fourth year at an accredited M.D. or D.O. degree-granting institution. Preference is given to minority candidates and those who have primary interests in services related to HIV/AIDS and substance abuse and its relationship to the mental health or the psychological well being of ethnic minorities. Applicants should be interested in a psychiatry, internal medicine, pediatrics, or research career. They must be interested in participating in a program that includes intense training in HIV mental health (including neuropsychiatry), a clinical and/or research experience working with a mentor, and participation in the Committee on AIDS of the American Psychiatric Association (APA). U.S. citizenship is required.

Financial data A stipend is provided (amount not specified).

Duration 1 year.

Additional information The heart of the program is in establishing a mentor relationship at 1 of 5 sites, becoming involved with a cohort of medical students interested in HIV medicine/psychiatry, participating in an interactive didactic/experimental learning program, and developing expertise in areas related to ethnic minority mental health research or psychiatric services. Students selected for the program who are not APA members automatically receive membership.

Number awarded Varies each year.

Deadline March of each year.

[657]
MINORITY MEDICAL STUDENT SUMMER EXTERNSHIP IN ADDICTION PSYCHIATRY

American Psychiatric Association
Attn: Department of Minority and National Affairs
1000 Wilson Boulevard, Suite 1825
Arlington, VA 22209-3901
(703) 907-8653   Toll Free: (888) 35-PSYCH
Fax: (703) 907-7852   E-mail: mking@psych.org
Web: www.psych.org/Resources/OMNA/MFP.aspx

Summary To provide funding to Asian American and other minority medical students who are interested in working on a research externship during the summer with a mentor who specializes in addiction psychiatry.

Eligibility This program is open to minority medical students who have a specific interest in services related to substance abuse treatment and prevention. Minorities include American Indians, Alaska Natives, Native Hawaiians, Asian Americans, Hispanic/Latinos, and African Americans. Applicants must be interested in working with a mentor who specializes in addiction psychiatry. Work settings provide an emphasis on working clinically with or studying underserved minority populations and issues of co-occurring disorders, substance abuse treatment, and mental health disparity. Most of them are in inner-city or rural settings.

Financial data Externships provide $1,500 for travel expenses to go to the work setting of the mentor and up to another $1,500 for out-of-pocket expenses directly related to the conduct of the externship.

Duration 1 month during the summer.

Additional information Funding for this program is provided by the Substance Abuse and Mental Health Services Administration (SAMHSA).

Number awarded 10 each year.

Deadline February of each year.

[658]
MINORITY VISITING STUDENT AWARDS PROGRAM

Smithsonian Institution
Attn: Office of Fellowships
470 L'Enfant Plaza, Suite 7102
P.O. Box 37012, MRC 902
Washington, DC 20013-7012
(202) 633-7070   Fax: (202) 633-7069
E-mail: siofg@si.edu
Web: www.si.edu/ofg/Applications/MIP/MIPapp.htm

Summary To provide funding to Asian American and other minority graduate students interested in conducting research at the Smithsonian Institution.

Eligibility This program is open to members of U.S. minority groups underrepresented in the Smithsonian's scholarly programs. Applicants must be advanced graduate students interested in conducting research in the Institution's disciplines and in the museum field.

Financial data Students receive a grant of $550 per week.

Duration Up to 10 weeks.

Additional information Recipients must carry out independent research projects in association with the Smithsonian's research staff. Eligible fields of study currently include animal behavior, ecology, and environmental science (including an emphasis on the tropics); anthropology (including archaeology); astrophysics and astronomy; earth sciences and paleobiology; evolutionary and systematic biology; history of science and technology; history of art (especially American, contemporary, African, Asian, and 20th-century art); American crafts and decorative arts; social and cultural history of the United States; and folklife. Students are required to be in residence at the Smithsonian for the duration of the fellowship.

Number awarded Varies each year.

Deadline January of each year for summer and fall residency; September of each year for spring residency.

[659]
MINORU YASUI MEMORIAL SCHOLARSHIP

Japanese American Citizens League
Attn: National Scholarship Awards
1765 Sutter Street
San Francisco, CA 94115
(415) 921-5225   Fax: (415) 931-4671
E-mail: jacl@jacl.org
Web: www.jacl.org/edu/scholar.htm

Summary To provide financial assistance for graduate study in selected fields to members of the Japanese American Citizens League (JACL).

Eligibility This program is open to JACL members who are attending or planning to attend an accredited college or university as a graduate student. Applicants must submit information on their involvement in JACL and a 2-page essay on a topic that changes annually but relates to Japanese Americans. Selection is based on academic record, extracurricular activities, financial need, and community involvement. Preference is given to applicants with a strong interest in human and civil rights; fields of study may also include sociology, law, or education.

Financial data   Stipends generally average approximately $2,000.

Duration   1 year; nonrenewable.

Number awarded   At least 1 each year.

Deadline   March of each year.

[660]
MIRIAM WEINSTEIN PEACE AND JUSTICE EDUCATION AWARD

Philanthrofund Foundation
Attn: Scholarship Committee
1409 Willow Street, Suite 210
Minneapolis, MN 55403-3251
(612) 870-1806   Toll Free: (800) 435-1402
Fax: (612) 871-6587   E-mail: info@PfundOnline.org
Web: www.pfundonline.org/scholarships.html

Summary   To provide financial assistance to Asian American and other minority students from Minnesota who are associated with gay, lesbian, bisexual, and transgender (GLBT) activities and interested in working on a degree in education.

Eligibility   This program is open to residents of Minnesota and students attending a Minnesota educational institution who are members of a religious, racial, or ethnic minority. Applicants must be self-identified as GLBT or from a GLBT family and have demonstrated a commitment to peace and justice issues. They may be attending or planning to attend trade school, technical college, college, or university (as an undergraduate or graduate student). Preference is given to students who have completed at least 2 years of college and are working on a degree in education. Selection is based on the applicant's 1) affirmation of GLBT identity or commitment to GLBT communities; 2) participation and leadership in community and/or GLBT activities; and 3) service as role model, mentor, and/or adviser for the GLBT community.

Financial data   The stipend is $3,000. Funds must be used for tuition, books, fees, or dissertation expenses.

Duration   1 year.

Number awarded   1 each year.

Deadline   January of each year.

[661]
MLA/NLM SPECTRUM SCHOLARSHIPS

Medical Library Association
Attn: Awards, Grants, and Scholarships
65 East Wacker Place, Suite 1900
Chicago, IL 60601-7246
(312) 419-9094   Fax: (312) 419-8950
E-mail: info@mlahq.org
Web: www.mlanet.org

Summary   To provide financial assistance to Asian Americans and members of other minority groups interested in preparing for a career as a medical librarian.

Eligibility   This program is open to members of minority groups (African Americans, Hispanics, Asian, Native Americans, and Pacific Islanders) who are attending library schools accredited by the American Library Association (ALA). Applicants must be interested in preparing for a career as a health sciences information professional.

Financial data   The stipend is $3,250.

Duration   1 year.

Additional information   This program, established in 2001, is jointly sponsored by the Medical Library Association (MLA) and the National Library of Medicine (NLM) of the U.S. National Institutes of Health (NIH). It operates as a component of the Spectrum Initiative Scholarship program of the ALA.

Number awarded   2 each year.

Deadline   February of each year.

[662]
MLA SCHOLARSHIP FOR MINORITY STUDENTS

Medical Library Association
Attn: Professional Development Department
65 East Wacker Place, Suite 1900
Chicago, IL 60601-7246
(312) 419-9094, ext. 28   Fax: (312) 419-8950
E-mail: mlapd2@mlahq.org
Web: www.mlanet.org/awards/grants/minstud.html

Summary   To assist Asian American and other minority students interested in preparing for a career in medical librarianship.

Eligibility   This program is open to racial minority students (Asians, African Americans, Hispanics, Native Americans, or Pacific Islander Americans) who are entering an ALA-accredited graduate program in librarianship or who have completed less than half of their academic requirements for the master's degree in library science. They must be interested in preparing for a career in medical librarianship. Selection is based on academic record, letters of reference, professional potential, and the applicant's statement of career objectives. U.S. or Canadian citizenship or permanent resident status is required.

Financial data   The stipend is $5,000.

Duration   1 year.

Additional information   This scholarship was first awarded in 1973.

Number awarded   1 each year.

Deadline   November of each year.

[663]
MULTICULTURAL ADVERTISING INTERN PROGRAM

American Association of Advertising Agencies
Attn: Manager of Diversity Programs
405 Lexington Avenue, 18th Floor
New York, NY 10174-1801
(212) 850-0732   Toll Free: (800) 676-9333
Fax: (212) 682-2028   E-mail: maip@aaaa.org
Web: www2.aaaa.org

Summary   To provide Asian American and other minority students with summer work experience in advertising agencies and to present them with an overview of the agency business.

Eligibility   This program is open to U.S. citizens and permanent residents who are Black/African American, Asian/Asian American, Pacific Islander, Hispanic, North American Indian/Native American, or multiracial and either 1) college juniors, seniors, or graduate students at an accredited college or university, or 2) students at any academic level attending a portfolio school of the sponsor. Applicants may be majoring in any field, but they must be able to demonstrate a serious commitment to preparing for a career in advertising. They must have a GPA of 3.0 or higher. Students with a cumulative GPA of 2.7 to 2.9 are encouraged to apply, but they must complete an additional essay question.

Financial data Interns are paid a salary of at least $70 per day. If they do not live in the area of their host agencies, they may stay in housing arranged by the sponsor. They are responsible for a percentage of the cost of housing and materials.

Duration 10 weeks during the summer.

Additional information Interns may be assigned duties in the following departments: account management, broadcast production, media buying/planning, creative (art direction or copywriting), digital/interactive technologies, print production, strategic/account planning, or traffic. The portfolio schools are the AdCenter at Virginia Commonwealth University, the Creative Circus and the Portfolio Center in Atlanta, the Miami Ad School, the University of Texas at Austin, Pratt Institute, the Minneapolis College of Art and Design, and the Art Center College of Design in Pasadena, California.

Number awarded 70 to 100 each year.

Deadline December of each year.

[664]
NAPABA LAW FOUNDATION SCHOLARSHIPS

National Asian Pacific American Bar Association
Attn: NAPABA Law Foundation
1612 K Street, N.W., Suite 1400
Washington, DC 20006
(202) 775-9555   Fax: (202) 775-9333
E-mail: foundation@napaba.org
Web: www.napaba.org

Summary To provide financial assistance to law students interested in serving the Asian Pacific American community.

Eligibility This program is open to students at ABA-accredited law schools in the United States. Applicants must demonstrate leadership potential to serve the Asian Pacific American community upon graduation. Along with their application, they must submit a 500-word essay that covers 1) the most significant experiences in their background that have shaped and demonstrated their commitment to serving the needs of Asian Pacific Americans; and 2) how they intend to serve the needs of the Asian Pacific American community in their future legal career. Selection is based on demonstrated commitment to and interest in pro bono, public interest, and/ or public service legal work; financial need; leadership potential; maturity and responsibility; and commitment to serving the needs of the Asian Pacific American community.

Financial data The stipend is $2,500 or $2,000.

Duration 1 year.

Additional information These scholarships were first awarded in 1995. In 2003, 1 of the scholarships was named the Chris Nakamura Scholarship in honor of a leader of the Asian Pacific American legal community in Arizona.

Number awarded 8 to 10 each year: 1 at $2,500 (the Chris Nakamura Scholarship) and the remainder at $2,000.

Deadline September of each year.

[665]
NASP MINORITY SCHOLARSHIP

National Association of School Psychologists
Attn: Education and Research Trust
4340 East-West Highway, Suite 402
Bethesda, MD 20814
(301) 657-0270, ext. 234   Toll Free: (866) 331-NASP
Fax: (301) 657-0275   TDD: (301) 657-4155
E-mail: kbritton@naspweb.org
Web: www.nasponline.org/about_nasp/minority.aspx

Summary To provide financial assistance to Asian Americans and other minority graduate students who are members of the National Association of School Psychologists (NASP) and enrolled in a school psychology program.

Eligibility This program is open to minority students who are NASP members enrolled in a regionally-accredited school psychology program in the United States. Applicants must have a GPA of 3.0 or higher. Doctoral candidates are not eligible. Applications must be accompanied by 1) a resume that includes undergraduate and/or graduate schools attended, awards and honors, student and professional activities, work and volunteer experiences, research and publications, workshops or other presentations, and any special skills, training, or experience, such as bilingualism, teaching experience, or mental health experience; 2) a statement, up to 1,000 words, of professional goals; 3) at least 2 letters of recommendation, including at least 1 from a faculty member from their undergraduate or graduate studies (if a first-year student) or at least 1 from a faculty member of their school psychology program (if a second- or third-year student); 4) a completed financial statement; 5) an official transcript of all graduate course work (first-year students may submit an official undergraduate transcript); 6) other personal accomplishments that the applicant wishes to be considered; and 7) a letter of acceptance from a school psychology program for first-year applicants. U.S. citizenship is required.

Financial data The stipend is $5,000 per year.

Duration 1 year; may be renewed up to 2 additional years.

Number awarded Varies each year; recently, 4 of these scholarships were awarded.

Deadline October of each year.

[666]
NATIONAL ASSOCIATION OF BOND LAWYERS GOVERNMENTAL AFFAIRS SUMMER ASSOCIATE PROGRAM

National Association of Bond Lawyers
Attn: Governmental Affairs Office
601 13th Street, N.W., Suite 800 South
Washington, DC 20005-3875
(202) 682-1498   Fax: (202) 637-0217
E-mail: internship@nabl.org
Web: www.nabl.org/about/Governmental-Affairs.html

Summary To provide an opportunity for law students, especially Asian Americans and those from other diverse backgrounds, to learn about municipal bond law during a summer internship at the Governmental Affairs Office of the National Association of Bond Lawyers (NABL) in Washington, D.C.

Eligibility This program is open to students currently enrolled in law school and interested in municipal bond law;

diverse candidates are especially encouraged to apply. Applicants must be interested in a summer internship at the NABL Governmental Affairs Office in Washington, D.C. They should be able to demonstrate a high regard for honesty, integrity, and professional ethics; excellent organization, time management, and coordination skills and judgment; strong interpersonal skills; ability to communicate effectively, both orally and in writing; strong personal computer and data processing skills; proven attention to detail; a basic knowledge of the structure of government; and an ability to work effectively in member-driven associations.

Financial data The stipend is $4,000.

Duration 3 months during the summer.

Number awarded 1 each year.

Deadline May of each year.

[667]
NATIONAL DEFENSE SCIENCE AND ENGINEERING GRADUATE FELLOWSHIP PROGRAM

American Society for Engineering Education
Attn: NDSEG Fellowship Program
1818 N Street, N.W., Suite 600
Washington, DC 20036-2479
(202) 331-3516   Fax: (202) 265-8504
E-mail: ndseg@asee.org
Web: ndseg.asee.org

Summary To provide financial assistance to doctoral students (especially Asian/Pacific Islander Americans, other minorities, and students with disabilities) who are working on a degree in areas of science and engineering that are of military importance.

Eligibility This program is open to U.S. citizens and nationals entering or enrolled in the early stages of a doctoral program in aeronautical and astronautical engineering; biosciences, including toxicology; chemical engineering; chemistry; civil engineering; cognitive, neural, and behavioral sciences; computer and computational sciences; electrical engineering; geosciences, including terrain, water, and air; materials science and engineering; mathematics; mechanical engineering; naval architecture and ocean engineering; oceanography; or physics, including optics. Applications are particularly encouraged from women, members of ethnic minority groups (American Indians, African Americans, Hispanics or Latinos, Native Hawaiians, Alaska Natives, Asians, and Pacific Islanders), and persons with disabilities. Selection is based on all available evidence of ability, including academic records, letters of recommendation, and GRE scores.

Financial data The annual stipend is $30,500 for the first year, $31,000 for the second year; and $31,500 for the third year; the program also pays the recipient's institution full tuition and required fees (not to include room and board). Medical insurance is covered up to $1,000 per year. An additional allowance may be considered for a student with a disability.

Duration 3 years, as long as satisfactory academic progress is maintained.

Additional information This program is sponsored by the Army Research Office, the Air Force Office of Scientific Research, and the Office of Naval Research. Recipients do not incur any military or other service obligation. They must attend school on a full-time basis.

Number awarded Approximately 200 each year.

Deadline January of each year.

[668]
NATIONAL KOREAN PRESBYTERIAN WOMEN GRANTS

National Korean Presbyterian Women
c/o Kyo Mo Chung, Moderator
2309 Misty Haven Lane
Plano, TX 75093
(214) 821-8776   E-mail: jungbang@gmail.com
Web: www.pcusa.org/korean/org-nkpw.htm

Summary To provide financial assistance to Korean American women preparing for ministry in the Presbyterian Church.

Eligibility This program is open to second-generation Korean American women who are entering their third semester of full-time study at a Presbyterian seminary. Selection is based on academic ability and leadership skills.

Financial data The stipend is $1,000.

Duration 1 year.

Deadline May of each year.

[669]
NATIONAL MEDICAL FELLOWSHIPS EMERGENCY SCHOLARSHIP FUND

National Medical Fellowships, Inc.
Attn: Scholarship Program
347 Fifth Avenue, Suite 510
New York, NY 10016
(212) 483-8880   Toll Free: (877) NMF-1DOC
Fax: (212) 483-8897   E-mail: info@nmfonline.org
Web: www.nmfonline.org/programs.php

Summary To provide financial assistance to Vietnamese, Cambodians, and other minority medical students who are facing financial emergencies.

Eligibility This program is open to U.S. citizens who are enrolled in the third or fourth year of an accredited M.D. or D.O. degree-granting program in the United States and are facing extreme financial difficulties because of unforeseen training-related expenses. Applicants must be African Americans, Mexican Americans, Native Hawaiians, Alaska Natives, American Indians, Vietnamese, Cambodians, or mainland Puerto Ricans who permanently reside in the United States. They must be interested in primary care practice in underserved communities.

Financial data Assistance ranges up to $20,000.

Duration Awards are available semi-annually.

Additional information This program was established in 2008, with support from the Kellogg Foundation.

Number awarded Varies each year; recently, 3 of these scholarships were awarded.

Deadline August of each year.

[670]
NATIONAL MEDICAL FELLOWSHIPS NEED-BASED SCHOLARSHIP PROGRAM

National Medical Fellowships, Inc.
Attn: Scholarship Program
347 Fifth Avenue, Suite 510
New York, NY 10016
(212) 483-8880   Toll Free: (877) NMF-1DOC
Fax: (212) 483-8897   E-mail: info@nmfonline.org
Web: www.nmfonline.org/programs.php

Summary   To provide financial assistance to Vietnamese, Cambodians, and other underrepresented minority medical students who can demonstrate financial need.

Eligibility   This program is open to U.S. citizens enrolled in the first or second year of an accredited M.D. or D.O. degree-granting program in the United States. Applicants must be African Americans, Mexican Americans, Native Hawaiians, Alaska Natives, American Indians, Vietnamese, Cambodians, or mainland Puerto Ricans who permanently reside in the United States. Along with their application, they must submit a 600-word essay on their motivation for a career in medicine and their personal and professional goals over the next 10 years. Selection is based primarily on financial need.

Financial data   The amount of the award depends on the student's total resources (including parental and spousal support), cost of education, and receipt of additional scholarships; recently, individual awards ranged from $1,000 to $10,000 per year.

Duration   1 year for first-year students; may be renewed for the second year only.

Number awarded   Varies each year; recently, 70 of these scholarships were awarded.

Deadline   August of each year.

[671]
NATIONAL MINORITY STEM FELLOWSHIPS

Educational Advancement Alliance, Inc.
Attn: National Minority STEM Fellowship Program
4548 Market Street, Suite LL-04
Philadelphia, PA 19139
(215) 895-4003   E-mail: info@nmsfp.org
Web: www.nmsfp.org

Summary   To provide financial assistance to Asian Americans and other minority residents of designated states who are working on a master's degree in fields of science, technology, engineering, or mathematics (STEM) at colleges in those states.

Eligibility   This program is open to U.S. citizens who are residents of Delaware, Maryland, New Jersey, Pennsylvania, or Washington, D.C. Members of cultural, racial, geographic, and socioeconomic backgrounds that are currently underrepresented in graduate education and especially encouraged to apply; those are defined to include Hispanics or Latinos, American Indians or Alaska Natives, Asians, Native Hawaiians or other Pacific Islanders, or Blacks. Applicants must be enrolled full time at colleges or universities in those states and working on a master's degree in a field of STEM, including physics, chemistry, non-medical biology, mathematics, computer science, or environmental science. Their degree requirements must include a research thesis. Students working on other graduate degrees (e.g., joint B.S./M.S., M.B.A.,

D.V.M., M.D., joint M.D./Ph.D., J.D., joint J.D./Ph.D.) are not eligible. Along with their application, they must submit a 1,000-word essay on their qualifications for the fellowship and their career goals, college transcripts, information on extracurricular activities, a copy of their GRE scores, 3 letters of recommendation, and information on their financial situation.

Financial data   The program provides a stipend of $18,000 per year and up to $20,500 per year as tuition support.

Duration   2 years.

Additional information   This program is funded by the U.S. Department of Energy Office of Science and administered by the Educational Advancement Alliance, Inc.

Number awarded   Up to 40 each year.

Deadline   March of each year.

[672]
NCAA ETHNIC MINORITY POSTGRADUATE SCHOLARSHIP PROGRAM

National Collegiate Athletic Association
Attn: Office for Diversity and Inclusion
1802 Alonzo Watford Sr. Drive
P.O. Box 6222
Indianapolis, IN 46206-6222
(317) 917-6222   Fax: (317) 917-6888
E-mail: tstrum@ncaa.org
Web: www.ncaa.org

Summary   To provide funding to Asian American and other minority graduate students who are interested in preparing for a career in intercollegiate athletics.

Eligibility   This program is open to members of minority groups who have been accepted into a program at a National Collegiate Athletic Association (NCAA) member institution that will prepare them for a career in intercollegiate athletics (athletics administrator, coach, athletic trainer, or other career that provides a direct service to intercollegiate athletics). Applicants must be U.S. citizens, have performed with distinction as a student body member at their respective undergraduate institution, and be entering the first semester or term of full-time postgraduate study. Selection is based on the applicant's involvement in extracurricular activities, course work, commitment to preparing for a career in intercollegiate athletics, and promise for success in that career. Financial need is not considered.

Financial data   The stipend is $6,000; funds are paid to the college or university of the recipient's choice.

Duration   1 year; nonrenewable.

Number awarded   13 each year.

Deadline   November of each year.

[673]
NCVAA/VABASC SCHOLARSHIP

National Conference of Vietnamese American Attorneys
c/o Dominque N. Thieu
Thieu Virtual Law Group
17220 Newhope Street, Suite 218
Fountain Valley, CA 92708
(714) 822-6093   Fax: (714) 274-7179
E-mail: dnt@thieulaw.com
Web: www.ncvaa.org/scholarship.html

Summary To provide financial assistance to law students who have been involved in the Vietnamese American community.

Eligibility This program is open to students currently enrolled at law schools in the United States. Applicants must have a record of involvement in the Vietnamese American community. Along with their application, they must submit an 800-word essay that covers 1) their involvement, in any public service or leadership role, within the Vietnamese American community; 2) what they see as a pressing concern facing the Vietnamese American community and how they see themselves contributing to or engaging in that issue; and 3) their experience in overcoming socioeconomic, cultural, or other barriers.

Financial data A stipend is awarded (amount not specified).

Duration 1 year.

Additional information This scholarship is offered jointly by the National Conference of Vietnamese American Attorneys (NCVAA) and the Vietnamese American Bar Association of Southern California (VABASC).

Number awarded Up to 3 each year.

Deadline October of each year.

[674]
NEW JERSEY LIBRARY ASSOCIATION DIVERSITY SCHOLARSHIP

New Jersey Library Association
4 Lafayette Street
P.O. Box 1534
Trenton, NJ 08607
(609) 394-8032   Fax: (609) 394-8164
E-mail: ptumulty@njla.org
Web: www.njla.org/honorsawards/scholarship

Summary To provide financial assistance to New Jersey residents who are Asian Americans or members of other minority groups and interested in working on a graduate or postgraduate degree in public librarianship at a school in any state.

Eligibility This program is open to residents of New Jersey and individuals who have worked in a New Jersey library for at least 12 months. Applicants must be members of a minority group (African American, Asian/Pacific Islander, Latino/Hispanic, or Native American/Native Alaskan). They must be enrolled or planning to enroll at an ALA-accredited school of library science in any state to work on a graduate or postgraduate degree in librarianship. Along with their application, they must submit an essay of 150 to 250 words explaining their choice of librarianship as a profession. An interview is required. Selection is based on academic ability and financial need.

Financial data The stipend is $1,300.

Duration 1 year.

Number awarded 1 each year.

Deadline February of each year.

[675]
NEW MEXICO DIVERSITY FELLOWSHIPS IN ENVIRONMENTAL LAW

American Bar Association
Attn: Section of Environment, Energy, and Resources
321 North Clark Street
Chicago, IL 60654-7598
(312) 988-5602   Fax: (312) 988-5572
E-mail: jonusaid@staff.abanet.org
Web: www.abanet.org

Summary To provide funding to Asian American and other law students from traditionally underrepresented groups who are interested in working on a summer project in environmental, energy, or natural resources law in New Mexico.

Eligibility This program is open to first- and second-year law students and third-year night students who are residents of New Mexico or residents of other states with a demonstrated interest in practicing law in New Mexico. Preference is given to students at law schools in New Mexico. Applicants must be members of minority and traditionally underrepresented groups preparing for a career in environmental, energy, or natural resources law. They must be interested in working during the summer at a government agency or public interest organization in New Mexico. Selection is based on interest in environmental and natural resource issues, academic record, personal qualities, and leadership abilities.

Financial data The stipend is $5,000.

Duration 8 to 10 weeks during the summer.

Additional information This program is supported by the New Mexico Environment Department.

Number awarded 1 each year.

Deadline February of each year.

[676]
NEW YORK MINORITY FELLOWSHIP IN ENVIRONMENTAL LAW

American Bar Association
Attn: Section of Environment, Energy, and Resources
321 North Clark Street
Chicago, IL 60654-7598
(312) 988-5602   Fax: (312) 988-5572
E-mail: jonusaid@staff.abanet.org
Web: www.abanet.org

Summary To provide funding to Asian American and other law students from underrepresented groups who are interested in working on a summer project related to environmental, energy, or natural resources law in New York.

Eligibility This program is open to first- and second-year law students and third-year night students who are African American, Latino, Native American, Alaskan Native, Asian, or Pacific Islander. Applicants may be enrolled at a law school in New York or be residents of New York and enrolled at a law school in another state. They must be interested in a summer internship at a government agency or public interest organization in New York in the field of environmental, energy, or natural resources law. Selection is based on interest in environmental issues, academic record, personal qualities, financial need, and leadership abilities.

Financial data The stipend is $6,000.

Duration At least 10 weeks during the summer.

Additional information This program is cosponsored by the Environmental Law Section of the New York State Bar Association and the Committee on Environmental Law of the New York City Bar Association.

Number awarded 1 or more each year.

Deadline November of each year.

[677]
NEXSEN PRUET DIVERSITY SCHOLARSHIPS

Nexsen Pruet
Attn: Diversity Scholarship
1230 Main Street, Suite 700
P.O. Drawer 2426
Columbia, SC 29202-2426
(803) 771-8900   Fax: (803) 727-1469
E-mail: diversity@nexsenpruet.com
Web: www.nexsenpruet.com/firm-diversity.html

Summary To provide financial assistance to Asian Americans and other minority students attending designated law schools in North and South Carolina.

Eligibility This program is open to minority students currently enrolled in the first year at the University of North Carolina School of Law, University of South Carolina School of Law, Wake Forest University School of Law, North Carolina Central University School of Law, Charleston School of Law, or Charlotte School of Law. Applicants must be interested in practicing law in North or South Carolina after graduation. Along with their application, they must submit information on their academic achievements; their contributions to promoting diversity in their community, school, or work environment; and their ability to overcome challenges in the pursuit of their goals. They must also submit essays of 250 words each on 1) their reasons for preparing for a legal career; 2) their interest in the private practice of law in North Carolina and/or South Carolina; 3) any obstacles, including but not limited to financial obstacles, that the scholarship will help them overcome; and 4) what they see as potential obstacles, issues, and opportunities facing new minority lawyers.

Financial data The stipend is $3,000 per year.

Duration 1 year; recipients may reapply.

Additional information Recipients are considered for summer employment in an office of the firm after completion of their first year of law school.

Number awarded Varies each year; recently, 3 of these scholarships were awarded.

Deadline October of each year.

[678]
NINA C. LEIBMAN FELLOWSHIP

California Women's Law Center
5700 Wilshire Boulevard, Suite 460
Los Angeles, CA 90036
(323) 951-1041   Fax: (323) 951-9870
E-mail: info@cwlc.org
Web: www.cwlc.org

Summary To provide summer work experience at the California Women's Law Center (CWLC) in Los Angeles to Asian American and other graduate students (including males and individuals with disabilities) who are working on a degree in media-related fields.

Eligibility This program is open to students who are currently working on a graduate degree in film studies, television studies, or communications. Applicants must have a record of interest in media issues affecting the civil rights of women and girls. They must be able to demonstrate strong research, writing, and problem-solving skills; excellent communication skills; and the ability to work independently, take direction, and follow through on assignments. Along with their application, they must submit a proposal for a summer research project on representation of women and/or girls in various media, representation of gender roles in various media, or treatment of women in either the creative or business side of media employment. Projects can focus on a single medium or compare 2 or more media. They must include the development of concrete advocacy strategies that can be implemented by the fellow over the summer and/or continued by CWLC following the fellowship. Men, persons with disabilities, the elderly, and people of color are encouraged to apply.

Financial data The stipend is $4,500; an additional $500 is available for purchase of project materials and supplies.

Duration 10 weeks during the summer.

Additional information This program was established in 2006.

Number awarded 1 each year.

Deadline May of each year.

[679]
NORTH AMERICAN DOCTORAL FELLOWSHIPS

The Fund for Theological Education, Inc.
Attn: North American Doctoral Fellows Program
825 Houston Mill Road, Suite 100
Atlanta, GA 30329
(404) 727-1450   Fax: (404) 727-1490
Web: www.fteleaders.org/pages/NAD-fellowships

Summary To provide financial assistance to Asian American and other underrepresented racial and ethnic minority students enrolled in a doctoral program in religious or theological studies.

Eligibility This program is open to continuing students enrolled full time in a Ph.D. or Th.D. program in religious or theological studies. Applicants must be citizens or permanent residents of the United States or Canada who are racial or ethnic minority students traditionally underrepresented in graduate education (e.g., African Americans, Asian Americans, Native Hawaiians, Native Americans, Alaska Natives, Hispanics). D.Min. students are ineligible. Preference is given to students nearing completion of their degree. Selection is based on commitment to teaching and scholarship, academic achievement, capacity for leadership in theological scholarship, and financial need.

Financial data Stipends range from $5,000 to $10,000 per year, depending on financial need.

Duration 1 year; may be renewed up to 2 additional years.

Additional information Funding for this program is provided by the National Council of Churches, proceeds from the book *Stony the Road We Trod: African American Biblical Interpretation,* an endowment from the Hearst Foundation, and the previously established FTE Black Doctoral Program supported by Lilly Endowment, Inc.

Number awarded Varies each year; recently, 12 of these fellowships were awarded.

Deadline February of each year.

[680]
NORTH CAROLINA DIVERSITY FELLOWSHIPS IN ENVIRONMENTAL LAW

American Bar Association
Attn: Section of Environment, Energy, and Resources
321 North Clark Street
Chicago, IL 60654-7598
(312) 988-5602   Fax: (312) 988-5572
E-mail: jonusaid@staff.abanet.org
Web: www.abanet.org

Summary To provide funding to Asian American and other law students from traditionally underrepresented groups who are interested in working on a summer project related to environmental, energy, or natural resources law in North Carolina.

Eligibility This program is open to first- and second-year law students and third-year night students who are members of underrepresented and underserved groups, such as minority or low-income populations. Students may be residents of any state and attending school in any state; preference is given to residents of North Carolina and to students who are enrolled at law schools in North Carolina or who have a strong interest in the state. Applicants must be interested in a summer internship at a government agency or public interest organization in North Carolina and working on an environmental project. Selection is based on interest in environmental issues, academic record, personal qualities, and leadership abilities.

Financial data The stipend is $5,000.

Duration 8 to 10 weeks during the summer.

Additional information This program is cosponsored by the Environment, Energy and Natural Resources Law Section of the North Carolina Bar Association.

Number awarded 2 each year.

Deadline February of each year.

[681]
NORTHEASTERN REGION KOREAN AMERICAN SCHOLARSHIPS

Korean American Scholarship Foundation
Northeastern Region
c/o James Lee, Scholarship Committee Chair
472 11th Street, Room 202
Palisades Park, NJ 07650
E-mail: Jae.h.shin@us.hsbc.com
Web: www.kasf.org/application_set.html

Summary To provide financial assistance to Korean American students from any state who are working on an undergraduate or graduate degree in any field at a school in northeastern states.

Eligibility This program is open to Korean American students who are currently enrolled in a college or university in a northeastern state as a full-time undergraduate or graduate student. Applicants may reside anywhere in the United States, as long as they attend school in the northeastern region: Connecticut, Maine, Massachusetts, New Hampshire, New Jersey, New York, Rhode Island, and Vermont. Selection

is based on academic achievement, school activities, community service, and financial need.

Financial data Stipends range from $1,000 to $2,000.

Duration 1 year; renewable.

Number awarded Varies each year; recently, 54 of these scholarships were awarded.

Deadline June of each year.

[682]
OLIVER GOLDSMITH, M.D. SCHOLARSHIP

Kaiser Permanente Southern California
Attn: Resident Recruitment and Outreach
393 East Walnut Street
Pasadena, CA 91188
Toll Free: (877) 574-0002   Fax: (626) 405-6581
E-mail: socal.residency@kp.org
Web: residency.kp.org

Summary To provide financial assistance to Asian American and other medical students who will help bring diversity to the profession.

Eligibility This program is open to students entering their third or fourth year of allopathic or osteopathic medical school. Applicants must have demonstrated their commitment to diversity through community service, clinical volunteering, or research. They may be attending medical school in any state, but they must intend to practice in southern California and they must be available to participate in a mentoring program and a clinical rotation at a Kaiser Permanente facility in that region.

Financial data The stipend is $5,000.

Duration 1 year.

Additional information These scholarships were first awarded in 2004.

Number awarded 12 each year.

Deadline February of each year.

[683]
OLIVER W. HILL SCHOLARSHIP

LeClairRyan
Attn: Director, Recruiting and Diversity
Riverfront Plaza, East Tower
951 East Byrd Street, Eighth Floor
Richmond, VA 23219
(804) 783-7597   Fax: (804) 783-2294
E-mail: george.braxton@leclairryan.com
Web: www.leclairryan.com

Summary To provide financial assistance to Asian Americans and other students of color at law schools in Virginia and Washington, D.C.

Eligibility This program is open to students of color who have completed at least 1 semester at a law school in Virginia or Washington, D.C. Applicants must be planning to practice in Virginia after graduation. They must have a GPA of 2.5 or higher. Along with their application, they must submit a 2,000-word essay presenting their ideas of pursuing social justice through the law.

Financial data The stipend is $5,000.

Duration 1 year.

Additional information This program was established in 2009.

Number awarded 1 each year.

Deadline March of each year.

[684]
OLYMPIA BROWN AND MAX KAPP AWARD

Unitarian Universalist Association
Attn: Ministerial Credentialing Office
25 Beacon Street
Boston, MA 02108-2800
(617) 948-6403   Fax: (617) 742-2875
E-mail: mco@uua.org
Web: www.uua.org/giving/awardsscholarships/57793.shtml

Summary To provide financial assistance to Unitarian Universalist (UU) candidates for the ministry (particularly Asian Americans and other students of color) who submit a project on an aspect of Universalism.

Eligibility This program is open to students currently enrolled full or at least half time in a UU ministerial training program with aspirant or candidate status. Applicants are primarily citizens of the United States or Canada. Along with their application, they may submit a paper, sermon, or a special project on an aspect of Unitarian Universalism. Priority is given first to those who have demonstrated outstanding ministerial ability and secondarily to students with the greatest financial need (especially persons of color).

Financial data The stipend is $2,500.

Duration 1 year.

Number awarded 1 each year.

Deadline April of each year.

[685]
OPERATION JUMP START III SCHOLARSHIPS

American Association of Advertising Agencies
Attn: AAAA Foundation
405 Lexington Avenue, 18th Floor
New York, NY 10174-1801
(212) 682-2500   Toll Free: (800) 676-9333
Fax: (212) 682-2028   E-mail: ameadows@aaaa.org
Web: www2.aaaa.org

Summary To provide financial assistance to Asian American and other multicultural art directors or copywriters interested in working on an undergraduate or graduate degree in advertising.

Eligibility This program is open to African Americans, Asian Americans, Hispanic Americans, and Native Americans who are U.S. citizens or permanent residents. Applicants must be incoming graduate students at 1 of 6 designated portfolio schools or full-time juniors at 1 of 2 designated colleges. They must be able to demonstrate extreme financial need, creative talent, and promise. Along with their application, they must submit 10 samples of creative work in their respective field of expertise.

Financial data The stipend is $5,000 per year.

Duration Most awards are for 2 years.

Additional information Operation Jump Start began in 1997 and was followed by Operation Jump Start II in 2002. The current program began in 2006. The 6 designated portfolio schools are the AdCenter at Virginia Commonwealth University, the Creative Circus in Atlanta, the Portfolio Center in Atlanta, the Miami Ad School, the University of Texas at Austin, and Pratt Institute. The 2 designated colleges are the Min-

neapolis College of Art and Design and the Art Center College of Design at Pasadena, California.

Number awarded 20 each year.

Deadline Deadline not specified.

[686]
ORANGE COUNTY ASIAN AMERICAN BAR FOUNDATION SCHOLARSHIPS

Orange County Asian American Bar Foundation
Attn: Administrator
P.O. Box 6130
Newport Beach, CA 92658
(949) 440-6700, ext. 254   Fax: (714) 784-4016
E-mail: ocaaba@gmail.com
Web: www.ocaaba.org

Summary To provide financial assistance to students from any state who are enrolled at law schools in southern California and have been active in the Asian American community.

Eligibility This program is open to students from any state who are in their first or second year of law school in southern California. Evening students in their third year of study are also eligible. Applicants must submit a 1,000-word statement on their involvement (in any public service or leadership role) within the Asian American community, their reason for attending law school, and whether or how they expect to use their legal education to contribute to the community. Selection is based on the applicant's service to, and/or leadership in, the Asian American community and commitment to continue providing such service and/or leadership.

Financial data The stipend is $1,000.

Duration 1 year.

Number awarded 2 each year.

Deadline April of each year.

[687]
OREGON DIVERSITY FELLOWSHIPS IN ENVIRONMENTAL LAW

American Bar Association
Attn: Section of Environment, Energy, and Resources
321 North Clark Street
Chicago, IL 60654-7598
(312) 988-5602   Fax: (312) 988-5572
E-mail: jonusaid@staff.abanet.org
Web: www.abanet.org

Summary To provide funding to Asian American and other law students from traditionally underrepresented groups who are interested in working on a summer project related to environmental, energy, or natural resources law in Oregon.

Eligibility This program is open to first- and second-year law students and third-year night students who are members of underrepresented and underserved groups, such as minority or low-income populations. Students may be residents of any state and attending school in any state; preference is given to residents of Oregon and to students who are enrolled at law schools in Oregon or who have a strong interest in the state. Applicants must be interested in a summer internship at a government agency or public interest organization in Oregon and working on a project in the fields of environmental, energy, or natural resources law. Selection is based on interest in environmental issues, academic record, personal qualities, and leadership abilities.

Financial data The stipend is $5,000.

Duration 8 to 10 weeks during the summer.

Additional information This program is cosponsored by the Affirmative Action Program of the Oregon State Bar.

Number awarded 1 each year.

Deadline January of each year.

[688]
OREGON STATE BAR CLERKSHIP STIPENDS

Oregon State Bar
Attn: Affirmative Action Program
16037 S.W. Upper Boones Ferry Road
P.O. Box 231935
Tigard, OR 97281-1935
(503) 431-6338
Toll Free: (800) 452-8260, ext. 338 (within OR)
Fax: (503) 598-6938   E-mail: eyip@osbar.org
Web: www.osbar.org/aap

Summary To provide summer job opportunities for Asian American and other law students in Oregon, especially those who will help the Oregon State Bar achieve its Affirmative Action objectives.

Eligibility This program is open to students currently enrolled in the first or second year of law school (or third year of a 4-year program). Applicants are not required to be enrolled at a law school in Oregon, but they must demonstrate a commitment to practice in the state. Preference is given to students who will contribute to the Oregon State Bar's Affirmative Action Program and "increase the diversity of the Oregon bench and bar to reflect the diversity of the people of Oregon." They must be interested in working in a law office during the summer; the employment should be in Oregon, although exceptions will be made if the job offers the student special experience not available within the state. Along with their application, they must submit 1) a personal statement on their history of disadvantage or barriers to educational advancement, personal experiences of discrimination, extraordinary financial obligations, composition of immediate family, extraordinary health or medical needs, and languages in which they are fluent as well as barriers they have experienced because English is a second language; and 2) a state bar statement on why they chose to attend an Oregon law school (if relevant); if they are not committed but are considering practicing in Oregon, what would help them to decide to practice in the state; and how they will improve the quality of legal service or increase access to justice in Oregon. Selection is based on financial need (30%), the personal statement (25%), the state bar statement (25%), community activities (10%), and employment history (10%).

Financial data This program pays a stipend of $7.00 per hour; the employer must then at least match that stipend.

Duration 12 weeks during the summer.

Additional information The selected students are responsible for finding work under this program.

Number awarded Approximately 20 each year.

Deadline January of each year.

[689]
OREGON STATE BAR SCHOLARSHIPS

Oregon State Bar
Attn: Affirmative Action Program
16037 S.W. Upper Boones Ferry Road
P.O. Box 231935
Tigard, OR 97281-1935
(503) 431-6338
Toll Free: (800) 452-8260, ext. 338 (within OR)
Fax: (503) 598-6938   E-mail: eyip@osbar.org
Web: www.osbar.org/aap

Summary To provide financial assistance to Asian Americans and other entering and continuing law students from any state, especially those who will help the Oregon State Bar achieve its Affirmative Action objectives.

Eligibility This program is open to students entering or continuing at 1 of the law schools in Oregon (Willamette, University of Oregon, and Lewis and Clark). Preference is given to students who will contribute to the Oregon State Bar's Affirmative Action Program to "increase the diversity of the Oregon bench and bar to reflect the diversity of the people of Oregon." Applicants must submit 1) a personal statement on their history of disadvantage or barriers to educational advancement, personal experiences of discrimination, extraordinary financial obligations, composition of immediate family, extraordinary health or medical needs, and languages in which they are fluent as well as barriers they have experienced because English is a second language; and 2) a state bar statement on why they chose to attend an Oregon law school; if they are not committed but are considering practicing in Oregon, what would help them to decide to practice in the state; and how they will improve the quality of legal service or increase access to justice in Oregon. Selection is based on financial need (30%), the personal statement (25%), the state bar statement (25%), community activities (10%), and employment history (10%).

Financial data The stipend is $2,000 per year. Funds are credited to the recipient's law school tuition account.

Duration 1 year; recipients may reapply.

Number awarded 10 each year.

Deadline March of each year.

[690]
OREGON-IDAHO CONFERENCE UMC ETHNIC MINORITY LEADERSHIP AWARDS

United Methodist Church-Oregon-Idaho Conference
Attn: Campus Ministries and Higher Education Ministry
  Team
1505 S.W. 18th Avenue
Portland, OR 97201-2524
(503) 226-7031   Toll Free: (800) J-WESLEY
Web: www.umoi.org/pages/detail/45

Summary To provide financial assistance to Asian Americans and other minorities who are Methodists from Oregon and Idaho and interested in attending a college or graduate school in any state.

Eligibility This program is open to members of ethnic minority groups (African American, Native American, Asian, Pacific Islander, or Hispanic) who have belonged to a congregation affiliated with the Oregon-Idaho Conference of the United Methodist Church (UMC) for at least 1 year. Applicants must be enrolled or planning to enroll full time as an undergraduate or graduate student at a 2- or 4-year college or university in any state. Along with their application, they must submit personal statements on 1) their faith development; and 2) where they sense God is calling the church in the present and future. Selection is based primarily on demonstrated leadership excellence and/or the potential for leadership excellence in the UMC and in community projects or activities, but other factors, including financial need, are also considered.

Financial data The stipend is $750.

Duration 1 year.

Number awarded 1 each year.

Deadline April of each year.

[691]
ORGANIC CHEMISTRY GRADUATE STUDENT FELLOWSHIPS

American Chemical Society
Division of Organic Chemistry
1155 16th Street, N.W.
Washington, DC 20036
(202) 872-4401　　Toll Free: (800) 227-5558, ext. 4401
E-mail: division@acs.org
Web: www.organicdivision.org/?nd=graduate_fellowship

Summary To provide funding for research to members of the Division of Organic Chemistry of the American Chemical Society (particularly Asian Americans, other minorities, and women) who are working on a doctoral degree in organic chemistry.

Eligibility This program is open to members of the division who are entering the third or fourth year of a Ph.D. program in organic chemistry. Applicants must submit 3 letters of recommendation, a resume, and a short essay on a research area of their choice. U.S. citizenship or permanent resident status is required. Selection is based primarily on evidence of research accomplishment. Applications from women and minorities are especially encouraged.

Financial data The stipend is $26,000; that includes $750 for travel support to present a poster of their work at the National Organic Symposium.

Duration 1 year.

Additional information This program was established in 1982. It includes the Emmanuil Troyansky Fellowship. Current corporate sponsors include Eli Lilly, Pfizer, Roche, GlaxoSmithKline, Genentech, Organic Reactions, Organic Syntheses, Boehringer Ingelheim, and Amgen.

Number awarded Varies each year; recently, 10 of these fellowships were awarded.

Deadline May of each year.

[692]
ORGANIZATION OF CHINESE AMERICANS INTERNSHIP PROGRAM

Organization of Chinese Americans, Inc.
1322 18th Street, N.W.
Washington, DC 20036-1803
(202) 223-5500　　Fax: (202) 296-0540
E-mail: oca@ocanational.org
Web: www.ocanational.org

Summary To provide an opportunity for Asian Pacific American college and graduate students to gain summer work experience through the Organization of Chinese Americans (OCA).

Eligibility This program is open to college and graduate students who have a demonstrated interest in civil rights, Asian Pacific American issues, and public affairs. Applicants must be interested in working at the OCA national office, in a Congressional office, or in a federal agency. Along with their application, they must submit a resume, an academic transcript, an essay on why they want to participate in the internship, and 2 letters of reference. Selection criteria emphasize oral and written communication skills.

Financial data A stipend is paid (amount not specified).

Duration 10 weeks in the summer, at the OCA national office, at a Congressional office, or at a federal agency; 10 weeks in the fall, winter, or spring at the OCA national office.

Additional information At the OCA national office, general internships and development internships are available year round. Public policy, technical, communications and public relations, and scholarship services internships are available only in the summer.

Number awarded Varies each year.

Deadline March of each year for summer; July of each year for fall; November of each year for winter or spring.

[693]
PANGARAP SCHOLARSHIP

Filipino Lawyers of Washington
c/o Jeri Gonzales
Evergreen Healthcare
12040 N.E. 128th Street, MS 115
Kirkland, WA 98034
(425) 899-1000　　E-mail: jeri.gonzales@gmail.com
Web: www.filipinolawyers.org/Default.aspx?pageId=772590

Summary To provide financial assistance to students from any state who are enrolled at law schools in Washington and have a record of service to the Filipino community.

Eligibility This program is open to residents of any state currently enrolled at law schools in Washington. Applicants must have demonstrated a significant commitment to community service, particularly service to the Filipino or Filipino American community. Along with their application, they must submit a 2-page essay on what they see as a challenge facing the Filipino American community and what they feel they can do to help overcome that challenge as an attorney. Selection is based on the essay, academic achievement, work experience, activities, post-law school goals, and service to the Filipino or Filipino American community.

Financial data The stipend is $500.

Duration 1 year.

Number awarded 1 each year.

Deadline September of each year.

[694]
PATRICK D. MCJULIEN MINORITY GRADUATE SCHOLARSHIP

Association for Educational Communications and
  Technology
Attn: ECT Foundation
1800 North Stonelake Drive, Suite 2
Bloomington, IN 47408
(812) 335-7675   Toll Free: (877) 677-AECT
Fax: (812) 335-7678
Web: www.aect.org/Foundation/Awards/McJulien.asp

Summary To provide financial assistance to Asian American and other minority members of the Association for Educational Communications and Technology (AECT) working on a graduate degree in the field of educational communications and technology.

Eligibility This program is open to AECT members who are members of minority groups. Applicants must be full-time graduate students enrolled in a degree-granting program in educational technology at the master's (M.S.), specialist (Ed.S.), or doctoral (Ph.D., Ed.D.) levels. They must have a GPA of 3.0 or higher.

Financial data A stipend is awarded (amount not specified).

Duration 1 year.

Number awarded 1 each year.

Deadline July of each year.

[695]
PAUL D. WHITE SCHOLARSHIP

Baker Hostetler LLP
Attn: Attorney Recruitment and Development Manager
PNC Center
1900 East Ninth Street, Suite 3200
Cleveland, OH 44114-3482
(216) 621-0200   Fax: (216) 696-0740
E-mail: ddriscole@bakerlaw.com
Web: www.bakerlaw.com/firmdiversity/scholarship

Summary To provide financial assistance and summer work experience to Asian American and other minority law school students.

Eligibility This program is open to first- and second-year law students of African American, Hispanic, Asian American, or American Indian descent. Selection is based on law school performance, demonstrated leadership abilities (as evidenced by community and collegiate involvement), collegiate academic record, extracurricular activities, work experience, and a written personal statement.

Financial data The program provides a stipend of $7,500 for the scholarship and a paid summer clerkship with the sponsoring firm. To date, the firm has expended nearly $2.0 million in scholarships and clerkships.

Duration 1 year, including the following summer.

Additional information This program was established in 1997. Clerkships may be performed at any of the firm's offices in Chicago, Cincinnati, Cleveland, Columbus, Costa Mesa, Denver, Houston, Los Angeles, New York, Orlando, or Washington, D.C.

Number awarded 1 or more each year.

Deadline January of each year.

[696]
PAUL P. VOURAS DISSERTATION RESEARCH GRANT

Association of American Geographers
Attn: Grants and Awards
1710 16th Street, N.W.
Washington, DC 20009-3198
(202) 234-1450   Fax: (202) 234-2744
E-mail: grantsawards@aag.org
Web: www.aag.org/cs/grants/dissertation

Summary To provide funding to members of the Association of American Geographers, especially Asian Americans and other minorities, who are preparing dissertations in geography.

Eligibility This program is open to doctoral students who have been members of the association for at least 1 year, have completed all Ph.D. requirements except the dissertation, and will not have earned the doctorate by the time of the award. The applicant's dissertation supervisor must certify eligibility. Preference is given to minority applicants.

Financial data Grants are approximately $500.

Duration 1 year.

Number awarded 1 or more each year.

Deadline December of each year.

[697]
PBS&J ACHIEVEMENT SCHOLARSHIP

Conference of Minority Transportation Officials
Attn: National Scholarship Program
818 18th Street, N.W., Suite 850
Washington, DC 20006
(202) 530-0551   Fax: (202) 530-0617
Web: www.comto.org/news-youth.php

Summary To provide financial assistance to Asian American and other minority high school seniors, undergraduates, and graduate students interested in studying the field of transportation.

Eligibility This program is open to minority graduating high school seniors, current undergraduates, and graduate students interested in the field of transportation. Applicants must be enrolled or planning to enroll full time at an accredited college, university, or vocational/technical institution. They must have a GPA of 2.0 or higher. Along with their application, they must submit a cover letter with a 500-word statement of career goals. Financial need is not considered in the selection process. U.S. citizenship is required.

Financial data The stipend is $4,000. Funds are paid directly to the recipient's college or university.

Duration 1 year.

Additional information The Conference of Minority Transportation Officials (COMTO) was established in 1971 to promote, strengthen, and expand the roles of minorities in all aspects of transportation. This program is sponsored by the engineering, architecture, and sciences company PBS&J. Recipients are expected to attend the COMTO National Scholarship Luncheon.

Number awarded 1 or more each year.

Deadline April of each year.

[698]
PERKINS COIE DIVERSITY STUDENT FELLOWSHIPS

Perkins Coie LLP
Attn: Chief Diversity Officer
131 South Dearborn Street, Suite 1700
Chicago, IL 60603-5559
(312) 324-8593   Fax: (312) 324-9400
E-mail: TCropper@perkinscoie.com
Web: www.perkinscoie.com/diversity/Diversity.aspx

Summary To provide financial assistance and work experience to Asian American and other law students who reflect the diversity of communities in the country.

Eligibility This program is open to students enrolled in the first year of a J.D. program at an ABA-accredited law school. Applicants must contribute meaningfully to the diversity of the law school student body and the legal profession. Diversity is defined broadly to include members of racial, ethnic, disabled, and sexual orientation minority groups, as well as those who may be the first person in their family to pursue higher education. Applicants must submit a 1-page personal statement that describes their unique personal history, a legal writing sample, a current resume, and undergraduate and law school transcripts. They are not required to disclose their financial circumstances, but a demonstrated need for financial assistance may be taken into consideration.

Financial data The stipend is $7,500.

Duration 1 year.

Additional information Fellows are also offered a summer associateship at their choice of the firm's offices in Anchorage, Bellevue, Boise, Chicago, Dallas, Los Angeles, Madison, Palo Alto, Phoenix, Portland, San Diego, San Francisco, Seattle, or Washington, D.C.

Number awarded Varies each year; recently, 7 of these fellowships were awarded.

Deadline January of each year.

[699]
PGA TOUR DIVERSITY INTERNSHIP PROGRAM

PGA Tour, Inc.
Attn: Minority Internship Program
100 PGA Tour Boulevard
Ponte Vedra Beach, FL 32082
(904) 285-3700
Web: www.pgatour.com/company/internships.html

Summary To provide summer work experience to Asian American and other undergraduate and graduate students who are interested in learning about the business side of golf and will contribute to diversity in the profession.

Eligibility This program is open to students who either have completed at least their sophomore year at an accredited 4-year college or university or are enrolled in graduate school. Applicants should be able to enrich the PGA Tour and its partnering organizations through diversity. They must have a GPA of 2.8 or higher. International students are eligible if they are legally permitted to work in the United States. Although all interns work in the business side of golf, the ability to play golf or knowledge of the game is not required for many positions.

Financial data Interns receive competitive wages and up to $500 for travel expenses to orientation in Ponte Vedra Beach, Florida or their initial work location. Depending on position and location, other benefits include subsidized housing, discounts on company merchandise, access to company training seminars, and possible golf privileges.

Duration Most assignments are for 10 to 12 weeks during the summer.

Additional information This program was established in 1992. Positions are available in accounting, corporate marketing, business development, international TV, information systems, event management, tournament services, tournament operations, retail licensing, sales, human resources, new media, and other areas within the PGA Tour. Most assignments are in Ponte Vedra Beach, Florida.

Number awarded Approximately 30 each year.

Deadline February of each year.

[700]
PHI DELTA PHI BALFOUR MINORITY SCHOLARSHIP PROGRAM

Phi Delta Phi International Legal Fraternity
1426 21st Street, N.W., First Floor
Washington, DC 20036
(202) 223-6801   Toll Free: (800) 368-5606
Fax: (202) 223-6808   E-mail: info@phideltaphi.org
Web: www.phideltaphi.org

Summary To provide financial assistance to Asian Americans and other minorities who are members of Phi Delta Phi International Legal Fraternity.

Eligibility All ethnic minority members of the legal fraternity are eligible to apply for this scholarship. Selection is based on participation, ethics, and scholastics.

Financial data The stipend is $3,000.

Duration 1 year.

Additional information This scholarship was established in 1997. Funding for this scholarship comes from the Lloyd G. Balfour Foundation.

Number awarded 1 each year.

Deadline October of each year.

[701]
PHILIPPINE NURSES ASSOCIATION OF AMERICA SCHOLARSHIP

Philippine Nurses Association of America
c/o Antonio B. Jayoma, Scholarship Committee Chair
3360 Chardonnay Drive
Brownsville, TX 78526
(956) 345-6042   E-mail: antoniojayoma@yahoo.com
Web: www.mypnaa.org

Summary To provide financial assistance for graduate study to members of the Philippine Nurses Association of America (PNAA).

Eligibility This program is open to PNAA members who are enrolled or admitted at an accredited program for a master's degree in nursing, post-master's study, or doctoral degree. Applicants must be endorsed by their PNAA chapter president. Along with their application, they must submit a 150-word essay on how this scholarship will help them attain their goals. Selection is based on that essay (10%), academic record (10%), 3 letters of recommendation (20%), work experience (10%), education and certification (10%), publications and research papers (10%), community activities and leadership roles (10%), professional affiliation (10%), and awards and achievements (10%).

Financial data   The stipend is $1,000 per year.

Duration   1 year; may be renewed, provided the recipient maintains a GPA of 3.0 or higher.

Number awarded   Varies each year; recently, 6 of these scholarships were awarded.

Deadline   April of each year.

[702]
PHYSICAL AND LIFE SCIENCES DIRECTORATE INTERNSHIPS

Lawrence Livermore National Laboratory
Physical and Life Sciences Directorate
Attn: Education Coordinator
7000 East Avenue, L-418
Livermore, CA 94550
(925) 422-0455   E-mail: hutcheon3@llnl.gov
Web: www-pls.llnl.gov

Summary   To provide an opportunity for undergraduate and graduate students (particularly Asian Americans, other minorities, and women) to work on summer research projects within the Physical and Life Sciences Directorate (PLS) of Lawrence Livermore National Laboratory (LLNL).

Eligibility   This program is open to full-time undergraduate and graduate students who are interested in working on research projects within the PLS Directorate of LLNL. Openings are currently available in chemistry (organic, inorganic, synthetic, analytical, computational, nuclear, and environmental) and materials science (theory, simulation and modeling, synthesis and processing, materials under extreme conditions, dynamic materials science, metallurgy, nuclear fuels, optical materials, and surface science). Applicants must have a GPA of 3.0 or higher. Selection is based on academic record, aptitude, research interests, and recommendations of instructors. Women and minorities are encouraged to apply.

Financial data   The stipend is $14 to $20 per hour for undergraduates or $4,100 to $4,900 per month for graduate students. Living accommodations and arrangements are the responsibility of the intern.

Duration   2 or 3 months, during the summer.

Number awarded   Varies each year.

Deadline   February of each year.

[703]
PNAO SCHOLARSHIP AWARD

Philippine Nurses Association of Ohio
c/o Audrey T. Godoy, President
15227 Scarlet Oak Trail
Strongsville, OH 44149
(216) 312-0510   E-mail: atgrn@roadrunner.com
Web: www.pnao.org/awards_scholarships.html

Summary   To provide financial assistance to students who have a tie to the Philippine Nurses Association of Ohio (PNAO) and are working on an undergraduate or graduate degree at a school of nursing in any state.

Eligibility   This program is open to residents of Ohio and the Philippines who are of at least 50% Filipino ethnicity and an associate member of PNAO, a relative of a member, or recommended by a member. Applicants must be enrolled in an undergraduate or graduate nursing program at a school in

any state. They must have a GPA of 3.0 or higher and be able to demonstrate financial need. Along with their application, they must submit a 1-page essay on their vision of nursing.

Financial data   The stipend is $500.

Duration   1 year.

Number awarded   2 each year.

Deadline   July of each year.

[704]
PORTER PHYSIOLOGY DEVELOPMENT AWARDS

American Physiological Society
Attn: Education Office
9650 Rockville Pike, Room 3111
Bethesda, MD 20814-3991
(301) 634-7132   Fax: (301) 634-7098
E-mail: education@the-aps.org
Web: www.the-aps.org

Summary   To provide research funding to Asian Americans and other minorities who are members of the American Physiological Society (APS) and interested in working on a doctoral degree in physiology.

Eligibility   This program is open to U.S. citizens and permanent residents who are members of racial or ethnic minority groups (Hispanic or Latino, American Indian or Alaska Native, Asian, Black or African American, or Native Hawaiian or other Pacific Islander). Applicants must be currently enrolled in or accepted to a doctoral program in physiology at a university as full-time students. They must be APS members. Selection is based on the applicant's potential for success (academic record, statement of interest, previous awards and experiences, letters of recommendation); applicant's proposed training environment (including quality of preceptor); and applicant's research and training plan (clarity and quality).

Financial data   The stipend is $28,300. No provision is made for a dependency allowance or tuition and fees.

Duration   1 year; may be renewed for 1 additional year and, in exceptional cases, for a third year.

Additional information   This program is supported by the William Townsend Porter Foundation (formerly the Harvard Apparatus Foundation). The first Porter Fellowship was awarded in 1920. In 1966 and 1967, the American Physiological Society established the Porter Physiology Development Committee to award fellowships to minority students engaged in graduate study in physiology.

Number awarded   Varies each year; recently, 8 of these fellowships were awarded.

Deadline   January of each year.

[705]
PORTLAND CHAPTER AAJA SCHOLARSHIPS

Asian American Journalists Association-Portland Chapter
c/o Amy Hsuan, Co-President
The Oregonian
1320 S.W. Broadway
Portland, OR 97201
(503) 997-4909   Fax: (503) 294-4193
E-mail: amyhsuan@news.oregonian.com
Web: chapters.aaja.org/Portland/scholar.html

Summary   To provide financial assistance to undergraduate and graduate journalism students in Oregon and southwestern Washington who have been involved in the Asian American community.

Eligibility This program is open to high school seniors, undergraduates, and graduate students who live or attend school in Oregon or southwestern Washington. Applicants must be enrolled or planning to enroll full time in a journalism program and be able to demonstrate involvement in the Asian American community. Along with their application, they must submit an essay (up to 750 words) on how they became interested in journalism or how they see themselves contributing to the Asian American community. They must also submit work samples (print: up to 3 articles; radio: up to 3 different stories on standard audio tapes; television: up to 3 different stories on a VHS tape; photojournalism: a portfolio of up to 15 entries). Selection is based on scholastic ability, commitment to journalism, sensitivity to Asian American issues as demonstrated by community involvement, journalistic ability, and financial need.

Financial data Stipends up to $2,000 are available.

Duration 1 year.

Number awarded 1 each year.

Deadline April of each year.

[706]
POST-BACCALAUREATE TRAINING IN DISPARITIES RESEARCH GRANTS

Susan G. Komen Breast Cancer Foundation
Attn: Grants Department
5005 LBJ Freeway, Suite 250
Dallas, TX 75244
(972) 855-1616   Toll Free: (866) 921-9678
Fax: (972) 855-1640
E-mail: helpdesk@komengrantsaccess.org
Web: ww5.komen.org

Summary To provide funding to graduate students (particularly Asian Americans and other minorities) who are interested in conducting research related to disparities in breast cancer outcomes.

Eligibility This program provides support to students enrolled in a master's, combined master's/doctoral, or doctoral degree program. Applications must be submitted by a full-time faculty member at their institution who is currently conducting research on disparities in breast cancer outcomes. Neither the students nor the faculty mentors are required to be U.S. citizens or residents. The application must describe a training program that combines didactic course work and hands-on laboratory, clinical, and/or public health research. The training program must ensure that all students at all levels will develop the analytic, research, scientific, clinical, and public health skills critical for them to effectively explore the basis for differences in breast cancer outcomes and to develop and translate research discoveries into clinical and public health practice to eliminate those disparities. Strong preference is given to involving trainees from populations adversely affected by disparities in breast cancer outcomes.

Financial data The grant is $45,000 per student per year for direct costs only.

Duration 2 years; a third year may be approved, based on an assessment of first-year progress.

Number awarded Varies each year; recently, 5 of these grants were awarded.

Deadline Pre-applications must be submitted by the end of September of each year; full applications are due in November.

[707]
PREDOCTORAL FELLOWSHIP IN MENTAL HEALTH AND SUBSTANCE ABUSE SERVICES

American Psychological Association
Attn: Minority Fellowship Program
750 First Street, N.E.
Washington, DC 20002-4242
(202) 336-6127   Fax: (202) 336-6012
TDD: (202) 336-6123   E-mail: mfp@apa.org
Web: www.apa.org

Summary To provide financial assistance to doctoral students (especially Asian/Pacific Islander Americans and other minorities) who are committed to providing mental health and substance abuse services to ethnic minority populations.

Eligibility Applicants must be U.S. citizens or permanent residents, enrolled full time in an accredited doctoral program, and committed to a career in psychology related to ethnic minority mental health and substance abuse services. Members of ethnic minority groups (African Americans, Hispanics/Latinos, American Indians, Alaskan Natives, Asian Americans, Native Hawaiians, and other Pacific Islanders) are especially encouraged to apply. Preference is given to students specializing in clinical, school, and counseling psychology. Students of any other specialty will be considered if they plan careers in which their training will lead to delivery of mental health or substance abuse services to ethnic minority populations. Selection is based on commitment to ethnic minority health and substance abuse services, knowledge of ethnic minority psychology or mental health issues, the fit between career goals and training environment selected, potential to become a culturally competent mental health service provider as demonstrated through accomplishments and goals, scholarship and grades, and letters of recommendation.

Financial data The stipend varies but is based on the amount established by the National Institutes of Health for predoctoral students; recently that was $21,600 per year.

Duration 1 academic or calendar year; may be renewed for up to 2 additional years.

Additional information Funding is provided by the U.S. Substance Abuse and Mental Health Services Administration.

Number awarded Varies each year.

Deadline January of each year.

[708]
PREDOCTORAL RESEARCH TRAINING FELLOWSHIPS IN EPILEPSY

Epilepsy Foundation
Attn: Research Department
8301 Professional Place
Landover, MD 20785-2237
(301) 459-3700   Toll Free: (800) EFA-1000
Fax: (301) 577-2684   TDD: (800) 332-2070
E-mail: grants@efa.org
Web: www.epilepsyfoundation.org

Summary To provide funding to doctoral candidates (especially Asian Americans, other minorities, women, and individuals with disabilities) who are interested in conducting dissertation research on a topic related to epilepsy.

Eligibility This program is open to full-time graduate students working on a Ph.D. in biochemistry, genetics, neuroscience, nursing, pharmacology, pharmacy, physiology, or psychology. Applicants must be conducting dissertation research on a topic relevant to epilepsy under the guidance of a mentor with expertise in the area of epilepsy investigation. Applications from women, members of minority groups, and people with disabilities are especially encouraged. U.S. citizenship is not required, but the project must be conducted in the United States. Selection is based on the relevance of the proposed work to epilepsy, the applicant's qualifications, the mentor's qualifications, the scientific quality of the proposed dissertation research, the quality of the training environment for research related to epilepsy, and the adequacy of the facility.

Financial data The grant is $20,000, consisting of $19,000 for a stipend and $1,000 to support travel to attend the annual meeting of the American Epilepsy Society.

Duration 1 year.

Additional information Support for this program, which began in 1998, is provided by many individuals, families, and corporations, especially the American Epilepsy Society, Abbott Laboratories, Ortho-McNeil Pharmaceutical, and Pfizer Inc.

Number awarded Varies each year.

Deadline August of each year.

[709]
PUBLIC HONORS FELLOWSHIPS OF THE OREGON STATE BAR

Oregon State Bar
Attn: Affirmative Action Program
16037 S.W. Upper Boones Ferry Road
P.O. Box 231935
Tigard, OR 97281-1935
(503) 431-6338
Toll Free: (800) 452-8260, ext. 338 (within OR)
Fax: (503) 598-6938   E-mail: eyip@osbar.org
Web: www.osbar.org/aap

Summary To provide law students in Oregon with summer work experience in public interest law, especially Asian Americans and others who will help the Oregon State Bar achieve its Affirmative Action objectives.

Eligibility This program is open to students at Oregon's law schools (Willamette, University of Oregon, and Lewis and Clark) who are not in the first or final year of study. Each school may nominate up to 5 students. Nominees must have demonstrated a career goal in public interest or public sector law. Preference is given to students who will contribute to the Oregon State Bar's Affirmative Action Program and "increase the diversity of the Oregon bench and bar to reflect the diversity of the people of Oregon." They must be interested in working in a law office during the summer; the employment should be in Oregon, although exceptions will be made if the job offers the student special experience not available within the state. Along with their application, they must submit 1) a personal statement on their history of disadvantage or barriers to educational advancement, personal experiences of discrimination, extraordinary financial obligations, composition of immediate family, extraordinary health or medical needs, and languages in which they are fluent as well as barriers they have experienced because English is a second language; and 2) a state bar statement on why they chose to attend an Oregon law school; if they are not committed but are considering practicing in Oregon, what would help them to decide to practice in the state; and how they will improve the quality of legal service or increase access to justice in Oregon. From the nominees of each school, 2 students are selected on the basis of financial need (30%), the personal statement (25%), the state bar statement (25%), and public service (20%). The information on those students is forwarded to prospective employers in Oregon and they arrange to interview the selectees.

Financial data Fellows receive a stipend of $4,800.

Duration 3 months during the summer.

Additional information There is no guarantee that all students selected by the sponsoring organization will receive fellowships at Oregon law firms.

Number awarded 6 each year: 2 from each of the law schools.

Deadline Each law school sets its own deadline.

[710]
PUBLIC INTEREST INTERNSHIPS

National Asian Pacific American Bar Association
Attn: NAPABA Law Foundation
1612 K Street, N.W., Suite 1400
Washington, DC 20006
(202) 775-9555   Fax: (202) 775-9333
E-mail: foundation@napaba.org
Web: www.napaba.org

Summary To provide funding to law students interested in a summer internship at a public interest organization that serves the Asian Pacific American community.

Eligibility Applications for grants must be submitted by public interest organizations that provide either direct legal services or impact litigation on behalf of the Asian Pacific American community. Once host organizations have been selected, the National Asian Pacific American Bar Association (NAPABA) Law Foundation solicits applicants through its website, newsletter, and Facebook page. Interested law students apply directly to host organizations, which select 3 to 5 finalists. The NAPABA Law Foundation then selects the students who will work as interns at each host organization.

Financial data The host organization receives a grant of $6,000; all funds must be used as salary for the intern. The host organization is responsible for any administrative fees, payroll processing fees, federal withholding, taxes, etc.

Duration 10 weeks during the summer.

Additional information These internships were first awarded in 2011.

Number awarded At least 2 each year.

Deadline Potential host organizations must submit their applications by October of each year. Interested students must apply by March of each year.

[711]
PUBLIC INTEREST LAW INITIATIVE SUMMER INTERNSHIPS

Public Interest Law Initiative
c/o Foley & Lardner
321 North Clark Street, 28th Floor
Chicago, IL 60610-4764
(312) 832-5127   Fax: (312) 467-6367
E-mail: pili@pili-law.org
Web: www.pili-law.org/internships.htm

Summary To provide a summer internship opportunity at public interest law agencies in the Chicago area to Asian Americans and other minority law students.

Eligibility This program is open to students in their first or second year at law schools across the country. Applicants must be interested in working at a public interest law agency in the Chicago area during the summer. The program is especially interested in recruiting a diverse group of interns; applicants should provide information about their minority status and foreign language fluency.

Financial data The stipend is $5,000.

Duration 10 weeks during the summer.

Additional information The Public Interest Law Initiative (PILI) established this program in 1977. Some of the 50 agencies where interns are assigned include the AIDS Legal Council of Chicago, Environmental Law and Policy Center of the Midwest, Lawyers' Committee for Better Housing, and National Immigrant Justice Center. PILI recruits applicants, funds stipends, and acts as a clearinghouse, but the agencies select the interns.

Number awarded Varies each year.

Deadline March of each year.

[712]
RACE RELATIONS MULTIRACIAL STUDENT SCHOLARSHIP

Christian Reformed Church
Attn: Office of Race Relations
2850 Kalamazoo Avenue, S.E.
Grand Rapids, MI 49560-0200
(616) 241-1691   Toll Free: (877) 279-9994
Fax: (616) 224-0803   E-mail: crcna@crcna.org
Web: www.crcna.org/pages/racerelations_scholar.cfm

Summary To provide financial assistance to Asian American and other undergraduate and graduate minority students interested in attending colleges related to the Christian Reformed Church in North America (CRCNA).

Eligibility Students of color in the United States and Canada are eligible to apply. Normally, applicants are expected to be members of CRCNA congregations who plan to pursue their educational goals at Calvin Theological Seminary or any of the colleges affiliated with the CRCNA. Students who have no prior history with the CRCNA must attend a CRCNA-related college or seminary for a full academic year before they are eligible to apply for this program. Students entering their sophomore year must have earned a GPA of 2.0 or higher as freshmen; students entering their junior year must have earned a GPA of 2.3 or higher as sophomores; students entering their senior year must have earned a GPA of 2.6 or higher as juniors.

Financial data First-year students receive $500 per semester. Other levels of students may receive up to $2,000 per academic year.

Duration 1 year.

Additional information This program was first established in 1971 and revised in 1991. Recipients are expected to train to engage actively in the ministry of racial reconciliation in church and in society. They must be able to work in the United States or Canada upon graduating and must consider working for 1 of the agencies of the CRCNA.

Number awarded Varies each year; recently, 31 students received a total of $21,000 in support.

Deadline March of each year.

[713]
RACIAL ETHNIC SUPPLEMENTAL GRANTS

Presbyterian Church (USA)
Attn: Office of Financial Aid for Studies
100 Witherspoon Street, Room M-052
Louisville, KY 40202-1396
(502) 569-5224   Toll Free: (888) 728-7228, ext. 5224
Fax: (502) 569-8766   E-mail: finaid@pcusa.org
Web: www.pcusa.org/financialaid/programs/grant.htm

Summary To provide financial assistance to Asian American and other minority graduate students who are Presbyterian Church (USA) members interested in preparing for church occupations.

Eligibility This program is open to racial/ethnic graduate students (Asian American, African American, Hispanic American, Native American, or Alaska Native) who are enrolled full time at a PCUSA seminary or accredited theological institution approved by their Committee on Preparation for Ministry. Applicants must be working on 1) an M.Div. degree and enrolled as an inquirer or candidate by a PCUSA presbytery, or 2) an M.A.C.E. degree and preparing for a church occupation. They must be PCUSA members, U.S. citizens or permanent residents, able to demonstrate financial need, and recommended by the financial aid officer at their theological institution. Along with their application, they must submit a 1,000-word essay on what they believe God is calling them to do in ministry.

Financial data Stipends range from $500 to $1,000 per year. Funds are intended as supplements to students who have been awarded a Presbyterian Study Grant but still demonstrate remaining financial need.

Duration 1 year; may be renewed up to 2 additional years.

Number awarded Varies each year.

Deadline June of each year.

[714]
RAILROAD AND MINE WORKERS MEMORIAL SCHOLARSHIP

Japanese American Citizens League
Attn: National Scholarship Awards
1765 Sutter Street
San Francisco, CA 94115
(415) 921-5225   Fax: (415) 931-4671
E-mail: jacl@jacl.org
Web: www.jacl.org/edu/scholar.htm

Summary To provide financial assistance for graduate study in any field to members of the Japanese American Citizens League (JACL).

Eligibility This program is open to JACL members who are attending or planning to attend an accredited college or university as a graduate student. Applicants must submit information on their involvement in JACL and a 2-page essay on a topic that changes annually but relates to Japanese Americans. Selection is based on that essay, academic history, extracurricular activities, JACL involvement, scholastic honors, and a letter of recommendation.

Financial data Stipends generally average approximately $2,000.

Duration 1 year; nonrenewable.

Number awarded At least 1 each year.

Deadline March of each year.

[715]
RALPH K. FRASIER SCHOLARSHIP

Porter Wright Morris & Arthur LLP
Huntington Center
41 South High Street
Columbus, OH 43215
(614) 227-2000   Toll Free: (800) 533-2794
Fax: (614) 227-2100
Web: www.porterwright.com/diversity_statement

Summary To provide financial assistance and summer work experience to Asian American and other minority students from any state who are enrolled at designated law schools in Ohio.

Eligibility This program is open to minority students enrolled in the first year at the following law schools: Ohio State University Moritz College of Law, Capital University Law School, Case Western Reserve University School of Law, Cleveland-Marshall College of Law, University of Cincinnati College of Law, University of Dayton School of Law, and University of Toledo College of Law. Applicants must submit undergraduate and law school transcripts, a resume, and an essay in the form of a legal memorandum on a hypothetical law case. They must also indicate their choice of the sponsoring firm's offices in Cleveland and Columbus for a summer clerkship.

Financial data The program provides a competitive salary for the summer clerkship and a stipend of $5,000 for the second year of law school.

Duration 1 year.

Additional information This program was established in 2005.

Number awarded 2 each year: 1 for a clerkship in Cleveland and 1 for a clerkship in Columbus.

Deadline January of each year.

[716]
RALPH W. SHRADER DIVERSITY SCHOLARSHIPS

Armed Forces Communications and Electronics Association
Attn: AFCEA Educational Foundation
4400 Fair Lakes Court
Fairfax, VA 22033-3899
(703) 631-6149   Toll Free: (800) 336-4583, ext. 6149
Fax: (703) 631-4693   E-mail: scholarship@afcea.org
Web: www.afcea.org

Summary To provide financial assistance to Asian American and other minority master's degree students in fields related to communications and electronics.

Eligibility This program is open to U.S. citizens working on a master's degree at an accredited college or university in the United States. Applicants must be enrolled full time and studying computer science, computer technology, engineering (chemical, electrical, electronic, communications, or systems), mathematics, physics, management information systems, or a field directly related to the support of U.S. national security or intelligence enterprises. At least 1 of these scholarships is set aside for a woman or a minority. Selection is based primarily on academic excellence.

Financial data The stipend is $3,000. Funds are paid directly to the recipient.

Duration 1 year.

Additional information This program is sponsored by Booz Allen Hamilton.

Number awarded Up to 5 each year, at least 1 of which is for a woman or minority candidate.

Deadline February of each year.

[717]
RAMA SCHOLARSHIP FOR THE AMERICAN DREAM

American Hotel & Lodging Educational Foundation
Attn: Manager of Foundation Programs
1201 New York Avenue, N.W., Suite 600
Washington, DC 20005-3931
(202) 289-3181   Fax: (202) 289-3199
E-mail: ahlef@ahlef.org
Web: www.ahlef.org/content.aspx?id=19820

Summary To provide financial assistance to Asian American and other minority undergraduate and graduate students working on a degree in hotel management at designated schools.

Eligibility This program is open to U.S. citizens and permanent residents enrolled as full-time undergraduate or graduate students with a GPA of 2.5 or higher. Applicants must be attending 1 of 13 designated hospitality management schools, which select the recipients. Preference is given to students of Asian-Indian descent and other minority groups and to JHM Hotel employees and their dependents.

Financial data The stipend varies at each of the participating schools, but ranges from $1,000 to $3,000.

Duration 1 year.

Additional information This program was established by JHM Hotels, Inc. in 1998. The participating institutions are Bethune-Cookman College, California State Polytechnic University at Pomona, Cornell University, Florida International

University, Georgia State University, Greenville Technical College, Howard University, Johnson & Wales University (Providence, Rhode Island), New York University, University of Central Florida, University of Houston, University of South Carolina, and Virginia Polytechnic Institute and State University.

Number awarded Varies each year; recently, 20 of these scholarships were awarded. Since the program was established, it has awarded more than $491,000 to 287 recipients.

Deadline April of each year.

[718]
RAYMOND L. OCAMPO JR. SCHOLARSHIP

Filipino Bar Association of Northern California
268 Bush Street, Suite 2928
San Francisco, CA 94104
E-mail: fbancinfo@gmail.com
Web: www.fbanc.org/law-students

Summary To provide financial assistance to entering or continuing law students who are interested in serving the Filipino American community.

Eligibility This program is open to currently-enrolled and entering law students who have a tie to the Filipino American community and intend to provide legal services to that community after graduation from law school. Applicants must submit a current transcript or admit letter, a resume, and a 2-page essay on why they want to become a lawyer and what the sponsor can do to get Filipinos interested in a law career. An interview may be required.

Financial data The stipend is $2,500.

Duration 1 year.

Additional information This program was established in 2000 as a result of a gift from Raymond L. Ocampo, Jr., who founded the Filipino Bar Association of Northern California in 1980.

Number awarded 1 each year.

Deadline March of each year.

[719]
RDW GROUP, INC. MINORITY SCHOLARSHIP FOR COMMUNICATIONS

Rhode Island Foundation
Attn: Funds Administrator
One Union Station
Providence, RI 02903
(401) 427-4017   Fax: (401) 331-8085
E-mail: lmonahan@rifoundation.org
Web: www.rifoundation.org

Summary To provide financial assistance to Asian Americans and other undergraduate and graduate students of color in Rhode Island who are interested in preparing for a career in communications at a school in any state.

Eligibility This program is open to undergraduate and graduate students at colleges and universities in any state who are Asian Americans or other Rhode Island residents of color. Applicants must intend to work on a degree in communications (including computer graphics, art, cinematography, or other fields that would prepare them for a career in advertising). They must be able to demonstrate financial need and a commitment to a career in communications. Along with their application, they must submit an essay (up to 300 words) on the impact they would like to have on the communications field.

Financial data The stipend ranges from $1,000 to $2,500 per year.

Duration 1 year; recipients may reapply.

Additional information This program is sponsored by the RDW Group, Inc.

Number awarded 1 each year.

Deadline April of each year.

[720]
REAL PROPERTY LAW SECTION MINORITY FELLOWSHIP

The New York Bar Foundation
One Elk Street
Albany, NY 12207
(518) 487-5651   Fax: (518) 487-5699
E-mail: foundation@tnybf.org
Web: www.tnybf.org/restrictedfunds.htm

Summary To provide an opportunity for Asian American and other minority residents of any state attending law school in New York to gain summer work experience at a public interest organization that represents tenants in local landlord/tenant cases.

Eligibility This program is open to minority students from any state who are enrolled at a law school in New York state. Students must be interested in working during the summer for a public interest legal organization in the state that represents tenants in local landlord/tenant cases. Applications must be submitted by the organization, which must be located in New York City or on Long Island.

Financial data The stipend is $3,333.

Duration 8 weeks during the summer.

Additional information This program was established in 2007 by the Real Property Law Section of the New York State Bar Association. It is administered by The New York Bar Foundation.

Number awarded 1 or more each year.

Deadline October of each year.

[721]
REED SMITH DIVERSE SCHOLARS PROGRAM

Reed Smith LLP
Attn: U.S. Director of Legal Recruiting
2500 One Liberty Place
1650 Market Street
Philadelphia, PA 19103
(215) 851-8100   E-mail: dlevin@reedsmith.com
Web: diversity.reedsmith.com

Summary To provide financial assistance and summer work experience to Asian American and other law students who are committed to diversity.

Eligibility This program is open to students completing their first year of law school. Applicants must be able to demonstrate a record of academic excellence and a commitment to diversity, inclusion, and community. Along with their application, they must submit 500-word statements on 1) the goals of diversity and inclusion in the legal profession and how their life experiences will enable them to contribute to those goals; and 2) their community involvement and/or volunteer efforts.

Financial data The stipend is $10,000. Recipients are also offered a summer associate position at their choice of 8 of the firm's U.S. offices after completion of their second year of law school.

Duration 1 year (the second year of law school).

Additional information The firm established this program in 2008 as part of its commitment to promote diversity in the legal profession.

Number awarded Several each year.

Deadline July of each year.

[722]
RESOURCES FOR THE FUTURE SUMMER INTERNSHIPS

Resources for the Future
Attn: Internship Coordinator
1616 P Street, N.W., Suite 600
Washington, DC 20036-1400
(202) 328-5008   Fax: (202) 939-3460
E-mail: IC@rff.org
Web: www.rff.org

Summary To provide internships to undergraduate and graduate students (particularly Asian Americans, other minorities, and women) who are interested in working on research projects in public policy during the summer.

Eligibility This program is open to undergraduate and graduate students (with priority to graduate students) interested in an internship at Resources for the Future (RFF). Applicants must be working on a degree in the social and natural sciences and have training in economics and quantitative methods or an interest in public policy. They should display strong writing skills and a desire to analyze complex environmental policy problems amenable to interdisciplinary methods. The ability to work without supervision in a careful and conscientious manner is essential. Women and minority candidates are strongly encouraged to apply. Both U.S. and non-U.S. citizens are eligible, if the latter have proper work and residency documentation.

Financial data The stipend is $375 per week for graduate students or $350 per week for undergraduates. Housing assistance is not provided.

Duration 10 weeks during the summer; beginning and ending dates can be adjusted to meet particular student needs.

Deadline March of each year.

[723]
REVEREND H. JOHN YAMASHITA MEMORIAL SCHOLARSHIP

Japanese American Citizens League
Attn: National Scholarship Awards
1765 Sutter Street
San Francisco, CA 94115
(415) 921-5225   Fax: (415) 931-4671
E-mail: jacl@jacl.org
Web: www.jacl.org/edu/scholar.htm

Summary To provide financial assistance for graduate study in any field to members of the Japanese American Citizens League (JACL).

Eligibility This program is open to JACL members who are attending or planning to attend an accredited college or uni-

versity as a graduate student. Applicants must submit information on their involvement in JACL and a 2-page essay on a topic that changes annually but relates to Japanese Americans. Selection is based on that essay, academic history, extracurricular activities, JACL involvement, scholastic honors, and a letter of recommendation.

Financial data Stipends generally average approximately $2,000.

Duration 1 year; nonrenewable.

Number awarded At least 1 each year.

Deadline March of each year.

[724]
RICHARD AND HELEN BROWN COREM SCHOLARSHIPS

United Church of Christ
Parish Life and Leadership Ministry Team
Attn: COREM Administrator
700 Prospect Avenue East
Cleveland, OH 44115-1100
(216) 736-2113   Toll Free: (866) 822-8224, ext. 2113
Fax: (216) 736-3783
Web: www.ucc.org/seminarians/ucc-scholarships-for.html

Summary To provide financial assistance to Asian American and other minority seminary students who are interested in becoming a pastor in the United Church of Christ (UCC).

Eligibility This program is open to students at accredited seminaries who have been members of a UCC congregation for at least 1 year. Applicants must work through 1 of the member bodies of the Council for Racial and Ethnic Ministries (COREM): United Black Christians (UBC), Ministers for Racial, Social and Economic Justice (MRSEJ), Council for Hispanic Ministries (CHM), Pacific Islander and Asian American Ministries (PAAM), or Council for American Indian Ministries (CAIM). They must 1) have a GPA of 3.0 or higher, 2) be enrolled in a course of study leading to ordained ministry, 3) be in care of an association or conference at the time of application, and 4) demonstrate leadership ability through participation in their local church, association, conference, or academic environment.

Financial data Stipends are approximately $10,000 per year.

Duration 1 year.

Number awarded Varies each year; recently, 4 scholarships were awarded by UBC, 3 by MRSEJ, and 2 by CHM.

Deadline Deadline not specified.

[725]
RICHARD D. HAILEY AAJ LAW STUDENT SCHOLARSHIPS

American Association for Justice
Attn: Minority Caucus
777 Sixth Street, N.W., Suite 200
Washington, DC 20001
(202) 965-3500, ext. 8302
Toll Free: (800) 424-2725, ext. 8302
Fax: (202) 965-0355
E-mail: brandon.grubesky@justice.org
Web: www.justice.org/cps/rde/xchg/justice/hs.xsl/1737.htm

Summary To provide financial assistance for law school to Asian American and other minority student members of the American Association for Justice (AAJ).

Eligibility This program is open to Asian American, African American, Hispanic, Native American, and biracial members of the association who are entering the first, second, or third year of law school. Applicants must submit a 500-word essay on how they meet the selection criteria: commitment to the association, involvement in student chapter and minority caucus activities, desire to represent victims, interest and proficiency of skills in trial advocacy, and financial need.

Financial data The stipend is $1,000.

Duration 1 year.

Additional information The American Association for Justice was formerly the Association of Trial Lawyers of America.

Number awarded Up to 6 each year.

Deadline May of each year.

[726]
ROBERT T. MATSUI ANNUAL WRITING COMPETITION

Asian Pacific American Bar Association Educational Fund
P.O. Box 2209
Washington, DC 20013-2209
Fax: (202) 408-4400   E-mail: aefboard@gmail.com
Web: www.aefdc.com/?page_id=93

Summary To recognize and reward law students who submit outstanding articles on topics of interest to the Asian Pacific American legal community.

Eligibility This competition is open to law students in the United States. Applicants must submit an original law review article, up to 10,000 words in length, that has not been published. The topic must relate to Asian Pacific Americans and the law.

Financial data The award is $1,500.

Duration The award is presented annually.

Additional information This competition was established in 2005. The winning entry is published by the *Asian Pacific American Law Journal* at the University of California, Los Angeles School of Law.

Number awarded 1 each year.

Deadline May of each year.

[727]
ROY H. POLLACK SCHOLARSHIP

Unitarian Universalist Association
Attn: Ministerial Credentialing Office
25 Beacon Street
Boston, MA 02108-2800
(617) 948-6403   Fax: (617) 742-2875
E-mail: mco@uua.org
Web: www.uua.org

Summary To provide financial assistance to seminary students (especially Asian American and other minority students) who are preparing for the Unitarian Universalist (UU) ministry.

Eligibility This program is open to seminary students who are enrolled full or at least half time in their second or third year in a UU ministerial training program with aspirant or candidate status. Applicants are generally citizens of the United States or Canada. Priority is given first to those who have demonstrated outstanding ministerial ability and secondarily to students with the greatest financial need (especially persons of color).

Financial data The stipend ranges from $1,000 to $11,000 per year.

Duration 1 year.

Number awarded Varies each year; recently, 2 of these scholarships were awarded.

Deadline April of each year.

[728]
R.P. AND J.L. CARR SOCIAL JUSTICE SCHOLARSHIP

Organization of Chinese Americans-Wisconsin Chapter
Attn: Scholarship Committee
P.O. Box 301
Dousman, WI 53118
(414) 258-2410   E-mail: ocawischolarship@yahoo.com
Web: www.ocawi.org

Summary To provide financial assistance to graduate students who are members of the Wisconsin Chapter of the Organization of Chinese Americans (OCA-WI) and interested in working on a degree in a field related to peace and social justice.

Eligibility This program is open to OCA-WI members who are enrolled or planning to enroll full time in a graduate program at an accredited college or university in any state. Applicants must be interested in working on a degree in a field related to peace and social justice (e.g., law, public policy, political science, community development). Along with their application, they must submit a 2-page personal statement that describes themselves, their field of study, pertinent personal history, and professional plans. U.S. citizenship or permanent resident status is required.

Financial data The stipend is $2,000.

Duration 1 year.

Number awarded 1 each year.

Deadline April of each year.

[729]
RUDEN MCCLOSKY DIVERSITY SCHOLARSHIP PROGRAM

Community Foundation of Sarasota County
Attn: Scholarship Manager
2635 Fruitville Road
P.O. Box 49587
Sarasota, FL 34230-6587
(941) 556-7156   Fax: (941) 556-7157
E-mail: mimi@cfsarasota.org
Web: www.cfsarasota.org/Default.aspx?tabid=263

Summary To provide financial assistance to Asian American and other minority students from any state attending designated law schools (most of which are in Florida).

Eligibility This program is open to racial and ethnic minority students from any state who are members of groups traditionally underrepresented in the legal profession. Applicants must be entering their second year of full-time study at the University of Florida Levin College of Law, Florida State University College of Law, Stetson University College of Law, Nova Southeastern University Shepard Broad Law Center,

St. Thomas University School of Law, Florida A&M University College of Law, Howard University College of Law, Texas Southern University Thurgood Marshall School of Law, Florida Coastal School of Law, Florida International University College of Law, or Barry University Dwayne O. Andreas School of Law. They must have a GPA of 2.6 or higher. Along with their application, they must submit a 1,000-word personal statement that describes their personal strengths, their contributions through community service, any special or unusual circumstances that may have affected their academic performance, or their personal and family history of educational or socioeconomic disadvantage; it must include their plans for practicing law in Florida after graduation. Applicants may also include information about their financial circumstances if they wish to have those considered in the selection process. U.S. citizenship or permanent resident status is required.

Financial data   The stipend is $2,500 per semester.

Duration   1 semester (the spring semester of the second year of law school); may be renewed 1 additional semester (the fall semester of the third year).

Additional information   This program is sponsored by the Florida law firm Ruden McClosky, which makes the final selection of recipients, and administered by the Community Foundation of Sarasota County.

Number awarded   1 or more each year.

Deadline   July of each year.

[730]
RYU FAMILY FOUNDATION SCHOLARSHIP GRANTS

Ryu Family Foundation, Inc.
186 Parish Drive
Wayne, NJ 07470
(973) 692-9696   Fax: (973) 692-0999
Web: www.seolbong.org

Summary   To provide financial assistance to Korean and Korean American students in the Northeast who are working on an undergraduate or graduate degree in any field.

Eligibility   This program is open to Korean Americans (U.S. citizens) and Koreans (with or without permanent resident status). Applicants must be enrolled full time and working on an undergraduate or graduate degree; have a GPA of 3.5 or higher; be able to document financial need; and be either residing or attending college in 1 of the following 10 northeastern states: Connecticut, Delaware, Maine, Massachusetts, New Hampshire, New Jersey, New York, Pennsylvania, Rhode Island, or Vermont. Along with their application, they must submit a 500-word essay on a subject that changes annually; recently, students were asked to present their opinion of the future of the United States.

Financial data   A stipend is awarded (amount not specified). Checks are made out jointly to the recipient and the recipient's school.

Duration   1 year; may be renewed.

Deadline   November of each year.

[731]
SABA FOUNDATION PUBLIC INTEREST FELLOWSHIPS

South Asian Bar Association of Northern California
Attn: SABA Foundation
P.O. Box 2733
San Francisco, CA 94126
(415) 894-9442   E-mail: president@southasianbar.org
Web: www.southasianbar.org/saba-foundation/fellowship

Summary   To provide summer work experience in public interest law that will benefit the South Asian community of northern California, especially to students at law schools in the area.

Eligibility   This program is open to students from any state enrolled at an ABA-accredited law school at least part time who can demonstrate dedication and commitment to public interest work benefiting the South Asian community in northern California. Strong preference is given to applicants enrolled at law schools in northern California and employed at an organization in the area doing work that directly impacts the South Asian community. Selection is based on academic merit, participation in extracurricular and community activities, professional training, and financial need. Interviews may be required.

Financial data   The stipend is $3,000 or $2,500.

Duration   Summer months.

Additional information   This program started in 2005.

Number awarded   Varies each year; recently, 7 of these fellowships were awarded: 1 at $3,000 and 6 at $2,500.

Deadline   March of each year.

[732]
SAJA SCHOLARSHIPS

South Asian Journalists Association
c/o Aseem Chhabra, Awards Committee Chair
4315 46th Street, Apartment E10
Sunnyside, NY 11104-2015
E-mail: chhabs@aol.com
Web: www.saja.org/programs/scholarships

Summary   To provide financial assistance for undergraduate and graduate study to journalism students of south Asian descent.

Eligibility   This program is open to students of south Asian descent (including Bangladesh, Bhutan, India, Maldives, Nepal, Pakistan, and Sri Lanka; Indo-Caribbeans are also eligible). Applicants must be serious about preparing for a journalism career and must provide evidence they plan to do so through courses, internships, or freelancing. They may be 1) high school seniors about to enroll in an accredited college or university; 2) current students in an accredited college or university in the United States or Canada; or 3) students enrolled or about to enter a graduate program in the United States or Canada. Applicants with financial hardship are given special consideration. Selection is based on interest in journalism, writing skills, participation in the sponsoring organization, reasons for entering journalism, and financial need.

Financial data   The stipends are $1,000 for high school seniors, $1,500 for current college students, or $2,000 for graduate students.

Duration   1 year.

Additional information Recipients are expected to give back to the South Asian Journalists Association (SAJA) by volunteering at the annual convention or at other events during the year.

Number awarded 4 each year: 1 to a high school senior entering college, 1 to a current college student, and 2 to graduate students.

Deadline March of each year.

[733]
SANDIA MASTER'S FELLOWSHIP PROGRAM

Sandia National Laboratories
Attn: Staffing Department 3535
MS-1023
P.O. Box 5800
Albuquerque, NM 87185-1023
(505) 844-3441   Fax: (505) 844-6636
E-mail: empsite@sandia.gov
Web: www.sandia.gov/careers/fellowships.html

Summary To enable Asian American and other minority students to obtain a master's degree in engineering or computer science and also work at Sandia National Laboratories.

Eligibility This program is open to minority (Asian, American Indian, Black, or Hispanic) students who have a bachelor's degree in engineering or computer science and a GPA of 3.2 or higher. Participants must apply to 3 schools jointly selected by the program and themselves. They must be prepared to obtain a master's degree within 1 year. The fields of study (not all fields are available at all participating universities) include computer science, electrical engineering, mechanical engineering, civil engineering, chemical engineering, nuclear engineering, materials sciences, and petroleum engineering. Applicants must be interested in working at the sponsor's laboratories during the summer between graduation from college and the beginning of their graduate program, and then following completion of their master's degree. U.S. citizenship is required.

Financial data Participants receive a competitive salary while working at the laboratories on a full-time basis and a stipend while attending school.

Duration 1 year.

Additional information During their summer assignment, participants work at the laboratories, either in Albuquerque, New Mexico or in Livermore, California. Upon successful completion of the program, they return to Sandia's hiring organization as a full-time member of the technical staff. This program began in 1968. Application to schools where students received their undergraduate degree is not recommended. After the schools accept an applicant, the choice of a school is made jointly by the laboratories and the participant.

Number awarded Varies each year; since the program began, more than 350 engineers and computer scientists have gone to work at Sandia with master's degrees.

Deadline Deadline not specified.

[734]
SBE DOCTORAL DISSERTATION RESEARCH IMPROVEMENT GRANTS

National Science Foundation
Attn: Directorate for Social, Behavioral, and Economic Sciences
4201 Wilson Boulevard, Room 905N
Arlington, VA 22230
(703) 292-8700   Fax: (703) 292-9083
TDD: (800) 281-8749
Web: www.nsf.gov/funding/pgm_summ.jsp?pims_id=13453

Summary To provide partial support to doctoral candidates (particularly Asian Americans, other minorities, women, and individuals with disabilities) who are conducting dissertation research in areas of interest to the Directorate for Social, Behavioral, and Economic Sciences (SBE) of the National Science Foundation (NSF).

Eligibility Applications may be submitted through regular university channels by dissertation advisers on behalf of graduate students who have advanced to candidacy and have begun or are about to begin dissertation research. Students must be enrolled at U.S. institutions, but they need not be U.S. citizens. The proposed research must relate to SBE's Division of Behavioral and Cognitive Sciences (archaeology, cultural anthropology, geography and spatial sciences, linguistics, or physical anthropology); Division of Social and Economic Sciences (decision, risk, and management science; economics; law and social science; methodology, measurement, and statistics; political science; sociology; or science, technology, and society); Division of Science Resources Statistics (research on science and technology surveys and statistics); or Office of Multidisciplinary Activities (science and innovation policy). Women, minorities, and persons with disabilities are strongly encouraged to apply.

Financial data Grants have the limited purpose of providing funds to enhance the quality of dissertation research. They are to be used exclusively for necessary expenses incurred in the actual conduct of the dissertation research, including (but not limited to) conducting field research in settings away from campus that would not otherwise be possible, data collection and sample survey costs, payments to subjects or informants, specialized research equipment, analysis and services not otherwise available, supplies, travel to archives, travel to specialized facilities or field research locations, and partial living expenses for conducting necessary research away from the student's U.S. academic institution. Funding is not provided for stipends, tuition, textbooks, journals, allowances for dependents, travel to scientific meetings, publication costs, dissertation preparation or reproduction, or indirect costs.

Duration Up to 2 years.

Number awarded 200 to 300 each year. Approximately $2.5 million is available for this program annually.

Deadline Deadline dates for the submission of dissertation improvement grant proposals differ by program within the divisions of the SBE Directorate; applicants should obtain information regarding target dates for proposals from the relevant program.

[735]
SCCLA SCHOLARSHIPS AND FELLOWSHIPS

Southern California Chinese Lawyers Association
Attn: SCCLA Foundation
P.O. Box 861959
Los Angeles, CA 90086-1959
Web: www.sccla.org/about_foundation.php

Summary To provide financial assistance and work experience to Asian Pacific American students from any state enrolled at law schools in southern California.

Eligibility This program is open to Asian Pacific American students at law schools in southern California. Applicants for scholarships may be in any year of law school, including entering first-year students and fourth-year evening students. They must also be interested in serving a clerkship at the Asian Pacific American Legal Center in Los Angeles for 10 to 15 hours per semester. Selection is based on academic accomplishment, financial need, and potential contribution to the Chinese American community.

Financial data The stipend is $1,500 for fellowships or $1,000 for scholarships.

Duration 1 year.

Additional information This program includes the following named scholarships: the Ming Y. Moy Memorial Scholarship, the Justice Elwood Lui Scholarship, the Lee Gum Low Presidential Scholarship, and the Margaret and Ned Good Scholarships.

Number awarded Varies each year; recently, 15 of these scholarships and fellowships were awarded.

Deadline February of each year.

[736]
SCHOLARSHIPS FOR MINORITY ACCOUNTING STUDENTS

American Institute of Certified Public Accountants
Attn: Academic and Career Development Division
220 Leigh Farm Road
Durham, NC 27707-8110
(919) 402-4931   Fax: (919) 419-4705
E-mail: MIC_Programs@aicpa.org
Web: www.aicpa.org/members/div/career/mini/smas.htm

Summary To provide financial assistance to Asian Americans and other minorities interested in studying accounting at the undergraduate or graduate school level.

Eligibility This program is open to minority undergraduate and graduate students, enrolled full time, who have a GPA of 3.3 or higher (both cumulatively and in their major) and intend to pursue a C.P.A. credential. Undergraduates must have completed at least 30 semester hours, including at least 6 semester hours of a major in accounting. Graduate students must be working on a master's degree in accounting, finance, taxation, or a related program. Applicants must be U.S. citizens or permanent residents and student affiliate members of the American Institute of Certified Public Accountants (AICPA). The program defines minority students as those whose heritage is Black or African American, Hispanic or Latino, Native American, or Asian American.

Financial data Stipends range from $1,500 to $3,000 per year. Funds are disbursed directly to the recipient's school.

Duration 1 year; may be renewed up to 3 additional years or until completion of a bachelor's or master's degree, whichever is earlier.

Additional information This program is administered by The Center for Scholarship Administration, E-mail: allison-lee@bellsouth.net. The most outstanding applicant for this program is awarded the Stuart A. Kessler Scholarship for Minority Students.

Number awarded Varies each year; recently, 94 students received funding through this program.

Deadline March of each year.

[737]
SCHWABE, WILLIAMSON & WYATT SUMMER ASSOCIATE DIVERSITY SCHOLARSHIP

Schwabe, Williamson & Wyatt, Attorneys at Law
Attn: Attorney Recruiting Administrator
1211 S.W. Fifth Avenue, Suite 1500-2000
Portland, OR 97204
(503) 796-2889   Fax: (503) 796-2900
E-mail: dcphillips@schwabe.com
Web: www.schwabe.com/recruitdiversity.aspx

Summary To provide financial assistance and summer work experience in Portland, Oregon to Asian American and other law students who will contribute to the diversity of the legal profession.

Eligibility This program is open to first-year students working on a J.D. degree at an ABA-accredited law school. Applicants must 1) contribute to the diversity of the law school student body and the legal community; 2) possess a record of academic achievement, capacity, and leadership as an undergraduate and in law school that indicates promise for a successful career in the legal profession; and 3) demonstrate a commitment to practice law in the Pacific Northwest upon completion of law school. They must be interested in a paid summer associateship at the sponsoring law firm's office in Portland, Oregon. Along with their application, they must submit a resume, undergraduate and law school transcripts, a legal writing sample, and a 1- to 2-page personal statement explaining their interest in the scholarship and how they will contribute to diversity in the legal community.

Financial data The program provides a paid summer associateship during the summer following completion of the first year of law school and an academic scholarship of $7,500 to help pay tuition and other expenses during the recipient's second year of law school.

Duration 1 year.

Number awarded 1 each year.

Deadline January of each year.

[738]
SECTION OF BUSINESS LAW DIVERSITY CLERKSHIP PROGRAM

American Bar Association
Attn: Section of Business Law
321 North Clark Street
Chicago, IL 60654-7598
(312) 988-5588   Fax: (312) 988-5578
E-mail: businesslaw@abanet.org
Web: www.abanet.org/buslaw/students/clerkship.shtml

Summary To provide summer work experience in business law to Asian American and other student members of the American Bar Association (ABA) and its Section of Business Law who will help the section to fulfill its goal of promoting diversity.

Eligibility This program is open to first- and second-year students at ABA-accredited law schools who are interested in a summer business court clerkship. Applicants must 1) be a member of an underrepresented group (student of color, woman, student with disabilities, gay, lesbian, bisexual, or transgender); or 2) have overcome social or economic disadvantages, such as a physical disability, financial constraints, or cultural impediments to becoming a law student. They must be able to demonstrate financial need. Along with their application, they must submit a 500-word essay that covers why they are interested in this clerkship program, what they would gain from the program, how it would positively influence their future professional goals as a business lawyer, and how they meet the program's criteria. Membership in the ABA and its Section of Business Law are required.

Financial data The stipend is $6,000.

Duration Summer months.

Additional information This program began in 2008. Assignments vary, but have included the Philadelphia Commerce Court, the Prince George's District Court in Upper Marlboro, Maryland, and the Delaware Court of Chancery.

Number awarded 9 each year.

Deadline January of each year.

[739]
SEO CORPORATE LAW PROGRAM

Sponsors for Educational Opportunity
Attn: Career Program
55 Exchange Place
New York, NY 10005
(212) 979-2040   Toll Free: (800) 462-2332
Fax: (646) 706-7113
E-mail: careerprogram@seo-usa.org
Web: www.seo-usa.org/Career/Corporate_Law

Summary To provide summer work experience to Asian Americans and other students of color interested in studying corporate law.

Eligibility This program is open to students of color who are college seniors or recent graduates planning to attend law school in the United States. Applicants must be interested in a summer internship at a participating law firm that specializes in corporate law. They should be able to demonstrate analytical and quantitative skills, interpersonal and community skills, maturity, and a cumulative GPA of 3.0 or higher. Along with their application, they must submit 1) information on their extracurricular and employment experience; 2) an essay of 75 to 100 words on how the program area to which they are applying related to their professional goals; and 3) an essay of 250 to 400 words on either an example of a time when they had to operate outside their "comfort zone" or their definition of success. Personal interviews are required.

Financial data Interns receive a competitive stipend.

Duration 10 weeks during the summer.

Additional information This program was established in 1980. Most internships are available in New York City or Washington, D.C.

Number awarded Varies each year.

Deadline December of each year.

[740]
SHEILA SUEN LAI SCHOLARSHIP OF LIBRARY AND INFORMATION SCIENCE

Chinese American Librarians Association
c/o Ying Xu, Scholarship Committee Chair
California State University at Los Angeles
University Library 2014
Los Angeles, CA 90032-8300
(323) 343-3959   E-mail: yxu1@calstatela.edu
Web: www.cala-web.org/node/216

Summary To provide financial assistance to Chinese American students interested in working on a graduate degree in library or information science.

Eligibility This program is open to students enrolled full time in an accredited library school in North America and working on a master's or doctoral degree. Applicants must be of Chinese nationality or Chinese descent. They must submit verification of admission to an accredited graduate program as a full-time student and/or proof of current full-time enrollment status, a curriculum vitae, a personal statement, an official transcript, and 3 letters of recommendation.

Financial data The stipend is $500.

Duration 1 year.

Additional information The program was established in 1989.

Number awarded 1 each year.

Deadline March of each year.

[741]
SHO SATO MEMORIAL SCHOLARSHIP

Japanese American Citizens League
Attn: National Scholarship Awards
1765 Sutter Street
San Francisco, CA 94115
(415) 921-5225   Fax: (415) 931-4671
E-mail: jacl@jacl.org
Web: www.jacl.org/edu/scholar.htm

Summary To provide financial assistance to student members of the Japanese American Citizens League (JACL) who are interested in preparing for a career in law.

Eligibility This program is open to JACL members who are currently enrolled or planning to enroll at an accredited law school. Applicants must submit information on their involvement in JACL and a 2-page essay on a topic that changes annually but relates to Japanese Americans. Selection is based on that essay, academic history, extracurricular activities, JACL involvement, scholastic honors, and a letter of recommendation.

Financial data Stipends generally average approximately $2,000.

Duration 1 year; nonrenewable.

Number awarded 1 each year.

Deadline March of each year.

[742]
SHRI RAM ARORA AWARD

The Minerals, Metals & Materials Society
Attn: TMS Foundation
184 Thorn Hill Road
Warrendale, PA 15086-7514
(724) 776-9000, ext. 229   Toll Free: (800) 759-4867
Fax: (724) 776-3770   E-mail: foundation@tms.org
Web: www.tms.org/Foundation/TFactivities.aspx

Summary To provide funding to graduate students and postdoctoral scholars of Indian origin who are interested in educational activities in materials science and engineering.

Eligibility This program is open to graduate students working on a degree in materials science or a related field and postdoctoral scholars actively involved in materials research. First priority is given to applicants living in India; if there are no qualified candidates from India, applicants of Indian heritage currently residing in the United States or other countries are considered. Applicants must be younger than 30 years of age. Along with their application, they must submit a statement that describes the purpose for which the award is being sought, including details on how this activity will contribute to their career plans and their aspiration to a leadership role in the materials science and engineering profession.

Financial data The award is $2,500, including a cash grant of $1,000 to be used at the recipient's discretion and $1,500 for travel, accommodation, and registration expenses to attend the annual meeting of The Minerals, Metals & Materials Society (TMS).

Duration The award is presented annually.

Additional information This award was first presented in 2000.

Number awarded 1 each year.

Deadline June of each year.

[743]
SIDLEY DIVERSITY AND INCLUSION SCHOLARSHIP

Sidley Austin LLP
Attn: Scholarships
One South Dearborn
Chicago, IL 60603
(312) 853-7000   Fax: (312) 853-7036
E-mail: scholarship@sidley.com
Web: www.sidley.com

Summary To provide financial assistance and work experience to Asian American and other law students who come from a diverse background.

Eligibility The program is open to students entering their second year of law school; preference is given to students at schools where the sponsor conducts on-campus interviews or participates in a resume collection. Applicants must have a demonstrated ability to contribute meaningfully to the diversity of the law school and/or legal profession. Along with their application, they must submit a 500-word essay that includes their thoughts on and efforts to improve diversity, how they might contribute to the sponsor's commitment to improving diversity, and their interest in practicing law at a global firm and specifically the sponsor. Selection is based on academic achievement and leadership qualities.

Financial data The stipend is $15,000.

Duration 1 year.

Additional information These scholarships were first offered in 2011. Recipients are expected to participate in the sponsor's summer associate program following their second year of law school. They must apply separately for the associate position. The firm has offices in Chicago, Dallas, Los Angeles, New York, Palo Alto, San Francisco, and Washington, D.C.

Number awarded A limited number are awarded each year.

Deadline Applications are accepted throughout the fall recruiting season.

[744]
SIDNEY B. WILLIAMS, JR. INTELLECTUAL PROPERTY LAW SCHOOL SCHOLARSHIPS

American Intellectual Property Law Education Foundation
485 Kinderkamack Road
Oradell, NJ 07649
(201) 634-1870   Fax: (201) 634-1871
E-mail: admin@aiplef.org
Web: www.aiplef.org/scholarships/sidney_b_williams

Summary To provide financial assistance to Asian American and other minority law students who are interested in preparing for a career in intellectual property law.

Eligibility This program is open to members of minority groups currently enrolled in or accepted to an ABA-accredited law school. Applicants must be U.S. citizens with a demonstrated intent to engage in the full-time practice of intellectual property law. Along with their application, they must submit a 250-word essay on how this scholarship will make a difference to them in meeting their goal of engaging in the full-time practice of intellectual property law and why they intend to do so. Selection is based on 1) demonstrated commitment to developing a career in intellectual property law; 2) academic performance at the undergraduate, graduate, and law school levels (as applicable); 3) general factors, such as leadership skills, community activities, or special accomplishments; and 4) financial need.

Financial data The stipend is $10,000 per year. Funds may be used for tuition, fees, books, supplies, room, board, and a patent bar review course.

Duration 1 year; may be renewed if the recipient maintains a GPA of 2.0 or higher.

Additional information This program, which began in 2002, is administered by the Thurgood Marshall Scholarship Fund, 80 Maiden Lane, Suite 2204, New York, NY 10038, (212) 573-8487, Fax: (212) 573-8497, E-mail: srogers@tmcfund.org. Additional funding is provided by the American Intellectual Property Law Association, the American Bar Association's Section of Intellectual Property Law, and the Minority Corporate Counsel Association. Recipients are required to join and maintain membership in the American Intellectual Property Law Association.

Number awarded Varies each year; recently, 12 of these scholarships were awarded.

Deadline March of each year.

[745]
SMITHSONIAN MINORITY STUDENT INTERNSHIP

Smithsonian Institution
Attn: Office of Fellowships
Victor Building, Suite 9300, MRC 902
P.O. Box 37012
Washington, DC 20013-7012
(202) 633-7070　　　　　　Fax: (202) 633-7069
E-mail: siofg@si.edu
Web: www.si.edu/ofg/Applications/MIP/MIPapp.htm

Summary To provide Asian American and other minority undergraduate or graduate students with the opportunity to work on research or museum procedure projects in specific areas of history, art, or science at the Smithsonian Institution.

Eligibility Internships are offered to minority students who are actively engaged in graduate study at any level or in upper-division undergraduate study. An overall GPA of 3.0 or higher is generally expected. Applicants must be interested in conducting research in specified fields of interest to the Smithsonian.

Financial data The program provides a stipend of $550 per week; travel allowances may also be offered.

Duration 10 weeks during the summer or academic year.

Additional information Eligible fields of study currently include animal behavior, ecology, and environmental science (including an emphasis on the tropics); anthropology (including archaeology); astrophysics and astronomy; earth sciences and paleobiology; evolutionary and systematic biology; history of science and technology; history of art (especially American, contemporary, African, Asian, and 20th-century art); American crafts and decorative arts; social and cultural history of the United States; and folklife.

Number awarded Varies each year.

Deadline January of each year for summer or fall; September of each year for spring.

[746]
SOCIETY FOR THE STUDY OF SOCIAL PROBLEMS RACIAL/ETHNIC MINORITY GRADUATE SCHOLARSHIP

Society for the Study of Social Problems
Attn: Executive Officer
University of Tennessee
901 McClung Tower
Knoxville, TN 37996-0490
(865) 689-1531　　　　　　Fax: (865) 689-1534
E-mail: sssp@utk.edu
Web: www.sssp1.org/index.cfm/m/261

Summary To provide funding to Asian American and other minority members of the Society for the Study of Social Problems (SSSP) who are interested in conducting research for their doctoral dissertation.

Eligibility This program is open to SSSP members who are Black or African American, Hispanic or Latino, Asian or Asian American, Native Hawaiian or other Pacific Islander, or American Indian or Alaska Native. Applicants must have completed all requirements for a Ph.D. (course work, examinations, and approval of a dissertation prospectus) except the dissertation. They must have a GPA of 3.25 or higher and be able to demonstrate financial need. Their field of study may be any of the social and/or behavioral sciences that will enable them to expand their perspectives in the investigation into social problems. U.S. citizenship or permanent resident status is required.

Financial data The stipend is $12,000. Additional grants provide $500 for the recipient to 1) attend the SSSP annual meeting prior to the year of the work to receive the award, and 2) attend the meeting after the year of the award to present a report on the work completed.

Duration 1 year.

Number awarded 1 each year.

Deadline January of each year.

[747]
SOCIETY OF AMERICAN ARCHIVISTS MOSAIC SCHOLARSHIPS

Society of American Archivists
Attn: Chair, Awards Committee
17 North State Street, Suite 1425
Chicago, IL 60602-3315
(312) 606-0722　　　　　Toll Free: (866) 722-7858
Fax: (312) 606-0728　　　E-mail: info@archivists.org
Web: www2.archivists.org

Summary To provide financial assistance to Asian American and other minority students who are working on a graduate degree in archival science.

Eligibility This program is open to minority graduate students, defined as those of American Indian/Alaska Native, Asian, Black/African American, Hispanic/Latino, or Native Hawaiian/other Pacific Islander descent. Applicants must be enrolled or planning to enroll in a graduate program or a multi-course program in archival administration. They may have completed no more than half of the credit requirements for a degree. Along with their application, they must submit a 500-word essay outlining their interests and future goals in the archives profession. U.S. or Canadian citizenship or permanent resident status is required.

Financial data The stipend is $5,000.

Duration 1 year.

Additional information This scholarship was first awarded in 2009.

Number awarded 2 each year.

Deadline February of each year.

[748]
SOCIETY OF PEDIATRIC PSYCHOLOGY DIVERSITY RESEARCH GRANT

American Psychological Association
Attn: Division 54 (Society of Pediatric Psychology)
c/o John M. Chaney
Oklahoma State University
Department of Psychology
407 North Murray
Stillwater, OK 74078
(405) 744-5703　　　　E-mail: john.chaney@okstate.edu
Web: www.societyofpediatricpsychology.org

Summary To provide funding to graduate students and postdoctorates who 1) belong to the Society of Pediatric Psychology (especially Asian Americans and members of other diverse groups) and 2) are interested in conducting research on diversity aspects of pediatric psychology.

Eligibility This program is open to current members of the society who are graduate students, fellows, or early-career (within 3 years of appointment) faculty. Applicants must be interested in conducting pediatric psychology research that features diversity-related variables, such as race or ethnicity, gender, culture, sexual orientation, language differences, socioeconomic status, and/or religiosity. Along with their application, they must submit a 2,000-word description of the project, including its purpose, methodology, predictions, and implications; a detailed budget; a current curriculum vitae, and (for students) a curriculum vitae of the faculty research mentor and a letter of support from that mentor. Selection is based on relevance to diversity in child health (5 points), significance of the study (5 points), study methods and procedures (10 points), and investigator qualifications (10 points).

Financial data Grants up to $1,000 are available. Funds may not be used for convention or meeting travel, indirect costs, stipends of principal investigators, or costs associated with manuscript preparation.

Duration The grant is presented annually.

Additional information The Society of Pediatric Psychology is Division 54 of the American Psychological Association (APA). This grant was first presented in 2008.

Number awarded 1 each year.

Deadline September of each year.

[749]
SOCIETY OF TOXICOLOGY/DR. LAXMAN DESAI GRADUATE STUDENT BEST ABSTRACT AWARD

Society of Toxicology
Attn: Association of Scientists of Indian Origin Special
  Interest Group
1821 Michael Faraday Drive, Suite 300
Reston, VA 20190-5348
(703) 438-3115   Fax: (703) 438-3113
E-mail: sothq@toxicology.org
Web: www.toxicology.org/ai/af/awards.aspx

Summary To recognize and reward graduate student members of the Society of Toxicology (SOT) who are of Indian origin and present outstanding papers at the annual meeting.

Eligibility This award is available to graduate students of Indian origin who are members of SOT and its Association of Scientists of Indian Origin (ASIO). Candidates must have an accepted abstract of a research poster or platform presentation for the SOT annual meeting. Along with the abstract, they must submit a short curriculum vitae and a recommendation letter by their academic adviser outlining their role in the research.

Financial data A plaque and a cash award (amount not specified) are presented.

Duration The award is presented annually.

Additional information This award was established in 2009.

Number awarded 1 each year.

Deadline January of each year.

[750]
SOUTH ASIAN BAR ASSOCIATION OF NEW YORK PUBLIC INTEREST FELLOWSHIPS

South Asian Bar Association of New York
c/o Moh Sharma, Vice President of Public Interest
  Fellowship
P.O. Box 1057
New York, NY 10163
(860) 916-8384   E-mail: sabanyfellowship@yahoo.com
Web: www.sabany.org/fellowships

Summary To provide funding to law students from any state who have ties to the South Asian community and have accepted an unpaid summer internship in New York.

Eligibility This program is open to first- and second-year students at law schools in any state who have accepted an unpaid public interest legal internship in New York state or the New York City metropolitan region (including Bergen, Essex, Hudson, Middlesex, Morris, Passaic, and Union counties in New Jersey and Fairfield County in Connecticut). Applicants must either 1) be of south Asian descent, or 2) have accepted an internship that specifically focuses on the needs of the local south Asian community. Selection is based on a 200-word job description that includes the mission of the host organization and the community it serves (40 points), a 500-word personal statement that explains why they selected the proposed internship and their interest in public service law (50 points), and financial need (10 points).

Financial data The stipend is $4,000.

Duration At least 10 weeks during the summer.

Additional information These fellowships were first awarded in 2004.

Number awarded Varies each year; recently, 5 of these fellowships were awarded.

Deadline March of each year.

[751]
SOUTH ASIAN BAR ASSOCIATION OF WASHINGTON DC PUBLIC INTEREST FELLOWSHIPS

South Asian Bar Association of Washington DC
c/o Padma Shah
P.O. Box 65349
Washington, DC 20035
(202) 363-2620   Fax: (202) 363-3490
E-mail: secretary@sabadc.org
Web: www.sabadc.org/public.php

Summary To provide funding to students from any state enrolled at law schools in the Washington, D.C. area who have accepted an unpaid internship and are either south Asians or interested in the south Asian community.

Eligibility This program is open to first- and second-year students from any state who are enrolled at law schools in the Washington, D.C. area. Applicants must have accepted an unpaid legal internship in the area. They must either 1) be of south Asian descent, or 2) have accepted an internship that specifically focuses on the needs of the local south Asian community. The internship must relate to public interest law and may be with a nonprofit organization, legal services organization, district attorney or public defender, government agency, or public service law firm. Along with their application, they must submit an essay that covers their previous service and/or plans to serve the South Asian community in the District of Columbia area, why they believe public interest work is important or relevant to the South Asian community, and a description of the organization where they will be working and the community it serves. Selection is based on that essay, commitment to public service, academic achievement, and financial need.

Financial data Recently, the stipend was $2,000.

Duration Summer months.

Number awarded Up to 3 each year.

Deadline May of each year.

[752]
SOUTHERN REGION KOREAN AMERICAN SCHOLARSHIPS

Korean American Scholarship Foundation
Southern Region
c/o Professor Myung Hoon Kim, Scholarship Committee
  Chair
1500 Chipping Court
Rosewell, GA 30076
(770) 274-5059   Fax: (770) 551-7097
E-mail: southern@kasf.org
Web: www.kasf.org/application_set.html

Summary To provide financial assistance to Korean American students from any state who are working on or planning to work on an undergraduate or graduate degree in any field at a school in southern states.

Eligibility This program is open to Korean American students who are currently enrolled in a college or university in the southern states as full-time undergraduate or graduate students. Applicants may reside anywhere in the United States as long as they attend school in the southern region: Alabama, Arkansas, Florida, Georgia, Louisiana, Mississippi, Oklahoma, South Carolina, Tennessee, and Texas. Selection is based on academic achievement, school activities, community service, and financial need.

Financial data Stipends are $1,000 for undergraduate, graduate, or professional students or $500 for high school seniors.

Duration 1 year; renewable.

Number awarded Varies each year; recently, 39 of these scholarships were awarded.

Deadline May of each year.

[753]
SOUTHERN REGIONAL EDUCATION BOARD DISSERTATION AWARDS

Southern Regional Education Board
Attn: Coordinator, Program and Scholar Services
592 Tenth Street N.W.
Atlanta, GA 30318-5776
(404) 879-5569   Fax: (404) 872-1477
E-mail: doctoral.scholars@sreb.org
Web: www.sreb.org/page/1113/types_of_awards.html

Summary To provide funding to Asian American and other minority students who wish to complete a Ph.D. dissertation, especially in fields of science, technology, engineering, or mathematics (STEM), while in residence at a university in the southern states.

Eligibility This program is open to U.S. citizens and permanent residents who are members of racial/ethnic minority groups (Native Americans, Hispanic Americans, Asian Americans, and African Americans) and have completed all requirements for a Ph.D. except the dissertation. Preference is given to students in STEM disciplines with particularly low minority representation, although all academic fields are eligible. Applicants must be in a position to write full time and must expect to complete their dissertation within the year of the fellowship. Eligibility is limited to individuals who plan to become full-time faculty members at a southern institution upon completion of their doctoral degree. The program does not include students working on other doctoral degrees (e.g., M.D., D.B.A., D.D.S., J.D., D.V.M., Ed.D., Pharm.D., D.N.P., D.P.T.).

Financial data Fellows receive waiver of tuition and fees (in or out of state), a stipend of $20,000, a $500 research allowance, and reimbursement of expenses for attending the Compact for Faculty Diversity's annual Institute on Teaching and Mentoring.

Duration 1 year; nonrenewable.

Additional information This program was established in 1993 as part of the Compact for Faculty Diversity, supported by the Pew Charitable Trusts and the Ford Foundation.

Number awarded Varies each year.

Deadline February of each year.

[754]
SPECTRUM SCHOLARSHIP PROGRAM

American Library Association
Attn: Office for Diversity
50 East Huron Street
Chicago, IL 60611-2795
(312) 280-5048   Toll Free: (800) 545-2433, ext. 5048
Fax: (312) 280-3256   TDD: (888) 814-7692
E-mail: spectrum@ala.org
Web: www.ala.org

Summary To provide financial assistance to Asian American and other minority students interested in working on a degree in librarianship.

Eligibility This program is open to ethnic minority students (African American or Black, Asian, Native Hawaiian or other Pacific Islander, Latino or Hispanic, and American Indian or Alaska Native). Applicants must be U.S. or Canadian citizens or permanent residents who have completed no more than a third of the requirements for a master's or school library media degree. They must be enrolled full or part time at an ALA-accredited school of library and information studies or an ALA-recognized NCATE school library media program. Selection is based on academic leadership, outstanding service, commitment to a career in librarianship, statements indicating the nature of the applicant's library and other work experience, letters of reference, and personal presentation.

Financial data The stipend is $5,000.

Duration 1 year; nonrenewable.

Additional information This program began in 1998. It is administered by a joint committee of the American Library Association (ALA).

Number awarded Varies each year; recently, 69 of these scholarships were awarded.

Deadline February of each year.

[755]
SREB DOCTORAL AWARDS

Southern Regional Education Board
Attn: Coordinator, Program and Scholar Services
592 Tenth Street N.W.
Atlanta, GA 30318-5776
(404) 879-5569   Fax: (404) 872-1477
E-mail: doctoral.scholars@sreb.org
Web: www.sreb.org/page/1113/types_of_awards.html

Summary   To provide financial assistance to Asian American and other minority students who wish to work on a doctoral degree, especially in fields of science, technology, engineering, or mathematics (STEM), at designated universities in the southern states.

Eligibility   This program is open to U.S. citizens and permanent residents who are members of racial/ethnic minority groups (Native Americans, Hispanic Americans, Asian Americans, and African Americans) and have or will receive a bachelor's or master's degree. Applicants must be entering or enrolled in the first year of a Ph.D. program at an accredited college or university. They must indicate an interest in becoming a college professor at an institution in the South. The program does not support students working on other doctoral degrees (e.g., M.D., D.B.A., D.D.S., J.D., D.V.M., Ed.D., Pharm.D., D.N.P., D.P.T.). Preference is given to applicants in STEM disciplines with particularly low minority representation, although all academic fields are eligible.

Financial data   Scholars receive a waiver of tuition and fees (in or out of state) for up to 5 years, an annual stipend of $20,000 for 3 years, an annual allowance for professional development activities, and reimbursement of travel expenses to attend the Company for Faculty Diversity's annual Institute on Teaching and Mentoring.

Duration   Up to 5 years.

Additional information   This program was established in 1993 as part of the Compact for Faculty Diversity, supported by the Pew Charitable Trusts and the Ford Foundation.

Number awarded   Varies each year; recently, the program was supporting more than 300 scholars. Since its founding, it has supported more than 900 scholars at 83 institutions in 29 states.

Deadline   February of each year.

[756]
STANFORD CHEN INTERNSHIP GRANTS

Asian American Journalists Association
Attn: Student Programs Coordinator
5 Third Street, Suite 1108
San Francisco, CA 94103
(415) 346-2051, ext. 102   Fax: (415) 346-6343
E-mail: programs@aaja.org
Web: www.aaja.org/programs/internships

Summary   To provide supplemental grants to student members of the Asian American Journalists Association (AAJA) working as interns at small or medium-size news organizations.

Eligibility   This program is open to AAJA members who are college juniors, seniors, or graduate students with a serious intent to prepare for a career in journalism (print, online, broadcast, or photography). Applicants must have already secured an internship with a print company (daily circulation

less than 100,000) or broadcast company (market smaller than the top 50). Along with their application, they must submit a 200-word essay on the kind of experience they expect as an intern at a small to medium-size media company, their career goals, and why AAJA's mission is important to them; a resume; verification of the internship; a letter of recommendation; and a statement of financial need.

Financial data   The grant is $1,750. Funds are to be used for living expenses or transportation.

Duration   Summer months.

Additional information   This program was established in 1998.

Number awarded   1 each year.

Deadline   April of each year.

[757]
STOEL RIVES FIRST-YEAR DIVERSITY FELLOWSHIPS

Stoel Rives LLP
Attn: Professional Development and Diversity Manager
900 S.W. Fifth Avenue, Suite 2600
Portland, OR 97204
(503) 294-9496   Fax: (503) 220-2480
E-mail: lddecker@stoel.com
Web: www.stoel.com/diversity.aspx?Show=2805

Summary   To provide financial assistance to Asian American and other law students who bring diversity to the profession and are interested in a summer associate position with Stoel Rives.

Eligibility   This program is open to first-year law students who contribute to the diversity of the student body at their law school and who will contribute to the diversity of the legal community. Applicants must be willing to accept a summer associate position at Stoel Rives offices in Boise, Portland, and Seattle. Selection is based on academic excellence, leadership, community service, interest in practicing in the Pacific Northwest, and financial need.

Financial data   The program provides a stipend of $7,500 to help defray expenses of law school and a salaried summer associate position.

Duration   1 year.

Additional information   This program began in 2004.

Number awarded   3 each year: 1 each in Boise, Portland, and Seattle.

Deadline   January of each year.

[758]
STUDENT JOURNALISM AWARDS

South Asian Journalists Association
c/o Aseem Chhabra, Awards Committee Chair
4315 46th Street, Apartment E10
Sunnyside, NY 11104-2015
E-mail: chhabs@aol.com
Web: www.saja.org/programs/awards

Summary   To recognize and reward outstanding reporting on any subject by undergraduate and graduate students of south Asian origin.

Eligibility   Eligible to be considered for these awards are print, broadcast, new media, and photographic works submitted by south Asian students in the United States or Canada (on any subject). Entries must have been completed as part of a class assignment.

Financial data Prizes are $500 for the winner and $250 for the finalists.

Duration The competition is held annually.

Number awarded 3 each year.

Deadline March of each year.

[759]
SUMMER TRANSPORTATION INTERNSHIP PROGRAM FOR DIVERSE GROUPS

Department of Transportation
Attn: Summer Transportation Internship Program for Diverse Groups
HAHR-40, Room E63-433
1200 New Jersey Avenue, S.E.
Washington, DC 20590
(202) 366-2907   E-mail: lafayette.melton@dot.gov
Web: www.fhwa.dot.gov/education/stipdg.htm

Summary To enable Asian American undergraduate, graduate, and law students, as well as those from other diverse groups, to gain work experience during the summer at facilities of the U.S. Department of Transportation (DOT).

Eligibility This program is open to all qualified applicants, but it is designed to provide women, persons with disabilities, and members of diverse social and ethnic groups with summer opportunities in transportation. Applicants must be U.S. citizens currently enrolled in a degree-granting program of study at an accredited institution of higher learning at the undergraduate (community or junior college, university, college, or Tribal College or University) or graduate level. Undergraduates must be entering their junior or senior year; students attending a Tribal or community college must have completed their first year of school; law students must be entering their second or third year of school. Students who will graduate during the spring or summer are not eligible unless they have been accepted for enrollment in graduate school. The program accepts applications from students in all majors who are interested in working on transportation-related topics and issues. Preference is given to students with a GPA of 3.0 or higher. Undergraduates must submit a 1-page essay on their transportation interests and how participation in this program will enhance their educational and career plans and goals. Graduate students must submit a writing sample representing their educational and career plans and goals. Law students must submit a legal writing sample.

Financial data The stipend is $4,000 for undergraduates or $5,000 for graduate and law students. The program also provides housing and reimbursement of travel expenses from interns' homes to their assignment location.

Duration 10 weeks during the summer.

Additional information Assignments are at the DOT headquarters in Washington, D.C., a selected modal administration, or selected field offices around the country.

Number awarded 80 to 100 each year.

Deadline January of each year.

[760]
SYNOD OF LAKES AND PRAIRIES RACIAL ETHNIC SCHOLARSHIPS

Synod of Lakes and Prairies
Attn: Committee on Racial Ethnic Ministry
2115 Cliff Drive
Eagen, MN 55122-3327
(651) 357-1140   Toll Free: (800) 328-1880
Fax: (651) 357-1141 E-mail: mkes@lakesandprairies.org
Web: www.lakesandprairies.org

Summary To provide financial assistance to Asian Americans and other minority residents of the Presbyterian Church (USA) Synod of Lakes and Prairies who are studying for the ministry at a seminary in any state.

Eligibility This program is open to members of Presbyterian churches who reside within the Synod of Lakes and Prairies (Iowa, Minnesota, Nebraska, North Dakota, South Dakota, and Wisconsin). Applicants must be members of ethnic minority groups studying for the ministry in the Presbyterian Church (USA) or a related ecumenical organization. They must be in good academic standing, making progress toward a degree, and able to demonstrate financial need. Along with their application, they must submit essays of 200 to 500 words each on 1) their vision for the church, and either 2) how their school experience will prepare them to work in the church, or 3) the person who most influenced their commitment to Christ.

Financial data Stipends range from $850 to $3,500.

Duration 1 year.

Number awarded Varies each year; recently, 9 of these scholarships were awarded.

Deadline September of each year.

[761]
SYNOD OF THE COVENANT ETHNIC THEOLOGICAL SCHOLARSHIPS

Synod of the Covenant
Attn: Ministries in Higher Education
1911 Indianwood Circle, Suite B
Maumee, OH 43537-4063
(419) 754-4050
Toll Free: (800) 848-1030 (within MI and OH)
Fax: (419) 754-4051
Web: www.synodofthecovenant.org

Summary To provide financial assistance to Asian Americans and other minorities working on a master's degree at an approved Presbyterian theological institution (with priority given to Presbyterian applicants from Ohio and Michigan).

Eligibility This program is open to ethnic individuals enrolled full time in church vocations programs at approved Presbyterian theological institutions. Priority is given to Presbyterian applicants from the states of Michigan and Ohio. Financial need is considered in the selection process.

Financial data Students may be awarded a maximum of $1,500 on initial application. They may receive up to $2,000 on subsequent applications, with evidence of continuing progress. Funds are made payable to the session for distribution.

Duration Students are eligible to receive scholarships 1 time per year, up to a maximum of 5 years.

Number awarded Varies each year.

Deadline August of each year for fall semester; January of each year for spring semester.

[762]
TAIWON SUHR JOURNALISM SCHOLARSHIP

Philip Jaisohn Memorial Foundation
Attn: Education and Scholarship Committee
6705 Old York Road
Philadelphia, PA 19126
(215) 224-2000 Fax: (215) 224-9164
E-mail: jaisohnhouse@gmail.com
Web: jaisohn.org

Summary To provide financial assistance to Korean American undergraduate and graduate students who are working on a degree in journalism.

Eligibility This program is open to Korean American undergraduate and graduate students who are currently enrolled at a college or university in the United States. Applicants must be working on a degree in journalism. They must be able to demonstrate academic excellence, leadership and service to their school and community, and financial need. Along with their application, they must submit an essay on either "Who is Dr. Jaisohn to Me," or "The Significance of Dr. Jaisohn's Ideal to Korean Americans." They must also submit a brief statement on how they can contribute to and be involved in the activities of the Philip Jaisohn Memorial Foundation.

Financial data The stipend is $1,000.

Duration 1 year.

Number awarded 1 each year.

Deadline November of each year.

[763]
TARGETED OPPORTUNITY PROGRAM (TOPJOBS)

Wisconsin Office of State Employment Relations
Attn: Division of Affirmative Action Workforce Planning
101 East Wilson Street, Fourth Floor
P.O. Box 7855
Madison, WI 53707-7855
(608) 267-1005 Fax: (608) 267-1020
E-mail: Claire.Dehnert@wisconsin.gov
Web: oser.state.wi.us/category.asp?linkcatid=342

Summary To provide an opportunity for Asian Americans, other minorities, women, and persons with disabilities to gain summer work experience with agencies of the state of Wisconsin.

Eligibility This program is open to women, ethnic/racial minorities (Black or African American, Asian, Native Hawaiian or other Pacific Islander, American Indian or Alaska Native, or Hispanic or Latino), and persons with disabilities. Applicants must be juniors, seniors, or graduate students at an accredited 4-year college or university or second-year students in the second year of a 2-year technical or vocational school program. They must be 1) Wisconsin residents enrolled full time at a school in Wisconsin or any other state, or 2) residents of other states who are enrolled full time at a school in Wisconsin.

Financial data Most internships provide a competitive stipend.

Duration Summer months.

Additional information This program was established in 1974. Relevant fields of study include, but are not limited to, the liberal arts and sciences (e.g., history, mathematics, library science, political science, philosophy, physics, psychology, social services, social work, sociology, women's studies); agriculture and natural resources (e.g., animal and dairy science, biology, botany, chemistry, geography, entomology, environmental studies, horticulture, landscape architecture, microbiology, plant pathology, soil science, urban planning, water resources management, wildlife ecology); business (e.g., accounting, business management, economics, finance, human resources, marketing, public administration, real estate); criminal justice; education; health care (including nursing); engineering; information systems and computers; journalism and communications; and law.

Number awarded Varies each year. Since the program was established, it has placed more than 2,500 students with more than 30 different agencies and universities throughout the state.

Deadline February of each year.

[764]
TEACHER QUEST SCHOLARSHIP

Brown Foundation for Educational Equity, Excellence and Research
Attn: Scholarship Committee
1515 S.E. Monroe
Topeka, KS 66615
(785) 235-3939 Fax: (785) 235-1001
E-mail: brownfound@juno.com
Web: brownvboard.org

Summary To provide financial assistance to Asian American and other undergraduate or graduate students of color who are interested in preparing for a teaching career.

Eligibility This program is open to members of minority groups who are enrolled at least half time at an institution of higher education with an accredited teacher education program. Applicants must be enrolled at the undergraduate, graduate, or post-baccalaureate level and have a GPA of 3.0 or higher. Along with their application, they must submit brief essays on 1) their involvement in school, community, and/or other activities and how those activities have prepared them to be an educator; 2) why they aspire to a career in education, their goals, and the level at which they plan to teach; and 3) how they think *Brown v. Board of Education* has influenced their own life experiences. Selection is based on the essays; GPA; school, community, and leisure activities; career plans and goals in education; and recommendations.

Financial data The stipend is $1,000 per year.

Duration 2 years.

Additional information The first Brown Foundation Scholarships were awarded in 1989. The current program replaced the Brown Foundation Academic Scholarships in 2009.

Number awarded Varies each year; recently, 5 of these scholarships were awarded.

Deadline March of each year.

[765]
TEXAS CHAPTER SCHOLARSHIPS

Asian American Journalists Association-Texas Chapter
c/o Scott Nishimura, Scholarship Committee Chair
Fort Worth Star-Telegram
P.O. Box 1870
Fort Worth, TX 76115
(817) 390-7808   E-mail: snishimura@star-telegram.com
Web: www.aajatexas.org/programs/student-programs

Summary To provide financial assistance to students from designated southwestern states who are working on an undergraduate or graduate degree in journalism and can demonstrate an awareness of Asian American issues.

Eligibility This program is open to graduating high school seniors, undergraduates, and graduate students who are either 1) residents of Arkansas, Louisiana, New Mexico, Oklahoma, or Texas; or 2) attending or planning to attend an accredited college or university in those states. Applicants are not required to be members of the Asian American Journalists Association (AAJA) when they apply. Along with their application, they must submit a 250-word autobiography that explains why they are interested in a career in journalism, a 500-word essay on the role of ethnic diversity in news coverage (both for the subjects of the news events and also the journalists involved), their most recent official transcript, 2 letters of recommendation, and a resume. Work samples to be submitted are 3 legible clips from print journalism students; 3 to 5 prints or slides with captions or descriptions from print photojournalism students; 2 taped VHS or DVD excerpts with corresponding scripts from television broadcast students; 2 edited VHS or DVD excepts from television photojournalism students; 3 taped cassette excerpts with corresponding scripts from radio broadcast students; or 3 legible online articles from web journalism students. Selection is based on commitment to the field of journalism, awareness of Asian American issues, journalistic ability, and scholastic ability.

Financial data The stipend is $1,000.

Duration 1 year.

Additional information Scholarship winners are also given a 1-year free membership in the AAJA Texas chapter.

Number awarded 2 each year.

Deadline May of each year.

[766]
TEXAS LIBRARY ASSOCIATION SPECTRUM SCHOLARSHIP

Texas Library Association
Attn: Director of Administration
3355 Bee Cave Road, Suite 401
Austin, TX 78746-6763
(512) 328-1518   Toll Free: (800) 580-2TLA
Fax: (512) 328-8852   E-mail: tla@txla.org
Web: www.txla.org

Summary To provide additional funding to Asian American and other students at schools of library and information studies in Texas who have received a Spectrum Scholarship for minorities from the American Library Association (ALA).

Eligibility This program is open to recipients of ALA Spectrum Scholarships who are enrolled in a master's degree program in library and information studies at a Texas university. Applicants must be African American, Latino or Hispanic, Asian or Pacific Islander, or Native American. They must be members of the Texas Library Association (TLA) and agree to work for 2 years in a Texas library following completion of their master's degree requirements.

Financial data The stipend is $2,000.

Duration 1 year.

Number awarded 1 or more each year.

Deadline January of each year.

[767]
TEXAS YOUNG LAWYERS ASSOCIATION MINORITY SCHOLARSHIP PROGRAM

Texas Young Lawyers Association
Attn: Minority Involvement Committee
1414 Colorado, Suite 502
P.O. Box 12487
Austin, TX 78711-2487
(512) 427-1529   Toll Free: (800) 204-2222, ext. 1529
Fax: (512) 427-4117   E-mail: btrevino@texasbar.com
Web: www.tyla.org

Summary To provide financial assistance to Asian Americans, other minorities, and women residents of any state who are attending law school in Texas.

Eligibility This program is open to members of recognized minority groups, including but not limited to women, African Americans, Hispanic Americans, Asian Americans, and Native Americans. Applicants must be attending an ABA-accredited law school in Texas. Along with their application, they must submit a 2-page essay on either 1) the role the minority attorney should play in the community and profession, or 2) how attorneys, specifically minority attorneys, can improve the image of the legal profession. Selection is based on academic performance, merit, participation in extracurricular activities inside and outside law school, and financial need.

Financial data The stipend is $1,000.

Duration 1 year.

Number awarded 9 each year: 1 at each accredited law school in Texas.

Deadline October of each year.

[768]
THOMAS G. NEUSOM SCHOLARSHIPS

Conference of Minority Transportation Officials
Attn: National Scholarship Program
818 18th Street, N.W., Suite 850
Washington, DC 20006
(202) 530-0551   Fax: (202) 530-0617
Web: www.comto.org/news-youth.php

Summary To provide financial assistance for college or graduate school to Asian American and other members of the Conference of Minority Transportation Officials (COMTO).

Eligibility This program is open to undergraduate and graduate students who have been members of COMTO for at least 1 year. Applicants must be working on a degree in a field related to transportation with a GPA of 2.5 or higher. Along with their application, they must submit a cover letter with a 500-word statement of career goals. Financial need is not considered in the selection process. U.S. citizenship is required.

Financial data The stipend is $5,500. Funds are paid directly to the recipient's college or university.

Duration 1 year.

Additional information COMTO was established in 1971 to promote, strengthen, and expand the roles of minorities in all aspects of transportation. Recipients are expected to attend the COMTO National Scholarship Luncheon.

Number awarded 2 each year.

Deadline April of each year.

[769]
THOMAS T. HAYASHI MEMORIAL SCHOLARSHIP

Japanese American Citizens League
Attn: National Scholarship Awards
1765 Sutter Street
San Francisco, CA 94115
(415) 921-5225 Fax: (415) 931-4671
E-mail: jacl@jacl.org
Web: www.jacl.org/edu/scholar.htm

Summary To provide financial assistance to student members of the Japanese American Citizens League (JACL) who are interested in preparing for a career in law.

Eligibility This program is open to JACL members who are currently enrolled or planning to enroll at an accredited law school. Applicants must submit information on their involvement in JACL and a 2-page essay on a topic that changes annually but relates to Japanese Americans. Selection is based on that essay, academic history, extracurricular activities, JACL involvement, scholastic honors, and a letter of recommendation. Special consideration is given to applicants who demonstrate an interest in entering the legal profession as a means of securing justice for the disadvantaged.

Financial data Stipends generally average approximately $2,000.

Duration 1 year; nonrenewable.

Number awarded 1 each year.

Deadline March of each year.

[770]
THOMPSON HINE DIVERSITY SCHOLARSHIP PROGRAM

Thompson Hine LLP
Attn: Manager of New Lawyer Recruiting
3900 Key Center
127 Public Square
Cleveland, OH 44114-1291
(216) 566-5500 Fax: (216) 566-5800
E-mail: info@thompsonhine.com
Web: www.thompsonhine.com

Summary To provide financial assistance and work experience to Asian American and other minority law students from any state who have been accepted as a summer associate with the law firm of Thompson Hine.

Eligibility This program is open to second-year law students who are members of minority groups as defined by the Equal Employment Opportunity Commission (Native American or Alaskan Native, Asian or Pacific Islander African American or Black, or Hispanic). Applicants must first be offered a summer associateship at an office of Thompson Hine in Atlanta, Cincinnati, Cleveland, Columbus, Dayton, New York, or Washington, D.C. Along with their application,

they must submit a writing sample (a legal brief or memorandum prepared for their first-year legal writing course or a prior employer), law school and undergraduate transcripts, a current resume, and a list of at least 2 references.

Financial data The stipend is $10,000. Funds are paid to the student after completing the summer associateship and may be used for tuition and other law school expenses during the third year.

Duration 1 year.

Number awarded 1 each year.

Deadline August of each year.

[771]
THZ FO FARM SCHOLARSHIP

Hawai'i Community Foundation
Attn: Scholarship Department
827 Fort Street Mall
Honolulu, HI 96813
(808) 537-6333 Toll Free: (888) 731-3863
Fax: (808) 521-6286
E-mail: scholarships@hcf-hawaii.org
Web: www.hawaiicommunityfoundation.org/scholarships

Summary To provide financial assistance to Hawaii residents of Chinese descent who are interested in working on an undergraduate or graduate degree in gerontology at a school in any state.

Eligibility This program is open to high school seniors, high school graduates, and college students in Hawaii who are of Chinese ancestry and interested in studying gerontology as full-time undergraduate or graduate students at a college or university in any state. Applicants must be able to demonstrate academic achievement (GPA of 2.7 or higher), good moral character, and financial need. Along with their application, they must submit a short statement indicating their reasons for attending college, their planned course of study, their career goals, and what community service means to them.

Financial data The amounts of the awards depend on the availability of funds and the need of the recipient. Recently, the average value of all scholarships awarded by the foundation was $2,041.

Duration 1 year.

Number awarded Varies each year; recently, 6 of these scholarships were awarded.

Deadline February of each year.

[772]
TONGAN CULTURAL SOCIETY SCHOLARSHIPS

Hawai'i Community Foundation
Attn: Scholarship Department
827 Fort Street Mall
Honolulu, HI 96813
(808) 537-6333 Toll Free: (888) 731-3863
Fax: (808) 521-6286
E-mail: scholarships@hcf-hawaii.org
Web: www.hawaiicommunityfoundation.org/scholarships

Summary To provide financial assistance to Hawaii residents of Tongan ancestry who are interested in attending college or graduate school in the state.

Eligibility This program is open to Hawaii residents of Tongan ancestry who are enrolled in or planning to enroll in an accredited college or university in Hawaii. Applicants must be full-time undergraduate or graduate students and able to demonstrate academic achievement (GPA of 2.7 or higher), good moral character, and financial need. Along with their application, they must submit a short statement indicating their reasons for attending college, their planned course of study, their career goals, and what community service means to them.

Financial data The amounts of the awards depend on the availability of funds and the need of the recipient. Recently, the average value of all scholarships awarded by the foundation was $2,041.

Duration 1 year.

Number awarded Varies each year; recently, 3 of these scholarships were awarded.

Deadline February of each year.

[773]
TONKON TORP FIRST-YEAR DIVERSITY FELLOWSHIP PROGRAM

Tonkon Torp LLP
Attn: Director of Attorney Recruiting
1600 Pioneer Tower
888 S.W. Fifth Avenue
Portland, OR 97204
(503) 221-1440   Fax: (503) 972-3760
E-mail: Loree.Devery@tonkon.com
Web: www.tonkon.com/Careers/-1LDiversityFellowship.html

Summary To provide financial assistance and summer work experience in Portland, Oregon to Asian American and other first-year minority law students.

Eligibility This program is open to members of racial and ethnic minority groups who are currently enrolled in their first year at an ABA-accredited law school. Applicants must be able to demonstrate 1) a record of academic achievement that indicates a strong likelihood of a successful career during the remainder of law school and in the legal profession; 2) a commitment to practice law in Portland, Oregon following graduation from law school; and 3) an ability to contribute meaningfully to the diversity of the law school student body and, after entering the legal profession, the legal community. They are not required to disclose their financial circumstances, but a demonstrated need for financial assistance may be taken into consideration.

Financial data The recipient is offered a paid summer associateship at Tonkon Torp in Portland, Oregon for the summer following the first year of law school and, depending on the outcome of that experience, may be invited for a second summer following the second year of law school. Following the successful completion of that second associateship, the recipient is awarded an academic scholarship of $7,500 for the third year of law school.

Duration The program covers 2 summers and 1 academic year.

Additional information For 2 weeks during the summer, the fellow works in the legal department of Portland General Electric Company, Oregon's largest electric utility and a client of the sponsoring firm.

Number awarded 1 each year.

Deadline January of each year.

[774]
TOWNSEND AND TOWNSEND AND CREW DIVERSITY SCHOLARSHIP

Townsend and Townsend and Crew LLP
Attn: Diversity Committee
Two Embarcadero Center, Eighth Floor
San Francisco, CA 94111-3834
(415) 576-0200   Fax: (415) 576-0300
Web: www.townsend.com/Who/Who-Diversity

Summary To provide financial assistance to Asian Americans, other minorities, and women students who are attending law school to prepare for a career in patent law.

Eligibility This program is open to students enrolled at ABA-accredited law schools who are women or members of minority groups that have historically been underrepresented in the field of patent law (American Indians/Alaskan Natives, Blacks/African Americans, Hispanics/Latinos, and Asian Americans/Pacific Islanders). Applicants must have an undergraduate or graduate degree in a field that will help prepare them for a career in patent law (e.g., life sciences, engineering). They must have a demonstrated commitment to preparing for a career in patent law in a city in which the sponsoring law firm has an office. Selection is based on academic performance; work experience related to science, engineering, or patent law; community service; and demonstrated leadership ability.

Financial data The stipend is $2,000 per year.

Duration 1 year; recipients may reapply.

Additional information This program was established in 2005. Townsend and Townsend and Crew has offices in San Francisco, Palo Alto (California), Denver, Walnut Creek (California), San Diego, Seattle, Tokyo, and Washington, D.C.

Number awarded Varies each year; recently, 11 of these scholarships were awarded.

Deadline April of each year.

[775]
TRAILBLAZER SCHOLARSHIPS

Conference of Minority Transportation Officials
Attn: National Scholarship Program
818 18th Street, N.W., Suite 850
Washington, DC 20006
(202) 530-0551   Fax: (202) 530-0617
Web: www.comto.org/news-youth.php

Summary To provide financial assistance to Asian Americans and other minority undergraduate and graduate students working on a degree in a field related to transportation.

Eligibility This program is open to undergraduate and graduate students who are working on a degree in a field related to transportation with a GPA of 2.5 or higher. Along with their application, they must submit a cover letter with a 500-word statement of career goals. Financial need is not considered in the selection process. U.S. citizenship is required.

Financial data The stipend is $2,500. Funds are paid directly to the recipient's college or university.

Duration 1 year.

Additional information The Conference of Minority Transportation Officials (COMTO) was established in 1971 to promote, strengthen, and expand the roles of minorities in all aspects of transportation. Recipients are expected to attend the COMTO National Scholarship Luncheon.

Number awarded 2 each year.

Deadline April of each year.

[776]
UNITARIAN UNIVERSALIST ASSOCIATION INCENTIVE GRANTS

Unitarian Universalist Association
Attn: Ministerial Credentialing Office
25 Beacon Street
Boston, MA 02108-2800
(617) 948-6403   Fax: (617) 742-2875
E-mail: mco@uua.org
Web: www.uua.org

Summary To provide financial aid to Asian Americans and other persons of color who the Unitarian Universalist Association is interested in attracting to the ministry.

Eligibility These grants are offered to Asian Americans and other persons of color who are the type of applicants the association is particularly interested in attracting to Unitarian Universalist ministry (to promote racial, cultural, or class diversity). Applicants must be in their first year of study. Decisions regarding potential recipients are made in consultation with the schools. Selection is based on merit.

Financial data A stipend is awarded (amount not specified).

Duration 1 year; nonrenewable.

Additional information In subsequent years, recipients may apply for the association's General Financial Aid Grants.

Number awarded Varies each year.

Deadline April of each year.

[777]
UNITED METHODIST WOMEN OF COLOR SCHOLARS PROGRAM

United Methodist Church
Attn: General Board of Higher Education and Ministry
Office of Loans and Scholarships
1001 19th Avenue South
P.O. Box 340007
Nashville, TN 37203-0007
(615) 340-7344   Fax: (615) 340-7367
E-mail: umscholar@gbhem.org
Web: www.gbhem.org/loansandscholarships

Summary To provide financial assistance to Asian American Methodist women, and other women of color, who are working on a doctoral degree to prepare for a career as an educator at a United Methodist seminary.

Eligibility This program is open to women of color (have at least 1 parent who is African American, African, Hispanic, Asian, Native American, Alaska Native, or Pacific Islander) who have an M.Div. degree. Applicants must have been active, full members of a United Methodist Church for at least 3 years prior to applying. They must be enrolled full time in a degree program at the Ph.D. or Th.D. level to prepare for a career teaching at a United Methodist seminary.

Financial data The maximum stipend is $10,000 per year.

Duration 1 year; may be renewed up to 3 additional years.

Number awarded Varies each year; recently, 10 of these scholarships were awarded.

Deadline January of each year.

[778]
UPS/NAPABA LAW FOUNDATION GOLD MOUNTAIN SCHOLARSHIPS

National Asian Pacific American Bar Association
Attn: NAPABA Law Foundation
1612 K Street, N.W., Suite 1400
Washington, DC 20006
(202) 775-9555   Fax: (202) 775-9333
E-mail: foundation@napaba.org
Web: www.napaba.org

Summary To provide financial assistance to law students who are the first in their family to attend law school and interested in serving the Asian Pacific American community.

Eligibility This program is open to students at ABA-accredited law schools in the United States who are the first in their family to attend law school. Applicants must demonstrate leadership potential to serve the Asian Pacific American community upon graduation. Along with their application, they must submit a 500-word essay that covers 1) the most significant experiences in their background that have shaped and demonstrated their commitment to serving the needs of Asian Pacific Americans; and 2) how they intend to serve the needs of the Asian Pacific American community in their future legal career. Selection is based on demonstrated commitment to and interest in pro bono, public interest, and/or public service legal work; financial need; and commitment to serving the needs of the Asian Pacific American community. U.S. citizenship or permanent resident status is required.

Financial data The stipend is $2,500.

Duration 1 year.

Additional information This program is supported by the UPS Foundation.

Number awarded 2 each year.

Deadline September of each year.

[779]
USA FUNDS ACCESS TO EDUCATION SCHOLARSHIPS

Scholarship America
Attn: Scholarship Management Services
One Scholarship Way
P.O. Box 297
St. Peter, MN 56082
(507) 931-1682   Toll Free: (800) 537-4180
Fax: (507) 931-9168   E-mail: scholarship@usafunds.org
Web: www.usafunds.org

Summary To provide financial assistance to undergraduate and graduate students, especially Asian Americans, other minorities, and students with physical disabilities.

Eligibility This program is open to high school seniors and graduates who plan to enroll or are already enrolled in full- or half-time undergraduate or full-time graduate course work at an accredited 2- or 4-year college, university, or vocational/technical school. GED recipients are also eligible. Up to 50% of the awards are targeted at students who have a documented physical disability or are a member of an ethnic minority group, including but not limited to Native Hawaiian,

Alaskan Native, Black/African American, Asian, Pacific Islander, American Indian, Hispanic/Latino, or multiracial. Residents of all 50 states, the District of Columbia, Puerto Rico, Guam, the U.S. Virgin Islands, and all U.S. territories and commonwealths are eligible. Applicants must also be U.S. citizens or eligible noncitizens and come from a family with an annual adjusted gross income of $35,000 or less. In addition to financial need, selection is based on past academic performance and future potential, leadership and participation in school and community activities, work experience, career and educational aspirations and goals, and unusual personal or family circumstances.

Financial data The stipend is $1,500 per year for full-time undergraduate or graduate students or $750 per year for half-time undergraduate students. Funds are paid jointly to the student and the school.

Duration 1 year; may be renewed until the student receives a final degree or certificate or until the total award to a student reaches $6,000, whichever comes first. Renewal requires the recipient to maintain a GPA of 2.5 or higher.

Additional information This program, established in 2000, is sponsored by USA Funds.

Number awarded Varies each year; recently, a total of $3.2 million was available for this program.

Deadline February of each year.

[780]
VAID FELLOWSHIPS

National Gay and Lesbian Task Force
Attn: The Task Force Policy Institute
80 Maiden Lane, Suite 1504
New York, NY 10038
(212) 604-9830   Fax: (212) 604-9831
E-mail: ngltf@ngltf.org
Web: www.thetaskforce.org

Summary To provide work experience to undergraduate and graduate students or professionals (especially Asian Americans and other minorities) who are interested in participating in the leadership of people of color in the progressive movement for gay, lesbian, bisexual, and transgender (GLBT) equality.

Eligibility Applicants must be enrolled in a degree program at least half time as a law, graduate, or undergraduate student or have successfully completed a law, graduate, or undergraduate degree within the preceding 12 months. They should have 1) a desire to work in a multicultural environment where commitment to diversity based on race, ethnic origin, gender, age, sexual orientation, and physical ability is an important institutional value; 2) demonstrated leadership in progressive and/or GLBT communities; 3) extensive research, writing, and critical thinking skills; 4) knowledge of, and commitment to, GLBT issues; and 5) computer proficiency in word processing, database work, e-mail, and Internet research. The program supports and recognizes the leadership of people of color and other emerging leaders in public policy, legal, and social science research.

Financial data The stipend ranges from $200 to $400 per week ($10 per hour). Fellows are responsible for their own housing and living expenses.

Duration Summer fellowships are 40 hours per week and spring/fall fellowships are 20 hours per week.

Additional information The Policy Institute of the National Gay and Lesbian Task Force (NGLTF), founded in 1995, is the largest think tank in the United States engaged in research, policy analysis, and strategic action to advance equality and understanding of GLBT people. Its primary programs are the racial and economic justice initiative, the family policy program, and the aging initiative. In addition to their primary roles of providing research and analysis, all 3 programs work closely with NGLTF colleagues in Washington, D.C. and other allies on advocacy and legislative efforts to actively change laws and policies affecting GLBT people.

Number awarded 3 fellows are selected each session.

Deadline April for the summer, July for the fall, and November for the spring.

[781]
VAMA SCHOLARSHIP PROGRAM

Vietnamese American Medical Association
Attn: Scholarship Committee
4108 Surfside Court
Arlington, TX 76016
(682) 667-1016   Fax: (817) 468-1852
E-mail: scholarship@vamausa.org
Web: vamausa.org/cms2/index.php/scholarships

Summary To provide financial assistance to medical students with an interest in serving the Vietnamese American community.

Eligibility This program is open to students enrolled in their third year at an accredited medical school in the United States. Applicants must be able to demonstrate a strong interest in serving the Vietnamese American community when they complete their training. Along with their application, they must submit a letter from the financial aid office of their medical school verifying the amount of other assistance they are receiving, a letter of recommendation, their medical school transcript, and a 600-word essay describing the reason why they wish to serve Vietnamese communities in the United States, including the specific location where they plan to practice. Preference is given to applicants who demonstrate the greatest financial need.

Financial data The stipend is $1,000.

Duration 1 year.

Number awarded Varies each year.

Deadline June of each year.

[782]
VARNUM DIVERSITY AND INCLUSION SCHOLARSHIPS FOR LAW STUDENTS

Varnum LLP
Attn: Scholarships
333 Bridge Street N.W.
P.O. Box 352
Grand Rapids, MI 49501-0352
(616) 336-6620   Fax: (616) 336-7000
E-mail: ewskaggs@varnumlaw.com
Web: www.varnumlaw.com

Summary To provide financial assistance to Asian American and other law students from Michigan who will contribute to diversity in the legal profession.

Eligibility This program is open to Michigan residents accepted or currently enrolled at an accredited law school in any state or residents of other states attending an accredited Michigan law school. Applicants must be members of an ethnic or racial minority or demonstrate a significant commitment to issues of diversity and inclusion. They must have a GPA of 3.0 or higher. Along with their application, they must submit a 750-word statement on their efforts to promote greater ethnic or racial diversity and inclusion within the legal profession and/or their community.

Financial data   The stipend is $4,000.

Duration   1 year.

Number awarded   2 each year.

Deadline   January of each year.

[783]
VIETNAMESE AMERICAN BAR ASSOCIATION OF NORTHERN CALIFORNIA SCHOLARSHIPS

Vietnamese American Bar Association of Northern
  California
c/o Quyen Ta, President
Keker & Van Nest LLP
710 Sansome Street
San Francisco, CA 94111
(415) 391-5400   Fax: (415) 397-7188
E-mail: vabancinfo@gmail.com
Web: www.vabanc.org

Summary   To provide financial assistance to law students who are committed to serving the Vietnamese American community.

Eligibility   This program is open to law students from any state who can demonstrate a commitment to serving the Vietnamese American community and financial need. Applicants must submit an 800-word personal statement on 1) what they see as a pressing concern facing the Vietnamese American community and how they see themselves contributing to or engaging in such an issue; and/or 2) their contributions to or activism within the Vietnamese American community; and/or 3) their experiences in overcoming socioeconomic and/or other barriers.

Financial data   The stipend is $1,000.

Duration   1 year.

Additional information   This program began in 2002.

Number awarded   3 each year.

Deadline   June of each year.

[784]
VIETNAMESE AMERICAN BAR ASSOCIATION OF THE GREATER WASHINGTON DC AREA SCHOLARSHIP

Vietnamese American Bar Association of the Greater
  Washington DC Area
33 Eighth Street, N.E.
Washington, DC 20002
E-mail: vabadc@gmail.com
Web: www.vabadc.com

Summary   To provide financial assistance to students at law schools in the greater Washington, D.C. area who are committed to serving the Vietnamese American community.

Eligibility   This program is open to residents of any state who are currently enrolled at a law school in the greater Washington, D.C. area. Applicants must be able to demonstrate a commitment to serving the Vietnamese American

community. Along with their application, they must submit a 750-word essay on 1 of the following topics: 1) how they plan to serve the needs of Vietnamese Americans in their legal career; 2) their experiences in serving the Vietnamese American community; or 3) how they have overcome barriers in their life to achieve their academic and/or career goals.

Financial data   The stipend is $1,000.

Duration   1 year.

Additional information   This program was established in 2009.

Number awarded   2 each year.

Deadline   February of each year.

[785]
VINCENT CHIN SCHOLARSHIP

Asian American Journalists Association
Attn: Student Programs Coordinator
5 Third Street, Suite 1108
San Francisco, CA 94103
(415) 346-2051, ext. 102   Fax: (415) 346-6343
E-mail: programs@aaja.org
Web: www.aaja.org/programs/scholarships

Summary   To provide financial assistance to student members of the Asian American Journalists Association (AAJA) who are high school seniors, undergraduates, or graduate students and interested in preparing for a career in journalism.

Eligibility   This program is open to AAJA members who are working or planning to work full time on an undergraduate or graduate degree in journalism. Applicants must submit a 500-word essay on their involvement or interest in the Asian American community and how, if they are awarded this scholarship, they would keep Vincent Chin's memory alive through their journalism work. Print applicants must submit up to 4 photocopied or printed articles; broadcast applicants must submit up to 3 stories (total length less than 10 minutes) copied on CDs; photojournalism applicants must submit a portfolio with no more than 10 entries. Selection is based on academic achievement, commitment to journalism, sensitivity to Asian American and Pacific Islander issues, demonstrated journalistic ability, and financial need.

Financial data   The stipend is $500.

Duration   1 year.

Number awarded   1 each year.

Deadline   May of each year.

[786]
VINSON & ELKINS DIVERSITY FELLOWSHIPS

Vinson & Elkins L.L.P.
Attn: Attorney Initiatives Assistant
1001 Fannin Street, Suite 2500
Houston, TX 77002-6760
(713) 758-2222   Fax: (713) 758-2346
Web: www.velaw.com/careers/law_students.aspx?id=602

Summary   To provide financial assistance to Asian American and other minority law students who are interested in working in a law firm setting.

Eligibility   This program is open to students who are entering the second year at an ABA-accredited law school and are members of a racial or ethnic group that has been historically underrepresented in the legal profession (Asian, American

Indian/Alaskan Native, Black/African American, Hispanic/Latino, multiracial, or Native Hawaiian or other Pacific Islander). Applicants must be able to demonstrate a strong undergraduate and law school record, excellent writing skills, and an interest in working in a law firm setting.

Financial data The stipend is $3,500 per year.

Duration 2 years (the second and third year of law school).

Additional information Fellows are also considered for summer associate positions at the sponsor's offices in Austin, Dallas, or Houston following their first year of law school.

Number awarded 4 each year.

Deadline January of each year.

[787]
VIRGINIA TEACHING SCHOLARSHIP LOAN PROGRAM

Virginia Department of Education
Division of Teacher Education and Licensure
Attn: Director of Teacher Education
P.O. Box 2120
Richmond, VA 23218-2120
(804) 371-2475 Toll Free: (800) 292-3820
Fax: (804) 786-6759
E-mail: JoAnne.Carver@doe.virginia.gov
Web: www.doe.virginia.gov

Summary To provide funding to upper-division and graduate students in Virginia (particularly Asian Americans and other minorities) who are interested in a career in teaching.

Eligibility This program is open to Virginia residents who are enrolled full or part time as a sophomore, junior, senior, or graduate student in a state-approved teacher preparation program in Virginia with a GPA of 2.7 or higher. Applicants must agree to engage in full-time teaching following graduation in 1) designated teacher shortage areas within Virginia; 2) a school with a high concentration of students eligible for free or reduced lunch; 3) within a school division with a shortage of teachers; 4) in a rural or urban region of the state with a teacher shortage; or 5) in a career and technical education discipline. Males interested in teaching in the elementary grades and people of color in all teaching areas also qualify.

Financial data The scholarship/loan is $3,720 per year. Loans are forgiven at the rate of $1,000 for each semester the recipient teaches in designated teacher shortage areas. If the recipient fails to fulfill the teaching service requirement, the loan must be repaid with interest.

Duration 1 year; may be renewed 1 additional year.

Additional information Critical shortage teaching areas in Virginia are currently identified as all areas of special education (severe disturbances, hearing impairment, learning disabilities, mental retardation, severe disabilities, visual impairment, early childhood special education, emotional disturbance, and speech and language disorders), career and technical education (including technology education, trade and industrial education, business education, and family and consumer sciences), mathematics (6-12), foreign language (preK-12), English (6-12), middle school (6-8), elementary education (preK-6), science (6-12), health and physical education (preK-12), and school counselor (preK-12).

Number awarded Varies each year; recently, 265 of these scholarship/loans were granted, including 111 in elementary education, 14 in English, 8 in foreign languages, 2 in history and social science, 18 in mathematics, 22 in middle grades, 2 in science, 30 in special education, 20 for males in elementary grades, 4 for males in middle grades, and 34 for people of color.

Deadline Deadline not specified.

[788]
WALTER O. SPOFFORD, JR. MEMORIAL INTERNSHIP

Resources for the Future
Attn: Coordinator for Academic Programs
1616 P Street, N.W., Suite 600
Washington, DC 20036-1400
(202) 328-5008 Fax: (202) 939-3460
E-mail: spofford-award@rff.org
Web: www.rff.org/About_RFF/Pages/default.aspx

Summary To provide summer internships to minority and other graduate students interested in working on Chinese environmental issues at Resources for the Future (RFF).

Eligibility This program is open to first- or second-year graduate students in the social or natural sciences. Applicants must have a special interest in Chinese environmental issues and outstanding policy analysis and writing skills. They must be interested in an internship in Washington, D.C. at RFF. Women and minority candidates are strongly encouraged to apply. Both U.S. and non-U.S. citizens (especially Chinese students) are eligible, if the latter have proper work and residency documentation.

Financial data The stipend is $375 per week. Housing assistance is not provided.

Duration The duration of the internship depends on the intern's situation.

Number awarded 1 each year.

Deadline February of each year.

[789]
WARNER NORCROSS & JUDD LAW SCHOOL SCHOLARSHIP

Grand Rapids Community Foundation
Attn: Education Program Officer
185 Oakes Street S.W.
Grand Rapids, MI 49503-4008
(616) 454-1751, ext. 103 Fax: (616) 454-6455
E-mail: rbishop@grfoundation.org
Web: www.grfoundation.org/scholarships

Summary To provide financial assistance to Asian Americans and other minorities from Michigan who are attending law school.

Eligibility This program is open to students of color who are attending or planning to attend an accredited law school. Applicants must be residents of Michigan or attending law school in the state. They must be U.S. citizens or permanent residents and have a GPA of 2.5 or higher. Financial need is considered in the selection process.

Financial data The stipend is $5,000. Funds are paid directly to the recipient's institution.

Duration 1 year.

Additional information Funding for this program is provided by the law firm Warner Norcross & Judd LLP.

Number awarded 1 each year.

Deadline March of each year.

[790]
WASHINGTON DIVERSITY FELLOWSHIPS IN ENVIRONMENTAL LAW

American Bar Association
Attn: Section of Environment, Energy, and Resources
321 North Clark Street
Chicago, IL 60654-7598
(312) 988-5602   Fax: (312) 988-5572
E-mail: jonusaid@staff.abanet.org
Web: www.abanet.org

Summary To provide funding to Asian American and other law students from underrepresented groups who are interested in working on a summer project in environmental, energy, or resources law in Washington.

Eligibility This program is open to first- and second-year law students and third-year night students who are members of underrepresented and underserved groups, such as minority or low-income populations. Students may be residents of any state and attending school in any state; preference is given to residents of Washington and to students who are enrolled at law schools in Washington or who have a strong interest in the state. Applicants must be interested in working during the summer at a government agency or public interest organization on a project in Washington in the fields of environmental, energy, or resources law. Selection is based on interest in environmental issues, academic record, personal qualities, and leadership abilities.

Financial data The stipend is $5,000.

Duration 8 to 10 weeks during the summer.

Number awarded 1 each year.

Deadline February of each year.

[791]
WATSON MIDWIVES OF COLOR SCHOLARSHIP

American College of Nurse-Midwives
Attn: ACNM Foundation, Inc.
8403 Colesville Road, Suite 1550
Silver Spring, MD 20910-6374
(240) 485-1850   Fax: (240) 485-1818
Web: www.midwife.org/foundation_award.cfm

Summary To provide financial assistance for midwifery education to Asian Americans and other students of color who belong to the American College of Nurse-Midwives (ACNM).

Eligibility This program is open to ACNM members of color who are currently enrolled in an accredited basic midwife education program and have successfully completed 1 academic or clinical semester/quarter or clinical module. Applicants must submit a 150-word essay on their 5-year midwifery career plans and a 100-word essay on their intended future participation in the local, regional, and/or national activities of the ACNM. Selection is based on leadership potential, financial need, academic history, and potential for future professional contribution to the organization.

Financial data The stipend is $3,000.

Duration 1 year.

Number awarded Varies each year; recently, 3 of these scholarships were awarded.

Deadline March of each year.

[792]
WEST AMERICA CHAPTER SCHOLARSHIP AWARDS

Phi Tau Phi Scholastic Honor Society-West America Chapter
c/o Nai-Chang Yeh, President
California Institute of Technology
Kavli Nanoscience Institute
128 Sloan Annex, Mail Code 114-36
1200 East California Boulevard
Pasadena, CA 91125
(626) 395-4313   E-mail: ncyeh@caltech.edu
Web: phitauphi.org

Summary To provide financial assistance to upper-division and graduate students of Chinese heritage from any state at colleges and universities in southern California.

Eligibility This program is open to juniors, seniors, and graduate students from any state enrolled at accredited institutions of higher education in southern California. Applicants must be of Chinese heritage or have a demonstrated interest in Chinese and culture. They must have a GPA of 3.4 or higher. Along with their application, they must submit a 1-page essay on their professional goals, achievements, and interest in Chinese culture. Financial need is not considered in the selection process.

Financial data The stipend is $1,000.

Duration 1 year.

Additional information Phi Tau Phi, first organized in 1921 in China and reestablished in 1964 in the United States, is a relatively small honor society of scholars, mainly of Chinese heritage, in various disciplines of science, technology, art, and the humanities.

Number awarded 4 or more each year.

Deadline August of each year.

[793]
WESTERN REGION KOREAN AMERICAN SCHOLARSHIPS

Korean American Scholarship Foundation
Western Region
Attn: Scholarship Committee
3540 Wilshire Boulevard, Suite 920
Los Angeles, CA 90010
(213) 380-KASF   Fax: (213) 380-KASF
E-mail: western@kasf.org
Web: www.kasf.org/application_set.html

Summary To provide financial assistance to Korean American students from any state who are working on or planning to work on an undergraduate or graduate degree in any field at a school in western states.

Eligibility This program is open to Korean American students who are high school seniors, undergraduates, or graduate students. Applicants may be residents of any state as long as they are attending or planning to attend school full time in the western region (Alaska, Arizona, California, Colorado, Hawaii, Idaho, Montana, Nevada, New Mexico, Oregon, Utah, Washington, or Wyoming). They must have a GPA of 3.0 or higher. Selection is based on academic achievement, community service, school activities, and financial need.

Financial data Stipends are at least $2,000.

Duration 1 year; renewable.

Number awarded Varies each year; recently, 37 of these scholarships were awarded.

Deadline May of each year.

[794]
WILEY W. MANUEL LAW FOUNDATION SCHOLARSHIPS

Wiley W. Manuel Law Foundation
c/o Law Offices of George Holland
1970 Broadway, Suite 1030
Oakland, CA 94612
(510) 465-4100
Web: wileymanuel.org/index.html

Summary To provide financial assistance to Asian American and other minority students from any state enrolled at law schools in northern California.

Eligibility This program is open to minority students entering their third year at law schools in northern California. Applicants should exemplify the qualities of the late Justice Wiley Manuel, the first African American to serve on the California Supreme Court. Along with their application, they must submit a 250-word essay on why they should be awarded this scholarship. Financial need is also considered in the selection process.

Financial data The stipend is approximately $1,500.

Duration 1 year.

Number awarded Varies each year; recently, 12 of these scholarships were awarded.

Deadline September of each year.

[795]
WILLIAM K. SCHUBERT M.D. MINORITY NURSING SCHOLARSHIP PROGRAM

Cincinnati Children's Hospital Medical Center
Attn: Office of Diversity and Inclusion, MLC 9008
3333 Burnet Avenue
Cincinnati, OH 45229-3039
(513) 803-6416   Toll Free: (800) 344-2462
Fax: (513) 636-5643   TDD: (513) 636-4900
E-mail: owen.burke@cchmc.org
Web: www.cincinnatichildrens.org

Summary To provide financial assistance to Asian Americans and members of other underrepresented groups interested in working on a bachelor's or master's degree in nursing to prepare for licensure in Ohio.

Eligibility This program is open to members of groups underrepresented in the nursing profession (males, American Indians or Alaska Natives, Blacks or African Americans, Hawaiian Natives or other Pacific Islanders, Hispanics or Latinos, or Asians). Applicants must be enrolled or accepted in a professional bachelor's or master's registered nurse program at an accredited school of nursing to prepare for initial licensure in Ohio. They must have a GPA of 2.75 or higher. Along with their application, they must submit a 750-word essay that covers 1) their long-range personal, educational, and professional goals and why they chose nursing as a profession; 2) any unique qualifications, experiences, or special talents that demonstrate their creativity; and 3) if they are able to pay any college expenses through work and how their work experience has contributed to their personal development.

Financial data The stipend is $2,750 per year.

Duration 1 year. May be renewed up to 3 additional years for students working on a bachelor's degree or 1 additional year for students working on a master's degree; renewal requires that students maintain a GPA of 2.75 or higher.

Number awarded 1 or more each year.

Deadline April of each year.

[796]
WILLIAM RUCKER GREENWOOD SCHOLARSHIP

Association for Women Geoscientists
Attn: AWG Foundation
12000 North Washington Street, Suite 285
Thornton, CO 80241
(303) 412-6219   Fax: (303) 253-9220
E-mail: office@awg.org
Web: www.awg.org/EAS/scholarships.html

Summary To provide financial assistance to Asian American and other minority women from any state working on an undergraduate or graduate degree in the geosciences at a college in the Potomac Bay region.

Eligibility This program is open to minority women who are residents of any state and currently enrolled as full-time undergraduate or graduate geoscience majors at an accredited, degree-granting college or university in Delaware, the District of Columbia, Maryland, Virginia, or West Virginia. Selection is based on the applicant's 1) participation in geoscience or earth science educational activities, and 2) potential for leadership as a future geoscience professional.

Financial data The stipend is $1,000. The recipient also is granted a 1-year membership in the Association for Women Geoscientists (AWG).

Duration 1 year.

Additional information This program is sponsored by the AWG Potomac Area Chapter.

Number awarded 1 each year.

Deadline April of each year.

[797]
WINSTON & STRAWN DIVERSITY SCHOLARSHIP PROGRAM

Winston & Strawn LLP
Attn: Attorney Recruitment Assistant
35 West Wacker Drive
Chicago, IL 60601-9703
(312) 558-5600   Fax: (312) 558-5700
E-mail: diversityscholarship@winston.com
Web: www.winston.com

Summary To provide financial assistance to Asian American and other diverse law students who are interested in practicing in a city in which Winston & Strawn LLP has an office.

Eligibility This program is open to second-year law students who self-identify as a member of 1 of the following groups: American Indian or Alaska Native, Asian or Pacific Islander, Black or African American, or Hispanic or Latino. Applicants must submit a resume, law school transcript, and 500-word personal statement. Selection is based on 1) interest in practicing law after graduation in a large law firm in a city in which Winston & Strawn has an office (currently, Charlotte, Chicago, Los Angeles, New York, San Francisco, and Washington, D.C.); 2) law school and undergraduate record, including academic achievements and involvement in extra-curricular activities; 3) demonstrated leadership skills; 4) and interpersonal skills.

Financial data   The stipend is $10,000.

Duration   1 year (the third year of law school).

Additional information   This program began in 2001.

Number awarded   3 each year.

Deadline   October of each year.

[798]
WISCONSIN LIBRARY ASSOCIATION DIVERSITY SCHOLARSHIP

Wisconsin Library Association
Attn: Scholarship Committee
5250 East Terrace Drive, Suite A1
Madison, WI 53718-8345
(608) 245-3640   Fax: (608) 245-3646
E-mail: wla@scls.lib.wi.us
Web: www.wla.lib.wi.us/scholarships/diversity.htm

Summary   To provide financial assistance to Asian Americans, other minorities, and physically-challenged residents of Wisconsin who are working on a master's degree in library and information science or library media at a school in the state.

Eligibility   This program is open to members of underrepresented groups, defined as racial and ethnic minorities (African Americans, Latinos or Hispanics, Asians and Pacific Islanders, or Native Americans and Alaskan Natives) and physically-challenged people who are residents of Wisconsin. Applicants must have been admitted to a master's degree program in library and information science or in library media at a college or university in Wisconsin. Along with their application, they must submit a 500-word essay describing 1) their background, experience, and career plans in the library profession, and 2) what this scholarship will mean to them. Selection is based on past academic performance, experience and background in library and library-related work, career plans in the library profession, and need and desire for the scholarship.

Financial data   The stipend is $850.

Duration   1 year.

Number awarded   1 each year.

Deadline   September of each year.

[799]
WISCONSIN MINORITY TEACHER LOANS

Wisconsin Higher Educational Aids Board
131 West Wilson Street, Suite 902
P.O. Box 7885
Madison, WI 53707-7885
(608) 267-2212   Fax: (608) 267-2808
E-mail: Mary.Kuzdas@wisconsin.gov
Web: heab.state.wi.us/programs.html

Summary   To provide funding to Asian Americans and other minorities in Wisconsin who are interested in teaching in Wisconsin school districts with large minority enrollments.

Eligibility   This program is open to residents of Wisconsin who are African Americans, Hispanic Americans, American Indians, or southeast Asians (students who were admitted to the United States after December 31, 1975 and who are a former citizen of Laos, Vietnam, or Cambodia or whose ancestor

was a citizen of 1 of those countries). Applicants must be enrolled at least half time as juniors, seniors, or graduate students at an independent or public institution in the state in a program leading to teaching licensure and have a GPA of 2.5 or higher. They must agree to teach in a Wisconsin school district in which minority students constitute at least 29% of total enrollment or in a school district participating in the inter-district pupil transfer program. Financial need is not considered in the selection process.

Financial data   forgivable loans are provided up to $2,500 per year. For each year the student teaches in an eligible school district, 25% of the loan is forgiven; if the student does not teach in an eligible district, the loan must be repaid at an interest rate of 5%.

Duration   1 year; may be renewed 1 additional year.

Additional information   Eligible students should apply through their school's financial aid office.

Number awarded   Varies each year.

Deadline   Deadline dates vary by institution; check with your school's financial aid office.

[800]
WMACCA CORPORATE SCHOLARS PROGRAM

Washington Metropolitan Area Corporate Counsel
   Association, Inc.
Attn: Executive Director
P.O. Box 2147
Rockville, MD 20847-2147
(301) 881-3018   E-mail: Ilene.Reid@wmacca.com
Web: www.wmacca.org

Summary   To provide a summer internship in the metropolitan Washington, D.C. area to Asian Americans and other students at law schools in the area who will contribute to the diversity of the profession.

Eligibility   This program is open to students entering their second or third year of part- or full-time study at law schools in the Washington, D.C. metropolitan area (including suburban Maryland and all of Virginia). Applicants must be able to demonstrate how they contribute to diversity in the legal profession, based not only on ideas about gender, race, and ethnicity, but also on concepts of socioeconomic background and their individual educational and career path. They must be interested in working during the summer at a sponsoring private corporation and nonprofit organizations in the Washington, D.C. area. Along with their application, they must submit a personal statement of 250 to 500 words explaining why they qualify for this program, a writing sample, their law school transcript, and a resume.

Financial data   The stipend is at least $9,000.

Duration   10 weeks during the summer.

Additional information   The Washington Metropolitan Area Corporate Counsel Association (WMACCA) is the local chapter of the Association of Corporate Counsel (ACC). It established this program in 2004 with support from the Minority Corporate Counsel Association (MCCA).

Number awarded   Varies each year; recently, 11 of these internships were awarded.

Deadline   January of each year.

[801]
WOLVERINE BAR FOUNDATION SCHOLARSHIP

Wolverine Bar Association
Attn: Wolverine Bar Foundation
645 Griswold, Suite 961
Detroit, MI 48226-4017
(313) 962-0250   Fax: (313) 962-5906
E-mail: wbaoffice@ameritech.net
Web: www.wbadirect.org

Summary To provide financial assistance for law school to Asian Americans and other minorities in Michigan.

Eligibility This program is open to minority law students who are either currently enrolled in a Michigan law school or are Michigan residents enrolled in an out-of-state law school. Applicants must be in at least their second year of law school. Selection is based on financial need, merit, and an interview.

Financial data The stipend is at least $1,000.

Duration 1 year; nonrenewable.

Additional information The Wolverine Bar Association was established by a number of African American attorneys during the 1930s. It was the successor to the Harlan Law Club, founded in 1919 by attorneys in the Detroit area who were excluded from other local bar associations in Michigan.

Number awarded 1 or more each year.

Deadline April of each year.

[802]
WOMBLE CARLYLE SCHOLARS PROGRAM

Womble Carlyle Sandridge & Rice, PLLC
Attn: Director of Entry-Level Recruiting and Development
301 South College Street, Suite 3500
Charlotte, NC 28202-6037
(704) 331-4900   Fax: (704) 331-4955
E-mail: wcsrscholars@wcsr.com
Web: www.wcsr.com/firm/diversity

Summary To provide financial assistance and summer work experience to Asian Americans and other diverse students at designated law schools.

Eligibility This program is open to students at designated law schools who are members of underrepresented groups. Applicants must be able to demonstrate solid academic credentials, personal or professional achievement outside the classroom, and significant participation in community service. Along with their application, they must submit a 300-word essay on their choice of 2 topics that change annually but relate to the legal profession. They must also submit a brief statement explaining how they would contribute to the goal of creating a more diverse legal community.

Financial data The stipend is $4,000. Recipients are also offered summer employment at an office of the sponsoring law firm. Salaries are the same as the firm's other summer associates in each office.

Duration 1 year (the second year of law school); may be renewed 1 additional year.

Additional information This program was established in 2004. The eligible law schools are North Carolina Central University School of Law (Durham, North Carolina), University of North Carolina at Chapel Hill School of Law (Chapel Hill, North Carolina), Duke University School of Law (Durham, North Carolina), Wake Forest University School of Law (Winston-Salem, North Carolina), University of South Carolina School of Law (Columbia, South Carolina), Howard University School of Law (Washington, D.C.), University of Virginia School of Law (Charlottesville, Virginia), University of Georgia School of Law (Athens, Georgia), Georgia Washington University Law School (Washington, D.C.), Emory University School of Law (Atlanta, Georgia), and University of Maryland School of Law (Baltimore, Maryland). The sponsoring law firm has offices in Atlanta (Georgia), Baltimore (Maryland), Charlotte (North Carolina), Greensboro (North Carolina), Greenville (South Carolina), Raleigh (North Carolina), Research Triangle Park (North Carolina), Tysons Corner (Virginia), Washington (D.C.), Wilmington (Delaware), and Winston-Salem (North Carolina).

Number awarded Varies each year; recently, 9 of these scholarships were awarded.

Deadline May of each year.

[803]
WORLD COMMUNION SCHOLARSHIPS

United Methodist Church
General Board of Global Ministries
Attn: Scholarship Office
475 Riverside Drive, Room 1351
New York, NY 10115
(212) 870-3787   Toll Free: (800) UMC-GBGM
E-mail: scholars@gbgm-umc.org
Web: new.gbgm-umc.org

Summary To provide financial assistance to Asian Americans, other minorities, and foreign students who are interested in attending graduate school to prepare for leadership in promoting the goals of the United Methodist Church.

Eligibility This program is open to 1) students from Methodist churches in nations other than the United States, and 2) members of ethnic and racial minorities in the United States. Applicants must have applied to or been admitted to a master's, doctoral, or professional program at a university or seminary in the United States. They should be planning to return to their communities to work in furthering Christian mission, whether that be in the local church, the neighborhood clinic, the state rural development office, or the national office on education. Financial need must be demonstrated.

Financial data The stipend ranges from $250 to $12,500, depending on the recipient's related needs and school expenses.

Duration 1 year.

Additional information These awards are funded by the World Communion Offering received in United Methodist Churches on the first Sunday in October.

Number awarded 5 to 10 each year.

Deadline November of each year.

[804]
XEROX TECHNICAL MINORITY SCHOLARSHIP PROGRAM

Xerox Corporation
Attn: Technical Minority Scholarship Program
150 State Street, Fourth Floor
Rochester, NY 14614
(585) 422-7689   E-mail: xtmsp@rballiance.com
Web: www.xeroxstudentcareers.com

Summary To provide financial assistance to Asian Americans and other minorities interested in undergraduate or graduate education in the sciences and/or engineering.

Eligibility This program is open to minorities (people of African American, Asian, Pacific Islander, Native American, Native Alaskan, or Hispanic descent) working full time on a bachelor's, master's, or doctoral degree in chemistry, computing and software systems, engineering (chemical, computer, electrical, imaging, manufacturing, mechanical, optical, or software), information management, laser optics, materials science, physics, or printing management science. Applicants must be U.S. citizens or permanent residents with a GPA of 3.0 or higher and attending a 4-year college or university.

Financial data Stipends range from $1,000 to $10,000.

Duration 1 year.

Number awarded Varies each year, recently, 125 of these scholarships were awarded.

Deadline September of each year.

[805]
YOUNG SOO CHOI STUDENT SCHOLARSHIP AWARD

Society of Toxicology
Attn: Korean Toxicologists Association in America Special
  Interest Group
1821 Michael Faraday Drive, Suite 300
Reston, VA 20190-5348
(703) 438-3115   Fax: (703) 438-3113
E-mail: sothq@toxicology.org
Web: www.toxicology.org/ai/af/awards.aspx

Summary To provide financial assistance to Korean students who are working on a graduate degree in toxicology.

Eligibility This program is open to Korean students (having been born in Korea or, if born in the United States, having 1 or more parents of Korean descent) who are enrolled or planning to enroll in a graduate program in toxicology or in a field of biomedical science related to toxicology. Applicants must submit a description of their graduate program (including any research conducted or planned), copies of any abstracts prepared for presentations at professional meetings, a brief statement indicating how the scholarship will assist in their graduate training, and a letter of recommendation from their mentor. Selection is based on merit and financial need.

Financial data A stipend is awarded (amount not specified).

Duration 1 year.

Additional information This program was established in 2008.

Number awarded 1 each year.

Deadline January of each year.

Professionals/
Postdoctorates

Listed alphabetically by program title and described in detail here are 120 grants, awards, educational support programs, residencies, and other sources of "free money" available to professionals and postdoctorates of Asian origins (including those of subcontinent Asian and Pacific Islander descent). This funding can be used to support research, creative activities, formal academic classes, training courses, and/or residencies in the United States.

[806]
AAPI CREATIVE WRITING COMPETITION

American Association of Physicians of Indian Origin
Attn: Medical Students, Residents and Fellows Section
600 Enterprise Drive, Suite 108
Oak Brook, IL 60523
(630) 990-2277   Fax: (630) 990-2281
E-mail: preselect@aapimsr.org
Web: www.aapimsr.org

Summary To recognize and reward members of the American Association of Physicians of Indian Origin (AAPI) who submit outstanding samples of creative writing, poetry, or photography.

Eligibility This competition is open to members of the Medical Students, Residents and Fellows (MSRF) section and the Young Physician's Section (YPS) of the AAPI. Applicants must submit 1) original writings, up to 1,000 words in length, on a medically-related topic, including stories based on real life experiences, travel-related stories, personal experiences on campus, or innovative management of patients; 2) poems, up to 50 lines, related to the medical experience, whether from the point of view of a health care worker, a patient, or simply an observer; or 3) photographs, not necessarily medically-related, that may capture an interesting scene, mood, or moment in life.

Financial data Prizes in each category are $500 for first, $400 for second, and $300 for third.

Duration The competition is held annually.

Additional information This competition was first held in 2011.

Number awarded 9 each year: 3 in each category.

Deadline April of each year.

[807]
ABE FELLOWSHIP PROGRAM

Social Science Research Council
Attn: Japan Program
One Pierrepont Plaza, 15th Floor
Brooklyn, NY 11201
(212) 377-2700   Fax: (212) 377-2727
E-mail: abe@ssrc.org
Web: www.ssrc.org/fellowships/abe-fellowship

Summary To provide funding to postdoctoral scholars (particularly Asian Americans, other minorities, and women) who are interested in conducting research on contemporary policy-relevant affairs in Japan.

Eligibility This program is open to citizens of the United States and Japan as well as to nationals of other countries who can demonstrate strong and serious long-term affiliations with research communities in Japan or the United States. Applicants must have a Ph.D. or the terminal degree for their field, or have attained an equivalent level of professional experience. They should be interested in conducting multidisciplinary research on topics of pressing global concern. Currently, research must focus on the 3 themes of traditional and nontraditional approaches to security and diplomacy, global and regional economic issues, or the role of civil society. Previous language training is not a prerequisite for this fellowship. Minorities and women are particularly encouraged to apply.

Financial data The terms of the fellowship include a base award and funds to pay supplementary research and travel expenses as necessary for completion of the research project.

Duration The program provides support for 3 to 12 months over a 24-month period.

Additional information Fellows are expected to affiliate with an American or Japanese institution appropriate to their research aims. In addition to receiving fellowship awards, fellows attend annual Abe Fellows Conferences, which promote the development of an international network of scholars concerned with research on contemporary policy issues. Funds are provided by the Japan Foundation's Center for Global Partnership. Fellows should plan to spend at least one-third of their tenure abroad in Japan or the United States.

Deadline August of each year.

[808]
AIR FELLOWS PROGRAM

American Educational Research Association
1430 K Street, N.W., Suite 1200
Washington, DC 20005
(202) 238-3200   Fax: (202) 238-3250
E-mail: fellowships@aera.net
Web: www.aera.net

Summary To provide an opportunity for junior scholars in the field of education (especially Asian American and other minority scholars) to engage in a program of research and advanced training while in residence in Washington, D.C.

Eligibility This program is open to early scholars who received a Ph.D. or Ed.D. degree within the past 3 years in a field related to education and educational processes. Applicants must be proposing a program of intensive research and training in Washington, D.C. Selection is based on past academic record, writing sample, goal statement, range and quality of research experiences, other relevant work or professional experiences, potential contributions to education research, and references. A particular goal of the program is to increase the number of minority professionals conducting advanced research or providing technical assistance. U.S. citizenship or permanent resident status is required.

Financial data Stipends range from $45,000 to $50,000 per year.

Duration Up to 2 years.

Additional information This program, jointly sponsored by the American Educational Research Association (AERA) and the American Institutes for Research (AIR), was first offered for 2006. Fellows rotate between the 2 organizations and receive mentoring from recognized researchers and practitioners in a variety of substantive areas in education.

Number awarded Up to 3 each year.

Deadline December of each year.

[809]
AIR FORCE OFFICE OF SCIENTIFIC RESEARCH BROAD AGENCY ANNOUNCEMENT

Air Force Office of Scientific Research
Attn: Directorate of Academic and International Affairs
875 North Randolph Street, Room 3112
Arlington, VA 22203-1954
(703) 696-9738   Fax: (703) 696-9733
E-mail: afosr.baa@afosr.af.mil
Web: www.wpafb.mil/afrl/afosr

Summary   To provide funding to investigators (particularly those at minorities serving institutions) who are interested in conducting scientific research of interest to the U.S. Air Force.

Eligibility   This program is open to investigators qualified to conduct research in designated scientific and technical areas. The general fields of interest include 1) aerospace, chemical, and materials sciences; 2) physics and electronics; 3) mathematics, information, and life sciences; 4) discovery challenge thrusts; and 5) other innovative research concepts. Assistance includes grants to university scientists, support for academic institutions, contracts for industry research, cooperative agreements, and support for basic research in Air Force laboratories. Because the Air Force encourages the sharing and transfer of technology, it welcomes proposals that envision cooperation among 2 or more partners from academia, industry, and Air Force organizations. It particularly encourages proposals from small businesses, Historically Black Colleges and Universities (HBCUs), other Minority Institutions (MIs), and minority researchers.

Financial data   The amounts of the awards depend on the nature of the proposals and the availability of funds. Recently, grants averaged approximately $150,000 per year.

Duration   Grants range up to 5 years.

Additional information   Contact the Air Force Office of Scientific Research for details on particular program areas of interest. Outstanding principal investigators on grants issued through this program are nominated to receive Presidential Early Career Awards for Scientists and Engineers.

Number awarded   Varies each year; recently, this program awarded approximately 1,650 grants and contracts to applicants at about 450 academic institutions and industrial firms.

Deadline   Each program area specifies deadline dates.

[810]
AMERICAN ASSOCIATION OF CHINESE IN TOXICOLOGY AND CHARLES RIVER BEST ABSTRACT AWARD

Society of Toxicology
Attn: American Association of Chinese in Toxicology
  Special Interest Group
1821 Michael Faraday Drive, Suite 300
Reston, VA 20190-5348
(703) 438-3115   Fax: (703) 438-3113
E-mail: sothq@toxicology.org
Web: www.toxicology.org/ai/af/awards.aspx

Summary   To recognize and reward graduate student and postdoctoral members of the Society of Toxicology (SOT) who are of Chinese ethnic origin and present outstanding papers at the annual meeting.

Eligibility   This award is available to SOT members who are graduate students or postdoctoral fellows of Chinese descent (having 1 or more parents of Chinese descent). Candidates must have an accepted abstract for the SOT annual meeting. Along with the abstract, they must submit a cover letter outlining the significance of the work to the field of toxicology.

Financial data   The prizes are $500 for first, $300 for second, and $200 for third.

Duration   The prizes are presented annually.

Number awarded   3 each year.

Deadline   December of each year.

[811]
AMERICAN ASSOCIATION OF OBSTETRICIANS AND GYNECOLOGISTS FOUNDATION SCHOLARSHIPS

American Gynecological and Obstetrical Society
Attn: American Association of Obstetricians and
  Gynecologists Foundation
409 12th Street, S.W.
Washington, DC 20024-2188
(202) 863-1649   Fax: (202) 554-0453
E-mail: clarkins@acog.org
Web: www.agosonline.org/aaogf/index.asp

Summary   To provide funding to physicians (especially Asian Americans, other minorities, and women) who are interested in a program of research training in obstetrics and gynecology.

Eligibility   Applicants must have an M.D. degree and be eligible for the certification process of the American Board of Obstetrics and Gynecology (ABOG). They must be interested in participating in research training conducted by 1 or more faculty mentors at an academic department of obstetrics and gynecology in the United States or Canada. the research training may be either laboratory-based or clinical, and should focus on fundamental biology, disease mechanisms, interventions or diagnostics, epidemiology, or translational research. There is no formal application form, but departments must supply a description of the candidate's qualifications, including a curriculum vitae, bibliography, prior training, past research experience, and evidence of completion of residency training in obstetrics and gynecology; a comprehensive description of the proposed training program; a description of departmental resources appropriate to the training; a detailed mentoring plan; a list of other research grants, training grants, or scholarships previously or currently held by the applicant; and a budget. Applicants for the scholarship cosponsored by the Society for Maternal-Fetal Medicine (SMFM) must also be members or associate members of the SMFM. Women and minority candidates are strongly encouraged to apply. Selection is based on the scholarly, clinical, and research qualifications of the candidate; evidence of the candidate's commitment to an investigative career in academic obstetrics and gynecology in the United States or Canada; qualifications of the sponsoring department and mentor; overall quality of the mentoring plan, and quality of the research project. Preference may be given to applications from candidates training in areas currently underrepresented in academic obstetrics and gynecology (e.g., urogynecology, family planning).

Financial data   The grant is $100,000 per year, of which at least $5,000 but not more than $15,000 must be used for employee benefits. In addition, sufficient funds to support travel to the annual fellows' retreat must be set aside. The balance of the funds may be used for salary, technical support, and supplies. The grant co-sponsored by the SMFM must be matched by an institutional commitment of at least $30,000 per year.

Duration 1 year; may be renewed for 2 additional years, based on satisfactory progress of the scholar.

Additional information Scholars must devote at least 75% of their effort to the program of research training.

Number awarded 2 each year: 1 co-sponsored by ABOG and 1 co-sponsored by SMFM.

Deadline June of each year.

[812]
AMERICAN ASSOCIATION OF PHYSICIANS OF INDIAN ORIGIN NATIONAL RESEARCH COMPETITION

American Association of Physicians of Indian Origin
Attn: Medical Students, Residents and Fellows Section
600 Enterprise Drive, Suite 108
Oak Brook, IL 60523
(630) 990-2277   Fax: (630) 990-2281
E-mail: preselect@aapimsr.org
Web: www.aapimsr.org

Summary To recognize and reward members of the American Association of Physicians of Indian Origin (AAPI) who submit outstanding research abstracts for presentation at the annual conference.

Eligibility This competition is open to members of the Medical Students, Residents and Fellows (MSRF) section and the Young Physician's Section (YPS) of the AAPI. Applicants must submit abstracts of research for presentation at the AAPI annual conference. Abstracts should be limited to 500 words with sections on background, methods, results, conclusions, and (for basic science articles) clinical relevance. Applicants must attend the conference where finalists are chosen for a poster and an 8-minute oral presentation.

Financial data Prizes are $1,000 for first and $750 for second.

Duration The competition is held annually.

Number awarded 2 each year.

Deadline April of each year.

[813]
AMERICAN COUNCIL OF LEARNED SOCIETIES FELLOWSHIPS

American Council of Learned Societies
Attn: Office of Fellowships and Grants
633 Third Avenue
New York, NY 10017-6795
(212) 697-1505   Fax: (212) 949-8058
E-mail: fellowships@acls.org
Web: www.acls.org/programs/acls

Summary To provide research funding to scholars in all disciplines of the humanities and the humanities-related social sciences, especially Asian Americans, other minorities, and women.

Eligibility This program is open to scholars at all stages of their careers who received a Ph.D. degree at least 2 years previously. Established scholars who can demonstrate the equivalent of the Ph.D. in publications and professional experience may also qualify. Applicants must be U.S. citizens or permanent residents who have not had supported leave time for at least 2 years prior to the start of the proposed research. Appropriate fields of specialization include, but are not limited to, American studies; anthropology; archaeology; art and architectural history; classics; economics; film; geography; history; languages and literatures; legal studies; linguistics; musicology; philosophy; political science; psychology; religious studies; rhetoric, communication, and media studies; sociology; and theater, dance, and performance studies. Proposals in those fields of the social sciences are eligible only if they employ predominantly humanistic approaches (e.g., economic history, law and literature, political philosophy). Proposals in interdisciplinary and cross-disciplinary studies are welcome, as are proposals focused on a geographic region or on a cultural or linguistic group. Awards are available at 3 academic levels: full professor, associate professor, and assistant professor. Applications are particularly invited from women and members of minority groups.

Financial data The maximum grant is $60,000 for full professors and equivalent, $40,000 for associate professors and equivalent, or $35,000 for assistant professors and equivalent. Normally, fellowships are intended as salary replacement and may be held concurrently with other fellowships, grants, and sabbatical pay, up to an amount equal to the candidate's current academic year salary.

Duration 6 to 12 months.

Additional information This program is supported in part by funding from the Ford Foundation, the Andrew W. Mellon Foundation, the National Endowment for the Humanities, the William and Flora Hewlett Foundation, and the Rockefeller Foundation.

Number awarded Approximately 57 each year: 17 at the full professor level, 18 at the association professor level, and 22 at the assistant professor level.

Deadline September of each year.

[814]
AMERICAN GASTROENTEROLOGICAL ASSOCIATION RESEARCH SCHOLAR AWARDS

American Gastroenterological Association
Attn: AGA Research Foundation
Research Awards Manager
4930 Del Ray Avenue
Bethesda, MD 20814-2512
(301) 222-4012   Fax: (301) 654-5920
E-mail: awards@gastro.org
Web: www.gastro.org/aga-foundation/grants

Summary To provide research funding to investigators (especially Asian Americans and other minorities or women) who are interested in developing an independent career in an area of gastroenterology, hepatology, or related fields.

Eligibility Applicants must hold full-time faculty positions at North American universities or professional institutes at the time of application. They should be early in their careers (fellows and established investigators are not appropriate candidates). Candidates with an M.D. degree must have completed clinical training within the past 5 years and those with a Ph.D. must have completed their degree within the past 5 years. Membership in the American Gastroenterological Association (AGA) is required. Selection is based on significance, investigator, innovation, approach, environment, relevance to AGA mission, and evidence of institutional commitment. Women, minorities, and physician/scientist investigators are strongly encouraged to apply.

Financial data The grant is $60,000 per year. Funds are to be used for project costs, including salary, supplies, and equipment but excluding travel. Indirect costs are not allowed.

Duration 2 years; a third year of support may be available, contingent upon availability of funds and a competitive review.

Additional information At least 70% of the recipient's research effort should relate to the gastrointestinal tract or liver.

Number awarded 1 or more each year.

Deadline September of each year.

[815]
ANDREW W. MELLON FOUNDATION/ACLS RECENT DOCTORAL RECIPIENTS FELLOWSHIPS

American Council of Learned Societies
Attn: Office of Fellowships and Grants
633 Third Avenue
New York, NY 10017-6795
(212) 697-1505   Fax: (212) 949-8058
E-mail: fellowships@acls.org
Web: www.acls.org/programs/rdr

Summary To provide funding to recent recipients of doctoral degrees in all disciplines of the humanities and the humanities-related social sciences (particularly Asian Americans, other minorities, and women) who need funding to advance their scholarly career.

Eligibility This program is open to recent recipients of a doctoral degree in a humanities or humanities-related social science discipline. Applicants must have been 1) a recipient of an Andrew W. Mellon Foundation/ACLS Dissertation Completion Fellowship in the previous year; 2) designated as an alternate in that fellowship program; or 3) a recipient of a dissertation completion fellowship in another program of national stature (e.g., Whiting, AAUW, Newcombe). They must be seeking funding to position themselves for further scholarly advancement, whether or not they hold academic positions. Appropriate fields of specialization include, but are not limited to, American studies; anthropology; archaeology; art and architectural history; classics; economics; film; geography; history; languages and literatures; legal studies; linguistics; musicology; philosophy; political science; psychology; religious studies; rhetoric, communication, and media studies; sociology; and theater, dance, and performance studies. Proposals in those fields of the social sciences are eligible only if they employ predominantly humanistic approaches (e.g., economic history, law and literature, political philosophy). Proposals in interdisciplinary and cross-disciplinary studies are welcome, as are proposals focused on any geographic region or on any cultural or linguistic group. Applications are particularly invited from women and members of minority groups.

Financial data The stipend is $30,000.

Duration 1 academic year. Grantees may accept this fellowship during the 2 years following the date of the award.

Additional information This program, which began in 2007, is supported by funding from the Andrew W. Mellon Foundation and administered by the American Council of

Learned Societies (ACLS). Fellows may not teach during the tenure of the fellowship. If they have a faculty position, they may use the fellowship to take research leave. Fellows who do not have a full-time position may choose to affiliate with a humanities research center or conduct research independently.

Number awarded 25 each year.

Deadline November of each year.

[816]
APA/SAMHSA MINORITY FELLOWSHIP PROGRAM

American Psychiatric Association
Attn: Department of Minority and National Affairs
1000 Wilson Boulevard, Suite 1825
Arlington, VA 22209-3901
(703) 907-8653   Toll Free: (888) 35-PSYCH
Fax: (703) 907-7852   E-mail: mking@psych.org
Web: www.psych.org/Resources/OMNA/MFP.aspx

Summary To provide educational enrichment to Asian American and other minority psychiatrists-in-training and stimulate interest in providing quality and effective services to minorities and the underserved.

Eligibility This program is open to residents who are in at least their second year of psychiatric training, members of the American Psychiatric Association (APA), and U.S. citizens or permanent residents. A goal of the program is to develop leadership to improve the quality of mental health care for members of ethnic minority groups (American Indians, Native Alaskans, Asian Americans, Native Hawaiians, Native Pacific Islanders, African Americans, and Hispanics/Latinos). Applicants must be interested in working with a component of the APA that is of interest to them and relevant to their career goals. Along with their application, they must submit a 2-page essay on how the fellowship would be utilized to alter their present training and ultimately assist them in achieving their career goals. Selection is based on commitment to serve ethnic minority populations, demonstrated leadership abilities, awareness of the importance of culture in mental health, and interest in the interrelationship between mental health/illness and transcultural factors.

Financial data Fellows receive a monthly stipend (amount not specified) and reimbursement of transportation, lodging, meals, and incidentals in connection with attendance at program-related activities. They are expected to use the funds to enhance their own professional development, improve training in cultural competence at their training institution, improve awareness of culturally relevant issues in psychiatry at their institution, expand research in areas relevant to minorities and underserved populations, enhance the current treatment modalities for minority patients and underserved individuals at their institution, and improve awareness in the surrounding community about mental health issues (particularly with regard to minority populations).

Duration 1 year; may be renewed 1 additional year.

Additional information Funding for this program is provided by the Substance Abuse and Mental Health Services Administration (SAMHSA). As part of their assignment to an APA component, fellows must attend the fall component meetings in September and the APA annual meeting in May. At those meeting, they can share their experiences as residents and minorities and discuss issues that impact on minority populations. This program is an outgrowth of the fellowships that were established in 1974 under a grant from the National Institute of Mental Health in answer to concerns about the underrepresentation of minorities in psychiatry.

Number awarded Varies each year; recently, 16 of these fellowships were awarded.

Deadline January of each year.

[817]
APAICS SUMMER INTERNSHIPS

Asian Pacific American Institute for Congressional
Studies
Attn: Summer Internship Program
1001 Connecticut Avenue, N.W., Suite 530
Washington, DC 20036
(202) 296-9200   Fax: (202) 296-9236
E-mail: apaics@apaics.org
Web: www.apaics.org

Summary To provide an opportunity for undergraduate students with an interest in issues affecting the Asian Pacific Islander American communities to work in Washington, D.C. during the summer.

Eligibility This program is open to Asian American and Pacific Islander students currently enrolled in an accredited undergraduate institution; recent (within 90 days) graduates are also eligible. Applicants must be able to demonstrate interest in the political process, public policy issues, and Asian American and Pacific Islander community affairs; leadership abilities; and oral and written communication skills. They must be 18 years of age or older; U.S. citizens or permanent residents; and interested in working in Congress, federal agencies, or institutions that further the mission of the Asian Pacific American Institute for Congressional Studies (APAICS). Preference is given to students who have not previously had an internship in Washington, D.C.

Financial data The stipend is $2,500 for interns from the continental United States or $3,000 for interns from Hawaii.

Duration 8 weeks, starting in June.

Number awarded Varies each year; recently, 9 interns were selected for this program.

Deadline January of each year.

[818]
ASIAN AMERICAN STUDIES VISITING SCHOLAR AND VISITING RESEARCHER PROGRAM

University of California at Los Angeles
Institute of American Cultures
Asian American Studies Center
3230 Campbell Hall
P.O. Box 951546
Los Angeles, CA 90095-1546
(310) 825-2974   Fax: (310) 206-9844
Web: www.gdnet.ucla.edu/iacweb/pstweber.htm

Summary To provide funding to scholars interested in conducting research in Asian American studies at UCLA's Asian American Studies Center.

Eligibility Applicants must have completed a doctoral degree in Asian American or related studies. They must be interested in teaching or conducting research at UCLA's Asian American Studies Center. Visiting Scholar appointments are available to people who currently hold permanent

academic appointments; Visiting Researcher appointments are available to newly-degree scholars. UCLA faculty, students, and staff are not eligible. U.S. citizenship or permanent resident status is required.

Financial data Fellows receive a stipend of $32,000 to $35,000 (depending on rank, experience, and date of completion of the Ph.D.), health benefits, and up to $4,000 in research support. Visiting Scholars are paid through their home institution; Visiting Researchers receive their funds directly from UCLA.

Duration 9 months, beginning in October.

Additional information Fellows must teach or do research in the programs of the center. The award is offered in conjunction with UCLA's Institute of American Cultures (IAC).

Number awarded 1 each year.

Deadline January of each year.

[819]
ASIAN PACIFIC AMERICAN INSTITUTE FOR CONGRESSIONAL STUDIES FELLOWSHIP PROGRAM

Asian Pacific American Institute for Congressional
Studies
Attn: Fellowship Program
1001 Connecticut Avenue, N.W., Suite 530
Washington, DC 20036
(202) 296-9200   Fax: (202) 296-9236
E-mail: apaics@apaics.org
Web: www.apaics.org

Summary To provide an opportunity for recent graduates with an interest in issues affecting the Asian Pacific American community to work in the Executive or Legislative branch of the federal government or a nonprofit agency.

Eligibility Applicants must have completed a graduate or bachelor's degree from an accredited educational institution. They must have a demonstrated interest in the political process, public policy, and Asian Pacific American community affairs; relevant work or internship experience; evidence of leadership abilities; oral and written communication skills; a cumulative GPA of 3.0 or higher; and an interest in gaining work experience with the federal government or a nonprofit agency in Washington, D.C. U.S. citizenship or permanent resident status is required. Along with their application, they must submit a 750-word essay on the role of the Congressional Asian Pacific American Caucus (CAPAC) and why they want to be a part of it.

Financial data The stipend is $20,000. Funds are intended to cover housing and personal expenses. A separate stipend covers basic health insurance, and round-trip air transportation is provided.

Duration 9 months, starting in September.

Additional information This program is supported by Anheuser-Busch and by Wal-Mart Stores.

Number awarded Varies each year; recently, 4 of these fellowships were awarded.

Deadline March of each year.

[820]
BEHAVIORAL SCIENCES POSTDOCTORAL FELLOWSHIPS IN EPILEPSY

Epilepsy Foundation
Attn: Research Department
8301 Professional Place
Landover, MD 20785-2237
(301) 459-3700   Toll Free: (800) EFA-1000
Fax: (301) 577-2684   TDD: (800) 332-2070
E-mail: grants@efa.org
Web: www.epilepsyfoundation.org

Summary To provide funding to postdoctorates in the behavioral sciences (especially Asian Americans, other minorities, women, and individuals with disabilities) who wish to pursue research training in an area related to epilepsy.

Eligibility Applicants must have received a Ph.D. or equivalent degree in a field of social science, including (but not limited to) sociology, social work, anthropology, nursing, or economics. They must be interested in receiving additional research training to prepare for a career in clinical behavioral aspects of epilepsy. Academic faculty holding the rank of instructor or above are not eligible, nor are graduate or medical students, medical residents, permanent government employees, or employees in private industry. Because these fellowships are designed as training opportunities, the quality of the training plans and environment are considered in the selection process. Other selection criteria include the scientific quality of the proposed research, a statement regarding the relevance of the research to epilepsy, the applicant's qualifications, the preceptor's qualifications, adequacy of the facility, and related epilepsy programs at the institution. Applications from women, members of minority groups, and people with disabilities are especially encouraged. U.S. citizenship is not required, but the research must be conducted in the United States.

Financial data Grants up to $40,000 are available.

Duration 1 year.

Number awarded Varies each year.

Deadline March of each year.

[821]
BEYOND MARGINS AWARD

PEN American Center
Attn: Beyond Margins Coordinator
588 Broadway, Suite 303
New York, NY 10012
(212) 334-1660, ext. 108   Fax: (212) 334-2181
E-mail: nick@pen.org
Web: www.pen.org/page.php/prmID/280

Summary To recognize and reward outstanding Asian Americans and other authors of color.

Eligibility This award is presented to an author of color (African, Arab, Asian, Caribbean, Latino, and Native American) whose book-length writings were published in the United States during the current calendar year. Works of fiction, literary nonfiction, biography/memoir, and other works of literary character are strongly preferred. U.S. citizenship or residency is not required. Nominations must be submitted by publishers or agents.

Financial data The prize is $1,000.

Duration The prizes are awarded annually.

Number awarded 5 each year.

Deadline December of each year.

[822]
BYRD FELLOWSHIP PROGRAM

Ohio State University
Byrd Polar Research Center
Attn: Fellowship Committee
Scott Hall Room 108
1090 Carmack Road
Columbus, OH 43210-1002
(614) 292-6531   Fax: (614) 292-4697
Web: bprc.osu.edu/byrdfellow

Summary To provide funding to postdoctorates (particularly Asian Americans, other minorities, women, veterans, and individuals with disabilities) who are interested in conducting research on the Arctic or Antarctic areas at Ohio State University.

Eligibility This program is open to postdoctorates of superior academic background who are interested in conducting advanced research on either Arctic or Antarctic problems at the Byrd Polar Research Center at Ohio State University. Applicants must have received their doctorates within the past 5 years. Each application should include a statement of general research interest, a description of the specific research to be conducted during the fellowship, and a curriculum vitae. Women, minorities, Vietnam-era veterans, disabled veterans, and individuals with disabilities are particularly encouraged to apply.

Financial data The stipend is $40,000 per year; an allowance of $3,000 for research and travel is also provided.

Duration 18 months.

Additional information This program was established by a major gift from the Byrd Foundation in memory of Rear Admiral Richard Evelyn Byrd and Marie Ames Byrd, his wife. Except for field work or other research activities requiring absence from campus, fellows are expected to be in residence at the university for the duration of the program.

Deadline October of each year.

[823]
CAMS SCHOLARSHIP PROGRAM

Chinese American Medical Society
Attn: Jerry Huo, Scholarship Committee
41 Elizabeth Street, Suite 403
New York, NY 10013
(212) 334-4760   Fax: (212) 965-1876
E-mail: jerryhuomd@gmail.com
Web: www.camsociety.org/scholarshipprogram.html

Summary To provide financial assistance to Chinese and Chinese American students who are working on a degree in medicine or dentistry.

Eligibility This program is open to Chinese or Chinese American students who are currently enrolled in the first, second, or third year at an approved medical or dental school in the United States. Applicants must submit a personal statement that includes their career goals, a current vitae, 2 letters of recommendation, and documentation of financial need. Special consideration is given to applicants with research projects relating to health care of the Chinese.

Financial data The scholarships range from $1,000 to $1,500.

Duration 1 year; recipients may reapply.

Additional information This program includes the Esther Lim Memorial Scholarship established in 1989, the Ruth Liu Memorial Scholarship established in 1996, and the American Center for Chinese Medical Sciences Scholarship established in 2004 upon the dissolution of that organization. Recipients who do not complete their planned study, research, or teaching must make a prorated refund to the society.

Number awarded Varies; recently, 3 to 5 scholarships have been awarded each year.

Deadline April of each year.

[824]
CAREER DEVELOPMENT GRANTS

American Association of University Women
Attn: AAUW Educational Foundation
301 ACT Drive, Department 60
P.O. Box 4030
Iowa City, IA 52243-4030
(319) 337-1716, ext. 60   Fax: (319) 337-1204
E-mail: aauw@act.org
Web: www.aauw.org

Summary To provide financial assistance to women (particularly Asian American and other minority women) who are seeking career advancement, career change, or reentry into the workforce.

Eligibility This program is open to women who are U.S. citizens or permanent residents, have earned a bachelor's degree, received their most recent degree more than 4 years ago, and are making career changes, seeking to advance in current careers, or reentering the work force. Applicants must be interested in working toward a master's degree, second bachelor's or associate degree, professional degree (e.g., M.D., J.D.), certification program, or technical school certificate. They must be planning to undertake course work at an accredited 2- or 4-year college or university (or a technical school that is licensed, accredited, or approved by the U.S. Department of Education). Special consideration is given to women of color and women pursuing credentials in nontraditional fields. Support is not provided for prerequisite course work or for Ph.D. course work or dissertations. Selection is based on demonstrated commitment to education and equity for women and girls, reason for seeking higher education or technical training, degree to which study plan is consistent with career objectives, potential for success in chosen field, documentation of opportunities in chosen field, feasibility of study plans and proposed time schedule, validity of proposed budget and budget narrative (including sufficient outside support), and quality of written proposal.

Financial data Grants range from $2,000 to $12,000. Funds may be used for tuition, fees, books, supplies, local transportation, dependent child care, or purchase of a computer required for the study program.

Duration 1 year, beginning in July; nonrenewable.

Additional information The filing fee is $35.

Number awarded Varies each year; recently, 47 of these grants, with a value of $500,000, were awarded.

Deadline December of each year.

[825]
CENTER FOR ADVANCED STUDY IN THE BEHAVIORAL SCIENCES RESIDENTIAL POSTDOCTORAL FELLOWSHIPS

Center for Advanced Study in the Behavioral Sciences
Attn: Secretary and Program Coordinator
75 Alta Road
Stanford, CA 94305-8090
(650) 321-2052   Fax: (650) 321-1192
E-mail: secretary@casbs.org
Web: www.casbs.org

Summary To provide funding to behavioral scientists (especially Asian Americans, other minorities, and women) who are interested in conducting research at the Center for Advanced Study in the Behavioral Sciences in Stanford, California.

Eligibility Eligible to be nominated for this fellowship are scientists and scholars from this country or abroad who show exceptional accomplishment or promise in the core social and behavioral disciplines: anthropology, economics, political science, psychology, or sociology; applications are also accepted from scholars in a wide range of humanistic disciplines, education, linguistics, and the biological sciences. Selection is based on standing in the field rather than on the merit of a particular project under way at a given time. A special effort is made to promote diversity among the scholars by encouraging participation from groups that often have been overlooked in academia: younger scholars, women, minorities, international scholars, and scholars whose home universities are not research-oriented.

Financial data The stipend is based on the fellow's regular salary for the preceding year, with a cap of $60,000. In most cases, the fellow contributes to the cost of the stipend with support from sabbatical or other funding source.

Duration From 9 to 11 months.

Additional information Fellows must be in residence in a community within 10 miles of the center for the duration of the program.

Number awarded Approximately 45 each year.

Deadline February of each year.

[826]
CENTER FOR ASIAN AMERICAN MEDIA FUNDING

Center for Asian American Media
Attn: Media Fund Director
145 Ninth Street, Suite 350
San Francisco, CA 94103
(415) 863-0814, ext. 122   Fax: (415) 863-7428
E-mail: mediafund@asianamericanmedia.org
Web: caamedia.org/filmmaker-resources/funding

Summary To provide funding to producers of public television programs that relate to the Asian American experience.

Eligibility This program is open to independent producers who are interested in developing and finishing public television programs on Asian American issues. Grants are available in 2 categories: 1) production funds, for projects at the production and/or post-production state, and 2) completion funds, for projects in the final post-production phase. Applicants must have previous film or television experience as demonstrated by a sample tape and must have artistic, budgetary, and editorial control. They must be 18 years of age or older and citizens or legal residents of the United States. All programs must be standard broadcast length and in accordance with PBS broadcast specifications. Ineligible projects include those: for which the exclusive domestic television broadcast rights are not available; are in the script development stage; intended solely for theatrical release or commercial in nature; in which applicant is commissioned, employed, or hired by a commercial or public television station; which use funds raised from investors and have a commercial financing structure in place; that are thesis projects or student films co- or solely owned or copywritten, or editorially or fiscally controlled by the school; that are foreign-based, owned, or controlled; or that are industrial or promotional projects. In the selection process, the following questions are considered: is the story idea compelling, engaging, original, and well-conceived; is the visual/stylistic treatment effective and distinctive; can the project be completed with a realistic timeline; will the project appeal not only to Asian American viewers, but also to a broader television audience; and does the sample tape show the skills and/or potential of the applicant to complete the proposed project.

Financial data Grants range from $20,000 to $50,000.

Additional information This program was formerly known as the National Asian American Telecommunications Association Media Fund Grants. Funding is provided by the Corporation for Public Broadcasting.

Number awarded 5 to 10 grants are awarded each year.

Deadline May of each year.

[827]
CENTER ON BUDGET AND POLICY PRIORITIES INTERNSHIPS

Center on Budget and Policy Priorities
Attn: Internship Coordinator
820 First Street, N.E., Suite 510
Washington, DC 20002
(202) 408-1080   Fax: (202) 408-1056
E-mail: internship@cbpp.org
Web: www.cbpp.org/jobs/index.cfm?fa=internships

Summary To provide work experience at the Center on Budget and Policy Priorities (CBPP) in Washington, D.C. to undergraduates, graduate students, and recent college graduates, especially Asian Americans or other minorities, women, and international students.

Eligibility This program is open to undergraduates, graduate students, and recent college graduates who are interested in public policy issues affecting low-income families and individuals. Applicants must be interested in working at CBPP in the following areas: media, federal legislation, health policy, housing policy, international budget project, Food Stamps, national budget and tax policy, outreach campaigns, state budget and tax policy, welfare reform, and income support. They should have research, fact-gathering, writing, analytic, and computer skills and a willingness to do administrative as well as substantive tasks. Women, international students, and minorities are encouraged to apply.

Financial data Hourly stipends are $8.50 for undergraduates, $9.50 for interns with a bachelor's degree, $10.50 for graduate students, $12.50 for interns with a master's or law degree, and $12.50 to $15.50 for doctoral students (depend-

ing on progress towards completion of degree requirements, relevant course work, and research).

Duration 1 semester; may be renewed.

Additional information The center specializes in research and analysis oriented toward practical policy decisions and produces analytic reports that are accessible to public officials at national, state, and local levels, to nonprofit organizations, and to the media.

Number awarded Varies each semester; recently, 5 interns were appointed for a fall semester.

Deadline February of each year for summer internships; June of each year for fall internships; October of each year for spring internships.

[828]
CHANG-LIN TIEN EDUCATION LEADERSHIP AWARDS

Asian Pacific Fund
225 Bush Street, Suite 590
San Francisco, CA 94104
(415) 433-6859   Toll Free: (800) 286-1688
Fax: (415) 433-2425   E-mail: info@asianpacificfund.org
Web: www.asianpacificfund.org

Summary To recognize and reward Asian American administrators at colleges and universities who demonstrate outstanding leadership in higher education.

Eligibility This award is available to Asian Americans who are currently serving at the level of dean (or a position of comparable responsibility) or higher at a 4-year public or private college or university in the United States. Nominees should have demonstrated scholarly achievement, administrative experience, pride in their Asian and American heritage, dedication to excellence, and commitment to providing access to academic institutions for a diverse population of students. Self-nominations are not accepted.

Financial data Awards consist of an unrestricted grant of $10,000.

Duration The awards are presented annually.

Additional information These awards were first presented in 2007 to honor Dr. Chang-Lin Tien, the first Asian American to head a major research university as chancellor of UC Berkeley from 1990 to 1997.

Number awarded 2 each year.

Deadline Nominations must be submitted by October of each year.

[829]
CHARLES A. RYSKAMP RESEARCH FELLOWSHIPS

American Council of Learned Societies
Attn: Office of Fellowships and Grants
633 Third Avenue
New York, NY 10017-6795
(212) 697-1505   Fax: (212) 949-8058
E-mail: fellowships@acls.org
Web: www.acls.org/programs/ryskamp

Summary To provide research funding to advanced assistant professors (particularly Asian American and other minority or women professors) in all disciplines of the humanities and the humanities-related social sciences.

Eligibility This program is open to advanced assistant and untenured associate professors in the humanities and related social sciences. Applicants must have successfully completed their institution's last reappointment review before tenure review. They must have a Ph.D. or equivalent degree and be employed at an academic institution in the United States. Appropriate fields of specialization include, but are not limited to, American studies; anthropology; archaeology; art and architectural history; classics; economics; film; geography; history; languages and literatures; legal studies; linguistics; musicology; philosophy; political science; psychology; religious studies; rhetoric, communication, and media studies; sociology; and theater, dance, and performance studies. Proposals in those fields of the social sciences are eligible only if they employ predominantly humanistic approaches (e.g., economic history, law and literature, political philosophy). Proposals in interdisciplinary and cross-disciplinary studies are welcome, as are proposals focused on any geographic region or on any cultural or linguistic group. Applicants are encouraged to spend substantial periods of their leaves in residential interdisciplinary centers, research libraries, or other scholarly archives in the United States or abroad. Applications are particularly invited from women and members of minority groups.

Financial data Fellows receive a stipend of $64,000, a grant of $2,500 for research and travel, and the possibility of an additional summer's support, if justified by a persuasive case.

Duration 1 academic year (9 months) plus an additional summer's research (2 months) if justified.

Additional information This program, first available for the 2002-03 academic year, is supported by funding from the Andrew W. Mellon Foundation.

Number awarded Up to 12 each year.

Deadline September of each year.

[830]
CHIPS QUINN SCHOLARS PROGRAM

Freedom Forum
Attn: Chips Quinn Scholars Program
555 Pennsylvania Avenue, N.W.
Washington, DC 20001
(202) 292-6271   Fax: (202) 292-6275
E-mail: kcatone@freedomforum.org
Web: www.chipsquinn.org

Summary To provide work experience to Asian American and other minority college students or recent graduates who are majoring in journalism.

Eligibility This program is open to students of color who are college juniors, seniors, or recent graduates with journalism majors or career goals in newspapers. Candidates must be nominated or endorsed by journalism faculty, campus media advisers, editors of newspapers, or leaders of minority journalism associations. Along with their application, they must submit a resume, transcripts, 2 letters of recommendation, and an essay of 200 to 500 words on why they want to be a Chips Quinn Scholar. Reporters must also submit 6 samples of published articles they have written; photographers must submit 10 to 20 photographs on a CD. Applicants must have a car and be available to work as a full-time intern during the spring or summer. U.S. citizenship or permanent resident

status is required. Campus newspaper experience is strongly encouraged.

Financial data Students chosen for this program receive a travel stipend to attend a Multimedia training program in Nashville, Tennessee prior to reporting for their internship, a $500 housing allowance from the Freedom Forum, and a competitive salary during their internship.

Duration Internships are for 10 to 12 weeks, in spring or summer.

Additional information This program was established in 1991 in memory of the late John D. Quinn Jr., managing editor of the *Poughkeepsie Journal*. Funding is provided by the Freedom Forum, formerly the Gannett Foundation. After graduating from college and obtaining employment with a newspaper, alumni of this program are eligible to apply for fellowship support to attend professional journalism development activities.

Number awarded Approximately 70 each year. Since the program began, more than 1,200 scholars have been selected.

Deadline October of each year.

[831]
CLAIRE M. FAGIN FELLOWSHIP

American Academy of Nursing
Attn: Geriatric Nursing Capacity Program
888 17th Street, N.W., Suite 800
Washington, DC 20006
(202) 777-1170   Fax: (202) 777-0107
E-mail: bagnc@aannet.org
Web: www.geriatricnursing.org

Summary To provide funding to nurses (particularly Asian American and other minority nurses) who are interested in a program of postdoctoral research training in geriatric nursing.

Eligibility This program is open to registered nurses who hold a doctoral degree in nursing and have a faculty position as an assistant or associate professor at a school of nursing. Recent doctorates in nursing are also eligible. Priority is given to those who received a Ph.D. within the past 7 years. Applicants must demonstrate evidence of commitment to a career in geriatric nursing and education and the potential to develop into independent investigators. They must submit 1) a professional development plan that identifies activities intended to prepare the applicant in research, teaching, and leadership; and 2) a geriatric nursing research project consistent with their interests and previous research or clinical experience, including a mentor who is a geriatric nurse scientist and with whom they will work. Selection is based on potential for substantial long-term contributions to the knowledge base in geriatric nursing; leadership potential; evidence of commitment to a career in academic geriatric nursing; and evidence of involvement in educational, research, and professional activities. U.S. citizenship or permanent resident status is required. Members of underrepresented minority groups (American Indians, Alaska Natives, Asians, Blacks or African Americans, Hispanics or Latinos/Latinas, Native Hawaiians or other Pacific Islanders) are especially encouraged to apply.

Financial data The stipend is $60,000 per year. An additional $5,000 is available to fellows whose research includes the study of pain in the elderly.

Duration 2 years.

Additional information This program began in 2001 with funding from the John A. Hartford Foundation. In 2004, the Atlantic Philanthropies of New York City provided additional support and the Mayday Fund added funding for scholars who focus on the study of pain in the elderly.

Number awarded Varies each year; recently, 9 of these fellowships were awarded.

Deadline January of each year.

[832]
COLLABORATIVE RESEARCH FELLOWSHIPS

American Council of Learned Societies
Attn: Office of Fellowships and Grants
633 Third Avenue
New York, NY 10017-6795
(212) 697-1505   Fax: (212) 949-8058
E-mail: fellowships@acls.org
Web: www.acls.org

Summary To provide funding for collaborative research to scholars (especially Asian American or other minority and women scholars) in any discipline of the humanities and the humanities-related social sciences.

Eligibility This program is open to teams of 2 or more scholars interested in collaborating on a single, substantive project. The project coordinator must have an appointment at a U.S.-based institution of higher education; other project members may be at institutions outside the United States or may be independent scholars. Appropriate fields of specialization include, but are not limited to, American studies; anthropology; archaeology; art and architectural history; classics; economics; film; geography; history; languages and literatures; legal studies; linguistics; musicology; philosophy; political science; psychology; religious studies; rhetoric, communication, and media studies; sociology; and theater, dance, and performance studies. Proposals in those fields of the social sciences are eligible only if they employ predominantly humanistic approaches (e.g., economic history, law and literature, political philosophy). Proposals in interdisciplinary and cross-disciplinary studies are welcome, as are proposals focused on a geographic region or on a cultural or linguistic group. Applications are particularly invited from women and members of minority groups.

Financial data The amount of the grant depends on the number of collaborators, their academic rank, and the duration of research leaves. Funding for salaries is provided at the rate of $60,000 for full professors, $40,000 for associate professors, or $35,000 for assistant professors. An additional $20,000 may be provided for collaboration funds (e.g., travel, materials, research assistance). The maximum amount for any single project is $140,000.

Duration Up to 24 months.

Additional information This program, established in 2008, is supported by funding from the Andrew W. Mellon Foundation.

Number awarded Up to 7 each year.

Deadline September of each year.

[833]
DANIEL H. EFRON RESEARCH AWARD

American College of Neuropsychopharmacology
Attn: Executive Office
5034-A Thoroughbred Lane
Brentwood, TN 37027
(615) 324-2360   Fax: (615) 523-1715
E-mail: acnp@acnp.org
Web: www.acnp.org/programs/awards.aspx

Summary To recognize and reward young scientists (especially Asian American or other minority and women scientists) who have conducted outstanding basic or translational research in neuropsychopharmacology.

Eligibility This award is available to scientists who are younger than 50 years of age. Nominees must have made an outstanding basic or translational contribution to neuropsychopharmacology. The contribution may be preclinical or work that emphasizes the relationship between basic and clinical research. Selection is based on the quality of the contribution and its impact on advancing neuropsychopharmacology. Membership in the American College of Neuropsychopharmacology (ACNP) is not required. Nomination of women and minorities is highly encouraged.

Financial data The award consists of an expense-paid trip to the ACNP annual meeting, a monetary honorarium, and a plaque.

Duration The award is presented annually.

Additional information This award was first presented in 1974.

Number awarded 1 each year.

Deadline Nominations must be submitted by June of each year.

[834]
DEPARTMENT OF HOMELAND SECURITY SMALL BUSINESS INNOVATION RESEARCH GRANTS

Department of Homeland Security
Homeland Security Advanced Research Projects Agency
Attn: SBIR Program Manager
Washington, DC 20528
(202) 254-6768   Toll Free: (800) 754-3043
Fax: (202) 254-7170   E-mail: elissa.sobolewski@dhs.gov
Web: www.dhs.gov/files/grants/gc_1247254058883.shtm

Summary To support small businesses (especially those owned by Asian Americans or other minorities, disabled veterans, and women) that have the technological expertise to contribute to the research and development mission of the Department of Homeland Security (DHS).

Eligibility For the purposes of this program, a "small business" is defined as a firm that is organized for profit with a location in the United States; is in the legal form of an individual proprietorship, partnership, limited liability company, corporation, joint venture, association, trust, or cooperative; is at least 51% owned and controlled by 1 or more individuals who are citizens or permanent residents of the United States; and has (including its affiliates) fewer than 500 employees. The primary employment of the principal investigator must be with the firm at the time of award and during the conduct of the proposed project. Preference is given to women-owned small business concerns, service-disabled veteran small business concerns, veteran small business concerns, and socially and economically disadvantaged small business concerns. Women-owned small business concerns are those that are at least 51% owned by a woman or women who also control and operate them. Service-disabled veteran small business concerns are those that are at least 51% owned by a service-disabled veteran and controlled by such a veteran or (for veterans with permanent and severe disability) the spouse or permanent caregiver of such a veteran. Veteran small business concerns are those that are at least 51% owned by a veteran or veterans who also control and manage them. Socially and economically disadvantaged small business concerns are at least 51% owned by an Indian tribe, a Native Hawaiian organization, a Community Development Corporation, or 1 or more socially and economically disadvantaged individuals (African Americans, Hispanic Americans, Native Americans, Asian Pacific Americans, or subcontinent Asian Americans). The project must be performed in the United States. Currently, DHS has 7 research priorities: explosives; border and maritime security; command, control, and interoperability; human factors; infrastructure and geophysical; chemical and biological; and domestic nuclear detection. Selection is based on the soundness, technical merit, and innovation of the proposed approach and its incremental progress toward topic or subtopic solution; the qualifications of the proposed principal investigators, supporting staff, and consultants; and the potential for commercial application and the benefits expected to accrue from this commercialization.

Financial data Grants are offered in 2 phases. In phase 1, awards normally range up to $100,000 (or $150,000 for domestic nuclear detection); in phase 2, awards normally range up to $750,000 (or $1,000,000 for domestic nuclear detection).

Duration Phase 1 awards may extend up to 6 months; phase 2 awards may extend up to 2 years.

Number awarded Varies each year; recently, 61 Phase 1 awards were granted.

Deadline February of each year.

[835]
DEPARTMENT OF TRANSPORTATION SMALL BUSINESS INNOVATION RESEARCH GRANTS

Department of Transportation
Attn: Research and Innovative Technology Administration
John A. Volpe National Transportation Systems Center
55 Broadway, Kendall Square
Cambridge, MA 02142-1093
(617) 494-2051   Fax: (617) 494-2370
E-mail: leisa.moniz@dot.gov
Web: www.volpe.dot.gov/sbir/index.html

Summary To support small businesses (especially those owned by Asian Americans or other minorities, veterans, and women) that have the technological expertise to contribute to the research and development mission of the Department of Transportation.

Eligibility For the purposes of this program, a "small business" is defined as a firm that is organized for profit with a location in the United States; is in the legal form of an individual proprietorship, partnership, limited liability company, corporation, joint venture, association, trust, or cooperative; is at least 51% owned and controlled by 1 or more individuals who are citizens or permanent residents of the United States; and

has (including its affiliates) fewer than 500 employees. The primary employment of the principal investigator must be with the firm at the time of award and during the conduct of the proposed project. Preference is given to 1) women-owned small business concerns; 2) veteran-owned small businesses; and 3) socially and economically disadvantaged small business concerns. Women-owned small business concerns are those that are at least 51% owned by a woman or women who also control and operate them. Veteran-owned small businesses are those that are at least 51% owned and controlled by 1 or more veterans. Socially and economically disadvantaged small business concerns are at least 51% owned by an Indian tribe, a Native Hawaiian organization, or 1 or more socially and economically disadvantaged individuals (African Americans, Hispanic Americans, Native Americans, Asian Pacific Americans, or subcontinent Asian Americans). The project must be performed in the United States. Selection is based on scientific and technical merit, the feasibility of the proposal's commercial potential, the adequacy of the work plan, qualifications of the principal investigator, and adequacy of supporting staff and facilities, equipment, and data.

Financial data Support is offered in 2 phases. In phase 1, awards normally do not exceed $100,000 (for both direct and indirect costs); in phase 2, awards normally do not exceed $750,000 (including both direct and indirect costs).

Duration Phase 1 awards may extend up to 6 months; phase 2 awards may extend up to 2 years.

Number awarded Varies each year; recently, DOT planned to award 16 of these grants: 1 to the Federal Aviation Administration, 3 to the Federal Highway Administration, 1 to the Pipeline and Hazardous Materials Safety Administration, 2 to the National Highway and Traffic Safety Administration, 3 to the Federal Transit Administration, and 6 to the Federal Railroad Administration.

Deadline November of each year.

[836]
DIGITAL INNOVATION FELLOWSHIPS

American Council of Learned Societies
Attn: Office of Fellowships and Grants
633 Third Avenue
New York, NY 10017-6795
(212) 697-1505   Fax: (212) 949-8058
E-mail: fellowships@acls.org
Web: www.acls.org/programs/digital

Summary To provide funding to scholars (particularly Asian American or other minority and women scholars) who are interested in conducting digitally-based research in the humanities and the humanities-related social sciences.

Eligibility This program is open to scholars who have a Ph.D. in any field of the humanities or the humanistic social sciences. Applicants must be interested in conducting research projects that utilize digital technologies intensively and innovatively. Projects might include, but are not limited to, new digital tools that further humanistic research (such as digital research archives or innovative databases), research that depends on or is greatly enhanced by the use of such tools, the representation of research that depends on or is greatly enhanced by the use of such tools, or some combination of those features. The program does not support creative works (e.g., novels or films), textbooks, straightforward translations, or purely pedagogical projects. U.S. citizenship or permanent resident status is required. Applications are particularly invited from women and members of minority groups. Selection is based on scholarly excellence (the project's intellectual ambitions and technological underpinnings), the project's likely contribution as a digital scholarly work to humanistic study, satisfaction of technical requirements for completing a successful research project, degree and significance of preliminary work already completed, extent to which the proposed project would promote teamwork and collaboration, and the project's articulation with local infrastructure.

Financial data Fellows receive a stipend of $60,000 and up to $25,000 for project costs.

Duration 1 academic year.

Additional information This program, first available for the 2006-07 academic year, is supported by funding from the Andrew W. Mellon Foundation.

Number awarded Up to 6 each year.

Deadline September of each year.

[837]
DISTINGUISHED CHINESE TOXICOLOGIST LECTURESHIP AWARD

Society of Toxicology
Attn: American Association of Chinese in Toxicology
  Special Interest Group
1821 Michael Faraday Drive, Suite 300
Reston, VA 20190-5348
(703) 438-3115   Fax: (703) 438-3113
E-mail: sothq@toxicology.org
Web: www.toxicology.org/ai/af/awards.aspx

Summary To recognize and reward members of the Society of Toxicology (SOT) who are of Chinese ethnic origin and have made outstanding contributions to the field.

Eligibility This award is available to SOT members who are of Chinese ethnic origin. Nominees should have contributed significantly to the science of toxicology and have an exemplary professional life. Nominations must be submitted by at least 2 members of the American Association of Chinese in Toxicology Special Interest Group (AACT-SIG) of SOT.

Financial data The award consists of a plaque and a $500 stipend.

Duration The award is presented annually.

Additional information The winner delivers an award lecture at an AACT-SIG session of the SOT annual meeting.

Number awarded 1 each year.

Deadline Nominations must be submitted by October of each year.

[838]
DOCTORAL FELLOWSHIPS IN LAW AND SOCIAL SCIENCE

American Bar Foundation
Attn: Administrative Assistant for Academic Affairs and
  Research Administration
750 North Lake Shore Drive
Chicago, IL 60611-4403
(312) 988-6548   Fax: (312) 988-6579
E-mail: alynch@abfn.org
Web: www.americanbarfoundation.org

Summary To provide research funding to scholars (particularly Asian American and other minority scholars) who are completing or have completed doctoral degrees in fields related to law, the legal profession, and legal institutions.

Eligibility This program is open to Ph.D. candidates in the social sciences who have completed all doctoral requirements except the dissertation. Applicants who have completed the dissertation are also eligible. Doctoral and proposed research must be in the general area of sociolegal studies or in social scientific approaches to law, the legal profession, or legal institutions and legal processes. Applications must include 1) a dissertation abstract or proposal with an outline of the substance and methods of the research; 2) 2 letters of recommendation; and 3) a curriculum vitae. Minority candidates are especially encouraged to apply.

Financial data The stipend is $27,000. Fellows may request up to $1,500 to reimburse expenses associated with research, travel to meet with advisers, or travel to conferences at which papers are presented. Relocation expenses of up to $2,500 may be reimbursed on application.

Duration 12 months, beginning in September.

Additional information Fellows are offered access to the computing and word processing facilities of the American Bar Foundation and the libraries of Northwestern University and the University of Chicago. This program was established in 1996. Fellowships must be held in residence at the American Bar Foundation. Appointments to the fellowship are full time; fellows are not permitted to undertake other work.

Number awarded 1 or more each year.

Deadline December of each year.

[839]
DORA AMES LEE LEADERSHIP DEVELOPMENT FUND

United Methodist Church
General Board of Global Ministries
Attn: United Methodist Committee on Relief
475 Riverside Drive, Room 1522
New York, NY 10115
(212) 870-3871   Toll Free: (800) UMC-GBGM
E-mail: jyoung@gbgm-umc.org
Web: gbgm-umc.org/health/doralee.cfm

Summary To provide financial assistance to Methodists and other Christians of Asian or Native American descent who are preparing for a career in a health-related field.

Eligibility This program is open to undergraduate and graduate students along with college graduates who are U.S. citizens of Asian American or Native American descent. Applicants must be professed Christians, preferably United Methodists. They must be attending a college or university to enter or continue in a health-related field. Financial need is considered in the selection process.

Financial data The stipend is $2,000.

Duration 1 year.

Additional information This program was established in 1980.

Number awarded 5 each year.

Deadline June of each year.

[840]
DR. DHARM SINGH POSTDOCTORAL FELLOW/ YOUNG INVESTIGATOR BEST ABSTRACT AWARD

Society of Toxicology
Attn: Association of Scientists of Indian Origin Special
  Interest Group
1821 Michael Faraday Drive, Suite 300
Reston, VA 20190-5348
(703) 438-3115   Fax: (703) 438-3113
E-mail: sothq@toxicology.org
Web: www.toxicology.org/ai/af/awards.aspx

Summary To recognize and reward postdoctoral members of the Society of Toxicology (SOT) who are of Indian origin and present outstanding papers at the annual meeting.

Eligibility This award is available to postdoctoral fellows of Indian origin who are members of SOT and its Association of Scientists of Indian Origin (ASIO). Candidates must have an accepted abstract of a research poster or platform presentation for the SOT annual meeting. Along with the abstract, they must submit a short curriculum vitae and a recommendation letter by their current mentor outlining their role in the research.

Financial data A plaque and a cash award (amount not specified) are presented.

Duration The award is presented annually.

Additional information This award was established in 2008.

Number awarded 1 each year.

Deadline January of each year.

[841]
DR. SUZANNE AHN AWARD FOR CIVIL RIGHTS AND SOCIAL JUSTICE FOR ASIAN AMERICANS

Asian American Journalists Association
Attn: Professional Programs Coordinator
5 Third Street, Suite 1108
San Francisco, CA 94103
(415) 346-2051, ext. 107   Fax: (415) 346-6343
E-mail: MarciaS@aaja.org
Web: www.aaja.org/programs/awards

Summary To recognize and reward Asian American and other journalists who have published or broadcast outstanding coverage of Asian American civil rights and social justice issues.

Eligibility This award is presented to journalists for excellence in coverage of civil rights of Asian Americans and/or issues of social justice for Asian Americans. Nominees do not need to be members of the Asian American Journalists Association (AAJA). Their work must have been published (in newspapers, news services, web sites, magazines, books) or broadcast (on radio or TV). Nominations must be accompanied by supporting materials (up to 5 articles, 10 photographs, 1 book, 1 CD, or 1 DVD) and a 1-page summary of the work. Submissions in other languages must come with an English translation.

Financial data The award consists of $5,000 and a plaque.

Duration The award is presented annually.

Additional information This award, first presented in 2003, is named for a Korean American physician, neurologist,

and inventor. Nominations by nonmembers of AAJA must be accompanied by a $25 entry fee.

Number awarded 1 each year.

Deadline April of each year.

[842]
EARLY CAREER POSTDOCTORAL FELLOWSHIPS IN EAST EUROPEAN STUDIES

American Council of Learned Societies
Attn: Office of Fellowships and Grants
633 Third Avenue
New York, NY 10017-6795
(212) 697-1505   Fax: (212) 949-8058
E-mail: fellowships@acls.org
Web: www.acls.org/grants/Default.aspx?id=534

Summary To provide funding to postdoctorates (particularly Asian American or other minority and women postdoctorates) who are interested in conducting original research in the social sciences and humanities relating to eastern Europe.

Eligibility This program is open to U.S. citizens and permanent residents who hold a Ph.D. degree or equivalent as demonstrated by professional experience and publications. Priority is given to scholars in the early part of their careers; tenured faculty are not eligible. Applicants must be interested in conducting research in the social sciences or humanities relating to Albania, Bosnia and Herzegovina, Bulgaria, Croatia, Czech Republic, Estonia, Hungary, Former Yugoslav Republic of Macedonia, Kosovo, Latvia, Lithuania, Montenegro, Poland, Romania, Serbia, Slovakia, or Slovenia. Projects comparing more than 1 country in eastern Europe or relating eastern European societies to those of other parts of the world are also supported. Selection is based on the scholarly merit of the proposal, its importance to the development of eastern European studies, and the scholarly potential and accomplishments of the applicant. Applications are particularly invited from women and members of minority groups.

Financial data Up to $25,000 is provided as a stipend. Funds are intended primarily as salary replacement, but they may be used to supplement sabbatical salaries or awards from other sources.

Duration 6 to 12 consecutive months.

Additional information This program is sponsored jointly by the American Council of Learned Societies, (ACLS) and the Social Science Research Council, funded by the U.S. Department of State under the Research and Training for Eastern Europe and the Independent States of the Former Soviet Union Act of 1983 (Title VIII) but administered by ACLS. Funds may not be used in western Europe.

Number awarded Varies each year; recently, 3 of these fellowships were awarded.

Deadline November of each year.

[843]
EAST EUROPEAN LANGUAGE GRANTS TO INDIVIDUALS FOR SUMMER STUDY

American Council of Learned Societies
Attn: Office of Fellowships and Grants
633 Third Avenue
New York, NY 10017-6795
(212) 697-1505   Fax: (212) 949-8058
E-mail: fellowships@acls.org
Web: www.acls.org/grants/Default.aspx?id=540

Summary To provide financial support to graduate students, professionals, and postdoctorates (particularly Asian Americans, other minorities, and women) who are interested in studying eastern European languages during the summer.

Eligibility Applicants must have completed at least a 4-year college degree. They must be interested in a program of training in the languages of eastern Europe, including Albanian, Bosnian-Croatian-Serbian, Bulgarian, Czech, Estonian, Hungarian, Latvian, Lithuanian, Macedonian, Polish, Romanian, Slovak, or Slovene. The language course may be at the beginning, intermediate, or advanced level. Normally, requests for beginning and intermediate level training should be for attendance at intensive courses offered by institutions in the United States; proposals for study at the advanced level are ordinarily for courses in eastern Europe. Applications are particularly encouraged from women and members of minority groups.

Financial data Grants up to $2,500 are available.

Duration Summer months.

Additional information This program, reinstituted in 2002, is supported by the U.S. Department of State under the Research and Training for Eastern Europe and the Independent States of the Former Soviet Union Act of 1983 (Title VIII).

Number awarded Approximately 15 each year.

Deadline January of each year.

[844]
E.E. JUST ENDOWED RESEARCH FELLOWSHIP FUND

Woods Hole Marine Biological Laboratory
Attn: Research Award Coordinator
7 MBL Street
Woods Hole, MA 02543-1015
(508) 289-7173   Fax: (508) 457-1924
E-mail: researchawards@mbl.edu
Web: www.mbl.edu/research/summer/awards_general.html

Summary To provide funding to Asian American and other minority scientists who wish to conduct summer research at the Woods Hole Marine Biological Laboratory (MBL).

Eligibility This program is open to minority faculty members who are interested in conducting summer research at the MBL. Applicants must submit a statement of the potential impact of this award on their career development. Fields of study include, but are not limited to, cell biology, developmental biology, ecology, evolution, microbiology, neurobiology, physiology, regenerative biology, and tissue engineering.

Financial data The fellowship supports a minority scientist's participation in research at MBL. Recently, grants averaged $1,500.

Duration At least 6 weeks during the summer.

Number awarded 1 each year.

Deadline December of each year.

[845]
EINSTEIN POSTDOCTORAL FELLOWSHIP PROGRAM

Smithsonian Astrophysical Observatory
Attn: Chandra X-Ray Center
Einstein Fellowship Program Office
60 Garden Street, MS4
Cambridge, MA 02138
(617) 496-7941   Fax: (617) 495-7356
E-mail: fellows@head.cfa.harvard.edu
Web: cxc.harvard.edu/fellows

Summary To provide funding to recent postdoctoral scientists (especially Asian American or other minority and women scientists) who are interested in conducting research related to high energy astrophysics missions of the National Aeronautics and Space Administration (NASA).

Eligibility This program is open to postdoctoral scientists who completed their Ph.D., Sc.D., or equivalent doctoral degree within the past 3 years in astronomy, physics, or related disciplines. Applicants must be interested in conducting research related to NASA Physics of the Cosmos program missions: Chandra, Fermi, XMM-Newton and International X-Ray Observatory, cosmological investigations relevant to the Planck and JDEM missions, and gravitational astrophysics relevant to the LISA mission. They must be citizens of the United States or English-speaking citizens of other countries who have valid visas. Women and minorities are strongly encouraged to apply.

Financial data Stipends are approximately $64,500 per year. Fellows may also receive health insurance, relocation costs, and moderate support (up to $16,000 per year) for research-related travel, computing services, publications, and other direct costs.

Duration 3 years (depending on a review of scientific activity).

Additional information This program, which began in 2009 with funding from NASA, incorporates the former Chandra and GLAST Fellowship programs.

Number awarded Up to 10 each year.

Deadline November of each year.

[846]
ELSEVIER PILOT RESEARCH AWARDS

American Gastroenterological Association
Attn: AGA Research Foundation
Research Awards Manager
4930 Del Ray Avenue
Bethesda, MD 20814-2512
(301) 222-4012   Fax: (301) 654-5920
E-mail: awards@gastro.org
Web: www.gastro.org/aga-foundation/grants

Summary To provide funding to new or established investigators (particularly Asian Americans, other minorities, and women) for pilot research projects in areas related to gastroenterology or hepatology.

Eligibility Applicants must have an M.D., Ph.D., or equivalent degree and a full-time faculty position at an accredited North American institution. They may not hold grants for projects on a similar topic from other agencies. Individual membership in the American Gastroenterology Association (AGA) is required. The proposal must involve obtaining new data that can ultimately provide the basis for subsequent grant applications for more substantial funding and duration in gastroenterology- or hepatology-related areas. Women and minority investigators are strongly encouraged to apply. Selection is based on novelty, importance, feasibility, environment, commitment of the institution, and overall likelihood that the project will lead to more substantial grant applications.

Financial data The grant is $25,000 per year. Funds may be used for salary, supplies, or equipment. Indirect costs are not allowed.

Duration 1 year.

Additional information This award is sponsored by Elsevier Science.

Number awarded 1 each year.

Deadline January of each year.

[847]
EPILEPSY FOUNDATION RESEARCH GRANTS PROGRAM

Epilepsy Foundation
Attn: Research Department
8301 Professional Place
Landover, MD 20785-2237
(301) 459-3700   Toll Free: (800) EFA-1000
Fax: (301) 577-2684   TDD: (800) 332-2070
E-mail: grants@efa.org
Web: www.epilepsyfoundation.org

Summary To provide funding to junior investigators (especially Asian Americans, other minorities, women, and individuals with disabilities) who are interested in conducting research that will advance the understanding, treatment, and prevention of epilepsy.

Eligibility Applicants must have a doctoral degree and an academic appointment at the level of assistant professor in a university or medical school (or equivalent standing at a research institution or medical center). They must be interested in conducting basic or clinical research in the biological, behavioral, or social sciences related to the causes of epilepsy. Faculty with appointments at the level of associate professor or higher are not eligible. Applications from women, members of minority groups, and people with disabilities are especially encouraged. U.S. citizenship is not required, but the research must be conducted in the United States. Selection is based on the scientific quality of the research plan, the relevance of the proposed research to epilepsy, the applicant's qualifications, and the adequacy of the institution and facility where research will be conducted.

Financial data The grant is $50,000 per year.

Duration 1 year; recipients may reapply for 1 additional year of funding.

Additional information Support for this program is provided by many individuals, families, and corporations, especially the American Epilepsy Society, Abbott Laboratories, Ortho-McNeil Pharmaceutical, and Pfizer Inc.

Number awarded Varies each year.

Deadline August of each year.

[848]
EQUAL JUSTICE WORKS FELLOWSHIPS

Equal Justice Works
2120 L Street, N.W., Suite 450
Washington, DC 20037-1541
(202) 466-3686   Fax: (202) 429-9766
E-mail: fellowships@equaljusticeworks.org
Web: www.equaljusticeworks.org

Summary To provide funding to graduating law students and recent law school graduates (especially Asian Americans, other minorities, and individuals with disabilities) who are committed to public interest law and interested in working on projects at selected nonprofit legal services organizations.

Eligibility This program is open to third-year law students and recent law graduates. Third-year law students must be able to graduate and begin the fellowship by September following the application. Candidates must 1) be graduating or have graduated from a law school that is an Equal Justice Works member, and 2) be interested in working at a nonprofit host legal services organization that has been selected to participate in this program. Host organizations must have been approved to offer a project that involves legal advocacy on behalf of disenfranchised individuals or groups or issues that are not adequately represented by some aspect of our legal system. Advocacy may entail a wide range of approaches, including, but not limited to, community legal education and training, organizing, direct services, litigation, transactional work, and administrative efforts. The project must address the legal needs of individuals or communities in the United States or its territories. Preference is given to projects that are designed to impact a large number of people, create programs that can be replicated in other communities, and create lasting institutions or programs. The organizations where the applicants propose to conduct their projects are evaluated on the basis of their history of accomplishments; how the project fits into their priorities; their commitment and ability to provide training, support, and supervision throughout the fellowship; and their commitment and ability to provide health insurance and other standard employee fringe benefits to the fellow during the fellowship. Candidates are evaluated on the basis of their demonstrated or stated commitment to public interest law generally and specifically to the community in which they are planning to work; their professional, volunteer, and/or subject matter expertise; and their commitment and ability to fulfill the full term of the program. Preference is given to candidates who will bring a diverse perspective to their project and the legal profession; applications are strongly encouraged from people who 1) are from diverse cultural and experiential backgrounds; 2) have disabilities; 3) are from diverse ethnic, racial, religious, and socioeconomic backgrounds, work experiences, national origins, sexual orientations, and ages.

Financial data Fellows receive the normal salary paid by their host organization. This program provides a grant of $39,000 per year as a contribution to the stipend, and the host organization is expected to pay the difference if its normal salary is higher. They are also expected to provide health insurance and standard fringe benefits. Fellows are eligible to apply to the Equal Justice Works Loan Repayment Assistance Program (LRAP), which repays a portion of their educational debts.

Duration 2 years.

Additional information This program began in 1992. Additional funding provided by the Open Society Institute permitted its expansion in 1997.

Number awarded Varies each year. At any given time, approximately 100 fellows are receiving support from this program.

Deadline September of each year.

[849]
FASSE/CUFA INQUIRY GRANT

National Council for the Social Studies
Attn: Program Manager, External Relations
8555 16th Street, Suite 500
Silver Spring, MD 20910-2844
(301) 588-1800, ext. 106   Fax: (301) 588-2049
E-mail: excellence@ncss.org
Web: www.socialstudies.org/getinvolved/awards/fasse-cufa

Summary To provide funding to faculty and graduate student members of the National Council for the Social Studies (NCSS), particularly Asian Americans and other minorities who are interested in conducting research projects in "citizenship education."

Eligibility This program is open to members of the council who are assistant, associate, or full professors or graduate students with the demonstrated support of a university mentor/adviser. Graduate student applicants must have a mentor/adviser who is also an NCSS member. Researchers from all groups, including underrepresented groups, are encouraged to apply. They must be interested in a project in "citizenship education" that affirms social, cultural, and racial diversity and that addresses issues of equality, equity, and social justice. Proposals that address aims for citizen action are preferred. All proposals should be relevant to school, university, or community-based educational settings. They should either 1) serve student bodies that are socially, culturally, and racially diverse; or 2) involve teachers or prospective teachers who work or will work with diverse student populations. They can address a range of educational levels and settings, from K-12 to collegiate levels, and from school to community settings.

Financial data Grants up to $10,000 are available.

Duration Funded projects must be completed within 1 academic year.

Additional information This program is sponsored by the College and University Faculty Assembly (CUFA) and the Fund for the Advancement of Social Studies Education (FASSE), established by the NCAA in 1984.

Number awarded 1 every 2 or 3 years.

Deadline June of the years in which grants are offered.

[850]
FELLOWSHIP PROGRAM IN MEASUREMENT

American Educational Research Association
1430 K Street, N.W., Suite 1200
Washington, DC 20005
(202) 238-3200   Fax: (202) 238-3250
E-mail: fellowships@aera.net
Web: www.aera.net

Summary To provide an opportunity for junior scholars in the field of education (particularly Asian Americans, other minorities, and women) who are interested in engaging in a program of research and advanced training while in residence at Educational Testing Service (ETS) in Princeton, New Jersey.

Eligibility This program is open to junior scholars and early career research scientists in fields and disciplines related to education research. Applicants must have completed their Ph.D. or Ed.D. degree within the past 3 years. They must be proposing a program of intensive research and training at the ETS campus in Princeton, New Jersey in such areas as educational measurement, assessment design, psychometrics, statistical analyses, large-scale evaluations, and other studies directed to explaining student progress and achievement. A particular goal of the program is to increase the involvement of women and underrepresented minority professionals in measurement, psychometrics, assessment, and related fields. U.S. citizenship or permanent resident status is required.

Financial data The stipend is $50,000 per year. Fellows also receive relocation expenses and ETS employee benefits.

Duration Up to 2 years.

Additional information This program is jointly sponsored by the American Educational Research Association (AERA) and ETS.

Number awarded Up to 2 each year.

Deadline December of each year.

[851]
FELLOWSHIP TO FACULTY TRANSITION AWARDS

American Gastroenterological Association
Attn: AGA Research Foundation
Research Awards Manager
4930 Del Ray Avenue
Bethesda, MD 20814-2512
(301) 222-4012   Fax: (301) 654-5920
E-mail: awards@gastro.org
Web: www.gastro.org/aga-foundation/grants

Summary To provide funding to physicians (especially Asian Americans, other minorities, and women) who are interested in research training in an area of gastrointestinal, liver function, or related diseases.

Eligibility This program is open to trainee members of the American Gastroenterological Association (AGA) who have an M.D. or equivalent degree and a gastroenterology-related fellowship at an accredited institution. Applicants must be committed to an academic career; have completed at least 1 year of research training at their current institution; have a commitment from their home institution for a full-time faculty position; and have a preceptor who will supervise their research activities and serve as a mentor. Women and minority investigators are strongly encouraged to apply. Selection is based on the candidate's promise for future success, feasibility and significance of the proposal, attributes of the candidate, record and commitment of the sponsors, and institutional and laboratory environment.

Financial data The grant is $40,000 per year. Funds are to be used as salary support for the recipient. Indirect costs are not allowed.

Duration 2 years.

Additional information Fellows must devote 70% effort to research related to the gastrointestinal tract or liver.

Number awarded 2 each year.

Deadline August of each year.

[852]
FELLOWSHIPS IN SCIENCE AND INTERNATIONAL AFFAIRS

Harvard University
John F. Kennedy School of Government
Belfer Center for Science and International Affairs
Attn: Fellowship Coordinator
79 John F. Kennedy Street
Cambridge, MA 02138
(617) 495-8806　　　　　　　　Fax: (617) 495-8963
E-mail: bcsia_fellowships@ksg.harvard.edu
Web: belfercenter.ksg.harvard.edu/fellowships

Summary To provide funding to professionals, postdoctorates, and doctoral students (especially Asian Americans, other minorities, and women) who are interested in conducting research in areas of concern to the Belfer Center for Science and International Affairs at Harvard University in Cambridge, Massachusetts.

Eligibility The postdoctoral fellowship is open to recent recipients of the Ph.D. or equivalent degree, university faculty members, and employees of government, military, international, humanitarian, and private research institutions who have appropriate professional experience. Applicants for predoctoral fellowships must have passed their general examinations. Lawyers, economists, political scientists, those in the natural sciences, and others of diverse disciplinary backgrounds are also welcome to apply. The program especially encourages applications from women, minorities, and citizens of all countries. All applicants must be interested in conducting research in 1 of the 3 major program areas of the center: 1) the International Security Program (ISP), including Religion in International Affairs; 2) the Science, Technology, and Public Policy Program (STPP), including information and communications technology, energy and water policy, managing the atom project, and the energy technology innovation policy research group; 3) and the Dubai initiative.

Financial data The stipend is $34,000 for postdoctoral research fellows or $20,000 for predoctoral research fellows. Health insurance is also provided.

Duration 10 months.

Number awarded A limited number each year.

Deadline January of each year.

[853]
FIRST BOOK GRANT PROGRAM FOR MINORITY SCHOLARS

Louisville Institute
Attn: Executive Director
1044 Alta Vista Road
Louisville, KY 40205-1798
(502) 992-5432　　　　　　　　Fax: (502) 894-2286
E-mail: info@louisville-institute.org
Web: www.louisville-institute.org/Grants/programs.aspx

Summary To provide funding to Asian Americans and other scholars of color who are interested in completing a major research and book project that focuses on an aspect of Christianity in North America.

Eligibility This program is open to members of racial/ethnic minority groups (African Americans, Hispanics, Native Americans, Asian Americans, Arab Americans, and Pacific Islanders) who have an earned doctoral degree (normally the Ph.D. or Th.D.). Applicants must be a pre-tenured faculty member in a full-time, tenure-track position at an accredited institution of higher education (college, university, or seminary) in North America. They must be able to negotiate a full academic year free from teaching and committee responsibilities in order to engage in a scholarly research project leading to the publication of their first (or second) book focusing on an aspect of Christianity in North America. Selection is based on the intellectual quality of the research and writing project, its potential to contribute to scholarship in religion, and the potential contribution of the research to the vitality of North American Christianity.

Financial data The grant is $40,000. Awards are intended to make possible a full academic year of sabbatical research and writing by providing up to half of the grantee's salary and benefits for that year. Funds are paid directly to the grantee's institution, but no indirect costs are allowed.

Duration 1 academic year; nonrenewable.

Additional information The Louisville Institute is located at Louisville Presbyterian Theological Seminary and is supported by the Lilly Endowment. These grants were first awarded in 2003. Grantees may not accept other awards that provide a stipend during the tenure of this award, and they must be released from all teaching and committee responsibilities during the award year.

Number awarded Varies each year; recently, 4 of these grants were awarded.

Deadline January of each year.

[854]
FREDERICK BURKHARDT RESIDENTIAL FELLOWSHIPS FOR RECENTLY TENURED SCHOLARS

American Council of Learned Societies
Attn: Office of Fellowships and Grants
633 Third Avenue
New York, NY 10017-6795
(212) 697-1505　　　　　　　　Fax: (212) 949-8058
E-mail: fellowships@acls.org
Web: www.acls.org/programs/burkhardt

Summary To provide funding to scholars (especially Asian Americans, other minorities, and women) in all disciplines of the humanities and the humanities-related social sciences who are interested in conducting research at designated residential centers.

Eligibility This program is open to citizens and permanent residents of the United States who achieved tenure in a humanities or humanities-related social science discipline at a U.S. institution within the past 4 years. Applicants must be interested in conducting research at 1 of 12 participating residential centers in the United States or abroad. Appropriate fields of specialization include, but are not limited to, American studies; anthropology; archaeology; art and architectural history; classics; economics; film; geography; history; languages and literatures; legal studies; linguistics; musicology; philosophy; political science; psychology; religious studies;

rhetoric, communication, and media studies; sociology; and theater, dance, and performance studies. Proposals in those fields of the social sciences are eligible only if they employ predominantly humanistic approaches (e.g., economic history, law and literature, political philosophy). Proposals in interdisciplinary and cross-disciplinary studies are welcome, as are proposals focused on a geographic region or on a cultural or linguistic group. Applications are particularly invited from women and members of minority groups.

Financial data The stipend is $75,000. If that stipend exceeds the fellow's normal academic year salary, the excess is available for research and travel expenses.

Duration 1 academic year.

Additional information This program, which began in 1999, is supported by funding from the Andrew W. Mellon Foundation. The participating residential research centers are the National Humanities Center (Research Triangle Park, North Carolina), the Center for Advanced Study in the Behavioral Sciences (Stanford, California), the Institute for Advanced Study, Schools of Historical Studies and Social Science (Princeton, New Jersey), the Radcliffe Institute for Advanced Study at Harvard University (Cambridge, Massachusetts), the American Antiquarian Society (Worcester, Massachusetts), the John W. Kluge Center at the Library of Congress (Washington, D.C.), the Folger Shakespeare Library (Washington, D.C.), the Newberry Library (Chicago, Illinois), the Huntington Library, Art Collections, and Botanical Gardens (San Marino, California), the American Academy in Rome, Collegium Budapest, and Villa I Tatti (Florence, Italy).

Number awarded Up to 9 each year.

Deadline September of each year.

[855]
GAIUS CHARLES BOLIN DISSERTATION AND POST-MFA FELLOWSHIPS

Williams College
Attn: Dean of the Faculty
Hopkins Hall, Third Floor
P.O. Box 141
Williamstown, MA 01267
(413) 597-4351   Fax: (413) 597-3553
E-mail: gburda@williams.edu
Web: dean-faculty.williams.edu/graduate-fellowships

Summary To provide financial assistance to Asian Americans and members of other underrepresented groups who are interested in teaching courses at Williams College while working on their doctoral dissertation or building their post-M.F.A. professional portfolio.

Eligibility This program is open to members of underrepresented groups, including ethnic minorities, first-generation college students, women in predominantly male fields, and scholars with disabilities. Applicants must be 1) doctoral candidates in any field who have completed all work for a Ph.D. except for the dissertation; or 2) artists who completed an M.F.A. degree within the past 2 years and are building their professional portfolio. They must be willing to teach a course at Williams College. Along with their application, they must submit a full curriculum vitae, a graduate school transcript, 3 letters of recommendation, a copy of their dissertation prospectus or samples of their artistic work, and a description of their teaching interests within a department or program at

Williams College. U.S. citizenship or permanent resident status is required.

Financial data Fellows receive $33,000 for the academic year, plus housing assistance, office space, computer and library privileges, and a research allowance of up to $4,000.

Duration 2 years.

Additional information Bolin fellows are assigned a faculty advisor in the appropriate department. This program was established in 1985. Fellows are expected to teach a 1-semester course each year. They must be in residence at Williams College for the duration of the fellowship.

Number awarded 3 each year.

Deadline November of each year.

[856]
GANNETT AWARD FOR INNOVATION IN WATCHDOG JOURNALISM

Asian American Journalists Association
Attn: Professional Programs Coordinator
5 Third Street, Suite 1108
San Francisco, CA 94103
(415) 346-2051, ext. 107   Fax: (415) 346-6343
E-mail: MarciaS@aaja.org
Web: www.aaja.org/programs/awards/gannett/

Summary To recognize and reward members of the Asian American Journalism Association (AAJA) who have used digital tools in their role as a community's watchdog.

Eligibility This award is available to full members of AAJA who have used digital tools to complete spot news, editorials, news analysis, columns, or features. Submitted work must have involved innovation that has contributed to the journalist's role as a community's watchdog; special consideration is given to journalism that helps a community understand and address important issues. Criteria for evaluating innovation include interactivity, creation of new tools, innovative adaptation of existing tools, and creative use of a digital medium. Submission of work by a team of reporters is accepted.

Financial data The award is $5,000.

Duration The award is presented annually.

Additional information This award is sponsored by the Gannett Foundation.

Number awarded 1 each year.

Deadline April of each year.

[857]
GEORGE A. STRAIT MINORITY SCHOLARSHIP ENDOWMENT

American Association of Law Libraries
Attn: Chair, Scholarships Committee
105 West Adams Street, Suite 3300
Chicago, IL 60603
(312) 939-4764   Fax: (312) 431-1097
E-mail: scholarships@aall.org
Web: www.aallnet.org/services/sch_strait.asp

Summary To provide financial assistance to Asian American and other minority college seniors or college graduates who are interested in becoming law librarians.

Eligibility This program is open to college graduates with meaningful law library experience who are members of minority groups and intend to have a career in law librarianship. Applicants must be degree candidates at an ALA-accredited library school or an ABA-accredited law school. Along with their application, they must submit a personal statement that discusses their interest in law librarianship, reason for applying for this scholarship, career goals as a law librarian, etc.

Financial data The stipend is $3,500.

Duration 1 year.

Additional information This program, established in 1990, is currently supported by Thomson West.

Number awarded Varies each year; recently, 5 of these scholarships were awarded.

Deadline March of each year.

[858]
GERTRUDE AND MAURICE GOLDHABER DISTINGUISHED FELLOWSHIPS

Brookhaven National Laboratory
Attn: Dr. Kathleen Barkigia
Building 460
P.O. Box 5000
Upton, NY 11973-5000
(631) 344-4467   E-mail: Barkigia@bnl.gov
Web: www.bnl.gov/hr/goldhaber.asp

Summary To provide funding to postdoctoral scientists (especially Asian Americans, other minorities, and women) who are interested in conducting research at Brookhaven National Laboratory (BNL).

Eligibility This program is open to scholars who are no more than 3 years past receipt of the Ph.D. and are interested in working at BNL. Candidates must be interested in working in close collaboration with a member of the BNL scientific staff and qualifying for a scientific staff position at BNL upon completion of the appointment. The sponsoring scientist must have an opening and be able to support the candidate at the standard starting salary for postdoctoral research associates. The program especially encourages applications from minorities and women.

Financial data The program provides additional funds to bring the salary to $75,000 per year.

Duration 3 years.

Additional information This program is funded by Battelle Memorial Institute and the State University of New York at Stony Brook.

Number awarded Up to 8 each year.

Deadline August of each year.

[859]
GILBERT F. WHITE POSTDOCTORAL FELLOWSHIP PROGRAM

Resources for the Future
Attn: Coordinator for Academic Programs
1616 P Street, N.W., Suite 600
Washington, DC 20036-1400
(202) 328-5008   Fax: (202) 939-3460
E-mail: white-award@rff.org
Web: www.rff.org/About_RFF/Pages/default.aspx

Summary To provide funding to postdoctoral researchers (especially Asian Americans, other minorities, and women) who wish to devote a year to scholarly work at Resources for the Future (RFF) in Washington, D.C.

Eligibility This program is open to individuals in any discipline who have completed their doctoral requirements and are interested in conducting scholarly research at RFF in social or policy science areas that relate to natural resources, energy, or the environment. Teaching and/or research experience at the postdoctoral level is preferred but not essential. Individuals holding positions in government as well as at academic institutions are eligible. Women and minority candidates are strongly encouraged to apply.

Financial data Fellows receive an annual stipend (based on their academic salary) plus research support, office facilities at RFF, and an allowance of up to $1,000 for moving or living expenses. Fellowships do not provide medical insurance or other RFF fringe benefits.

Duration 11 months.

Additional information Fellows are assigned to an RFF research division: the Energy and Natural Resources division, the Quality of the Environment division, or the Center for Risk, Resource, and Environmental Management. Fellows are expected to be in residence at Resources for the Future for the duration of the program.

Number awarded 1 each year.

Deadline February of each year.

[860]
GLORIA E. ANZALDUA BOOK PRIZE

National Women's Studies Association
Attn: Book Prizes
7100 Baltimore Avenue, Suite 203
College Park, MD 20740
(301) 403-0407   Fax: (301) 403-4137
E-mail: nwsaoffice@nwsa.org
Web: www.nwsa.org/awards/index.php

Summary To recognize and reward Asian American and other members of the National Women's Studies Association (NWSA) who have written outstanding books on women of color and transnational issues.

Eligibility This award is available to NWSA members who submit a book that was published during the preceding year. Entries must present groundbreaking scholarship in women's studies that makes a significant multicultural feminist contribution to women of color and/or transnational studies.

Financial data The award provides an honorarium of $1,000 and lifetime membership in NWSA.

Duration The award is presented annually.

Additional information This award was first presented in 2008.

Number awarded 1 each year.

Deadline April of each year.

[861]
GRADUATE STUDENTS OF ASIAN/ASIAN-AMERICAN/PACIFIC-ISLANDER DESCENT STUDENT ESSAY AWARD

National Women's Studies Association
Attn: Women of Color Caucus
7100 Baltimore Avenue, Suite 203
College Park, MD 20740
(301) 403-0407   Fax: (301) 403-4137
E-mail: nwsaoffice@nwsa.org
Web: www.nwsa.org/students/scholarships/woccguide.php

Summary To recognize and reward Asian American/Pacific Islander graduate students and recent postdoctorates who are members of the National Women's Studies Association (NWSA) and submit outstanding essays on feminist issues.

Eligibility This competition is open to women of Asian, Asian American, or Pacific Islander descent who are currently enrolled in a graduate or professional program. Recipients of Ph.D.s who completed their degree requirements within the past year are also eligible. Applicants must submit a scholarly essay that provides critical theoretical discussions and/or analyses of issues and experiences of women and girls of Asian, Asian American, or Pacific Islander descent in the United States and throughout the Diaspora. They must be members of the NWSA.

Financial data The award is $500.

Duration The award is presented annually.

Number awarded 1 each year.

Deadline May of each year.

[862]
HEALTH AND AGING POLICY FELLOWSHIPS

Columbia University College of Physicians and Surgeons
Attn: Department of Psychiatry
Deputy Director, Health and Aging Policy Fellows
1051 Riverside Drive, Unit 9
New York, NY 10032
(212) 543-6213   Fax: (212) 543-6021
E-mail: healthandagingpolicy@columbia.edu
Web: www.healthandagingpolicy.org

Summary To provide an opportunity for health professionals (especially Asian Americans and members of other underrepresented groups) who have an interest in aging and policy issues and are interested in working as legislative assistants in Congress or at other sites.

Eligibility This program is open to physicians, nurses, and social workers who have a demonstrated commitment to health and aging issues and a desire to be involved in health policy at the federal, state, or local levels. Other professionals with clinical backgrounds (e.g., pharmacists, dentists, clinical psychologists) working in the field of health and aging are also eligible. Preference is given to professionals early or midway through their careers. Applicants must be interested serving as residential fellows by participating in the policy-making process on either the federal or state level as legislative assistants in Congress or as professional staff members in executive agencies or policy organizations. A non-residential track is also available to applicants who wish to work on a policy project throughout the year at relevant sites. The program seeks to achieve racial, ethnic, gender, and discipline diversity; members of groups that historically have been underrepresented are strongly encouraged to apply. Selection is based on commitment to health and aging issues and improving the health and well being of older Americans, potential for leadership in health policy, professional qualifications and achievements, impact of the fellowship experience on the applicant's career, and interpersonal and communication skills. U.S. citizenship or permanent resident status is required.

Financial data For residential fellows, the stipend depends on their current base salary, to a maximum of $120,000 per year; other benefits include a travel allowance for pre-fellowship arrangements and to fellowship-related meetings, a relocation grant of up to $3,500, and up to $400 per month for health insurance. For non-residential fellows, grants provide up to $30,000 to cover related fellowship and travel costs.

Duration 9 to 12 months; fellows may apply for a second year of participation.

Additional information This program, which began in 2009, operates in collaboration with the American Political Science Association Congressional Fellowship Program. Funding is provided by The Atlantic Philanthropies. The John Heinz Senate Fellowship Program, an activity of the Teresa and H. John Heinz III Foundation, supports 1 fellow to work in the Senate. In addition, the Centers for Disease Control and Prevention Health Aging Program sponsors 1 non-residential fellow to work with its staff in Atlanta, Georgia.

Number awarded Varies each year; recently, 4 residential and 5 non-residential fellowships were awarded.

Deadline May of each year.

[863]
HORIZON PHARMA STUDENT ABSTRACT PRIZES

American Gastroenterological Association
Attn: AGA Research Foundation
Research Awards Manager
4930 Del Ray Avenue
Bethesda, MD 20814-2512
(301) 222-4012   Fax: (301) 654-5920
E-mail: awards@gastro.org
Web: www.gastro.org/aga-foundation/grants

Summary To recognize and reward Asian American and other students at any level who submit outstanding abstracts for presentation during Digestive Disease Week (DDW).

Eligibility This program is open to high school, undergraduate, premedical, predoctoral, and medical students and medical residents (up to and including postgraduate year 3) who have performed original research related to gastroenterology and hepatology. Postdoctoral fellows, technicians, visiting scientists, and M.D. research fellows are not eligible. Applicants must submit an abstract on their research and must be the designated presenter or first author of the abstract. They must be sponsored by a member of the American Gastroenterological Association (AGA). Travel awards are presented to authors of outstanding abstracts to enable them to attend DDW. After presentation of the papers at DDW, the most outstanding abstracts receive prizes. Selection is based on novelty, significance of the proposal, clarity of the abstract, and contribution of the student. Women and minority students are strongly encouraged to apply.

Financial data The prizes are $1,000; the travel awards are $500.

Duration Awards and prizes are presented annually.

Additional information This award is sponsored by Horizon Pharma.

Number awarded 8 travel awards are presented each year. Of the 8 awardees, 3 receive additional prizes of $1,000.

Deadline February of each year.

[864]
HUBBLE FELLOWSHIPS

Space Telescope Science Institute
Attn: Hubble Fellowship Program Office
3700 San Martin Drive
Baltimore, MD 21218
(410) 338-4574   Fax: (410) 338-4211
E-mail: rjallen@stsci.edu
Web: www.stsci.edu

Summary To provide funding to recent postdoctoral scientists (particularly Asian Americans, other minorities, and women) who are interested in conducting research related to the Hubble Space Telescope or related missions of the National Aeronautics and Space Administration (NASA).

Eligibility This program is open to postdoctoral scientists who completed their doctoral degree within the past 3 years in astronomy, physics, or related disciplines. Applicants must be interested in conducting research related to NASA Cosmic Origins missions: the Hubble Space Telescope, Herschel Space Observatory, James Webb Space Telescope, Stratospheric Observatory for Infrared Astronomy, or the Spitzer Space Telescope. They may be of any nationality, provided that all research is conducted at U.S. institutions and that non-U.S. nationals have valid visas. Research may be theoretical, observational, or instrumental. Women and members of minority groups are strongly encouraged to apply.

Financial data Stipends are $58,500 for the first year, $59,500 for the second year, and $60,500 for the third year. Other benefits may include health insurance, relocation costs, and support for travel, equipment, and other direct costs of research.

Duration 3 years: an initial 1-year appointment and 2 annual renewals, contingent on satisfactory performance and availability of funds.

Additional information This program, funded by NASA, began in 1990 and was limited to work with the Hubble Space Telescope. A parallel program, called the Spitzer Fellowship, began in 2002 and was limited to work with the Spitzer Space Telescope. In 2009, those programs were combined into this single program, which was also broadened to include the other NASA Cosmic Origins missions. Fellows are required to be in residence at their host institution engaged in full-time research for the duration of the grant.

Number awarded Varies each year; recently, 17 of these fellowships were awarded.

Deadline June of each year.

[865]
ILLINOIS MINORITY REAL ESTATE SCHOLARSHIP

Illinois Association of Realtors
Attn: Illinois Real Estate Educational Foundation
522 South Fifth Street
P.O. Box 2607
Springfield, IL 62708
Toll Free: (866) 854-REEF   Fax: (217) 241-9935
E-mail: lclayton@iar.org
Web: www.ilreef.org/Scholarships.htm

Summary To provide financial assistance to Illinois residents who Asian or members of other minority groups and preparing for a career in real estate.

Eligibility This program is open to residents of Illinois who are African American, Hispanic or Latino, Native American, or Asian. Applicants must be interested in preparing for a career in real estate by pursuing: 1) courses to meet Illinois salesperson license requirements; 2) course work to meet Illinois broker license requirement; 3) course work required for Illinois appraisal licensing/certification; 4) professional development unrelated to obtaining license/certification; or 5) an undergraduate or graduate program of study. Along with their application, they must submit information on their employment history, transcripts, evidence of financial need, and an essay that describes their career goals and explains why they believe they should receive scholarship assistance through this program.

Financial data The maximum stipend is $500.

Duration Funds must be used within 24 months of the award date.

Deadline Applications may be submitted at any time, but they must be received at least 12 weeks prior to the beginning of the school term for which financial assistance is requested.

[866]
INTERNATIONAL AND AREA STUDIES FELLOWSHIPS

American Council of Learned Societies
Attn: Office of Fellowships and Grants
633 Third Avenue
New York, NY 10017-6795
(212) 697-1505   Fax: (212) 949-8058
E-mail: fellowships@acls.org
Web: www.acls.org/programs/acls

Summary To provide funding to postdoctoral scholars (particularly Asian Americans, other minorities, and women) who are interested in conducting humanities-related research on the societies and cultures of Asia, Africa, the Middle East, Latin America and the Caribbean, eastern Europe, and the former Soviet Union.

Eligibility This program is open to U.S. citizens and residents who have lived in the United States for at least 3 years. Applicants must have a Ph.D. degree and not have received supported research leave time for at least 3 years prior to the start of the proposed research. They must be interested in conducting humanities and humanities-related social science research on the societies and cultures of Asia, Africa, the Middle East, Latin America and the Caribbean, eastern Europe, or the former Soviet Union. Selection is based on the intellectual merit of the proposed research and the likelihood that it will produce significant and innovative scholarship. Applications are particularly invited from women and members of minority groups.

Financial data The maximum grant is $60,000 for full professors and equivalent, $40,000 for associate professors and equivalent, or $35,000 for assistant professors and equivalent. These fellowships may not be held concurrently with another major fellowship.

Duration 6 to 12 months.

Additional information This program is jointly supported by the American Council of Learned Societies (ACLS) and the Social Science Research Council (SSRC), with funding provided by the National Endowment for the Humanities (NEH).

Number awarded Up to 10 each year.
Deadline September of each year.

[867]
JAMES A. RAWLEY PRIZE

Organization of American Historians
Attn: Award and Committee Coordinator
112 North Bryan Street
Bloomington, IN 47408-4141
(812) 855-7311   Fax: (812) 855-0696
E-mail: khamm@oah.org
Web: www.oah.org/awards/awards.rawley.index.html

Summary To recognize and reward Asian American and other authors of outstanding books dealing with race relations in the United States.

Eligibility This award is presented to the author of the outstanding book on the history of race relations in America. Entries must have been published during the current calendar year.

Financial data The award is $1,000 and a certificate.

Duration The award is presented annually.

Additional information This award was established in 1990.

Number awarded 1 each year.

Deadline September of each year.

[868]
JAMES H. DUNN, JR. MEMORIAL FELLOWSHIP PROGRAM

Office of the Governor
Attn: Department of Central Management Services
503 William G. Stratton Building
Springfield, IL 62706
(217) 524-1381   Fax: (217) 558-4497
TDD: (217) 785-3979
Web: www.ilga.gov/commission/lru/internships.html

Summary To provide recent college graduates (especially Asian Americans, other minorities, women, and individuals with disabilities) with work experience in the Illinois Governor's office.

Eligibility This program in open to residents of any state who have completed a bachelor's degree and are interested in working in the Illinois Governor's office or in various agencies under the Governor's jurisdiction. Applicants may have majored in any field, but they must be able to demonstrate a substantial commitment to excellence as evidenced by academic honors, leadership ability, extracurricular activities, and involvement in community or public service. Along with their application, they must submit 1) a 500-word personal statement on the qualities or attributes they will bring to the program, their career goals or plans, how their selection for this program would assist them in achieving those goals, and what they expect to gain from the program; and 2) a 1,000-word essay in which they identify and analyze a public issue that they feel has great impact on state government. A particular goal of the program is to achieve affirmative action through the nomination of qualified minorities, women, and persons with disabilities.

Financial data The stipend is $2,611 per month.

Duration 1 year, beginning in August.

Additional information Assignments are in Springfield and, to a limited extent, in Chicago or Washington, D.C.

Number awarded Varies each year.

Deadline February of each year.

[869]
JAPANESE MEDICAL SOCIETY OF AMERICA SCHOLARSHIPS

Japanese Medical Society of America, Inc.
100 Park Avenue, Suite 1600
New York, NY 10017
(212) 351-5038   Fax: (212) 351-5047
E-mail: info@jmsa.org
Web: www.jmsa.org

Summary To provide funding to Japanese American medical school students, residents, and fellows who are interested in working on a project.

Eligibility This program is open to Japanese Americans who are currently enrolled as medical students, residents, or fellows. Applicants must be proposing to conduct a project that will benefit the Japanese Medical Society of America (JMSA) and the Japanese community. Along with their application, they must submit a 1-page essay about themselves and what they will do to contribute to the JMSA. Selection is based on academic excellence and interest in JMSA.

Financial data Stipends depend on the availability of funds, but have ranged from $2,500 to $20,000. Support is provided primarily for tuition, but a portion of the funds may be used to carry out the proposed project.

Duration 1 year.

Additional information This program receives support from a number of sponsors, including the Honjo Foundation, Nishioka Foundation, Mitsui USA, and Toyota USA. Examples of past projects include a service to connect elderly Japanese American patients with health care, a medical blog in Japanese detailing the experiences of a medical student in America, and a collaborative web site to connect Japanese and American medical students.

Number awarded Varies each year; recently, 11 of these scholarships were awarded.

Deadline December of each year.

[870]
JOEL ELKES RESEARCH AWARD

American College of Neuropsychopharmacology
Attn: Executive Office
5034-A Thoroughbred Lane
Brentwood, TN 37027
(615) 324-2360   Fax: (615) 523-1715
E-mail: acnp@acnp.org
Web: www.acnp.org/programs/awards.aspx

Summary To recognize and reward young scientists (particularly Asian Americans, other minorities, and women) who have contributed outstanding clinical or translational research to neuropsychopharmacology.

Eligibility This award is available to scientists who are younger than 50 years of age. Nominees must have made an outstanding clinical or translational contribution to neuropsychopharmacology. The contribution may be based on a single discovery or a cumulative body of work. Emphasis is placed on contributions that further understanding of self-regulatory processes as they affect mental function and behavior in disease and well-being. Membership in the American College of Neuropsychopharmacology (ACNP) is not required. Nomination of women and minorities is highly encouraged.

Financial data The award consists of an expense-paid trip to the ACNP annual meeting, a monetary honorarium, and a plaque.

Duration The award is presented annually.

Additional information This award was first presented in 1986.

Number awarded 1 each year.

Deadline Nominations must be submitted by June of each year.

[871]
JOHN V. KRUTILLA RESEARCH STIPEND

Resources for the Future
Attn: Coordinator for Academic Programs
1616 P Street, N.W., Suite 600
Washington, DC 20036-1400
(202) 328-5088   Fax: (202) 939-3460
E-mail: krutilla-award@rff.org
Web: www.rff.org/About_RFF/Pages/default.aspx

Summary To provide funding for research related to environmental and resource economics to scholars, particularly Asian American or other minority and women scholars.

Eligibility This program is open to scholars who received their doctoral degree within the past 5 years. Applicants must be interested in conducting research related to environmental and resource economics. They must submit a short description of the proposed research, a curriculum vitae, and a letter of recommendation. Women and minority candidates are strongly encouraged to apply.

Financial data The grant is $9,000.

Duration 1 year.

Additional information This award was first presented in 2006.

Number awarded 1 each year.

Deadline February of each year.

[872]
JUDITH L. WEIDMAN RACIAL ETHNIC MINORITY FELLOWSHIP

United Methodist Communications
Attn: Communications Resourcing Team
810 12th Avenue South
P.O. Box 320
Nashville, TN 37202-0320
(615) 742-5481   Toll Free: (888) CRT-4UMC
Fax: (615) 742-5485   E-mail: scholarships@umcom.org
Web: crt.umc.org/interior.asp?ptid=1&mid=6891

Summary To provide work experience to Methodists who are Asian American or members of other minority groups and interested in a communications career.

Eligibility This program is open to United Methodists of racial ethnic minority heritage who are interested in preparing for a career in communications with the United Methodist Church. Applicants must be recent college or seminary graduates who have broad communications training, including work in journalism, mass communications, marketing, public relations, and electronic media. They must be able to under-

stand and speak English proficiently and to relocate for a year. Selection is based on Christian commitment and involvement in the life of the United Methodist Church; achievement as revealed by transcripts, GPA, letters of reference, and work samples; study, experience, and evidence of talent in the field of communications; clarity of purpose and goals for the future; desire to learn how to be a successful United Methodist conference communicator; and potential leadership ability as a professional religion communicator for the United Methodist Church.

Financial data The stipend is $30,000 per year. Benefits and expenses for moving and professional travel are also provided.

Duration 1 year, starting in July.

Additional information This program was established in 1998. Recipients are assigned to 1 of the 63 United Methodist Annual Conferences, the headquarters of local churches within a geographic area. At the Annual Conference, the fellow will be assigned an experienced communicator as a mentor and will work closely with that mentor and with United Methodist Communications in Nashville, Tennessee. Following the successful completion of the fellowship, United Methodist Communications and the participating Annual Conference will assist in a search for permanent employment within the United Methodist Church but cannot guarantee a position.

Number awarded 1 each year.

Deadline March of each year.

[873]
JULIUS AXELROD MENTORSHIP AWARD

American College of Neuropsychopharmacology
Attn: Executive Office
5034-A Thoroughbred Lane
Brentwood, TN 37027
(615) 324-2360   Fax: (615) 523-1715
E-mail: acnp@acnp.org
Web: www.acnp.org/programs/awards.aspx

Summary To recognize and reward members of the American College of Neuropsychopharmacology (ACNP), especially Asian Americans, other minorities, and women who have demonstrated outstanding mentoring of young scientists.

Eligibility This award is available to ACNP members who have made an outstanding contribution to neuropsychopharmacology by mentoring and developing young scientists into leaders in the field. Nominations must be accompanied by letters of support from up to 3 people who have been mentored by the candidate. Nomination of women and minorities is highly encouraged.

Financial data The award consists of a monetary honorarium and a plaque.

Duration The award is presented annually.

Additional information This award was first presented in 2004.

Number awarded 1 each year.

Deadline Nominations must be submitted by June of each year.

[874]
KAPPA OMICRON NU NEW INITIATIVES GRANTS

Kappa Omicron Nu
Attn: Awards Committee
4990 Northwind Drive, Suite 140
East Lansing, MI 48823-5031
(517) 351-8335   Fax: (517) 351-8336
E-mail: dmitstifer@kon.org
Web: www.kon.org/awards/grants.html

Summary To provide financial assistance to Asian American and other members of Kappa Omicron Nu, an honor society in home economics, who are interested in conducting research.

Eligibility This program is open to 1) individual members of the society, and 2) research teams where the leader is a member of the society. Applicants must be interested in conducting research in family and consumer sciences or any of its related specializations. The research approach should be integrative in nature and make connections across specializations to pursue problems or questions. Special consideration is given to research that studies the cultural and religious differences that affect leadership, especially Hispanic, Asian, and Native American. Another topic of interest is the exploration of how minority students "strike out on their own" in career development.

Financial data The maximum grant is $3,000.

Duration 1 year; multi-year funding may be accomplished by including a multi-year management plan in the initial proposal and reporting successful accomplishment of previous objectives annually.

Additional information Funding for these grants is provided by the New Initiatives Fund of Kappa Omicron Nu.

Number awarded 1 or more each year.

Deadline February of each year.

[875]
KOREAN TOXICOLOGISTS ASSOCIATION IN AMERICA BEST PRESENTATIONS BY GRADUATE STUDENT AND POSTDOCTORAL TRAINEE AWARD

Society of Toxicology
Attn: Korean Toxicologists Association in America Special
   Interest Group
1821 Michael Faraday Drive, Suite 300
Reston, VA 20190-5348
(703) 438-3115   Fax: (703) 438-3113
E-mail: sothq@toxicology.org
Web: www.toxicology.org/ai/af/awards.aspx

Summary To recognize and reward graduate students and postdoctoral trainees who present outstanding papers during a session of the Korean Toxicologists Association in America (KTAA) at the annual meeting of the Society of Toxicology (SOT).

Eligibility This award is available to graduate students and postdoctoral trainees who have an accepted abstract of a research poster or platform presentation for a KTAA session at the SOT annual meeting. Along with the abstract, they must submit a letter of nomination from their major adviser.

Financial data A plaque and a cash award (amount not specified) are presented.

Duration The awards are presented annually.

Additional information These awards are presented jointly by KTAA and the Korean Institute of Toxicology (KIT).

Number awarded 2 each year.

Deadline January of each year.

[876]
LAURENCE R. FOSTER MEMORIAL GRADUATE SCHOLARSHIP

Oregon Student Assistance Commission
Attn: Grants and Scholarships Division
1500 Valley River Drive, Suite 100
Eugene, OR 97401-2146
(541) 687-7395   Toll Free: (800) 452-8807, ext. 7395
Fax: (541) 687-7414   TDD: (800) 735-2900
E-mail: awardinfo@osac.state.or.us
Web: www.osac.state.or.us/osac_programs.html

Summary To provide financial assistance to residents of Oregon (particularly Asian Americans and other minorities) who are interested in enrolling in graduate school in any state to prepare for a public health career.

Eligibility This program is open to residents of Oregon who are enrolled at least half time at a college or university in any state to prepare for a career in public health (not private practice). Applicants must be either a college graduate currently working in public health or enrolled as graduate students in that field. Preference is given to applicants from diverse environments. Along with their application, they must submit brief essays on 1) what public health means to them; 2) the public health aspect they intend to practice and the health and population issues impacted by that aspect; and 3) their experience living or working in diverse environments.

Financial data Stipend amounts vary; recently, they were at least $4,167.

Duration 1 year.

Additional information This program is administered by the Oregon Student Assistance Commission (OSAC) with funds provided by the Oregon Community Foundation.

Number awarded Varies each year; recently, 6 undergraduate and graduate scholarships were awarded.

Deadline February of each year.

[877]
LEADERSHIP IN ACTION INTERNSHIP

Leadership Education for Asian Pacifics, Inc.
Attn: Executive Assistant
327 East Second Street, Suite 226
Los Angeles, CA 90012
(213) 485-1422, ext. 4119   Fax: (213) 485-0050
E-mail: nyap@leap.org
Web: leap.org/empower_lia.html

Summary To provide college students and recent graduates from any state with an opportunity to gain leadership experience through a summer internship at a community based organization (CBO) within the Asian and Pacific Islander nonprofit sector in southern California.

Eligibility This program is open to residents of any state who have completed at least 2 years of college or are recent graduates. Applicants must be able to demonstrate prior experience in Asian or Pacific Islander communities, a passion for learning and growing their leadership skills, and an interest in gaining work experience at an Asian and Pacific

Islander nonprofit CBO. Along with their application, they must submit a 1-page statement on the types of experience they have had in leadership and community involvement, how their experience has contributed to their role in the Asian and Pacific Islander community, and what they hope to gain from this internship experience. Selection is based on demonstrated leadership, community service, interpersonal skills, written and verbal communication skills, maturity and professional demeanor, and GPA.

Financial data Interns receive a stipend of $2,000 upon completion of the program.

Duration 8 weeks during the summer. During each week, interns spend 4 days at their assigned CBO and 1 day at LEAP headquarters.

Additional information This program began in 1998.

Number awarded Varies each year; since the program began, it has placed 109 interns with 38 CBOs in southern California.

Deadline March of each year.

[878]
LEE & LOW BOOKS NEW VOICES AWARD

Lee & Low Books
95 Madison Avenue, Suite 1205
New York, NY 10016
(212) 779-4400   Fax: (212) 683-1894
E-mail: general@leeandlow.com
Web: www.leeandlow.com/p/new_voices_award.mhtml

Summary To recognize and reward outstanding unpublished children's picture books by Asian Americans and other writers of color.

Eligibility The contest is open to writers of color who are residents of the United States and who have not previously published a children's picture book. Writers who have published in other venues, (e.g., children's magazines, young adult fiction and nonfiction) are eligible. Manuscripts previously submitted to the sponsor are not eligible. Submissions should be no more than 1,500 words and must address the needs of children of color by providing stories with which they can identify and relate and that promote a greater understanding of each other. Submissions may be fiction or nonfiction for children between the ages of 5 and 12. Folklore and animal stories are not considered. Up to 2 submissions may be submitted per entrant.

Financial data The award is a $1,000 cash grant plus the standard publication contract, including the standard advance and royalties. The Honor Award winner receives a cash grant of $500.

Duration The competition is held annually.

Additional information This program was established in 2000. Manuscripts may not be sent to any other publishers while under consideration for this award.

Number awarded 2 each year.

Deadline October of each year.

[879]
LIBRARY OF CONGRESS JUNIOR FELLOWS PROGRAM

Library of Congress
Library Services
Attn: Junior Fellows Program Coordinator
101 Independence Avenue, S.E., Room LM-642
Washington, DC 20540-4600
(202) 707-0901   Fax: (202) 707-6269
E-mail: jrfell@loc.gov
Web: www.loc.gov/hr/jrfellows/index.html

Summary To provide summer work experience at the Library of Congress (LC) to upper-division students, graduate students, and recent graduates (particularly those who are Asian Americans, other minorities, women, and individuals with disabilities).

Eligibility This program is open to U.S. citizens with subject expertise in the following areas: American history, including veterans and military history; American popular culture; area studies (African, Asian, European, Hispanic, Middle Eastern); bibliographic description and access; film, television, and radio; folklife; geography and maps; history of photography; history of popular and applied graphic arts, architecture, and design; manuscript collections processing; music; preservation and conservation; rare books and manuscripts; science, technology, and business; serials and government publications and newspapers; or sound recordings. Applicants must 1) be juniors or seniors at an accredited college or university, 2) be graduate students, or 3) have completed their degree in the past year. Applications from women, minorities, and persons with disabilities are particularly encouraged. Selection is based on academic achievement, letters of recommendation, and an interview.

Financial data Fellows are paid a taxable stipend of $300 per week.

Duration 3 months, beginning in either May or June. Fellows work a 40-hour week.

Additional information Fellows work with primary source materials and assist selected divisions at LC in the organization and documentation of archival collections, production of finding aids and bibliographic records, preparation of materials for preservation and service, completion of bibliographical research, and digitization of LC's historical collections.

Number awarded Varies each year; recently, 6 of these internships were awarded.

Deadline March of each year.

[880]
LLOYD LACUESTA BROADCAST NEWS GRANT

Asian American Journalists Association
Attn: Student Programs Coordinator
5 Third Street, Suite 1108
San Francisco, CA 94103
(415) 346-2051, ext. 102   Fax: (415) 346-6343
E-mail: programs@aaja.org
Web: www.aaja.org/programs/internships

Summary To provide a supplemental grant to male members of the Asian American Journalists Association (AAJA) working as a summer intern at a television broadcasting company.

Eligibility This program is open to male AAJA members who are full-time college students or recent college graduates. Applicants must have secured a summer internship at a television broadcasting company before they apply. Along with their application, they must submit a 200-word essay on why they want to prepare for a career in broadcast journalism, what they want to gain from the experience, and why AAJA's mission is important to them; a letter of recommendation; a resume; proof of age (at least 18 years); verification of an internship; and statement of financial need.

Financial data The grant is $1,000. Funds are to be used for living expenses or transportation.

Duration Summer months.

Number awarded 1 each year.

Deadline May of each year.

[881]
LONG RANGE ANNUAL FUNDING OPPORTUNITY ANNOUNCEMENT FOR NAVY AND MARINE CORPS SCIENCE, TECHNOLOGY, ENGINEERING & MATHEMATICS (STEM) PROGRAMS

Office of Naval Research
Attn: Code 03R
875 North Randolph Street, Suite 1410
Arlington, VA 22203-1995
(703) 696-4111   E-mail: kam.ng1@navy.mil
Web: www.onr.navy.mil

Summary To provide financial support to investigators (particularly those working at minority serving institutions) who are interested in conducting long-range science, technology, engineering, or mathematics (STEM) projects on topics related to the U.S. Navy.

Eligibility This program is open to faculty and staff from academia (colleges and universities), middle and high schools, nonprofit organizations, and industry. Applicants must be interested in conducting long-range projects in STEM fields that offer potential for advancement and improvement of Navy and Marine Corps operations. The projects should help fulfill the mission of the program to foster an interest in, knowledge of, and study in STEM to ensure an educated and well-prepared work force that meets naval and national competitive needs. Applicants at Historically Black Colleges and Universities (HBCUs) and Minority Institutions (MIs) are encouraged to submit proposals and join others in submitting proposals.

Financial data Grants range up to $200,000 per year.

Duration 12 to 36 months.

Number awarded Varies each year; recently, a total of $10 million was available for this program.

Deadline Full proposals must be submitted by September of each year.

[882]
LONG RANGE BROAD AGENCY ANNOUNCEMENT FOR NAVY AND MARINE CORPS SCIENCE AND TECHNOLOGY

Office of Naval Research
Attn: Acquisition Department, Code BD255
875 North Randolph Street
Arlington, VA 22203-1995
(703) 696-2570   Fax: (703) 696-3365
E-mail: misale.abdi@navy.mil
Web: www.onr.navy.mil

Summary To provide financial support to minority and other investigators interested in conducting long-range science and technology research on topics of interest to the U.S. Navy and Marine Corps.

Eligibility This program is open to researchers from academia (colleges and universities) and industry. Applicants must be interested in conducting long-range projects in fields of science and technology that offer potential for advancement and improvement of Navy and Marine Corps operations. The proposed research must relate to 1 of the following topic areas: 1) expeditionary maneuver warfare and combating terrorism; 2) command, control communications, computers, intelligence, surveillance, and reconnaissance; 3) ocean battlespace sensing; 4) sea warfare and weapons; 5) warfighter performance; and 6) naval air warfare and weapons. Researchers at Historically Black Colleges and Universities (HBCUs) and Minority Institutions (MIs) are encouraged to submit proposals and join others in submitting proposals.

Financial data Grant amounts depend on the nature of the proposal.

Number awarded Varies each year.

Deadline White papers must be submitted in November of each year.

[883]
MANY VOICES RESIDENCIES

Playwrights' Center
2301 East Franklin Avenue
Minneapolis, MN 55406-1024
(612) 332-7481   Fax: (612) 332-6037
E-mail: info@pwcenter.org
Web: www.pwcenter.org/fellows_voices.php

Summary To provide funding to Asian American and other playwrights of color in Minneapolis who are interested in spending a year at the Playwrights' Center in Minneapolis.

Eligibility This program is open to playwrights of color who are citizens or permanent residents of the United States and have been residents of Minnesota for at least 1 year. Applicants must be interested in playwriting and creating theater in a supportive artist community at the Playwrights' Center. They may be beginning playwrights (with little or no previous playwriting experience) or emerging playwrights (with previous playwriting experience and/or training). Selection is based on the applicant's commitment, proven talent, and artistic potential.

Financial data Beginning playwrights receive a $1,000 stipend, $250 in play development funds, and a structured curriculum of playwriting instruction and dramaturgical support. Emerging playwrights receive a $3,600 stipend, $1,000 in play development funds, and dramaturgical support.

Duration 9 months, beginning in October.

Additional information This program, which began in 1994, is funded by the Jerome Foundation. Fellows must be in residence at the Playwrights' Center for the duration of the program.

Number awarded 5 each year: 2 beginning playwrights and 3 emerging playwrights.

Deadline February of each year.

[884]
MARIE F. PETERS AWARD

National Council on Family Relations
Attn: Ethnic Minorities Section
1201 West River Parkway, Suite 200
Minneapolis, MN 55454-1115
(763) 781-9331   Toll Free: (888) 781-9331
Fax: (763) 781-9348   E-mail: info@ncfr.com
Web: www.ncfr.org/sections/em/section-awards

Summary To recognize and reward Asian American and other members of the National Council on Family Relations (NCFR) who have made significant contributions to the area of ethnic minority families.

Eligibility This award is available to members of NCFR who have demonstrated excellence in the area of ethnic minority families. Selection is based on leadership and/or mentoring, scholarship and/or service, research, publication, teaching, community service, contribution to the ethnic minorities section, and contribution to the NCFR.

Financial data The award is $500 and a plaque.

Duration The award is granted biennially, in odd-numbered years.

Additional information This award, which was established in 1983, is named after a prominent Black researcher and family sociologist who served in many leadership roles in NCFR. It is sponsored by the Ethnic Minorities Section of NCFR.

Number awarded 1 every other year.

Deadline April of odd-numbered years.

[885]
MARTIN LUTHER KING, JR. MEMORIAL
SCHOLARSHIP FUND

California Teachers Association
Attn: Human Rights Department
1705 Murchison Drive
P.O. Box 921
Burlingame, CA 94011-0921
(650) 552-5446   Fax: (650) 552-5002
E-mail: scholarships@cta.org
Web: www.cta.org

Summary To provide financial assistance for college or graduate school to Asian Americans and other minorities who are members of the California Teachers Association (CTA), children of members, or members of the Student CTA.

Eligibility This program is open to members of racial or ethnic minority groups (African Americans, American Indians/ Alaska Natives, Asians/Pacific Islanders, and Hispanics) who are 1) active CTA members; 2) dependent children of active, retired, or deceased CTA members; or 3) members of Student CTA. Applicants must be interested in preparing for a teaching career in public education or already engaged in such a career.

Financial data Stipends vary each year; recently, they ranged from $1,000 to $4,000.

Duration 1 year.

Number awarded Varies each year; recently, 12 of these scholarships were awarded: 4 to CTA members, 6 to children of CTA members, and 2 to Student CTA members.

Deadline March of each year.

[886]
MINORITY ENTREPRENEURS SCHOLARSHIP
PROGRAM

International Franchise Association
Attn: IFA Educational Foundation
1501 K Street, N.W., Suite 350
Washington, DC 20005
(202) 662-0784   Fax: (202) 628-0812
E-mail: mbrewer@franchise.org
Web: www.franchise.org/Scholarships.aspx

Summary To provide financial assistance to Asian Americans, other minorities, and adult entrepreneurs enrolled in academic or professional development programs related to franchising.

Eligibility This program is open to 1) college students enrolled at an accredited college or university, and 2) adult entrepreneurs who have at least 5 years of business ownership or managerial experience. Applicants must be U.S. citizens and members of a minority group (defined as African Americans, American Indians, Hispanic Americans, and Asian Americans). Students should be enrolled in courses or programs relating to business, finance, marketing, hospitality, franchising, or entrepreneurship. Adult entrepreneurs should be enrolled in professional development courses related to franchising, such as those recognized by the Institute of Certified Franchise Executives (ICFE). All applicants must submit a 500-word essay on why they want the scholarship and their career goals. Financial need is not considered in the selection process.

Financial data The stipend is $3,000.

Duration 1 year.

Additional information This program is cosponsored by the IFA Educational Foundation and Marriott International.

Number awarded 5 each year.

Deadline June of each year.

[887]
MINORITY FACULTY DEVELOPMENT
SCHOLARSHIP AWARD IN PHYSICAL THERAPY

American Physical Therapy Association
Attn: Honors and Awards Program
1111 North Fairfax Street
Alexandria, VA 22314-1488
(703) 684-APTA   Toll Free: (800) 999-APTA
Fax: (703) 684-7343   TDD: (703) 683-6748
E-mail: executivedept@apta.org
Web: www.apta.org

Summary To provide financial assistance to Asian American and other minority faculty members in physical therapy who are interested in working on a doctoral degree.

Eligibility This program is open to U.S. citizens and permanent residents who are members of the following minority groups: African American or Black, Asian, Native Hawaiian or other Pacific Islander, American Indian or Alaska Native, or Hispanic/Latino. Applicants must be full-time faculty members, teaching in an accredited or developing professional physical therapist education program, who will have completed the equivalent of 2 full semesters of post-professional doctoral course work. They must possess a license to practice physical therapy in a U.S. jurisdiction and be enrolled as a student in an accredited post-professional doctoral program whose content has a demonstrated relationship to physical therapy. Along with their application, they must submit a personal essay on their professional goals, including their plans to contribute to the profession and minority services. Selection is based on 1) commitment to minority affairs and services; 2) commitment to further the physical therapy profession through teaching and research; and 3) scholastic achievement.

Financial data A stipend is awarded (amount not specified).

Duration 1 year.

Additional information This program was established in 1999.

Number awarded 1 or more each year.

Deadline November of each year.

[888]
NASA ASTROBIOLOGY PROGRAM MINORITY INSTITUTION RESEARCH SUPPORT

United Negro College Fund Special Programs
 Corporation
Attn: NASA Astrobiology Program
6402 Arlington Boulevard, Suite 600
Falls Church, VA 22042
(703) 205-7641   Toll Free: (800) 530-6232
Fax: (703) 205-7645   E-mail: portal@uncfsp.org
Web: www.uncfsp.org

Summary To provide an opportunity for Asian American and other faculty at Minority Serving Institutions (MSIs) to work on a summer research project in partnership with an established astrobiology investigator.

Eligibility This program is open to full-time tenured or tenure-track faculty members at MSIs who have a Ph.D., Sc.D., or equivalent degree in a field of STEM (science, technology, engineering, or mathematics). Applicants must be interested in conducting a summer research project on a topic related to astrobiology. They must identify an established investigator of the National Aeronautics and Space Administration (NASA) Astrobiology Program who has agreed to serve as host researcher. Eligible fields of study include biology, microbiology, astronomy, planetary science, astrochemistry, astrophysics, geology, geochemistry, or geobiochemistry. U.S. citizenship or permanent resident status is required.

Financial data Fellows receive a stipend of $10,000 and an additional grant of $5,000 to cover travel, lodging, and living expenses.

Duration 10 weeks during the summer.

Additional information This program is funded by NASA and administered by the United Negro College Fund Special Programs Corporation.

Number awarded Varies each year.

Deadline March of each year.

[889]
NATIONAL ALUMNI CHAPTER GRANTS

Kappa Omicron Nu
Attn: Awards Committee
4990 Northwind Drive, Suite 140
East Lansing, MI 48823-5031
(517) 351-8335   Fax: (517) 351-8336
E-mail: dmitstifer@kon.org
Web: www.kon.org/awards/grants.html

Summary To provide financial assistance to Asian Americans and other members of Kappa Omicron Nu, an honor society in family and consumer sciences, who are interested in conducting research.

Eligibility This program is open to 1) individual members of the society, and 2) research teams where the leader is a member of the society. Applicants must be interested in conducting research in family and consumer sciences or any of its related specializations. The research approach should be integrative in nature and shall make connections across specializations to pursue problems or questions. Special consideration is given to research that studies the cultural and religious differences affecting leadership, Hispanic, Asian, and Native Americans are encouraged to apply. Another topic of interest is the exploration of how minority students "strike out on their own" in career development.

Financial data The grant is $1,000.

Duration 1 year; multi-year funding may be accomplished by including a multi-year management plan in the initial proposal and reporting successful accomplishment of previous objectives annually.

Additional information Funding for these grants is provided by the National Alumni Chapter of Kappa Omicron Nu.

Number awarded 1 or more each year.

Deadline February of each year.

[890]
NEW JERSEY LIBRARY ASSOCIATION DIVERSITY SCHOLARSHIP

New Jersey Library Association
4 Lafayette Street
P.O. Box 1534
Trenton, NJ 08607
(609) 394-8032   Fax: (609) 394-8164
E-mail: ptumulty@njla.org
Web: www.njla.org/honorsawards/scholarship

Summary To provide financial assistance to New Jersey residents who are Asian Americans or members of other minority groups and interested in working on a graduate or postgraduate degree in public librarianship at a school in any state.

Eligibility This program is open to residents of New Jersey and individuals who have worked in a New Jersey library for at least 12 months. Applicants must be members of a minority group (African American, Asian/Pacific Islander, Latino/Hispanic, or Native American/Native Alaskan). They must be enrolled or planning to enroll at an ALA-accredited school of library science in any state to work on a graduate or postgraduate degree in librarianship. Along with their application, they must submit an essay of 150 to 250 words explaining their choice of librarianship as a profession. An interview is required. Selection is based on academic ability and financial need.

Financial data The stipend is $1,300.

Duration 1 year.

Number awarded 1 each year.

Deadline February of each year.

[891]
NEW YORK PUBLIC LIBRARY FELLOWSHIPS

American Council of Learned Societies
Attn: Office of Fellowships and Grants
633 Third Avenue
New York, NY 10017-6795
(212) 697-1505   Fax: (212) 949-8058
E-mail: fellowships@acls.org
Web: www.acls.org/programs/acls

Summary To provide funding to postdoctorates (particularly Asian American or other minority and women postdoctorates) who are interested in conducting research at the Dorothy and Lewis B. Cullman Center for Scholars and Writers of the New York Public Library.

Eligibility This program is open to scholars at all stages of their careers who received a Ph.D. degree at least 2 years previously. Established scholars who can demonstrate the equivalent of the Ph.D. in publications and professional experience may also qualify. Applicants must be U.S. citizens or permanent residents who have not had supported leave time for at least 2 years prior to the start of the proposed research. Appropriate fields of specialization include, but are not limited to, American studies; anthropology; archaeology; art and architectural history; classics; economics; film; geography; history; languages and literatures; legal studies; linguistics; musicology; philosophy; political science; psychology; religious studies; rhetoric, communication, and media studies; sociology; and theater, dance, and performance studies. Proposals in the fields social science fields are eligible only if they employ predominantly humanistic approaches (e.g., economic history, law and literature, political philosophy). Proposals in interdisciplinary and cross-disciplinary studies are welcome, as are proposals focused on any geographic region or on any cultural or linguistic group. Applicants must be interested in conducting research at the New York Public Library's Dorothy and Lewis B. Cullman Center for Scholars and Writers. Women and members of minority groups are particularly invited to apply.

Financial data The stipend is $60,000.

Duration 9 months, beginning in September.

Additional information This program was first offered for 1999-2000, the inaugural year of the center. Candidates must also submit a separate application that is available from the New York Public Library, Humanities and Social Sciences Library, Dorothy and Lewis B. Cullman Center for Scholars and Writers, Fifth Avenue and 42nd Street, New York, NY 10018-2788, E-mail: csw@nypl.org. Fellows are required to be in continuous residence at the center and participate actively in its activities and programs.

Number awarded Up to 5 each year.

Deadline September of each year.

[892]
NICKELODEON WRITING FELLOWSHIP PROGRAM

Nickelodeon Animation Studios
Attn: Nick Writing Fellowship
231 West Olive Avenue
Burbank, CA 91502
(818) 736-3663   E-mail: info.writing@nick.com
Web: www.nickwriting.com

Summary To provide an opportunity for young writers and animators (especially those of Asian American or other minority descent) to gain experience working at Nickelodeon Animation Studio in Burbank, California.

Eligibility This program is open to writers, whether experienced or not, who are at least 18 years of age. Applicants must submit a spec script, 1-page resume, and half-page biography. The spec script may be either live action (half hour television script based on a current television series) or animation (11- or 30-minute script based on a current animated television series). Scripts should focus on comedy. The program encourages applications from culturally and ethnically diverse writing talent.

Financial data This is a salaried position.

Duration Up to 1 year, divided into 3 phases: a 6-week audition phase in which the fellows write 1 spec script and their talent and progress are evaluated to determine if they are qualified to remain in the program; a 10-week development phase in which they write 1 spec script and are integrated into the activities of the production and development department; and a 34-week placement phase in which they write another spec script and pitch 1 original idea.

Number awarded Up to 4 each year.

Deadline February of each year.

[893]
NIDA CAREER DEVELOPMENT AWARD

American Academy of Child and Adolescent Psychiatry
Attn: Department of Research, Training, and Education
3615 Wisconsin Avenue, N.W.
Washington, DC 20016-3007
(202) 966-7300   Fax: (202) 966-2891
E-mail: research@aacap.org
Web: www.aacap.org/cs/awards

Summary To provide funding to child and adolescent psychiatrists (particularly Asian Americans, other minorities, and women) who are interested in a program of mentored training in addiction-related research focused on children and adolescents.

Eligibility This program is open to qualified child and adolescent psychiatrists who intend to established careers as independent investigators in mental health and addiction research. Applicants must design a career development and research training program in collaboration with a research mentor. The program may include prevention; early intervention or treatment research; epidemiology; etiology; genetics, gene-environment interactions, or pharmacogenetics; developmental risk factors; psychiatric comorbidity; medical comorbidity including HIV, Hepatitis C, and STD risk reduction; pathophysiology; services research; special populations (minorities, pregnancy, juvenile justice); health disparities; or imaging studies. U.S. citizenship, nationality, or permanent resident status is required. Women and minority candidates are especially encouraged to apply.

Financial data Grants provide salary support for 75% of the recipient's salary (up to $90,000 plus fringe benefits) and $50,000 per year to cover research and training costs.

Duration Up to 5 years.

Additional information This program is co-sponsored by the American Academy of Child and Adolescent Psychiatry (AACAP) and the National Institute on Drug Abuse (NIDA) as a K12 program of the National Institutes of Health (NIH).

Number awarded 1 or more each year.

Deadline Letters of intent must be submitted in early January of each year; completed applications are due the following March.

[894]
OFFICE OF NAVAL RESEARCH YOUNG INVESTIGATOR PROGRAM

Office of Naval Research
Attn: Code 03R
875 North Randolph Street, Suite 1409
Arlington, VA 22203-1995
(703) 696-4111   E-mail: William.lukens1@navy.mil
Web: www.onr.navy.mil/Education-Outreach.aspx

Summary To provide funding to academic scientists and engineers (particularly those at minority serving institutions) who are interested in conducting research on topics of interest to the U.S. Navy.

Eligibility This program is open to U.S. citizens, nationals, and permanent residents holding tenure-track faculty positions at U.S. universities who received their graduate degrees (Ph.D. or equivalent) within the preceding 5 years. Applicants must be proposing to conduct research relevant to 1 of the divisions within the Office of Naval Research: expeditionary warfare and combating terrorism; command, control communications, computers, intelligence, surveillance, and reconnaissance; ocean battlespace sensing; sea warfare and weapons; warfighter performance; and naval air warfare and weapons. Selection is based on 1) past performance, demonstrated by the significance and impact of previous research, publications, professional activities, awards, and other recognition; 2) a creative proposal, demonstrating the potential for making progress in a listed priority research area; and 3) a long-term commitment by the university to the applicant and the research. Researchers at Historically Black Colleges and Universities (HBCUs) and Minority Institutions (MIs) are encouraged to submit proposals and join others in submitting proposals.

Financial data Awards up to $170,000 per year are available.

Duration 3 years.

Additional information Approximately 2 recipients of these awards are also nominated to receive Presidential Early Career Awards for Scientists and Engineers to provide an additional 2 years of funding.

Number awarded Approximately 18 each year.

Deadline December of each year.

[895]
OKURA MENTAL HEALTH LEADERSHIP FOUNDATION FELLOWSHIP

American Psychological Foundation
750 First Street, N.E.
Washington, DC 20002-4242
(202) 336-5843   Fax: (202) 336-5812
E-mail: foundation@apa.org
Web: www.apa.org/apf/funding/okura-fellow.aspx

Summary To provide funding to members of the Asian American Psychological Association (AAPA) who are interested in conducting projects related to the Asian American and Pacific Islander (AAPI) community.

Eligibility This program is open to AAPA members who are interested in conducting psychological projects that will benefit the AAPI community. The emphasis of the program rotates among support for training initiatives (2013), support for service and practice initiatives (2014), and support for research (2015). Applicants must be within 10 years of completing their doctoral degree and be affiliated with a nonprofit organization. Selection is based on conformance with stated program goals and requirements; innovative and potential impact qualities; competence and capability of project leaders; and quality, viability, and promise of the proposed work.

Financial data The grant is $20,000.

Duration The grant is presented annually.

Additional information This program, established in 2009, is administered on behalf of AAPA by the American Psychological Foundation (APF), with funding provided by the Okura Mental Health Leadership Foundation.

Number awarded 1 each year.

Deadline September of each year.

[896]
ONLINE BIBLIOGRAPHIC SERVICES/ TECHNICAL SERVICES JOINT RESEARCH GRANT

American Association of Law Libraries
Attn: Online Bibliographic Services Special Interest
   Section
105 West Adams Street, Suite 3300
Chicago, IL 60603
(312) 939-4764   Fax: (312) 431-1097
E-mail: aallhq@aall.org
Web: www.aallnet.org/sis/obssis/research/funding.htm

Summary To provide funding to members of the American Association of Law Libraries (AALL), especially Asian Americans, other minorities, and women who are interested in conducting a research project related to technical services.

Eligibility This program is open to AALL members who are technical services law librarians. Preference is given to members of the Online Bibliographic Services and Technical Services Special Interest Sections, although members of other special interest sections are eligible if their work relates to technical services law librarianship. Applicants must be interested in conducting research that will enhance law librarianship. Women and minorities are especially encouraged to apply. Preference is given to projects that can be completed in the United States or Canada, although foreign research projects are given consideration.

Financial data Grants range up to $1,000.

Duration 1 year.
Number awarded 1 or more each year.
Deadline June of each year.

[897]
PATSYLU PRIZE

International Alliance for Women in Music
c/o Pamela Marshall, Search for New Music Competition
 Coordinator
38 Dexter Road
Lexington, MA 02420
E-mail: snm@iawm.org
Web: www.iawm.org/oppsComp_snm.htm

Summary To recognize and reward outstanding musical compositions by members of the International Alliance for Women in Music (IAWM) who are Asian American, other women of color, or lesbians.

Eligibility This competition is open to women composers who are women of color and/or lesbians and whose music has not yet been recorded or published. Applicants must submit a composition of a work in any medium that is unpublished, has no plans to be recorded, and has won no prior awards. A standard CD or DVD of the work must accompany the submission. Contestants must be IAWM members or willing to join at the time of entry.

Financial data The prize is $500.
Duration The competition is held annually.
Number awarded 1 each year.
Deadline March of each year.

[898]
PAUL HOCH DISTINGUISHED SERVICE AWARD

American College of Neuropsychopharmacology
Attn: Executive Office
5034-A Thoroughbred Lane
Brentwood, TN 37027
(615) 324-2360   Fax: (615) 523-1715
E-mail: acnp@acnp.org
Web: www.acnp.org/programs/awards.aspx

Summary To recognize and reward members of the American College of Neuropsychopharmacology (ACNP), especially Asian Americans, other minorities, and women who have a record of outstanding service to the organization.

Eligibility This award is available to ACNP members who have made unusually significant contributions to the College. The emphasis of the award is on service to the organization, not on teaching, clinical, or research accomplishments. Any member or fellow of ACNP may nominate another member. Nomination of women and minorities is highly encouraged.

Financial data The award consists of an expense-paid trip to the ACNP annual meeting, a monetary honorarium, and a plaque.
Duration The award is presented annually.
Additional information This award was first presented in 1965.
Number awarded 1 each year.
Deadline Nominations must be submitted by June of each year.

[899]
PAUL TOBENKIN MEMORIAL AWARD

Columbia University
Attn: Graduate School of Journalism
Mail Code 3809
2950 Broadway
New York, NY 10027-7004
(212) 854-5377   Fax: (212) 854-7837
E-mail: am494@columbia.edu
Web: www.journalism.columbia.edu

Summary To recognize and reward outstanding newspaper writing that reflects the spirit of Paul Tobenkin, who fought all his life against racial and religious hatred, bigotry, bias, intolerance, and discrimination.

Eligibility Materials reflecting the spirit of Paul Tobenkin may be submitted by newspaper reporters in the United States, editors of their publications, or interested third parties. The items submitted must have been published during the previous calendar year in a weekly or daily newspaper.

Financial data The award is $1,000 plus a plaque.
Duration The award is presented annually.
Additional information This award was first presented in 1961,.
Number awarded 1 each year.
Deadline February of each year.

[900]
POSTDOCTORAL FELLOWSHIP IN MENTAL HEALTH AND SUBSTANCE ABUSE SERVICES

American Psychological Association
Attn: Minority Fellowship Program
750 First Street, N.E.
Washington, DC 20002-4242
(202) 336-6127   Fax: (202) 336-6012
TDD: (202) 336-6123   E-mail: mfp@apa.org
Web: www.apa.org/pi/mfp/psychology/postdoc/index.aspx

Summary To provide financial assistance to minority and other postdoctoral scholars interested in a program of research training related to providing mental health and substance abuse services to ethnic minority populations.

Eligibility This program is open to U.S. citizens and permanent residents who received a doctoral degree in psychology in the last 5 years. Applicants must be interested in participating in a program of training under a qualified sponsor for research, delivery of services, or policy related to substance abuse and its relationship to the mental health or psychological well-being of ethnic minorities. Members of ethnic minority groups (African Americans, Hispanics/Latinos, American Indians, Alaskan Natives, Asian Americans, Native Hawaiians, and other Pacific Islanders) are especially encouraged to apply. Selection is based on commitment to a career in ethnic minority mental health service delivery, research, or policy; qualifications of the sponsor; the fit between career goals and training environment selected; merit of the training proposal; potential demonstrated through accomplishments and goals; appropriateness to goals of the program; and letters of recommendation.

Financial data The stipend depends on the number of years of research experience and is equivalent to the standard postdoctoral stipend level of the National Institutes of

Health (recently ranging from $38,496 for no years of experience to $53,112 for 7 or more years of experience).

Duration 1 academic or calendar year; may be renewed for 1 additional year.

Additional information Funding is provided by the U.S. Substance Abuse and Mental Health Services Administration.

Number awarded Varies each year.

Deadline January of each year.

[901]
POSTDOCTORAL FELLOWSHIPS OF THE MINORITY SCHOLAR-IN-RESIDENCE PROGRAM

Consortium for Faculty Diversity at Liberal Arts Colleges
c/o DePauw University
Academic Affairs Office
305 Harrison Hall
7 East Larabee Street
Greencastle, IN 46135
(765) 658-6595   E-mail: jgriswold@depauw.edu
Web: www.depauw.edu

Summary To make available the facilities of liberal arts colleges to Asian American and other minority scholars who recently received their doctoral/advanced degree.

Eligibility This program is open to African American, Asian American, Hispanic American, and Native American scholars in the liberal arts and engineering who received the Ph.D. or M.F.A. degree within the past 5 years. Applicants must be interested in a residency at a participating institution that is part of the Consortium for a Strong Minority Presence at Liberal Arts Colleges. They must be U.S. citizens or permanent residents.

Financial data Fellows receive a stipend equivalent to the average salary paid by the host college to beginning assistant professors. Modest funds are made available to finance the fellow's proposed research, subject to the usual institutional procedures.

Duration 1 year.

Additional information The following schools are participating in the program: Agnes Scott College, Bard College at Simon's Rock, Bowdoin College, Bryn Mawr College, Carleton College, Centre College, College of Wooster, Colorado College, Denison University, DePauw University, Dickinson College, Gettysburg College, Goucher College, Grinnell College, Hamilton College, Harvey Mudd College, Haverford College, Hobart and William Smith Colleges, Kalamazoo College, Lafayette College, Lawrence University, Luther College, Macalester College, Mount Holyoke College, Muhlenberg College, New College of Florida, Oberlin College, Pomona College, Reed College, Rhodes College, University of Richmond, Scripps College, St. Olaf College, Sewanee: The University of the South, Skidmore College, Smith College, Southwestern University, Swarthmore College, Trinity College, Vassar College, Wellesley College, Whitman College, and Willamette University. Fellows are expected to teach at least 1 course in each academic term of residency, participate in departmental seminars, and interact with students.

Number awarded Varies each year.

Deadline November of each year.

[902]
POSTDOCTORAL RESEARCH TRAINING FELLOWSHIPS IN EPILEPSY

Epilepsy Foundation
Attn: Research Department
8301 Professional Place
Landover, MD 20785-2237
(301) 459-3700   Toll Free: (800) EFA-1000
Fax: (301) 577-2684   TDD: (800) 332-2070
E-mail: grants@efa.org
Web: www.epilepsyfoundation.org

Summary To provide funding for a program of postdoctoral training to academic physicians and scientists (particularly Asian Americans, other minorities, women, and individuals with disabilities) who are committed to epilepsy research.

Eligibility Applicants must have a doctoral degree (M.D., Sc.D., Ph.D., or equivalent) and be a clinical or postdoctoral fellow at a university, medical school, research institution, or medical center. They must be interested in participating in a training experience and research project that has potential significance for understanding the causes, treatment, or consequences of epilepsy. The program is geared toward applicants who will be trained in research in epilepsy rather than those who use epilepsy as a tool for research in other fields. Equal consideration is given to applicants interested in acquiring experience either in basic laboratory research or in the conduct of human clinical studies. Academic faculty holding the rank of instructor or higher are not eligible, nor are graduate or medical students, medical residents, permanent government employees, or employees of private industry. Applications from women, members of minority groups, and people with disabilities are especially encouraged. U.S. citizenship is not required, but the project must be conducted in the United States. Selection is based on scientific quality of the proposed research, a statement regarding its relevance to epilepsy, the applicant's qualifications, the preceptor's qualifications, and the adequacy of facility and related epilepsy programs at the institution.

Financial data The grant is $45,000. No indirect costs are covered.

Duration 1 year.

Additional information Support for this program is provided by many individuals, families, and corporations, especially the American Epilepsy Society, Abbott Laboratories, Ortho-McNeil Pharmaceutical, and Pfizer Inc. The fellowship must be carried out at a facility in the United States where there is an ongoing epilepsy research program.

Number awarded Varies each year.

Deadline August of each year.

[903]
PRESIDENTIAL EARLY CAREER AWARDS FOR SCIENTISTS AND ENGINEERS

National Science and Technology Council
Executive Office of the President
Attn: Office of Science and Technology Policy
725 17th Street, Room 5228
Washington, DC 20502
(202) 456-7116   Fax: (202) 456-6021
Web: www.ostp.gov

Summary To recognize and reward the nation's most outstanding young science and engineering faculty members (particularly those who are Asian Americans other minorities, women, and individuals with disabilities) by providing them with additional research funding.

Eligibility Eligible for these awards are U.S. citizens, nationals, and permanent residents who have been selected to receive research grants from other departments of the U.S. government. Recipients of designated research grant programs are automatically considered for these Presidential Early Career Awards for Scientists and Engineers (PECASE). Most of the participating programs encourage applications from racial/ethnic minority individuals, women, and persons with disabilities.

Financial data Awards carry a grant of at least $80,000 per year.

Duration 5 years.

Additional information The departments with research programs that nominate candidates for the PECASE program are: 1) the National Aeronautics and Space Administration, which selects recipients of Early Career Awards based on exceptionally meritorious proposals funded through the traditional research grant process or the unsolicited proposal process; 2) the Department of Veterans Affairs, which nominates the most meritorious recipients of Veterans Health Administration Research Awards in the categories in medical research, rehabilitation research, and health services research; 3) the National Institutes of Health, which nominates the most meritorious investigators funded through its First Independent Research Support and Transition (FIRST) Awards and NIH Individual Research Project Grants (R01) programs; 4) the Department of Energy, which nominates staff members of the national laboratories and the most meritorious recipients of the DOE–Energy Research Young Scientist Awards and DOE–Defense Programs Early Career Scientist and Engineer Awards; 5) the Department of Defense, which nominates outstanding recipients of the Office of Naval Research Young Investigator Program, the Air Force Office of Scientific Research Broad Agency Program, and the Army Research Office Young Investigator Program; 6) the Department of Agriculture, which nominates staff scientists from the Agricultural Research Service, the most meritorious investigators funded through the National Research Initiative Competitive Grants Program (NRICGP) New Investigator Awards, and staff scientists of the Forest Service; 7) the Department of Commerce, which nominates outstanding staff members of the National Oceanic and Atmospheric Administration and the National Institute of Standards and Technology; 8) the Department of Transportation, which nominates the most qualified and innovative researchers in its University Transportation Centers and University Research Institutes programs; and 9) the National Science Foundation, which selects its nominees from the most meritorious investigators funded through the Faculty Early Career Development (CAREER) Program. For a list of the names, addresses, and telephone numbers of contact persons at each of the participating agencies, contact the Office of Science and Technology Policy.

Number awarded Varies each year; recently, 85 of these awards were granted.

Deadline Deadline not specified.

[904]
R. ROBERT & SALLY D. FUNDERBURG RESEARCH AWARD IN GASTRIC CANCER

American Gastroenterological Association
Attn: AGA Research Foundation
Research Awards Manager
4930 Del Ray Avenue
Bethesda, MD 20814-2512
(301) 222-4012   Fax: (301) 654-5920
E-mail: awards@gastro.org
Web: www.gastro.org/aga-foundation/grants

Summary To provide funding to established investigators (especially Asian Americans, other minorities, and Women) who are working on research that enhances fundamental understanding of gastric cancer pathobiology.

Eligibility This program is open to faculty at accredited North American institutions who have established themselves as independent investigators in the field of gastric biology, pursuing novel approaches to gastric mucosal cell biology, including the fields of gastric mucosal cell biology, regeneration and regulation of cell growth, inflammation as precancerous lesions, genetics of gastric carcinoma, oncogenes in gastric epithelial malignancies, epidemiology of gastric cancer, etiology of gastric epithelial malignancies, or clinical research in diagnosis or treatment of gastric carcinoma. Applicants must be individual members of the American Gastroenterological Association (AGA). Women and minority investigators are strongly encouraged to apply. Selection is based on the novelty, feasibility, and significance of the proposal. Preference is given to novel approaches.

Financial data The grant is $50,000 per year. Funds are to be used for the salary of the investigator. Indirect costs are not allowed.

Duration 2 years.

Number awarded 1 each year.

Deadline September of each year.

[905]
RALPH J. BUNCHE AWARD

American Political Science Association
1527 New Hampshire Avenue, N.W.
Washington, DC 20036-1206
(202) 483-2512   Fax: (202) 483-2657
E-mail: apsa@apsanet.org
Web: www.apsanet.org/content_4129.cfm

Summary To recognize and reward outstanding scholarly books on ethnic/cultural pluralism.

Eligibility Eligible to be nominated (by publishers or individuals) are scholarly political science books issued the previous year that explore issues of ethnic and/or cultural pluralism.

Financial data The award is $1,000.

Duration The award is presented annually.

Additional information This award was first presented in 1978.

Number awarded 1 each year.

Deadline January of each year for nominations from individuals; February of each year for nominations from publishers.

[906]
RECOGNITION AWARDS PROGRAM

American Epilepsy Society
342 North Main Street
West Hartford, CT 06117-2507
(860) 586-7505   Fax: (860) 586-7550
E-mail: ctubby@aesnet.org
Web: www.aesnet.org/research/research-awards

Summary To provide funding to investigators (particularly Asian Americans, other minorities, and women) who are interested in conducting research related to epilepsy.

Eligibility This program is open to active scientists and clinicians working in any aspect of epilepsy. Candidates must be nominated by their home institution and be at the level of associate professor or professor. There are no geographic restrictions; nominations from outside the United States and North America are welcome. Nominations of women and members of minority groups are especially encouraged. Selection is based on pioneering research, originality of research, quality of publications, research productivity, relationship of the candidate's work to problems in epilepsy, training activities, other contributions in epilepsy, and productivity over the next decade; all criteria are weighted equally.

Financial data The grant is $10,000. No institutional overhead is allowed.

Additional information This program was established in 1991.

Number awarded 2 each year.

Deadline August of each year.

[907]
RESEARCH AND TRAINING FELLOWSHIPS IN EPILEPSY FOR CLINICIANS

Epilepsy Foundation
Attn: Research Department
8301 Professional Place
Landover, MD 20785-2237
(301) 459-3700   Toll Free: (800) EFA-1000
Fax: (301) 577-2684   TDD: (800) 332-2070
E-mail: clinical_postdocs@efa.org
Web: www.epilepsyfoundation.org

Summary To provide funding to clinically-trained professionals (particularly Asian Americans, other minorities, women, and individuals with disabilities) who are interested in gaining additional training in order to develop an epilepsy research program.

Eligibility Applicants must have an M.D., D.O., Ph.D., D.S., or equivalent degree and be a clinical or postdoctoral fellow at a university, medical school, or other appropriate research institution. Holders of other doctoral-level degrees (e.g., Pharm.D., D.S.N.) may also be eligible. Candidates must be interested in a program of research training that may include mechanisms of epilepsy, novel therapeutic approaches, clinical trials, development of new technologies, or behavioral and psychosocial impact of epilepsy. The training program may consist of both didactic training and a supervised research experience that is designed to develop the necessary knowledge and skills in the chosen area of research and foster the career goals of the candidate. Academic faculty holding the rank of instructor or higher are not eligible, nor are graduate or medical students, medical residents, permanent government employees, or employees of private industry. Applica-

tions from women, members of minority groups, and people with disabilities are especially encouraged. U.S. citizenship is not required, but the project must be conducted in the United States. Selection is based on the quality of the proposed research training program, the applicant's qualifications, the preceptor's qualifications, and the adequacy of clinical training, research facilities, and other epilepsy-related programs at the institution.

Financial data The grant is $50,000 per year. No indirect costs are provided.

Duration Up to 2 years.

Additional information Support for this program is provided by many individuals, families, and corporations, especially the American Epilepsy Society, Abbott Laboratories, Ortho-McNeil Pharmaceutical, and Pfizer Inc. Grantees are expected to dedicate at least 50% of their time to research training and conducting research.

Number awarded Varies each year.

Deadline September of each year.

[908]
ROBERT WOOD JOHNSON HEALTH POLICY FELLOWSHIPS

Institute of Medicine
Attn: Health Policy Fellowships Program
500 Fifth Street, N.W.
Washington, DC 20001
(202) 334-1506   Fax: (202) 334-3862
E-mail: mmichnich@nas.edu
Web: www.healthpolicyfellows.org

Summary To provide an opportunity to health professionals and behavioral and social scientists (particularly Asian Americans and other scientists from diverse backgrounds) who are interested in participating in the formulation of national health policies while in residence at the Institute of Medicine (IOM) in Washington, D.C.

Eligibility This program is open to mid-career professionals from academic faculties and nonprofit health care organizations who are interested in experiencing health policy processes at the federal level. Applicants must have a background in allied health professions, biomedical sciences, dentistry, economics or other social sciences, health services organization and administration, medicine, nursing, public health, or social and behavioral health. They must be sponsored by the chief executive office of an eligible nonprofit health care organization or academic institution. Selection is based on potential for leadership in health policy, potential for future growth and career advancement, professional achievements, interpersonal and communication skills, and individual plans for incorporating the fellowship experience into specific career goals. U.S. citizenship or permanent resident status is required. Applications are especially encouraged from candidates with diverse backgrounds.

Financial data Total support for the Washington stay and continuing activities may not exceed $165,000. Grant funds may cover salary support at a level of up to $94,000 plus fringe benefits. Fellows are reimbursed for relocation expenses to and from Washington, D.C. No indirect costs are paid.

Duration The program begins in September with an orientation that includes meeting with key executive branch officials responsible for health activities, members of Congress and their staffs, and representatives of health interest groups; also included in the orientation period are seminars on health economics, major federal health and health research programs, the Congressional budget process, background on the major current issues in federal health policy, and the politics and process of federal decision-making. In November, the fellows join the American Political Science Association Congressional Fellowship Program for sessions with members of Congress, journalists, policy analysts, and other experts on the national political and governmental process. During that stage, fellows make contact with Congressional or executive branch offices involved in health issues and negotiate their working assignments. Those assignments begin in January and end in August, with an option for extending through the legislative term (which normally ends in October or early November). Fellows then return to their home institutions, but they receive up to 2 years of continued support for further development of health policy leadership skills.

Additional information This program, initiated in 1973, is funded by the Robert Wood Johnson Foundation.

Number awarded Up to 6 each year.

Deadline November of each year.

[909]
RUBY YOSHINO SCHAAR PLAYWRIGHT AWARD

Japanese American Citizens League-New York Chapter
75 Grove Street, Number 2
Bloomfield, NJ 07003
(973) 680-1441   Fax: (973) 680-1441
E-mail: lckimura@worldnet.att.net
Web: www.jacl.org/edu/yosh-award.htm

Summary To recognize and reward outstanding Japanese American playwrights.

Eligibility This award is available to U.S. or Canadian citizens of Japanese descent who are playwrights and sponsored by a member or chapter of the Japanese American Citizens League. Applicants must have had at least 1 of their plays presented in a public forum, such as an established theater, workshop, or formal reading. They must submit a manuscript for a play that has not been theatrically produced. Selection is based on dramatic excellence and insight into the Japanese American or Canadian experience.

Financial data The award is $3,000.

Duration 1 every other year, in even-numbered years.

Additional information This award, established in 1984, is named in memory of a former Japanese American Citizens League chapter president and executive director.

Number awarded 1 every even-numbered year.

Deadline April of even-numbered years.

[910]
SALLY C. TSENG PROFESSIONAL DEVELOPMENT GRANT

Chinese American Librarians Association
c/o Lian Ruan, Professional Development Grant
  Committee
University of Illinois
Head Librarian, Illinois Fire Service Institute
11 Gerty Drive
Champaign, IL 61820
(217) 265-6107   E-mail: ruan@illinois.edu
Web: www.cala-web.org/node/205

Summary To provide funding to members of the Chinese American Librarians Association (CALA) who are interested in conducting a research project.

Eligibility This program is open to full-time librarians of Chinese descent who have been CALA members for at least 2 years. Applicants must be interested in conducting a research project in library and information science for which they are qualified and which will result in the advancement of their professional status. Preference is given to members with 15 or fewer years of professional library experience.

Financial data The grant is $1,000.

Duration 1 year.

Number awarded 1 or 2 each year.

Deadline March of each year.

[911]
SAM CHU LIN BROADCAST NEWS GRANT

Asian American Journalists Association
Attn: Student Programs Coordinator
5 Third Street, Suite 1108
San Francisco, CA 94103
(415) 346-2051, ext. 102   Fax: (415) 346-6343
E-mail: programs@aaja.org
Web: www.aaja.org/programs/internships

Summary To provide a supplemental grant to student and other members of the Asian American Journalists Association (AAJA) working as a summer intern at a radio or television broadcasting company.

Eligibility This program is open to AAJA members who are full-time college students or recent college graduates. Applicants must have secured a summer internship at a television or radio broadcasting company before they apply. Along with their application, they must submit a 200-word essay on why they want to prepare for a career in broadcast journalism, what they want to gain from the experience, and why AAJA's mission is important to them; a letter of recommendation; a resume; proof of age (at least 18 years); verification of an internship; and statement of financial need.

Financial data The grant is $2,500. Funds are to be used for living expenses or transportation.

Duration Summer months.

Number awarded 1 each year.

Deadline May of each year.

[912]
SARA WHALEY BOOK PRIZE

National Women's Studies Association
Attn: Book Prizes
7100 Baltimore Avenue, Suite 203
College Park, MD 20740
(301) 403-0407   Fax: (301) 403-4137
E-mail: nwsaoffice@nwsa.org
Web: www.nwsa.org/awards/index.php

Summary To recognize and reward members of the National Women's Studies Association (NWSA), particularly Asian American and other women of color, who have written outstanding books on topics related to women and labor.

Eligibility This award is available to NWSA members who submit a book manuscript that relates to women and labor, including migration and women's paid jobs, illegal immigration and women's work, impact of AIDS on women's employment, trafficking of women and women's employment, women and domestic work, or impact of race on women's work. Both senior scholars (who have a record of publication of at least 2 books and published the entry within the past year) and junior scholars (who have a publication contract or a book in production) are eligible. Women of color of American or international origin are encouraged to apply.

Financial data The award is $2,000.

Duration The awards are presented annually.

Additional information This award was first presented in 2008.

Number awarded 2 each year: 1 to a senior scholar and 1 to a junior scholar.

Deadline April of each year.

[913]
SHEILA SUEN LAI RESEARCH GRANT

Asian Pacific American Librarians Association
Attn: Executive Director
University of California at Santa Barbara
Davidson Library
Santa Barbara, CA 93106
(805) 893-8067   E-mail: colmenar@library.ucsb.edu
Web: www.apalaweb.org/awards/sslgrant.htm

Summary To provide research funding to members of the Asian Pacific American Librarians Association (APALA).

Eligibility Eligible to apply are APALA members in good standing who have belonged for at least 1 year prior to applying. Applicants must have an M.L.S. or M.L.I.S. degree and currently be employed in a professional position in library science or a related field. They must be U.S. citizens or permanent residents. Current recipients of other APALA grants or scholarships are not eligible for this award. A complete grant application must contain a cover letter, a resume or curriculum vitae, a detailed statement of intended research activities, including a budget (up to 5 pages), and, optionally, letters of recommendation or institutional commitment of resources.

Financial data Grants range up to $1,000.

Duration Grants are awarded annually.

Additional information Funds cannot be used to attend professional association conferences.

Number awarded 1 or more each year.

Deadline February of each year.

[914]
SHRI RAM ARORA AWARD

The Minerals, Metals & Materials Society
Attn: TMS Foundation
184 Thorn Hill Road
Warrendale, PA 15086-7514
(724) 776-9000, ext. 229   Toll Free: (800) 759-4867
Fax: (724) 776-3770   E-mail: foundation@tms.org
Web: www.tms.org/Foundation/TFactivities.aspx

Summary To provide funding to graduate students and postdoctoral scholars of Indian origin who are interested in educational activities in materials science and engineering.

Eligibility This program is open to graduate students working on a degree in materials science or a related field and postdoctoral scholars actively involved in materials research. First priority is given to applicants living in India; if there are no qualified candidates from India, applicants of Indian heritage currently residing in the United States or other countries are considered. Applicants must be younger than 30 years of age. Along with their application, they must submit a statement that describes the purpose for which the award is being sought, including details on how this activity will contribute to their career plans and their aspiration to a leadership role in the materials science and engineering profession.

Financial data The award is $2,500, including a cash grant of $1,000 to be used at the recipient's discretion and $1,500 for travel, accommodation, and registration expenses to attend the annual meeting of The Minerals, Metals & Materials Society (TMS).

Duration The award is presented annually.

Additional information This award was first presented in 2000.

Number awarded 1 each year.

Deadline June of each year.

[915]
SOCIETY OF PEDIATRIC PSYCHOLOGY DIVERSITY RESEARCH GRANT

American Psychological Association
Attn: Division 54 (Society of Pediatric Psychology)
c/o John M. Chaney
Oklahoma State University
Department of Psychology
407 North Murray
Stillwater, OK 74078
(405) 744-5703   E-mail: john.chaney@okstate.edu
Web: www.societyofpediatricpsychology.org

Summary To provide funding to graduate students and postdoctorates who 1) belong to the Society of Pediatric Psychology (especially Asian Americans and members of other diverse groups) and 2) are interested in conducting research on diversity aspects of pediatric psychology.

Eligibility This program is open to current members of the society who are graduate students, fellows, or early-career (within 3 years of appointment) faculty. Applicants must be interested in conducting pediatric psychology research that features diversity-related variables, such as race or ethnicity, gender, culture, sexual orientation, language differences, socioeconomic status, and/or religiosity. Along with their application, they must submit a 2,000-word description of the project, including its purpose, methodology, predictions, and implications; a detailed budget; a current curriculum vitae, and (for students) a curriculum vitae of the faculty research mentor and a letter of support from that mentor. Selection is based on relevance to diversity in child health (5 points), significance of the study (5 points), study methods and procedures (10 points), and investigator qualifications (10 points).

Financial data Grants up to $1,000 are available. Funds may not be used for convention or meeting travel, indirect costs, stipends of principal investigators, or costs associated with manuscript preparation.

Duration The grant is presented annually.

Additional information The Society of Pediatric Psychology is Division 54 of the American Psychological Association (APA). This grant was first presented in 2008.

Number awarded 1 each year.

Deadline September of each year.

[916]
SUBSTANCE ABUSE FELLOWSHIP PROGRAM

American Psychiatric Association
Attn: Department of Minority and National Affairs
1000 Wilson Boulevard, Suite 1825
Arlington, VA 22209-3901
(703) 907-8653   Toll Free: (888) 35-PSYCH
Fax: (703) 907-7852   E-mail: mking@psych.org
Web: www.psych.org/Resources/OMNA/MFP.aspx

Summary To provide educational enrichment to Asian American and other minority psychiatrists-in-training and stimulate their interest in providing quality and effective services related to substance abuse to minorities and the underserved.

Eligibility This program is open to psychiatric residents who are members of the American Psychiatric Association (APA) and U.S. citizens or permanent residents. A goal of the program is to develop leadership to improve the quality of mental health care for members of ethnic minority groups (American Indians, Native Alaskans, Asian Americans, Native Hawaiians, Native Pacific Islanders, African Americans, and Hispanics/Latinos). Applicants must be in at least their fifth year of a substance abuse training program approved by an affiliated medical school or agency where a significant number of substance abuse patients are from minority and underserved groups. They must also be interested in working with a component of the APA that is of interest to them and relevant to their career goals. Along with their application, they must submit a 2-page essay on how the fellowship would be utilized to alter their present training and ultimately assist them in achieving their career goals. Selection is based on commitment to serve ethnic minority populations, demonstrated leadership abilities, awareness of the importance of culture in mental health, and interest in the interrelationship between mental health/illness and transcultural factors.

Financial data Fellows receive a monthly stipend (amount not specified) and reimbursement of transportation, lodging, meals, and incidentals in connection with attendance at program-related activities. They are expected to use the funds to enhance their own professional development, improve training in cultural competence at their training institution, improve awareness of culturally relevant issues in psychiatry at their institution, expand research in areas relevant to minorities and underserved populations, enhance the current treatment

modalities for minority patients and underserved individuals at their institution, and improve awareness in the surrounding community about mental health issues (particularly with regard to minority populations).

Duration 1 year; may be renewed 1 additional year.

Additional information Funding for this program is provided by the Substance Abuse and Mental Health Services Administration (SAMHSA). As part of their assignment to an APA component, fellows must attend the fall component meetings in September and the APA annual meeting in May. At those meeting, they can share their experiences as residents and minorities and discuss issues that impact minority populations. This program is an outgrowth of the fellowships that were established in 1974 under a grant from the National Institute of Mental Health in answer to concerns about the underrepresentation of minorities in psychiatry.

Number awarded Varies each year; recently, 3 of these fellowships were awarded.

Deadline January of each year.

[917]
SUSAN G. KOMEN BREAST CANCER FOUNDATION POSTDOCTORAL FELLOWSHIP

Susan G. Komen Breast Cancer Foundation
Attn: Grants Department
5005 LBJ Freeway, Suite 250
Dallas, TX 75244
(972) 855-1616   Toll Free: (866) 921-9678
Fax: (972) 855-1640
E-mail: helpdesk@komengrantsaccess.org
Web: ww5.komen.org

Summary To provide funding to postdoctoral fellows (particularly Asian Americans and other minorities) who are interested in pursuing research training related to breast cancer.

Eligibility This program is open to postdoctorates who are no more than 5 years past completion of their Ph.D. or, if an M.D., no more than 3 years past completion of clinical fellowship or 5 years past completion of residency. Applicants may not hold any current faculty appointments and may not currently be or have been a fellow for the same sponsor. They are not required to be U.S. citizens or residents. A principal investigator who is a full-time faculty member at the same institution must sponsor the applicant. Currently, proposals must focus on 4 types of research training activities: 1) basic research that substantially advances progress in breast cancer research and will lead to future reductions in breast cancer incidence and/or mortality; 2) translational research that expands skills and expertise in the application of laboratory, clinical, and applied disciplines to research that translates laboratory, clinical, and/or population discoveries into new clinical tools and applications leading to reductions of breast cancer incidence and/or mortality; 3) clinical research for physicians who wish to pursue a career path that blends patient care with high impact, clinical, and/or translational breast cancer research; expands their skills; positions them for independent careers as physician scientists; and supports high quality research concepts; or 4) disparities research that expands skills and expertise in research exploring the basis for differences in breast cancer outcomes and the translation of this research into clinical and public health practice interventions, particularly among junior scientists from populations affected by breast cancer disparities. The program is especially interested in providing training support for minority scientists; a portion of available funds are designated for minority fellows.

Financial data   The grant is $60,000 per year for direct costs only.

Duration   2 years; a third year may be approved, based on an assessment of first-year progress.

Number awarded   Varies each year; recently, 56 of these fellowships were awarded.

Deadline   Pre-applications must be submitted in September of each year; full applications are due in January.

[918]
TRAINEESHIPS IN AIDS PREVENTION STUDIES (TAPS) PROGRAM POSTDOCTORAL FELLOWSHIPS

University of California at San Francisco
Attn: Center for AIDS Prevention Studies
50 Beale Street, Suite 1300
San Francisco, CA 94105
(415) 597-9260   Fax: (415) 597-9213
E-mail: Rochelle.Blanco@ucsf.edu
Web: www.caps.ucsf.edu

Summary   To provide funding to scientists (especially Asian American and other minority scientists) who are interested in conducting HIV prevention research.

Eligibility   This program is open to U.S. citizens, nationals, and permanent residents who have a Ph.D., M.D., or equivalent degree. Applicants must be interested in a program of research training at CAPS in the following areas of special emphasis in AIDS research: epidemiological research, studies of AIDS risk behaviors, substance abuse and HIV, primary prevention interventions, research addressing minority populations, studies of HIV-positive individuals, policy and ethics, international research, and other public health and clinical aspects of AIDS. Recent postdoctorates who have just completed their training as well as those who are already faculty members in academic or clinical departments are eligible. Members of minority ethnic groups are strongly encouraged to apply.

Financial data   Stipends depend on years of relevant postdoctoral experience, based on the NIH stipend scale for Institutional Research Training Grants (currently ranging from $37,740 for fellows with no relevant postdoctoral experience to $52,068 to those with 7 or more years of experience). Other benefits include a computer, travel to at least 1 annual professional meeting, health insurance, and other required support. The costs of the M.P.H. degree, if required, are covered.

Duration   2 or 3 years.

Additional information   The TAPS program is designed to ensure that at the end of the training each fellow will have: 1) completed the M.P.H. degree or its equivalent; 2) taken advanced courses in research methods, statistics, and other topics relevant to a major field of interest; 3) participated in and led numerous seminars on research topics within CAPS, as well as in the formal teaching programs of the university; 4) designed several research protocols and completed at least 1 significant research project under the direction of a faculty mentor; and 5) made presentations at national or international meetings and submitted several papers for publication.

Number awarded   Varies each year.

Deadline   November of each year.

[919]
TRAINING PROGRAM FOR SCIENTISTS CONDUCTING RESEARCH TO REDUCE HIV/STI HEALTH DISPARITIES

University of California at San Francisco
Attn: Center for AIDS Prevention Studies
50 Beale Street, Suite 1300
San Francisco, CA 94105
(415) 597-4976   Fax: (415) 597-9213
E-mail: jackie.ramos@ucsf.edu
Web: www.caps.ucsf.edu

Summary   To provide funding to scientists (particularly Asian American and other minority scientists) who are interested in obtaining additional training at the University of California at San Francisco (UCSF) Center for AIDS Prevention Studies (CAPS) for HIV prevention research in minority communities.

Eligibility   This program is open to scientists in tenure-track positions or investigators in research institutes who have not yet obtained research funding from the U.S. National Institutes of Health (NIH) or equivalent. Applicants must be interested in a program of activity at CAPS to improve their programs of HIV-prevention research targeting vulnerable ethnic minority populations. They must be eligible to serve as principal investigators at their home institutions. Selection is based on commitment to HIV social and behavioral research, prior HIV prevention research with communities and community-based organizations targeting communities with high levels of health disparities (e.g., communities with a high proportion of disadvantaged or disabled persons, racial and ethnic minority communities), creativity and innovativeness for a pilot research project to serve as a preliminary study for a subsequent larger R01 grant proposal to NIH or other suitable funding agency, past experience conducting research and writing papers, quality of letters of recommendation from colleagues and mentors, and support from the home institution (e.g., time off for research, seed money). A goal of the program is to increase the number of minority group members among principal investigators funded by NIH and other agencies.

Financial data   Participants receive 1) a monthly stipend for living expenses and round-trip airfare to San Francisco for each summer, and 2) a grant of $25,000 to conduct preliminary research before the second summer to strengthen their R01 application.

Duration   6 weeks during each of 3 consecutive summers.

Additional information   This program is funded by the NIH National Institute of Child Health and Human Development (NICHHD) and National Institute on Drug Abuse (NIDA).

Number awarded   Approximately 4 each year.

Deadline   January of each year.

[920]
UCSB LIBRARY FELLOWSHIP PROGRAM

University of California at Santa Barbara
Attn: Associate University Librarian, Human Resources
Davidson Library
Santa Barbara, CA 93106-9010
(805) 893-3841   Fax: (805) 893-7010
E-mail: bankhead@library.ucsb.edu
Web: www.library.ucsb.edu/hr/fellowship.html

Summary To provide an opportunity for recent library school graduates, especially Asian Americans and members of other underrepresented groups, to serve in the library system at the University of California at Santa Barbara (UCSB).

Eligibility This program is open to recent graduates of library schools accredited by the American Library Association. Applicants must be interested in a postgraduate appointment at UCSB. They must have a knowledge of and interest in academic librarianship and a strong desire for professional growth. Members of underrepresented groups are encouraged to apply.

Financial data Fellows are regular (but temporary) employees of the university and receive the same salary and benefits as other librarians at the assistant librarian level ($46,164 to $48,029 per year).

Duration 2 years.

Additional information The program began in 1985. Fellows spend time in at least 2 different departments in the library, serve on library committees, attend professional meetings, receive travel support for 2 major conferences, and participate in the Librarians' Association of the University of California.

Number awarded 1 each year.

Deadline January of each year.

[921]
VAID FELLOWSHIPS

National Gay and Lesbian Task Force
Attn: The Task Force Policy Institute
80 Maiden Lane, Suite 1504
New York, NY 10038
(212) 604-9830   Fax: (212) 604-9831
E-mail: ngltf@ngltf.org
Web: www.thetaskforce.org

Summary To provide work experience to undergraduate and graduate students or professionals (especially Asian Americans and other minorities) who are interested in participating in the leadership of people of color in the progressive movement for gay, lesbian, bisexual, and transgender (GLBT) equality.

Eligibility Applicants must be enrolled in a degree program at least half time as a law, graduate, or undergraduate student or have successfully completed a law, graduate, or undergraduate degree within the preceding 12 months. They should have 1) a desire to work in a multicultural environment where commitment to diversity based on race, ethnic origin, gender, age, sexual orientation, and physical ability is an important institutional value; 2) demonstrated leadership in progressive and/or GLBT communities; 3) extensive research, writing, and critical thinking skills; 4) knowledge of, and commitment to, GLBT issues; and 5) computer proficiency in word processing, database work, e-mail, and Internet research. The program supports and recognizes the leadership of people of color and other emerging leaders in public policy, legal, and social science research.

Financial data The stipend ranges from $200 to $400 per week ($10 per hour). Fellows are responsible for their own housing and living expenses.

Duration Summer fellowships are 40 hours per week and spring/fall fellowships are 20 hours per week.

Additional information The Policy Institute of the National Gay and Lesbian Task Force (NGLTF), founded in 1995, is the largest think tank in the United States engaged in research, policy analysis, and strategic action to advance equality and understanding of GLBT people. Its primary programs are the racial and economic justice initiative, the family policy program, and the aging initiative. In addition to their primary roles of providing research and analysis, all 3 programs work closely with NGLTF colleagues in Washington, D.C. and other allies on advocacy and legislative efforts to actively change laws and policies affecting GLBT people.

Number awarded 3 fellows are selected each session.

Deadline April for the summer, July for the fall, and November for the spring.

[922]
VITO MARZULLO INTERNSHIP PROGRAM

Office of the Governor
Attn: Department of Central Management Services
503 William G. Stratton Building
Springfield, IL 62706
(217) 524-1381   Fax: (217) 558-4497
TDD: (217) 785-3979
Web: www.ilga.gov/commission/lru/internships.html

Summary To provide recent college graduates (particularly Asian Americans, other minorities, women, and individuals with disabilities) with work experience in the Illinois Governor's office.

Eligibility This program is open to residents of Illinois who have completed a bachelor's degree and are interested in working in the Illinois Governor's office or in various agencies under the Governor's jurisdiction. Applicants may have majored in any field, but they must be able to demonstrate a substantial commitment to excellence as evidenced by academic honors, leadership ability, extracurricular activities, and involvement in community or public service. Along with their application, they must submit 1) a 500-word personal statement on the qualities or attributes they will bring to the program, their career goals or plans, how their selection for this program would assist them in achieving those goals, and what they expect to gain from the program; and 2) a 1,000-word essay in which they identify and analyze a public issue that they feel has great impact on state government. A particular goal of the program is to achieve affirmative action through the nomination of qualified minorities, women, and persons with disabilities.

Financial data The stipend is $2,611 per month.

Duration 1 year, beginning in August.

Additional information Assignments are in Springfield and, to a limited extent, in Chicago or Washington, D.C.

Number awarded Varies each year.

Deadline February of each year.

[923]
W.E.B. DUBOIS FELLOWSHIP PROGRAM

Department of Justice
National Institute of Justice
Attn: W.E.B. DuBois Fellowship Program
810 Seventh Street, N.W.
Washington, DC 20531
(202) 514-6205   E-mail: Marilyn.Moses@usdoj.gov
Web: www.nij.gov

Summary To provide funding to junior investigators (particularly Asian Americans and other minorities) who are interested in conducting research on "crime, violence and the administration of justice in diverse cultural contexts."

Eligibility This program is open to investigators who have a Ph.D. or other doctoral-level degree (including a legal degree of J.D. or higher). Applicants should be early in their careers. They must be interested in conducting research that relates to specific areas that change annually but relate to criminal justice policy and practice in the United States. The sponsor strongly encourages applications from diverse racial and ethnic backgrounds. Selection is based on quality and technical merit; impact of the proposed project; capabilities, demonstrated productivity, and experience of the applicant; budget; dissemination strategy; and relevance of the project for policy and practice.

Financial data Grants range up to $100,000. Funds may be used for salary, fringe benefits, reasonable costs of relocation, travel essential to the project, and office expenses not provided by the sponsor. Indirect costs are limited to 20%.

Duration 6 to 12 months; fellows are required to be in residence at the National Institute of Justice (NIJ) for the first 2 months and may elect to spend all or part of the remainder of the fellowship period either in residence at NIJ or at their home institution.

Number awarded 1 each year.

Deadline January of each year.

[924]
WILLIAM WOO INTERNSHIP FUND

Asian American Journalists Association
Attn: Student Programs Coordinator
5 Third Street, Suite 1108
San Francisco, CA 94103
(415) 346-2051, ext. 102   Fax: (415) 346-6343
E-mail: programs@aaja.org
Web: www.aaja.org/programs/internships

Summary To provide a supplemental grant to student and other members of the Asian American Journalists Association (AAJA) working as a summer intern at a print or online journalism company.

Eligibility This program is open to AAJA members who are full-time college students or recent college graduates. Applicants must have secured a summer internship at a print or online company before they apply. Along with their application, they must submit a 200-word essay on why they want to prepare for a career in print or online journalism, what they want to gain from the experience, and why AAJA's mission is important to them; a letter of recommendation; a resume; proof of age (at least 18 years); verification of an internship; and statement of financial need.

Financial data The grant is $1,000. Funds are to be used for living expenses or transportation.

Duration Summer months.

Additional information This program began in 2006.

Number awarded 1 each year.

Deadline May of each year.

[925]
WOMEN'S STUDIES IN RELIGION PROGRAM

Harvard Divinity School
Attn: Director of Women's Studies in Religion Program
45 Francis Avenue
Cambridge, MA 02138
(617) 495-5705   Fax: (617) 495-8564
E-mail: wsrp@hds.harvard.edu
Web: www.hds.harvard.edu/wsrp

Summary To encourage and support scholars (especially Asian American or other minority and women scholars) who are interested in conducting research on the relationship between religion, gender, and culture.

Eligibility This program is open to minority and other scholars who have a Ph.D. in the field of religion. Candidates with primary competence in other humanities, social sciences, and public policy fields who have a serious interest in religion and religious professionals with equivalent achievements are also eligible. Applicants should be proposing to conduct research projects at Harvard Divinity School's Women's Studies in Religion Program (WSRP) on topics related to the history and function of gender in religious traditions, the institutionalization of gender roles in religious communities, or the interaction between religion and the personal, social, and cultural situations of women. Appropriate topics include feminist theology, biblical studies, ethics, women's history, and interdisciplinary scholarship on women in world religions. Selection is based on the quality of the applicant's research prospectus, outlining objectives and methods; its fit with the program's research priorities; the significance of the contribution of the proposed research to the study of religion, gender, and culture, and to its field; and agreement to produce a publishable piece of work by the end of the appointment.

Financial data The stipend is $45,000; health insurance and reimbursement of some expenses are also provided.

Duration 1 academic year, from September to June.

Additional information This program was founded in 1973. Fellows at the WSRP devote the majority of their appointments to individual research projects in preparation for publication, meeting together regularly for discussion of research in process. They also design and teach new courses related to their research projects and offer a series of lectures in the spring. Recipients are required to be in full-time residence at the school while carrying out their research project.

Number awarded 5 each year. The group each year usually includes at least 1 international scholar, 1 scholar working on a non-western tradition, 1 scholar of Judaism, and 1 minority scholar.

Deadline October of each year.

Indexes

Program Title Index

If you know the name of a particular funding program open to Asian Americans and want to find out where it is covered in the directory, use the Program Title Index. Here, program titles are arranged alphabetically, word by word. To assist you in your search, every program is listed by all its known names or abbreviations. In addition, we've used an alphabetical code (within parentheses) to help you determine if the program is aimed at you: U = Undergraduates;   G = Graduate Students;   P = Professionals/Postdoctorates. Here's how the code works: if a program is followed by (U) 241, the program is described in the Undergraduates section, in entry 241. If the same program title is followed by another entry number—for example, (P) 901—the program is also described in the Professionals/Postdoctorates section, in entry 901. Remember: the numbers cited here refer to program entry numbers, not to page numbers in the book.

U–Undergraduates   **G–Graduate Students**   **P–Professionals/Postdoctorates**

U–Undergraduates   **G–Graduate Students**   **P–Professionals/Postdoctorates**

U–Undergraduates   **G–Graduate Students**   **P–Professionals/Postdoctorates**

James A. Rawley Prize, (P) 867

James B. Morris Scholarship, (U) 187, (G) 579

James Bok Wong and Betty KC Yeow Scholarship. *See* Chinese American Citizens Alliance Foundation Scholarships, entry (U) 75

James Carlson Memorial Scholarship, (U) 188, (G) 580

James E. Webb Internships, (U) 189, (G) 581

James Echols Scholarship, (U) 190, (G) 582

James H. Dunn, Jr. Memorial Fellowship Program, (P) 868

James J. Wychor Scholarships, (U) 191

Japanese American Bar Association Educational Foundation Scholarships, (G) 583

Japanese American Citizens League/Kenji Kasai Memorial Scholarship. *See* JACL/Kenji Kasai Memorial Scholarship, entry (U) 185

Japanese American Veterans Association Memorial Scholarships. *See* JAVA Memorial Scholarships, entries (U) 192, (G) 585

Japanese Medical Society of America Scholarships, (G) 584, (P) 869

JAVA Memorial Scholarships, (U) 192, (G) 585

Je Hyun Kim Scholarship. *See* Korean-American Scientists and Engineers Association Undergraduate Scholarships, entry (U) 208

Jean Lu Student Scholarship Award, (G) 586

Jeanne Spurlock Minority Medical Student Clinical Fellowship in Child and Adolescent Psychiatry, (G) 587

Jeanne Spurlock Research Fellowship in Substance Abuse and Addiction for Minority Medical Students, (G) 588

Jeffrey Campbell Graduate Fellows Program, (G) 589

Jensen Scholarship. *See* Herbert Jensen Scholarship, entry (U) 164

J.K. Fukushima Scholarship for Seminarians, (U) 193, (G) 590

J.K. Sasaki Memorial Scholarships, (G) 591

J.L. Carr Social Justice Scholarship. *See* R.P. and J.L. Carr Social Justice Scholarship, entry (G) 728

Jo Ann Ota Fujioka Scholarship. *See* Dr. Jo Ann Ota Fujioka Scholarship, entry (U) 117

Joe Allman Scholarship, (U) 194

Joe Morozumi Scholarship. *See* AABA Law Foundation Scholarships, entry (G) 385

Joel Elkes Research Award, (P) 870

John and Muriel Landis Scholarships, (U) 195, (G) 592

John F. Aiso Scholarship. *See* Japanese American Bar Association Educational Foundation Scholarships, entry (G) 583

John Stanford Memorial WLMA Scholarship, (G) 593

John V. Krutilla Research Stipend, (P) 871

Johnson Health Policy Fellowships. *See* Robert Wood Johnson Health Policy Fellowships, entry (P) 908

Johnson & Johnson Campaign for Nursing's Future-American Association of Colleges of Nursing Minority Nurse Faculty Scholars Program, (G) 594

Johnson, Jr. Scholarship Program. *See* Lloyd M. Johnson, Jr. Scholarship Program, entry (G) 630

Johnson West Michigan Diversity Law School Scholarship. *See* Miller Johnson West Michigan Diversity Law School Scholarship, entry (G) 650

Joseph Ichiuji Memorial Scholarship. *See* JAVA Memorial Scholarships, entries (U) 192, (G) 585

Joseph L. Fisher Doctoral Dissertation Fellowships, (G) 595

Josephine Forman Scholarship, (G) 596

JTBF Judicial Externship Program, (G) 597

Judge Edward Y. Kakita Scholarship, (G) 598

Judge Robert M. Takasugi Fellowships for Public Interest Law, (G) 599

Judge William M. Marutani Fellowship, (G) 600

Judicial Externship Program. *See* JTBF Judicial Externship Program, entry (G) 597

Judicial Intern Opportunity Program, (G) 601

Judith L. Weidman Racial Ethnic Minority Fellowship, (P) 872

Judy Young Scholarship. *See* Drs. Poh Shien and Judy Young Scholarship, entry (U) 119

Julius and Eleanor Sue Scholarship. *See* Chinese American Citizens Alliance Foundation Scholarships, entry (U) 75

Julius Axelrod Mentorship Award, (P) 873

June Uejima Memorial Scholarship. *See* Deni and June Uejima Memorial Scholarship, entry (U) 108

Jung Memorial Scholarship. *See* Chinese American Citizens Alliance Foundation Scholarships, entry (U) 75

Jung Scholarship. *See* Chinese American Citizens Alliance Foundation Scholarships, entry (U) 75

Just Endowed Research Fellowship Fund. *See* E.E. Just Endowed Research Fellowship Fund, entry (P) 844

Just the Beginning Foundation Judicial Externship Program. *See* JTBF Judicial Externship Program, entry (G) 597

Justice Elwood Lui Scholarship. *See* SCCLA Scholarships and Fellowships, entry (G) 735

Justice John F. Aiso Scholarship. *See* Japanese American Bar Association Educational Foundation Scholarships, entry (G) 583

Justice Stephen K. Tamura Scholarship. *See* Japanese American Bar Association Educational Foundation Scholarships, entry (G) 583

Justin Haruyama Ministerial Scholarship, (G) 602

Justine E. Granner Memorial Scholarship, (U) 196

K

Kaiser Permanente Colorado Diversity Scholarship Program, (U) 197, (G) 603

Kajiwara Memorial Scholarship. *See* Kenji Kajiwara Memorial Scholarship, entry (U) 204

Kakita Scholarship. *See* Judge Edward Y. Kakita Scholarship, entry (G) 598

Kalpana Chawla Scholarship Award, (G) 604

Kamikawa Memorial Scholarship. *See* JAVA Memorial Scholarships, entries (U) 192, (G) 585

Kansas ESOL/Bilingual Education Scholarship, (U) 198

Kansas Ethnic Minority Scholarship Program, (U) 199

Kansas SPJ Minority Student Scholarship, (U) 200

Kapp Award. *See* Olympia Brown and Max Kapp Award, entry (G) 684

Kappa Omicron Nu National Alumni Chapter Grants. *See* National Alumni Chapter Grants, entry (P) 889

Kappa Omicron Nu New Initiatives Grants, (P) 874

Karas Memorial Fellowship. *See* International Radio and Television Society Summer Fellowship Program, entries (U) 182, (G) 576

Kasai Memorial Scholarship. *See* JACL/Kenji Kasai Memorial Scholarship, entry (U) 185

Kashiwahara Scholarship. *See* Ken Kashiwahara Scholarship, entry (U) 203

Kathy Mann Memorial Scholarship, (U) 201

Kathy Woodall Minority Student Scholarship. *See* Don Sahli–Kathy Woodall Minority Student Scholarship, entry (U) 114

U–Undergraduates   **G–Graduate Students**   **P–Professionals/Postdoctorates**

U–Undergraduates   **G–Graduate Students**   **P–Professionals/Postdoctorates**

Sponsoring Organization Index

The Sponsoring Organization Index makes it easy to identify agencies that offer financial aid to Asian Americans. In this index, the sponsoring organizations are listed alphabetically, word by word. In addition, we've used an alphabetical code (within parentheses) to help you identify the intended recipients of the funding offered by the organizations: U = Undergraduates; G = Graduate Students; P = Professionals/Postdoctorates. For example, if the name of a sponsoring organization is followed by (U) 241, a program sponsored by that organization is described in the Undergraduate section, in entry 241. If that sponsoring organization's name is followed by another entry number—for example, (G) 950—the same or a different program sponsored by that organization is described in the Professionals/Postdoctorates section, in entry 950. Remember: the numbers cited here refer to program entry numbers, not to page numbers in the book.

U–Undergraduates   **G–Graduate Students**   **P–Professionals/Postdoctorates**

U–Undergraduates   **G–Graduate Students**   **P–Professionals/Postdoctorates**

Scholarship America, (U) 53, 352, 354, (G) 779
Schwabe, Williamson & Wyatt, Attorneys at Law, (G) 737
Science Applications International Corporation, (U) 316-317
Scotts Company, (U) 318
Seattle Foundation, (U) 47
Sidley Austin LLP, (G) 743
Smithsonian Astrophysical Observatory, (P) 845
Smithsonian Institution. Freer and Sackler Galleries, (U) 302
Smithsonian Institution. Office of Fellowships, (U) 189, 323, (G) 581, 658, 745
Social Science Research Council, (G) 488, 490, 520, (P) 807, 842, 866
Society for Maternal-Fetal Medicine, (P) 811
Society for the Study of Social Problems, (G) 746
Society of American Archivists, (G) 596, 747
Society of Manufacturing Engineers, (U) 67, 125, (G) 506
Society of Professional Journalists. Kansas Professional Chapter, (U) 200
Society of Professional Journalists. Western Washington Chapter, (U) 271
Society of Toxicology, (G) 395, 501, 586, 617, 749, 805, (P) 810, 837, 840, 875
Sociologists for Women in Society, (G) 416, 516
Sodexo USA, (U) 148
Soo Yuen Benevolent Association, (U) 324
South Asian Bar Association of New York, (G) 750
South Asian Bar Association of Northern California, (G) 731
South Asian Bar Association of Washington DC, (G) 751
South Asian Journalists Association, (U) 83, 130, 307, 329, (G) 466, 512, 732, 758
Southern California Chinese Lawyers Association, (G) 735
Southern Regional Education Board, (G) 753, 755
Southwestern Sociological Association, (G) 416
Space Telescope Science Institute, (P) 864
Sponsors for Educational Opportunity, (U) 319, (G) 739
Stafford King Wiese Architects, (U) 154
State Bar of California, (G) 448, 450
State Bar of Texas, (G) 573
State University of New York at Stony Brook, (P) 858
Stoel Rives LLP, (G) 757
StraightForward Media, (U) 328
Student Conservation Association, Inc., (U) 102, (G) 478
Susan G. Komen Breast Cancer Foundation, (G) 706, (P) 917

T
Target Stores, (U) 40
Tennessee Education Association, (U) 114
Tennessee Student Assistance Corporation, (U) 337
Teresa and H. John Heinz III Foundation, (P) 862
Texas Library Association, (G) 766
Texas Young Lawyers Association, (G) 767
Thai Alliance in America, (U) 339
Thompson Hine LLP, (G) 770
Thomson West, (G) 544, (P) 857
Thurgood Marshall Scholarship Fund, (G) 744
Tonkon Torp LLP, (G) 773
Townsend and Townsend and Crew LLP, (G) 774
Toyota Motor Sales, U.S.A., Inc., (G) 584, (P) 869

U
Unitarian Universalist Association, (G) 480-481, 635, 684, 727, 776

United Church of Christ, (G) 390, 724
United Health Foundation, (U) 345
United Methodist Church. Arkansas Conference, (U) 28, (G) 412
United Methodist Church. California-Pacific Annual Conference, (G) 468
United Methodist Church. General Board of Discipleship, (U) 303
United Methodist Church. General Board of Global Ministries, (U) 115, (G) 499, 803, (P) 839
United Methodist Church. General Board of Higher Education and Ministry, (U) 156, 346, (G) 550, 777
United Methodist Church. General Commission on Archives and History, (G) 596
United Methodist Church. Oregon-Idaho Conference, (U) 275, (G) 690
United Methodist Communications, (U) 219, (P) 872
United Methodist Foundation of Arkansas, (U) 113, (G) 496
United Methodist Foundation of South Indiana, (U) 113, (G) 496
United Methodist Foundation of Western North Carolina, (U) 113, (G) 496
United Methodist Higher Education Foundation, (U) 113, (G) 496
United Negro College Fund, (U) 151, (G) 630
United Negro College Fund Special Programs Corporation, (U) 131, 179, (G) 513, 572, (P) 888
United States Tennis Association, (U) 120
UnitedHealthcare, (U) 348
University of California at Los Angeles. Center for Information as Evidence, (G) 494
University of California at Los Angeles. Institute of American Cultures, (P) 818
University of California at San Francisco. Center for AIDS Prevention Studies, (P) 918-919
University of California at Santa Barbara. Library, (P) 920
UPS Foundation, (U) 44, 347, 350-351, (G) 778
U.S. Air Force. Office of Scientific Research, (G) 667, (P) 809, 903
U.S. Army. Judge Advocate General's Corps, (G) 415
U.S. Army. Research Office, (G) 667, (P) 903
U.S. Centers for Disease Control and Prevention, (G) 459, (P) 862
U.S. Central Intelligence Agency, (U) 71, 79
U.S. Defense Intelligence Agency, (U) 105
U.S. Department of Agriculture. Agricultural Research Service, (P) 903
U.S. Department of Agriculture. Cooperative State Research, Education, and Extension Service, (P) 903
U.S. Department of Agriculture. Forest Service, (P) 903
U.S. Department of Commerce. National Institute of Standards and Technology, (P) 903
U.S. Department of Commerce. National Oceanic and Atmospheric Administration, (P) 903
U.S. Department of Defense, (G) 667
U.S. Department of Education. Office of Postsecondary Education, (U) 179, (G) 572
U.S. Department of Energy. Office of Biological and Environmental Research, (U) 153, (G) 546
U.S. Department of Energy. Office of Defense Programs, (P) 903
U.S. Department of Energy. Office of Science, (G) 671
U.S. Department of Homeland Security, (P) 834
U.S. Department of Housing and Urban Development, (G) 564
U.S. Department of Justice. National Institute of Justice, (P) 923
U.S. Department of State, (U) 110, (G) 485, 488, 504, 520, (P) 842-843
U.S. Department of Transportation, (U) 331, (G) 759, (P) 903

U–Undergraduates   **G–Graduate Students**   **P–Professionals/Postdoctorates**

Residency Index

Some programs listed in this book are set aside for Asian Americans who are residents of a particular state or region. Others are open to applicants wherever they may live. The Residency Index will help you pinpoint programs available in your area as well as programs that have no residency restrictions at all (these are listed under the term "United States"). To use this index, look up the geographic areas that apply to you (always check the listings under "United States"), jot down the entry numbers listed for the recipient level that applies to you (Undergraduates, Graduate Students, or Professionals/Postdoctorates), and use those numbers to find the program descriptions in the directory. To help you in your search, we've provided some "see" and "see also" references in the index entries. Remember: the numbers cited here refer to program entry numbers, not to page numbers in the book.

A

Alaska: **Undergraduates,** 47. *See also* Northwestern states; United States

Alexandria, Virginia: **Undergraduates,** 366. *See also* Virginia

American Samoa: **Undergraduates,** 40, 148, 312, 345, 356. *See also* United States

Anne Arundel County, Maryland: **Undergraduates,** 366. *See also* Maryland

Arizona: **Undergraduates,** 41, 164, 194, 311. *See also* United States

Arkansas: **Undergraduates,** 28-29, 338; **Graduate Students,** 412-413, 765. *See also* Southern states; United States

Arlington County, Virginia: **Undergraduates,** 366. *See also* Virginia

B

Belmont County, Ohio: **Undergraduates,** 297. *See also* Ohio

Burnett County, Wisconsin: **Undergraduates,** 129. *See also* Wisconsin

C

California: **Undergraduates,** 38-39, 41, 47, 54-57, 64-65, 75, 77, 82, 97, 100, 144, 154, 190, 214, 231, 310, 324, 327, 345, 356, 360, 372; **Graduate Students,** 428, 449-451, 454, 464-465, 476, 497, 582, 636; **Professionals/Postdoctorates,** 885. *See also* United States

California, southern: **Graduate Students,** 468. *See also* California

Calvert County, Maryland: **Undergraduates,** 366. *See also* Maryland

Charles County, Maryland: **Undergraduates,** 366. *See also* Maryland

Clark County, Washington: **Undergraduates,** 42, 150. *See also* Washington

Colorado: **Undergraduates,** 41, 86-87, 109, 197; **Graduate Students,** 603. *See also* United States

Columbiana County, Ohio: **Undergraduates,** 297. *See also* Ohio

Connecticut: **Undergraduates,** 14, 92-93, 95, 138, 158, 183, 305; **Graduate Students,** 524, 730. *See also* Northeastern states; United States

D

Delaware: **Undergraduates,** 211, 305; **Graduate Students,** 671, 730. *See also* Northeastern states; Southeastern states; Southern states; United States

District of Columbia. *See* Washington, D.C.

F

Fairfax County, Virginia: **Undergraduates,** 366. *See also* Virginia

Falls Church, Virginia: **Undergraduates,** 366. *See also* Virginia

Fauquier County, Virginia: **Undergraduates,** 366. *See also* Virginia

Florida: **Undergraduates,** 98, 145-146, 356; **Graduate Students,** 535-536. *See also* Southeastern states; Southern states; United States

Frederick County, Maryland: **Undergraduates,** 366. *See also* Maryland

G

Georgia: **Undergraduates,** 41, 143, 176. *See also* Southeastern states; Southern states; United States

Guam: **Undergraduates,** 40, 148, 230, 312, 345, 352, 356; **Graduate Students,** 468, 633, 779. *See also* United States

H

Harrison County, Ohio: **Undergraduates,** 297. *See also* Ohio

Hawaii: **Undergraduates,** 17, 45, 47, 72, 89, 96, 136, 141-142, 159, 165, 207, 259, 342-343, 349; **Graduate Students,** 468, 473, 509, 529, 551, 557, 771-772. *See also* United States

Howard County, Maryland: **Undergraduates,** 366. *See also* Maryland

Tenability Index

Some programs listed in this book can be used only in specific cities, counties, states, or regions. Others may be used anywhere in the United States. The Tenability Index will help you locate funding that is restricted to a specific area as well as funding that has no tenability restrictions (these are listed under the term "United States"). To use this index, look up the geographic areas where you'd like to go (always check the listings under "United States"), jot down the entry numbers listed for the recipient group that represents you (Undergraduates, Graduate Students, Professionals/Postdoctorates), and use those numbers to find the program descriptions in the directory. To help you in your search, we've provided some "see" and "see also" references in the index entries. Remember: the numbers cited here refer to program entry numbers, not to page numbers in the book.

A

Alabama: **Undergraduates,** 325; **Graduate Students,** 472, 752. *See also* Southern states; United States; names of specific cities and counties

Alameda County, California: **Graduate Students,** 623. *See also* California

Alaska: **Undergraduates,** 371; **Graduate Students,** 793. *See also* United States; names of specific cities

Albuquerque, New Mexico: **Graduate Students,** 733. *See also* New Mexico

Allentown, Pennsylvania: **Graduate Students,** 489; **Professionals/Postdoctorates,** 901. *See also* Pennsylvania

Amherst, Massachusetts: **Undergraduates,** 125; **Graduate Students,** 506, 533. *See also* Massachusetts

Ann Arbor, Michigan: **Graduate Students,** 494, 537. *See also* Michigan

Appleton, Wisconsin: **Graduate Students,** 489; **Professionals/Postdoctorates,** 901. *See also* Wisconsin

Arizona: **Undergraduates,** 371; **Graduate Students,** 793. *See also* United States; names of specific cities and counties

Arkansas: **Undergraduates,** 29, 325, 338; **Graduate Students,** 413, 752, 765. *See also* Southern states; United States; names of specific cities and counties

Athens, Georgia: **Graduate Students,** 802. *See also* Georgia

Atlanta, Georgia: **Undergraduates,** 274, 298; **Graduate Students,** 435, 530, 610, 685, 717, 770, 802. *See also* Georgia

Austin, Texas: **Undergraduates,** 274; **Graduate Students,** 435, 494, 685, 786. *See also* Texas

B

Baltimore, Maryland: **Graduate Students,** 489, 802; **Professionals/Postdoctorates,** 901. *See also* Maryland

Bergen County, New Jersey: **Graduate Students,** 750. *See also* New Jersey

Berkeley, California: **Graduate Students,** 537. *See also* California

Big Rapids, Michigan: **Undergraduates,** 292. *See also* Michigan

Blacksburg, Virginia: **Undergraduates,** 298; **Graduate Students,** 717. *See also* Virginia

Bloomington, Indiana: **Graduate Students,** 431. *See also* Indiana

Boise, Idaho: **Graduate Students,** 757. *See also* Idaho

Boston, Massachusetts: **Undergraduates,** 125; **Graduate Students,** 494, 506, 640. *See also* Massachusetts

Brunswick, Maine: **Graduate Students,** 489; **Professionals/Postdoctorates,** 901. *See also* Maine

Bryn Mawr, Pennsylvania: **Graduate Students,** 489; **Professionals/Postdoctorates,** 901. *See also* Pennsylvania

Buies Creek, North Carolina: **Undergraduates,** 292. *See also* North Carolina

Burbank, California: **Professionals/Postdoctorates,** 892. *See also* California

C

California: **Undergraduates,** 19, 38, 55-57, 75, 77, 82, 100, 144, 190, 214, 231, 244, 310, 327, 345, 371-372; **Graduate Students,** 396, 448, 450-451, 454, 464-465, 472, 476, 479, 582, 636, 652, 735, 793; **Professionals/Postdoctorates,** 885. *See also* United States; names of specific cities and counties

California, northern: **Undergraduates,** 289; **Graduate Students,** 385, 427, 640, 731, 794. *See also* California

California, southern: **Undergraduates,** 32, 68, 218, 370; **Graduate Students,** 419, 560, 614, 686, 792; **Professionals/Postdoctorates,** 877. *See also* California

Cambridge, Massachusetts: **Graduate Students,** 528, 530; **Professionals/Postdoctorates,** 852, 854, 925. *See also* Massachusetts

Canton, New York: **Graduate Students,** 589. *See also* New York

Carlisle, Pennsylvania: **Graduate Students,** 489; **Professionals/Postdoctorates,** 901. *See also* Pennsylvania

Chapel Hill, North Carolina: **Graduate Students,** 494, 802. *See also* North Carolina

Subject Index

There are hundreds of specific subject fields covered in this directory. Use the Subject Index to identify these topics, as well as the recipient level supported (Undergraduates, Graduate Students, or Professionals/Postdoctorates) by the available funding programs. To help you pinpoint your search, we've included many "see" and "see also" references. Since a large number of programs are not restricted by subject, be sure to check the references listed under the "General programs" heading in the subject index (in addition to the specific terms that directly relate to your interest areas); hundreds of funding opportunities are listed there that can be used to support activities in any subject area   although the programs may be restricted in other ways. Remember: the numbers cited in this index refer to program entry numbers, not to page numbers in the book.

A

A.V. *See* Audiovisual materials and equipment

Academic librarianship. *See* Libraries and librarianship, academic

Accounting: **Undergraduates,** 3, 15-16, 53, 61, 79, 107, 132, 145, 178, 189, 230, 285, 295, 304, 314, 319, 335, 354, 357; **Graduate Students,** 570, 581, 633, 699, 736, 763. *See also* Finance; General programs

Acquired Immunodeficiency Syndrome. *See* AIDS

Acting. *See* Performing arts

Actuarial sciences: **Undergraduates,** 258. *See also* General programs; Statistics

Addiction. *See* Alcohol use and abuse; Drug use and abuse

Administration. *See* Business administration; Management; Personnel administration; Public administration

Adolescents: **Graduate Students,** 587-588; **Professionals/ Postdoctorates,** 893. *See also* Child development; General programs

Advertising: **Undergraduates,** 5, 18, 21, 88, 183, 210, 222, 256, 274, 299; **Graduate Students,** 394, 435, 620, 663, 685, 719. *See also* Communications; General programs; Marketing; Public relations

Aeronautical engineering. *See* Engineering, aeronautical

Aerospace engineering. *See* Engineering, aerospace

Aerospace sciences. *See* Space sciences

Affirmative action: **Undergraduates,** 177. *See also* Equal opportunity; General programs

African studies: **Undergraduates,** 220; **Graduate Students,** 626; **Professionals/Postdoctorates,** 866, 879. *See also* General programs; Humanities

Aged and aging: **Undergraduates,** 342; **Graduate Students,** 497, 624, 771; **Professionals/Postdoctorates,** 862. *See also* General programs; Social sciences

Agribusiness: **Undergraduates,** 26, 138; **Graduate Students,** 524. *See also* Agriculture and agricultural sciences; Business administration; General programs

Agricultural engineering. *See* Engineering, agricultural

Agriculture and agricultural sciences: **Undergraduates,** 50, 138, 209, 335; **Graduate Students,** 524, 763. *See also* Biological sciences; General programs

Agrimarketing and sales. *See* Agribusiness

Agronomy: **Undergraduates,** 26. *See also* Agriculture and agricultural sciences; General programs

AIDS: **Graduate Students,** 624; **Professionals/ Postdoctorates,** 918-919. *See also* Disabilities; General programs; Medical sciences

Albanian language. *See* Language, Albanian

Alcohol use and abuse: **Graduate Students,** 624, 643, 707; **Professionals/Postdoctorates,** 900, 916. *See also* Drug use and abuse; General programs; Health and health care

American history. *See* History, American

American literature. *See* Literature, American

American studies: **Graduate Students,** 403; **Professionals/ Postdoctorates,** 813, 815, 829, 832, 854, 891. *See also* General programs; Humanities

Animal science: **Undergraduates,** 323, 335; **Graduate Students,** 658, 745, 763. *See also* General programs; Sciences; names of specific animal sciences

Animation: **Professionals/Postdoctorates,** 892. *See also* Filmmaking; General programs

Anthropology: **Undergraduates,** 49, 323; **Graduate Students,** 403, 434, 658, 734, 745; **Professionals/Postdoctorates,** 813, 815, 820, 825, 829, 832, 854, 891. *See also* General programs; Social sciences

Antitrust and trade regulation: **Graduate Students,** 539. *See also* General programs; Law, general

Applied arts. *See* Arts and crafts

Aquatic sciences. *See* Oceanography

Archaeology: **Undergraduates,** 102, 323; **Graduate Students,** 403, 478, 658, 734, 745; **Professionals/Postdoctorates,** 813, 815, 829, 832, 854, 891. *See also* General programs; History; Social sciences

Architectural engineering. *See* Engineering, architectural

Religion and religious activities: **Undergraduates,** 113, 193, 233, 296, 303, 330; **Graduate Students,** 390, 403, 422, 436, 468, 480-481, 496, 507, 514-515, 528, 590-591, 602, 632, 635, 668, 679, 684, 712-713, 724, 727, 760-761, 776-777; **Professionals/Postdoctorates,** 813, 815, 829, 832, 852-854, 872, 891, 925. *See also* General programs; Humanities; Philosophy

Religious reporting: **Undergraduates,** 219. *See also* Broadcasting; General programs; Journalism; Religion and religious activities

Respiratory therapy: **Undergraduates,** 167. *See also* General programs; Health and health care

Restaurants. *See* Food service industry

Retailing. *See* Sales

Risk management: **Graduate Students,** 734. *See also* Actuarial sciences; Business administration; Finance; General programs

Romanian language. *See* Language, Romanian

S

Safety studies: **Undergraduates,** 44, 111, 186; **Graduate Students,** 493, 578. *See also* Engineering, general; General programs

Sales: **Undergraduates,** 171, 285, 319, 368; **Graduate Students,** 441, 699. *See also* General programs; Marketing

School counselors. *See* Counselors and counseling, school

School libraries and librarians. *See* Libraries and librarianship, school

School psycholgists. *See* Psychology, school

Schools. *See* Education

Science education. *See* Education, science and mathematics

Science reporting: **Undergraduates,** 250. *See also* Broadcasting; General programs; Journalism; Sciences

Science, history. *See* History, science

Sciences: **Undergraduates,** 78, 80, 131, 151, 208, 253, 263, 317; **Graduate Students,** 513, 619, 671, 753, 755; **Professionals/Postdoctorates,** 858, 881-882, 894, 903. *See also* General programs; names of specific sciences

Secondary education. *See* Education, secondary

Secret service. *See* Intelligence service

Securities law: **Graduate Students,** 539. *See also* General programs; Law, general

Security, national: **Graduate Students,** 528, 716; **Professionals/Postdoctorates,** 834, 852. *See also* General programs; Military affairs

Serbo-Croatian language. *See* Language, Serbo-Croatian

Sexuality: **Undergraduates,** 130; **Graduate Students,** 512. *See also* General programs; Medical sciences; Social sciences

Sight impairments. *See* Visual impairments

Slovak language. *See* Language, Slovak

Slovene language. *See* Language, Slovene

Social sciences: **Undergraduates,** 301, 330, 353; **Graduate Students,** 403, 488, 490, 495, 520, 722, 746, 780, 788; **Professionals/Postdoctorates,** 807, 813, 815, 829, 832, 836, 838, 842, 854, 859, 866, 891, 908, 921. *See also* General programs; names of specific social sciences

Social services: **Undergraduates,** 13, 330, 335; **Graduate Students,** 763. *See also* General programs; Public service; Social work

Social studies: **Graduate Students,** 525; **Professionals/Postdoctorates,** 849. *See also* General programs; Social sciences

Social work: **Undergraduates,** 49, 62, 110, 335; **Graduate Students,** 434, 456, 485, 643, 763; **Professionals/Postdoctorates,** 820, 862. *See also* General programs; Social sciences

Sociology: **Undergraduates,** 49, 335; **Graduate Students,** 403, 416, 434, 516, 659, 734, 763; **Professionals/Postdoctorates,** 813, 815, 820, 825, 829, 832, 854, 884, 891. *See also* General programs; Social sciences

Soils science: **Undergraduates,** 26, 335; **Graduate Students,** 763. *See also* Agriculture and agricultural sciences; General programs; Horticulture

Songs. *See* Music

South American studies. *See* Latin American studies

Soviet studies: **Graduate Students,** 520; **Professionals/Postdoctorates,** 866. *See also* European studies; General programs; Humanities

Space sciences: **Graduate Students,** 604; **Professionals/Postdoctorates,** 809. *See also* General programs; Physical sciences

Special education. *See* Education, special

Speech impairments: **Graduate Students,** 401. *See also* Disabilities; General programs; Speech therapy

Speech pathology: **Undergraduates,** 359; **Graduate Students,** 787. *See also* General programs; Medical sciences; Speech impairments; Speech therapy

Speech therapy: **Undergraduates,** 167; **Graduate Students,** 401. *See also* General programs; Health and health care; Speech impairments

Sports. *See* Athletics

Sports reporting: **Undergraduates,** 211. *See also* Broadcasting; General programs; Journalism

Spying. *See* Intelligence service

Stage design. *See* Performing arts

Statistics: **Undergraduates,** 53; **Graduate Students,** 566, 734; **Professionals/Postdoctorates,** 850. *See also* General programs; Mathematics

Structural engineering. *See* Engineering, structural

Substance abuse. *See* Alcohol use and abuse; Drug use and abuse

Surgery: **Undergraduates,** 197; **Graduate Students,** 603. *See also* General programs; Medical sciences

Surveying: **Undergraduates,** 136. *See also* General programs

Systems engineering. *See* Engineering, systems

T

Taxation: **Undergraduates,** 61, 178, 314; **Graduate Students,** 570, 736. *See also* Economics; General programs; Public administration

Teaching. *See* Education

Technology: **Undergraduates,** 80, 106; **Graduate Students,** 484, 528, 671, 694, 734, 753, 755; **Professionals/Postdoctorates,** 852, 881-882, 894. *See also* Computer sciences; General programs; Sciences

Teenagers. *See* Adolescents

Telecommunications: **Undergraduates,** 181; **Graduate Students,** 575. *See also* Communications; General programs; Radio; Television

Television: **Undergraduates,** 88, 144, 181, 220-221, 239, 285; **Graduate Students,** 575, 626, 642, 678, 699; **Professionals/Postdoctorates,** 826, 879. *See also* Communications; Filmmaking; General programs

Calendar Index

Since most funding programs have specific deadline dates, some may have already closed by the time you begin to look for money. You can use the Calendar Index to identify which programs are still open. To do that, go to the recipient category (Undergraduates, Graduate Students, or Professionals/Postdoctorates) that interests you, think about when you'll be able to complete your application forms, go to the appropriate months, jot down the entry numbers listed there, and use those numbers to find the program descriptions in the directory. Keep in mind that the numbers cited here refer to program entry numbers, not to page numbers in the book.